People and Computers XXI
HCI... but not as we know it

Volume 2

People and Computers XXI
HCI... but not as we know it

Volume 2

Proceedings of HCI 2007
The 21st British HCI Group Annual Conference
University of Lancaster, UK
3–7 September 2007

Devina Ramduny-Ellis and Dorothy Rachovides

 BCS

BCS
Publishing and Information Products
First Floor, Block D
North Star House
North Star Avenue
Swindon
SN2 1FA
UK
www.bcs.org

ISBN 978-1-902505-95-4

British Cataloguing in Publication Data.
A CIP catalogue record for this book is available at the British Library.
All trademarks, registered names etc. acknowledged in this publication are to be the property of their respective owners.

Disclaimer:
The views expressed in this book are of the author(s) and do not necessarily reflect the views of BCS except where explicitly stated as such. Although every care has been taken by the authors and BCS in the preparation of the publication, no warranty is given by the authors or BCS as publisher as to the accuracy or completeness of the information contained within it and neither the authors nor BCS shall be responsible or liable for any loss or damage whatsoever arising by virtue of such information or any instructions or advice contained within this publication or by any of the aforementioned.

Typeset by
Sunrise Setting Ltd

Contents

Papers are listed in alphabetical order of first author surname under each section

Student Papers

Posters

Interactive Experience

Panels

Organisational Overviews

Workshops

Tutorials

HCI Practice Day

Doctoral Consortium

Preface:
"HCI… but not as we know it" – Volume 2

As the British HCI conference has reached its 21st year, it has earned its status as being a conference with a mind of its own – a bit provocative and looking to the future. This is what we have tried to reflect in the Volume 2 proceedings. Short papers are an ideal forum for work in progress and late breaking results. This year we have also included a number of papers that are more thought-provoking, both for the future of HCI and our own practices. As such, this Volume captures exactly what "not as we know it" represents: papers that are all trying to say something new and different, whether at a theoretical level or in terms of research carried out in non-traditional areas or using novel methodologies. The present papers also complement very effectively the full papers presented in Volume 1, and are categorised under the same themes for presentation at the conference: *Creative and Aesthetic Experiences, Everyday Interaction, Communicating and Sharing Experiences, Mobile and Remote Interaction, Tracking Usability Issues, From Theory to Technique, HCI: Surveying the Domain,* and *Extending HCI.*

As well as the 31 short papers and 8 student papers, Volume 2 also includes posters, interactive experiences, panels, organisational overviews, workshops, and tutorials, in addition to papers associated with the HCI practice day and the doctoral consortium. All of these events are at the heart of the conference as they give us the buzz, get us talking in a more informal way about our work, and provide opportunities to present and discuss work that is not yet finalised in the form of a full paper.

All submissions for Volume 2 have been rigorously reviewed using the same process that was applied to the full papers that were submitted to Volume 1. Submissions received an average of four external reviews and were then subjected to further meta-reviewing.

Producing Volume 2 has been the joint effort of the authors, reviewers, category co-chairs and the entire organising committee who contributed much time and effort. We would like to thank all contributors – without you this conference would not exist.

We hope that the essence of British HCI's 21st birthday has been communicated to you through this Volume.

Devina Ramduny-Ellis
Dorothy Rachovides

July 2007

HCI 2007 Committee

Conference Chairs	Tom Ormerod *Lancaster University, UK*
	Corina Sas *Lancaster University, UK*
Fairy Godfather	Alan Dix *Lancaster University, UK*
General Scientific Co-Chair	Russell Beale *University of Birmingham, UK*
Full Papers Chairs	Linden Ball *Lancaster University, UK*
	Angela Sasse *University College London, UK*
Short Papers Chairs	Devina Ramduny-Ellis *Lancaster University, UK*
	Dorothy Rachovides *University of Surrey, UK*
Webmasters	Peter Bagnall *Lancaster University, UK*
	Jane Holt *Lancaster University, UK*
HCI Practice Chair	Laura Cowen *IBM United Kingdom Ltd, UK*
Tutorials Chairs	Willem-Paul Brinkman *Brunel University, UK*
	Steve Draper *University of Glasgow, UK*
Workshops Chairs	Dimitris Rigas *University of Bradford, UK*
	Anke Dittmar *University of Rostock, Germany*
Posters Chairs	Andrew Howes *University of Manchester, UK*
	Marc Fabri *Leeds Metropolitan University, UK*
Panels Chairs	Janet Finlay *Leeds Metropolitan University, UK*
	Timo Jokela *University of Oulu, Finland*
Interactive Experience Chair	Simon Lock *Lancaster University, UK*
Student Papers Chairs	Janet Read *University of Central Lancashire, UK*
	Claire O'Malley *University of Nottingham, UK*
Laboratory & Organisational Overviews	Pamela Briggs *Northumbria University, UK*
	Tom McEwan *Napier University, UK*
Doctoral Consortium Chairs	Lachlan MacKinnon *University of Abertay Dundee, UK*
	Stephen Payne *University of Manchester, UK*
Sponsorship	Tom Ormerod *Lancaster University, UK*
Publicity	Tom McEwan *Napier University, UK*
	Keith Mitchell *Lancaster University, UK*
Exhibition Manager	Patrick Olivier *Newcastle University, UK*
Treasurer	Alan Dix *Lancaster University, UK*
Technical Support	Peter Bagnall *Lancaster University, UK*
	Peter Phillips *Lancaster University, UK*
Student Volunteers	Stavros Asimakopoulos *Lancaster University, UK*
	Jane Holt *Lancaster University, UK*
British HCI Group Liaison	Janet Finlay *Leeds Metropolitan University, UK*
	Adrian Williamson *Graham Technology plc, UK*
	Fintan Culwin *London South Bank University, UK*
HCI 2008 Liaison	David England *Liverpool John Moores University, UK*
HCI 2006 Liaison	Nick Bryan-Kinns *Queen Mary, University of London, UK*
	Pat Healey *Queen Mary, University of London, UK*
Conference Administration & Social Programme	Jenny Harding *Lancaster University, UK*
	Chris Needham *Lancaster University, UK*

The Reviewers

Abate	Umberto	University of Sussex
Agarwal	Pragya	University College London
Al Hashimi	Sama'a	Middlesex University
Aliakseyeu	Dima	Technical University Eindhoven
Amaldi	Paola	Middlesex University
Anastassova	Margarita	CREATE-NET
Anceaux	Francoise	University Valenciennes
Andre	Paul	University of Southampton
Asadi Nikooyan	Ali	Amirkabir University of Technology
Asimakopoulos	Stavros	Lancaster University
Atkinson	Matthew	Loughborough University
Baber	Chris	University of Birmingham
Back	Jonathan	University College London
Bagnall	Peter	Lancaster University
Balbo	Sandrine	University of Melbourne
Ball	Linden	Lancaster University
Barboni	Eric	IRIT – LIIHS
Bardzell	Jeffrey	Indiana University
Bardzell	Shaowen	Indiana University
Beale	Russell	University of Birmingham
Bednarik	Roman	University of Joensuu
Ben Ammar	Mohamed	Université de Sfax
Bennett	Emily	University of Portsmouth
Bevan	Emma	University of Cambridge
Bissett	Andy	Sheffield Hallam University
Boardman	Richard	Google
Bonini	Deirdre	Usability Consultant at Yuseo, Paris
Bourguet	Marie-Luce	Queen Mary, University of London
Bowerman	Chris	University of Sunderland
Boyd Davis	Stephen	Middlesex University
Brejcha	Jan	Charles University Prague
Bremner	Fiona	General Dynamics Canada
Briggs	Pamela	Northumbria University
Brinkman	Willem-Paul	Brunel University
Bryan-Kinns	Nick	Queen Mary, University of London
Brys	Catherine	University of Glasgow
Busse	Daniela	Microsoft Corp.
Cairns	Paul	University College London
Calvillo Gámez	Eduardo	University College London
Carelli	Izaura Maria	Universidade Estadual do Oeste do Paraná
Cereijo Roibas	Anxo	University of Brighton
Chickerur	Satyadhyan	Sona College of Technology
Choi	Youngmi	University of Melbourne
Clark	Lillian	University of York
Coninx	Karin	Universiteit Hasselt
Cowen	Laura	IBM UK Ltd
Cramer	Henriette	Universiteit van Amsterdam
Crease	Murray	NRC-IIT
Creed	Chris	University of Birmingham

Crerar	Dr Alison	Napier University
Cunliffe	Daniel	University of Glamorgan
Dempster	Euan	University of Abertay, Dundee
Dittmar	Anke	University of Rostock
Dix	Alan	Lancaster University
Dogan	Huseyin	BAE Systems
Draper	Steve	University of Glasgow
Dubois	Emmanuel	IRIT – LIIHS
Dubois	Jean-Marc	Université Victor Segalen Bordeaux
Dunlop	Mark	University of Strathclyde
Eales	Jim	Middlesex University
Eibl	Maximilian	Technical University Chemnitz
Ellis	Geoffrey	Lancaster University
Elsweiler	David	University of Strathclyde
England	David	Liverpool John Moores University
Fabri	Marc	Leeds Metropolitan University
Farrell	Vivienne	Swinburne University
Feinman	Alexander	Charles River Analytics, Inc.
Fenley	Sue	University of Reading
Fields	Bob	Middlesex University
Fincher	Sally	University of Kent
Finlay	Janet	Leeds Metropolitan University
Folmer	Eelke	Rijks Universiteit Groningen
Ford	Gabrielle	University of KwaZulu-Natal
Fröhlich	Peter	Telecommunications Research Center Vienna
Frauenberger	Christopher	KUG, University of Music and Dramatic Arts Graz
Gardner	Peter	University of Leeds
Gauffre	Guillaume	IRIT - Toulouse
Geven	Arjan	CURE - Center for Usability Research and Engineering
Ghaoui	Claude	Liverpool John Moores University
Ghosh	Gautam	Userminded Ltd, Norway
Gilleade	Kiel	Lancaster University
Gillham	Robert	Amberlight Partners Ltd
Goodman	Dr Joy	University of Cambridge
Griffiths	Lee	University of Salford
Gul	Leman Figen	The University of Newcastle
Hürst	Wolfgang	Albert-Ludwigs-Universität Freiburg
Harrison	Chandra	University of York
Healey	Pat	Queen Mary, University of London
Heishman	Ricci	George Mason University
Helgeson	Bo	Blekinge Institute of Technology
Hey	Elliott	IBM Ease of Use Group
Hickey	Seamus	University of Oulu
Higson	Irene	Heriot-Watt University
Hoffmann	Hans-Juergen	Darmstadt University of Technology
Holmlid	Stefan	Human Centered Systems
Holt	Jane	Lancaster University
Hone	Kate	Brunel University
Horton	Matthew	University of Central Lancashire
Howes	Andrew	University of Manchester
Hughes	Baden	University of Melbourne
Hulme	Romeo	
Iqbal	Rahat	Faculty of Engineering and Computing
Iqbal	Shamsi	University of Illinois, Urbana-Champaign

Isokoski	Poika	University of Tampere
Jain	Jhilmil	Hewlett Packard Labs
Jeffcoate	Judith	University of Buckingham
Jillbert	Julius	Hasanuddin University
Jokela	Timo	University of Oulu
Jomhari	Nazean	University of Manchester
Jones	Christian	University of the Sunshine Coast
Joyce	Kev	Hutchison Whampoa Ltd
Költringer	Thomas	Vienna University of Technology
Kantamneni	Satyam	PayPal Corp. (an eBay Company)
Karagiannidis	Charalampos	University of Thessaly
Karam	Maria	Ryerson University
Katifori	Akrivi	National and Capodistrian University of Athens
Kemp	Elizabeth	Massey University
Ketola	Pekka	Nokia
Kettley	Sarah	Napier University
Klante	Palle	Pixelpark AG
Klein	Peter	User Interface Design GmbH
Lárusdóttir	Marta	Reykjavik University
Lancaster	Thomas	UCE Birmingham
Law	Effie Lai-Chong	ETH Zürich
Lawson	Shaun	University of Lincoln
Lepouras	Georgios	University of Peloponnese
Leuchter	Sandro	Fraunhofer Institute for Information and Data Processing
Lilley	Mariana	University of Hertfordshire
Lock	Simon	Lancaster University
Loudon	Gareth	University of Wales Institute, Cardiff
Lumsden	Jo	National Research Council of Canada
Macaulay	Catriona	University of Dundee Interaction Design Lab
MacKinnon	Lachlan	University of Abertay Dundee
Mahlke	Sascha	Technische Universität Berlin
Mandl	Thomas	Universität Hildesheim
Mann	Phebe	The Open University
Mansoux	Benoit	LIG
Martin	Beth	US Department of Health and Human Services
Masoodian	Masood	University of Waikato
Mazzone	Emanuela	University of Central Lancashire
McAllister	Graham	Queen's University Belfast
McCrindle	Dr Rachel	University of Reading
McEwan	Tom	Napier University
McGookin	David	University of Glasgow
Memmel	Thomas	University of Konstanz
Metatla	Oussama	Queen Mary, University of London
Millard	Nicola	BT
Montgomery Masters	Michelle	University of Strathclyde
Moore	David	Leeds Metropolitan University
Morse	David	The Open University
Nørgaard	Mie	University of Copenhagen
Nair	Rahul	University of California at Berkeley
Nascimento Souto	Patricia Cristina	Loughborough University
Neil	Stuart	University of Wales Institute, Cardiff
Nicol	Tony	University of Central Lancashire
Nielsen	Lene	Copenhagen Business School, CBS
Nilsson	Maria	University of Skovde

Noel	Sylvie	Communications Research Centre
Nonaka	Hidetoshi	Hokkaido University
Nosseir	Ann	Strathclyde
Olivier	Patrick	University of Newcastle Upon Tyne
O'Malley	Claire	University of Nottingham
Ormerod	Tom	Lancaster University
Paelke	Volker	University of Hannover
Papatzanis	George	QMUL
Payne	Stephen	University of Manchester
Perera	Dharani	Deakin University
Peter	Christian	Fraunhofer IGD Rostock
Phillips	Peter	Lancaster University
Pickering	Emma	Ordnance Survey
Pinto da Luz	Rodolfo	Centro Universitário Unieuro
Plimmer	Beryl	University of Auckland
Ploderer	Bernd	University of Melbourne
Pohl	Margit	University of Technology Vienna
Prasad R	Venkatesha	WMC, TUDelft
Purchase	Helen	Glasgow University
Rønne Jakobsen	Mikkel	University of Copenhagen
Rachovides	Dorothy	University of Surrey
Raisamo	Jukka	University of Tampere
Ramaswamy	Sreeramen	Human Factors International
Ramduny-Ellis	Devina	Lancaster University
Raymaekers	Chris	Hasselt University
Read	Janet	University of Central Lancashire
Rebelo	Irla Bocianoski	UNIEURO - Cetro Universitário Euroamericana/Brasília/Brazil
Reed	Darren	University of York
Reeves	Nina	University of Gloucestershire Business School
Reeves	Stuart	University of Nottingham
Renaud	Karen	GUCSD
Renshaw	Tony	Leeds Metropolitan University
Rigas	Dimitris	University of Bradford
Roberts	Dave	IBM
Romano	Daniela	The Department of Computer Science
Romero	Natalia	Eindhoven University of Technology
Rose	Tony	Russell Rose Consulting
Roth	Patrick	University of Geneva
Russo	Angelina	Queensland University of Technology
Sainz Salces	Fausto	Universidad Carlos III Madrid
Salber	Daniel	Joost Technologies B.V.
Salovaara	Antti	Helsinki Institute for Information Technology
Santos	Lucinio	IBM Corporation
Sari	Eunice	University of Art and Design Helsinki
Sas	Corina	Lancaster University
Sasse	M. Angela	University College London
Schatz	Raimund	Telecommunications Research Center, Vienna
Schmettow	Martin	University Passau
Scott	Suzanne	University of Dundee
Sener	Bahar	Middle East Technical University
Sheridan	Jennifer G.	Lancaster University
Sim	Gavin	University of Central Lancashire
Simi	Maria	Università di Pisa
Slack	Frances	Sheffield Hallam University

Soosay	Meg	Leeds Metropolitan University
Storer	Tim	University of St Andrews
Strom	Georg	University of Copenhagen
Stumpf	Simone	Oregon State University, Corvallis
Terrier	Patrice	Université de Toulouse & CNRS
Thapliyal	Mathura	HNB Garhwal University, Srinagar(Garhwal)
Thimbleby	Harold	University of Wales Swansea
Tomitsch	Martin	Vienna University of Technology
Tsuji	Bruce	Human Oriented Technology Lab
Turner	Phil	Napier University
Turner	Susan	Napier University
Upton	Mark	EDS
Van den Ende	Nele	Philips Research
Vanderdonckt	Jean	Université Catholique de Louvain
Vasalou	Asimina	Imperial College London
Venkatesha Murthy	Sudhindra	
Venters	Colin C.	University of Manchester
Wall	Steven	University of Surrey
Ward	Robert	University of Huddersfield
Warr	Andrew	University of Oxford
Whitelock	Denise	The Open University
Widjaja	Ivo	University of Melbourne
Wild	Peter	University of Cambridge
Wilson	Judy	Middlesex University
Wilson	Max	University of Southampton
Xu	Diana	University of Central Lancashire
Zaphiris	Panayiotis	City University

Short Papers

Blogs, Reflective Practice and Student-Centered Learning

Russell Beale
Advanced Interaction Group
School of Computer Science
University of Birmingham
Edgbaston, Birmingham
B15 2TT, UK
Tel: +44 (0) 121 414 3729

R.Beale@cs.bham.ac.uk

ABSTRACT

Blogging can be used to enhance education by encouraging reflective practice. We present a study in which a final year HCI course was constructed around regular blogging activity. We discuss the role of blogs in providing a social mechanism for the student body and in acting as a conduit between classroom and practical examples. We analyze the blogs from a quantitative and qualitative perspective, and show that the students found it a useful and effective addition to their learning.

Categories and Subject Descriptors

H5. Information interfaces and presentation (e.g., CHI)

General Terms

Experimentation, Human Factors

Keywords

Blogging, education, cultural probe, reflective practice.

1. BLOGS AS AN EDUCATIONAL TOOL

Weblogs have become very popular recently [8, 13], as a fast, easy to use way of sharing your thoughts with others on the internet. Weblogs (or blogs) are temporally ordered personal commentaries published on the internet, and cover a wide range of topics from the personal diary through to news sites, political comment, technical and social issues, and gossip [7]. Because of their web-based nature, they encourage external referencing to other internet sites, allowing bloggers (people who blog) to comment on news, others opinions – in fact, on anything that they come across in the wide world of the web. Often, bloggers find other bloggers who share similar views or interests, and highly interlinked communities grow up, sharing information and opinions [9, 10]. Blogging technologies have made the publication of blogs much simpler, enabling users to create usable, aesthetically pleasing websites with no prior knowledge of HTML, opening up the world of blogging to any user who wants to participate [1, 10]. Because blogs are designed to be read, and are referenced by other bloggers who are often

regarded as colleagues or friends, they encourage frequent, often daily, postings.

The engagement that many users have with their blogs has not gone unnoticed by educationalists [11, 15], who have seen them as a potential way to engage students more fully with the topic. They appear to have potential as tools for supporting student sharing of information, for engaging them with the subject by using cool new technology and relating their work to the outside world, and, by the very nature of the blogging activity, supporting reflective practice [4, 14]. Reflective practice is an approach to learning that encourages thought about what has been experienced and seen, which can then drive new theories and investigations to test those theories, leading to new experiences that may, or may not, validate the original ideas. This leads to them being modified, extended, and refined, and the cycle continues. This is shown in Figure 2, derived from Kolb [6].

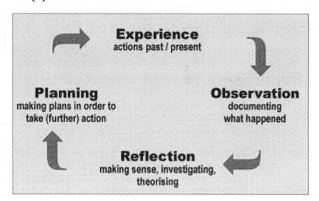

Figure 2: Reflective practice: its place in the learning cycle

Originating in the nursing sphere, and originally focused on aiding learning from practical subjects, reflective practice has a place within more conventional education; its encouragement of students to consider the implications of what they see, to investigate how what they know relates to practical issues, to find examples that prove or disprove a particular approach; all are important aspects in moving students through the four stages of education and awareness that have usefully characterized as: unconscious incompetence, conscious incompetence, conscious competence, unconscious competence. In HCI practice, this equates to a transition from uninformed programming through to experienced 'craft' practitioners/researchers/ designers who instinctively do 'good' things. In order to encourage reflective practice, we therefore need to support the main elements of the learning cycle within the context of any course. Blogging appears to offer this opportunity.

From an activity perspective, blogs encourage regular postings, which forces bloggers to think about what it is they are to write about. Being an internet activity, blogs encourage exploration of the internet and hence give users a wider experience of many issues that are of relevance to HCI – website usability, design, new technologies, social impact of systems, and so on. In order to blog about such things, users need to experience them, observe them in detail, and then distill their thoughts, views and observations into meaningful comment. They may encounter opinions or experiences that challenge their current notions of the world, or of a particular HCI issue, or a previously held belief about something (in itself a good thing) and will then have to plan other explorations or activities in order to better understand what they have observed. This cycle of experience, observation, reflection leading to theorizing and understanding, or to looking into things further, maps directly onto the reflective practice cycle.

From a social and pedagogical perspective, blogging provides two advantages. The first is that it can support a sense of community amongst the students. They can read and comment on other students postings, and can learn from both experiences that others have discovered, and from the insights of their peers regarding those experiences. In this way, exceptional students can forge into the unknown, being opinionated, making deep insightful comments on the state of the world, the role of HCI, or anything else, whilst the weaker students are pulled along in their wake, reading and learning, able to make their own sense of things in their own time. In addition, by making their work semi-public, students can see the sort of activities done by other students and hence have transparency on the amount of work that is required. Because others can also see their level of activity or inactivity, peer pressure should exert an influence and encourage them to maintain at least an acceptable level of input into their blogging activities. Even without the student undertaking any additional research work or internet exploration, the act of forcing them to write a blog entry means that they have to consider what they wish to say, and hence it forces them to think, even for a short time, about HCI in some context or other. In addition, the creation of a blog on the topic is akin to the student creating a portfolio relating to HCI issues, and portfolio development is known to be useful in developing deeper insights in the learning process [3].

Because blogging is relatively new, it also represents a 'cool' technology, and playing with such approaches feels much less like learning than reading books or doing exercises, and hence it engages more students more readily. As an accessible Internet technology, requiring nothing more than a web browser and internet access, it also allows students to contribute to their blogs whenever they are able, at times to suit them: in the world of the modern student, this is becoming increasingly important as many of them have to undertake paid work for a large number of hours and being able to fit aspects of their learning around the work that pays for their courses is crucial.

It therefore seems that blogging should be able to support reflective practice, which should have the effect of connecting the work done in the lecture room with experiences the students have had in the outside world, and reinforcing the progression from episodic experiences of HCI in the classroom to a more detailed semantic understanding of the issues in context.

2. COURSE COHORT, DESIGN AND PEDAGOGY

The students in this study were computing students, who had opted to do a newly-offered HCI course as a follow-up to an introductory course done the previous year. The main goal of the course was to engage people with the subject of HCI – to provide them with the prompts to understand and challenge both technical systems and non-technical ones. We worked with a cohort of 36 students, all of whom were on the HCI course. 26 of the students were final year undergraduates and 10 of them were Masters students; all had previously undertaken at least one undergraduate introductory level course in HCI.

We firstly undertook a simplistic enquiry into what it was valid for the course to cover, by asking the students to identify what they felt HCI was about. The results, unsurprisingly, reflect their previous exposure to HCI, which is scaffolded on aspects of the ACM curriculum. After this discussion, we gave the students input to designing the course by identifying the main areas of interest to them, allowing them to define the areas of the course that they felt to be critical for them, to provide them with a tailored HCI experience that met both their needs and their interests. The course focused on the user-centered design lifecycle, discussing theories tools and techniques as we encountered different aspects.

Pedagogically, the course was constructed around four simultaneous strands of blended learning[2]: lectures, directed reading, a mini-project, and blogging. The lectures covered the main principles of the topics within the course, giving the key information and concepts to the students, but with a primary focus of motivating them to follow these up in their own time outside of the lectures. To support this, we offered a set of directed readings on related topics, mainly web-based for easy access. In addition, the students did a mini-project to experience user-centered design from start to evaluated prototype, and had directed reading on issues related to the lecture structure outlined above. The final piece in the pedagogy was to get them to create and maintain a blog on HCI issues. For this investigation, they were asked to blog on any HCI issues that they considered to be relevant. This work was not directed in any way – we left the choice of topic up to them. The aim was to explicitly get them to cover and integrate wider material into the work covered in the lectures. Implicitly, the process encouraged reflective practice, helping them evaluate their learning, and develop it in new directions.

3. QUANTITATIVE ANALYSIS OF BLOGS

We have analysed the blogs produced by the students, counting the entries and looking at the sizes of postings. Of the 36 blogs, six contained either no information of any substance at all, or were corrupt, or refused to be analysed. Of the 30 blogs analysed in detail, there were 827 individual posts (an average of 27.56 posts per blog – over the period of 11 weeks of the course that equates to 2.51 posts per week: more than the 2 per week we suggested was necessary, providing the first evidence that this was a popular approach with the students). The average posting had 179.89 words, with a standard deviation of 179.77. Clearly this is not too useful: a more relevant measure is the median count of 137 words; the modal value was 50 words. Three blog entries had word counts of greater than 1000 – these discussed blogging and communities of practice (1073 words); the ethics of blogging (2671 words); and design approaches in the construction industry (1032 words). A graph of word count versus number of posts with that count is shown in Figure 3 – the >1000 word blogs are omitted for clarity. Of these 827 posts, 180 (22%) of them referred to other blogs, either those of fellow students (the majority) or to other bloggers. 404 (49%) had references to non-blog URL's – other websites – whilst 483 (58%) had references to either blog or other websites. This fits with a common pattern of usage of blogs, in that a majority of the postings refer to other events on the web or in the blogosphere that are commented on or referred to by the blogger.

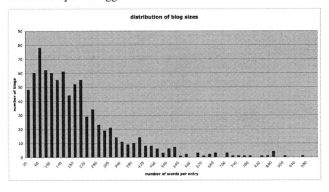

Figure 3: Distribution of blog sizes

404 posts (42%) of posts had no references to other websites at all. These posts tended to be either direct reflections (or summaries) of a lecture, or reporting on their user-centered design project. The students were explicitly asked to report on the progress of their project in their blog, which clearly affected the statistics on external references, but had clear pedagogical purpose in that it allowed them to present their concepts and ideas to their fellow students and to receive comment and feedback on their design from their peers, and to write about experiences, observations, reflections and plans (the reflective practice cycle).

We wanted to understand the students' approach to blogging, and in particular whether they treated writing about other people's blogs differently to writing about other websites. To address this, we examined those postings that referred to blogs and those that examined other websites, and undertook a student-t test to determine if there was a significant difference in posting size between these two categories. The results showed conclusively that we could not reject the null hypothesis, that *there was no difference between the posting size for the different categories*. In other words, there is no statistically significant difference between the size of posting that was created that refers to a blog entry compared to referring to something on an conventional website. We can (loosely) conclude from this that the students viewed other blogs and other websites as not hugely different to each other, and worthy of roughly similar comment.

Comments in blogs allow us to investigate the extent to which the students received feedback on their opinions and views, and how much of a dialogue and community grew up around the blogs. None of the instructors on the course made comments in the blogs. The statistics are as follows. There were a total of 136 comments: the mean number of comments is 0.164, $\sigma=0.562$; the maximum number of comments is 4. There were 52 posts (6.3%) with one comment, 20 (2.4%) with two, 8 (1.0%) with three, and 5 posts (0.6%) with 4 comments. This suggests that the students didn't hugely use commenting; there are rarely long 'comment' conversations, and most posts are uncommented on. Conversely, it is still an activity that has a level of participation that is not trivial, and validates the point that students could get wider input on their ideas and that blogging helped build communications.

4. QUALITIATIVE ANALYSIS

By providing the students with the freedom to investigate anything that they felt to be relevant to HCI, and the tools to allow them to share their perspective with us, we are also able

to use the blog as a cultural probe [5], using it to discover their perspectives on what HCI is about, what it covers, its scope and perspective, as they perceive it.

In order to understand the results from a qualitative perspective, we have borrowed techniques from a grounded theory approach[12], categorizing the topics within the blogs by the main issue that they address. Where an entry doesn't fit into an existing category, a new category is created and the entry recorded under that. Most entries appear in only one category; a few are classified under two categories where this is clearly sensible. Therefore, the total number of blog entries is slightly less than the sum of numbers in the categories, but not by much.

Some of the main categories we found in the analysis were: *blogging, practical project, design examples, HCI examples, new technology, software, privacy, cool sites, input devices, comedy, gaming, creativity, Microsoft, elderly/disabled, mobile, website design, politics, education, futuristic systems, security, social comment, lecture material, legal, personal, operating systems, other.*

Blogging, and *practical project* were discussed with far greater frequency than the other topics, though this is unsurprising: students were self-reflective about their blogging activities, and the reminders given in lectures would have created a greater awareness of blogging issues; as for project discussions, they were expected to commentate on these in their blogs as time progressed and so we would expect their to be ongoing postings about these issues. These project postings proved popular with the students, who felt that exposing their work to their peers allowed the others to see what efforts they were putting in, as well as allowing a wider audience to comment and discuss their new concepts. Typically they reported on the key stages of the development: creativity and concept generation, user discussions about possible designs, settling on the design/product type, questionnaires on functionality and usability, prototype tests, redesign, and conclusions – sometimes in separate postings, sometimes combining more than one topic. Whilst we did not quantitatively analyze the size of just these postings, observation and reading of the blogs suggests that postings on project topics were significantly larger than other postings.

For the other topics, what is interesting is the range of things that the students discussed, and that they felt was relevant to HCI. However, most of these topics were at least mentioned in at least one of the lectures, suggesting that the students did not often bring completely new concepts into the domain and discuss them. Interestingly, particularly in the domain of design examples and interaction examples, they found and commented on *new* examples of (usually poor) design that they criticized effectively. For example, one student comments on a vending machine:

"*Kick the stupid machine:* Fast service, easy to use. You simply put a coin in the machine and make your selection. No need for running to a store to get what you want. You have the solution just next to you. Chocolates, crisps, soft-drinks, condoms. Anything you need, whenever you need it. But I still HATE these machines, both for technical and psychological reasons.To be honest the first time I tried to use one was a few months ago. I don't know why, I guess I just never needed to use one before. Anyway, the first experience I had with a vending machine it was quite 'painful'. I wanted a coke, so I went near the machine and put some coins in it, without bothering reading the instructions and pressed my selection. And here we go...."

As an example of the range of issues on which they reflected, he is an example of a somewhat philosophical musing on design for print:

"What's the measure of well design print media? What is the measure of well designed print media? Is it Appropriateness? Beauty? One can claim that it is all and none of the above. The trouble with print media is that it is extremely difficult to turn a set of words and ideas into a physical object that will express them effectively[…]."

The posts of some students clearly influenced others, thus providing evidence for both the social aspects of learning that blogging was supposed to engender, and (in this case) for reflective disagreement. ("Jat" is a student on the course)

"Whilst reading Jat's post about the interface of rss, I began to think of why rss might not have become hugely popular. Just because it is new is a valid reason but it isn't enough. Jat went on to say that simplicity is the key when it comes to accessing rss updates from sites. But I think I disagree with some of this…"

It is important to note that these and the other topics that received coverage are not directly those that you would obtain from the course outline and description: these topics are more focused on specifics that occurred in lectures or were key issues at the time of them blogging. This provides some evidence that the students were linking their classwork to the real world, seeing HCI in the wild as well as in an educational context.

5. COURSE EVALUATION

Being a new course, previous years' results were not available for comparison, so we compared the course to the other modules taken by the students. Questionnaires were distributed, based on a 0-4 scale, with 0 bad and 4 excellent. The course achieved a 100% return rate of questionnaires. It was well received: Scores of 3.25 on value (c.f. average score on other modules of 2.27), 3.5 on interest (c.f. 2.3), 3.31 on web support (c.f. 2.12) and 3.35 on happiness with choice (c.f. 2.38). Value, difficulty level, amount learnt, speed, clarity, interest, handout quantity, handout clarity, usefulness of web support, appropriateness of exercises, and happiness of choice were all better than the average on other modules.

6. CONCLUSIONS

We found the use of blogs to be an effective tool for supporting students in reflective practice, for connecting their classroom experiences to the outside world, and for allowing them to receive greater feedback from their colleagues on their practical design exercise than they might otherwise have done. The students enjoyed the approach, and gave the course high satisfaction marks overall, suggesting that blogging is an effective, engaging approach for supporting other educational practices.

7. ACKNOWLEDGMENTS

I would like to thank Peter Lonsdale, who taught part of the HCI course and made valuable comments on the blogging activities; Rob Goldsmith who wrote the software to do the blog analysis; and to the final year students who participated in this study.

8. REFERENCES

[1] Beale, R., Mobile blogging: experiences of technologically led design. in *CHI'06 extended abstracts on Human factors in computing systems: Experience reports*, (Montreal, Canada, 2006), ACM Press, 225-230.

[2] Bonk, C. and Graham, C. *The Handbook of Blended Learning : Global Perspectives, Local Designs*. Pfeiffer, 2005.

[3] Fernsten, L. and Fernsten, J. Portfolio assessment and reflection: enhancing learning through effective practice. *Reflective Practice, 6* (2).(2005), 303-309.

[4] Fiedler, S., Personal webpublishing as a refective conversational tool for self-organized learning. in *BlogTalks*, (Vienna, Austria, 2003), 190-216.

[5] Gaver, B., Dunne, T. and Pacenti, E. Design: Cultural probes. *interactions, 6* (1).(1999), 21-29.

[6] Kolb, D.A. *Experiential Learning: experience as the source of learning and development*. Prentice-Hall, New Jersey, 1984.

[7] Kumar, R., Novak, J., Raghavan, P. and Tomkins, A. Structure and evolution of blogspace *Commun. ACM 47* (12).(2004), 35-39

[8] McGann, R. The Blogosphere By the Numbers. http://www.clickz.com/stats/sectors/traffic_patterns/article.php/3438891.

[9] Nardi, B.A., Schiano, D.J. and Gumbrecht, M. Blogging as social activity, or, would you let 900 million people read your diary? . in *Proceedings of the 2004 ACM conference on Computer supported cooperative work* ACM Press, Chicago, Illinois, USA 2004 222-231

[10] Nardi, B.A., Schiano, D.J., Gumbrecht, M. and Swartz, L. Why we blog *Commun. ACM 47* (12).(2004), 41-46

[11] Oravec, J.A. Blending by Blogging: weblogs in blended learning initatives. *Journal of Educational Media, 28* (2-3).(2003), 225-233.

[12] Pidgeon, N.F., Turner, B.A. and Blockley, D.I. The use of Grounded Theory for conceptual analysis in knowledge elicitation. *Int.J.Man-Machine Studies, 35*.(1991), 151-173.

[13] Rainie, L. The state of blogging, The Pew Internet & American Life Project, 2005.

[14] Schon, D.A. *The Reflective Practitioner*. UK:Maurice Temple Smith Ltd., 1983.

[15] Williams, J.B. and Jacobs, J. Exploring the use of blogs as learning spaces in the higher education sector. *Australasian Journal of Educational Technology, 20* (2).(2004), 232-247.

Erotic Life as a New Frontier in HCI

Olav W. Bertelsen & Marianne Graves Petersen
University of Aarhus, Department of Computer Science
Aabogade 34, DK-8200 Aarhus N,
Denmark
{olavb, mgraves}@daimi.au.dk

ABSTRACT

In this paper we discuss how information technology impacts erotic life. This has been a neglected issue in most of the literature, even the literature on IT in the home. We argue that current IT, in particular in the home, tends to marginalize erotic aspects of life, through developing domestic technology, without considering how it impacts conditions for erotic life in the home. We suggest the need for a counter discourse in HCI, and we outline a number of theoretical and empirical perspectives, which can contribute to establish erotic life as a new frontier in HCI.

Categories and Subject Descriptors
H.1.2 User/Machine Systems.

General Terms
Design, Human Factors.

Keywords
Erotic life, aesthetics, communication, visibility and invisibility, interactive spaces, life quality, workplace rationality.

1. INTRODUCTION
The field of HCI is increasingly becoming interested in the field of the home as a site for design of technology. This has been seen as an interesting site, since it provokes the rationalities of designing for a workplace [7][18], the domain out of which HCI was born and has developed from. However, apart from the CHI 2006 workshop [6], a perspective on sex and eroticism is almost totally absent. To clarify, we see erotic life as embracing a spectrum from the erotic atmosphere (or ambience) via the light flirt, to the concrete conditions for realizing the sexual intercourse.

Basically, there are two ways of looking at how domestic design influences everyday erotic life. One approach is to focus on designing interactive technologies to support erotic experiences, and a second strategy is to look at how the design of mundane everyday technologies influences conditions for erotic life. Some people do involve interactive technology in their erotic life, but so far this area has received very little

attention from the HCI research community; [6] is one example though.

The second issue we cannot escape as a community, but so far we see only few attempts in this direction. As an example, there is an increasing interest in introducing sensor technologies in the home, e.g. to infer availability status [11]. Such systems impact conditions for exercising erotic life, but this issue is not even touched upon nor linked to the issue of availability. Thus, as technology becomes more and more ubiquitous, we have to consider erotic life as part of our understanding of human-computer interaction, in order to avoid designing sterile deserts.

In much research on domestic computing, it seems as if the ideals of efficiency and the focus on tasks seamlessly has drifted into the domestic computing area [18], even though there have been a number of warnings against this tendency [18][7]. The focus on erotic life is a useful provocation in maturing the field of HCI to truly embrace the characteristics of home life and felt life [13], as it inherently provoke ideals from the workplace, as this is perhaps the most inefficient and non-work activity taking place in a domestic context.

In designing IT-based artefacts various quality criteria may apply. One example is effectiveness, efficiency and satisfaction as laid out in the usability standards. However, going back to the birth of participatory design, some higher level values was proposed as the ideals to work from with respect to technology design. These included the ideal of improved life quality [9]. More recently, it has been pointed out how this perspective is relevant, if not urgently needed in the development of future domestic technology too [12]. Thus if we are willing to take a broader perspective, it is hard not to adopt quality of life as a basic principle. Already well-established accounts on humanistic psychology have hinted that sexual satisfaction is important for a complete life. More recent positions have also established a well functioning sexual life as an important aspect of a "good life" [23]. Thus, adopting a perspective of life quality in technology development implies that quality of erotic life should also be accounted for.

Most approaches to technology mediated erotic activity in the past seem to have centered around futuristic concepts such as cyber sex, where sexual activities would be carried out in virtual reality with the users hooked up via direct stimulation of erogenous zones. In contrast, we aim to look into eroticism, and sexual practice, as aspects of everyday life not necessarily directly designed for in the development of information technology, but still changed massively as technology is becoming present in the private and intimate sphere. A recent investigation suggested that couples that have television in their bedroom have sexual intercourse half as often as those who do not [20]. On the other hand the TV set can also be used for watching pornography as inspiration or as part of the sexual activity. So obviously, the issue is complex, and technology can serve as an enabler as well as a disabler. That is, sometimes the effects of the new technologies are positive, but most often it seems that intimacy is jeopardized as these workplace centric technologies invade private life. This is a problem, as it seems that many of the new technologies entering into the private space (in combination with an intensified working life) are significant factors in making sexual life difficult for many couples today. What is striking in the context of HCI, however, is that investigations on how technology design influences our erotic life, let alone make way for new erotic experiences, is almost completely absent from the research field. With this paper, we propose to start such investigation. As a first step towards a foundation for erotic life in HCI, we outline and discuss a series of relevant themes.

2. AESTHETICS IN EROTIC LIFE

Recently, the field of HCI has opened up to cover new perspectives like emotion and aesthetics. This is partly a result of acknowledging that the increasing permeation of technology into everyday life creates a need for new perspectives to understand, design and evaluate human-computer interaction. Several authors have pointed out that aesthetics is becoming a necessary and integral part of HCI [3] [4] [14] [19] [22]. This turn is not only motivated by the fact that HCI is becoming relevant in new settings, but as much in a theoretical need to understand the dynamics of the use situation [2][4].

Eroticism has been a central concept in modern aesthetic theory denoting the non-interpretable and immediate counterpoint to the hermeneutic [5]. Erotic experience has also been a key theme in many artworks. As in Baudelaire's poem "to a passer-by":

A lightning flash... then night! Fleeting beauty
By whose glance I was suddenly reborn,
Will I see you no more before eternity? [1]

This excerpt of the poem points to the erotic moment as being fundamentally mysterious and contingent. The moment is irreversible and irretrievable and cannot be captured by reasoning. This erotic moment results in an instantaneous reshaping of the two involved persons. The erotic glance is out in the open, to be seen by anyone, but only perceivable for the relevant other person. The poem highlights the intensity of the experience that is shared between these two people only. It is a secret layer in an everyday, public situation that for the involved man and women is a unique experience. Where the modern aesthetics represented by Baudelaire emphasizes the unique and shocking, even if it is achieved by glancing out of the tram, the current aesthetic wave in HCI is to a large extend based on a pragmatist approach emphasizing the bodily mundane [14][19][21].

Aesthetics is potentially a fruitful perspective for understanding the more sensitive aspects of computing [14]. From this perspective it has been highlighted how interaction design should consider all human senses and the whole body in the design.

From the pragmatists perspective, Shusterman [21], points out that aesthetic experience offers a fruitful perspective on erotic experience. In opposition to the awkward way western society treats sex and eroticism, he argues that western modernity at large tends to treat sex in a distinctly medical rather than aesthetic perspective. As an alternative he promotes aesthetic experience as a basis for understanding erotic life: "…seeing erotic experience as aesthetic experience has more than theoretical consequences. It can inspire us to greater aesthetic appreciation of our sexual experience, and consequently, to

more artistic and aesthetically rewarding performance in our erotic behavior, which surely forms one important dimension of the art of living". [[21] p. 227].

3. INTIMACY IN FAMILY LIFE

Within the fields of sociology and psychology, a number of investigations have been undertaken around human erotic life. The challenge for HCI is to investigate these with the aim of pointing to implications for technology design, or alternatively perform new investigations that address the relation between erotic experiences and technology design. Looking to established HCI-based research of home life, design patterns have been suggested as a fruitful approach to draw implications from empirical studies of domestic life for technology design [7]. However, until now the patterns developed have not covered intimate and erotic situations.

Broader studies of modern family life can also point to findings relevant for future technology design. A recent Danish survey around the changing conditions for family life [8] highlighted how postmodern family life, where people are part of multiple and changing social groups and possibly live in changing and network families, make an improved pressure on the family as a site for true intimate relations:

"… establishing close relationships based on common experiences demands much more of the family members. In other words, family members can no longer be guided by traditions. In order to lead a fulfilling family life, its members will need to rely increasingly on their capacity to reflect continuously on their social relationships and actively to construct commonality" [8].

The family becomes a kind of specialized sanctuary for intimacy. While this holds for the family as a whole, this must also concern the partners. Domestic computing research around connecting, people who live apart, to some extend addresses this issue [17]. However, the paradigm of anything, anywhere anyhow is a double-edged sword in this respect, as it holds for lovers as well as for others, and thus may seriously interfere with intimate situations. Furthermore, it has been pointed out that the increasing fraction of families where both adults work full time tend to shift their relationship into one where negotiations around time, and the right to work more and more hours take up a lot of attention [7] [8]. In an American context, Hochschild [11] has illustrated how people seem to be caught in a time trap when work becomes family and family becomes work. At work, there is a focus on self-realization and social relationship with colleagues, whereas home life concentrates on the practical tasks, which need to be accomplished and which are increasingly outsourced.

Thus, a design approach to addressing this challenge is to design for unexpected openings, illogical combinations, which can support erotic impulses and erotic play. The coarse example would be to have a random four hour power outage two times each week (this "approach" at least proved to work during world war two).

4. COMMUNICATION IN EROTIC LIFE

According to the general sexology literature, inability to communicate seems to be the most common reason for divorce and other problems in intimate relationships [13]. The ability to communicate is not necessarily of key importance in the early phases of a relationship, when sexual tension and the attraction of the opposite are drawing the couple together, but communication patterns established early in the relationship are important later on [ibid]. Differences in vocabulary and the lack of experience in talking about sex are obvious sources for problems in maintaining a sexual relationship. The literature on marriage counseling also points to the general mode of communication as often being problematic, e.g. communication patterns developed between siblings, focusing on blaming the other part, or patterns focusing on winning the argument lead to problems when applied in the relationship.

Interactive technologies present in the home impact communication in several ways. The discussion on the time trap [11] indicates that communication has degenerated into negotiation, substituting intimate communication with technical rationality. The constant opportunity to communicate with people outside the home and the constant stream of media contents seems to be negative factors as pointed out above. A low-tech approach would be to reduce the impact of the disabling technologies, e.g. by cutting off the media stream and by defining specific time slots for external communication. Along the same lines, defining time slots for talking together, or having a shared diary could compensate for the missing communication.

An intimate communications perspective provides a clear departure away form the hegemony of technical rationality, helping the erotic back from its exiled position as residual category.

5. VISIBILITY OF EROTIC LIFE

Invisibility is a key factor in ambient technology; the rationale being that with myriads of devices it is required that the technology minds itself without users' intervention. Criticizing this naïve position, the Palcom project [10] has set out from the assumption that technology that just does its' thing independently of users control will not work properly in non-standard situations. The challenge of making systems that provide invisibility with visibility is critical in such situations. As the Palcom project primarily focuses on architectures for ambient computing they take the visibility-invisibility tension in a quite literal and technical meaning. The visibility–invisibility tension is not, however, only a technical issue but also, a personal and relational issue.

The tension between visibility and invisibility is important to erotic life in at least two ways. Firstly, it is related to possible excitements around exhibitionist and voyeuristic flavored experiments. Secondly, it is related to intimacy being exclusive to the involved then requiring a "safe space" and at the same time excluding others. The exploration of this tension in relation to erotic life may provide new insights and strategies for handling visibility and invisibility in general..

6. EROTIC LIFE AS FUN

Among the selected findings in a survey of the world sexology literature in 2000, WHO Senior Policy Advisor, Judith Mackay pointed out the following:

"WHERE IS THE FUN? It was surprisingly difficult to find cheerful aspects of sex. Most of what is measured is negative - teenage abortions, diseases, child prostitutes, harsh laws, sex crimes such as rape, harassment and stalking. Even the success of sex education is usually measured by the avoidance of unwanted pregnancies and STIs, not by whether children grow up to have a fulfilling sex life." [15]

Our attempts to find inspiration in the sexology literature, lead to similar conclusion. Indeed also our own analysis as presented here in terms of the diagnosis of how erotic life has become a

residual category under the hegemonic status of technical rationality, how the inability to communicate leads to marital problems, etc has also focused on the negative. It is, however, important to note that our argument is twofold; in arguing for a discourse in interaction design that both reduces the negative impacts technology and support design of technology that can inspire and enhance erotic life.

7. CONCLUSIONS

We have pointed to the complex relation between information technology and erotic life as impacting the quality of human life. Thereby, we claim that this complex should be addressed as a new frontier for HCI. The discussions above open a number of themes that will be relevant for HCI in addressing erotic life. Below we conclude the discussion by outlining the elements of a disciplinary discourse in HCI regarding erotic life

Theoretically and intellectually, we point to perspectives that can frame this complex issue in the field of HCI. Both the pragmatic and the modernist aesthetics have something to offer in this direction. Most importantly, the aesthetic turn breaks fundamentally with the dominating status of technical rationality. For this new discourse, it is also important to integrate knowledge from medical, sociological, sexology, and therapeutic practice dealing with erotic life and its conditions in modern families. There are opportunities for focusing on communication around erotic experiences and for investigating the tension between technologies that are invisible and visible in use. Finally, the emerging interest in designing for fun in HCI can serve to frame a new perspective on designing for erotic life, and the conditions for exercising this in a playful way, rather than the prevalent medical approaches to problems in erotic life, as is highly prevalent in the western world. It is important, also, to realize that many issues related to sex and information technology are not necessarily part of HCI; e.g. various forms of abuse, or the diffusion of pornography through the Internet.

The starting point, for the erotic life-oriented HCI design approach we will suggest, is that we don't think that IT necessarily should have a role in peoples sexual life. Because, however, current technologies do have a negative effect in many cases these effects should be counterbalanced by deliberate design for erotic life. We should avoid solutions that make erotic life difficult, e.g. by extending workplace rationality into the home, and aim for solutions that provide enablers for erotic life activities, e.g. by providing privileged room for intimate communication. We also suggest that designing opportunities for playfulness, unforeseen fun and inventiveness in erotic life activities is important, as a way to help people maintain focus on their marital relation.

Methodically, HCI and interaction design for erotic life is a challenge. We are faced with new criteria that most established methods do not address, and because intimacy is intimate and private, it is by nature difficult for outsiders to observe. We expect that many established methods that address open design situations, like rapid prototyping with users and participant observation studies will be awkward to apply in this new field. Other approaches such as dairy based studies, and qualitative interviews are more promising, but should be adapted to the fact that most people consider sex and erotic life very private. Close collaboration with marriage counselors may also be a fruitful method in particular if combined with rapid cycles of design, use and redesign of IT-solutions.

These difficulties also impact the possible approaches to evaluation and validation. The criteria for success are hard to define, as a good erotic life most likely cannot be measured in terms of the frequencies of sexual intercourse in the couple, or other exact measures. For HCI to succeed in this new field collaboration with, and integration of knowledge from other disciplines is important. This may also be a challenge to those disciplines. E.g. medical sexology tends to rely exclusively on epidemiological approaches that are less suited for generating an understanding of the dynamics of intimate relations and the creation of erotic moments. Thus, design for erotic life, will probably provoke development in other disciplines.

For HCI in general erotic life is important in unfolding the experience oriented turn, in addressing the situation of use in a broader perspective, and in provoking the refinement of methods.

8. ACKNOWLEDGMENTS

We thank Sofie Beck participating in developing this perspective, and we thank colleagues and students who have helped mature this perspective through engaging and provoking discussions.

9. REFERENCES

[1] Baudelaire, C., (1857). *Les Fleurs du Mal.*

[2] Bertelsen O. W. (2006). Tertiary Artefactness at the interface, In Fishwick, P. (ed.) *Aesthetic Computing.* MIT-Press.

[3] Bertelsen, O. W. and S. Pold (2004). Criticism as an approach to interface aesthetics. *Proc. NordiCHI 2004.* Tampere, Finland, ACM Press.

[4] Bolter, J. D. and D. Gromala (2003). *Windows and mirrors: interaction design, digital art and the myth of transparency.* Cambridge, MA, MIT-Press.

[5] Breinbjerg, M. (2003). At lytte til verden - mellem hermeneutik og erotik (To listen to the world – between hermeneutics and eroticism). *Autograf - tidsskrift for ny musik,* Aarhus Unge Tonekunstnere.

[6] Brewer, J., Kaye, J., Williams, A., Wyche, S. (2006). Sexual interactions: why we should talk about sex in HCI. *CHI '06 Extended Abstracts* ACM Press, 1695-1698.

[7] Crabtree, A., Hemmings, T., and Rodden, T. (2002). Pattern-based support for interactive design in domestic settings. *Proc. DIS '02.* ACM Press.

[8] Dencik, L (2001) Living in Modern Times: Implications for the Lives of Children and their Families. Opening plenary lecture at the International Conference of the International Commission on Couple and Family Relations, Stockholm. http://www.baff.ruc.dk/Reports/pdf_reports/no4.pdf

[9] Ehn. P., Eriksson, B., Eriksson, M., Frenckner, K., and Sundblad, Y. (1984). *Utformning av Datorstödd Ombrytning för dagstidninger* (Development of Computer Supported Typesetting for Newspapers). Graphic Systems, Göteborg.

[10] Grönvall, E., Marti, P., Pollini, A., Rullo, A., Bertelsen, O. W. (2005). Palpable Time for Heterogeneous Care Communities. *Proc. Critical Computing, Aarhus 2005.* ACM Press.

[11] Hochschild, A.R. (1999). *The time trap - when work becomes home and home becomes work.* NY: Amacom.

[12] Iversen, O. S., Kanstrup, A., and Petersen M. G. (2004). On Emancipation, Quality & Democracy in Design. *Proc of NordiCHI 2004.*

[13] LeVay, S. & Valente, S. M. (2006). *Human Sexuality.* Sunderland MA: Sinauer Associates.

[14] McCarthy, J. and Wright, P. (2004). *Technology as Experience.* MIT Press.

[15] Mackay, J. (2000). Global Sex: Sexuality and sexual practices around the world. *5th Congress of the European Federation of Sexology, Berlin, 29 June - 2 July 2000.* http://www2.hu-berlin.de/sexology/GESUND/ARCHIV/PAP_MAC.HTM#S3

[16] Nagel, K. S., Hudson, J. M., and Abowd, G. D. 2004. Predictors of availability in home life context-mediated communication. *Proc. CSCW '04.* ACM Press, 497-506.

[17] Petersen, M. G. (2007). Squeeze: Designing for Playful Experiences among co-located People in Homes. *CHI2007 (work in progress).* ACM Press.

[18] Petersen, M. G. (2004). Remarkable Computing – the Challenge of Designing for the Home. *CHI '04 Extended Abstracts s,* ACM Press, pp. 1445-1448.

[19] Petersen, M.G., Iversen, O., Krogh, P., Ludvigsen, M. (2004). Aesthetic Interaction - A pragmatic aesthetics of interactive systems. *Proc DIS2004,* ACM Press.

[20] Politiken (Article in Danish Newspaper) 17.1.2006 "A TV in the Bedroom stops the lust".

[21] Shusterman, R. (2006). Aesthetic Experience: From Analysis to Eros. *J. of Aest. & Art Crit. 64:2,* Spring 2006.

[22] Udsen, L.E. and Jørgensen, A.H. (2005). The aesthetic turn: unravelling recent aesthetic approaches to human-computer interaction. *Digital Creativity,* 16 (4): 205-216.

[23] Ventegodt, S. (1998). Sex and the Quality of Life in Denmark *Archives of Sexual Behaviour, 27(3), pp 295-230.*

An Empirical Investigation into Dual-Task Trade-offs while Driving and Dialing

Duncan P. Brumby
Department of Computer Science
Drexel University
Philadelphia, PA 19140 USA

Brumby@cs.drexel.edu

Dario D. Salvucci
Department of Computer Science
Drexel University
Philadelphia, PA 19140 USA

Salvucci@cs.drexel.edu

Andrew Howes
Manchester Business School
University of Manchester
Manchester, M15 6PB UK

HowesA@Manchester.ac.uk

ABSTRACT

Engaging in a secondary task, such as dialing a cell phone, while driving a car has been found to have a deleterious effect on driver performance. A point often overlooked though is that people can potentially vary the extent to which these two tasks are interleaved (i.e., attention can be returned to driving more or less often while dialing). To investigate this idea of strategic variability in multitasking behavior, an experiment was conducted in a driving simulator in which participants were instructed to focus on dialing as quickly as possible or on steering as safely as possible. It was found that participants drove more safely when encouraged to do so. However, driving safely necessarily brought about an increase in the total time to complete the dialing task because of frequent task interleaving. In contrast, there was a significant increase in the lateral deviation of the car from the lane centre when participants were encouraged to complete the dialing task as quickly as possible. These results suggest that contrary to existing advice, the total time that the driver is distracted is less important to safety than the strategy used for interleaving secondary and primary tasks. In particular, there may be value in designing mobile devices that facilitate short bursts of interaction for in-car use because allowing drivers to make additional glances back to the road while actively working on a concurrent secondary task might help to elevate some of the effects of distracted driving.

Categories and Subject Descriptors

H.5.2 [**Information Interfaces and Presentation**] User Interfaces: Evaluation/methodology; K.4.1 [Computers and Society] Public Policy Issues: Human safety; H.1.2 [Models and Principles] User/Machine Systems: Human factors.

General Terms

Experimentation, Human Factors.

1. INTRODUCTION

Mobile computing devices are increasingly ubiquitous in society with technology-rich environments replete with "infotainment" systems for work and pleasure. In many of these environments, interaction with such systems occurs while the person is performing another task. One multitasking environment that has garnered a great deal of attention is that

occupied by the driver of a car. Many studies of driver distraction have painted a rich picture of how interaction with various secondary devices can impair performance (e.g., [11,13]), with by far the most attention given to distraction resulting from cellular phone use (e.g., [1,8,10]).

Because of the dangers of using a cell phone while driving, legislation has been introduced in many countries (including Australia, France, Germany, Japan, Russia, Singapore, and the UK; for a complete list see, [15]) banning drivers from using a handheld device while driving. Despite these legal deterrents, which often carry a substantial fine and other penalties, people continue to use their phones while driving. For instance, compliance with the UK ban has slipped from 90% from its introduction in 2003 to around 75% in 2007; that is, today there are some 10 million UK motorists who admit to using a phone while driving, even though this activity is against the law [14].

Given that it is difficult to make people stop engaging in secondary tasks while driving, there may be substantial value in developing a better understanding of how people multitask. For instance, this knowledge might be useful for providing guidance on how mobile devices might be better designed to make their use by the driver of a car less egregious. One proposed heuristic for secondary-task interaction states that it should be possible to complete a stand-alone task on an in-car device in less than 15 seconds [5]. This 15-second rule, which is set out in a draft Society of Automotive Engineers standard [12] for car manufacturers and designers of in-car devices, is based on the logic that the more time a driver spends on a secondary task, the higher the risk of adversely affecting driver performance. However, some researchers, most notably Tijerina et al. [13], have argued that the 15-second rule is a poor predictor of driver distraction effects across a variety of tasks.

Cognitive modeling has provided researchers another way to better understand multitasking behavior. While recent cognitive models have accounted for many performance measures of human driver behavior under single- and dual-task conditions [8,9,10], these efforts have not attempted to capture possible strategic variability in multitasking behavior. To capture such strategic variability, Brumby, Howes, and Saluvcci [2,3,4] have adopted a *cognitive constraint modeling* (CCM, [6]) approach. This CCM approach focuses on understanding the constraints on the interaction between the driver and the task environment, and allows for objective functions to represent desired trade-offs in relation to critical performance variables (e.g., tradeoffs between secondary-task time and driver performance).

In particular, Brumby, Howes, and Salvucci [2] consider the task of dialing a cell phone number while driving. In this task, a driver might dial all digits at once without returning attention to driving, or might dial digits singly, returning to driving after each digit. Between these two extremes exist a plethora of alternative ways to complete the task (i.e., whether to switch back to driving between each pair of key-presses). The model evaluated each strategy within this space of possible strategies making predictions for driver performance (lateral deviation) and total time to complete the dialing task. This analysis showed that while interleaving tasks more often might increase task time it should also lead to safer performance on the driving task because of the decrease in time between consecutive updates of steering control. Moreover, this analysis suggests that, contrary to the advice given above, the total time that the driver is distracted is less important to safety than the strategy used for completing a secondary task while driving.

Previous studies of driver distraction [1,8,10,11,13] have generally not attempted to understand possible strategic variability in human behavior while multitasking; therefore it is an open question whether people indeed exhibit the type of strategic variability in behavior explored by Brumby et al.'s [2,3,4] modeling analysis. In this paper we present an experiment that was designed to investigate dual-task trade-offs while dialing a cell phone and steering a car. In particular, the aim of the study was to test the idea that changing the task objective from focusing on dialing as quickly as possible to focusing on steering as safely as possible should have effects on relevant task performance measures.

2. METHOD

2.1 Participants
Participants were eight students (two female) at Drexel University, aged between 20- and 32-years ($M = 23$-years). All participants were experienced drivers who had held a valid US driving license for at least 2 years, and who owned and regularly used a car. All participants also owned and regularly used a cell phone. Participants were paid $10 for taking part in the experiment, which took approximately one hour.

2.2 Materials
2.2.1 Driving Task and Setup
The experiment was conducted in a fixed-base driving simulator at Drexel University. The simulator includes the front half of a Nissan 240sx with standard steering and pedal controls. These controls connect to a Macintosh desktop computer that runs the simulation and data collection software. The driving simulation was developed in The Open Racing Car Simulator (TORCS, available at http://torcs.sourceforge.net/) and was projected onto an 8-foot wide screen in front of the simulator vehicle, resulting in a roughly 48° field of view. The simulated driving environment used in the study was a simple highway-like environment, except that there were no other vehicles on the road. Drivers navigated the middle of a straight three-lane highway, where construction cones discouraged them from moving toward or into the outer two lanes.

The driving task required participants to control the steering of the car only; participants were not required to use the acceleration or brake pedals because the simulator maintained the car at a constant speed (described below). While this type of driving task is much simpler than a real-world driving environment, the motivation for focusing on steering control was two-fold. First, steering control directly affects lateral deviation, which serves as an important proxy for driving safety. Second, given normal speed control, drivers may slow down on their own accord while engaged in the dialing task. To control for this potential confound, we forced participants to drive at a particular speed so that the effect of driving speed on lateral deviation might be directly inferred.

2.2.2 Dialing Task and Setup
The dialing task used a Sony Ericsson Z710i phone. Hardware integration with the Macintosh desktop computer running the

simulation and data collection software was achieved through a wireless Bluetooth connection. Software from Salling (available at http://www.salling.com/Clicker/) was used to develop an application to display experimental prompts, enter digits on the phone's screen, and send log event information to the experimental software running on the Macintosh desktop.

For the dialing task, participants entered a 10-digit sequence of numbers, which followed the typical structure of a North American phone number (i.e., *XXX-XXX-XXXX*). This number entry task was preceded by a select key-press representing a "power-on" function and was followed by a second select key-press representing a "send" function, to initiate the call — giving 12 key-presses in total. All participants entered the same phone number throughout the experiment. The number was based on a local Drexel University phone number (*215-895-XXXX*) so would be somewhat familiar to participants prior to the experiment. In this way, the aim was to simulate the situation where people might enter a familiar and often dialed phone number while driving.

2.3 Experimental Design and Procedure
At the beginning of the experiment, participants were given an overview of the experiment, in which they were informed that they would be required to dial a cell phone while driving a simulated car. A demonstration was given by the experimenter on how to use the cell phone; in particular, it was expressed to the participant that the phone number had to be entered correctly in order to end a trial and that a backspace key on the device could be used to delete incorrect digit entries from the phone's display.

Participants were given a practice period (approx. 5 minutes), in which they familiarized themselves with the device and practiced entering the phone number. In order to minimize the possible impact of learning effects on dual-task performance, participants entered the same phone number throughout the familiarization period. The main part of the study began once participants were well practiced at entering the number sequence correctly on the cell phone.

2.3.1 Single-task conditions
For the dialing task, participants completed two blocks of five trials under single-task conditions. Participants were instructed to enter the phone number as quickly and accurately as possible. A trial started when the participant pressed the select key on the phone. A trial ended only when the participant again pressed the select key after correctly entering the phone number. At the end of each trial, participants received feedback showing the time taken to enter the number (in seconds). At the end of a block of five trials, the average dial time for that block of trials was presented to the participant.

If an incorrect key-press was made, participants had to delete the incorrect digit from the cell phone's display, and then re-enter the correct digit — only when the correct sequence of digits was entered would the phone number be accepted and the trial end. Moreover, feedback reflected the total time to complete the trial. In this way, participants were explicitly discouraged from making errors by designing the dialing task such that it had a built-in speed-accuracy trade-off — that is, making an error incurred a time cost in terms of deleting the incorrect key and re-entering the correct one. We found that this significantly reduced the number of errors made in dual-task conditions from those in an earlier pilot study, where participants were found to strategically make errors in order to terminate a trial where they lost control of the car while dialing. All error trials were later excluded from analysis (albeit unknown to the participant).

After the participant had completed two blocks of single-task dialing, they were introduced to the driving task. Participants were informed that the driving task did not require them to use the accelerator or brake pedal and that the car would travel at a consistent speed. They were told that the aim of the task was to drive the car as close to the centre of the centre lane as possible. Participants were given a practice session to familiarize themselves with steering the car within the roadway.

Following the practice session, the driving task was performed at both a slow driving speed where participants drove the car at a constant speed of 35 mph (~56 kph) and also a fast driving speed where participants drove the car at a constant speed of 55 mph (~87 kph). For each of the two driving speeds, participants completed two blocks of five trials. Participants were instructed to keep the car as close to lane centre as possible (minimizing lateral deviation) over a 10-second period of driving. At the end of each trial, participants received feedback information showing the root mean square error (RMSE) lateral deviation of the car from lane centre over the trial. Again, at the end of a block of five trials, the average lateral deviation for that block of trials was also presented. Finally, before the next trial could start, participants were notified by the experimental software to centre the car in the lane; the message persisted until the car was within +/- 0.20 meters from the lane centre, ensuring that the car was in a central location at the start of each trial.

2.3.2 Dual-task conditions
For dual-task conditions the structure of the dialing task and the driving task remained the same as that described above. The only difference was that once the car was close to lane centre, the participant started a dual-task trial by pressing the select key on the phone. The trial ended when the participant pressed the select key again after correctly entering the phone number.

The primary aim of the experiment was to determine the consequences of varying task objective and driving speed in dual-task condition for dial time and lateral deviation. The experiment followed a 2 x 2 x 4 (task objective x driving speed x trial block) completely within-subjects design. In order to manipulate the task objective, participants were given instructions to focus on either completing the dialing task as quickly as possible (minimizing dial time) or keeping the car as close to the centre of the lane as possible (minimizing lateral deviation). At the end of a given trial, participants received feedback aimed at emphasizing the focus performance variable (i.e., showing the dial time or lateral deviation achieved for that trial; note that feedback was not provided for the non-focus performance variable). In order that a participant adjusts to a particular task objective, conditions were blocked together, such that a participant completed a series of 40 dual-task trials where they focused on the dialing task and then completed a series of 40 dual-task trials where they focused on the steering task. The order in which each condition was completed was counterbalanced between participants, such that half of the participants in the study focused on minimizing dial time and then focused on minimized the cars lateral deviation, and vice-versa for the other half of participants.

The experiment also manipulated driving speed. This manipulation was again counter-balanced between participants, such that within each task objective condition, half of the participants completed the slow speed (35 mph) condition before the fast speed (55 mph) condition, and vice-versa for the other half of participants. Finally, participants completed four blocks of five trials of each of the dual-task experimental conditions described above. In total, participants completed 80 dual-task trials (5 trials x 4 blocks x 2 task objective x 2 speeds of car), where each condition was partially counter-balanced between participants.

3. RESULTS
Analysis focused on performance between the different dual-conditions. In particular, we were interested in the time taken to correctly dial the phone number and RMSE lateral deviation of the car from the centre of the lane. For statistical analysis a 2x2 (task objective x car speed) repeated-measures ANOVA was used. (Due to space limitations we do not present an analysis of differences in performance over each block of trials.) As a point of contrast, we also present dual-task performance in the context of single-task performance.

Relatively few trials were excluded from the analysis because of participant error on the dialing task. Recall that participants were discouraged from making an error on the dialing task because correcting it incurred additional time costs. From a total of 160 single-task dialing trials, only 4 (2.5%) were excluded because of error; from a total of 640 dual-task trials, 37 (5.78%) trials were excluded because of error. These low error rates suggest that participants were competent users of the cell phone and also learnt the number during the familiarization period prior to the study.

Figure 1 shows the time to enter the phone number in single-task and dual-task conditions under varying task objectives. It can be seen in the figure that participants adjusted their dual-task strategy dependent on the task objective – when participants focused on the dialing task, dial time in the dual-task condition was more or less equivalent to dial time in the single-task condition. Whereas, when participants focused on the steering task, dialing time was slower in the dual-task condition than in the single-task condition. In dual-task conditions, dialing time was significantly faster when the objective was to focus on the dialing task than when the objective was to focus on the steering task, $F(1,7)=25.83$, $p<.001$, $MSE=2.65$. Driving speed did not have a significant effect on dial time, $F(1,7)=3.33$, $p=.11$, $MSE=.80$, nor was there a significant interaction, $F(1,7)=2.66$, $p=.15$, $MSE=.44$.

Figure 2 shows the RMSE lateral deviation of the vehicle for single-task and dual-task conditions under varying task objectives and driving speeds. It is clear from the figure that driving speed had an effect on lateral deviation. In the single-task condition, lateral deviation from lane centre was less when the car was traveling at a slow speed than at a fast speed, $t(7)=5.41$, $p<.001$. There was a similar main effect of driving speed on lateral deviation in dual-task conditions, $F(1,7)=35.06$, $p<.001$, $MSE=.01$.

While it is clear from Figure 2 that participants adjusted their dual-task strategy based on the task objective, the most interesting aspect of the data is the clear interaction effect between task objective and driving speed on lateral deviation in dual-task conditions. In particular, when participants focused on the driving task, lateral deviation in the dual-task condition was more or less equivalent to that in the single-task condition. Whereas, when participants focused on the dialing task, lateral deviation was greater in the dual-task condition than in the single-task condition, but only at the faster driving speed.

Statistical analysis found a main effect of task objective on lateral deviation: Lateral deviation was greater when the objective was to focus on the dialing task compared to when it was to focus on the steering task, $F(1,7)=5.04$, $p=.06$, $MSE=.01$. But there was also a significant trend for the task objective x driving speed interaction effect, $F(1,7)=3.64$, $p=.09$, $MSE=.01$. Follow-up tests of the simple effects of task objective at each driving speed showed that when driving at a fast speed lateral deviation was greater when participants focused on the dialing task rather than the steering task, $F(1,7)=5.30$, $p=.05$. However, at a slow driving speed there was not a significant simple effect of task objective on lateral deviation, $F(1,7)=.002$, $p=.96$.

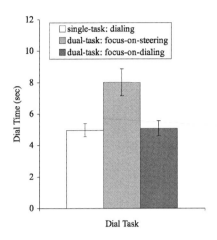

Figure 1: Time to enter the phone number in single-task and dual-task conditions under varying task objectives. Error bars represent 95% confidence intervals. (Dial-time is averaged over slow and fast driving speeds, because there was no effect of driving speed on dialing time.)

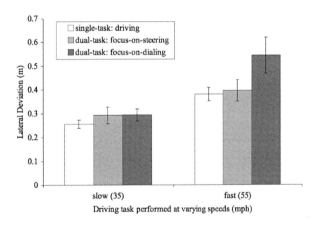

Figure 2: RMSE lateral deviation in single-task and dual-task conditions under varying task objectives and driving speeds. Error bars represent 95% confidence intervals.

4. DISCUSSION

We have presented preliminary results from an experiment that investigated dual-task trade-offs while driving and dialing. These results clearly demonstrate that under dual-task conditions people can adjust their strategy dependent on varying task objectives but that this necessarily has consequences for the other tasks performance. When participants were instructed to focus on minimizing dial time, they dialed the number as fast as when entering it while not driving. When participants were instructed to focus on minimizing the lateral deviation of the car from the lane centre, they steered the car just as well as when they were not distracted by the dialing task. These strategy shifts had consequences for the other variable in dual-task conditions: Dial-time increased when participants focused on steering, and lateral deviation increased when participants focused on dialing (though only when the car was being driven at a faster speed). These data support the idea of psychological bottlenecks that limit the degree of parallelism between performing multiple tasks while driving (see also, [7]).

Implications can be drawn from the results of the study presented here for the design of mobile devices that could be used by the driver of a car. Given that it is difficult to make people stop engaging in secondary tasks while driving, efforts might be directed towards understanding how to better design mobile devices to make their use by a driver less dangerous. While a common metric for determining secondary-task safety is the total time it takes to complete a task on the device [5,12], our results suggest instead that there is value in simply encouraging drivers to pay greater attention to how they are driving while performing a secondary task. The total time that the driver is distracted is less important than the extent to which the driver is encouraged to make quick glances back to the road while actively working on the secondary task. This suggests that designing mobile devices that facilitate short bursts of interaction as opposed to requiring long stretches of interaction help to alleviate the effects of distracted driving.

5. ACKNOWLEDGMENTS

This research was supported by National Science Foundation grant #IIS-0426674. We would like to thank Dan Markley and Mark Zuber for their exquisite hacking of the TORCS software and integration of the cell phone using Salling software. We also thank the four anonymous reviewers for providing comments for improving this paper.

6. REFERENCES

[1] Briem, V., & Hedman, L.R. (1995). Behavioral effects of mobile telephone use during simulated driving. *Ergonomics, 38,* 2536–2562.

[2] Brumby, D.P., Howes, A., & Salvucci, D.D. (2007). A cognitive constraint model of dual-task trade-offs in a highly dynamic driving task. In *Proceedings of the SIGCHI Conference on Human Factors in Computing Systems (CHI 2007)* (pp. 233-242). New York, NY: ACM Press.

[3] Brumby, D.P., Salvucci, D.D., & Howes, A. (2007). Dialing while driving? A bounded rational analysis of concurrent multi-task behavior. To appear in *Proceedings of the 8th International Conference on Cognitive Modeling.* Ann Arbor, MI.

[4] Brumby, D.P., Salvucci, D.D., Mankowski, W., & Howes, A. (2007). A cognitive constraint model of the effects of portable music-player use on driver performance. To appear in *Proceedings of the Human Factors and Ergonomics Society 51st Annual Meeting.* Santa Monica, CA: HFES.

[5] Green, P. (1999). The 15-Second Rule for Driver Information Systems. *ITS America Ninth Annual Meeting Conference Proceedings,* Washington, D.C.: ITS America.

[6] Howes, A., Vera, A., & Lewis, R.L. (2007). Bounding rational analysis: Constraints on asymptotic performance. In W.D. Gray (Ed.) *Integrated Models of Cognitive Systems* (pp. 403–413). New York, NY: Oxford University Press.

[7] Levy, J., Pashler, H., & Boer, E. (2006). Central interference in driving: Is there any stopping the psychological refractory period? *Psychological Science, 17,* 228-235.

[8] Salvucci, D.D. (2001). Predicting the effects of in-car interface use on driver performance: An integrated model approach. *International Journal of Human-Computer Studies, 55,* 85-107.

[9] Salvucci, D. D., & Gray, R. (2004). A two-point visual control model of steering. *Perception, 33,* 1233-1248.

[10] Salvucci, D.D., & Macuga, K.L. (2002). Predicting the effects of cellular-phone dialing on driver performance. *Cognitive Systems Research, 3,* 95-102.

[11] Salvucci, D.D., Markley, D., Zuber, M., & Brumby, D.P. (2007). iPod distraction: Effects of portable music-player use on driver performance. In *Proceedings of the SIGCHI Conference on Human Factors in Computing Systems (CHI 2007)* (pp. 243-250). New York, NY: ACM Press.

[12] Society of Automotive Engineers (1998). *SAE Standard for Navigation and Route Guidance Function Accessibility While Driving (SAE 2364),* Committee Draft of November 23, Warrendale, PA: Society of Automotive Engineers.

[13] Tijerina, L., Johnston, S., Parmer, E., & Winterbottom, M.D. (2000). *Driver distraction with route guidance systems* (Technical Report DOT HS 809-069). East Liberty, OH: NHTSA.

[14] "Careless talk", available at http://news.bbc.co.uk/2/hi/uk_news/magazine/6382077.stm

[15] "Countries that ban cell phones while driving", available at http://www.cellular-news.com/car_bans/

Habitats: A Simple Way to Bridge Artifacts, Professions, and Theories in Ubiquitous Design

Martin Brynskov

Center for Interactive Spaces, University of Aarhus
Aabogade 34, DK-8200 Aarhus N
Denmark
brynskov@daimi.au.dk

Gunnar Kramp

Aarhus School of Architecture
Noerreport 20, DK-8000 Aarhus C
Denmark
gunnar.kramp@aarch.dk

ABSTRACT

This paper briefly shows how product designers as well as information system designers may use the habitat framework as a tool to inform their understanding of the pervasive computing systems they are designing. This is done by (1) introducing the basic elements of habitats, (2) analyzing and comparing two empirical case-studies, one about life and death (emergency response at major incidents) and one about playfulness (children's pervasive play and gaming), and (3) discussing the usefulness of using habitats. The result is a number of real-world examples where we argue that using habitats as a simple common ground seems to be useful for professionals coming from quite different traditions.

Categories and Subject Descriptors

H.1.2 **[Models and Principles]**: User/Machine Systems – *human factors, human information processing*.

General Terms

Design, Human Factors, Theory.

Keywords

Design support, design principles, interdisciplinary work, pervasive healthcare, pervasive play and gaming

1. INTRODUCTION

Our interest in this paper is to demonstrate some shared characteristics between work and play involving wireless networked devices. The reason for doing so is partly because designing pervasive technologies is still a field that is poorly understood, partly because we want to explore theories and methods—preferably simple ones—that can be shared among very diverse professional backgrounds, in this case industrial design and computer science/human-computer interaction.

The motive for sharing our experiences using habitats grew out of frustration while working in multidisciplinary teams that lacked a shared set of concepts and vocabulary to set the stage for design discussions about ubiquitous systems. Wishing to move beyond ad hoc, emergent, team-specific idiosyncrasies, we retrospectively used habitats to reformulate two design cases, one about rescue work and one about pervasive playfulness.

2. HABITATS: THREE PERSPECTIVES

The notion of habitats originally comes from biology as a definition of the relationship between the population of a specific species and a specific environment. The basic idea is that a habitat supports its inhabitants.

Wireless networked technology is an expander of our natural habitat. Hot spots in cities for accessing the internet is an obvious example of a habitat which supports its inhabitants, and where the relationship between its users and the environment is inseparable.

The expanded environment has thus given the need for clarification resulting for example in discussions regarding space and place (cf. Harrison and Dourish [6]). However space and place discussions do not take into consideration the root of the discussion as it relates to the world as we understand it today; as a configuration of places in a surrounding space. This understanding is related to our everyday physical world where places can be located by coordinates and space can be configured in 3D coordinate systems. By discussing space and place we constrain ourselves to the physical world of space and time in physics. Accordingly, habitats provide a much richer approach to describing, analyzing, and designing for wireless technology and leaps over the dichotomy of space-place discussions and into the fundamental relationship between ourselves and the our environment.

Our inspirational source is work done by May and Kristensen [9] where they introduce the notion of "Habitats for the Digitally Pervasive World". May and Kristensen conceive habitats as something that specifies some kind of locality, they comprise inhabitants and they provide support to their inhabitants. They identify three types of habitats: the physical, the informational, and the conceptual habitat. Others have developed the habitat concept further into a more consistent framework to support analysis and design of ubicomp systems [3, 1]. The fundamental feature of the habitat framework is that it offers three perspectives on a habitat in which activities take place. While the previous literature on (digital) habitats has been confusing the 'habitat' as a whole with the three perspectives, we refer to habitats only to denote the compound concept (except when quoting others).

- A *habitat* is a chunk of space-time that is designed or has evolved to support a delimited set of activities by offering physical artifacts and information sources useful for conducting the activities.

From this definition, it follows that a habitat should be characterized along three dimensions. These three dimensions of a habitat are called perspectives or parts:

- The *physical* perspective: the physical boundaries and qualities of the habitat including artifacts.

- The *informational* perspective: the signs (digital and non-digital) available to participants (access and reference area).

- The *pragmatic* perspective: the action affordances offered by the habitat and the role-requirements.

Habitats are structured around activities. Activities consist of actions subsumed under a shared goal, and participants play roles in relation to actions and activities.

2.1 Physical Perspective

The physical aspect is what Gibson [5] defines as medium, substances, and surfaces. While Gibson's description is very concrete, another—and in our view more helpful—definition is: the part of the habitat where the activities of the inhabitants take place, i.e. the physical perspective. Physical parts of a habitat can thus be, e.g., a car, a farmers field, an office, and physical parts can be nested in each other. For example an office can be nested in a building, a building can be nested in at town and so forth, providing physical scale.

2.2 Informational Perspective

A hotspot in a city is part of a habitat. The range of the wireless network may define the extent of the habitat. However, while the technology defines the extent of the habitat, there is also a qualitative aspect, namely the information which is conveyed in the habitat. May and Kristensen give an example of an email system as an "informational habitat." But while May and Kristensen see the email system as a habitat in itself, we follow the definition above and see the hotspot through different perspectives. Thus the hotspot may been seen both from the physical perspective and the informational perspective.

In the informational perspective, Brynskov and Andersen [3] distinguishes between the *access* area and the *reference* area. The access area is the area where the inhabitants have access to the information, while the reference area is the object of the information. The access area and the reference area are connected through a medium. For example, the hotspot area is the access area and the internet is the reference area which is connected through a medium such as a laptop.

2.3 Pragmatic Perspective

Brynskov and Andersen [3] have a slightly different approach than May and Kristensen as they instead of "conceptual habitats" use the notion of "pragmatic habitats," which are characterized by being a "shared mental space" which sets the boundaries for the inhabitants behavior. In practice this means that there are habitats where skills, knowledge, obligations and rights of the inhabitants are defined implicitly or explicitly, and which are necessary to possess or comply with in order to be a inhabitant in the habitat. Brynskov and Andersen argue that the pragmatic perspective cannot be separated from intentions and expectations, thus resulting in what they call *potential* activity and *realized* activity. It follows that the pragmatic perspective can consist of potential activities defined as roles, while the realized activity is the potential activity realized by a person or digital agent, thus becoming the filler of the role. This relation between potential and realized activity becomes important, as can be seen in the later examples, because the informational perspective often will facilitate either a remote filler of a realized activity and/or facilitate that several users can join efforts to fill one role.

3. A COMMON STAGE

In the following we present two simple uses of the habitat framework in creating a foundation for staging the activities taking place in the world of wireless networked technology. While others have developed the framework in more depth and detail, we only apply it to our design cases to see what can be gained from thinking in terms of habitats. The link between the two cases is only that they are faced with somewhat similar

problems as a consequence of designing ubicomp systems.

Activities involving wireless networked technologies often increase complexity due to multiple actors, physical and digital constraints, and the distributed use of artifacts. An activity taking place in one situation can have a profound impact on another situation in another setting. This complexity is furthermore worsened by the number of professions and theories involved in the design process.

The habitat framework presented here is not to be interpreted as a complete formula for making successful design solutions in the complex domain of ubiquitous computing. It should rather be understood as a model for distilling the activities taking place at different levels, in order to provide simplicity for design, while still retaining important distinctions that often characterize ubiquitous computing systems. As a consequence, habitats need to be complemented by other methods and disciplines as we shall see. The framework merely offers a common stage to be populated by a range of artifacts, professions, and theories.

3.1 Habitat Analyses of Two Case Examples

We provide a brief analysis of illustrative examples from two cases: (A) a prototype of the "biomonitor" [7] which is used at major incident sites to provide vital information about wounded victims, and (B) a prototype of a pervasive game called DARE! [4], in which children can use mobile phones and pervasive technologies to compose and send challenges to each other, e.g. to take a picture of something. These experiences with habitat analyses of the biomonitor and the game are described from the perspectives of an industrial designer and an HCI person respectively.

A habitat can be defined as a place which supports the activities of its inhabitants, and the inhabitants relationship to the habitat can be defined as one or several roles. When a major incident occurs, e.g. a railroad accident or an earthquake, the place where it happens is not a habitat for the victims. On the contrary, it is significant that the reason for the accident will be because something in the environment has not supported the activity taking place. For example that a railway does not support two trains running towards the same point on one track.

What needs to be done for the rescue personnel at the arrival is to try to force the incident site into a state where the habitat supports the rescue activities taking place. This transformation is not trivial. The physical environment is non-predictable, the different communities of practice seldom work together under these conditions, and the people in charge may never have met in person before. Furthermore, communication between personnel, coordination of resources etc. is complex and, finally, it all takes places with an overhanging time pressure. There seems to be a general acceptance of the term "the golden hour" [8], which implies that chances of recovering from a serious trauma are significantly better if the patient is treated within an hour from the time of the accident.

Similarly, when a group of children engaged in the DARE! game move between locations, the interaction potential changes. DARE! is a simple social activity that consists of three phases: composition, performance, and evaluation of a dare. The motive behind this kind of playfulness is to provide a pervasive platform which supports humor, friendly conflict, and identity construction. In some places the children have time and opportunity to challenge each other and to take interesting pictures, while in other situations it is less desirable or possible.

A way of trying to get an overview of people, artifacts, and communication technologies is to utilize the notion of habitats. We have in the example below (Figure 1) classified the organi-

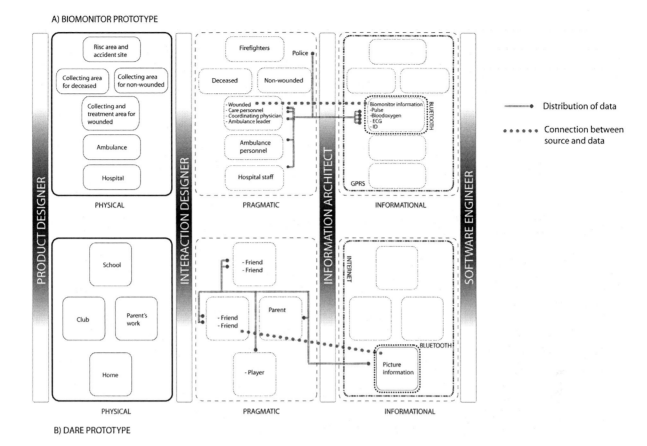

Figure 1. Habitat analyses of two cases: (A) the biomonitor prototype and (B) the DARE! game prototype.

zation of both the major incident case and the pervasive play case in the three perspectives: the physical, the informational, and the pragmatic perspective in order to provide an overview of the use of biomonitors on an incident site and of a simple picture dare. The four vertical bars, illustrate the "positioning" of product design, interaction design, information architecture, and software engineering in relation to the three perspectives. Evidently, these positions are in reality much more intertwined and complex, but we use the illustration to show how the three perspectives on the habitat can encompass the involved professions.

3.1.1 Physical perspective

If we compare the play scenario to the emergency response, we see a similarity in the fact that none of designers (general rescue operations procedure planners and dare composers) know exactly what situation their designed activity will play out in. In fact, they can count on the unexpected to play a major role. The difference is, however, that the emergency response activity has a much clearer procedure that ties the rules and roles to physical space. The participants also know that everyone (at least the professionals) will do their best to adhere to the plan. Dares, on the other hand, involve a constant element of surprise and competition. There are dares that are classics, but overall, even they are just a few stable elements in an ever-changing chain of exchanges. On a general level, dares may or may not be tied to designated parts of physical space.

The consequences of this on design is that both systems should support adaptation to the physical surroundings. But there are differences. The emergence response system should pay close attention to the ideal that is laid out in the detailed procedures in order that safety and accountability is given first priority. The

game, on the other hand, should highlight opportunities for fun and social exchange. The first part of a habitat analysis highlights the physical properties of the habitat and show how people, artifacts, and places are related to each other. The actual appearance may be naturalistic, e.g. projected onto a real map, or abstract, focusing only on relationships and accessibility. The two examples in Figure 1 are abstract. In the case of the biomonitor, they show how the different zones of the incident site are separated, and in the play scenario they show the different places that kids visit throughout a regular school day.

3.1.2 Informational perspective

The informational aspects of the dare activities consist of the digital information in the system as well as of whatever information that may be left in the physical environment. Such non-digital or analog information includes physical markers of tags, bystanders informing or helping the performer, and simple signs, e.g. "Camera phones not allowed". Simply the fact the we force ourselves to consider how information that is not modeled in the system at all may play a role in the activities is important. It opens up the space for thinking creatively both at system design time and subsequently at dare design time.

An analysis of the informational habitat also visualizes the relationships between where information is actually accessible (the access areas, e.g. a screen or a tag) and what it refers to (the reference area, e.g. a person or a place). By mapping these areas we get a sense of where what is available. Again this may lead to a larger, more relevant decision space at both system design time and dare design time, potentially making way for better solutions.

The system should support reconfigurations of informational parts of habitats by allowing the participants to change and combine access and reference areas. By modeling this relationship in a habitat, the designers can explore and analyze issues that are problematic and need special attention or discover opportunities to provide flexible activity support.

In DARE!, one such situation may occur if the recipient of a challenge sees an opportunity to fulfill the requirements by enrolling proxies, e.g. a friend that is present somewhere close to an object that must be found or photographed. This could also be described as "realizing an activity by combining inhabitants to fill a role."

The other example shows what information that is made available by the biomonitor within the area for collecting and treating the wounded. It also shows in which other areas this information might potentially be useful, e.g. if a doctor is not physically present at the site but sits back in the hospital.

Again there are similarities and differences between the two cases. Both the emergency response work and DARE! will benefit from providing explicit support for altering the informational habitat in order to establish a situation that is desirable for some reason (e.g. using audio and video feeds to facilitate the joint effort of ambulance personnel and a hospital physician in a case where they cannot be physically co-located). The differences are mostly concerning of reliability and quality of service, but if a particular workaround is the only solution in a critical situation, it should certainly not be disregarded.

3.1.3 Pragmatic Perspective
The pragmatic aspects of habitats are characterized by the roles that are given and created. One interesting feature by looking at the play scenario is that it does not necessarily matter whether a role is played by a human being or an agent, e.g. a robot or a piece of software. One can easily imagine challenges where the clever recipient can enroll non-human agents in his or her efforts to meet the goal of the challenge.

This is not all that different from the emergency response situation, except emergency response is a mission-critical activity. People may die, if something goes wrong and a wrong decision is made. As a consequence, only roles that are more or less trivial may be filled by an autonomous agent—unless, maybe, that using an agent is the only way out. Then the desperate situation may warrant the user's enrollment of an autonomous agent. Such levels of control are well-known from the transport sector, e.g. airplanes and ships that change between fully automated, semi-automatic, and manual maneuvering [2].

Describing and mapping the pragmatic perspective of a habitat may very well draw on thick descriptions that are distilled into simpler models of the social configurations. These may be related to the physical perspective, as mentioned earlier. But they may also be considered in connection to the informational perspective. Figure 1 shows the pragmatic aspects of the two habitats as the distribution of roles in the physical space. This example does not distinguish between potential and realized activities.

4. CONCLUSION
In this paper, we have turned the attention towards the notion of habitats not only as a physical environment supporting its inhabitants, but also as an environment consisting of informational and pragmatic aspects. All three perspectives are related to our perceived world and the human scale centered around our activities. However, the existence of and relationships between the perspectives are not well recognized in current theories and methods as we still lack sufficient transparency across the domains of physical and digital design theories and methods to

include this in our solutions as users and designers. Nevertheless, we have used the notion of habitats as a foundation for framing activities in wireless networked environments in general and our two use cases specifically.

While initially frustrated, we have found the framework helpful in analyzing our work with pervasive and palpable computing. The set of concepts seem simple enough to be shared easily. The examples that we have highlighted above especially showed how it can be used to expose emergent use situations during design. However, habitats do not remove the need for more specific models, theories, and professional skills. Furthermore, although we have both worked separately on different projects, and one participant has never used the framework before, this is only a weak validation of the efficacy of using habitats. Just because our frustration was eased there is no guarantee that others will perceive habitats as helpful in ubiquitous design work.

It is our conclusion that even though the framework can be very simple, or maybe because of this, the subdivision of habitats into three perspectives—physical, informational, and pragmatic—can provide a helpful foundation for framing the stage of ubiquitous, pervasive, and palpable computing across disciplines. It is also our conclusion that more work is needed to mature the framework towards sustaining the balance of simplicity and power of expression as complexity of the design domain increases.

5. ACKNOWLEDGMENTS
We wish to thank our colleagues who worked with us on the two projects. We would also like to thank the anonymous reviewers for helpful comments. This work was supported by the Center for Interactive Spaces at the University of Aarhus (ISIS Katrinebjerg project #122) and the Palpable Computing EU project, PalCom (IST 002057).

6. REFERENCES
[1] Andersen, P.B. and Brynskov, M. The semiotics of smart appliances and pervasive computing. In: Gudwin, R. and Queiroz, J. (eds.) *Semiotics and Intelligent Systems Development*, Idea Group, Hershey, NJ, 2006, 211-255.

[2] Bødker, S. and Andersen, P.B. Complex Mediation. *Human-Computer Interaction*, 20 (4), 2005, 353-402.

[3] Brynskov, M. and Andersen, P.B. Habitats, Activities, and Signs. In *Proc. of Organisational Semiotics 2004*, INSTICC Press, 128-151.

[4] Brynskov, M. and Ludvigsen, M. Mock Games: A New Genre of Pervasive Play. In *Proc. of DIS 2006*, ACM Press.

[5] Gibson, J.J. *The Ecological Approach to Visual Perception*. Houghton Mifflin, Boston, 1979.

[6] Harrison, S. and Dourish, P. Re-place-ing space: The roles of space and place in collaborative systems. In *Proc. of CSCW 1996*, ACM Press, 67-76.

[7] Kramp, G., Kristensen, M., and Pedersen, J.F. Physical and digital design of the BlueBio biomonitoring system prototype, to be used in emergency medical response. In *Proc. of Pervasive Healthcare 2006*.

[8] Lerner, E.B. and Moscati, R.M. The Golden Hour: Scientific Fact or Medical "Urban Legend"? *Academic Emergency Medicine*, 8 (7), 2001, 758-760.

[9] May, D. and Kristensen, B.B. Habitats for the Digitally Pervasive World. In: Andersen, P.B. and Qvortrup, L. (eds.) *Virtual Applications: Applications with Virtual Inhabited 3D Worlds*, Springer, London, 2004.

Lessons Learned Implementing an Educational System in Second Life

Richard Stephen Clavering

Computing Department
Lancaster University
InfoLab21, LA1 4WA

richard@clavering.me.uk

Andrew Robert Nicols

Computing Department
Lancaster University
InfoLab21, LA1 4WA
+44 7751 204885

andrew@nicols.co.uk

ABSTRACT

Second Life is an online 3D virtual environment that offers interesting potential for use in education due to its widespread availability, flexibility, and its use of standard platforms and input devices. Given a broad design brief for a nine-week masters' student project of using Second Life for education, we explored a range of potential ways of using the environment, and designed and implemented a 3D turtle-graphics system. In this paper we present our findings together with a reflection on both the constraints that Second Life places on the range of educational uses worth pursuing, and the specific issues likely to be faced by researchers creating other such systems.

Categories and Subject Descriptors

K.3.0 [**Computer and Education**]: Computer Uses in Education – *computer assisted learning (CAI)*

H.5.1 [**Information Interfaces and Presentation**]: Multimedia Information Systems – *artificial, augmented and virtual realities*

General Terms

Design, Human Factors.

Keywords

Second Life, Virtual Learning Environment, Education, Collaborative Virtual Environments, Virtual Reality, Teaching.

1. INTRODUCTION

Second Life has gained both considerable popularity and widespread attention in the media. Of particular interest within academia are its potential education uses, which we investigated in a nine-week project as part of our Masters in HCI. Rather than exploring social uses within education [1], or uses for groups with special needs such as those with learning difficulties [3], we looked at using it for learning and supporting teaching with a broader audience. We first explored the breadth of the design space by producing a range of conceptual designs, and then developed one of them – a 3D version of a turtle-graphics system (see section 4) – into a

working prototype. While the turtle-graphics prototype is not particularly novel, the experience allows us to offer researchers interested in using Second Life insight in three main areas: a detailed view of what Second Life is and is not, and how it differs from other virtual environments (see section 2); the types of design that are likely to be feasible (section 3); and design constraints that only became apparent during implementation, which we think are generally applicable but can be ameliorated (section 5). Section 6 presents our conclusions: that Second Life can be an effective platform for rapid prototyping of 3D interfaces despite its flaws, but that the limitations imposed by the system will make it hard to go from a prototype to a high-quality finished product.

2. SECOND LIFE

Second Life is an online three-dimensional virtual world, accessed via a custom software client available on multiple platforms, and with over seven million registered user accounts world-wide (though fewer regular users). Unlike online role-playing games, to which it is often compared, there are no set objectives, and the world is controlled to a much greater degree by the users. At a high level, the rules of the world are fixed: the Havok Physics Engine[1] provides detailed and fairly realistic physics simulation within the world, including enforcing aspects of real-world physics that need not apply to a virtual world, for instance buildings in Second Life cannot be larger inside than outside. However, the range of buildings, vehicles, avatars and objects users see are created primarily by the users themselves. There is an in-world currency, the Linden Dollar, which is convertible at no cost to and from US dollars. Linden Dollars can be used to buy areas of land in the virtual world, on which they can create their own environments (called "sims"). Buildings and other objects can either be bought from other users, or constructed from scratch at no cost other than the time spent. Users retain all intellectual property rights for objects they create: when selling them to other users they may individually control whether the buyer will be able to resell, edit, or create copies of the object.

The wide range of complex objects seen in Second Life are created by users linking together varying numbers of "prims" – basic (primitive) 3D shapes such as cubes, spheres, and prisms, which can be freely resized and rotated, and the appearance set to either a colour or texture image. The "material" a prim is made of can also be chosen from a pre-set list (including steel, wood, etc.) and this influences how the Havok physics engine treats the prim, as do a number of special properties for such things as a prim not being subject to gravity, being intangible, and whether the item is temporary (and therefore automatically

---

[1] http://www.havok.com – Last retrieved 23rd May 2007

deleted soon after creation). Prims can be grouped together to make more complex shapes and have a number of objects and scripts added to their contents. Scripts are written in Linden Scripting Language (LSL), which is described by its creators as a cross between Java and C. LSL can be used to control objects, transfer currency between users, buy and sell objects, and to manage a range of other in-world activities. A number of features are built into the language to limit the potential load on servers, thereby enabling a fast and usable system for all users.

Avatars are used to represent the user in Second Life and many aspects of their appearance are highly configurable. Whilst the environment and avatar are both 3D objects within the Second Life World, some aspects of the user interface use conventional 2D dialogue windows overlaid on the 3D view. These include dialogues for performing activities such as localised chat, instant messaging, and search, and to display additional information such as the users' inventory and in world maps. Whereas objects can be built in the 3D world, it is not possible to modify the 2D elements of the interface or create new such elements. Input to both the 2D and 3D parts of the interface is via a standard keyboard and mouse, rather than specialised devices such as data gloves often found in virtual reality systems.

3. EXPLORING SECOND LIFE FOR EDUCATIONAL PURPOSES

Since Second Life became available to the public in 2003, it has found a growing popularity within the education sector. While many treat it as a game, it has encountered increased support from both educators and students who use it for a wide range of reasons, from running courses and classes in the environment to running research-based studies.

To improve the availability of Second Life for education, Linden Lab have provided a scheme named "Campus: Second Life", which allows college-level students in semester-long periods to borrow special areas of the environment for class-work and research. A second separate grid to be used solely by teenagers and schools, named "Teen Second Life" has been created. It attempts to provide a safer environment where strict regulation is enforced by Linden Lab employees. Educators are also invited to run classes and experiments within the Campus environment and, as of spring 2006, nineteen such events were running within the campus[2].

One of the most popular uses of Second Life in conjunction with education is as a social networking tool, enabling users to interact with one another and improve group dynamics, particularly within long-distance courses [1].

The ideas we considered were smaller in scope, due to the limited time available to us. They included a range of activities such as educational games and puzzles; models to explain scientific theories or engineering principles; and educational tools such as collaborative mind-mapping systems. Many of these are difficult to implement effectively because of unchangeable aspects of the Second Life environment, as explained below. For those ideas which were feasible, we often found that there was no obvious benefit in using Second Life rather than creating a tool in the physical world or using a 2D computer interface. A prime example of this were the educational games, and using Second Life for some of the

activities presently supported by virtual learning environments, such as distributing class notes and information, providing further sources of information and testing of students abilities. Similarly, we discarded the idea of a Second Life equivalent of a university open-day, in which potential students could explore a replica of the university campus, interact with staff and students, and find information about courses: course information is already readily available and more easily readable on the web. Interaction with other people, perhaps the most valuable part of such events, is much less rich in Second Life due to the restriction to text-based communication, and the lack of expressiveness of users' avatars. Additionally, requirements of virtual campuses have already been researched extensively [2].

We hoped to use Second Life's built-in Havok physics engine to implement educational tools, specifically simulations of real-world physics principles, reminiscent of the exhibits often found in science museums and similar to high-school science experiments. Examples might include electromagnetism, Newton's laws of motion, and conservation of momentum. While we believe that these would be worthwhile uses of the environment, and would give more feedback of the processes in action, the physics modelled by the Havok engine cannot be changed (e.g. by altering how collisions work, or the relative effects of gravity), even within private land owned by a user, and cannot be relied upon to be realistic enough for teaching science. Although the physics engine can be manipulated to have individual objects not subject to certain rules (such as gravity, or collision), there is no way to effect more detailed changes such as running in slow-motion.

While it might be possible to implement the physics for a simulation using LSL, there remain other issues restricting the usefulness of Second Life for such purposes. The inability to alter the available views of objects (e.g. to produce a cross-sectional diagram of an object) further restrict the environment for these uses, as does the difficulty of providing an interface to control the simulation: the 2D parts of the Second Life interface are not significantly extensible and lack the potential for either manipulation or customisation. Further, providing controls as Second Life objects would make for awkward interaction requiring the user to keep manipulating their field of view (or even moving their avatar) to get access to the controls as they moved it around the simulation.

A further idea we considered was to make use of the collaborative and graphical elements built in to Second Life by developing a multi-user mind-mapping tool. This tool was designed to enable users to share their ideas in a different, more creative manner. Although technically possible, we concluded that it could not be completed within the project time.

In the next section we present the idea we ultimately selected to develop: a 3D turtle-graphics system (shown in figure 1), selected for its proven educational value and the feasibility of its implementation.

4. THE TURTLE-GRAPHICS SYSTEM

Turtle-graphics is a simple model for drawing, using a metaphor of a turtle dragging its tail in the sand and thereby forming a line-art picture. The turtle is restricted to moving forward, turning, and raising or lowering its tail to fit with the metaphor; the commands to do so are usually issued using the Logo programming language. This combination has long been used in schools to teach children about computers and procedural thought (through procedural programming). Our idea was to implement a turtle-graphics system within Second

---

[2] http://forums.secondlife.com/showthread.php?t=88521 – Last retrieved 24th May 2007

**Figure 1. The turtle drawing in three dimensions with
the chat window / interactive shell shown.**

Life, and extending it to allow movement in all three dimensions (further breaking the metaphor, which was already stretched by the transition from physical turtle-shaped robots to on-screen turtles bearing little resemblance to their namesake). As well as the obvious benefits of being able to teach 3D graphics and geometry, and improving spatial thinking generally, we expected that using a 3D environment would make for a more challenging and engaging experience – hopefully improving the students' knowledge and skill retention. While time constraints prevented us from carrying out a thorough evaluation, the informal procedure we used did tend to support this.

The design and implementation of the turtle were largely conflated due to our lack of time and of detailed understanding of the capabilities of the platform. As implemented, the system consists of a platform/plane object which the turtle draw on in 2D (and is needed as an origin for the coordinate system which the turtle moves relative to). The turtle is represented as a simple half-cone, which is the simplest possible way of fully indicating the orientation (a full turtle model could be substituted given more time). Pictures are composed of a series of cylindrical objects left behind the turtle, analogous to the lines found in a 2D system. Code is necessarily distributed across all three classes of object.

To control the turtle we envisaged the classic combination of an interactive console for immediate control, and a separate method for writing and saving more complex procedures (such as a full code editor). The latter proved impossible to implement (as explained in the next section), but we were able to implement a limited console. The commands expected from 2D turtle graphics were used, including those for calling and defining procedures. Additionally we provided an undo command, and two additional rotation commands to allow

movement in the third dimension. Due to time limits, we did not provide a full expression language and mathematical operations (due to the increased complexity of parsing input).

We had hoped to experiment with features to further the 3D geometry teaching goals, such as showing axes for the different coordinate spaces introduced each time the turtle turned, and being able to have the system display angles between arbitrary line segments, but limited time prevented this.

5. CHALLENGES IN DESIGNING THE TURTLE

In designing and implementing the turtle we met several classes of problem that would be relevant to other researchers. The most significant of these, which are explained in greater detail below, are: the lack of overall documentation of the system, and the corresponding need to implement while still learning about the system; the lack of extensibility of the 2D elements of the Second Life interface; problems caused by the mechanisms for limiting resource usage; and the mixed benefits of built-in features such as animation.

As when designing for any new platform, it was difficult to develop a detailed initial design for the turtle prior to starting coding, due to our limited knowledge of the platform's capabilities and limitations. However this was more marked than when (e.g.) switching between different toolkits for 2D desktop applications, since there is no standard set of widgets for 3D interfaces. Instead one must experiment with Second Life's graphical tools for creating prims, and read the documentation for LSL. The documentation lacks any overview of what kinds of actions are possible, instead simply providing descriptions of individual library functions and some language concepts such as the first-class events, and the resource-limiting systems. LSL is a wholly procedural rather than object-oriented language – prims can communicate only through limited-length string messages (not via method calls). This results in a standard library that mixes expected basic functions such as those for array manipulation, and advanced functions for particle effects and for directing the physics engine. Overall, this leads to a style of development where the initial design is very abstract, with the details being decided only as implementation proceeds.

Being unable to extend the overlaid 2D elements of the Second Life interface proved to be the most significant problem in implementing our turtle, since entering Logo commands (either interactively or for defining procedures) is naturally suited to a 2D interface. Alternatives such as displaying the text on an in-world screen or board object would force the user to keep adjusting the camera or moving their avatar to switch between viewing their code and viewing the turtle. However, we found we could instead *repurpose* existing 2D overlays for our needs, and believe this could be a generally useful technique. In the case of the turtle this consisted of reusing the in-world chat system as a console for commanding the turtle: the turtle listens for all chat messages from nearby avatars, and attempt to parse them as Logo commands. The built-in chat history window in Second Life then functions as the command history of the interactive shell in a conventional turtle graphics implementations.

Repurposing interface elements in this way produces less than ideal results. As an example, providing good feedback for errors in Logo commands issued via the chat system is difficult because other users of Second Life my also be chatting near the turtle without intending to control it. We had to choose between issuing error messages for any message that wasn't a valid Logo command (including other users' conversations), which clutters the chat history, or silently ignoring errors, making it difficult for novice users to understand their mistakes. We briefly tried requiring all commands to be prefixed with "turtle" to distinguish them, but found to be too tedious for non-trivial use.

We also hoped to repurpose the existing script-editing window in Second Life for writing longer procedures or programs to control the turtle. It initially appeared that this should be feasible, at the acceptable cost of forcing users to use LSL syntax rather than Logo, but with the benefit of syntax colouring and free syntax error messages. However, running turtle scripts produced this way proved impossible, since LSL lacks any way of either evaluating code stored in a string, or executing a script by dragging it onto an object such as the turtle.

Resource-usage limits imposed by LSL, while admittedly necessary to prevent malicious or poorly-written scripts from interfering with all others on the same server, also cause considerable difficulties. Firstly, each script has a strict limit on the amount of memory it can use, and exceeding this usually results in stack–heap collision errors. This resulted in the "undo" command for our turtle having to retain only a very short history of commands. Considerable problems were also caused by built-in delays in certain library functions, including a few hundred milliseconds for each object instantiated, moved, resized or rotated. Delays also make coordination between different objects difficult (due to using message passing rather than blocking function calls), requiring manual delays to be inserted to keep the turtle's movements synchronised with the

creation of line-segments. In addition to delays, there is a second resource limitation mechanism called "energy", which accumulates over time and is used by some function calls. This appears only to be important for large objects (relative to avatar's sizes) that are "physical" (i.e. affected by gravity, and other rules of the Havok engine), and so was not relevant in our turtle system, and likely would not be in other educational tools.

The delay in built-in functions also allows Second Life to incorporate animation into movements and rotations: as objects are moved or resized using LSL, they are smoothly animated across the display. Whilst reducing the amount of work for a programmer, this introduces the possibility for additional confusion to the user. As an example, if the user would like to turn the turtle right by 270 degrees, Second Life will control the animation and instead turn it left by 90 degrees, potentially confusing users as to the current orientation of the turtle.

6. CONCLUSIONS
Overall, while Second Life does provides a rapid development environment for educational tools like our turtle, the constraints of the system such as the lack of extensibility of the 2D parts of the interface make the final designs of such tools suboptimal. Many of the built-in features such as animation and a detailed physics engine are a mixed blessing, since they cannot be controlled in detail, and some cannot be avoided. However, as Second Life continues to evolve this situation may improve.

The range of truly worthwhile educational applications of Second Life remains an open question. The efficacy of social uses of Second Life is hard to assess, which led us to instead explore uses involving small numbers of users, and largely ignoring the presence of an avatar. Many of the obvious ideas in this area such as explanatory interactive 3D models of Newton's laws of motion are difficult to implement well because of the lack of control of how objects are viewed, and how the physics engine operates, which we do not expect to change. Additionally, the use of keyboard and mouse interaction, while making the system more widely available, does exclude uses where tactile feedback is important.

7. ACKNOWLEDGMENTS
Our thanks to Nick Day and Can Zhao who were also members of the team designing the turtle, and to Corina Sas for her role as course director.

8. REFERENCES
[1] Childress, M., and Braswell, R. Using Massively Multiplayer Online Role-Playing Games for online learning. *Distance Education, 27,* 2 (Aug. 2006), 187-196.

[2] Prasolova-Førland, E. Analyzing place metaphors in different educational CVEs: Lessons learned. In *Proceedings of the IADIS International Conference on Cognition and Exploratory Learning in Digital Age (CELDA '05)* (Porto, Portugal, December 14-16 2005). IADIS Press, 2005, 325-332.

[3] Vera, L., Herrera, G., and Vived, E. Virtual reality school for children with learning difficulties. In *Proceedings of the 2005 ACM SIGCHI International Conference on Advances in computer entertainment technology (ACE '05)* (Valencia, Spain June 15-17). ACM Press, New York, NY, USA, 2005, 338–341.

Learning Beans: Design, Implementation & Evaluation

Fintan Culwin
CISE
London South Bank University
London SE1 0AA, UK
+44 (0)20 7815 7434

fintan@lsbu.ac.uk

ABSTRACT

This paper describes the use of statechart notation to design the pattern of behavior that a user will have when interacting with a learning bean. The larger context of a learning bean and the stakeholders that are involved in its deployment and use are also introduced, two beans are briefly described and the results of a user trial presented.

Categories and Subject Descriptors

D.2.2 [Software Engineering]: Design Tools and Techniques *modules and interfaces, object-oriented design methods, State-diagrams, user interface, human factors.*

General Terms

Algorithms, Design, Human Factors, Standardisation.

Keywords

learning objects, learning beans, learning activity management systems (lams), learning frameworks, usability.

1. INTRODUCTION

Learning objects have many conflicting definitions [1]. One consistent element of the definitions is that they have low granularity and so are focused upon one simple learning outcome. This is in accord with software objects whose intention was that object re-use would allow applications to be assembled like Lego bricks. This turned out not to be the case for the first generation of software objects [2] and has also not been the case for learning objects. Reuse is particularly important for educational resources as they can be very expensive to produce and tend not to be used outside the immediate environment they were developed in.

Second generation software objects, such as Java beans [3] promised greater potential reusability by defining a generic behavioral framework into which application specific objects could be placed. Learning beans [4] are an attempt to transfer this concept to the domain of learning objects. The learning bean behavioral framework provides a large range of patterns of possible learner interaction into which content specific learning objects can be plugged and specific patterns of interaction defined. This is comparable to Learning Activity

Management Systems (LAMS) [5] which, at a much higher level of granularity, separate the activities involved in learning from the content of what is learned.

The behavioral framework implemented in a learning bean is pedagogically promiscuous. That is; they are not wedded to any particular theory of how people learn, rather they are capable of being configured to implement a variety of particular behaviors within the framework.

The usability of the beans is central to their successful deployment and with such a low granularity they would have to have near walk-up capability. That is a learner should be able to interact with the bean efficiently and effectively with little or no instruction. In order to assure this requirement at the design stage the behavioral framework was designed using statechart notation [6]. Once this design had been completed and verified, the software interface between the framework and the content objects could be finalised.

The wider context of the bean's usability was also considered and three stakeholders were identified. The learner would need walk-up usability with a deployed bean. The learning interaction designer would be responsible for configuring and deploying the bean within a learning context. The learning object developer would need to design a separate, highly interactive, content bean which, by means of the software interface, could be plugged into the framework to produce a completed learning bean.

2. THE FRAMEWORK DESIGN

A slightly simplified design of the learning bean behavioral framework is presented using state transition diagram notation in Figure 1. A state transition diagram consists of states, shown in round edged boxes, and transitions, shown as labeled arrows connecting two states. The label is in two parts shown above and below a line, either of which may be omitted. The label above the line is an event which must occur for the transition to be considered. An empty event label means that the transition will be continually considered. The label below the line is the pre-condition which must be true for the transition to be followed. An empty pre-condition label is always true.

The initial state is shown as a solid circle, from which in this design there are two possibilities. If the bean is in *timed* mode it enters the *Timed Start* mode where the learner can use a *start* control to enter the *Content Bean* state. This is also the initial state when the bean is in the simpler *challenge* mode.

In the *Content Bean* state the learner will interact with the embedded interface until they are ready to *try* their solution to the challenge. When the user *tries* the outcome can be correct or incorrect, leading to either the *Solution Incorrect* or *Solution Correct* state respectively. From the *Solution Incorrect* state there are four possible transitions, the user can *try again*,

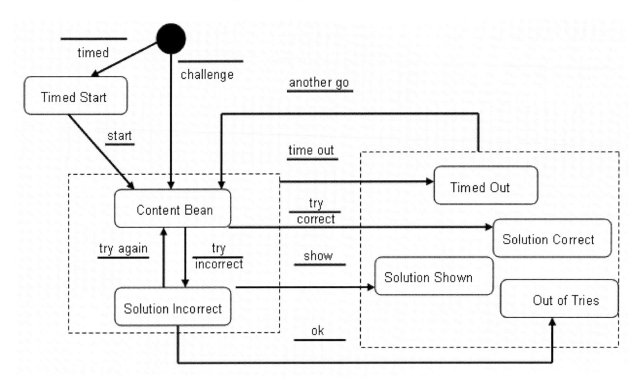

Figure 1 Behavioural Framework STD

if allowed, re-entering the *Content Bean* state. Alternatively the user can ask to *show* the solution, if allowed, and enter the *Solution Shown* state. If the learner has run out of tries and is not allowed to see a solution then they will be informed of this, and they can transit to the *Out of Tries* state by acknowledging the message with the *ok* control. The fourth transition can also be followed from the *Content Bean* state, as shown by the dashed superstate. This is the *time out* transition which can only occur if the interface is in timed mode and which leads to the *Timed Out* state. From the four possible states that lead from this superstate, the learner can request *another go* at a different challenge, if allowed, entering the *Content Bean* state again.

The textual description of the design given above is implicit in the notation. A design commentary would clarify the possible paths that could be followed through this behavioural framework. For example, a learning designer might decide that the learner could have an unlimited amount of time, but is only allowed one attempt and is never shown a solution. This would define a simple path through the diagram as *Content Bean* followed by either *Solution Correct*, or *Solution Incorrect* leading to *Out of Tries*.

A more complex possibility might be that the learner is allowed at most four tries to solve the challenge, with a five minute time out and a solution may be shown after two tries have been made. A detailed textual description of the possible paths through the framework could be made, but it should be obvious that this, and many other possible, behaviors could be afforded by the design.

The design implicitly shows all the behaviors that are possible. The relative simplicity of the design with only two superstates one with a *try/ try again* pattern of behaviour and one with four possible challenge terminations suggests that it will have the required walk-up usability. Moreover the design can be used during development and testing to ensure that the framework does have the correct patterns built into it.

A particular instance of the bean will have a content bean plugged into it and be configured for a particular pattern of behavior by an instructional designer. A utility that allows the instructional designer to accomplish this will be described below after two sample learning objects are shown.

3. TWO SAMPLE CONTENT BEANS
3.1 The Imperative Programming Bean
Figure 2 shows the imperative programming content bean in the *Solution Incorrect* state configured with a time constraint, a limit the number of tries and allowing a solution to be shown.

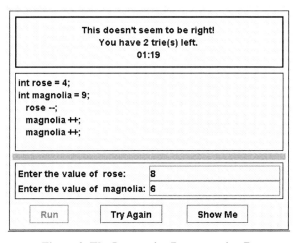

Figure 2. The Imperative Programming Bean

The imperative programming bean is concerned with affording the learner the opportunity to explore the manipulation of primitive integer variables in a C style programming language. The learner is invited to examine the code shown and predict the values of the variables after the code has executed; typing the values into the fields at the bottom of the content bean's interface. Each time the bean is re-presented a different challenge will be given in order to assure that deep, rather than shallow, learning occurs.

Although not strictly a required characteristic of a content learning bean this, and other objects produced as proofs of the concept, support progressive disclosure. The content bean shown in Figure 2 is intended for learners who are beginning to explore imperative concepts. It is restricted to two variables, small positive integer values, three lines of code and uses only of the post-increment and post-decrement operators. The instructional designer can progressively permit more cognitive complexity by increasing the number of variables, the range of values, the number of lines of code and the operators allowed. Programming beans concerned with selection and iteration have also been developed.

3.2 The Piano Music Bean

Figure 3 shows the piano music content bean in the *Content Bean* state configured with no time constraint and to not allow a solution to be shown.

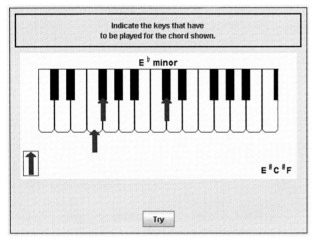

Figure 3. The Piano Music Bean

The user is required to drag and drop arrows, pointing to which keys they think have to be played for the chord specified. As with the imperative bean this bean supports progressive disclosure, allowing for ranges of complexity of chords. It can also be operated 'in reverse' where the learner has to name, using pull-down menus, a chord which is displayed.

In both of these beans, the area at the top where instruction is given and the area at the bottom where the buttons are shown are provided by the bean framework. The area in the middle is the context specific learning bean and it is the interactions in this area which comprise the *Content Bean* state on the state transition diagram. A learning object developer can, by using a defined software interface, produce a content bean for any topic provided only that it can generate challenges and decide if the learner has successfully completed the challenge set.

4. THE CONFIGURATION UTILITY

The instructional designer is responsible for preparing an instance of the bean and hosting it within a particular learning context. There are two parts to the configuration, configuration of the learning bean framework and of the content bean. The configuration utility for the bean framework is illustrated in Figure 4.

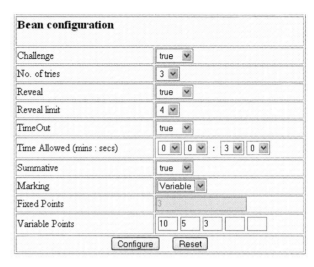

Figure 4. Learning bean framework configuration

Using this utility the instructional designer is able to specify the number of tries, if an answer is to be revealed, if so when the answer is revealed, if the bean is timed and if so how long is allowed. It is also possible to set the bean into non-challenge, explorative mode, and to prepare it for use in summative assessments. These latter two aspects are omitted from the design presented in section 2 for reasons of space.

Each content bean requires a specific configuration utility which can be presented to the instructional designer along with the framework utility. The configuration utility for the imperative bean is presented in Figure 5. This utility allows the complexity of the learner's task to be specified, with the range of operations chosen from the pull-down menu as shown.

Imperative Bean configuration	
Negative Values	false
Number of Variables	2
Number of Lines	3
Maximum Declaration Value	10
Maximum Mult/Div Value	5
Maximum Modulo Value	11
Capability	POST ONLY

Bean configuration
Challenge
No. of tries
Reveal
Reveal limit

POST ONLY
POST-PRE
ADD-SUB
ADD-SUB-SELF
ALL-BUT
ALL-MODULO
DIV-MOD
ALL-BUT-SELF
ALL-MOD-SELF
EVERYTHING

Figure 5. Imperative Bean Configuration Utility

When the instructional designer has configured both the framework and the content components of the bean, an instance of the configured bean can be launched in a separate window. This allows the instructional designer to interact with the bean as if they were the learner, in order to confirm that the configuration is as they intended. The window that contains the bean instance also contains the HTML APPLET tag together with the list of parameters that define the bean and its configuration. The instructional designer can copy and paste this tag into the location within the learning environment where it is needed. As the bean is written 100% in Java and the APPLET tag is part of the HTML standard this should assure wide deployability for the bean. The beans were also developed using java's internationalisation capability to further enhance their deployability.

5. LEARNER TRIAL

It is difficult if not impossible to differentiate the usability aspects of the framework from those of the embedded content bean in end-learner trials. Accordingly the beans were evaluated in their entirety, including both the framework and the content parts. Moreover the context for the use of these beans is pedagogic and the proof of their utility might be in the measured ability and, perhaps more importantly, confidence of the learner.

The learners involved in one trial were 17 second year undergraduate computing students who might be expected to be able and confident about their skills in the fundamental programming concepts of sequence, selection and iteration. However many studies [7] have indicated that this is rarely the case.

Table 1. End-learner trial of the programming beans

	pre test		post test	
	ability	confidence	ability	confidence
sequence	0.45	2.25	0.95	4.35
selection	0.4	3.15	0.8	4.25
iteration	0.2	1.95	0.65	3.85

The procedure consisted of a paper pre-test and post-test assessing the ability of the students to answer questions related to the concepts, scored 0, 1 or 2. This was accompanied by a five point Likart scale measuring their confidence in their ability to answer such questions. Following the pre-test each of the three beans was briefly demonstrated using a data projector.

The learners were then allowed 30 minutes to use six bean instances, two each of sequence, selection and iteration with one conceptually simple and one more complex. All beans were configured to allow an unlimited number of untimed attempts with no solution available. The students were reminded every ten minutes and asked to move onto the next pair of beans.

The intention had been that the investigator would log each request for help from the students which related to either unknown bugs or the usability of the beans, as distinct from conceptual issues relating to programming. In the event there were no requests for assistance of any kind from the students during the session and the inference was that the beans had satisfied the requirement for near walk-up usability.

The results of the trial are shown in Table 1. The ability measures are out of 2, with 2 being perfect performance. The confidence measures are out of 5, with 5 being highly confident. For all programming concepts both an improvement in ability and an improvement in confidence was demonstrated. This latter outcome is possibly more significant as confidence is a pre-requisite for effective learning [8].

This was a small scale limited duration study conducted in the institution and by the team who developed the beans. There is every possibility of a Hawthorne effect. However other in-house trials have demonstrated similar results and the beans are being widely used in several institutions attracting favourable comment from the tutors involved.

6. ACKNOWLEDGMENTS

The development of the beans was co-funded by London South Bank University and the Higher Education Academy subject centre for Information and Computer Sciences. The development of the beans was done by Gus Moratario under the direction of Fintan Culwin. This paper has a 8% and 12% overlap with two previous papers on learning beans [4,9] which can be attributed to a common technical vocabulary. The beans are available free of charge for non-commercial use at http://cise.lsbu.ac.uk/poples.

7. CONCLUSIONS

This paper has illustrated how a highly interactive behavioral framework can be designed by use of state transition notation and subsequently implemented. Two content beans were presented, provided proof of concept evidence that the separation of the generic pedagogic behavior from the learning topic specific behavior can be effected. In the wider context the beans are configured and deployed by an instructional designer and a configuration utility to assist in this was also described. Trials of the beans with learners indicated that the beans had accomplished their design requirement of walk-up usability and providing an effective and engaging learning environment.

8. REFERENCES

[1] McGreal R, *Learning Objects: A Practical Definition, an attempt to bring some sense to the definition of a LO.* International Journal of Instructional Technology & Distance Learning, 2004.

[2] Gabriel, Richard P., *Objects have failed. Notes for the OOPSLA 2002 panel discussion.* (Available at http://www.dreamsongs.com/NewFiles/ObjectsHaveFailed.pfd Accessed 25 June 2007), 2002.

[3] Sun, *Enterprise Java Bean White Paper.* (Available at http://java.sun.com/products/javabeans/docs/spec.html Accessed 25 June 2007), undated.

[4] Culwin F. *Beyond learning objects: Towards learning beans.* In R. Atkinson, C. McBeath et al (Eds), Beyond the comfort zone: Proceedings of the 21st ASCILITE Conference, 2004.

[5] Dalziel J *Implementing Learning Design: The Learning Activity Management System (LAMS).* In G.Crisp, et al (Eds), Interact, Integrate, Impact: Proceedings of the 20th ASCILITE Conference Adelaide, 2003.

[6] Culwin F. *The statechart design of a novel date input mechanism.* Italics V3 No 1 Jan 2004. Available at http://www.ics.heacademy.ac.uk/italics (Accessed 25 June 2007), 2004.

[7] McCracken M. et. al, *A multi-national, multi-institutional study of assessment of programming skills of first year CS students.* ACM SIGCSE Bulletin Vol 33 Issue 4, 2001.

[8] Norman, M. and Hyland, L., *The Role of Confidence in Lifelong Learning.* Educational Studies, Vol 29, No 2/3, 2003.

[9] Moratorio G & Culwin F *Three Programming Beans,* Proc. 7th Annual HEA/ICS Conference Dublin, 2006.

Designing for Appropriation

Alan Dix
Computing Department, InfoLab21
Lancaster University, Lancaster, LA1 4WA, UK
+44 1524 510 319

alan@hcibook.com
http://www.hcibook.com/alan/papers/HCI2007-appropriation/

ABSTRACT

Ethnographies often show that users appropriate and adapt technology in ways never envisaged by the designers, or even deliberately subverting the designers' intentions. As design can never be complete, such appropriation is regarded as an important and positive phenomenon. However designing for appropriation is often seen as an oxymoron; it appears impossible to design for the unexpected. In this paper we present some guidelines for appropriation based on our own experience and published literature and demonstrate their use in two case studies. You may not be able to design for the unexpected, but you can design to allow the unexpected.

Categories and Subject Descriptors

H.5.5 [Information Interfaces and Presentation]: HCI

General Terms

Design, Human Factors.

Keywords

appropriation, hackability, tailorability, guidelines.

1. INTRODUCTION

Appropriation is a common theme in ethnographies of new technology use and is often seen as an important sign of users' acceptance of technology. However, while much has been written about the *importance* of appropriation, it is far harder to find practical advice on how to *design* for appropriation.

Certainly reading accounts of appropriation can sensitize a designer to the issue, as do more theoretical works emphasizing the ecological fit of technology and the importance of technology being embedded into users' real work practices. However, even in Dourish's "Where the action is", probably one of the most well known texts in the area, the advice on '"Moving towards Design" is, quite reasonably, broad [9].

This paper was born out of the need to capture some of this knowledge more explicitly, particularly for my own students of HCI and because I was faced with writing about the issue for

the next edition of a textbook [6]. So I wanted a form, which whilst still open, gives directed design guidance. Being more specific is of course dangerous as one can be more wrong! So, these design guidelines are not presented to foreclose debate, but to present an incomplete but I hope useful practical contribution and also a departure point for ongoing discussion.

The next section will present a short description of appropriation for readers for whom it is not a familiar topic and also discuss the reasons why it is important, followed by a brief overview of some literature in the area. A set of design principles is then proposed drawn from the literature and my own experience. These are then illustrated by micro case studies showing how they have been applied in real designs.

2. ABOUT APPROPRIATION
2.1 What is Appropriation?

In ethnographies and field studies a frequent observation is that people do not 'play to the rules': they adapt and adopt the technology around them in ways the designers never envisaged. Think to your own experience: perhaps you have used a screwdriver to open a paint tin, or heavy textbook to prop open a door … or tried to open a bottle of wine without a corkscrew.

Improvisation is critical to 'getting things done'. Sometimes we have exactly the right tool to hand, but often the particular circumstances are not totally foreseen and we need to work with what we have to hand.

We see the same process of appropriation with digital technologies. Email is intended as a way to communicate with remote colleagues, but some people email themselves web links whilst browsing instead of using a bookmark, 'communicating' with themselves; others use email attachments as a way to share files with a colleague on the next desk.

These improvisations and adaptations around technology are not a sign of failure, things the designer forgot, but show that the technology has been domesticated, that the users understand and are comfortable enough with the technology to use it in their own ways. At this point we know the technology has become the users' own not simply what the designer gave to them. This is *appropriation*.

Appropriation may occur where there is no existing tool for the task, for example, the users mailing themselves a web link because bookmarks and email folders are distinct and they want to organise them together. It may also occur where there is an alternative method, but the appropriation is easier either at the moment or because of learning time, for example, using email for sharing files instead of configuring shared network folders.

2.2 Advantages of Appropriation

Appropriation is important for several reasons:

situatedness – The end point of design has been described in terms of *intervention* [6], not just an artefact or even the artefact and its immediate ways of interaction with it, but the way in which it changes the environment in which it is set. While each word processor may be the same, each office, home or laptop on a train is a different environment. We cannot expect to be able to understand each environment fully and to meet every possible task or need.

dynamics – Environments and needs change. Suppose we designed specifically for a particular work group in a particular office, and covered all eventualities for them. A month later, a year later, new people would have joined the group, the external business environment may have changed their focus, there may be additional software or furniture that changes the digital and physical workspace. Design for use must be design for change.

ownership – With appropriation comes a sense of ownership. This may simply be a feeling of control, users feeling they are doing things their own way. It may also be explicit: often people proudly show you the ways they use software and technology to achieve their purposes. These positive feelings can be as important as the things that are achieved.

Sometimes appropriation can be a form of *subversion*, deliberately using something in a way it was not intended, not just because of something the designer didn't think about, but in order to thwart its intentions. For example, in the days before mobile phones were ubiquitous, people often avoided paying the charge on a public payphone by saying something like: "when I'm ready to be picked up I'll ring twice on the phone and then hang up". Whether this is an advantage or disadvantage of appropriation depends on who you are!

This form of subversion is often seen in work contexts: a salesman might deliberately create a 'phantom order' and later withdraw it in order to ensure there is stock available for a loyal customer [1]. In this kind of setting the subversion is against the formal rules in the system, but may be working towards the same ultimate goal of making the best sales for the company.

2.3 Related Work

As noted, appropriation is a common theme in ethnographies of the workplace and the home. In their study of mobile phone use by teenagers, Carroll et al. proposed a framework, the *Technology Appropriation Cycle,* for understanding the *process* of technology appropriation [2]. They distinguish technology-as-designed (as provided by the designer) and technology-in-use (as embedded into the lives of users). These are then linked through a process of appropriation whereby technology is either never seriously considered (non-appropriation) or taken on board selected and adapted by users (appropriation), but even if appropriated may at some stage be rejected (dis-appropriation). Focus on process is also evident in other writings, for example several papers at the CHI2005 workshop on community appropriation [13].

In a DIS2004 keynote Tom Moran suggested several "trends supporting design": open standards, web architecture, portalization, freeform technologies [14]. These are focused more on the ability of end-users to hack or modify systems and are based on a long tradition of user-tailorable systems such as the Xerox Buttons interface [12]. His keynote prefigured the explosion in Web2.0 mashups, which have themselves triggered a fresh focus on 'hackable' systems [11].

3. GUIDELINES FOR APPROPRIATION

The idea of designing for appropriation almost seems like an oxymoron: "plan for the unexpected". However, whilst you cannot design for the unexpected, you can design so that people are more likely to be able to use what you produce for the unexpected – they do the final 'design' when the need arises.

The fact that design for appropriation is possible is made most clear by realising that some sorts of design make appropriation difficulty or impossible. Consider an espresso machine. It is so special purpose it is hard to imagine any alternative use. (Although human ingenuity is such that I expect a rush of emails telling me about alternative uses for espresso machines!) This also shows that design for appropriation is not always what is desired, the espresso machine does one thing very well indeed – why do any more with it.

However, explicit design guidance to allow appropriation is less clear. Here are some principles, but they should be taken as ways to encourage reflection, not a tick list to verify.

allow interpretation – Don't make everything in the system or product have a fixed meaning, but include elements where users can add their own meanings. For example, in MacOS you can associate colours with file, but there is no fixed meaning to a red file (maybe urgent, or problem) – it is the user who provides the interpretation. Similarly, in MacOS folders and Windows desktop you can position file icons freely. *Because* location does not mean anything to the system, the user is free to group files; perhaps have one corner of a folder window means "finished with". Similarly in a database system, a simple free text comment field allows users to add details the designer never considered, just like writing comments on a paper form.

provide visibility – Make the functioning of the system obvious to the users so that they can know the likely effects of actions and so make the system do what they would like. This is particularly important when the effects of actions are distant or at different time, for example in a collaborative application. Often systems, particularly networks, try to cover up or hide the underlying 'details'. This is fine so long as it is totally and permanently hidden, but often the details leak out (e.g., at the limits of wireless coverage). Users find their way round these problems if they are made clear (signal level bars on a mobile phone allow you to find better signal). The notion of 'seamful' design [3] deliberately exposes these 'seams' in coverage and connectivity in order to create games and applications. Note the common usability heuristic 'visibility of system status' usually refers to the *relevant* state; whereas it is often the *irrelevant* state and *internal process* that can be appropriated.

expose intentions – While appropriation can be very powerful, we have also seen that it can be used to subvert systems. Rather than trying to prevent such subversion the designer can deliberately aim to expose the intention behind the system. This means that (cooperative) users can choose appropriations that may subvert the rules of the system and yet still preserve the intent. For example, if logging into a system is a slow process, then one member of a work group may login once at the beginning of the day and then everyone else use the logged-in system. If the purpose of the login is security, then this may be fine so long as the machine is never left unattended, however if the purpose is to adapt the system to individual users then this appropriation would be inappropriate. Exposing the intentions behind a system can be a frightening thing – you cannot hide behind "well that's the way it works". However, doing this can make the assumptions explicit and if they are wrong then they need to be re-examined. In the login example, if the purpose is personalisation would it be possible to allow a single secure login but have a facility to quickly swap between users.

support not control – As a designer you want to do things right, to make them as efficient and optimal as possible. However, if you optimise for one task you typically make others more difficult. In some situations, such as very repetitive tasks, then designing explicitly for the task may be the correct thing to do, perhaps taking the user step by step through the activities. However, more often the tasks description is incomplete and approximate, in particular ignoring exceptions. Instead of designing a system *to do* the task you can instead design a system so that the task *can be done*. That is you provide the necessary functions so that the user can achieve the task, but not drive the user through the steps. Dourish describes this as "informal assemblage of steps rather than rote procedure driven by the system" [9]. Of course you still want the common tasks done efficiently and so you may provide fast paths, or wizards to perform frequent activities using the basic tools and operations … remembering of course visibility, making sure the user understands what is being done.

plugability and configuration – Related closely to the idea of support is to create systems where the parts can be plugged together in different ways by the user. Quoting from Dourish again "Users, not designers manage coupling" [9]. This is most obvious in programmable or scriptable systems and there is considerable work in making these more accessible to the user. This ability to plug-and-play components becomes a critical issue in ubiquitous computing and Newman et al. discuss the idea of recombinant computing [15] were systems are created bottom-up from small end-user combinable components. In more a traditional interface MacOS Automator allows the user to chain together small actions from different applications, so that, for example, you can create a workflow that takes a collection of images, sepia tints them, and then mails them all to a group of people from your address book. Similarly Yahoo! Pipes (pipes.yahoo.com) allow users to create and share mashups of RSS feeds and search results.

encourage sharing – People are proud of their appropriations of technology, so let them tell others about it! If one user learns a good trick for using an application or device, then this may be useful to others as well. Documentation can be enhanced by end-user contributed material; many web sites offer tips and advice on different software, and this can be designed as an integral part of a system, perhaps a 'tips' button that allows users to annotate functions with their favourite tricks. This could function across institutions making use of the communities of practice to which the user belongs. This sharing is even more important in the case of programmable systems. Even if the configuration or scripting is designed to be 'easy' it will still be only a small subset of users who actively script. However, if you make it easy for more confident or more technically adroit users to share with others then your product grows all on its own. The success of Xerox Buttons was an early example of this [12]. More recently, the MacOS Dashboard has this shareable quality, as does the Firefox architecture. Both allow the creation of plugins using a combination of small XML and HTML files and Javascript; importantly both have web sites dedicated to sharing these. As an online application, the Yahoo! Pipes interface not only allows sharing of complete pipes, but also makes it easy to see the graphical 'code' of pipes and hence copy and adapt them.

learn from appropriation – After a while one old, but broad bladed screwdriver becomes 'the' paint-tin opener. What was once a temporary use of a tool has become specialised. This crystalising of appropriation leads to a new tool and the entrepreneur might spot this, notice the particular kinds of screwdriver that made good paint-tin openers and then design a special purpose tool just for the job. By observing the ways in which technology has been appropriated, we may then redesign the technology to better support the newly discovered uses. This is a form of co-design where the users are considered an integral part of the design process. This closing of the *Technology Appropriation Cycle* has been called *design from appropriation* [2]. Of course any redesign should also take into account potential further appropriation. This learning from appropriation is particularly easy in some web applications (e.g. blogging or photosharing sites) where the results of users appropriation of the application are easily visible to the designers.

A common feature to these principles is openness, making things that allow themselves to be used in unexpected ways, echoing in some ways the idea in literature of an 'open' or 'writerly' text [4]. It is also to some extent about humility, knowing that you do not understand completely what will happen in real use, no matter how good your user-centred design process has been.

4. IN PRACTICE
We will now look at two micro case studies of how these principles work in practice. The first is a post hoc analysis of learning from appropriation and the latter an example of deliberate design for appropriation.

4.1 OnCue – Learn from Appropriation
OnCue is a desktop tool available during the dot.com years [5]. It appeared as a small floating tool palette and when the user copied or cut any text onCue examined it using primitive 'intelligence' to decide what kind of thing was in the clipboard and offered various web and desktop services that could use this kind of data; for example, a name might trigger a phone lookup.

An early and enthusiastic adopter was interviewed about his use of onCue. During the discussion it turned out that sometimes he had a name, postcode, or something that he wanted to use onCue to lookup, but it was not in a document to copy. So he opened an empty document in a text editor, typed into it and then copied the text. Only at that point did onCue fire up and offer suggestions. It was interesting that he did not consider this laborious process a major 'problem' partly because onCue was giving him sufficient value and partly, because (as noted earlier) he was rather proud of his workaround.

At the risk of hurting his pride (!) a redesign was suggested and in the second release of onCue clicking the onCue icon would open up a small search-engine-like type-in box beneath the onCue tool palette. We should note that this use of onCue had been entirely unforeseen by the designers (although in retrospect it seems obvious), and the redesign was entirely due to following the principle of '*learn from appropriation*'.

4.2 eCommerce Design for Appropriation
The second mini case study concerns a small eCommerce web site, although for commercial confidentiality some of the details have been altered. The system gathered online orders, but if the

order included books, where stock levels varied, payment was delayed until the book administrator could verify that all the books were in stock and only then charge the customer's card.

A few months after initial deployment the book administrator asked whether it was possible to make a modification to the administration system. When an order was not completed for some reason she wished to be able to indicate the reason explicitly, rather than leave it simply uncompleted. This was partly for her benefit, and partly to flag up such transactions for the finance staff. She suggested a simple 'incomplete' flag.

The requirement was straightforward; however, following the '*support not control*' principle it was decided not to create an interface feature that directly addressed the expressed need. Instead a more generic status flag with a number of different icons was added: stars, question mark, etc. In addition a notes field was added. Following the principle '*allow interpretation*' we did not prescribe a particular use of either of these, but left it to users to make their own use of the elements (see Fig 1.).

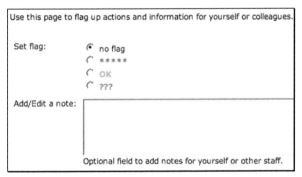

Figure 1. Fields for user interpretation

At first these were used only for the initial purpose, but over time we saw the use change. In particular, in early use, orders that were incomplete due to an out-of-stock book were simply labeled generically "book out of stock", whereas later these were marked with a different icon from other orders and the name of the book put in the notes field, acting as a sort of 'to do' showing which books needed reordering – the user had appropriated the system in a way that would have been impossible with a more task-focused, but closed design. Due to staff turn-over we were unable to discuss this, but is clear that the design was successful in allowing appropriation..

5. DISCUSSION

Arguably the design features suggested by the appropriation principles seem trivial. In fact, this is often the case, designs that are closed are often more apparently sophisticated, because they may do more for the user, but ultimately do not allow the users to do more for themselves. Good design for appropriation in practice however is clearly *not* trivial given the lack of suitable features in many systems and the results of innumerable ethnographies, hence the importance of *explicit* advice as well as case studies and vignettes.

It is evident from the case studies that design for appropriation (a) is possible, (b) can work and (c) is not so complex as it may appear. Clearly all systems have boundaries, but we can design them so that the space of possibilities for design by users in the context of use is expanded. In some situations, (e.g. safety critical systems) it is important for users to operate systems exactly as designed, hence the importance of '**expose intentions**' as users will inevitable bypass controls (as in Chernobyl) if they do not understand why they are there.

The guidelines are not new in that most can be found in some form embedded in the literature, for example, variants of the first two can be found (albeit buried somewhat) in [7]. However, I believe this is the first attempt to systematically extract this knowledge and to present it in an applicable form.

Validating design principles is hard as simple post-hoc evaluation is methodologically unsound [10]. However, a more thorough theoretical framework or model of appropriation would be valuable to both validate these principles and suggest future directions of study.

6. REFERENCES

[1] Ainger, A. and Maher, R. The 'Salesman's' Promise (CSCW in Sales). Chapter 5 in *Remote cooperation: CSCW issues for mobile and tele-workers.* A. Dix and R. Beale (eds.), Springer Verlag. 1996.

[2] Carroll, Jennie., Howard, S., Vetere, F., Peck, J. and Murphy, J. Identity, power and fragmentation in cyberspace: technology appropriation by young people. In *Proc. of Australian Conf. on Information Systems*, 2001.

[3] Chalmers, M. and Galani, A. Seamful Interweaving: Heterogeneity in the Theory and Design of Interactive Systems. In *Proc. DIS 2004*, ACM Press, 2004, 243-252.

[4] Cuddon, J. *The Penguin Dictionary of Literary Terms and Literary Theory*, 4th ed. Penguin, 1998.

[5] Dix, A., Beale, R. and Wood, A. Architectures to make simple visualisations using simple systems. In *Proc. AVI2000*, ACM Press, 2001, 51-60.

[6] Dix, A, Finlay, J., Abowd, G., and Beale, R. Chapter 5. Interaction design basics. *Human-Computer Interaction, 3rd ed..* Prentice Hall, 2004.

[7] Dourish, P. The appropriation of interactive technologies: some lessons from placeless documents. *Computer Supported Cooperative Work* 12, 4 (Sep. 2003), 465-490

[8] Dourish, P. *Where the Action Is: The Foundations of Embodied Interaction.* Cambridge: MIT Press, 2001.

[9] Dourish, P. Implications for Design. In *Proc. CHI 2006* (Montreal, Canada), ACM Press, 2006, 541-550.

[10] Ellis, G. and Dix, A. 2006. An explorative analysis of user evaluation studies in information visualisation. In *Proc. of BELIV '06*. ACM Press, New York, NY, 1-7.

[11] Galloway, A., Brucker-Cohen, J., Gaye, L., Goodman, E., and Hill, D. 2004. Design for hackability. In *Proc. DIS'04*. ACM Press, New York, NY, 2004, 363-366.

[12] MacLean, A., Carter, K., Lövstrand, L., and Moran, T.. User-tailorable systems: pressing the issues with buttons. In *Proc. CHI '90*. ACM Press, 1990, 175-182.

[13] March, W., Jacobs, M., and Salvador, T. Designing technology for community appropriation. In *Proc. CHI '05 Extended Abstracts*, ACM Press, 2005, 2126-2127

[14] Moran, T., Everyday Adaptive Design (keynote). DIS'02. http://www.sigchi.org/dis2002/

[15] Newman, M., Sedivy, J., Neuwirth, C., Edwards, W., Hong, J.., Izadi, S., Marcelo, K., and Smith, T. Designing for serendipity: supporting end-user configuration of ubiquitous computing environments. In *Proc. DIS'02*. ACM Press, 2002, 147-156.

Evaluating Advanced Interaction Techniques
for Navigating Google Earth

Dubois, E., Truillet, Ph., Bach, C.
IRIT – University of Toulouse 3
118, route de Narbonne
F – 31 062 Toulouse Cedex 9
+33 5 61 55 74 05

{Emmanuel.Dubois ; Philippe.Truillet ; Bach}@irit.fr

ABSTRACT

This paper presents the design and comparison of a mouse-based interaction technique (hereafter IT) and two advanced IT, used in public spaces to support navigation in a 3D space. The comparison is based on a composite evaluation, including performance and satisfaction aspects. These preliminary results demonstrate that the use of mixed IT in a public space do not result in more differences among user than a mouse-based IT. It also highlights the fact that performance and satisfaction have to be considered simultaneously since they appear to be two complementary aspects of an evaluation, especially in public space environment, where the performance is no longer the only dimension to consider.

Categories and Subject Descriptors

H.5.1 [Multimedia Information Systems]: Artificial, augmented and virtual realities. H.5.2 [User Interfaces]: Evaluation methodology, Interaction styles, User-centred design.

General Terms

Design, Experimentation, Human Factors.

Keywords

User-centred design, experimentation, augmented reality, mixed interactive techniques, user-testing.

1. INTRODUCTION

Recent developments have pushed human-computer interfaces beyond the traditional mouse/keyboard configuration, into novel and multiple display systems, multi-sensory and multi-modal interfaces and virtual and augmented reality. The use of these advances in the design of input and output devices is intended to increase the usability of the interaction techniques. Commensurate with this revolution, there has been a great deal of research into 1/ information visualisation including metaphors, 3D representation, views such as perspective walls or fisheye views and 2/ adapted interaction techniques (hereafter, IT) such as large screens, dedicated tools or mixed and augmented systems.

© Dubois, E., Truillet, P., Bach, C., 2007
Published by the British Computer Society
Volume 2 Proceedings of the 21st BCS HCI Group
Conference
HCI 2007, 3-7 September 2007, Lancaster University, UK
Devina Ramduny-Ellis & Dorothy Rachovides (Editors)

Visualisation exploits the user's visual acuity, cognitive abilities, expertise and experience. For instance, large displays can help to build situation awareness through a common understanding of the information presented and to facilitate coordination. To allow users' intuitive as well as collaborative exploration, interaction capabilities need to be improved so that access to the data and associated features become apparent.

However IT developed to take advantage of these considerations are rarely compared with previous results and their effectiveness is seldom quantified by user studies. To better understand the impact of these multiple factors, it is becoming crucial to develop new design guidelines and metrics for usability evaluation of these interactive systems and environments. Much research has focused on the development of visualisation toolkits [10], new dedicated devices ([2], [3], [11]) and new interaction techniques [13] on large displays. Nevertheless, the situation of use often includes critical environments such as medicine, military command posts or air traffic control in which the user has primarily to be high-performing.

In our work we are examining a slightly different kind of context: advanced interactive techniques in public spaces. Indeed, our work is part of a larger project that aims at developing mixed interaction techniques, such as tangible UI or Augmented and Mixed Reality UI, in the context of museums. The goal is to transform knowledge into an interactive experience that carries knowledge and involves the user deeply. Evaluating user's performance remains important because the user must not be slowed by the interaction technique. However, other aspects such as discovery, pleasure, integration, satisfaction and robustness are also relevant when evaluating interactive systems in such public spaces.

The goal of the present work is thus to include performance and users' satisfaction aspects in a comparison of different interaction techniques in a public space context of use. Our first hypothesis is that these two aspects are not necessarily correlated: similarly to ergonomic criteria, designer will always have to establish a compromise between these two design options. We consider that reducing the gulf of execution [8] is extremely important in such contexts. Our second hypothesis is that providing interaction techniques that clearly separate the available commands will have a positive impact on their use. Finally, we also believe that reducing the input articulatory distance by providing interaction techniques that require user's action in direct correlation to the command to apply, will help the user to rapidly adopt skills for manipulating the technique.

In the rest of the paper, we first present the concrete application we used the basis of this experiment. We then introduce the interactive techniques we developed to investigate the three hypotheses mentioned above. We finally detail the settings of our experiment and discuss the first major results.

2. MOUSE-BASED AND ADVANCED IN-TERACTION TECHNIQUES

Google Earth (GE) [4] is a free application that supports navigation, bookmarks and search onto satellite pictures of the Earth. Pictures, presented from a bird-eye view perpendicular to the surface of the globe, are mapped on a sphere representing the Earth. The point of view can be modified, thus providing the user with a pseudo 3D view on these images. In this experiment we only considered navigation features that can be activated without any use of the Google Earth menus, icons and navigation tool provided in the upper right corner of the standard application. Furthermore, semi-automated features such as "double-click" or "double-click and slide" are implemented but were excluded from our experiment settings. The next sections present how the available commands are accessible with the mouse and the two advanced interaction techniques that we developed.

2.1 GE manipulation with a mouse

A first set of commands is used to support translations of the displayed image of the earth. For example, in order to visualise a region of the globe situated on the left of the current screen, one must press the left mouse button, move the mouse to the right and release the mouse button: this results in a rotation of the globe from left to right (see Fig. 1). Likewise, translations of the mouse to the left, top or bottom result into displaying globe areas placed on the right, bottom or top of the current view, respectively. In addition, the use of the mouse wheel enables the user to modify the altitude of the bird-eye view: this corresponds to the definition of the zoom level on the images.

Figure 1: Effect on Google Earth of the mouse translation to the right while pressing the left mouse button.

The second set of commands considered in this experiment results in rotations of the displayed images. If the mouse cursor is in the upper half part of the displayed globe area, pressing the wheel mouse and then moving the mouse cursor horizontally to the left (resp. right), results in a counter-clockwise (resp. clockwise) rotation of the globe area as shown in fig. 2: this corresponds to a modification of the orientation of the North direction, and this behaviour is inverted if the mouse cursor is in the lower half part of the screen.

Finally pressing the scroll wheel and then vertically moving it down (resp. up), results in a diminution (resp. increase) of the angle between the point of view and the globe surface tangent (see fig.2): this corresponds to a modification of the viewpoint.

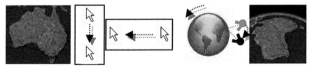

Figure 2: Effect on Google Earth of a combination of the horizontal and vertical translations of the mouse while pressing the scroll wheel.

2.2 GE-Stick

The first interaction technique we developed is called the Google-Earth Stick. This interaction technique is interesting for two reasons: first, it clearly separates the different available commands (one per sensor) and second, user's actions that have

to be performed are similar to the result of the command (turn the potentiometer to turn the earth, push the slider to zoom out, etc.) which should reduce the gulf of the execution (hypothesis 2).

It consists of a prop held in the user's hand and a board representing a compass rose. To perform the 4 translations, the user has to bring the prop close to one of the 4 directions represented on the compass rose (top, bottom, right and left). Bringing the prop close to one of the two areas present in the middle of this compass rose and tilting the prop up or down modifies the orientation of the point of view. Finally, there are two buttons on the prop: one can be turned with the thumb and forefinger to modify the orientation of the North axis and the second can be slid up or down to change the zoom. In a specific and predefined position, the "neutral zone", these buttons have no effect.

This technique is based on the Phidget sensors [9]: the prop includes an RFID reader, a potentiometer and a slider; on the reverse side of the board, RFID tags are fixed to detect the position of the prop on the board.

Figure 3: GE-Stick and the two sides of the board.

2.3 GE-Steering Board

The second interaction technique we developed is the Google-Earth Steering Board. This interaction technique is notable as, firstly, the user is no longer in direct contact with any device thus reducing the risk of damaging or stealing devices, especially in public contexts. Secondly, user's actions (move the board to the left) are directly applied to one of the domain concept: the viewpoint on the image (move the point of view to the left) which should reduce the input articulatory distance.

The same board as used with the GE-Stick now represents the position of the point of view on the images. Moving the board results in moving the point of view accordingly; a neutral zone also exists in which only rotations can be triggered.

Technically, the GE-Steering Board involves video-based tracking software [1] to localise the position of the reverse side of the board in the space. As illustrated in fig. 4 a camera for the detection of the board is positioned in front of the user.

3. EXPERIMENTAL SETTINGS

To investigate these techniques, we conducted an experiment comparing mouse interaction with GE-Stick and GE-Steering Board in navigation tasks.

3.1 Users and Material

14 users were involved in this experiment, 8 males and 6 females (29.6 years old, SD = 7.3). All of them are researchers in Computing Science, which means they are familiar with mouse use. The version of Google Earth we used is 4.0.2416 and it was displayed on a screen 2.1 m wide, 1.5 m high (2.56 m in diagonal): the picture was retro-projected on the screen. Users stood in front of the screen, at approximately 2 m. A table was

placed between them and the screen at 1.9 m. An area was defined on the table to represent the zone in which to manipulate the mouse; it also represented a vertical projection, onto the table, of the "neutral zone" defined for the GE-Steering Board: this area was 0.3 x 0.25 m.

A camcorder placed on the same side of the screen as the user, captured data displayed on the screen and the totality of the user's interaction (see fig. 4). On the other side of the screen, hidden from the user, two observers measured the duration of each task accomplished by the user and took notes about misuse of the interaction techniques.

Figure 4: Picture of the settings in front of the screen

3.2 Procedure

A pre-study usability evaluation session was performed on the three techniques and was based both on expert usability inspection and analyses of elementary interaction. These pre-experiment usability sessions were based on previous lessons learnt: cleaning up an ongoing evaluated IT avoids problems than can jeopardize user- testing and facilitates interpretation of results.

Each user was involved in a 3 phase process: training, measurement and interview. During the training phase, the goal was to teach to the user how to perform the ten different Google Earth commands involved in the experiment: six translations, including the zoom in and out, and 4 rotations. Users were informed that semi-automated zooming and moving with mouse are prohibited by experiment settings. The user received concise instruction from an experimenter before trying to achieve each command: the instruction was just composed of a description of the Google Earth command, e.g. "move toward the top of the screen", without any information explaining the link between the command and the interaction technique: the user had to discover by himself how to use the interaction technique. Before teaching the next command, users had no time limit and were asked to confirm whenever they thought they perfectly understood and controlled how to trigger the command. Observers behind the screen, recorded the duration of the different task taught to the user, with the different techniques. Each user had to go through this training with the mouse first: this technique constitutes our control technique; users were then trained on the GE-Stick and GE-Steering Board in a counterbalanced order. Finally, using the mouse only, cities involved in the measurement phase were shown to the user (Paris, New York, Nouméa).

During the second phase, users were informed that the time to perform the following tasks was measured. This measurement phase was based on a predefined scenario. The scenario was made of seven steps involving the ten Google Earth commands previously taught to the user: for example, users were all starting from Paris and the first step asked the user to "reach Liberty Island at an altitude of 400 m". Each step of the scenario was stated by the experimenter who explicitly mentioned when to start carrying out each step. Each user had to perform the scenario three times, with the three different interaction techniques, in the same order taught in the training phase.

During the last phase, users were interviewed about their experience with the application. The goal of this semi-guided questionnaire was to identify the preferred technique, the most complex one, and the best and worse aspects of each technique. These interviews were not recorded and the experimenter leading the interview was in charge of taking notes of the answers.

4. ASSESSMENT RESULTS
4.1 Satisfaction analysis

A semi-guided interview was used to determine for each user, the preferred IT, their feelings about the discovery process, the 3 strongest and weakest points of each techniques, the most efficient and the most constraining techniques, and finally the physical workload. In this paper, we focus on the user's preferred IT.

To identify preferred IT, participants were asked to rank ITs by preference order. A proportional score (range 0 to 20) was then extracted by summing the scores given by the users to each IT. According to this analysis the preferred IT is the GE-Steering Board (12.14) followed by the mouse (10.71) and GE-Stick (7.14). Preliminary interview analyses indicate that users prefer the GE-Steering Board because it allows a good level of presence and a feeling of omnipotence. Preference for the mouse seemed to be based on familiarity arising from everyday uses (habit).

This result tends to confirm our third hypothesis, that having to perform a user's action similarly to the behaviour of the command has a positive impact on the use of the IT.

4.2 Performance analysis

In order to complement the previous analyses, we conducted analyses on the duration of use of each IT (sum of the durations of the seven steps). This paper focuses on descriptive performance results based on means (M) and standard deviations (SD).

M and SD of the duration of use (in minutes) over the 14 users have been calculated for the mouse (M=5'19; SD=2'31), the GE-Stick (M=6'48; SD=0'53) and the GE-Steering Board (M=7'23; SD=2'13). It thus clearly appears that the performance order, based on the duration of use, is completely different from the preferred IT order. Significance of the difference has not been studied so far.

This result confirms our first hypothesis that performance and satisfaction are not necessarily correlated. It also illustrates the necessity of a composite evaluation (multi methods and domains) of advanced interaction techniques as mentioned by [7]. Beyond this first comparison between performance and satisfaction, a composite evaluation approach is also important to refine evaluation results: for example, the analysis of the SD identifies the GE-Stick as the most stable inter-users IT which confirm our second hypothesis that a strong differentiation of each command leads to more consistent inter-users performance; however this IT is the least preferred. These different nuances clearly show that a simple performance analysis is still insufficient to evaluate the quality of an advanced interaction technique.

Another performance result arises from the comparison of the SD of each IT. The SD represents the level of variability between users' performance when interacting with an IT: the smaller the variability, the more consistent the IT in terms of stability of use among different users. Unexpectedly, it appears that the SD of the two advanced ITs are equal (GE-Steering Board) or smaller (GE-Stick) than the SD of the mouse (control group). Since stability of use is one of the major factors of transferability of an IT to public spaces, because it positively affects consistency of use, this interesting result suggests that advanced interaction techniques are worth being further investigated and developed in such a context.

When considering the results in terms of M of duration of use, the better performance is accomplished with the mouse. However, we noticed during the experiment that, with mouse use, the speed of the image translations was directly correlated with the speed of the user's movement of the mouse, while with the two other ITs, the speed of the image translations is constant, even when user's movement are quicker or larger. Technical constraints caused these differences and further analysis based on the video-records will be conducted to define a ratio to correct the values obtained with the mouse on one hand and the two other ITs on the other hand, or to modify the link to the software application.

Additional preliminary analyses of the duration of each step of the scenario confirm results of pre-study usability evaluation sessions: some IT seems to be more appropriate for specific navigation commands. This result suggests it would be useful to perform a more detailed analysis of the duration of each step.

Finally, we have informally observed inter-user performance differences: this third axis will also be further investigated, especially from the point of view of a possible effect of IT presentation order. Indeed, we have identified that some users had difficulty understanding one experimental instruction during the measurement phase whereas they well understood the same instruction during the training phase. Each of these users had learnt to manipulate the GE-Stick before the GE-Steering Board. For now, we think that this situation could be a consequence of the cognitive workload due to GE-Stick training as mentioned in similar context by [12] for this kind of fragmented IT. Another hypothesis is that it could be a simple consequence of a misunderstood instruction. Finally, this may have been the result of a problem with the recruitment. Indeed, despite all the precautions that we have taken with the recruitment process, we observed, for one user, an important performance deviation (i.e. outside of M + 2 SD) that can be explained by user disabilities with orientation and 3D. These difficulties to control sample consistency are mentioned by other authors and led them to avoid some problematic user's profiles [5] or to use an elaborate specific recruitment process based on tests measuring participant's abilities to interact with Virtual Environments [6]. These points led us to take this subject out of the group.

5. CONCLUSION

This paper shows the main and most interesting results and questions of a first iteration of a larger user-centered evaluation process of advanced interaction techniques dedicated to public spaces. The first lesson learnt from this work is that that it is impossible to be satisfied by a performance evaluation on its own when assessing such advanced interaction techniques. A composite evaluation process is required: indeed reducing an evaluation to performance considerations may result in exclud-

ing other solutions better suited to the user's experience and satisfaction. Using composite evaluation will be useful to encourage the investigation of technical improvements of IT that are not the most efficient but that are the most appreciated by the users.

The composite evaluation conducted in our experiment and with our users sample, also shows that our prototypes could well be transferred to public spaces, because they appeared to be of better quality than mouse on various dimensions such as inter-users stability (GE-Stick) and our satisfaction measure (GE- Steering).

This paper only reports preliminary results of this experiment and further analyses of our data will address different hypotheses or open questions extracted from this iteration. We intend to focus on the identification of good and bad points of each technique according to the different steps of the scenario, the study of possible IT presentation order effect on IT learnability or cognitive workload (e.g. could be a warm topic in a multipoint exhibition context), the analysis of the recruitment process of participants (e.g. pre-test users' abilities and knowledge about Virtual Environment interaction required or not), and the improvement of the technical and software realisation of our advanced IT.

Further experiments will also be conducted to compare our advanced IT with other interaction techniques such as Wii-mote and to evaluate the usability of these techniques with other applications.

6. REFERENCES

[1] AR Toolkit web site: www.hitl.washington.edu/artoolkit

[2] Atlas Gloves, atlasgloves.org

[3] Frölich B., Plate J., The cubic mouse: a new device for three-dimentional input, CHI'2000, The Hague (Netherlands), p. 526-531

[4] Google Earth web site: http://earth.google.com/intl/en/

[5] Green, C. S. and Bavelier, D., Effect of action video games on the spatial distribution of visuospatial attention. Journal of experimental psychology: Human perception and performance, 32, pp. 1465-1478, 2006.

[6] Griffiths, G., Sharples, S., & Wilson, J. R., Performance of new participants in virtual environments: The Nottingham tool for assessment of interaction in virtual environments (NAIVE). International Journal of Human-Computer Studies, 64, 240–250., 2006.

[7] Hartson, H. R., Andre, T. S. and Williges, R. C., Criteria for evaluating usability evaluation methods. International Journal of HCI, 13, p. 373-410, 2001.

[8] Norman D., The Design of Everyday Things, MIT Press, 4th printing, 2001

[9] Phidgets web site: http://www.phidgets.com/

[10] KitWare, http://www.kitware.com/

[11] SpaceNavigator, www.3dconnexion.com/products/3a1d.php

[12] Stanney, K.M, Mourant, R. R. and Kennedy, R.S., Human Factors issues in Virtual Environments : a review of the literature. Presence : Teleoperators and Virtual Environments, 7, pp. 327-351, 1998.

[13] Tse E., Shen C., Greenberg S., Forlines C., Enabling Interaction with Single User Applications through Speech and Gestures on a Multi-User Tabletop, AVI '06, May 23-26, 2006, Venezia, Italy, pp. 336-34

Envisioning Future Mobile Spatial Applications

Peter Fröhlich, Rainer Simon, Elisabeth Muss, Andrea Stepan, Peter Reichl
Telecommunications Research Center Vienna (ftw.)
Donau-City-Str.1
1220 Vienna, Austria
+43/1/5052830-85

{froehlich, simon, muss, stepan, reichl}@ftw.at´

ABSTRACT

This paper presents two empirical investigations of future applications of mobile spatial interaction, i.e. the use of mobile phones as pointers to the real world. In situated interviews and a photo diary study, real-world objects of interest for referencing services were identified. Furthermore, envisioned services, their attractiveness and relevant usage situations were explored. The presented results of the study indicate that access to background information on buildings as well as spatially-related search and service access are highly attractive for future users, whereas spatially-related purchase, advertisement, gaming, and sharing is of less interest..

Categories and Subject Descriptors

H.5 Information Interfaces and Presentation (I.7); H5.2 User Interfaces: User-Centered Design.

General Terms

Measurement, Design, Economics, Experimentation, Human Factors.

Keywords

Mobile Spatial Interaction, Future applications, Innovation, Empirical user studies

1. INTRODUCTION

Ongoing advances in hardware and software technology are currently enabling researchers to develop new ways of interacting with digital information. One of the most intriguing ideas is 'mobile spatial interaction', i.e. to use your mobile phone as a pointing device to real world objects (see [1] for a detailed overview).

The Point-to-Discover project (p2d, [3], see Fig. 1) aims at realizing this vision by means of a combination of GPS, digital compass and tilt sensors. p2d is a joint academic/industry research project that explores the technologies behind this innovative concepts for how people might discover and access information about their immediate environment in the near future. Apart from technological challenges, namely hardware, platform and mobile client development, it is also a non-trivial task to identify suitable application scenarios.

When exploring future use, it is essential to adopt an empirical, human-centered approach to innovation, rather than relying on design intuition or technology-driven thinking (compare [2]). As is the case with many ubiquitous research endeavors, it is hard to elicit meaningful and valid input from users, simply because the concepts are so new and uncommon. Moreover, it is impossible to investigate mobile spatial interaction concepts in standard stationary laboratories, due to the close relationship to spontaneous behavior in outdoor real world contexts.

Figure 1. Accessing and annotating services referenced with surrounding objects: the p2d project

In our investigations we were addressing the following research questions:

1. How do people spontaneously envisage using p2d in a concrete setting? Which objects would they reference?

2. What would people like to do with p2d, i.e. which spatially-encoded services would they consider attractive?

3. In which situations would they be likely using p2d?

In the remainder of the paper, two user studies designed to find first answers to these questions are described in sections 2 and 3. Section 4 provides key results of both studies, which will then be discussed in section 5.

2. STUDY 1: SITUATED INTERVIEWS

In this study, a moderator accompanied a test participant for a 40 minute walk along a specified route through Vienna's 4th and 1st district. The route was chosen to include different building topologies (e.g. narrow streets vs. large squares) and building occupancies (e.g. residential area, shopping street, market place vs. squares and boulevard with historic buildings).

The sample comprised 10 participants with a mean age of 32 years, and was balanced regarding sex and professional status (2 employees, 1 freelancer, 2 housewives, 4 students). Their Internet usage averaged about 12 hours per week. While all participants owned a mobile phone, 6 had not yet surfed in the Internet with a mobile phone, 3 occasionally, and 1 regularly[1].

In the first part of the route, the participants were asked to spontaneously mention ideas related to objects in their surroundings. They were told to imagine that every surrounding object was already associated to information services. The participants were instructed to show each object they would use p2d for and to answer the questions summarized in Table 1.

Table 1. Questions asked for each referenced object in both user studies

	Question
1	Please name the object!
2	Please briefly describe the object!
3	Which service(s) would you like to use with regard to this object?
4 (Optional)	Please name situations in which the service could be attractive!
5	Please provide a rating of the attractiveness of the described service (5-point rating scale)!

In the second part of the route, the participants were asked to imagine they could annotate content with p2d, for example: notes to buildings or other objects in form of a personal diary, to participate in a community or like in Flickr to take pictures that recognize the position and orientation. The rest of the instruction was the same as in the first part.

After having completed the route, an interview was conducted. Additionally to demographic questions, the participants were asked to rate the attractiveness of a set of service categories for p2d (see Table 2). They could again optionally name situations in which they considered the service attractive. Audio recordings were made throughout the course of the study, and the objects that the participants pointed at were photographed.

3. STUDY 2: PHOTO DIARIES

While the situated interviews aimed at capturing people's initial thoughts about p2d application possibilities, we were also interested in a longer-term observation. For this purpose, we conducted an 'imaginative diary study'. The main concept was to ask users to take photos of surrounding objects in their everyday life, for which they would like to use p2d.

Also here, the sample recruitment (N=11) aimed at a balanced distribution of age (mean: 34), sex (5 female; 6 male) and professional status. The average time actively spent on the Internet was 12 hours per week. All persons owned a mobile device, however only 2 had already experiences with the mobile Internet.

To account for different contexts, motivations and daily procedures, the participants' background was varied: 2 tourists, 3 students during their semester, 1 teenager during school period, 1 person on a business trip, 2 commuters, 1 housewife, and 1 retired. All participants owned and frequently used a digital camera.

---
[1] The sample composition deliberately accounted for the low usage rate of mobile Internet in the Austrian/European population in 2007.

There were 3 phases: a briefing workshop, the trial phase, and the final interview. In the briefing workshop the participants were informed about p2d and its general application potential (based on the service categories shown in Table 2) and about the further course of the study.

For the following 2 weeks, they were asked to take about 30 pictures of objects they would be interested to reference with p2d. They were provided with a diary template, in which they could annotate their digital photographs, following the same question structure as in Study 1 (see Table 1). A follow-up call at the end of the first week aimed at monitoring the status of the participants' progress and, if needed, at reminding users to take photos. The final interview was conducted singularly with each participant, based on the photos and annotations in the diary, which had been sent to the moderator in advance.

Table 2. Service categories, serving as structure for the interviews in both studies

Service Category	Example
Background information to certain buildings or objects	Historical information
Spatially-related search	The next restaurant or the next taxi stand
Spatially-related access to information services	Public transport schedules or the program of the opera
Spatially-related advertisement	Pointing at McDonalds and participating in competitions
Spatially-related purchasing	Directly order special offers of a supermarket or find out the price of real estates
Spatially-related games	Find people with similar interests and know where they are, or for paper-chase
Spatially-related sharing	A mobile diary with comments to certain objects or a forum

4. RESULTS

The results described in this section are structured along the three research questions formulated at the end of section 1: object references, service attractiveness, and situational factors.

4.1 Object reference

4.1.1 Information access

In the situated interviews, an overall of 73 objects were mentioned as interesting pointing targets by the 10 participants. Only 2 of them were moving (tramway), the rest (71) were static. Most of the mentioned objects concerned commercial entities (47%) such as shops, restaurants etc, followed by entire buildings (36%) and others (19%) such as signs, streets etc.

In the photo diary study, the 11 participants all in all selected 318 objects. Compared to the situated interview study, the proportion of entire buildings (48%) was greater and the proportion of commercial entities (21%) was smaller. Moreover, there was a greater share of other object references, for example public transportation means, posters and signs, natural landmarks, and public spaces (31%, see a more detailed overview in Table 3).

Table 3. Object types selected by the participants of the photo diary study

Object type	Freq.	in %
Historical buildings (e.g. churches)	53	16.7
Shops	36	11.3
Institutions for sports or cultural activities	34	10.7
Means of transport (public and private)	24	7.5
Posters and signs	19	6.0
Educational institutions	17	5.3
Monuments	16	5.0
Residential houses	15	4.7
Landscape (e.g. rivers, mountains)	14	4.4
Companies	13	4.1
Restaurants	13	4.1
Public places (e.g. market places and parks)	13	4.1
Health care institutions	10	3.1
Architectural highlighting buildings	8	2.5
Hotels	6	1.9
Others	27	8.5

4.2 Service attractiveness

Service attractiveness was investigated in two ways. First, the participants had to state for each of the selected objects a specific service they would envision. During data analysis, the participants' ideas were allocated to the 7 service categories presented in Table 2. Fig. 2 summarizes the respective results for both studies.

The results from both studies are mostly similar in this regard. Most strikingly, spatially-related advertisement, gaming and sharing were not mentioned at all. The only notable difference was the higher prevalence of purchasing in the situated interview.

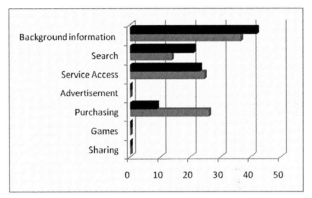

Figure 2. Percentage of p2d services referenced to objects. Grey bars represent situated interviews, black bars represent photo diary.

Second, in the final interviews of both studies, the participants directly provided attractiveness ratings for each of the 7 service categories. The results are presented in Fig. 3 below. Quite obviously there are two clusters of service categories: background information to buildings, spatially-related search and service access vs. spatially-related advertisement, purchasing, gaming, and sharing. Pairwise comparisons (Wilcoxon tests) between the service categories of the two clusters confirm this difference for both studies (p <.05), with the exception that in the situated interview the attractiveness difference between spatially-related purchasing and service access did not reach significance (p < .065).

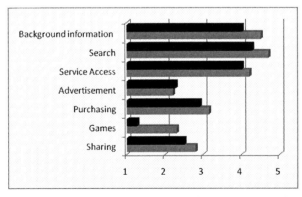

Figure 3. Attractiveness ratings for p2d service categories. Grey bars represent situated interviews, black bars represent photo diary.

4.1.2 Annotation

The participants had a much harder time when instructed to add or annotate their surroundings in the second part of the *situated interview* study. They regarded only 36 objects suitable for annotation, in contrast to 73 objects for information access. Furthermore, in about half of the cases (19 of 36) they were more interested in passive usage of user-generated content, such as tourist fora or restaurant review services, not in making annotations themselves. The ideas concerning active annotations can be summarized as follows:

- Reviews and recommendations of restaurants and shops for others, e.g. "This book shop currently has amazing sales offers! Check it out!" (mentioned 7 times)

- Reminiscences for oneself, such as reminders to a good restaurant, or notes about interesting places one had enjoyed (mentioned 4 times).

- Reminders for future events ("I am interested in the event announced on THIS poster"; mentioned once).

- Co-ordination between friends (noting an attractive real estate offer, in order to discuss with a friend whether one should move in; mentioned once)

- Background information for others, perhaps comparable to a mobile Wikipedia (mentioned twice)

- Initiation of discussions about topics of local interest, e.g. "This is a never ending construction site! It's a shame that they mutilate this place for such a long time" (mentioned once).

- Gathering sound recordings from each place (brought up by a musician).

4.3 Situational factors

For each of the referenced objects, the participants could optionally mention situations, in which they would most likely use p2d for that purpose. During data analysis, the mentioned situations were classified into 5 categories. Fig. 4 presents the percentage-wise allocation to these categories. The huge difference between the two studies regarding the general category may be ascribed to a stronger motivation of giving an answer when being accompanied by an interviewer than when filling out a diary on her own.

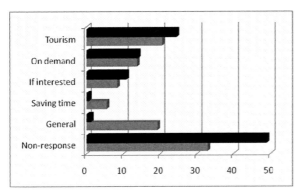

Figure 4. Percentage of situations mentioned during object referencing. Grey bars represent situated interviews, black bars represent photo diary.

5. DISCUSSION AND CONCLUSIONS

Two empirical studies have been conducted to explore the future use of mobile spatial interaction. The key results of both studies have shown to be consistent: the participants had strong interest in the – possibly more obvious and classic - uses of mobile spatial interaction (background information, search and service access), and were less comfortable with more advanced concepts, such as gaming, sharing, and also purchasing.

This finding is certainly due to the deliberate composition of a sample with an average openness to new technologies. We argue that, in order to envisage mass-market potential, user study samples should not have a strong bias towards early-adopters.

Participants did not appear to have a strong need for annotating content to places by means of mobile devices. More efficient methods for input on mobile devices appear to be indispensable increase acceptance of such services.

The study results helped to inform and ground the p2d design and implementation process. Instead of an initially planned pervasive game, we decided to build a mobile guide and information service, both enabling mobile search and background information to buildings. In this way, our focus has been shifted from innovating complete application concepts towards innovating *the access* to conventional services by location and orientation awareness.

The qualitative user comments, which could only partly be reported in this paper, provide important insights and still require further analysis. A consequent next step of our empirical innovation process is to conduct user studies with functional p2d prototypes, in order to further refine the application scenario.

We hope that the methodological approach presented may be adopted in other ubiquitous computing research endeavors. It provides a way to achieve contextually meaningful results, with moderate use of resources. It is of course true that investigations of this style are highly sensitive with regard to country-specific or even regional usage habits and motivations. It would therefore be worthwhile to replicate these studies in other (non-European) countries.

6. ACKNOWLEDGMENTS

This work is part of the ftw. projects p2d and SUPRA, funded by Mobilkom Austria, Siemens Austria and the Austrian competence centre program **K***plus*.

7. REFERENCES

[1] Fröhlich, P., Simon, R., Baillie, L., Roberts, J., and Murray-Smith, R. (2007). Mobile Spatial Interaction. Extended Abstracts of CHI 2007. ACM Press. Workshop website: http://msi.ftw.at

[2] Oulasvirta, A. (2005). Grounding the innovation of future technologies. An Interdisciplinary Journal on Humans in ICT Environments. Volume 1 (1), April 2005, 58-75.

[3] Point-to-Discover project (p2d): http://p2d.ftw.at

Thanks for the Memory

Harper, R.

Microsoft Research
JJ Thomson Av
Cambridge, UK
Tel+44 (0)1223 479824

R.Harper@microsoft.com

Randall, D.

Manchester Metropolitan University
Dep't of Sociology
Geoffrey Manton Building M16 5LL
Tel (+44) 161 247 3037

D.Randall@mmu.ac.uk

**Smythe, N., Evans, C.,
Heledd, L. & Moore, R.**

BBC Wales and BBC White City,
Shepard's Bush, London

First.surname@bbc.co.uk

ABSTRACT

This paper reports the trial of a memory prosthesis, SenseCam, as a resource for digital narratives. Over a period of one week, six participants were asked to use SenseCams to capture digital traces of their experiences, and to use the same to create 'story telling' materials for presentation. The study found that all users delighted in the devices, though the traces that the SenseCams produced were not analogues to their own memory. Instead, the data traces presented a picture of daily life which was at once different to the one recollected by participants and yet brought a sense of wonder, depth and felt-life that was enriching. Furthermore, SenseCam data enabled participants to create artistic and evocative stories about prosaic activities that would not normally merit being recounted. The paper will comment on the implications these findings have for memory prosthesis device design, and on the epistemological assumptions underscoring them.

Categories and Subject Descriptors

H5.m. Information interfaces and presentation (e.g., HCI): Miscellaneous.

General Terms

Design, Human Factors, Theory.

Keywords

Memory; memory prosthesis; sociology, psychology; digital narratives; wearable data capture; SenseCam.

1. INTRODUCTION

Technology and the conceptual frameworks that determine the function and meaning of that technology go hand in hand, one might say, though there is of course much discussion about which comes first: technology or concepts. Whatever the answer to this question - whether it is the technology or the idea that drives change - what is generally agreed is that the trajectory of the resulting marriage is fairly clear to discern. The merging of cameras with mobile phones, for example, has shifted what it means to be a photographer just as it has altered

© Harper, et al, 2007
Published by the British Computer Society
Volume 2 Proceedings of the 21st BCS HCI Group
Conference
HCI 2007, 3-7 September 2007, Lancaster University, UK
Devina Ramduny-Ellis & Dorothy Rachovides (Editors)

the value placed on captured images. Whereas once photographers were experts of sorts, their presence used to celebrate special events, and the images they captured displayed in honored locations (the mantelpieces, bedside cabinets etc), so now everyone is a photographer, every event is photographed and there is no knowing what will be displayed. The trajectory here is one that suggests that the relationship between images and special events is dissolving, as is too the relationship between the image and its honorific display. The scope and depth of research into this trajectory is, now, one might add, immense.

Sometimes, however, a conceptual shift can alter a perceived trajectory in new and exciting ways. For example, the massive reduction in the cost of digital memory and data capturing devices has lead some researchers to invent what they call memory aids or memory prostheses. MSRC's SenseCam is one such device. This consists of a camera, data storage chip and various other sensors, combined with a battery all embedded in a lightweight case about the size of a corporate ID badge, which can automatically capture and store about 3000 images. Currently various researchers are investigating the utility of SenseCams for this conception, building their enquiries around the framing concept of Qualia, and the idea that memory consists of some kind of internal mind's eye [1,2].

Whatever one thinks about this set of enquiries, this is not the only set of framing concepts that can guide the trajectory of use and development for devices like SenseCam. For instance, if one abandons the idea of memory as cognitive process and instead conceives of capturing images as a way of providing resources for digital story telling, then what something like SenseCam can do, how it is used, and hence how it might be developed, can shift.

It was just this possibility that we report on in this paper. More particularly, we report on the use of SenseCams by a set of six users who were asked to produce digital narratives over a one week period. The findings from this study have encouraged us to think that this particular conceptual shift is likely to produce dividends.

More especially, this paper will report that the 'narrative'(s) produced by SenseCam data traces are not ones that reflect the experience of living as typically thought about, reflected upon or remembered, by our user group at least. Instead, these traces are discontinuous with that experience. This does not mean that they contradict or correct 'lived memory'. It is rather that what is captured, what is seen and what is evoked is distinct. The paper will suggest that this is a benefit, at least for users if not historians. For these very differences created new values, new resources for narrative and self-understanding. These have distinctly appealing values to our users.

These findings are, we think, of profound importance, but space precludes full consideration of them here. The bulk of this paper will instead be devoted to reporting the research upon which these claims and the evidence for them were gathered, though it will end with some further elaboration of what these findings mean for memory prostheses and their conceptual underpinnings, whetherever they might be.

The paper will be organized as follows. Having described the study, it will then present the findings, breaking those into sections around the type of experience evoked. This will be followed by discussion of the implications, as just mentioned.

2. THE STUDY

The study was undertaken as part of a three year, DTI-EPSRC and commercially funded project, called PARTICIPATE. This primarily involves the BBC, BT, MSRC and the Universities of Nottingham and Bath. Part of the project entails investigating forms of data capture that allow ordinary users to 'participate' in new 'ubiquitous' computing experiences. SenseCams obviously fit under these auspices.

With this in mind, during Easter, 2007, the BBC arranged for six participants in South Wales to be given the use of MSRC SenseCams for one week. The BBC have been undertaking studies of and user oriented workshops for digital narratives for some time, so were well versed in how to make a success of such trials. More particularly, having each been given a SenseCam and laptop to run the associated application, each participant was given a brief on how the devices worked. To help the participants focus their endeavours, they were asked to perform simple tasks during the week, such as choosing one image per day and captioning it. The tasks were left vague, however, so as to maximise the degree of freedom participants felt they had. The subjects were then given some guidance as to what digital narratives might consist of, but were assured that in this instance the narratives they produced, whatever their quality, were not for broadcast.

At the end of the trial, participants were invited to a review meeting where a free discussion of their experiences took place. Each participant was invited to present some results in a form which they found suitable and, if they so desired, to make samples of SenseCam images and associated materials (such as notes, edited Media-player or I-Movie films), available at the review meeting and ultimately to the research team. The following findings derive from these materials.

2.1 Findings

Narratives can of course take many forms and indeed can be motivated by many desires: to broadcast one's identity, for example; to celebrate lives that might be otherwise ignored; and so on. But underneath all these purposes there is a sense in which a narrative will be empirical if it is anything at all. Hence, one's experience, one's bodily movement through space, one's moment-by-moment thoughts, all this and more may be thought of as the raw stuff of which narrative will be made, presumably, whatever their purposes. It seems perfectly reasonable to assume, therefore, that various sorts of digital devices can be brought to bear on the task of capturing this 'stuff' and making it available for the assembly of such things as digital narratives. Our research taught us that this is not such a straightforward proposition as it seems.

From the outset of the SenseCam feedback session, it became clear, as we have already noted, that SenseCam 'data' is not the analogue of experience. It is in various ways discontinuous yet empirically bound to it. This sounds contradictory, but as shall

become clear, there is a subtle but important set of possible relationships between the remembered experience before examination of SenseCam data and experience as recollected thereafter. These relationships have to do with such things as the difference between the 'stuff' that ought to be remembered and that which was not; between the 'stuff' which is never remembered because it lacks merit; between one's own 'stuff' the 'stuff' which is another's view and so could not be remembered; and so forth. Each of these dimensions has distinct characteristics and properties. Such dimensions became visible as we listened to our participants, each talking in turn and offering their own digital narrative(s). Accordingly, we present the main dimensions or 'properties of the past' separately, below, before bringing together an analysis.

2.1.1 Strangeness

First of all, then, and as we have just indicated, participants frequently expressed surprise at how their lives were, to a degree, rendered 'strange' by SenseCam images. At the minimal, this included 'noticings' of previously unremarked features:

N: I took it on holiday and 80% of the photos were of my boyfriend ... but what I loved about it was the way it caught his mannerisms and behaviour ... the way he'd be looking out the window or watching something else...the mannerisms ...

Sometimes, participants remarked on the way in which things they habitually took for granted looked different:

M:.. it was a bit like being in a silent movie ... you could see over the handlebars ... it made me look at things that I'd taken for granted in a different way ...

Part of the strangeness was also achieved because the SenseCams have fish eye lens cameras. This type of lens had been fitted since the original designers thought the images captured would be closer to those experienced. As it happens, this is quite opposite to the truth:

N. The fish eye lens makes everything look different but its quite cute, it's kind of more interesting..

2.1.2 Measuring a life

The strangeness that the SenseCam images induced also provided a different way of measuring what a day's activities had entailed. In particular SenseCam images provided a way of 'foregrounding' events that might otherwise have slipped from view. In the following, one participant talks about how a 'bad day' she'd had with her daughter had been utterly transformed in a single moment she was able to retrieve later. Her captioning of this moment had a poetic quality, one which moved all of the people in the discussion:

S: ... cos, I'd had like the worst day ever ... I just found it ..., she'd been driving me absolutely mad ... and we were in the playground and there was no-one there ... and she was ... she won't eat properly .. she's so small ...

Q: And what you've written, is that documenting [image of daughter next to a giraffe painted on the wall]...

S: Yeah, yeah, it was like the conversation we had ... it was like, 'but Mum, when ... when am I going to be bigger ...

We found that, typically, our participants remarked on the way that the images they reviewed made them see the mundane in new ways, ranging from noticing for the first time what the world looks like from between a pair of bicycle handlebars, through to the foregrounding of concerns, as in the above example, to the surprise evoked at seeing candid images of a child reacting to being 'caught' in some trivial way:

S:... I actually caught her on camera eating a dog biscuit and giving another one to the dog ... the guilt on her face ... I never ever could have got that if I was trying to take pictures ...

In various ways, then, the SenseCams brought the mundane to life, whether it was by simply seeing things another way, foregrounding what had previously been background issues, or capturing things (like a boyfriend's mannerisms) that would otherwise remain neglected.

2.1.3 Reflection

Seeing events in this way also provided opportunities for reflection. More than one participant talked about their surprise on discovering certain features of their lives they ordinarily seem to neglect, and in particular their realizations about certain mundane features to be discovered within them:

S: I noticed how much I was in the car ... how much you go shopping ... how much of your day is taken up by washing up ... you know ... you see quite a lot of the insides of my house ...

A: you look at newspapers and it's all about lifestyle ... that's why I like this ... it actually goes into the life you're leading ... the boring bits where you're not achieving status ... they turn out quite interesting ... it focuses on the things we don't [normally] reflect on ... you make a slightly different judgement ... it can be really reaffirming, to look back on a really nice day and say, oh, it was ok ...

It was striking the way in which respondents chose to talk about the ordinary and humdrum features of their lives. SenseCam images could be an excuse for celebration, to make the subjects humble about something, or to laugh at themselves. SenseCam images could even suggest a need for change:

M: No, what I would do is only put it on ... ... it's brought home to me that I need to change a few things ... it makes you rethink your life a little bit ... wear it for a week and you realise what you're doing with your life ... like a therapy...

2.1.4 'La Vie des Autres'

A further dimension of the experience evoked by SenseCam images was a heightened sense of the lives of others. At its most prosaic this simply meant seeing those others:

M. All the people you focus on normally are people who are present in your life, and the strangers ... you exclude them ... this brings the strangers back ...

Some participants asked partners, workmates and others to wear the camera.

I: I'd be interested in seeing other people's days .. I actually gave it to my housemate to see what he does at work ... the answer was, 'not much' ..

Through the lives of others was not the only way that SenseCams provided opportunities. Animate and inanimate objects alike provided vehicles for exploring different views:

I put it on a kite. We were in the park ... I wanted to know what it looks like when you fly . I'd love to know what that's like so I put it on a kite with some gaffer tape.It didn't work though!

Yeah, I wanted to put it on my dog. the world from his level ...

2.1.5 Creativity

Some uses can only be described as creative. Creativity here refers to both imagined and real uses of the devices. This was especially driven by a concern with the novel aesthetics of SenseCam images, such as related to the perspectival distortion the fish eye lens produced.

In one instance, a participant selected some images of a group of friend's ten-pin bowling which were, in their mind, meaningless but 'artistic':

M. Oh yeah, the bowling ones [images of a group of friends ten pin bowling] ... especially the arty ones , this one . I captioned this, 'great bowls of fire' ... I love those kind of abstract images

This suggests that, for our participants, one of the ways the past could be made interesting was through making it entirely unfamiliar, divorced if you like from the experience-as-experienced. Yet, part of the magic here would appear to be related to how this difference was made visible and more tractable by somehow being anchored in the recollection of the event itself. The delightful difference and artistic value of a 'creative view' was measured in terms of how far that view was from what the event was thought and experienced to be.

One desired feature of this tension between empirical facts and the artistic rendering of the same, between what some users said was the fragmentary vision of their existence and the idea that their existence had some narrative or linear form to it, was the possibility that, with SenseCam images of the past, or at least SenseCam traces of it, the past could be juggled up. Respondents juxtaposed, changed, organized images in ways that frequently challenged the linear flow of experience. In one case, a participant designed a film (taking six hours to complete it) which was shown to everyone else present. Afterwards he admited:

'It's not the way my week went ... I divided it up ... put things together so they would be interesting ...'

2.1.6 Reconceiving the Author - Subject

If strangeness, the neglected and the aesthetic, were part of the values that use of SenseCam gave vitality to and, if, further, the ability to juggle-up the narrative of life to create evocative stories was also a bonus, then it is not entirely surprising that, with a capture device that can work automatically, people should be less prone to editorialising before or during the event. Our subjects treated SenseCams as a producer of raw material and the values provided to the subjects were in large part up with the fact that the user(s) did not 'steer' or give planned voice to 'stuff' that was collected.

There was a key *social property* of SenseCams that lay behind this which several of the participants commented on. This had to do with how the devices transformed the role and the function of the author and the subject. Whereas photography (both classical and ephemeral, as mentioned at the outset) requires someone to take a picture and someone to be the subject of a picture, so SenseCams make this different. Automatic capture means it no longer matters who is who. This released some participants from the burden of making this distinction itself.

H. You know with this I don't worry about what the pictures look like; I am not involved, I mean I know I chose to wear it for the trial but you know I didn't feel as if I was taking pictures I didn't ask anyone to stand still and look right - I mean I did sometimes but not always and the thing about it is I feel much more free...

This in turn, so some participants remarked, made the events in question more 'natural' and less 'infected' (as one put it), by the presence of photography.

This has a paradoxical consequence, of course. When participants first started wearing SenseCams they had worried that they were making the world as a whole a subject. In some instances they had been especially worried about this because they had been in places where imaging was prohibited, such as in playgrounds. There, the very concept of author-subject was the salient along which concern arose. By the end of the week, however, at least some of the participants were delighting in the dissolution of this nexus. They were no longer the author. 'It' was.

3. Conclusion

There were, needless to say, other dimensions of experience that came out from our trial. Space precludes discussion of them all. We have focused on what we think are the most provocative and in particular on issues to do with the relationship between memory and memory prosthesis and to a lesser extent issues to do with the creation of personal narratives.

As regards the idea of digital memory. What we have seen is that the relationship between things-as-remembered-by-the-subjects-in-ordinary-ways and things-as-presented-by-the-SenseCams is complex. For one thing, SenseCam data captured things-that-might-have-been-remembered-but-not-intentionally and things-that-were-beyond-the-possibility-of-being-recalled-by-the-user-but-which,-when-presented-to-the-same-user,-somehow-provoked-a-recollection. Here we are thinking of the weird images, views from peculiar places, the faces that were there but not seen, and so on.

This awkward language alludes to the difficult and complex relationship between human memory and digital traces of action. We have seen that SenseCam data makes lived-experience, in various ways and in varying degrees, *strange* to the persons who had the relevant experiences in question. Strangeness here is not a negative thing, as we saw. Strangeness brings values of various kinds. The crux, it seems to us, is that in creating discongruent experiences to the one's imagined or recollected, SenseCams brought to bear ways of seeing that were not obviously the subject's own, but which were nevertheless empirically related to those experiences, though in complex ways.

It seems to us that it is precisely this complexity that is at issue when it comes to memory prosthesis. In our view, research which seeks to build prostheses on the assumption that human recollection is merely an empirical object is completely neglecting this complexity. This research tends to treat the problem as one of scope, extent, volume (albeit alloyed with operationalised definitions of types such as 'episodic' 'flash bulb', etc [3]). Once the data is there this research thinks it only a secondary (though sometimes difficult) task to recall it. Our study shows that this might be a wrong way of thinking about human memory and digital data traces.

Our reading of the evidence leads us to argue that whatever ones feeling about the concept of Qualia and related ideas, much of which are deeply contentious, what is clear from this research is that the past is not a place one merely recalls; the past is a place *one ventures into*. SenseCams are thus not merely capturing devices; they capture in particular ways. It is these particularities that gives them their unique value. A fish eye lens creates one way of exploring the past, for example; just as a passive capture technique offers another. Each design choice creates a particular vision on what the past was, can be seen as, and leads the 'user' to find evocative. In short, one should not think of devices like SenseCam as good or bad

analogues for human memory; as successful or failing memory prostheses. They are devices that, in their design, *makes the past in particular ways*. Hence, they should be designed with sensitivity to how that rendering occurs. What we have seen is that these renderings can offer delight, surprise, foreignness and strangeness in equal measure. We have seen too, how these renderings can shift even what it means be an 'author' (a photographer) of one's own life.

In these respects, we think this small trial ought to make us think differently about memory as an object of interest to HCI. This interest has been, up to now, pretty much solely driven by various forms of psychological behaviourism and-or cognitivism. The evidence here suggests that we ought to move toward a different view, one that is perhaps more sociological. In so doing it might lead us nearer to the view of memory expounded by the speech acts theorists and their pregenitors, the ordinary language philosophers such as Wittgenstein [4].

But even if we do, we also think that the findings ought to make us skeptical of the sociological view of memory which might seem more plausible and more closely allied to the idea of narrative. This holds that memory is a 'social construction' a kind of 'act', and that memories are 'stories' with political intentions. It seems to us that, although the findings do suggest that memory is a 'place one ventures to' and thus one 'acts out', they also suggest that devices like SenseCam make the past a broader, richer, less socially tidy place than one's 'sociological memory' would like. We say this because the sociology of memory literature emphasises the political and intentional arrangement of recollection. In this view, some events are selected to be honoured (by Cenotaphs for example) whilst others are forgotten. Following on from this, personal narratives of the past are designed to give especial credit to some events and not others. Yet our study shows that the 'felt-experience' and discongruent perspectives that SenseCam brings to the past, and the resources it provides for digitally mediated narratives about that past, show that the past is always a big place. What one does routinely, forgetfully, with forethought or with neglect, through habit and indifference, with boredom or with wonder, is not always tractable to social mores that dictate what ought to be recalled and what ought to be neglected. The past is an empirical place, to be sure, but just how and in what ways is up for us in the present, with our desire to tell stories or seek wonder, to explore. Choices about what we explore are not always political acts. Sometimes the past is merely a place one ventures into. It has been the purpose of this paper to show how even a small trial can show that this is so.

4. ACKNOWLEDGMENTS
Our thanks to all participants, and to a number of people who worked hard to make the technology work, notably A.Woolard, G.Morlais, J.Scott, G.Smyth.

5. REFERENCES
[1] Hodges, et al, 2006, SenseCam: a retrospective memory aid, *Proc.Ubicomp* 2006

[2] Sellen, A. et al, 'Do Life-Logging Technologies Support Memory for the Past? An Experimental Study Using SenseCam', *CHI 2007*, ACM Press, pp81-90.

[3] Connerton, P., How Societies Remember, Cambridge, CUP, 1989 Sellen, Connerton, P., *How Societies Remember, Cambridge*, CUP, 1989

[4] Ricoeur,P. *Memory, History, Forgetting*, 2004, Chicago.

Automatic vs. Manual Multi-Display Configuration

A Study of User Performance in a Semi-Cooperative Task Setting

Thomas Heider, Thomas Kirste
Institute of Computer Science
Rostock University, Germany
{th,tk}@informatik.uni-rostock.de

ABSTRACT

Emerging multi-display infrastructures provide users with a large number of (semi-) public and private displays. Selecting what information to present on which display here becomes a real issue, especially when multiple users with diverging interests have to be considered. This especially holds for *dynamic* ensembles of displays. Therefore, automatic assignment strategies might be useful, if they are able to provide the required assignment precision. We claim that it is possible to define such strategies, and show that it is able to assist users in solving specific tasks in multi-display environments at least as effectively as conventional manual assignment. Our claims are based on user performance data collected in the scope of a comparison study.

Categories and Subject Descriptors

H.5.2 [**Information Interfaces and Presentation**]: User Interfaces—*Evaluation/methodology*

Keywords

Multi-Display Environments, Pro-active Meeting Support

1. MULTI-DISPLAY ENVIRONMENTS

Multi-Display Environments (see e.g. the UbiComp 2004 workshop on Ubiquitous Display Environments [1] or the Ubicomp 2006 workshop on next generation conference rooms [2]) support collaborative problem solving and teamwork by providing multiple display surfaces for presenting information. Typical examples for such environments are meeting rooms, conference rooms, and "mission control centers".

One difficult task here is the *Display Mapping problem* – that is, deciding which information to present on what display in order to optimally satisfy the users' needs for information. While this task is more or less trivial in single-user, single-display situations, it becomes challenging in multi-user, multi-display settings: Users and displays are spatially dispersed so that the visibility of (semi-) public and private

displays varies across users. Also, information needs may vary across users, so that finding the "best" assignment of information to displays becomes a difficult problem.

Current approaches for controlling multi-display environments rely on manual assignment, using a suitable interactive interface, resolving conflicts by social protocols (negotiations). One example is the ModSlideShow system [3], which is designed to manage presentation slides on multiple displays. For assignment of content to displays, meeting participants drag-and-drop presentations from their note books to any of the available displays. Another similar system is the PointRight software developed for Stanford's Meyer Teamspace [4]. However, manual display assignment has to cope with the following problems:

- **Interest conflicts** between users might be solved faster by computer supported negotiation mechanism: Morris et al. [5] have already observed that social protocols do not always suffice for coordinating the use of shared resources, such as display surfaces, in teams – even in relatively simple situations. They suspect that the need for coordination may increase as the number of users, the number of documents, or the number or size of the surfaces increases. Indeed, they advocate the development of specific strategies for automatizing the negotiation process.

- The need for **dynamic realignment** of Display Mapping is caused by topic changes in the user population – in this situation, the user's focus of attention will be on the changing topic rather than on convincing the display infrastructure to change the topic.

Therefore, an automatic display assignment might be helpful in multi-display environments, specifically in multi-user settings. However, to our knowledge, it is not known if suitable automatic assignment heuristics can be found. This is the question we want to answer.

2. DISPLAY MAPPING QUALITY

A *display mapping* is a function m, which assigns documents to sets of displays. For a given document d, $m(d)$ gives the set of displays document d is assigned to. (It sometimes clearly makes sense to assign a document to more than one display.)

In order for automatic display mapping to be successful it is necessary to identify a well-defined quality measure that

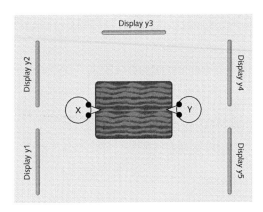

Figure 1: Experimental setup

sufficiently captures the users needs. Clearly, at least the following aspects seem reasonable:

Spatial Layout: For documents of high importance to a user, displays should be preferred that provide a good visibility for the user. Formally, this critierion m can be defined as

$$q_s(m) = \sum_{\substack{u \in U \\ d \in D}} impt(d, u) * \max_{y \in m(d)} vis(y, u) \qquad (1)$$

where $impt(d, u) \in [0 .. 1]$ denotes the importance of the document d to a user u, and $vis(y, u) \in [0 .. 1]$ the *visibility* of display y by user u. If a document is assigned to multiple displays, only the best one for a given user is considered when computing the quality for this user (this is the "max *vis*" term). We call this display "primary display".

Deriving a reliable estimation of *impt* in general may be a substantial challenge – however, there may be additional informations available that can be used as a surrogate (such as an agenda item listing a responsible person with a number of associated documents, etc.). In our test, we have used a manual importance assigment.

Temporal Continuity: When considering a display for a document, the system should prefer already existing assignments: Documents should not unnecessarily change their place. A relevant display shift occurs between two mappings, if a user's primary display for a document changes. We then try to minimize these shifts relative to the document's importance.

Based on these criteria, we have developed an algorithm that is able to automatically compute a display mapping for a set of users and documents (see [6] for more details).

3. EVALUATION
3.1 Experimental Design
The objective of our evaluation experiment was to compare the effect of manual and automatic display assignment on task performance. Our hypotheses is that automatic assignment , even using the straightforward quality measure outlined above, is able to provide the same quality as a manual assignment.

Specifically, we have measured the impact of manual vs. automatic display assignment on the performance of a team in solving a semi-cooperative task. In such tasks, the need of cooperation and joint use of information is not evident from the start, but rather arises while working on the task. We think that this kind of aspect pertains to many team processes, specifically in multidisciplinary teams.

Setup. Two-person teams had to solve a semi-cooperative set of comparison tasks as fast as possible. The two team members, X and Y, were given different agendas, each containing the description of an individual comparison. For X the task was to compare two documents A and B, for Y the task was to compare A and C. The task was a simple letter comparison, counting the number of differences in the two letter sequences contained in A and B resp. A and C. In addition, X and Y had to report time information and a random key from another document Time. The seemingly unrelated tasks for X and Y were linked into a cooperative task through the shared documents A and Time.

The experimental environment provided five projection based public displays (see Figure 1). Note that there are two pairs of displays exclusively visible to X and Y, respectively, and one display visible to both X and Y. For the experiments, every participant was given a simple user interface for document assignment. Manually assignment of a document to a display-surface is done through a simple "drag & drop". For automatic assignment, the user just associates an importance value with the documents.

As the agendas and task descriptions were mutually unknown, the sharing had to be discovered through a conflict in the manual assignment group. (In order to enforce resource conflicts in this simple setting, each document could only be displayed on one display at a time.)

For each experiment, we recorded the time required for completing the task, the number of interactions, and the solution correctness (percentage of letter differences found). After each task set, the subjects were asked to answer a questionnaire regarding user satisfaction. After both task sets, the subjects were asked to complete a final questionnaire regarding the comparison of the automatic and the manual assignment.

Participants. 24 voluntary subjects (19 male and 5 female) were recruited from staff members and students of the local university. The participants were between the ages of 20 and 41 and were used to computer systems. The participants were randomly grouped into 12 teams, 6 in group A and 6 in group M. The teams had to solve two sets of comparison tasks in sequence. Group A had to solve the first set using automatic assignment and the second set with manual assignment. The Group M was given the tasks in reverse order. In the evaluation of the results, we will call the first set "Initial Test" and the second "After Training", respectively.

Summary of experimental design

Group A:		Group M:	
First Task Set (Initial Test)	Second Task Set (After Training)	First Task Set (Initial Test)	Second Task Set (After Training)
Automatic	Manual	Manual	Automatic

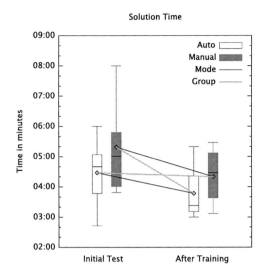
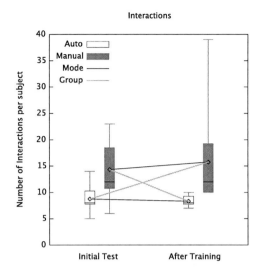

Figure 2: Boxplots of solution time vs. mode, overall (left) and interaction count vs. mode, (right)

Note. A goal of the experimental design has been to (I) explicitly provoke conflicts between the team members regarding the use of the available display space and (II) to enforce substantial changes in the set of documents currently important for a user. Clearly, display assignment becomes an issue only, once more relevant documents than displays are available (specifically, if different users have different sets of relevant documents), and once the set of currently relevant documents changes dynamically.

3.2 Results

Performance. On average all subjects needed 4:28 min to complete one set of a comparison task. When the teams were using automatic assignment, the average time was 4:08 min, while they required an average time of 4:49 min using manual assignment. The overall average number of interactions was 11.8, where the subjects needed 8.5 interactions on average with automatic and 15 interactions on average with manual assignment. The average solution correctness was 95%, for both manual and automatic assignment.

This indicates that the automatic assignment is superior to manual assignment, regarding time and interactions (a brief statistical validation for this claim is given further below).

An overview of the collected data is shown in the boxplots in Figure 2 and 3[1]. In these plots, "mode" refers to the display assignment mode (manual vs. automatic). In the per-task-set plots, grey lines connect the mean values of the two consecutive task sets of a group (Group A or Group M), black lines connect consecutive task sets using the same assignment mode.

As can be seen in Figure 2, left, for both task sets the solution time is shorter when using automatic assignment. In addition, Group M was able to solve the task substantially faster in the second set (i.e., when switching from manual to

---

[1]These boxplots show the minimum and maximum values, the 25% and 75% percentiles, the median (horizontal bar inside the box), and the mean (small circle inside the box).

automatic assignment), whereby Group A was not able to improve performance in the second set (i.e., switching from automatic to manual assignment). The number of interactions (Figure 2, right) is smaller for the automatic method in both sets. Interestingly, the interaction counts within a mode are almost identical in both sets. There was no training effect. This indicates, that the training (due to solving similar task in both sets) had no influence in using the system infrastructure. The training effect was limited to solving the key problem of comparing the letter sequences.

In the manual assignment mode, both groups initially had no idea that they needed to share documents. So they unwittingly "stole" the shared documents from each others "private" displays. It took a couple of interactions until the participants realized that they needed to cooperate and to assign some of the documents to a display visible to both users. This process of realization and negotiation was the reason for confusion and delay (manifesting itself in the higher solution time and interaction counts required in the manual mode). Interestingly, even the Group A did not realize that they had to share documents in the manual task set (second task set for Group A), although they might have been able to discover this fact in the first task set.

In the automatic assignment mode no such conflicts did arise as the system automatically displayed shared documents on a shared screen. If we use the number of interactions as indicator of occurred conflicts, the data shows that with the automatic mode the number of conflicts is considerably smaller than in the manual mode. A detailed survey of the log files showed that documents which had to be shared, very frequently were reassigned in the manual mode. This proves the presumption that resolving conflicts by social negotiation is – in some situations – inferior to a computer supported negotiation, which can be solved by an automatic assignment using a global quality function such as q.

User Satisfaction. For assessing user satisfaction, we used parts of the technology acceptance model (TAM). We in-

45

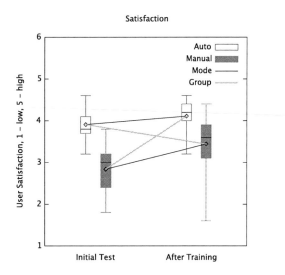

Figure 3: Boxplots of user satisfaction vs. mode

cluded the following items, each to be answered on a scale from 1 (strongly disagree) to 5 (strongly agree):

- The system is easy to use.

- The system helps in solving the task efficiently.

- It is easy to cooperate with the team partner.

- The system helps in solving team conflicts.

- I felt comfortable in using the system.

The final questionnaire used the same items, but with the request to compare both approaches, automatic and manual assignment, on a scale from 1 (manual assignment strongly preferred) to 5 (automatic assignment strongly preferred).

The distribution of the user satisfaction data (using per-questionaire averages) is shown in Figure 3. The overall user satisfaction is higher in the auto mode, for both task sets. In addition, user satisfaction *decreases* within a *group* when switching from auto to manual, while it *increases* when switching from manual to auto.

The correlation of the subjective user satisfaction with the objective data from the log files confirm our hypothesis that the automatic display assignment is superior to the manual assignment in multi-user, multi-display situations with conflicting and dynamic document sets.

For assessing the statistical validity of the results for solution time t, interaction count i, and overall satisfaction s, we have used a one-sided t-test (assuming unknown and not necessarily equal variances for the automatic and the manual test results). The null hypothesis in each case has been that the manual method is at least as good as the automatic method. The alternative hypothesis in each case is that automatic assignment is superior to manual assignment. As can bee seen from the results below, the null hypothesis can

be rejected in all cases. Therefore we conclude that automatic assignment for multi-user and multi-display situations is superior to manual assignment.

H_0	H_1	H_0 rejected at level
$t_{man} \leq t_{auto}$	$t_{man} > t_{auto}$	2.5%
$i_{man} \leq i_{auto}$	$i_{man} > i_{auto}$	0.5%
$s_{man} \geq s_{auto}$	$s_{man} < s_{auto}$	0.5%

4. SUMMARY

We have discussed the problem of assisting teams in effectively using multi-display environments for working together and we have addressed the question whether it is possible to find well-defined quality criteria for automatic display assignment.

We have proposed two criteria (spatial quality and temporal continuity). Our user studies show that – at least for specific scenarios – an automatic display assignment based on these heuristics can be at least as good as a manual assignment. Therefore, it proves that it is *possible* to successfully identify a set of quality criteria for automatic display assignment.

Indeed, we have even been able to show that automatic assignment enables teams to solve their tasks in a shorter time, with less conflicts between team members, and with greater satisfaction.

5. REFERENCES

[1] Alois Ferscha, Gerd Kortuem, and Antonio Krüger. Workshop on ubiquitous display environments. In *Proc. Ubicomp 2004*, Nottingham, England, Sep 7 2004.

[2] Maribeth Back et al. Workshop on ubiquitous display environmentssable ubiquitous computing in next generation conference rooms: design, architecture and evaluation. In *Ubicomp 2006*, Newport Beach, CA, USA, Sep 17 2006.

[3] Patrick Chiu, Qiong Liu, John S. Boreczky, Jonathan Foote, Don Kimber, Surapong Lertsithichai, and Chunyuan Liao. Manipulating and annotating slides in a multi-display environment. In *Human-Computer Interaction INTERACT '03: IFIP TC13 International Conference on Human-Computer Interaction*, 2003.

[4] Brad Johanson, Greg Hutchins, Terry Winograd, and Maureen Stone. Pointright: Experience with flexible input redirection in interactive workspaces. In *Proc. ACM Conference on User Interface and Software Technology (UIST2002)*, pages 227–234, Paris, France, 2002.

[5] Meredith R. Morris, Kathy Ryall, Chia Shen, Clifton Forlines, and Frederic Vernier. Beyond "social protocols": multi-user coordination policies for co-located groupware. In *CSCW '04: Proceedings of the 2004 ACM conference on Computer supported cooperative work*, pages 262–265, New York, NY, USA, 2004. ACM Press.

[6] Thomas Heider, Martin Giersich, and Thomas Kirste. Resource optimization in multi-display environments with distributed grasp. In *Proceedings of the First International Conference on Ambient Intelligence Developments (AmI.d'06)*, pages 60 – 76, Sophia Antipolis, France, September 19 - 22 2006. Springer.

Head-shaped Tangible Interface for Affective Expression

Christian Jacquemin
LIMSI-CNRS & Univ. Paris 11
BP 133, Batiment 508
91403 ORSAY, France
+33 1 69 85 81 11

FirstName.Name@limsi.fr

ABSTRACT

A head shaped resin with several holes and equipped with a camera is used for facial expression synthesis through intuitive multiple finger contacts and gestures. The calibration of the interface is presented together with an evaluation of its accuracy under different light and equipment conditions. Three experiments on using the interface for facial expression synthesis are described: a synthesis of emoticons and two modes of expressive animation by associating face zones with expressions of a 3D face. Evaluations confirm the usability of the interface and show that subjects have appreciated its nuanced and sensitive interaction modes.

Categories and Subject Descriptors

H.5.2 [**Information Interfaces and Presentation**]: User Interfaces – *Input devices and strategies.*

General Terms

Design, Human Factor.

Keywords

Tangible interfaces, Affective computing, Anthropomorphic interfaces.

1. INTRODUCTION

The use of anthropomorphic shapes for output interfaces is quite common (e.g. Embodied Conversational Agents), but it is more rare for tangible input interfaces. When compared with non human-shaped interfaces, anthropomorphic interfaces have the double advantage to be quite intuitive to handle, and to allow for immediate expressive and emotional communication. Intuitiveness is exploited in the doll's head interface of Hinckley et al. [1] for neurosurgical planning through brain visualization. The head shape of the interface provides the appropriate affordances for intuitive and efficient brain view selection. SenToy [2] takes advantage of our natural affective relationship with human body. It is a full body doll equipped with sensors so that players can engage an affective communication with the characters of a game by manipulating the toy.

The work presented here focuses on the head as a natural and intuitive tool for the capture of expressive gestures. We report

on the design of a low-cost input interface to affective communication through multi-point finger contacts. It is made of a head-shaped resin equipped with 42 holes and an internal video camera (Figure 1). The interface is used to control the facial animation of a virtual 3D model through finger contacts. The evaluations made through 45 minutes sessions with a panel of 22 subjects aged between 15 and 56 show that such an interface can offer an intuitive and efficient device for the expression of emotions.

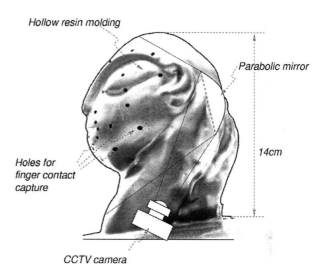

Figure 1. Cross-section of the Interface

2. MULTI-TOUCH FINGER CAPTURE

The purpose of the interface is to use the tangible affordances of a human head to control the expressions of an animated head. Real-time facial animation raises difficult issues because an expression is the result of the association of several local and fine actions called Action Units (AUs) by Friesen and Eckman [3]. We want the users to acquire quickly the production of AUs so that they can focus on their combinations. For this purpose, we have associated face parts with AUs such as *Lip Corner Depressor* or *Brow Lowerer*. The users can combine these elementary expressions through progressive muti-touch interaction with the interface. Through the interface we want users to be able to act simultaneously on several parts of the head, and to produce complex expressions by combining partially expressed elementary AUs..

The multi-touch capture of finger positions on the interface is made by a video camera inside the resin molding. Because of the small dimensions of the interface (approximately the height of a joystick), it is necessary to use a device for wide-angle video capture. The use of a concave mirror has been preferred to lenses because it makes the visual distortion independent of the camera, because it does not result in any loss of brightness and does not augment the camera size, and because it increases the distance between face and camera through reflection (figure 1).

For each of the holes used to capture finger positions, finger contact is recognized by computing the difference between the image brightness at calibration time and the brightness at capture time. Such an image processing technique allows for the simultaneous acquisition of all the finger positions (without recognition of the obturating fingers). The partial obturation of a hole by the fingers can result in the progressive expression of the associated emotion. Thus the tangible interface is a contact sensor that has the two expected properties: it is both gradual and multi-touch.

In order to accept slight changes in camera position and however preserve an accurate capture of light on head holes, the image capture can be calibrated. The camera image is presented to the user together with four anchors that must be placed on four specific holes (Figure 2.a). With the mouse, the user can drag the anchors so that they cover the corresponding holes (Figure 2.b). The correspondences between screen coordinates and hole locations are recomputed and the capture zones around holes (squares) are shown to the user so that she can evaluate the quality of the calibration and possibly makes additional adjustments (Figure 2.c).

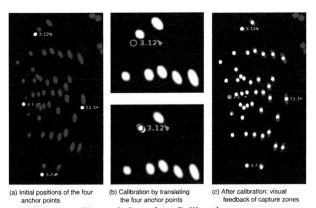

(a) Initial positions of the four anchor points   (b) Calibration by translating the four anchor points   (c) After calibration: visual feedback of capture zones

Figure 2. Interface Calibration.

The computation of image and hole center transformations relies on an homography: the geometric transformation that associates the initial view of the face, with the current view of the video camera. An homography is appropriate because camera motions are small rotations close to the center of view (they are due to the imperfect construction of the interface).

The matrix M for a 3D homography in homogenous coordinates is given by 8 floats. The values of the 4 initial and final locations A_i and A'_i of the calibration anchors result in a system of 8 equations with 8 unknowns that is solved by a Gaussian elimination:

$$\forall i \in 1..4 \begin{pmatrix} a'_{ix} \\ a'_{iy} \\ 1 \end{pmatrix} = \begin{pmatrix} m_{1,1} & m_{1,2} & m_{1,3} \\ m_{2,1} & m_{2,2} & m_{2,3} \\ m_{3,1} & m_{3,2} & 1 \end{pmatrix} \begin{pmatrix} a_{ix} \\ a_{iy} \\ 1 \end{pmatrix}$$

At calibration time, the gray level in each hole is recorded. During interaction, the new values of brightness are computed and each hole activation is proportional to the ratio between the current brightness, the one captured initially, and full darkness. Thus hole activation is a function of the opacity of a finger and of the strength with which a hole is obturated.

Figure 3 shows logs of the activation values (darknesses) of a hole and its neighbors at different light levels and with two equipments (black glove for the figure 3.a or bare hand for 3.b). The captured gesture is a finger that points at a hole, reaches its target and obturates it, and finally moves away. The time is the horizontal coordinate and the vertical coordinate is the level of obturation of each hole. The activation of the targeted hole (#3.4) is represented by a solid line. The concurrent activations of neighboring holes are represented by dotted lines, they result from shadowing effects of the fingers and hand palm. Hole #3.4 is the bottom center of the right eye, the coactivated holes (#3.6, #3.2, #3.12) correspond respectively to eye center, upper center, and right corner of the same eye.

Because of the finger translucency, the level of obturation with bare hand and strong light is weaker than with lower lighting conditions (figure 3.b), while it is constant with black gloves whatever the light intensity (figure 3.a). Whereas it may seem desirable to have a better obturation by using black gloves, wearing gloves has the drawback to increase the shadowing effect on neighboring holes: coactivated holes have closer values to #3.4 in Figure 3.a than in Figure 3.b. Bare hand manipluation has been preferred to gloves because it does not require an additional equipment, and because it reduces the level of undesirable shadows. In the case of bare hand manipulation, the results of Figure 3.b show that the better discrimination is obtained for strong light even though the obturation by the fingers is not very high (~0.2). At all light levels, the targeted hole is the most activated, but strong light yields better discrimination.

Obturation of point 3.4 and its neighbors

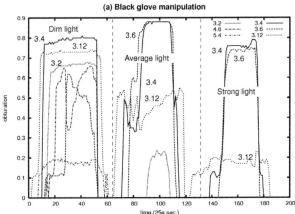

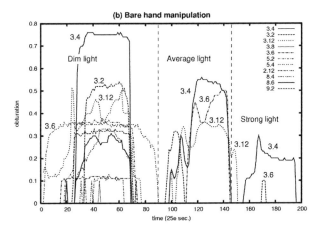

Figure 3. Hole activations with finger pointing at hole #3.4.

3. EXPERIMENTS

Among the multiple applications of this interface, we have chosen to focus on its use for facial animation. Animating a 3D face is a skilled activity, and we wanted to provide the users with a tool that would enable them to control easily the expressions of a synthetic face. The presence of undesirable coactivations of neighboring holes has oriented towards the use of face zones instead of individual holes for the mapping between finger contacts and expressions. For this purpose, we have divided the tangible interface into 6 zones and associated each zone with a predefined expression (an Action Unit of [3]): the forehead is associated with *raised brows*, the nose with *lower brows*, the eyes with *closed eyes*, the mouth with smile (*lip corner puller*), the jaws with *jaw drop*, and the chin with *lip corner depressor* (Figure 4.b). A similar mapping has been established between the face zones and emoticons (Figure 4.a).

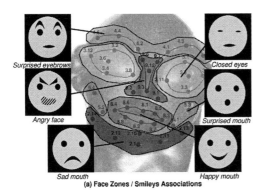

(a) Face Zones / Smileys Associations

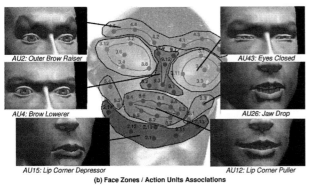

(b) Face Zones / Action Units Associations

Figure 4. Mapping between face zones and base expressions

We have designed two modes of facial animation: a *boolean exclusive mode*: only one basic expression can be activated at a time, and a *blended mode*: expressions can be gradually activated (from neutral face to full expression) and can be combined. Emoticons cannot be used in blended mode, this mode only concerns 3D facial expressions.

In order to evaluate the usability of the interface together with the user's pleasure, 22 volunteer subjects aged between 15 and 58 (average 29.1) have made a 45' experiment with on interactive facial animation. Figure 5 shows the experimental setup: the subject sits in front of the interface, manipulates it with her fingers, and tries to reproduce a model (top left of the screen) on an animated head or emoticon (center of the screen). The subject has two sheets that correspond to Figures 4.a and 4.b to help her memorize the mappings between face zones and emoticons or Action Units.
Each evaluation session consists of a presentation of the purpose of the interface by the experimenter and three

experiments. The first two experiments, are in the boolean exclusive mode (emoticons for experiment 1 and facial expressions for experiment 2). In these experiments, the subject is presented successively 15 random target emoticons or expressions and must reproduce them by touching the associated zone of the interface and holding the expression for half a second. Every time a target expression is reached, the next one is displayed until the last one.

Figure 5. Experimental setup

The third experiment is in the blended mode. Blended expressions can be produced by touching simultaneously and more or less strongly several zones. The resulting expression is the linear combination of the elementary expressions with weights computed from the zone activation values [4] (the activation of a zone is the level of the most occluded hole). For instance, the simultaneous activations of the jaw and mouth zones result in a combination of smile and lip protrusion. In this experiment, the subjects are asked to reproduce as accurately as possible each target blended expression and to decide by themselves when they are satisfied before turning to the next target.

Before starting each experiment, the subjects are asked to feel comfortable, to take as much time as they need to practice the interface in the current mode. They can hold the interface either facing them or oriented the other way.

4. EVALUATIONS

Quantitative evaluations rely on the time needed to reproduce a target expression. For the third experiment, we also use the error between the target and the produced expression. Tables 1 and 2 report the percentage of subjects at each expertise level by the average time taken to reach a target. These tables show that expert users tend to be quicker in the first experiment (emoticon). But the advantage of expert subjects tends to disappear in the second experiment, either because non expert subjects take longer to learn how to control the interface or because the additional difficulty due to the need to identify a target 3D expression before reproducing it (emoticons are easier to recognize) tends to leverage the completion speeds between expert and non expert users.

Table 1. Distribution of the subjects by average time and expertise (1st task)

Expertise:	Low	Average	High
0-5 sec.	33%	30%	**67%**
5-10 sec.	**56%**	**60%**	33%
> 10 sec.	11%	10%	0%

Table 2. Distribution of the subjects by average time and expertise (2nd task)

Expertise:	Low	Average	High
0-5 sec.	0%	20%	33%
5-10 sec.	**89%**	**70%**	**67%**
> 10 sec.	11%	10%	0%

The third experiment brings an additional difficulty: the subjects must combine zone activations to reach a blended expression. In order to take into account the quality of the produced expression, Table 3 reports, for each duration and for each level of expertise an average measure of the error between the achieved expression and the target one. The error is the sum of the distances between the coordinates of the face made by the user and the target face in the 6D space of blended expressions.

Due to the difficulty of the task, the time taken to reach the targets are longer than in the first two experiments. Table 3 shows that expert subjects get better quality, but they do not perform significantly faster than non expert subjects: low, average, and high experts have the respective average durations 27.2", 26.9", and 25.9".

Table 3. Error by average time and expertise (3rd task)

Expertise:	Low	Average	High
10-20 sec.	1.74	1.14	1.06
20-30 sec.	1.52	1.66	1.0
30-40 sec.	1.53	1.34	1.38
> 40 sec.	-	1.91	0.89

The qualitative evaluation is based on an anonymous questionnaire that contained questions about the expertise of the subjects, about the subjective level of difficulty and the pleasure of use, and about general thoughts on the interface and its possible applications. All the subjects but one have appreciated using the interface and have been deeply engaged in the experiments that were proposed.

Among the positive aspects of the interface, 12 subjects out of 22 appreciate the soft and sensitive tactile interaction with such arguments as *the possibility of nuanced control*, *it is touch friendly and natural based* or *the tactile interface and its reactivity*. The negative points concern the difficulties in the manipulation of the interface: the shadowing, the small distances between holes, and a lack of relief on the mouth.

In response to the question whether they could envision some applications to this interface, the subjects have been very positive. They have made many propositions such as graphical modeling, emoticons for chat or email, plastic surgery, telepresence and affective communication, interface for the blind and visually impaired people, theater, animation, embodied conversational agents...

Last, subjects were asked to comment freely on the interface. We just report one comment that is certainly representative of the impression given by such a device: *The contact of fingers on a face is a particular gesture that we neither often nor easily make (You do not let people easily touch your face). Luckily, this uncomfortable impression does not last very long. After a few trials, you feel like a sculptor working with clay...*

5. CONCLUSION

The interface presented in this paper was based on the idea that giving access to a tactile interaction with a head-shaped interface could engage users in a deep and sensitive experience. The results of the experiments show that usability is satisfactory even though some of the technical aspects could be improved. More importantly, the observation of the subjects and the analysis of the questionnaire confirm that users have experienced the interface as an appealing device for affective communication. Some of the users have even start talking with the interface *Come on! Close your mouth...* in situation where they could not make it look as they wished.

More applications should be conducted in the near future to evaluate the interface for interpersonal communication and telepresence. The first experiments reported here show that the characteristics of the device are a good starting point for further investigations in its use for affective communication.

6. ACKNOWLEDGEMENTS

Many thanks to Clarisse Beau, Vincent Bourdin, Laurent Pointal and Sébastien Rieublanc (LIMSI-CNRS) for their help in the design of the interface; Jean-Noël Montagné (Centre de Ressources Art Sensitif), Francis Bras, and Sandrine Chiri (Interface Z) for their help on sensitive interfaces; Catherine Pelachaud (Univ. Paris 8) for her help on ECAs. This work is supported by LIMSI-CNRS *Talking Head* action coordinated by Jean-Claude Martin.

REFERENCES

[1] K. Hinckley, R. Pausch, J. C. Goble, and N. F.Kassell. Passive real-world interface props for neurosurgical visualization. In *CHI '94 : Proceedings of the SIGCHI conference on Human factors in computing systems*, pages 452–458, New York, NY, USA, 1994. ACM Press.

[2] A. Paiva, G. Andersson, K. Höök, D. Mourao, M. Costa, and C. Martinho. Sentoy in Fantasya. Designing an affective sympathetic interface to a computer game. *Personal Ubiquitous Comput.*, 6(5-6):378–389, 2002.

[3] P. Ekman, and W.V. Friesen. Facial action coding system: *A technique for the measurement of facial movement.* Consulting Psychologists Press, Palo Alto, CA, USA, 1978.

[4] N. Tsapatsoulis, A. Raouzaiou, S. Kollias, R. Crowie, E. Douglas-Cowie. Emotion recognition and synthesis based on MPEG-4 FAPs. In I.S. Pandzic, R. Forchheimer, eds.: *MPEG-4 Facial Animation*. Wiley, Chichester, UK, 141–167, 2002.

Expert Habits vs. UI Improvements:
Re-Design of a Room Booking System

Per A. Jonasson [1]
Sigma Kudos Sweden AB [1]
Chalmers University of Technology
SE-412 96 Gothenburg
per.jonasson@sigmakudos.com

Morten Fjeld [2]
t2i Lab, www.t2i.se, CSE [2]
Chalmers University of Technology
SE-412 96 Gothenburg
morten@fjeld.ch

Aiko Fallas Yamashita [2,3]
SW Engineering and Management [3]
IT University of Gothenburg
SE-417 56 Gothenburg
aiko@ituniv.se

ABSTRACT

This paper presents the results of a case study examining prototyping as a method in re-designing a user interface (UI). In the case presented, a web-based room booking was re-designed. Running on a university web site, the existing system has caused much critique amongst its users. Their expectations for a new UI were increased ease of use, less effort required, and less time consumed. We prototyped a new UI using Visio and tested it with a small number of experienced and novice users. Our results partly favor the existing system and partly the new one. To our surprise, experienced users performed relatively poorer with the new UI considering their critique of the existing one. We found paper prototyping to be an efficient method to gain user feedback on usability issues and that a low-fidelity prototype does not automatically mean low-effort testing. We observed that visible-state UI elements can be demanding to test through paper prototyping.

Categories and Subject Descriptors

H.5.2 [**User Interfaces**]: Graphical user Interfaces (GUI), Prototyping, Evaluation/methodology, User-centered design

General Terms

Measurement, Design, Human Factors

Keywords

HCI, User interface design, low-fidelity prototyping, Visio, booking, booking systems, re-design.

1. INTRODUCTION

We present results of a case study examining prototyping as a method in re-designing a user interface (UI). In the case presented, we studied a web-based university room booking system [3]. Rooms offered by the system are generally small and intended for group work, seminars, and study sessions. The main reason for this choice of subject was frustration reported amongst users of the existing system. Re-design employing a low-fidelity approach combined with a user test of the re-

designed system involving a small number of participants is often referred to as paper prototyping [8]. Due to the small amount of empirical data, user tests most often do not include statistical analysis. The case presented aims to develop an understanding of some of the factors involved in re-designing and evaluating a UI for web-based room booking.

2. RELATED WORK

Prototyping in order to guide the re-design process has been examined for various fields such as commercial UIs [1] and UIs for young users [9]. Practitioners' understanding of fidelity in prototyping methods was addressed by McCurdy et al. [6]. User-centered prototyping and design was examined by Kiris [5]. So-called HCI patterns have been applied to the re-designed online booking systems [10]. As part of an undergraduate HCI course given by one of the authors, students developed and tested paper prototypes to guide a re-design of their course booking system (Fig. 1). In short, while literature covers low-fidelity prototyping, re-design, fidelity in prototyping, user-centered prototyping, and patterns for the re-design of online booking systems, we are not aware of works aiming to guide the re-design of web-based room booking services. The results presented here may contribute towards establishing such knowledge.

Figure 1. Developing (left) and testing (right) a paper prototype for re-design of a course booking system.

3. PROTOTYPING

In our work, prototyping was an iterative process with two cycles. First, we gathered requirements, re-designed the UI, designed a new GUI using Visio [7], and tested this using the three researchers involved in this project (see acknowledgements). Secondly, the outcome of the first cycle was used to refine the first-mentioned steps and then to carry out a real user test.

3.1 Requirements gathering

To gain knowledge about the constraints and requirements within the existing system as well as about typical users and their usage of the system, a few open interviews were conducted with students and staff of the Department of Computer Science, all experienced users of the system. This led to the following critique of the existing UI:

- Affordance: Lack of visibility of constraints in the system. Limitations are not visible until after an action has been taken and come in the form of error messages.

- Search: Difficult to book a room fitting a group's requirements because it is not possible to search for a room based on properties like time slot, size, and available equipment.

- Navigation: Difficult to find a room, as this requires browsing of a large schedule map and scrolling in both horizontal and vertical directions. This map is generally hard to navigate as identifiers for rooms and time slots can become hidden (see Fig. 2).

- Retrieval: Difficult to find a room booked by someone else, for instance, in the event of a group meeting.

- Cancellation: Difficult to cancel as users cannot easily access their own bookings. Instead, this is done by first accessing the room being reserved (provided the user remembers which room was reserved).

Figure 2. Existing UI: finding a free room.

To gain a greater understanding of general issues concerning booking systems, we reviewed a number of existing systems. These included travel booking systems, a generic commercial booking system, a library booking system, and several room booking systems related to universities. This review showed that most booking systems incorporate a notion of cost for the booking. These are either monetary and charged with each booking or related to access time. In both types of systems, it is important to make users aware of the cost issue. In a monetary system, a check-out cart usually presents costs and users approve the sum/fee to be charged. In an access time system, the cost usually consists of a limitation on the number of bookings that can be made at one time or over a period of time.

3.2 Re-design: developing the prototype

Based on input from the interviews as well as our own experience with the system, we performed a task analysis in the form of a use case model. The following attributes were identified as being central to the function of the system:

- Search: Finding a free room within the parameters of place, size, equipment, and free time. Finding existing bookings based on user or description.

- Booking management: Booking a room for a duration of time/time slot, finding own/others' bookings and canceling such bookings

- Easy access: Most lookup functions should be available without logging into the system, thereby speeding up access and not limiting the user base to only those with an account.

3.2.1 Constraints for the re-design

Working on an existing system we had to make a decision as to how far we were going to pursue the re-design task: either keep it at the very basic level, staying within the constraints of the existing system or suggest new types of functionality that would be beneficial to the users. We decided to stay close to the existing system's functionality (i.e. what is visible or imaginable through the existing UI), but with one exception: we added the element of room properties in order to make the task of searching for a free room more adaptable to users' real needs. This information could most likely be added to the room database with little effort.

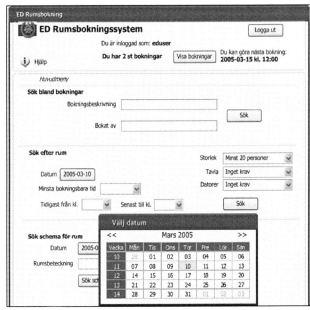

Figure 3. Re-designed UI: example screen of one of the functionalities of the system: "finding a free room".

3.2.2 Prototyping

A low-fidelity prototype was deemed sufficient for the level of user evaluation required by the project (see Fig. 3). In order to be able to work iteratively and perform rapid changes a paper prototype was created using Visio. The rationale for this was twofold: Visio contains a simple drag-and-drop-interface with predefined (Microsoft Windows) widgets for all interaction elements we wanted to use, and it was easily available to us through university licenses. Any modern HTML-editor would likely have sufficed, but since the design presents the internal state of the application to the user, such an approach would have resulted in severe page duplication. With Visio we could handle the subsections of the screen independently and create the various combinations without worrying about the overall state of a page (this was, at least, our intention). It also works better in the production of printouts needed for the paper prototype, including the frames for cutting, folding, and identifying the prototype pieces.

The screen images were configured in Visio for the different situations in the scenarios, assigned unique identifiers, printed, and then folded along the edges to have the widget identifier showing on the back. This should aid the human "computer" in choosing the correct prototype pieces to use for each scenario (see Fig. 4).

Figure 4. Paper prototype used in our study. More than 40 UI elements existed: windows, mouse-over texts, pop-ups, and dropdown menus.

3.2.3 Refinement of the prototype
As we tested the prototype with the three researchers involved in this project (see acknowledgements), a significant finding was the need for users to know their "current position" in the system ("click-hierarchy") in order to enable backward navigation. This resulted in the addition of so-called "breadcrumbs" [2]. Also, the selection method for room constraints (computer, white board etc.) was changed from Yes/No checkboxes to Drop-down choices, because the "Does not matter" alternative is important when expressing restrictions. We also identified the need to make certain texts in the prototype more understandable. With an accordingly refined prototype we then proceeded to the user test.

3.3 User test
The user test was carried out with an experimental leader, a human "computer", and five participants who were invited individually. Of the five participants there were three novice users and two experienced users of the existing room booking system. All subjects were highly computer literate. We prepared eight distinct tasks[1]. When creating and combining

---

[1] Eight tasks in the order presented (with operation(s)/state(s) required/encountered): i) book a room (search, login), ii) book a room (search, failure due to restriction), iii) find existing bookings, iv) book a room (from list), v) book a room (search), vi) unbook a room

tasks, we tried to define a natural and effective way through the system. Tasks were formulated as clearly as possible without making them too easy to perform. Based on a fixed order of the eight tasks, we prepared a complete script describing exactly how the human "computer" should work. The script contained both what the "computer" was supposed to do and the expected user interaction. The script was inspired by an action list of a cognitive walk-through [4]. The script ensured that every test was carried out in exactly the same way, ensuring the attainment of valid, comparable data.

The test procedure consisted of a first interview regarding previous knowledge and actual task solving, and a second interview regarding subjective ranking of the prototype. Each task was followed by a few additional questions to ensure task completion such as: "Are you sure that you have logged out?". In the second interview, users were asked about the quality and functions of the system, usability, and possible changes or improvements.

3.3.1 Objective results
For the test scenario's eight tasks, total task solving time was between 8.0 and 17.8 minutes, with a mean of 13 minutes. We emphasize that two novice participants accomplished the tasks in a shorter amount of time than the experienced participants.

3.3.2 Subjective results
Information presented in the header (as the user's status bar) was considered confusing and indistinct. Such information was meant to show the user the number of bookings made and when the system allows new bookings. Some participants were uncertain whether this concerned the number of bookings remaining or the number made. The information regarding when the next booking could be made was also unclear. The subjects offered proposals for combining the information and reformulating them for better comprehension.

A search function for bookings was appreciated by the participants. A "my bookings" function in the header (where the status bar of the user is visible) was considered a convenient way to verify and cancel bookings. The ability to view a room's schedule and then make or cancel a booking was also highly valued. Pop-ups that appeared due to system restrictions were appreciated and not considered annoying.

Participants stated that the paper prototype gave them a very good insight into the system. However, the human "computer" response time caused by the shuffling of prototype pieces was a bit too high.

4. DISCUSSION
For re-design projects, i.e. projects where there is a user base with previous application experience, it is helpful to think *small* in terms of the size of advancements, the number of changes, and the magnitude of changes being incorporated. Our most interesting finding was the lack of enthusiasm that participants with previous experience expressed towards the new design *despite* their lack of enthusiasm towards the older design. The simple explanation to this is habitual work patterns: despite a lousy UI, people tend to adapt and become "power users" for simple systems in little time, finding their way around the quirks and problems. A re-designed UI may break this mode of operation. Still, the power of habit is truly a factor to be considered when re-designing a UI. Our experience is similar to

---

(using calendar), vii) find a room booked for a specific course, and viii) logout.

that presented by Bryan-Kinns and Hamilton [1] where the need to adjust the experience along several dimensions (interaction, graphical, etc.) was noted. For re-design, an approach with small steps should be considered, which can teach existing users the benefits of the new design.

This problem also brings up the issue of learning: in order to test a UI there might be a need to instruct or teach the users the main principles behind it. However, this instruction can interfere with the testing as it may give away too much information about the issues for novice users. Since we thought that instructions could benefit expert and novice users differently, we decided to use a "no teaching" approach as much as possible, only informing the users of the existence of constraints and preconditions (e.g. that the scenarios would include a previous booking made by the same user). Interestingly, two out of three novice users performed *better* than the two experienced users, suggesting that the UI was generally usable (with some overall problems, see below), but that there was a discrepancy in usage mode from the existing system that could have hindered experienced users.

Although paper prototyping is a useful tool for testing ideas on a small set of users, there are issues of fidelity to be considered. We chose to use Visio because it would help us get started quickly and develop model content in greater depth. However, this was also a drawback because we added more details to the model than originally required. On the whole, a sketched prototype would likely have taken less time to complete despite the need to redraw duplicates. Walker [11] found that low- and high-fidelity prototypes are equally good at uncovering usability issues. This finding relates to the reported success of mixed-fidelity prototypes [6]. Our Visio model would probably have been more effective in a high-fidelity approach e.g. as the graphical basis for a simulation using PowerPoint or Flash.

Another problem we encountered with paper prototyping was making the status of UI elements clearly visible. Making this information visible required the human "computer" to shuffle pieces of the UI back and forth.

5. CONCLUSIONS AND FUTURE WORK

A main contribution to our understanding of re-design and paper prototyping of existing UIs was the finding that even a bad UI may have "committed" users. As such, a re-design may not be as simple or beneficial as initially hoped for. Furthermore, we conclude that it is important to consider habits of experienced users in the re-design of an existing system. Even if users do not like the existing system, they are still accustomed to it and designers have to take this into account. If a re-design diverges greatly from a current standard it must be well justified. The formulation of textual and graphical cues is important because any ambiguity can be misinterpreted by users. Some future work in order to help in understanding these issues may examine the learning process (i.e. the user workload) compared to the older system and considerations involving expert users and emotional attachment. Future studies using a larger number of participants may help in achieving more robust and relevant results.

Concerning paper prototyping as a method, we found that it is a convenient method for testing a new design. However, for the testing to run smoothly the system cannot be too complex. Our room booking system could be navigated in many different ways, producing an excessive amount of combinations to be taken into account. This resulted in our limiting the users, not allowing them to solve the problem their own way but only ours. Another problem with paper prototyping occurs when a visible system status must be updated frequently. Both of these problems resulted in a high workload for the person acting as the "computer", which was perceived by participants as increased response time.

6. ACKNOWLEDGEMENTS
Prototyping and re-design leading to this paper was done by Per A. Jonasson together with Linda Bööj and David Jonasson.

7. REFERENCES
[1] Bryan-Kimms, N., and Hamilton, F. 2002. One for all and all for one? Case studies of using prototypes in commercial projects. In *Proc. NordiCHI'02*, ACM, pp.91-100.

[2] Dix, A., Finlay, J., Abowd, G., Beale, R. *Human-Computer Interaction.* Pearson Education Ltd, 2004.

[3] ED Booking System, Chalmers, Gothenburg: www.ed.chalmers.se/bokningssystem

[4] Jurca, A. 2000. Consumer-centered interfaces: customizing online travel planning. In *Proc. CHI '00 Ext. Abstracts on Human Factors in Computing Systems*, ACM, pp. 93-94.

[5] Kiris, E. 2004. User-centered eService design and redesign. In *Proc. CHI 2004*, ACM, pp. 990-999.

[6] McCurdy, M., Connors, C., Pyrzak, Guy, Kanefsky, B., and A. Vera. 2006. Breaking the fidelity barrier: An examination of our current characterization of prototypes and an example of a mixed-fidelity success. In *Proc. CHI 2006*, pp. 1233-1242.

[7] Microsoft Office Visio 2003 Professional, Microsoft, 2003.

[8] Nielsen, J. 2003. Paper prototyping: Getting user data before you code. www.useit.com/alertbox/20030414.html

[9] Rettig, M. 1994. Prototyping for Tiny Fingers. In *Communications of the ACM*, 27(4), pp. 21-27.

[10] Teuber, C., Forbrig, P. 2004. Different types of patterns for online-booking systems. In *Proc. 3rd Annual Conference on Task models and diagrams*, pp 91-97.

[11] Walker, M., Takayama, L., and Landay, J. High-fidelity or low-fidelity, paper or computer medium? In *Proc. of the Human Factors and Ergonomics Society 46th Meeting: HFES2002*, pp. 661-665.

GazeSpace: Eye Gaze Controlled Content Spaces

Sven Laqua
University College London
Department of Computer Science
Gower Street
0044 (0)20 7679 0351

s.laqua@cs.ucl.ac.uk

Shane Udaraka Bandara
University College London
Department of Computer Science
Gower Street

shaneucl@yahoo.co.uk

M. Angela Sasse
University College London
Department of Computer Science
Gower Street
0044 (0)20 7679 7212

a.sasse@cs.ucl.ac.uk

ABSTRACT

In this paper, we introduce GazeSpace, a novel system utilizing eye gaze to browse content spaces. While most existing eye gaze systems are designed for medical contexts, GazeSpace is aimed at able-bodied audiences. As this target group has much higher expectations for quality of interaction and general usability, GazeSpace integrates a contextual user interface, and rich continuous feedback to the user. To cope with real-world information tasks, GazeSpace incorporates novel algorithms using a more dynamic gaze-interest threshold instead of static dwell-times. We have conducted an experiment to evaluate user satisfaction and results show that GazeSpace is easy to use and a "fun experience".

Categories and Subject Descriptors

H5.2 [**User Interfaces**]: Input devices and strategies.

General Terms

Design, Experimentation, Human Factors.

Keywords

Pointing and Selection, Eye Tacking, Eye Gaze Interaction, Eye Controlled User Interfaces

1. INTRODUCTION

For over 20 years people have used keyboards and mice as primary input devices for personal computers. With continuous advances in technology, novel forms of interaction are emerging. With the shift towards mobile and ubiquitous computing, touch screens are used in many scenarios. People use a pen or finger to control tablet PCs, PDAs, smart phones or public terminals. With advances in eye-tracking technology [1, 2, 3, 7, 8 and 10] and projects that reduce implementation costs [9], eye gaze may be the next interaction technique to break into mainstream usage.

Eye gaze interaction is commonly regarded as a potential complement, if not a replacement for traditional input techniques. However, when discussing input techniques for computing systems it is crucial to distinguish two main steps in the interaction process. As today's user interfaces (UI) mostly apply a desktop metaphor, users are required to point (e.g.: move a mouse) and select (e.g.: press a mouse button). It is important to consider this distinction when analyzing potential eye gaze interaction techniques. Many existing eye gaze systems demonstrate satisfying results for gaze-based pointing (or gaze-pointing). However, this only fulfills half of the requirement for the described "point and select" interactions. Successfully implementing the selection part of the interaction is more challenging than the pointing part. Current eye gaze systems commonly make use of static dwell-times to achieve this second part of the interaction process [1, 6, 7 and 10].

2. BACKGROUND

Most existing eye gaze systems are designed for medical contexts (e.g.: Tobii P10), where they enhance quality of life for people with disabilities, who cannot use traditional input techniques. The most common applications for patients are eye-typing to communicate with their surroundings and means to control their environment (e.g.: light switches, or motor controls for wheel chair). With increasing accuracy (resolution of gaze pointing), flexibility (freedom of head movements) and decreasing costs [9], applications "will soon be practical for able-bodied users" [3]. But as able-bodied audiences have much higher expectations for quality of interaction and general usability, challenges to beat traditional input methods and user interfaces arise. This partly explains why much of existing research focuses on rather abstract tasks when evaluating prototypes using dwell-time selection [1, 6 and 10].

Task complexity: Testing simple selection tasks ensures that limited cognitive effort is required. Although one can argue that simple selection tasks help modeling future scenarios, e.g. of selecting menu items, the abstract nature of these experiments often excludes the *cognitive component*: people need to look at a number of elements, make a choice, and then select the appropriate element. Experiments testing selection based on colour or single letters [10] minimize cognitive load and thus simplify task complexity. We hypothesize that more complex information tasks work less efficiently with static dwell times (H1). As complex tasks involve unique mental processes, they might require tailored activation times.

Research on more realistic use-cases, involving more complex tasks, commonly combines gaze-pointing with alternative means for selection (e.g.: hotkeys [3], speech [8] or even EMG clicking [2]). Due to space restrictions, we only discuss the most recent one: Kumar's EyePoint system [3] enables users to browse the World Wide Web by replacing mouse interactions with a combination of gaze-pointing and hotkeys for selection (using a keyboard). EyePoint proposes a "look-press-look-release action" to cope with accuracy limitations of current eye trackers when used with standard user interfaces. This incorporates (a) looking at an area of interest, (b) zooming into

4.1.3 Impact of Algorithms

The comparison of the two tested algorithms (SIA and DID) revealed a higher preference for the static interest accumulation algorithm (see Table 1). Interestingly, 35% of participants did not notice any difference in the user interface of the two sessions (apart from content). Participants favoring the SIA algorithm usually stated faster interactions as the reason.

Table 1. User preference of prototype versions

no difference noticed	35%
With static algorithm (SIA)	45%
With dynamic algorithm (DID)	20%

When looking at the questionnaire feedback, using algorithms as independent variable, superior ratings for the static interest accumulation (SIA) algorithm for *learnability* and for *interface & content* have been found (see Figure 6). Although the SIA algorithm was preferred, participants surprisingly rated it less accurate. However, it needs to be noted that these differences are not significant.

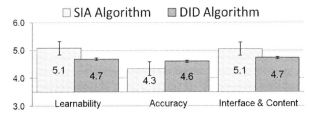

Figure 6. User satisfaction based on algorithm

5. CONCLUSIONS

We have not compared the GazeSpace system with traditional mouse-based input, as the main aim of this early study was to investigate initial user responses to the GazeSpace prototype. Results show that participants throughout liked user interface and interaction technique. As the most common complaint mentioned has been the speed of interaction, future work should test lower activation thresholds (*"if faster ... it would be fun and relaxing"*). Many participants preferred the SIA algorithm, as it resulted in faster activations. We consciously decided for longer activation thresholds in the beginning of the experiment to prevent high error rates. These could have negatively biased participant's general evaluation of this novel interaction technique. When using static dwell times for selection, speed of interaction and error rates will always influence each other. To compete with traditional input techniques, future eye gaze systems might require adaptive selection algorithms which can be tailored to individual users and task complexity.

Participants' comments such as "aesthetically pleasing", "user friendly" and "nice interface" further suggest that the user experience will be crucial when targeting future eye gaze systems at able-bodied audiences. The design of the user interfaces should complement the novelty of the interaction technique and rich feedback on the system's state will further complement the user experience. Although feedback on the general tracking state seems to be quite useful, findings suggest a redesign into a more subtle and less disturbing feedback feature.

Looking at algorithm performance mainly revealed a difference in interaction speed. Although not in the focus of this paper, some initial eye tracking analysis suggests no significant differences in fixation counts, gaze time or fixation durations

between SIA and DID. Further studies and more detailed analysis of the eye tracking data might enable a more detailed discrimination. It also appears crucial to experiment with different settings for gaze-interest-thresholds and timing values for the decay function.

6. FUTURE WORK

Besides improving current algorithms, further development of the GazeSpace prototype will focus on redesigning the layered architecture of the application to enable direct web access. Achieving this milestone will result in the ability to browse "live" blog spaces simply through eye gaze. To enable realistic blog-reading, GazeSpace will require the integration of scrolling functionality to cope with larger amounts of text. Previous research has confirmed that this is a feasible feature [3]. Another crucial aspect for the development of future eye gaze systems will be the required effort for correcting a false interaction. The easier it will be to correct an error (wrong selection), the more tolerant users should be.

7. REFERENCES

[1] Hansen, J. P. et al. Command Without a Click: Dwell Time Typing by Mouse and Gaze Selections. In *Proceedings of Ninth IFIP TC13 International Conference on Human-Computer Interaction (Interact '03)* (Zurich, Switzerland, Sept 1-5, 2003)

[2] Junker, A. M. and Hansen, J. P. Gaze Pointing and facial EMG clicking. In *2nd Conference on Communication by Gaze Interaction (COGAIN 2006)* (Turin, Italy, Sept 4-5, 2006)

[3] Kumar, M. et al. EyePoint: Practical Pointing and Selection Using Gaze and Keyboard. In *Proceedings of the SIGCHI conference on Human factors in computing systems (CHI '07)* (San Jose, CA, 2007).

[4] Laqua, S. and Brna, P. The Focus-Metaphor Approach: A Novel Concept for the Design of Adaptive and User-Centric Interfaces. In *Proc. Interact '05*, (Rome, Italy, 2005), 295-308.

[5] Laqua, S., Ogbechie, N. and Sasse, M. A. Contextualizing the Blogosphere: A Comparison of Traditional and Novel User Interfaces for the Web. In *Proc. 21st BCS HCI Group Conference (HCI '07)* (Lancaster, UK, 2007).

[6] Majaranta, P. et al. Effects of Feedback on Eye Typing with a Short Dwell Time. In *Proceedings of the Eye Tracking Research & Application Symposium (ETRA 2004)* (San Antonio, TX, 2004).

[7] Miniotas, D. et al. Eye Gaze Interaction with Expanding Targets. *In CHI'04 extended abstracts on Human factors in computing systems* (Vienna, Austria, 2004), 1255-1258.

[8] Miniotas, D. et al. Extending the Limits for Gaze Pointing through the Use of Speech. In *Information Technology and Control*, 2005, Vol. 34, No. 3, 225-230.

[9] openEyes. http://hcvl.hci.iastate.edu/cgi-bin/openEyes.cgi, last accessed on 24 May 2007.

[10] Silbert, L. E. and Jacob, R. J. K. Evaluation of Eye Gaze Interaction. In *Proceedings of the SIGCHI conference on Human factors in computing systems (CHI '00)* (The Hague, Netherlands, 2000), 281-288.

[11] Tobii P10. http://www.tobii.com//default.asp?sid=553, last accessed on 24 May 2007.

Contextualizing the Blogosphere: A Comparison of Traditional and Novel User Interfaces for the Web

Sven Laqua
University College London
Department of Computer Science
Gower Street
0044 (0)20 7679 0351

s.laqua@cs.ucl.ac.uk

Nnamdi Ogbechie
University College London
Department of Computer Science
Gower Street

nogbechie@googlemail.com

M. Angela Sasse
University College London
Department of Computer Science
Gower Street
0044 (0)20 7679 7212

a.sasse@cs.ucl.ac.uk

ABSTRACT

In this paper, we investigate how contextual user interfaces affect blog reading experience. Based on a review of previous research, we argue why and how contextualization may result in (H1) *enhanced blog reading experiences.* In an eyetracking experiment, we tested 3 different web-based user interfaces for information spaces. The StarTree interface (by Inxight) and the Focus-Metaphor interface are compared with a standard blog interface. Information tasks have been used to evaluate and compare task performance and user satisfaction between these three interfaces. We found that both contextual user interfaces clearly outperformed the traditional blog interface, both in terms of task performance as well as user satisfaction.

Categories and Subject Descriptors

H.5.2 [**User Interfaces**]: Graphical User interfaces

General Terms

Design, Experimentation, Human Factors.

Keywords

Blogging, Contextualization, Contextual User Interfaces, Focus + Context, Focus-Metaphor Interface, StarTree, Eye Tracking.

1. INTRODUCTION

The World Wide Web is increasingly about social interaction and collaboration. Blogging is a key activity in this *Social Web* enabling collective contributions of any type of information. Blogs have empowered millions of users to share their knowledge and experiences. But meaningful blogging experiences are as much about accessing information (reading) as they are about contributing information (writing). With one million new contributions being published every day [10], how much of this information is novel, meaningful and of interest for the reader? In a world of increasing information overload [8], efficient and effective strategies to manage information are essential.

The blogosphere (entirety of all blogs) faces the general problem of imbalance between ease of information contribution and meaningful information seeking. Millions of individual

authors create millions of small and unique blog sites, and compete for attention in this messy space. Every contribution to this universal conversation - the actual content of a blog post - is wrapped into an individual visual design and a tailored structure of information through means of categories or tags. The dynamic nature of blogs quickly buries older content in archives or at best category lists reflecting the individual mind sets of their authors. In a sense, blogs are much like streams of individual thoughts. The main problem with information spaces as dynamic as the blogosphere is information discovery [1]. Finding useful information can be hard and time-consuming often with a negative impact on the interaction experience.

Information-seeking behavior aiming beyond undirected browsing leads to clashes of readers' and authors' unique mental models (see Figure 1). When accessing content wrapped into layers of information structure, navigation and visual design, user's and author's unique mental models clash: To understand the content on a new web page, the user needs to extract meaning from the wrapping visual and structural layers (see Figure 1- left). The idea of contextual user interfaces like the Focus-Metaphor is to minimize noise caused by any wrapping layers and to achieve a seamless information experience much closer to the actual content (see Figure 1 - right). Rather than redesigning the user interface to provide a seamless and contextual **information experience**, current efforts are focused around "**search-based interaction**". However, traditional search only works well in a limited subset of information tasks and research suggests that "the perfect search engine is not enough" [11]. A step in the right direction is contextual search [5], concerned with serving more meaningful results to information queries, often by clustering results [12].

Contextual user interfaces aim to go a step further providing *improved orientation* on information spaces and leading to more *explorative interaction strategies.*

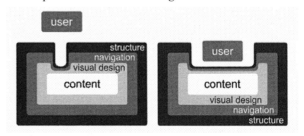

Figure 1. Standard vs. contextual interface design

Well-known user interface (UI) techniques to display information within context (also: focus + context) are Fisheye views [3] and Degree-of-Interest trees (DOI trees) [2]. Most focus + context implementations require well-defined information structures, and many try to display as much context as possible. This richness of context can help to understand large structures, relationships and to get a general overview. However, displaying all links (or knots in a tree) simultaneously can create visual noise in large information spaces, where too many displayed knots will create information overload within the context. In contrast, presenting limited information in a context more relevant to the individual user might create a more meaningful information experience.

Human knowledge is shaped by interpreting information through top-down and bottom-up processes. People derive meaning of contextual information from visual cues in the interface (bottom-up), but also from individual tasks that drive them (top-down) and from prior experience (top-down). These top-down processes should be appreciated as influencing factors in the interpretation and understanding of information - ultimately, suggesting that the contextual display of *information should be tailored to the individual.*

Current web-based user interfaces (UI) follow rigid and static visual designs, using grid and table-like layouts, where rows and columns blur the border between information, navigation and "noise". We believe that these print-like UIs do not work with personalized content. RSS feeds are an interesting example of new technology designed to cope with the above mentioned information problems. RSS is particularly used in the blogging context to provide personalized information delivery. But, when looking at phenomena like banner blindness [9] on websites or how large amounts of unread feeds commonly pile up in news readers (much like with emails), it becomes clear that traditional interfaces represent a burden to the user [7]. Research & design on the Focus-Metaphor interface (FMI) [6] aims to eliminate these problems. With the creation of a dynamic and customizable interface and a novel navigational approach, FMI provides seamless interaction aiming to improve the user's information experience (see Figure 1 – right).

2. EXPERIMENT

This paper reports an eyetracking experiment evaluating usability of different user interfaces for displaying blog-based information. A standard blog interface (Blog) has been used as baseline representing "traditional" layouts on the Web. This blog interface has been tested against the FMI, which uses a contextual visualisation of blog entries. To compare its performance, the FMI has been tested against Inxight's StarTree® interface (formerly known as Hyperbolic Browser, StarTree is a popular application using DOI trees). A within-subjects design has been used to test the same content and structure across all 3 interface versions. The content in this study covers NASA's "History of Space Flight". It consists of approx. 130 articles following a clear and hierarchical structure. Participants were given information tasks one at a time - 16 in total (e.g.: *"What was the weight of Gemini spacecraft?"*, *"What were the objectives of Skylab program?"* ...).

After answering one task (right or wrong), giving up or requiring too much time, participants were given the next task. Order of tasks has been randomized and sequence of interfaces counterbalanced between subjects. The study involved 6 participants (3 male, 3 female) with an average age of 21 years (all students). Using information tasks to simulate goal-driven blog reading sessions, *blog reading experience* is measured by task performance and user satisfaction.

Hypothesis: Using the contextual user interfaces (StarTree and FMI) may result in (H1) *enhanced blog reading experiences* (user preference). However, familiarity with traditional web layouts may result in (H2) *inferior task performance*

(completion time and error rate) of the contextual user interfaces compared to the blog interface.

2.1 Standard Blog Interface (BlogUI)

The blog environment used in the experiment deploys a Wordpress installation with a 2 column theme (see Figure 2). It is being used as reference to millions of blogs with similar "traditional" layouts in the blogosphere. The BlogUI provides a detailed hierarchically structured category list with an entry for each article. Each category contains all blog entries that are part of the according sub-tree of this hierarchy. Providing such a detailed category list in the BlogUI may help participants to (H2.1) *find the requested information more efficiently* (increased task performance).

Figure 2. Standard blog user interface (BlogUI)

2.2 StarTree® Interface (StarTree)

StarTree (see Figure 3) provides an alternative form of navigation aimed at *"illuminating relationships ... and large information hierarchies"* [4]. StarTree uses a dynamic navigation tree, displaying (nearly) all knots concurrently. Each knot correlates to a category in the BlogUI. When activating a knot (click or mouse over), the linked article is being displayed in the content section on the left. Providing the whole structure of the information space concurrently may result in (H2.2) *superior orientation in the information space for the StarTree* (increased task performance compared to the FMI).

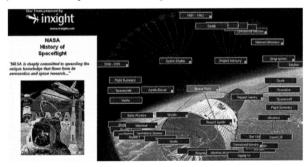

Figure 3. StarTree® user interface (by Inxight)

2.3 Focus-Metaphor Interface (FMI)

The Focus-Metaphor interface (FMI) provides dynamic and seamless interaction with the information space (see Figure 4). It combines contextual navigation with the actual display of information. The FMI could be interpreted as a fish-eye view mapped onto a StarTree-like structure encapsulating the complete content in each knot. Contextual interface elements are arranged around the primary content element which displays the selected article. The contextual elements function as navigation (activated through clicking) and provide previews onto the underlying content much like snippets on search engine result pages (SERP). Only "neighbors" of the currently active information are displayed as contextual navigation (all direct children plus the direct parent). When selecting a contextual element, its state changes: It enlarges into a content element and moves to the centre of the screen, replacing the previous element. The display of contextual elements is dynamically adapted to the new primary content element. The reduced display of hierarchy in the FMI may result in (H2.3) *inferior orientation for the FMI* (decreased task performance).

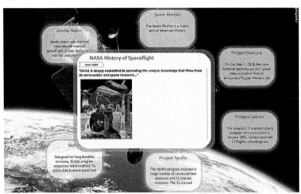

Figure 4. Focus-Metaphor interface (FMI)

2.4 Results

The analysis of user performance and user satisfaction in the next two sections reports the most important findings of the described study. Due to the limited number of participants, reporting will be focused around significant and some near-significant findings.

2.4.1 User Performance

Task performance was measured through completion time and error rate. Although overall task completion times did not reveal any significant differences, substantial differences have been found in the error rates across the three interfaces (see Table 1).

Error Rates: StarTree outperformed both BlogUI and FMI, showing significantly fewer errors than the BlogUI ($t_5 = 2.73$, $p < 0.021$). Differences between StarTree and FMI were not significant. When comparing FMI and BlogUI near-significant differences were found ($t_5 = 1.87$, $p < 0.061$). Paired t-tests were used.

Table 1. Error Rates (16 tasks in total)

	BlogUI	StarTree	FMI
tasks without error	7	11	11
Total errors	19	6	11
Average	**3.2**	**1.0**	**1.8**

Interestingly, 8 of the 11 errors in the FMI were caused by just 2 tasks (*"What year did Deke Slayton die?"* and *"When was Dr. Owen K. Garriott born?"*). The FMI only reveals direct context and questions did not reveal any further information (e.g.: which project these people where allocated to). As a result, when given these 2 tasks many participants could not find the right answers using the FMI due to the missing larger context. In general, participants had the most problems to find the right information using the BlogUI. Although a very detailed navigation with all available categories has been provided, participants struggled with a larger number of tasks.

More than half of the tasks (9 out of 16) caused problems to at least one of the participants using the BlogUI.

Gaze time: The analysis was conducted across all 16 tasks. No significant differences were found between the three interfaces. However, comparing gaze times for content and for navigation, significant differences were found within each of the interfaces (see Table 2). Participants spent more time using the navigation then skimming or reading text.

Table 2. Gaze time (time in seconds)

	BlogUI	StarTree	FMI
content	161	156	146
navigation	272	333	267
Significance of difference	$p < 0.027$	$p < 0.05$	$p < 0.002$
Total gaze time	**433**	**490**	**414**

Average Fixation Durations: Analysing average fixation durations revealed interesting differences between the three interfaces (see Figure 5). Near-significant differences were found between FMI and the other two interfaces for the navigational parts of experiment sessions (*FMI vs. StarTree:* $t_9 = 1.80$, $t < 0.053$; *FMI vs. BlogUI:* $t_{10} = 1.76$, $p < 0.054$). Moreover, the BlogUI showed a significant difference in average fixation durations between time spent on content and time spent navigating ($t_{10} = 2.01$, $p < 0.037$). In contrast, both StarTree and FMI showed much more similar average fixation durations across navigation and content. This could refer to a difference in cognitive load between standard web layouts (BlogUI) and contextual user interfaces (StarTree and FMI).

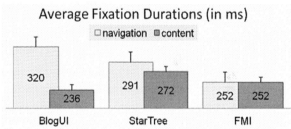

Figure 5. Average fixation durations when navigating and when reading (scanning content) (in ms)

2.4.2 User Satisfaction

Task performance alone can reveal objective differences between different user interfaces. But, to successfully introduce significant shifts in the user experience, users need to be in favour of these changes. To build a rich picture of participants' subjective preferences, a three-fold usability questionnaire has been used:

Section 1: To capture participants' overall reaction to the interface versions, 6 questions from the "Questionnaire for User Interface Satisfaction" (QUIS) have been used (e.g.: *"The system was: Frustrating – Satisfying"* - using a 6-point Likert scale). Both contextual interfaces show a significant difference to the baseline blog interface. Participants favour StarTree ($t_{10} = 2.81$, $p < 0.01$) and FMI ($t_{10} = 2.18$, $p < 0.03$) over the BlogUI.

Section 2: To evaluate aspects of ease of use, learnability and effectiveness, 15 usability questions (e.g.: *"Learning to navigate the system was easy"* - rated using a 6-point Likert scale) were used in this section. Again, both contextual interfaces excel the baseline BlogUI (*FMI:* $t_{10} = 3.42$, $p < 0.01$ and *StarTree:* $t_{10} = 2.94$, $p < 0.01$).

Section 3: The final four questions of the post-questionnaire asked participants to rank the interfaces directly (e.g.: *"Which interface did they like the most?"* - rated with 1st, 2nd and 3rd place). Figure 6 shows the results of Section 3 normalized for comparison with Section 1 and 2. Participants' direct ratings correlate with the results calculated from the first two sections, with the most interesting facts being:

- Nobody rated the BlogUI best.
- Half of the participants preferred the FMI; the other half preferred the StarTree.
- One user found the BlogUI the easiest to navigate, which might result from familiarity with blogs in general.
- Interestingly, the same user also rated the StarTree worst overall, behind the BlogUI in 2nd place.

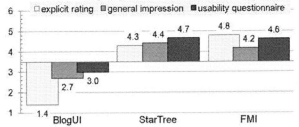

Figure 6. Results of all three sections of post-experiment usability questionnaire for BlogUI, StarTree and FMI

3. CONCLUSIONS

The limited scale of this study did not allow for a very detailed analysis of the eye tracking data. Nevertheless, some substantial conclusions could be drawn, despite its sample size. We argued that contextualization may lead to enhanced blog reading experiences (H1) and found strong evidence for this claim. Participant feedback shows clear preference for both contextual interfaces (StarTree and FMI). We further assumed that familiarity with traditional web layouts will improve task performance for the BlogUI (arguing that novelty has an inverse effect on task performance) (H2). This hypothesis has to be rejected. Although no clear differences could be found in the time it took participants to finish each session, error rates draw a clear picture. Especially StarTree outperformed the BlogUI benefitting from a superior overview of the blog space (H2.2). One participant noted that it was *"easy to find information even for a first time user"*. Although we assumed that providing a detailed, even hierarchically structured, category list in the BlogUI will help participants to answer the information tasks provided, we have to reject this hypothesis (H2.1), when comparing the results to the contextual interfaces. The clear structuring of articles through categories in the Blog UI could not be translated into a clear visual structure (see discussion on Figure 1). The reduced display of contextual information in the FMI was less successful (in terms of error rates) than StarTree, but superior to the BlogUI. We thus partly accept H2.3. The big increase (approx. 50%) in average fixation durations when navigating the BlogUI suggests increased cognitive load. This correlates with the reported problems participants had finding the right information. One participant wrote: *"the info is organized in an unclear way ... difficult to navigate through what is needed"*. This also correlates with participants' task performance (error rates) and their subjective responses (qualitative feedback).

4. FUTURE WORK

We are currently planning an extended version of the experiment, which will also involve a substantially higher number of participants. This experiment will enable a more detailed analysis of the eye tracking data and of individual tasks. Future work on the FMI prototype will add features to help users gaining a better overview of available information, but still maintaining current minimalist and clear visualization. This approach facilitates users' decision making and confidence in their judgment when faced with complex information tasks (to keep switch cost low). Moreover, future work will extend the FMI to visualize content from entire blog spaces. Spanning a multitude of related blogs, the FMI will be able to contextualize entries across individual blogs through means of categorization and other techniques. Intelligent linking of entries from various individual blogs will allow users to seamlessly explore entire blog spaces.

5. REFERENCES

[1] Brooks, C. H. and Nancy, M. Improved annotation of the blogosphere via autotagging and hierarchical clustering. In *Proceedings of the 15th international conference on World Wide Web (WWW '06)* (Edinburgh, Scotland, 2006). ACM Press, New York, NY, 2006, 625-632.

[2] Card, S. K. and Nation, D. Degree-of-Interest Trees: A Component of an Attention-Reactive User Interface. In *Proc. Advanced Visual Interfaces 2002*, ACM Press (2002), Trento, Italy.

[3] Furnas, G. W. Generalized Fisheye Views. In *Proc. CHI 1986*, ACM Press (1986), 16-23.

[4] Inxight StarTree. *http://www.inxight.com/products/sdks/st/* last accessed on 14 May 2007.

[5] Kraft, R. et al. (2006). Searching with Context. In *Proc. of International World Wide Web Conference (WWW '06)*, (Edinburgh, Scotland, 2006). ACM Press.

[6] Laqua, S. and Brna, P. The Focus-Metaphor Approach: A Novel Concept for the Design of Adaptive and User-Centric Interfaces. In *Proc. Interact 2005*, Springer (2005), 295-308.

[7] Lin, C.C. (2005): Optimal Web site reorganization considering information overload and search depth. In *European Journal of Operational Research*. Elsevier, Article in Press.

[8] Moreville, P. *Ambient Findability*. O'Reilly Media, Sebastopol, USA, 2005

[9] Norman, D. (1999): Banner Blindness, Human Cognition, and Web Design. In: *Internetworking*, Fourth Issue, 2.1, March 1999.

[10] Technorati. *http://www.technorati.com*, last accessed on 14 Jan 2007.

[11] Teevan, J. et al. The perfect search engine is not enough: a study of orienteering behavior in directed search. In *Proceedings of the SIGCHI conference on Human factors in computing systems (CHI '04)* (Vienna, Austria, 2004)

[12] Zeng, H. J. et al. Learning to Cluster Web Search Results. In *Proceedings of the 27th annual international ACM conference on Research and development in information retrieval (SIGIR '04)* (Sheffield, United Kingdom, 2004). ACM Press, New York, NY, 2004, 210-217

Bluetooth Friendly Names: Bringing Classic HCI Questions into the Mobile Space

Barry Lavelle, Daragh Byrne, Gareth J. F. Jones, Alan F. Smeaton
Centre for Digital Video Processing & Adaptive Information Cluster
Dublin City University
Dublin 9, Ireland

{barry.lavelle@eeng.dcu.ie}, {daragh.byrne, gareth.jones, alan.smeaton@computing.dcu.ie}

ABSTRACT

We explore the use of Bluetooth friendly names within the mobile space. Each Bluetooth-enabled device possesses a short string known as a 'friendly name' used to help identify a device to human users. In our analysis, we collected friendly names in use on 9,854 Bluetooth-enabled devices over a 7-month period. These names were then classified and the results analysed. We discovered that a broad range of HCI themes are applicable to the domain of Bluetooth friendly names, including previous work on personalisation, naming strategies and anonymity in computer mediated communication. We also found that Bluetooth is already being used as a platform for social interaction and communication amongst collocated groups and has moved beyond its original intention of file exchange.

Categories and Subject Descriptors

H.5.1 [Information Interfaces and Presentation]: Multimedia Information Systems; H.1.2 [User/Machine Systems]: Human Factors; H.5.2 [Information Interfaces and Presentation (e.g., HCI)]: User Interfaces; H.5.3 [Information Interfaces and Presentation]: Group and Organization Interfaces

General Terms

Design, Human Factors

Keywords

Bluetooth, friendly name, mobile phones, mobile computing.

1. INTRODUCTION

Bluetooth is a short-range wireless communications protocol designed to allow mobile devices to easily exchange information between one another. In order to facilitate this communication, each device is given a unique hardware id. This identifier is a 12 digit hexadecimal number and as such is not designed for human use but rather by a computer. To make the device easily identifiable by a person, each device can also be labeled with a short 'friendly name' which can be changed by the user at any point, and potentially many times over short spaces of time. Typically, out of the box, a mobile phone will use a default manufacturer friendly name normally comprised of the phone manufacturer's name and the model number.

Today there are over 1 billion Bluetooth equipped devices in use and it is expected that this number will double by 2009 [4]. Bluetooth is typically used on mobile phones, but it is not limited to them and can be used to interact with PDAs, computers, laptops, earpieces, keyboards and mice, for example. Bluetooth is typically enabled on personal devices, the overwhelming majority of which are portable and always in the presence of the owner. Bluetooth has a wide range of applications such as the exchange of personal contact information between phones and computers, exchange of pictures, video and other digital content and the synchronisation of personal information between portable and static computing devices.

Despite the technology's firm roots in the exchange of file-based media, we are increasingly seeing Bluetooth leveraged in more social applications. *Bluejacking*, for example, is a simple exploitation of the protocol to send unsolicited messages to Bluetooth enabled devices [17]. While essentially harmless, it can sometimes be used to socially engineer access to the recipient's device [3]. More recently some mobile applications have popularised the use of Bluetooth in social situations. The BlueTunA [1] application allows users to find music of interest on proximal Bluetooth enabled devices while Nokia 'Sensor' [10] and 'Serendipity' [6] are designed to enable socialising and dating amongst co-located groups. These solutions have, however, yet to gain mass adoption. As these applications gain traction, we expect that Bluetooth will rapidly transition from being seen as a file-exchange platform to a platform for social communication and interaction. There are however already small numbers of users leveraging Bluetooth for social interaction. This is typically achieved through the alteration of their friendly name to convey personal or demographic information, attracting others to interact with them (normally by sending a text message via Bluetooth.)

In this paper, we investigate the Bluetooth friendly name scheme as a means by which we can explore the degree to which Bluetooth is currently being used for social interaction. In our studies we uncovered novel and interesting applications of the Bluetooth friendly name, which stimulate further discussion of classic HCI research questions such as personalisation, the effects of anonymity and perspective in naming. We expect that in the next few years, with the anticipated greater adoption of Bluetooth, we will see it transition towards a new enabler of person-to-person computer mediated communication. These HCI issues are explored across a range of domains and will become more and more applicable to the mobile space as usage increases.

2. DATA GATHERING

Between August 2006 and February 2007 we collected a large log of Bluetooth data. A custom Java ME application was run continuously on a mobile phone during this period recording

63

each and every Bluetooth enabled device, which was encountered proximal to it. One person carried the mobile phone during their daily life, 24 hours per day, to naturally record Bluetooth encounters. Information recorded included the unique hardware ID of the device encountered along with the friendly name of that device (if available) and the timestamp of the encounter. Data was collected from a broad range of locations, however the majority were either on the University campus or in its vicinity, but also from trips abroad and visits to the city centre. Data was collected from a wide range of events including social events and conferences where high numbers of devices were encountered. At the end of the study, over 165,000 unique encounters with devices had been recorded over the 144 days. These encounters were recorded for 9,854 individual Bluetooth-enabled devices, which possessed 2,105 unique friendly names. Multiple devices possess the same friendly name and this explains the disparity in the two figures. Due to the nature of Bluetooth, demographic information could not be attributed to encountered devices or their users.

3. CLASSIFICATION

When the Bluetooth friendly names were analysed, each identifiable type was given a category to fit into a coding frame. By attempting to identify key attributes of the friendly names used to label devices, categories for coding were created. This activity was completed by two evaluators for inter-coder reliability [7]. This resulted in each of the encountered friendly names being assigned to one of 12 broad categories. The categories are outlined, with examples, in Table 1. A simple correlation co-efficient test showed 89% agreement between coders. The small degree of variance between coders demonstrates that the resulting framework was robust and the arrangement into categories was effective for the dataset.

4. RESULTS & DISCUSSION

The results, listed in Table 2, demonstrate some very interesting uses and issues relating to Bluetooth as a communication technology. The results are discussed in detail below.

4.1 Use of Manufacturer Default Name

From observational analysis, it was anticipated that a large proportion of the results would be found in the "Manufacturer Default" category. Almost 20% of all friendly names used were the manufacturer default and this correlates with the findings of previous studies which investigated vulnerabilities in Bluetooth [15]. It also highlights a problem for those wishing to interact with these devices. For example, in a crowded room, there may be several devices labeled "Nokia 6230i" so how does the user know which one they want to select? Additionally, it raises interesting questions about the general level of education of users about Bluetooth, and to why people are not personalising the friendly name on their devices. Are they, for example, unaware as to what Bluetooth is; that it is available and operating on their device; and that they can indeed customise the friendly name of their device?

4.2 Use of Person Name Combinations

The 'person name only' and 'person name and device' categories accounted for over 40% of the friendly names encountered. While one might expect that this is a reasonably unsurprising result, what is interesting about this category is the issues of naming for retrieval by self and others. Almost 26% of friendly names encountered specifically mentioned the type of device. There are two possible explanations for this. First and most simply, that the owner has multiple Bluetooth-enabled devices and wants to distinguish them clearly. Secondly, the owner may be attempting to specify as much detail about the

Table 1. Bluetooth Friendly Name Classification Categories and examples from the collected dataset.

Category Name	Explanation	Actual Example(s)
Manufacturer Default	Each manufacturer provides a default friendly name, which it is intended would be changed by the user. If the user is still using this name it is assigned to this category.	"Nokia 6230i", "BlackBerry 8100"
Person Name Only	When a user labels their device with their first (and/or last name) or some minor variation of this.	"Neil"
Person Name + Device	When a user labels their device with their first (and/or last name) and explicitly defines the type of Bluetooth device they own. This may simply involve defining the type but they may also provide the model number.	"John's Phone", "Alans Intel Mac"
Custom – Extravert	Those who labeled their device with something distinct, memorable and recognizable. The label was, also, deemed to be highly expressive.	"SWAT_SNIPER", "Beet Bopping Barry"
Custom – Intravert	Some of the labels given to a device appeared to be attempting to conceal as much information as possible. These include short strings, initials, blank names, or the use of punctuation solely as the name.	"DD", "?", "R.C."
Inviting Interaction	These names appear to be asking other Bluetooth users to engage in some activity with them. Often this is the exchange of files such as adult material.	"find me if u can", "Can u send me porn"
Declining Interaction	These names are explicitly declining any and all forms of interaction from other Bluetooth users. This may be perhaps as a result of *Bluejacking*.	"T630 Go Away", "F*** OFF!"
Provocative	These labels seemed to be designed to provoke annoyance, anger or some strong reaction but were not necessarily offensive in nature.	"Behind You!", "Your Ma!"
Offensive, Explicit or Sexual	These names, whether intentional or otherwise, have sexual connotations, and may be deemed to be offensive or explicit by someone viewing them. These include lewd and crass phrases and/or expletives.	"8 Inches", "9 Inches", "12 inches", "W***er",
Promotional	These friendly names are used to promote an event, company, product or a website.	"Traesti 4th Nov"
Popular Person / Character	These are devices which have been labeled using the name of a well-known person, such as a movie-star, or a popular fictional character such as from a TV show.	"Mel Gibson", "Ron Burgundy", "Batman"
Phone Number	User's belong to this category when they use a mobile phone number as their Bluetooth friendly name. These were recognized as starting with the typical dialing codes of 00353, +353, 086, 087 or 085 (the standard prefix dialing codes for mobile phones in Ireland)	"087 123 4567"

device to enable others to locate it with greater ease. The latter clearly relates to previous research on naming conventions. Pitman and Payne [12] explored such issues in relation to hierarchical file systems and naming of files for collaborative groups. They cited challenges to retrieval of files by name to be consistency and consensus of name choice, but also indicated that users adapt their naming strategies when they know they are intended for use by other people. It is likely that since Bluetooth is intended for communication, this will, to some degree, influence the naming strategy employed.

4.3 Use of Customisation (Introverted & Extraverted)

It was not anticipated that such a high proportion of encountered friendly names would be uniquely customised and personalised. 30% of all friendly names exhibited highly memorable "non-person" names (see Table 1 for explanation.) These names appeared to be counter-intuitive to general interactions and file exchanges envisaged for Bluetooth. It could be assumed that people seeking to interact with a specific device could anticipate a standard name, a name and device combination or a default device name, and so initially locating the intended device with a more expressive name might be more cumbersome. Alternatively, this result may indicate that the names in this category are, more often than not, designed for a subset of users (presumably close friends) who will easily recognise this nickname.

However, what it does clearly indicate is that the Bluetooth friendly names currently being used are very expressive and rich both in nature and language. It implies that these names have social importance and may be designed intentionally to be playful and meaningful within a collocated group or alternatively to replace some of the contextual cues, which are typically removed by computer-mediated communication. Pseudonyms are "*often chosen to hide explicitly identity yet simultaneously reveal a personal facet of the author*" [8]. This certainly appears to be the case in a large proportion of the Bluetooth friendly names encountered. Furthermore, a person may, for example, use this friendly name to influence their perception of others towards them within the mobile space. Previous studies have shown it not uncommon for users to alter their persona or even "gender swap" in computer-mediated communications (CMC) by presenting a particular image via the user's nickname [2]. Unfortunately the degree to which this may occur within the Bluetooth space is difficult to determine due to the inherent lack of demographic information afforded by the Bluetooth technology.

4.4 Use of Offensive, Explicit, Sexual and Provocative Names

Bluetooth like other forms of CMC lacks many contextual cues as to who the person behind the name is. Consequently, those interacting in this medium can gain greater social anonymity. Unlike traditional CMC, Bluetooth only allows interaction with devices proximate to the user (normally within 10m). Despite this, there is still difficulty in associating a person to a device, especially in crowded or public places. This preserves a relative degree of anonymity for the users and also removes features of social identity such as race, physical appearance and gender in interactions in the mobile space. It has been clearly demonstrated that this anonymity, combined with an absence of socio-emotional and contextual information, can often remove the social norms and conventions of face-to-face communication, opening the door to offensive or abusive language [9, 13, 14, 16]. Bluetooth brings this virtual

anonymity to a new context of interaction and we can see that people are clearly using offensive names within this domain (over 3% of all names.) This result seems to be in line with previous work by Bechar-Israeli [2] in which 4% of IRC chat users adopted nicknames relating to sex or provocation.

It is also conceivable that these names were not intended to be offensive or provocative by their owners, but rather humorous or engaging. Previous work by Kruger and Epley [10] demonstrates that within e-mail, people engaged in communication inherently apply their own perspective in interpreting the emotional state of the sender from the message's content. The inability of communicators to accurately discern the intended tones and emotions conveyed is worrisome, and the authors indicate that this problem is not limited to email communications, but rather a wide range of communication's media such as instant messaging. It is reasonable to assume that similar factors may operate in interpreting Bluetooth friendly names.

Table 2. Distribution of 2105 Friendly Names.

Category Name	Number	Percentage
Manufacturer Default	374	17.77
Person Name Only	350	16.63
Person Name + Device	540	25.65
Custom – Extravert	519	24.66
Custom – Intravert	130	6.18
Inviting Interaction	13	0.62
Declining Interaction	6	0.29
Provocative	25	1.19
Offensive, Explicit or Sexual	46	2.19
Promotional	40	1.90
Popular Person / Character	57	2.71
Own Phone Number	5	0.24

4.5 Use of Names for Interaction

Only a relatively small number of friendly names relate to inviting or declining interaction. This is, however, particularly important as it clearly demonstrates that Bluetooth is not simply a means of file exchange between users but it also, and already, mediates social communication between small numbers of users. While less than 1% of encountered friendly names were explicitly named for interaction purposes, it can safely be assumed that there are more than this 1% actually interacting via Bluetooth, but they just have their device labeled with names belonging to other categories. These friendly names appear to be used to encourage relative "strangers" to interact, as opposed to people known by the owner. Although the reasons for this are somewhat dubious, we found that several of the encountered friendly names in this category were asking other users to send them material of an adult nature. The remainder of these names were often playful in nature, some inviting others to "Pick me, Pick me."

A very small number of friendly names encountered were very clearly declining any interaction from other users (see Table 1 for examples). An interesting question here is why would users choose to expressly decline interaction from others by altering the Bluetooth Friendly name as opposed to simply switching off Bluetooth on their device?

The results in this category demonstrate that Bluetooth is being used over short ranges to allow people to communicate and interact socially. While this may currently be limited to a small subset of "early adopters," we anticipate that the social aspects of Bluetooth will increasingly be exploited, and that interactions via Bluetooth will increase over the next few years.

4.6 Use of Mobile Phone Numbers

Despite an extremely small number of user's belonging to this category, it does raise some serious concerns about personal security and privacy on mobile devices. Once the device has been labeled with a mobile number, personal information typically not exposed by Bluetooth is available to anyone within range of them. Perhaps the Bluetooth device owner is simply unaware that they have made their number available via Bluetooth. More worrying is that it may potentially leave them open to social engineering. Interestingly, using a numerically based friendly name may defeat the purpose of the friendly name concept. By replacing the 12 digit hardware ID with a phone number (between 10 and 14 digits in length and only even potentially recognisable to a small group of close associates), the Bluetooth device may no longer 'human readable' and may cause issues for those wishing to locate it and interact with it.

5. FUTURE WORK

We are currently collecting an extended set of Bluetooth friendly names and have several participants actively using the Bluetooth logging device. Once a sufficiently large and diverse set of data has been collected we will explore some of the issues outlined in this paper in greater detail. This is likely to involve the detailed lingual and affective analysis of the friendly names, which have been encountered. We are also considering means by which demographic information may be collected on Bluetooth users to add further value to this analysis. We also wish to explore the effect of setting and social context on choice of friendly name.

6. CONCLUSIONS

As Carroll [5] suggests a person's name choice reflects the idiosyncrasies of their own cognitive system. As expected a wide variety of friendly names for Bluetooth enabled devices were encountered. These fell into 12 broad categories and exhibited very interesting characteristics. Most interestingly, we can see that there appear to be three characteristics in the naming styles applied: first, the majority of users name with their own first and/or last name in order to allow broad interaction with the device (Person Name Combinations); second, some users seem to use nicknames to limit knowledge of ownership of the device to a small subset of users who will recognise the 'handle' or to preserve relative anonymity within the mobile space (Custom - Extravert); and finally, a very small number of users attempt to completely obfuscate their "friendly name" to completely maintain their anonymity and perhaps to avoid some interaction with others (Custom - Intravert).

We have also clearly demonstrated that these naming choices and conventions beg further and more detailed investigation, and that many HCI studies relating to personalisation, perspective, naming choices for self and others, anonymity, identity and computer mediated communication, will if not already, increasingly apply to Bluetooth and the mobile space as it evolves into a collocated social interaction platform.

7. ACKNOWLEDGMENTS

We would like to thank the Irish Research Council for Science, Engineering and Technology and Science Foundation Ireland under grant number 03/IN.3/I361 for support.

8. REFERENCES

[1] Baumann, S., Jung, B., Bassoli, A. and Wisniowski, M. BluetunA: let your neighbour know what music you like. In Extended Abstracts of Conference on Human factors in Computing Systems (CHI '07), (San Jose, USA, April 2007). ACM Press, New York, NY, 1941 – 1946.

[2] Bechar-Israeli, H. (1995) From <Bonehead> to <cLoNehEAd>: Nicknames, Play, and Identity on Internet Relay Chat, Journal of Computer-Mediated Communication, 1, 2 (Sept. 1995).

[3] Bialoglowy, M. Bluetooth Security Review, Part 1. (Apr. 2005) Retrieved from: http://www.securityfocus.com/infocus/1830

[4] Bluetooth SIG. Bluetooth Technology in Hands of One Billion. (Nov. 2006) Retrieved from: http://www.bluetooth.com/Bluetooth/SIG/Billion.htm

[5] Carroll, J.M. What's in a Name? An Essay in the Psychology of Reference. W. H. Freeman and Company, New York, 1985.

[6] Eagle, N. and Pentland, A. (2005), Social Serendipity: Mobilizing Social Software. IEEE Pervasive Computing, Special Issue: The Smart Phone. (April-June 2005), 28-34.

[7] Gwet, K. Handbook of Inter-Rater Reliability, Gaithersburg,StatAxis Publishing, 2001

[8] Jaffe, J.M., Lee Y.E., Huang, L. and Oshagan H. Gender, Pseudonyms, and CMC: Masking Identities and Baring Souls. Paper presented at the Annual Conference of the International Communication Association, (1995) Albuquerque, New Mexico. Available: http://research.haifa.ac.il/~jmjaffe/genderpseudocmc/.

[9] Kiesler, S., Siegel, J., and McGuire, T.W. Social psychological aspects of computer-mediated communication. American Psychologist, 39, 10 (1984), 1123-1134.

[10] Kruger, J., Epley, N., Parker, J. & Ng, Zhi-Wen (2005) Egocentrism Over Email: Can We Communicate as Wellas We Think? Journal of Personality and Social Psychology, 89, 6, (2005), 925-936.

[11] Nokia Europe. Nokia Sensor. (2005) Retrieved from: http://europe.nokia.com/A4144923

[12] Pitman, J. A. and Payne S. J. Creating names for retrieval by self and others. Behaviour & Information Technology, 25, 6 (Nov. – Dec. 2006), 489-496.

[13] Rice, R. E. The New Media: Communication, Research, and Technology. Beverly Hills, CA, Sage, 1984.

[14] Rice, R. E. Issues and concepts in research on computer-mediated communication systems. In J.A. Anderson (Ed.), Communication Yearbook 12 (pp. 436- 476). Newbury Park, CA, Sage, 1989.

[15] Solon, A. and Callaghan, M. (2006) Case Study on the Bluetooth Vulnerabilities in Mobile Devices. IJCSNS International Journal of Computer Science and Network Security, 6, 4 (April 2006), 125-129.

[16] Sproull, L., and Kiesler, S. Connections: New Ways of Working in the Networked Organization. Cambridge, MA MIT Press, 1991.

[17] Thom-Santelli, J., Ainslie, A. and Gay, G. Location, location, location: a study of bluejacking practices. In Extended Abstracts of Conference on Human factors in Computing Systems (CHI 2007), (San Jose, USA, April 2007). ACM Press, New York, NY, 2693 – 2698.

Investigating the Usability of PDAs with Ageing Users

Sheila Mc Carthy
University of Ulster at Magee
Northland Road, Derry BT48 7JL
Northern Ireland, UK
+44 (0)28 713 75157

McCarthy-S2@ulster.ac.uk

Heather Sayers
University of Ulster at Magee
Northland Road, Derry BT48 7JL
Northern Ireland, UK
+44 (0)28 713 75148

hm.sayers@ ulster.ac.uk

Paul McKevitt
University of Ulster at Magee
Northland Road, Derry BT48 7JL
Northern Ireland, UK
+44 (0)28 713 75433

p.mckevitt@ ulster.ac.uk

ABSTRACT

Mobile technologies have the potential to enhance the lives of ageing users, especially those who experience a decline in cognitive abilities. However, diminutive devices often perplex the aged and many HCI problems exist. This research ultimately aims to develop a mobile reminiscent application for ageing users entitled MemoryLane. This application will use artificial intelligent techniques to compose and convey excerpts from a lifetime's memories to the user in a multimodal storytelling format. The proposed deployment platform for MemoryLane is a Personal Digital Assistant (PDA). The initial stage of this research, a HCI pilot study was recently conducted with a sample of ageing users, the study aimed to investigate the usability of a PDA. This paper documents the methodologies employed in this pilot study and its subsequent results. The next stages of the research are also identified and discussed.

Categories and Subject Descriptors

K.4.2. [**Social Issues**]: Assistive technologies for persons with disabilities.

General Terms

Design, Human Factors.

Keywords

PDA, usability, HCI, elderly, cognitive decline, memory loss, gerontechnology, storytelling, MemoryLane.

1. INTRODUCTION

The ageing population is dramatically increasing, especially in the more economically developed countries of the world. According to the 2001 census the UK now has more people aged over 60 than under 16 years. 1.1 million people are now aged over 85, and by 2050 the number of centenarians is expected to have increased eighteen times [1]. Cognitive decline is part of the natural ageing process affecting individuals at varying rates, and catering for such a diverse

sector requires detailed analysis. Mobile computing is commonplace and offers the potential to be harnessed as a tool to assist many of these ageing people. However, many usability problems exist and this potential is very often not maximised. Mobile technologies can assist ageing users to live independently and maintain a high quality of life, in turn minimising the emotional and financial strain often caused by nursing home accommodation. The usability problems identified in this research will contribute to the development of a set of design guidelines which will aim to assist in the design of PDA based applications for ageing users. This research is underpinned by the larger research areas of gerontechnology and HCI usability studies.

1.1 Gerontechnology and HCI

Due to the increasing numbers of the ageing population, they have become the focus of much research designed to improve, prolong and enhance their lives. Gerontology is the study of ageing people and of the social, psychological and biological aspects of the ageing process itself, as distinct from the term Geriatrics, the study of the diseases which afflict ageing people. Gerontechnology, the merger between gerontology and technology is a newer genus, concerning itself with the utilisation of technological advancements to improve the health, mobility, communication, leisure and environment of ageing people. Therefore gerontechnology is heavily concerned with the ways in which ageing people interact with computers and technology. In a recent paper Zajicek [8] reflects upon established HCI research processes and identifies certain areas in which this type of research differs significantly from other research disciplines.

1.2 HCI Usability Studies

Myriad HCI usability studies are being conducted in the area of computers and ageing users, but substantially less are being conducted into the specifics of how ageing people interact with mobile devices, despite the fact that active researchers within this area have discussed the benefits of mobile devices to ageing people, and have highlighted the need to learn more to support designing for this genre [3]. An initial PDA usability study conducted by Siek et al. [6] compared differences in the interaction patterns of ageing users and younger users. This work attempted to ascertain whether ageing people, who may be subject to reduced cognitive abilities, could effectively use PDAs. This initial research was conducted with a small sample of 20 users, a control group of 10 younger users aged 25-35, and 10 older users aged 75-85 years and was restricted to the monitored analysis of the participants' abilities to perform 5 controlled interactive tests using a Palm Tungsten T3 PDA. The findings of this study failed to identify any major differences in the performance of the two groups possibly due to the fact that the ageing users group were allowed extra practice time privileges. Siek et al.'s work offered an early insight into the nature of the field work for this research.

2 METHODOLOGY AND DESIGN

The aim of this research is to develop a user-friendly PDA application called MemoryLane to assist ageing users recall past life events and memories as they experience the natural cognitive declines associated with the ageing process. The preferred deployment platform, a DELL Axim X51v PDA device is pictured beside an impression of the proposed MemoryLane prototype in Figure 1. The methodology adopted in this research is the User Sensitive Inclusive Design (USID) approach proposed by Newell and Gregor which focuses on universal usability. This new methodology extends User Centred Design by developing technological systems for everyone, to include those with disabilities and mutatis mutandis for other minority groups [5]. Close attention will also be paid to the findings that mutual inspiration is the most effective approach in developing new technology for ageing people [2] and the recent study by Zajicek [8] into the various aspects of HCI for ageing people. MemoryLane will be designed to support multimodal input via a touch screen and possible use of simple voice control commands. The benefits of multimodal interaction are widely acclaimed and the design of MemoryLane will assure a multimodal interface which will accommodate ageing users with different capabilities, expertise or expectations [4]. MemoryLane will also provide multimodal output in the form of images, video, audio and text to speech synthesis. It is thought that MemoryLane will incorporate a hybrid artificial intelligent system to compose life-caching data into appropriate and pleasing 'stories' for the user.

Figure 1: Dell Axim X51v PDA and an Impression of the Proposed MemoryLane Prototype

3 PILOT STUDY

The initial stage of this research began with a preliminary HCI pilot study conducted with a sample of older users and aimed at investigating the usability of a PDA. Prior to conducting interviews many preliminary visits were initially required to gain trust and build a rapport with the ageing participants. Silverman [7] recommends that when interacting with a sample, researchers should note all they see and hear and also how they behave and feel they are treated.

3.1 Sample Selection

The pilot study sample comprised 15 participants of apparent good health. The sample was aged between 55 and 82 years and included 6 males and 9 females. Participants were selected from four different sources, 6 attended an Age Concern centre, 3 were members of The University of the 3rd Age, 2 were day patients of a local Nursing Unit and the remaining 4 were selected at random from responses received from volunteers.

3.1.1 Personal Backgrounds

Of the 15 participants 14 were right-handed. No participants were colour-blind and 12 wore glasses. 5 admitted to

experiencing minor vision problems when viewing a TV or computer screen and 3 suffered from slight hearing loss. All but one participant lived in their own home and 13 agreed that they had more free time now than they used to have. 7 of the 15 reported that they had more disposable income than 10 years ago, 6 thought they had less. Most participants watched TV on a daily basis, the favoured programs ranging between soap operas news and weather, sports and documentaries. No one expressed a preference for technical or computer programs. 11 participants read on a daily basis, but none expressed a preference for reading any form of technical or computing literature.

3.2 Interviews & Questionnaires

Each participant was interviewed separately in a one-to-one structured interview format in familiar surroundings. The interviews involved completion of a detailed questionnaire, a demonstration of how to interact with a PDA by the researcher, followed by observation of participants' capability in attempting to complete pre-set interactive PDA tasks.

Initial research for the questionnaire design discovered that questions requiring prose type answers took participants too long to complete, during which they often became frustrated and seemed to prefer yes/no or tick box answers. Prose answers also proved ambiguous and often difficult to quantify, therefore the questionnaire followed the 5 point Likert- type scale giving participants 5 optional answers. The ensuing questionnaire was divided into sections A and B. Section A of the questionnaire was designed to acquire background information regarding participants' physical characteristics, socio-economic factors, perceived technical abilities, prior exposure to technology and personal opinions of modern day technology. Section B of the questionnaire was designed to be completed in conjunction with undertaking the interactive PDA tasks; this section determined the participant's ability to complete the set tasks and ascertained their HCI preferences. This section centered on questions regarding preferred interaction modalities and aspects and elements of the PDA hardware and software. As part of section B, participants were asked to attempt 6 basic tasks on the PDA as illustrated in Figure 2. This section of the interview was videotaped where possible, in conjunction with the participant's approval.

Figure 2: Participant Interacting with PDA

4 RESULTS

The following sub sections document the findings of the pilot study and are organised into sections which reflect the format of the questionnaire.

4.1 Technical Experience

Section A of the questionnaire details the levels of prior technical exposure and experience encountered by the 15 participants. Questions focused on participants' usage of household technical devices, with a view to investigating if those participants with increased exposure to technical devices found PDA interaction easier than their counterparts.

Phones were the first device under scrutiny, 8 participants had a regular corded home telephone, 6 owned regular cordless telephones and 9 used a mobile phone. When asked, no one rated their ability to use a mobile phone as 'excellent', 5 considered their ability as 'good' and 7 considered themselves as 'poor' phone users. All participants owned a TV, but only 4 had ever used Teletext. 8 participants owned both a VCR and DVD player and only 2 of the participants said that they did not use a remote control to operate these devices. This demonstrated that the majority of the participants were familiar with operating buttons on a basic hand-held device such as a remote control. The majority of participants said that they did not require any assistance with programming or operating household devices such as timers, alarms, radios and microwaves, however not all actually owned programmable devices. 4 said that they found such devices complex and did require assistance.

As expected, the findings of the pilot study concluded that those participants who owned and used a mobile phone were generally more predisposed to engaging with the PDA, as were those who extensively utilised their household appliances. Those participants who declared minimal usage of telephones, remotes and household devices tended to show more apprehension toward the PDA.

The main reason for computer use among this age bracket was for email purposes and the majority of users proclaimed to be self-taught. Only 5 participants owned their own computer and 3 used a computer on a daily basis. 9 said they had never used a computer; however 10 reported that they had access to a computer if desired. Only 1 participant had prior knowledge of a PDA, the remainder had never heard of them. Just half the participants said they were interested in learning about new technologies, and less than this thought it important for them to keep abreast with technological advances.

4.2 Computing Expertise

It was hypothesised that participants who regularly socialised with younger people (in the age bracket of 25 to 55) would have a higher exposure to modern day technologies than those who do not regularly socialise with people of this age, and would rate their own level of computer knowledge as significantly higher. However this generalisation proved not to be the case, as can be seen in Figure 3.

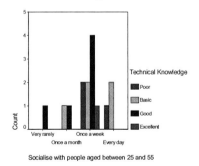

Figure 3: Technical Knowledge & Social Interaction

Participants who had the highest social interaction with younger people (on a daily basis) described their knowledge levels as merely poor and basic. Participants who socialised weekly with younger people were divided over rating their computing ability. 4 did describe their computing knowledge as good and 1 as excellent; however, 4 from this group also rated their knowledge as poor and basic. Participants who socialised on a monthly basis with 25 to 55 year olds described their

knowledge levels as basic and good. The remaining participants, who very rarely socialised with younger people, actually described their knowledge levels as good.

Participants' perceptions of their own expertise and knowledge was occasionally subjective, some rated themselves highly and later professed to having never used a computer or a mobile phone, while others, who often used computers, criticised their abilities and rated their knowledge as inferior; one even producing a mobile phone from his pocket to demonstrate how poorly he believed he used it. However, despite the differing impressions participants held of themselves, the findings indicate that in contrast to the hypothesis, regular contact between older and younger people does not seem to generate noteworthy increased knowledge of modern day technologies in the elderly.

It was further hypothesised that participants' previous occupations would have direct bearing on their perceived computing ability, where those with an academic background would display a heightened computing ability. However, as displayed in Figure 4, this again was not the case.

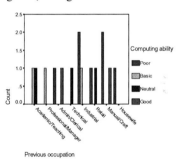

Figure 4: Background & Computing Ability

None of the participants, irrespective of previous occupation, rated their computing ability as 'excellent'. Participants with academic and managerial backgrounds rated their expertise as merely 'basic', with the highest ratings appearing from those with clerical and manual backgrounds. The poorer self-ratings came from those with clerical, industrial and manual backgrounds. Again these findings did not hold true with the hypothesis and were subject to participants' differing perceptions of their own prowess. These findings would seem to illustrate that there is no definite correlation between the previous occupations of this age group and their perceived computing abilities. Overall, due to the subjectivity of the participants and their lack of benchmarks for comparison, is awkward to quantify the competent levels of computer literacy among the sample. It would seem that the participants too had difficulty in accurately rating their own computing and technical abilities, a conundrum which may account for apprehension in embracing technology.

4.3 Interactive Tasks

Task 1 involved navigating a menu structure and locating 3 files containing text of various colours, features and sizes. The first file contained 15 lines of text written in different colours and participants were requested to select their preferred 5 text colours. The second file contained 6 lines of text written in various text styles and the participants were asked to rate their preferred 3. The third file contained 5 lines of text written in different text sizes, 8 to 16 and the participants were asked to select only one preferred text size. The participants had difficulty navigating the menu structure unaided; however the study found that the participants' preferred text colours were: black, red, navy, green and blue. They also preferred text in

69

'Normal' format, followed by embolden text and lastly underlined text and the preferred text size among participants was size 10 font. During this task 12 of the 15 were eventually able to use the on-screen scroll bar when aided. Task 2 required participants to locate and view 3 media files. The first was a photograph of the researcher, the second an audio clip of waltz music and the third a video file of line dancing. Participants were then asked to comment on how easily they could view and hear these files. Again, the participants had difficulty when attempting to navigate the menu structure and find and open the required media files. However, when found, all participants were able to see and hear the associated content.

Task 3 involved a dual interaction with a bespoke application called 'Button Press Task'. This task required participants to navigate through a 12 on screen buttons by firstly using the 5-way navigational button and then repeat the procedure using the stylus. Participants were asked to indicate their preferred mode of interaction. This task proved one of the more difficult for the participants, the majority found the 5-way navigational button extremely complex and small to use, and all preferred using the stylus (or their finger). Tasks 4 and 5 centred on text entry. Firstly participants were asked to enter their name via the onscreen keyboard, and then subsequently write their name using a free-hand format. The participants were asked to identify which method they preferred. The participants also experienced significant difficulty with this task and required considerable assistance, and not all participants were able to fully accomplish the task, of those who did the majority preferred the 'neatness' of the keyboard option to the 'vagueness' of the free-hand entry.

The final Task 6 instructed each participant to record and replay a simple voice message. Again, no participants were able to accomplish this task on their own, but when aided, participants were able to record and replay their own voice message on the PDA. For completeness the PDA's program buttons were also discussed as were the participants' preferences for screen orientation between portrait and landscape, where the majority preferred the PDA screen in portrait orientation. All participants found the menu structure difficult to navigate, and most found the PDA screen size easy to view but were evenly split over their preference for the interface usage of an icon or text. All participants were able to grip and hold the stylus. No one reported that the PDA felt heavy to carry, or awkward to hold.

5 CONCLUSIONS

It was clear from the outset that the participants found the PDA extremely complicated to use and had difficulty even knowing where to start; no one found the interface instinctive or intuitive. This was evidenced by the level of assistance requested and given. Despite the functionality of a PDA being demonstrated beforehand, not one of the participants could carry out even the most basic of tasks unaided. There was also a noticeable level of general disinterest in applications hosted on the PDA; none were of particular personal appeal to the participants. For example most thought that its functions as a calendar or diary were of little interest as they preferred a pen and diary. When asked, many agreed that they would certainly be more interested, and inclined to engage with the PDA if it provided an application of personal interest, such as MemoryLane. However, despite participants initially expressing concern about being unable to partake in the study due to their lack of computer knowledge, and the difficulties incurred during the tasks, many participants said they actually

enjoyed the experience of PDA interaction. Most felt that their skills would improve if they had more time with the PDA and some expressed a desire to learn more about a PDA given the desired surroundings and instructor. The portability of a PDA appealed to the majority of participants who remarked on it being 'small enough' to fit into a handbag or breast pocket. This would imply that many elderly users possess a genuine interest in engaging with mobile technologies and that a PDA has a certain appeal to many ageing, however, due to complex interfaces many choose not to experiment with such devices. These findings suggest that the interface for MemoryLane must strive to be simplistic, usable and intuitive to be successfully deployed on a PDA.

FUTURE WORK

This pilot study has paved the way for the next step in this research, a larger HCI requirements analysis will investigate how elderly people reminisce and recall past memories, this study will lead to the design and implementation of MemoryLane.

ACKNOWLEDGMENTS

The authors would like to express gratitude to Prof Mike McTear and Dr. Norman Alm for their input and to Dr. Kevin Curran and Professors Bryan Scotney and Sally McClean for their valuable advice and guidance. The authors would also like to extend appreciation to the pilot study participants who took the time to contribute to the research.

REFERENCES

[1] Directgov (2006), National Statistics, Census 2001, http://www.statistics.gov.uk/census/

[2] Eisma, R., Dickinson, A., Goodman, J., Mival, O., Syme, A. & Tiwari, L. (2003), Mutual Inspiration in the Development of New Technology for Ageing users, Include 2003, 252 - 259.

[3] Goodman, J., Brewster, S. & Gray, P. (2004), Older People, Mobile Devices and Navigation, HCI and the Older Population. Workshop at the British HCI 2004, Leeds, UK, Sep 2004, 13 - 14.

[4] Lazar, J., (2007), Universal Usability; Designing Computer Interfaces for Diverse Users, John Wiley & Sons Ltd., The Atrium, Southern Gate, Chichester, West Sussex, England

[5] Newell, A.F. & Gregor, P. (2000), User Sensitive Inclusive Design, ACM Conference on Universal Usability 2000, ACM Press, New York, USA, 39 - 44.

[6] Siek, K.A., Rogers, Y. & Connelly, K.H. (2005), Fat Finger Worries: How Older and Younger Users Physically Interact with PDAs, INTERACT 2005, eds. M.F. Costabile & F. Paterno, Springer Berlin, 267 - 280.

[7] Silverman, D., (2000), Doing Qualitative Research; A Practical Handbook, SAGE Publications Ltd, 6 Bonhill Street, London.

[8] Zajicek, M. (2006), Aspects of HCI research for elderly people, Universal Access in the Information Society, vol. Volume 5, Number 3, 279 – 286.

ALT Text and Basic Accessibility

Tom McEwan
Napier University, Edinburgh.
10 Colinton Road,
Edinburgh EH11 1PN, UK
+44 131 455 2793

t.mcewan@napier.ac.uk

Ben Weerts
Napier University, Edinburgh.
10 Colinton Road,
Edinburgh EH11 1PN, UK
+44 131 455 2793

benweerts@hotmail.com

ABSTRACT

Recent surveys have shown that the majority of websites are not accessible. Despite legal obligations and the importance of the internet for disabled people, most websites fail to reach a basic level of accessibility, yet web developers are not short of accessibility guidelines and recommendations. This preliminary study consists of a meta-review of web accessibility studies in order to identify a set of common barriers faced by the impaired. Automated testing, of websites created by recent multimedia graduates in their final semester, confirms these problems. In particular non-use, and incorrect use, of ALT (alternative) text emerges as the most frequent, basic error. We conclude that ALT is a litmus test of developers' attitudes towards accessibility and propose future work to identify how to understand and improve these attitudes

Categories and Subject Descriptors

H.5.4 Hypertext/Hypermedia. I.7.2 HTML

General Terms

Human Factors, Standardization, Legal Aspects.

Keywords

Web Development, accessibility compliance

1. INTRODUCTION

Despite standards (e.g. W3C standards), guidelines (e.g. Web Content Accessibility Guidelines) and laws (e.g. [1]) designed to ensure that all websites are accessible to all users, recent surveys (eg [7]) find that more than 80% of websites have accessibility problems. Ignorance alone does not explain this – it seems that accessibility is simply not a priority for (increasingly professionalised) web developers. The objective of this initial study is to identify the common reported accessibility problems, and to confirm whether they are present in the portfolios of new entrants to the profession. This will lead to future work with practitioners that will investigate why these standards, guidelines and laws do not lead to improvements in web development practice and to identify how to address this situation.

1.1 Web Accessibility

For those with access, the growth of the web has given us access to a multitude of services and information sources:

online banking, online shopping, vacation and travel planning, and instant messaging. These services make it possible for most people to do their daily activities online and without having to leave the house. For many the internet has become an indispensable and integral part of their daily lives [10]. For people with impairments, there are now many more options to access information and services than in the past. The visually impaired can listen to online newspapers and magazines, the physically impaired can shop online for goods even if they are unable to access existing shops, and so on. Many services and activities that were impossible or hard to do before for people with impairments can now be done online via assistive technologies (screen readers, voice browsers, alternative keyboards, speech recognition, etc) [24]. All of this, of course, assumes that website creators do not erect accessibility barriers that exclude categories of impaired users.

1.2 Legal Requirements

Many countries now have relevant legislation, though typically this is part of some general disability or equality legislation and not specific to web accessibility [21]. For example, part III of the UK Disability Discrimination Act 1995 (DDA) [1] requires providers of goods, facilities and services to avoid treating those with impairments "less favourably" than others, and to make "reasonable adjustments" to ensure access information and services (including websites). However, the DDA does not clearly state how accessibility should be achieved, and the term "reasonable adjustments" is vague and can lead to confusion. In the USA, the 1998 amendment [22] to Section 508 of the Rehabilitation Act establishes requirements for accessible websites for federal departments and agencies, to ensure that the disabled have the same access to, and use of, information as others. The EU's "eAccessibility" [9] encourages member states to use a "design for all" approach, to remove all barriers to accessing information and communication technologies (ICT), advocating compliance through accessibility certification. Some claim the majority of UK websites contravene the DDA [20], and, although there has, as yet, been no UK legal decision, in Australia, Maguire successfully sued the Sydney Organising Committee for the Olympic Games [3]. Given the global nature of the internet, however, it will be difficult to enforce some accessibility laws across national boundaries.

1.3 Accessibility in Practice

Despite the importance of the net for disabled people and the legal requirements, recent research [eg 7, 14, 16] reveals that the majority of websites are still not accessible. 81% of 1000 websites tested in 2004 [7] had accessibility failings, and tests with disabled users revealed that it is impossible for people with certain impairments to make use of the services provided. 94% of 200 Irish websites, across various sectors and service types, were found to be inaccessible [16]. A follow up study [21] found hope for improvement: the majority of the tested websites may still be inaccessible, but web developers are increasingly aware of accessibility issues). 95% of 162 British university homepages are inaccessible [13]. American studies [18, 20] of higher education websites suggest a partial improvement - websites are not completely inaccessible (40% achieve at least basic levels of accessibility), but are still far from fully accessible. We can conclude that the majority of the tested websites are not accessible, and two common problems emerge: disabled users find it difficult to use the provided online services, and, web developers are not sufficiently aware of, or do not prioritise, accessibility. The first viewpoint is clearly widely held. 93% of the blind users have difficulties using search engines [2]; on average, disabled people can only perform 76% of the tasks on websites [7]. The second viewpoint, however, seems to receive less analysis, so this study therefore will investigate why developers seem unaware of, or don't care about, the accessibility barriers they erect.

2. Meta-review

The current Web Content Accessibility Guidelines version 1.0 [27] (WCAG 1.0 – a second version, WCAG 2.0 [28] is not yet completed) provides 14 guidelines, each with one or more checkpoints, and split into 3 levels of priority. There are also 3 levels of conformance with the guidelines: levels A, AA and AAA, describing cumulative adherence to priorities 1, 1&2, 1&2&3 respectively.

We analysed 10 accessibility studies for the most frequently recurring accessibility errors. There are several ways of evaluating websites for compliance with WCAG1.0. At a very basic level an automatic software tool can be used to test for

compliance, though use of these tools alone does not guarantee accessibility [16] and the tools' users need to have a good understanding of WCAG and how the tool works [6]. Not all guidelines can be fully checked automatically for conformance, and a human expert has to test certain guidelines for compliance [16]. A combination of automatic and manual checking is required because manual testers might miss some errors that automatic tools would have found [21]. Improved measurement of accessibility can be achieved by including user simulation to help understand how the user interacts with the website, though it is very difficult for a non-disabled person to have the same experience as a disabled person. User evaluation is thought to give the best indication of accessibility - by getting experts and disabled users to give an in-depth evaluation of the website [21].

Each study had used WCAG 1.0 and one [14] also used Section 508 guidelines. All but one [11] used automated testing with Bobby (now called WebXact [23]) as their preferred testing tool. Some studies also used manual testing, user evaluation and/or simulation. Size varies from thirty [4] to one thousand [7] websites. We examined each study for three most frequently recurring accessibility errors they report, and these are listed in Table 1, which also presents details about each survey. In collating the most frequent accessibility errors, we disregarded the size of studies, since there was insufficient data to normalize them. The most common accessibility problems are, in order of frequency: No alternative (ALT) text for non-text elements; No titles for frames; Use of absolute sizing and positioning.

Title	Eval'n Method	Size	Most Common Barrier	2nd Most Common	3rd Most Common
Evaluation of consumer health website accessibility by users with sensory and physical disabilities [4]	Auto & manual	30	Provide ALT text for all images	If an image conveys important information beyond its ALT text, provide extended description.	Provide ALT content for each SCRIPT that conveys important information or functionality
The Web - Access and Inclusion for Disabled People [7]	Auto, manual, user simulation	1000	Provide a text equivalent for every non-text element	Ensure that foreground and background colours provide sufficient contrast	Ensure that pages are usable when scripts, (…) are turned off or not supported
A Review of Selected E-Recruiting Websites - Disability Accessibility Considerations [8]	Auto & User Simulation	41	Provide ALT text for all images	Provide ALT text for all image-type buttons in forms	Provide ALT text for all image map … (AREAs)
Usability of E-Government Web-Sites for People with Disabilities [11]	Manual	35	Provide a text equivalent for every non-text element	Organize documents so they may be read without style sheets	Identify row and column headers for data tables
Web site accessibility: a study of six genres [12]	Auto	549	Provide ALT text for all images	Provide a title for each frame	Provide ALT text for all image map … (AREAs)
Web Accessibility in the Mid-Atlantic United States: A Study of 50 Home Pages [14]	Auto & manual	50	Provide ALT text for all images	Ensure pages are usable when scripts, (…) are turned off or not supported	Ensure that all information conveyed with color is also available without color
Web site accessibility: an online sector analysis [15]	Auto	45	Use relative sizing and positioning	Identify the language of the text	Provide a summary for tables
WARP - Web Accessibility - Reporting Project - Ireland 2002 [16]	Auto	~ 200	Use of relative sizing & positioning	Provide ALT text for all images	Use a public text identifier in a DOCTYPE statement
The Accessibility of Web Pages for Mid-Sized College & Univ. Libraries [18]	Auto	190	Provide ALT text for all images	Provide ALT text for all image map hot–spots (AREAs)	Provide a title for each frame
An assessment of Web accessibility of UK accountancy firms [26]	Auto	72	Provide ALT text for all images	Provide a title for each frame	Provide ALT text for all image map hot-spots (AREAs)

Table 1: Review of Web Accessibility Studies

2.1 ALT text

Eight of the studies report the ALT text problem as the most frequent, and only one does not list it in the top three. There are many non-text elements which are only accessible to some users [19] through the ALT text: images, image map hot-spots, audio, video, graphical buttons, applets, animations, but images were reported to cause the most problems. The guidelines [27] state that a text equivalent must be provided and fulfil the same function for a disabled person as it does for a person without a disability. This ensures that users relying on assistive

technology, such as screen readers, can access the same information as others. If ALT text is absent, the screen reader cannot provide that access – it will either simply not inform the user of that image or it will convey other information (e.g. filename) [25].

There are admittedly a number of perspectives on ALT text – poor descriptions can be considered worse than none at all, and text should be succinct and accurate. If nothing else, however, something as simple to implement (and test for) as ALT does indicate the willingness of the developer to take accessibility into account. When determining appropriate alternative text for images, the purpose of the image should be considered first. Images can be used for a variety of purposes and each image type should use ALT text in a different way. One study [5] classifies five different categories of image (layout, decoration, navigation, supplement and content), with different ALT text suggestions for each, and the draft guidelines [28] makes similar recommendations. The same image will require different ALT text according to the reason for, and location of, its use. ALT text should be generated case by case and the diverse needs and capabilities of disabled users should be considered [16]. ALT text should also be kept as accurate and succinct possible. Unnecessarily long ALT text makes it more difficult for users of assistive technology to understand the website content [25, 26].

2.2 Other accessibility barriers

There are other common accessibility barriers found in these studies. Several [16, 18, 26] report "frame problems", in particular, frames without titles. Frames make it possible to display more than one web page in the same browser window, but are particularly problematic for the visually impaired, especially if frames are not meaningfully titled. The use of absolute sizing and positioning is another frequently recurring accessibility barrier [15, 16]. The size and position of HTML elements (text size, column widths, etc.) can be specified in *relative* units and then scaled according to the user's preferences for the browser. This is particularly useful for users with limited vision using standard browsing technology [16].

Other, less frequent accessibility barriers are reported in the above accessibility studies, although it is possible that their less frequent recurrence is due to the methodologies of the studies involved. Additionally a limitation of our approach is our focus on *frequency* rather than *seriousness* of these barriers. It is possible that certain common problems have little impact and are relatively easy to solve, while other less frequent problems can have a more serious impact.

3. Trainee Web Developers

We had access to an opportunistic sample – the websites produced by 40 final year undergraduates as an assessment for a Multimedia Technology module. By the time of our study, most of these students had graduated and either had, or were seeking, jobs as web developers, and kept their websites publicly available as an online portfolio. For the assessment they had to develop a publicly available website that contains an introduction screen, a menu, information on an e-learning application and the application itself. The students were asked to follow accessibility guidelines when designing the website, but accessibility itself is neither a module learning outcome nor a significant factor in the marks. All students had previously passed a Web Development module which required them to demonstrate basic understanding of web accessibility, and other HCI-related modules.

As final year students they are the web developers of the future –"destinations surveys" suggest most enter the web development industry after their course, mainly as developers. We hoped that their conformance to (at least) level A in WCAG 1.0 would be a good indication of the extent to which their previous learning remained with them and would inform future practice. The results were surprising and disappointing. Although it is possible that some took a strategic approach to assessment and deliberately ignored the guidelines, it would appear that most had not retained their earlier learning.

Given that some time had elapsed since the assessment was completed, not all sites were still publicly available. In total 30 websites were successfully evaluated for accessibility, using the same approach as others [12, 26] take, recording: WebXact approval or not; Priority 1 errors; and reported user checks. No manual checks were performed. 9 gained level A conformance, 2 gained level AA, 2 gained level AAA. The majority did not conform: 16 failed to meet any of the Priority Guidelines, 1 met Priority 2 but not Priority 1. Table 2 contains the priority 1 issues, the most basic level of accessibility. Almost all are ALT text-related. Given that only 4 students did better than level A conformance, Priority 2 and 3 issues were even more prevalent.

Table 2: Accessibility Error Frequency in Student Sites

	Explanation	sites	
1.1	Provide a text equivalent for images	12	P1
1.1	Provide a text equivalent for objects	10	P1
1.1	Provide a text equivalent for ASCII art	2	P1
12.1	Title each frame to facilitate frame identification and navigation	2	P1
6.2	Update equivalents for dynamic content when the dynamic content changes	1	P1

3.1 Limitations and Future Work

Although there is correlation between our future web developers practices and past studies into web accessibility, this could be in part due to our using the same automated testing method as used in most of the studies. WebXact is useful, but it has several limitations. It can only test for a certain number of WCAG 1.0 checkpoints and users must test the remaining checkpoints manually. It can't test the accessibility of scripts, cascading style sheets and secure websites. It occasionally reports false positive or false negative results [17, p42]. It also shows some difficulties with distinguishing between the impact of different appearances of the same type of error. But despite its limitations, WebXact has been the preferred accessibility tool of many accessibility studies [eg 8, 12, 13, 15, 16, 26], and using it here allows us to make comparisons with other studies. Also, our accessibility testing is limited to testing the homepage only, though this gateway is considered [14, p.7, 26] to be a good indicator of the overall accessibility of a website. If the homepage is not accessible then it will be difficult for a person with an impairment to access the rest of the website.

Accessibility is clearly a fundamental competency required by a web developer. In the British Computing Society's SFIAplus competency framework, the "Website Specialist" role definition includes (Ref: TSWBSP302) *"Is aware of the special requirements of the visually impaired and hard of hearing"*. In the next stage of our study we will explore such statements in interviews with professional web developers from a variety of companies. We hope to establish their level of understanding of, and sympathy towards, accessibility, and then to analyse their work processes for how, when, why and by whom, ALT text is written. We also want to identify whether customers prioritise accessibility, or even ask for it. We hope to identify when accessibility is tested/evaluated and by whom and when, and whether users with impairments are included as testers. We then plan to evaluate the usefulness of guidelines, and in particular WCAG 2.0, in order to suggest improvements to tools, training, working practices and competency definitions.

4. Conclusions

Repeated studies have shown that ALT text is the most fundamental accessibility problem in commercial website development. There may be other issues that have a greater impact on different groups of users, in different contexts, but despite (or perhaps because of) a variety of guidelines, this most basic form of accessibility compliance is achieved in a minority of websites.

While ALT text is not a panacea for accessibility, it may be a bell-weather for the developer's commitment to accessibility. It is the most frequently recurring failure to follow the most basic accessibility guidelines. As such it is often taught relatively early in university degree courses, yet this knowledge does not seem to stay with students as they move into practice. For the social inclusion of people with impairments, to ensure that university courses are fit for purpose, and for the professionalism of web development, it is vital to understand why ALT text remains problematic, and then provide redress.

5. REFERENCES

[1] British Government (1997). *Disability Discrimination Act 1995 (c. 50).* Retrieved June 14, 2006 from http://www.opsi.gov.uk/acts/acts1995/1995050.htm.

[2] Buzzi, M., Andronico, P. & Leporini, B. (2004) *Accessibility and Usability of Search Engine Interfaces: Preliminary Testing.* Retrieved July 8, 2006 from http://ui4all.ics.forth.gr/workshop2004/files/ui4all_proceedings /adjunct/accessibility/58.pdf.

[3] Carter, W. (2000). *Bruce Lindsay Maguire v Sydney Organising Committee for the Olympic Games.* Retrieved July 5, 2006 from http://www.humanrights.gov.au/disability_rights/decisions/comdec/2000/DD000120.htm.

[4] Chiang, M.F., & Starren, J. (2004). Evaluation of consumer health website accessibility by users with sensory and physical disabilities. *Proceedings of Medinfo 2004*; IOS Press, Amsterdam, 2004:1128-1132.

[5] Danino, N. & MacFarlane, S. (2001). Images on the Web: A suitable alternative. In J. Vanderdonckt, A. Blandford & A. Derycke (Eds.), *Interaction without frontiers, Volume II. 109-112.* Toulouse: Cépaduès-Éditions.

[6] Diaper, D. & Worman, L. (2003) Two Falls out of Three in the Automated Accessibility Assessment of World Wide Web Sites: A-Prompt v. Bobby. In P. Johnson. & P. Palanque (Eds.) *People and Computers XVII.* Springer-Verlag.

[7] Disability Rights Commission (DRC). (2004). *The Web: Access and Inclusion for Disabled People.* London: TSO.

[8] Erickson, W. & Bruyère, S. (2002) *A Review of Selected E-Recruiting Websites: Disability Accessibility Considerations. Cornell University.*

[9] European Commission. (2006). *eAccessibility.* Retrieved July 8, 2006 from http://europa.eu/scadplus/leg/en/lvb/l24226h.htm.

[10] Hoffman, D., Novak, T., & Peralta, M. (2004). Has the Internet become indispensable? *Communications of the ACM, 40*(2), 37-42.

[11] Huang, C. (2002). Usability of E-Government Web-Sites for People with Disabilities & Accessibility of E-Government Web-Sites in Taiwan. *Proceedings of the Annual Hawaii International Conference on System Sciences*, USA, 36, p147c.

[12] Jackson-Sanborn, E., Odess-Harnish, K., & Warren, N. (2002). Web site accessibility: a study of six genres. *Library Hi-Tech, 20*(3), 308-317.

[13] Kelly, B. (2002). *An Accessibility Analysis Of UK University Entry Points.* Retrieved June 29, 2006 from http://www.ariadne.ac.uk/issue33/web-watch/.

[14] Lazar, J., & et al. (2003). Web Accessibility in the Mid-Atlantic United States: A Study of 50 Home Pages. *Universal Access in the Information Society Journal, 2*(4), 331-341.

[15] Loiacono, E., & McCoy, S. (2004). Web site accessibility: an online sector analysis. *Information Technology & People, 17*(1), 87-101.

[16] McMullin, B. (2002). *WARP: Web Accessibility Reporting Project Ireland 2002 Baseline Study.* Retrieved June 11, 2006 from http://eaccess.rince.ie/white-papers/2002/warp-2002-00/warp-2002-00.pdf.

[17] Schmetzke, A. (2001). Web accessibility at university libraries and library schools. *Library Hi Tech, 19*(1), 35-49.

[18] Spindler, T. (2004). The Accessibility of Web Pages for Mid-Sized College and University Libraries. *Reference & User Services Quarterly, 42*(2), 149-154.

[19] Thatcher, J. et al. (2002). *Constructing accessible web sites.* Birmingham: Glasshaus.

[20] Thompson, T., Burgstahler, S. & Comden, D. (2003). *Research on Web Accessibility in Higher Education.* Retrieved July 7, 2006 from http://www.rit.edu/~easi/itd/itdv09n2/thompson.htm.

[21] Trulock, V. (2006). *A comparative investigation of the accessibility levels of Irish websites.* Unpublished MSc dissertation. Edinburgh, UK: Napier University.

[22] US Government. (1998, August). *Amendment to Section 508 of the Rehabilitation Act.* Retrieved July 4, 2006 from http://www.section508.gov/index.cfm?FuseAction=Content&ID=14.

[23] Watchfire WebXact. (n.d.). Retrieved March 31, 2007 from http://www.webxact.com/ .

[24] Web Accessibility in Mind (WebAIM). (n.d.(a)). *Introduction to Web Accessibility.* Retrieved July 6, 2006 from http://www.webaim.org/intro/.

[25] WebAIM. (n.d.(b)). *Creating Accessible Images.* Retrieved July 10, 2006 from http://www.webaim.org/techniques/images/alt_text.php.

[26] Williams, R. & Rattray, R. (2003). An assessment of web accessibility of UK accountancy firms. *Managerial Auditing Journal, 9*(16), 710-716.

[27] World Wide Web Consortium (W3C). (1999a). *Web Content Accessibility Guidelines 1.0.* Retrieved June 14, 2006 from http://www.w3.org/TR/WCAG10.

[28] W3C. (2006a). *Web Content Accessibility Guidelines 2.0.* Retrieved September 21, 2006 from http://www.w3.org/TR/WCAG20/Overview.html#contents.

Calling Time: An Effective and Affective Evaluation of Two Versions of the MIT Beer Game

Nicola Millard and
Rosalind Britton
British Telecommunications PLC
Adastral Park
Martlesham Heath, Ipswich, U.K.
<firstname.surname>@bt.com

ABSTRACT

Playing a business game needs to be both educational and entertaining. Thus, evaluation of the experience of playing games needs to incorporate both effective and affective dimensions. This experiment compared the experience of playing the conventional MIT beer game with a prototype electronic version, which had been developed to reduce the complexity and costs associated with the original game. It suggested design enhancements in terms of effective and affective dimensions of play.

General Terms

Human Factors.

Keywords

Design and evaluation methods, affective Human-Computer Interaction, business games.

1. WHAT IS THE BEER GAME?

A game with beer in the title sounds great fun – however, the only thing that the beer game lacks is real alcohol! The MIT 'Beer Game' is a role-playing simulation developed at MIT's Sloan School of Management in the early 1960s as part of Forrester's research [1, 2] on industrial systems dynamics. It illustrates the advantages of taking an integrated approach to managing a factory style production supply chain. It particularly demonstrates the value of sharing information across the various components of a supply chain and shows the long-term consequences of people's actions.

The objective of the game is to maximise customer service and profitability across the linked elements of the production of the beer – from the retailer to wholesaler to the beer factory. Each component in the supply chain has unlimited storage capacity and there is a fixed supply lead time and order delay time between each component. On each simulated week, each component in the supply chain tries to meet the demand of the downstream component. There is always a one-week delay in the upstream supply. Any orders that cannot be met are

recorded as backorders, and are met as soon as possible. No orders can be ignored, and all orders must eventually be fulfilled. There are "financial" penalties for shortages on backorders and held inventory

Chaos usually ensues as people go from boom to bust as they overestimate and then underestimate demand in the system [2]. Emotions generally run high as blame is usually attributed throughout the linked supply chain elements. Though each player is free to make their own decisions, the same patterns of behaviour emerge every time the game is played. This vividly demonstrates the powerful role of the 'system' in shaping behaviours.

2. IF IT AIN'T BROKE…

The traditional beer game has been played all over the world by thousands of people ranging from university students to company chief executive officers. However, the game relies on a specially designed games board, takes a lot of time to play and requires the services of a trained facilitator – and they can be thin on the ground or vastly overworked. So, a new prototype version of the beer game was designed using a Sensetable [3]. The Sensetable is a touch sensitive graphical user interface which is embedded into the top of a games table. This was designed to orchestrate player moves and drive the game forward without the need for a human facilitator.

The object of this experiment was to compare the experience of playing the conventional beer game with a prototype of the electronic beer game and suggest how the game could be improved in terms of both effective and affective dimensions of play.

3. PLAYING THE GAME.

The evaluation team ran two beer game sessions with two teams of eight players competing against each other. The first session was a conventional, facilitator run beer game using the game boards. The second was a non-facilitated version of the beer game using the Sensetable to drive action. Both teams played both conventional and electronic versions of the game.

Data was gathered on both the effective and affective aspects of game play in both sessions. This comprised of:

- Questionnaires that covered team working, facilitation, learning, satisfaction and usability.
- PrEmo questionnaires [4] gauging emotions evoked by each version of the game using an expressive cartoon character.
- Participant observation – with two observers embedded within each of the teams. They noted any

conversations and body language that they believed were of interest to either effective or affective elements of game play.

- Structured interviews with selected participants.

The conventional and PrEmo questionnaires plus the structured interviews were administered immediately after each of the two games sessions.

4. AFTERMATH.

4.1. Evaluation of Game Effect.

Data about the effectiveness of the games were primarily gained through the questionnaires, with additional data provided through participant observation and player interviews.

The percentage of people who thought that the electronic game encouraged teamworking was significantly less (48%) than with the conventional game (92%). This was reinforced by observations during the conventional game that interactions were taking place that were not directly related to play. The speed of the electronic game meant that energies were directed at the game board rather than at other members of the team, so less team interaction and general banter was occurring.

Similarly, learning was perceived to be less (54% said they had learned something from the conventional game verses 20% with the electronic). Again, the speed of the electronic game meant that there was faster strategising with much less thought or team discussion invested in the ordering process. One player randomly ordered 200 barrels and pressed return without blinking! (This is linked with less sense of stock movement in the electronic game, since this action in the physical game would necessitate the movement of a large number of coloured counters).

The facilitation was also singled out as being more effective with the human facilitator (86% agreed that facilitation was "about right", 14% thought that facilitation was "too little") than with the electronic direction (50% agreed it was "about right" and 50% "too little").

In terms of satisfaction, 85% said they would recommend the conventional game verses 50% with the electronic. 91% stated they found the conventional game mentally stimulating compared with 58% for the electronic.

On usability, the most significant difference was around understanding what to do next – with only 50% reporting problems with the conventional game (one player commented that he "had no idea what the strategy was") compared with 70% for the electronic version (players commented that "at least in the board game I thought I knew what I was doing - I'm pretty lost here!"). There was, in the electronic version, a tendency to press buttons randomly until something happened. This was not helped by the (lack of) sensitivity of the Sensetable to multiple finger touches.

This was also reflected by the data investigating the clarity and aesthetics of the information presented – with 86% reporting that the conventional game was clear and understandable and 71% rating presentation as attractive, compared with 42% and 57% with the electronic.

The electronic version of the game came out as marginally stronger than the conventional game in two dimensions: game duration and the player's perception of control.

The conventional game took 1 hour and 35 minutes to complete a cycle of 35 weeks. The electronic game took a mere 28 minutes to reach 35 weeks. 12% of players thought that the conventional game was too long, with 6% of players reporting that the electronic version was too lengthy. However, players reported that the impetus and sense of urgency in game play that was encouraged by the human facilitator was not evident in the electronic version.

50% of players reported that they felt more in control of the electronic version of the game against 42% with the conventional version. This is largely because the electronic game would not permit players to do things that were against the game's rules so players did not need to continually check whether they were doing the right thing, as they were in the conventional game.

4.2. Evaluation of Game Affect.

The PrEmo method [4] was chosen as a tool to evaluate the affective aspects of game play. PrEmo uses a number of cartoon characters arranged in a series of positive and negative semantic differentials to assess emotional reaction using user self report.

The PrEmo questionnaires unearthed a number of differences in the emotional reaction that the two games provoked (emotion labels have been added to the cartoon figures for clarity).

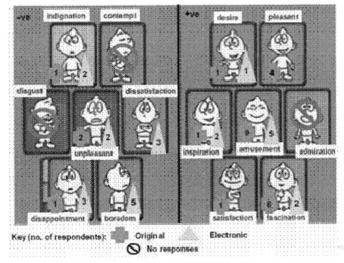

Figure 1: Results of PrEmo evaluation.

Of the total emotions reported using PrEmo:

The original game:

- 68% reported overall positive affect.
- 21% reported overall negative affect.
- The highest scores related to 'Amusement' and 'Fascination'.

The electronic game:

- 31% reported overall positive affect.
- 68% reported overall negative affect.
- The highest scores related to 'Amusement' and 'Boredom'.
- 3 people reported 'Dissatisfaction' with the game.

The affective data was reinforced by the participant observation. Body language in the conventional game was generally positive (i.e. forward posture with engagement in game playing). Observed instances of disengagement (often leaning back with arms folded) were usually borne out of frustration. Interestingly, frustration in the conventional game was frequently directed at other players, whereas frustration in the electronic game was almost exclusively directed at the system.

5. CONCLUSIONS AND DESIGN IMPLICATIONS.

One key result for both versions of the game is that they were perceived to be amusing – a key quality in a successful game. However, the levels of engagement (fascination vs. boredom) could not be sustained by the electronic game.

Although the electronic beer game seemed less effective in terms of dimensions such as teambuilding and learning, it did offer higher levels of perceived control to players. The usability of the electronic prototype did tend to cloud perceptions of effective play even though players stated that they found the conventional game "fiddly".

One of the biggest differences between the two versions of the game was the lack of facilitator influence in the electronic game. This caused the impetus for play to lag.

This combination of effective and affective evaluation was used to feed design recommendations into the electronic game technical team. These included:

- Improving the usability of the electronic game – in particular the sensitivity of the Sensetable, the clarity of the supply chain roles and the sense of game flow.
- A multimedia introduction to explain the basic concepts and rules of the beer game. To encourage interaction between players, the electronic game rules needed to emphasise the role of collaboration and strategy.
- Introduction of a more explicit facilitation mechanism (or at least a timer mechanism).
- Suggesting that more than one table is required and that, ideally, multiple tables should be networked together to encourage more competition/teambuilding to take place. One of the major problems with electronic version was that, due to the relative small size of the Sensetable, there was a restriction on the number of players that could interact with the table at any one time.
- Since players had less of a feeling of tangible stock movements in the electronic version of the game there was a suggestion that a more tangible interface, e.g. physical counters, could be used with the Sensetable.

It is acknowledged that there may have been some element of order effect bias introduced since the players experienced the original game first and then evaluated the electronic version in the light of the original. However, the time constraints of the evaluation project prevented the experiment being rerun with the electronic game being played first.

However, the experiment did prove the advantages of taking a multifaceted data capture approach combining traditional quantitative data with affective data in a game play environment. By doing this, the evaluation team got access to data which was relevant to the emotional experience of playing the game as well as practical usability data.

6. REFERENCES

[1] Forrester, J. W. (1958), "Industrial Dynamics: A Major Breakthrough for Decision Makers", *Harvard Business Review*, Vol. 36, No. 4, pp. 37-66.

[2] Sterman, J. D. (1989), "Modeling Managerial Behavior: Misperceptions of Feedback in a Dynamic Decision Making Environment," *Management Science,* Vol. 35, No. 3, pp. 321-339.

[3] Patten, J., Ishii, H., Hines, J., Pangaro, G., Sensetable: A Wireless Object Tracking Platform for Tangible User Interfaces, in Proceedings of Conference on Human Factors in Computing Systems (CHI '01), Seattle, Washington, USA, March 31 - April 5, 2001, ACM Press, pp.253-260.

[4] Desmet, P.M.A., Hekkert, P. and Jacobs, J.J. (2000), When a Car Makes You Smile: Development and Application of an Instrument to Measure Product Emotions, in Hoch, S.J. and Meyer, R.J. (eds), *Advances in Consumer Research*, 27, Provo, UT: Association of Consumer Research, 111-117.

Overcoming the Distance between Friends

Johanna Renny Octavia
User System Interaction
Eindhoven University of Technology
Den Dolech 2, 5600 MB, Eindhoven,
The Netherlands
j.r.octavia@tm.tue.nl

Elise van den Hoven
Department of Industrial Design
Eindhoven University of Technology
Den Dolech 2, 5600 MB, Eindhoven,
The Netherlands
e.v.d.hoven@tue.nl

Hans De Mondt
Research & Innovation, ReNA
Alcatel-Lucent
Copernicuslaan 50, B-2018, Antwerp,
Belgium
hans.de_mondt@alcatel-lucent.be

ABSTRACT

Staying in touch is a fundamental aspect in maintaining a long-distance relationship, whether it is in a family context or a friendship. An effective communication appliance can enable families or friends living apart to have a feeling of connectedness and help them to maintain their relationship despite the physical distance. This paper describes the results of an exploration study on people living far away from their families and friends, with a focus on how they stay in touch with their close friends and overcome the distance.

The targeted user group in this study is geographically and physically isolated people. A user study was conducted by means of a survey, focus group and interview. The results show that sharing problems and feelings between two remotely located friends is crucial. Consequently, the design goal was set to enable users to notify and physically comfort each other, in a subtle way, through a remote but shared experience, whenever a problem or feeling occurs.

Categories and Subject Descriptors

H.4.3 [**Information Systems Applications**]: Communications Applications; H.5.2 [**Information Interfaces and Presentation (e.g. HCI)**]: User Interfaces – *User-centred design*

General Terms

Design.

Keywords

Communication appliance, awareness, connectedness, long-distance relationship, tangible interaction, personal artefacts.

1. INTRODUCTION

Globalization has changed our world in so many different ways. One of the effects is the increasing migration of people from one country to another, which can have various reasons, such as having a new job, studying, or going on holiday. This phenomenon is resulting in a situation where families and friends live far away from one another, physically separated and geographically distributed.

Maintaining a long-distance relationship, whether between

family members or friends, faces many challenges. When physical separation occurs, there is a higher risk of relationship deterioration, which in turn may lead to relationship dissolution. Once one's relationship deteriorates, the possibility of losing friends is higher than losing family members. Family ties are for life, where as friends may come and go. Considering this, relationship maintenance between friends seems more challenging than between family members. In this paper, we focus on the exploration of long-distance relationships between close friends.

2. RELATED WORK

Technology-mediated communication plays a significant role in facilitating interpersonal communication (e.g. between family members, friends, couples) and group communication (e.g. among co-workers), when face-to-face communication is not viable. Much research has been done to explore how technology-mediated communication can support remotely located people to stay in touch and connected with each other. This form of communication ranges from emails, phones, and instant messaging applications to awareness systems.

Existing network communication technologies facilitate staying in touch with remote families or friends to some extent. Media such as email, instant messaging, and telephone, are considered content-oriented communication, focusing on conveying meaningful information. However, communication activities in daily life and social relationships involve much more than just the exchange of explicit information. Kuwabara [9] et al. proposed the concept of connectedness-oriented communication, which aims to foster a feeling of connectedness to maintain and enhance human social relationships. Liechti and Ichikawa [10] introduced the idea of affective awareness as a general sense of being close to families and friends. These studies support the idea that the communication media that are currently available do not fully support maintaining long-distance relationships.

One way to stay in touch is by means of an awareness system. An awareness system is a new form of technology-mediated communication that has been widely studied over the last decade. An awareness system is defined as a system that facilitates lightweight, emotional, informal forms of communication that help people to effortlessly maintain awareness of each other's whereabouts and activities [8]. If designed effectively, an awareness system provides connectedness and a sense of being close to one's family or friends.

Time-wise there are two types of communication: synchronous communication, then the interaction takes place in real time, and asynchronous communication, in that case the information exchanged is stored and can be accessed later when the receiving party feels the need.

In this respect awareness systems can be seen as a new type of communication medium that augments existing ones since it offers the possibility of having asynchronous communication before switching to synchronous communication.

Following the concept of connectedness-oriented communication [9], several works on awareness systems have focused in supporting people that are emotionally-close in maintaining their relationship while living physically separated by providing a feeling of connectedness. For example, family members (e.g. ASTRA [11] and Familyware [5]); couples (e.g. Feather and Scent [13] and Lover's Cup [2]); and close friends (e.g. Shaker [13] and FaintPop [9]). Most of these studies focus on staying in touch within a family context. Although some studies also try to cover staying in touch between friends [9,11,13], no study has ever focused completely on friends.

In line with the notion of supporting awareness and enhancing remote communication, there are several applications for awareness systems designed based on the idea of tangible interaction. PSyBench [1] facilitates remote users not only to collaborate in a shared physical workspace but also to have a strong feeling of each other's physical presence. InTouch [1] is designed to enable haptic interpersonal communication between remote users. More recently, Social Radio [4] is presented as a tangible awareness system that enables small intimate groups to stay in touch and mediate a feeling of connectedness among them through sharing personal music. Another example, Keep in Touch [12] enables remote couples to maintain intimacy by means of a fabric touchscreen. Tangible Interaction (TI) is a recent field that has been growing rapidly in the last few years. The idea behind it is that digital information is made accessible to users through everyday physical artefacts in their everyday environment.

Hoven and Eggen [6] presented an extension to the taxonomy of Ullmer and Ishii [14] by adding a category of TI with personal artefacts. Physical artefacts are categorized as personal when the artefact has a personal meaning to the user and most likely the user also owns the artefact. Using personal artefacts rather than generic ones in TI is argued to reduce the learning time for users since they already have a mental model regarding the personal artefact. Existing TI for awareness systems all use generic artefacts [1,4,12].

Hoven [7] incorporated the use of personal objects, namely souvenirs, in the design of a Digital Photo Browser, a TI application for supporting recollection of personal memories. It is suggested that using personal objects may give an affordance for users to interact with TI applications in a better way since a mental model already exists concerning the object and the associated digital information.

This paper presents the exploration phase of a study on staying in touch with physically separated friends. The study aims to design a connectedness-oriented communication appliance to support staying in touch and maintaining relationships, by means of tangible interaction and the use of personal artefacts.

3. EXPLORATION PHASE

The targeted user group in this study are people who move away from their friends. Being isolated can lead to loneliness and depression [3], which in the end might affect their well-being. Establishing contact with other people could alter this situation. Therefore, this group is considered to have a need for communication.

Two categories of isolation are studied. First, geographic isolation caused by a geographical distance, for example moving to a new place for work or study. Second, physical isolation caused by a certain physical condition, such as being in exile, displaced or very ill. In this study, expatriates and international students represent the first group; and asylum seekers represent the second group.

The exploration phase consists of two parts: a general exploration on long-distance relationships and a more focused continuation.

3.1 Long-Distance Relationship Exploration

To gather an initial understanding of the research problem, an online survey and a focus group session were carried with questions such as: What do people experience when living far away from their close friends? In what ways do they stay in touch? What kind of difficulties do they face with respect to communication? Does relationship deterioration occur? And what kind of personal artefacts do they have that are linked to their friends?

3.1.1 Survey

The online survey was aimed at both people who moved and people who stayed behind. The survey was distributed by snowball sampling via email and mouth-to-mouth advertisement. Valid responses were obtained from 101 participants (73% moved and 27% left behind, 59% female and 41% male, reason for moving: 52% study, 25% work, 15% follow family and 8% better living condition). From the survey, the main findings were:

- People who moved and those who are left behind both share similar feelings, such as finding it hard or difficult to be apart, missing the other, feeling distant, sad, and lonely. In addition, no significant differences are found when comparing the two groups on frequency of contact with each other, presence of personal artefacts, and self-proclaimed relationship deterioration.

- The major means of communication is email (92%), instant messaging (73%) and phones (68%).

- The type of information shared remains more or less the same compared to when they were physically close: personal matters (news, problems and feelings), work or study, family, and friends. However, the information is less detailed, they only share updates on old information or news.

- Talking, sharing, being together and doing things together, face-to-face meetings and having physical contact are important elements that a long-distance friendship misses.

- Relationship deterioration is experienced by half of the respondents (52%). After living far away for a certain period, they feel not as close as before, have less contact, share less information, and have less common things or shared experiences. The main reasons are that they are busy and living different lives.

- Half of the respondents (50%) have a personal artefact that relates to their close friend, mainly pictures and presents. They perceive the artefact as personal because it reminds them of how the close friend looks, of their great moments together, and brings back memories.

Knowing that the problems that people experienced, either when they moved away or stayed behind, are more or less similar, it was decided to focus on people who moved in the next steps of the study since we have easier access to this group of people.

3.1.2 Focus Group

Two focus group sessions were conducted. The first group (geographically-isolated) consisted of 2 males and 2 females; two of them were international students, 1 expatriate, and 1 expatriate's family member. The second group (physically-isolated) were 3 asylum seekers living in an asylum centre, two of them were male and 1 female. The main purpose of the focus group was to acquire a deeper understanding of the users and their requirements, and also to dive into the survey findings. Three research materials were used in the focus group: an introductory questionnaire, "a day in the life" video of two personas (representing each group), and participants' personal artefacts. Some of the main findings were:

- Time constraints, time difference, living different lives, different life styles, and different life rhythms are the main difficulties in staying in touch with close friends.

- The situation of being away from friends is more difficult for the asylum seekers since it is a permanent situation for them, and also the means of communication available are more limited. They also realize that their relationships are not likely to get weakened, as their close friends tend to have more understanding towards their condition.

- The feeling of envy sometimes hinders sharing experiences between geographically isolated participants with their close friends. However, having shared experiences, or sharing the same experience, is considered to be a very important element in a friendship. When friends no longer have shared experiences, over time they will drift apart. In the end, this may lead to relationship deterioration.

- Memories of prior shared experiences, special attention, something in common, and problems, are the things that make participants feel connected with their close friends.

Findings show that shared experiences turn out to be essential things that people miss in a long-distance friendship, which over time may cause the friendship to deteriorate. Therefore at this point, the research continued with a focus on facilitating a remote shared experience. It was also chosen only to proceed with the first group (expatriates, international students, and their accompanying family members), because these people, as well as their friends, will have easier access to the potential design solution, which will consist of technological equipment that is not readily available to all.

3.2 Shared Experiences Exploration

In this study, shared experience is described as the things that two or more close friends do together, not necessarily at the same time, but give them the same experience. Having many shared experiences is like glue that holds a friendship together. The main question raised in this phase is: What kind of experiences did people share when they still lived nearby? What kind of shared experiences would they like to have now even though they live far apart? And how do they manage to have shared experiences now?

3.2.1 Survey

Another online survey was carried out, by sending emails to people who participated in the previous survey. For this second survey, 32 people responded (78% female and 22% male, 50%

study, 34% work and 16% follow family). The main findings of the survey were:

- Sharing problems and feelings is the shared experience that most respondents had before and wished to have now. For a top five of shared experiences see Table 1.

Table 1. Top five shared experience that respondents had before and wished to have now

No.	Kind of shared experience	% of respondents (n=32)	
		Had	Wished
1	Sharing problems and feelings	88 %	78 %
2	Sharing jokes and funny stories	84 %	66 %
3	Going out for a drink or meal	81 %	56 %
4	Hanging out	75 %	50 %
5	Having physical contacts (hugs, shoulder pats)	69 %	50 %

- It is still possible to share problems, feelings, jokes and funny stories to some extent, by talking about them over the phone, chatting, or sharing via emails. For other shared experiences such as going out for a drink or meal and having physical contacts, are not feasible anymore until they visit each other. However, some people prefer making new friends as a remedy.

Even though the survey participants live far away from their close friends, the shared experience they miss most is to share problems and feelings. For that reason, the design in this research will be focusing on facilitating remote shared experience of sharing problems and feelings.

3.2.2 Interviews

To acquire more detailed and elaborate information on the experience of sharing problems and feelings, semi-structured interviews were conducted with 5 participants. Four of them were females and one male; three of them were international students, 1 expatriate, and 1 expatriate's family member. The main findings were:

- Knowing a friend's problems and feelings connects people emotionally and builds a stronger friendship. The problems and feelings shared are mainly big, life-related problems and deep, intense feelings that they normally only share with very close friends.

- When people are living near to one another and one has problems, they meet face-to-face, spend time together and talk the problems through. When living far away, synchronous communication (e.g. talking on the phone, chatting) is difficult because of time constraints, different time zones, and the fact that sharing problems requires an enormous amount of energy and time.

- When people are meeting each other, it is also easier to sense whenever their close friend is having a problem or not feeling well (through body language and facial expression). When living far away, sensing each other's current feelings is nearly impossible. Hence, people become less sensitive to the feelings of their close friends.

- People find it difficult to share big problems. They simply do not know how to start expressing their problem. They wish their close friends would instantly know and ask them what is wrong.

- People miss the physical contact they usually have with their close friends right after sharing their problems, such as hugs or simple comforting touches on the hands or shoulders. They said that sometimes they just wanted to be comforted and did not need to hear any solutions instantly.

3.3 Design Goals

This study focuses on designing an appliance to facilitate two close friends in sharing their problems and feelings over a distance. The thorough exploration described in this paper gave us sufficient understanding of the research problem to come up with the following two design goals:

1) People should be able to let their remote friend know that they have a problem or a particular feeling, without using any words, in a subtle way.

2) People should be able to give comfort physically to their remote friend.

4. CONCLUSIONS AND FUTURE WORK

We performed an exploration study to investigate how people stay in touch and maintain their long-distance friendships when they are living far away from their close friends. A shared experience is considered very important in a friendship as it brings a feeling of connectedness to one's close friends. Due to the distance, physically separated friends are more likely to have less shared experiences which over time may cause the relationship to deteriorate. Sharing problems and feelings is the shared experience that is highly missed in a long-distance friendship. The comprehensive exploration has led us to an interim conclusion that facilitating a remote experience of sharing problems and feelings between close friends is crucial. Two design goals have been identified: the design should enable users in a non-obtrusive way to *notify* each other, and *physically comfort* each other whenever a problem or feeling takes place.

The approach of this study is user-centred design, which means that after the completion of the user and requirements study, the conceptual design phase will take place. Subsequently, the selected design concept will be prototyped and followed by a user evaluation.

5. ACKNOWLEDGMENTS

We thank all the dedicated participants in this study and the Ambient Media team at Research & Innovation, ReNA, Alcatel-Lucent, in particular Marc Godon and Laurence Claeys, for their valuable contributions.

6. REFERENCES

[1] Brave, S., Ishii, H., and Dahley, A. Tangible Interfaces for Remote Collaboration and Communication. In *Proceedings of the 1998 ACM Conference on Computer Supported Cooperative Work (CSCW '98)* (Seattle, Washington, USA, November 14-18, 1998). ACM Press, 169-178.

[2] Chung, H., Lee, C.J., and Selker, T. Lover's Cups: Drinking Interfaces as New Communication Channels. In *Proceedings of the 2006 Conference on Human Factors in Computing Systems (CHI'06)* (Montréal, Québec, Canada, April 22-27, 2006). ACM Press, 375-380.

[3] Devito, J. *Human Communication*. New York, USA: Longman Publishing Group, 1997.

[4] Etter, R. and Röcker, C. A Tangible User Interface for Multi-User Awareness Systems. In: *Proceedings of the International Conference on Tangible and Embedded Interaction (TEI '07)* (Baton Rouge, Louisiana, USA, Feb15-17, 2007). ACM Press, 11-12.

[5] Go, K., Carroll, J.M., and Imamiya, A. Familyware: Communicating with Someone You Love. In *Proceedings of the IFIP TC9 WG9.3 International Conference on Home Oriented Informatics and Telematics (HOIT'00), "IF at Home: Virtual Influences on Everyday Life"* (Wolverhampton, UK, June 28-30, 2000). Information, Technology and Society, 125-140.

[6] Hoven, E. A. W. H. van den, and Eggen, B. Tangible Computing in Everyday Life: Extending Current Frameworks for Tangible User Interfaces with Personal Objects. In: P. Markopoulos et al. (Eds.), EUSAI 2004, LNCS 3295, 230–242.

[7] Hoven, E. A. W. H. van den, and Eggen, B. Digital Photo Browsing with Souvenirs. In: M. Rauterberg et al. (Eds.), Human-Computer Interaction-INTERACT'03, IOS Press, 2003, 1000-1003.

[8] IJsselsteijn, W.A., van Baren, J., and van Lanen, F. Staying in Touch: Social Presence and Connectedness through Synchronous and Asynchronous Communication Media. In: C. Stephanidis and J. Jacko (Eds.), Human-Computer Interaction: Theory and Practice (Part II), volume 2 of the Proceedings of HCI International 2003, 924-928.

[9] Kuwabara, K., Watanabe, T., Ohguro, T., Itoh, Y., and Maeda, Y. Connectedness Oriented Communication: Fostering a Sense of Connectedness to Augment Social Relationships. In *Proceedings of the 2002 Symposium on Applications and the Internet (SAINT '02)* (Nara, Japan, Jan 28-Feb 01, 2002). IEEE Computer Society, 2002, 186-193.

[10] Liechti, O. and Ichikawa, T. A Digital Photography Framework Enabling Affective Awareness in Home Communication. Personal Technologies 4 (1), 2000, 6-24.

[11] Markopoulos, P., Romero, N., van Baren, J., IJsselsteijn, W., de Ruyter, B., and Farshchian, B. Keeping in Touch with the Family: Home and Away with the ASTRA Awareness System. In *Proceedings of the 2004 Conference on Human Factors in Computing Systems (CHI'04)* (Vienna, Austria, April 24-29, 2004). ACM Press, 1351-1354.

[12] Motamedi, N. Keep in Touch: A Tactile-Vision Intimate Interface. In *Proceedings of the 1st International Conference on Tangible and Embedded Interaction (TEI'07)* (Baton Rouge, Louisiana, USA, February 15-17, 2007). ACM Press, 21-22.

[13] Strong, R. and Gaver, B. Feather, Scent and Shaker: Supporting Simple Intimacy. In Videos, Demos and Short Papers of CSCW '96. *Proceedings of the 1996 ACM Conference on Computer Supported Cooperative Work (CSCW '96)* (Boston, Massachusetts, USA, November 16-20, 1996). ACM Press, 29-30.

[14] Ullmer, B. and Ishii, H. Emerging framework for tangible user interfaces. IBM Systems Journal, 39 (3-4), 2000, 915-931.

Validating the Unified Theory of Acceptance and Use of Technology (UTAUT) Tool Cross-Culturally

Lidia Oshlyansky
University of Wales Swansea
Singleton Park
Swansea SA2 8PP
+44 1792 205678

lidiaosh@gmail.com

Paul Cairns
Dept of Computer Science
University of York
York Y010 5DD
+44 1904 434336

pcairns@cs.york.ac.uk

Harold Thimbleby
University of Wales Swansea
Singleton Park
Swansea SA2 8PP
+44 1792 205678

harold@thimbleby.net

ABSTRACT

HCI methods and tools are often used cross-culturally before being tested for appropriateness and validity. As new tools emerge, they must be cross-culturally validated to ensure that they work with all audiences, not just those in the country in which they were developed. This paper presents the validation of a technology acceptance model over nine culturally-diverse countries. The model validated is the Unified Theory of Acceptance and Use of Technology (UTAUT). The paper also explores ongoing analysis of the culture differences that emerge on UTAUT measures, and suggests avenues for future work.

Categories and Subject Descriptors

H.5.2 [**User interfaces**]: Evaluation/methodology

General Terms

Measurement, Reliability, Standardization, Verification.

Keywords

Cross-cultural, technology acceptance, UTAUT, validation.

1. INTRODUCTION

Particularly with website design and mobile devices, Human-Computer Interaction practitioners face the challenges of designing across cultures daily, but there is little in the way of proven, cross-culturally validated tools. Ongoing research has shown that differences do exist in the way subjects in different cultures respond to standard usability measurement techniques [3,6]. Standard HCI measurement tools have been shown to have cultural differences that can be missed if they are not carefully evaluated and considered [13].

HCI has often relied on cultural models to help explain differences found in various aspects of usability and interaction. For example, cultural models have been used to explain cross-cultural differences in technology acceptance, adoption and uptake [2,5,10]. However, models of cultural differences may not be applicable, or indeed valid, for use in the field [9,11,14].

"Technology acceptance," that is, people's attitude to the up-take and use of different technologies, has emerged as a strong candidate for cross-cultural validation of HCI tools. Previous research has undertaken some work to cross-culturally validate and culturally extend technology acceptance models, such as the Technology Acceptance Model (TAM) [4,7,15]. However, the Unified Theory of Acceptance and Use of Technology, UTAUT [16], is a more recent instrument, which is a synthesis of eight existing models of technology acceptance — including TAM. UTAUT also integrates elements from: Theory of Reasoned Action, Motivational Model, Theory of Planned Behaviour (TPB), a combined TAM and TPB model, Model of PC Utilization, Innovation Diffusion Theory, and Social Cognition Theory. The unification of these models provides UTAUT with eight constructs: Performance expectancy, Effort expectancy, Attitude towards using technology, Social influence, Facilitating conditions, Self-efficacy, Anxiety and Behavioural intention to use the system [16].

UTAUT has already been validated and applied in the field in English-speaking countries [1,16]. The present paper provides a cross-cultural validation.

2. PREPARING UTAUT

The aim of the present study was to collect data from countries around the world to cross-culturally validate the UTAUT tool. The data was collected from undergraduate and postgraduate students from all countries sampled. To make the questions on UTAUT accessible and applicable to all participants in the study, the general use of websites was queried, which ensured that all participants would have access to the technology in question. External factors, such as price and technology availability, would not interfere or skew confound the findings.

UTAUT is meant to be adjusted to fit the technology being queried [16], and therefore a certain amount of rewording is expected. Due to the nature of the questions being asked, and because this research did not seek to predict usage or acceptance of a particular application, certain measures on UTAUT were excluded. Behavioural intention to use was dropped, as it is intended as a predictor of use. Facilitating conditions was excluded specifically because the chosen technology, websites, would be available and accessible to all participants - making many of the questions on this construct redundant. The question, "Using the system is a bad/good idea" was dropped from Attitude towards using technology construct as it was not possible to make its wording suitable for the general question of website use.

These adjustments may of course influence the validity of the instrument, as measures are removed and questions changed.

To ensure that these changes have not affected the overall validity of UTAUT, an analysis of the data from English only speaking countries was done. As will be discussed in the Results section of this paper, these changes did not significantly influence the tool.

2.1 Translation

Once all questions were reworded, UTAUT was translated into six languages: Arabic (Saudi Arabian), Czech, Dutch, French, Greek, and Malay. Each translation was completed by at least two bilingual speakers, using the back-translation process. This process ensures that meaning and nuance are not lost, and that the translated versions of the questionnaires remain as true to the original as possible [12]. The translation process did not give rise to further modifications of the UTAUT tool.

3. PARTICIPANTS

Table 1. Per country participant sample summary

	Total sample	Reject data	Used sample	Male	Female	Mean age
Czech Republic	157	5	152	98	44	23.3
Greece	152	36	116	39	61	23.75
India	129	36	93	68	21	23.44
Malaysia	187	19	168	49	102	21.99
New Zealand	199	92	107	58	48	21.7
Saudi Arabia	123		91	36	46	24.19
South Africa	144	34	110	75	27	20.94
United Kingdom	242	125	117	53	61	25.68
United States	156	30	126	43	79	24.28
Totals	1489	286	1080	519	489	23.25

The translated questionnaires were distributed to university students in the Czech Republic, France, Greece, India, Malaysia, Netherlands, New Zealand, Saudi Arabia, South Africa, the United Kingdom, and to the United States. In all countries students were recruited from diverse Faculties including, Humanities, Science, Health Science, Medicine, Engineering, Computer Science, Business and Economics. No sample was represented by less than 5 academic disciplines.

A total of 1,570 questionnaires were returned. Only those countries returning close to 100 or more questionnaires were left in for analysis (table 1). This meant that the France (N=38) and the Netherlands (N=43) were not used in further analysis. Of the remaining sample, participants were kept in the analysis if their questionnaires were completed and no suspect data pattern was present; that is, questionnaires with more than five questions missing, patterns like 1234512345, or giving all one answer were discarded. Likewise, only native participants, those receiving primary, secondary and university education in the same country as where they were living, were used in the analysis to ensure a truly representative, homogeneous country sample. The sample was matched for age, education and access to technology and was equally balanced by gender. Table 1 summarises the data collected for those countries meeting the selection requirements.

4. DATA ANALYSIS

Large sets of data, such as the one collected here, can be difficult to understand without tools that assist in simplifying and summarising them. Factor analysis simplifies a matrix of correlations into more easily comprehensible factors. Factors, in turn, represent a summary of the relationship between sets of variables. Principal Component Analysis (PCA) was used here as it is a good method for exploring broad questions about the relationship between variables in large sets of data. Additionally, PCA makes no distributional assumptions about the data arising from the UTAUT cross-culturally unlike confirmatory factor analysis methods. If the UTAUT constructs are working across cultures - and indeed measuring technology acceptance - they will emerge as one omnibus factor in the analysis [16]. Variables measuring each individual construct should also group together on factors, showing that they measure a particular aspect of technology acceptance [8].

The determination of factors is not defined by the factor analysis method, but instead must be a result of judgment or heuristics. We have used the common guidelines [8] that factors are selected if their eigenvalues are 1 or more; variables having a loading of magnitude 0.3 or more are considered to have a significant influence on the factor especially in large samples such as this. Of course, where these heuristics are nearly met, we highlight this to give a more rounded and flexible picture.

Table 2: UTAUT Principal Component Analysis all countries

	1 (29.04)	2 (12.87)	3 (8.30)	4 (6.27)	5 (5.74)	6 (4.37)
Performance	0.32	-0.31	0.57	0.07	0.15	0.02
Performance	0.37	-0.42	0.54	0.11	0.22	0.05
Performance	0.43	-0.38	0.57	0.15	0.15	0.04
Performance	0.49	-0.32	0.43	0.16	-0.01	0.04
Effort	0.53	-0.38	-0.17	0.05	0.22	-0.05
Effort	0.65	-0.18	-0.37	0.05	0.32	-0.19
Effort	0.65	-0.23	-0.39	0.07	0.34	-0.21
Effort	0.65	-0.18	-0.36	0.07	0.32	-0.22
Attitude	0.54	-0.17	0.02	0.43	-0.32	0.09
Attitude	0.59	-0.07	-0.22	0.44	-0.44	0.13
Attitude	0.62	-0.10	-0.25	0.37	-0.39	0.09
Social	0.62	0.14	0.15	-0.22	-0.31	-0.37
Social	0.61	0.17	0.14	-0.14	-0.36	-0.33
Social	0.65	0.14	0.17	-0.40	-0.18	-0.15
Social	0.63	0.14	0.15	-0.49	-0.08	-0.08
Self-efficacy	0.63	-0.10	-0.20	-0.18	0.08	0.08
Self-efficacy	0.66	0.22	-0.08	-0.17	0.01	0.30
Self-efficacy	0.58	0.04	-0.06	-0.29	0.06	0.46
Self-efficacy	0.60	0.12	-0.11	-0.23	0.03	0.48
Anxiety	0.40	0.62	0.12	0.21	0.10	-0.07
Anxiety	0.19	0.68	0.14	0.20	0.26	0.02
Anxiety	0.27	0.77	0.12	0.24	0.16	0.04
Anxiety	0.29	0.74	0.13	0.22	0.17	-0.07

4.1 Analysis of UTAUT in all countries

The data for the English only language sample was analysed to ensure that the changes made to UTAUT had not affected its overall validity. This sample included New Zealand, the United Kingdom and the United States. South Africa and India were not included in this analysis because while English is used in higher education and in business it is not necessarily the only or first language of the participants. The component matrix for this analysis is not reproduced here, as it is very similar to the one presented for all countries in Table 2. Just as in the original devising and evaluation of UTAUT [16], the English-only data produces the first omnibus factor but with the exception of Anxiety.

The data was then analysed as one complete set to ascertain if UTAUT would work on a widely-heterogeneous sample. Table 2 presents the component matrix for the all-countries data set. The questions for each construct appear in the order in which they are presented in the questionnaire. The heading for each column lists the factor number, and the amount of variance account for that factor in brackets. The six factors selected account for over 66% of the overall variance in the data collected.

The analysis clearly shows the first factor is the general UTAUT factor. All UTAUT constructs load on factor 1, with the exception of Anxiety, which loads strongly on factor 2 (Table 2). Closer examination shows that, in fact, a further two of the Anxiety questions load almost at the 0.3 cut-off point in the all-countries analysis. Thus, we have confidence that UTAUT is working as expected. The only concerning question then is, why the Anxiety measure does not load on factor 1 in the English only analysis.

Table 3: UTAUT constructs emerging on factors 2, 3, 4

	Factor 2	Factor 3	Factor 4
Czech Republic	Attitude - Effort	Attitude - Effort - Performance Social	Attitude Performance
Greece	Anxiety - Performance	Effort - Performance	Attitude
India	Anxiety Attitude -	---	Attitude
Malaysia	Anxiety	Attitude Performance	Social -
New Zealand	Anxiety	Effort Performance -	Attitude Performance
Saudi Arabia	Anxiety Social	Effort Performance	---
South Africa	Anxiety - Performance	Anxiety Effort - Performance	Attitude -
United Kingdom	Anxiety - Effort	Effort - Performance	Attitude
United States	Anxiety	Performance	Attitude Social -

In the remaining factors, questions that measure UTAUT constructs (Performance, Effort Expectancy, Attitude, Social, Self-efficacy, and Anxiety) load, for the most part, in their sets. For example, Performance and Anxiety load on factor 2, Performance also loads with Effort on factor 3. However, in both Effort and Self-Efficacy, there is one question that does not load with the other questions on that scale. The Social and Self Efficacy constructs are both noted as being slightly awkward [16]. The Social construct is strongly influenced by gender, age and experience, while the effect of the Self-efficacy construct is partially captured by the Effort Expectancy construct [16]; this could be the reason for their lower loadings here. In the case of Effort, the missing question is loading factor 2 with the Performance measure. In the English only sample the missing Effort question falls just short of the .30 cut

off (.25) on factor 2. (This question rates, "Interacting with the website is clear and understandable.") In the case of the data collected here it seems that this question groups with those of Performance rather than Effort. This behaviour could be an artefact of the technology (the web) being queried and not of the UTAUT tool: people may relate to websites differently than other technologies, especially those that are not as ubiquitous and readily available.

The worst construct is Social. After loading on the omnibus factor 1, the Social construct is broken up over factors 4, 5 and 6. This may reflect Ventkatesth et al.'s original problems with the Social construct. Overall, then, this analysis of the entire dataset provides some confidence that the UTAUT tool works cross-culturally.

4.2 UTAUT analysis by country

An analysis of UTAUT country-by-country provided further evidence that the questionnaire is working as intended in each of the sample countries. Furthermore, translation did not hinder the performance of UTAUT. Factor 1 emerged as the omnibus factor in all countries, except India. In India the sample was small and male-dominant, which may account for the unexpected UTAUT performance in that sample.

As the first factor to emerge is always the UTAUT factor, it is most interesting to consider the remaining factors. Looking at the different UTAUT constructs that appear for each country on the subsequent factors provides a better understanding of specific cultural influence on technology acceptance. Instead of reproducing the component matrices for each country, Table 3 provides a summary of the UTAUT constructs that emerged on factors 2, 3 and 4 for each country. A minus sign after a construct indicates that it loads negatively on the factor rather than positively. The "---" indicates that no clear construct emerged on these factors for the country but rather the factor was made up of different questions from several different constructs.

Table 3 provides clear evidence that the UTAUT constructs continue to load together and work across the nine cultures sampled, even when the countries are examined independently. However, different constructs have different amounts of influence in each country. For example, the Social construct only emerges on factor 2 for the Saudi Arabia sample, which seems to indicate that social influence has greater weight on website acceptance in Saudi Arabia than in the other countries sampled. Anxiety, on the other hand, emerges on factor 2 in all countries except the Czech Republic. This may show that Anxiety is not a strong influence on website acceptance in the Czech Republic. The Effort and Performance constructs almost always emerge on factors 2 and 3 for all the countries (except India, whose sample was problematic). This could point to the overall, cross-cultural importance of these two constructs. The confused factors for India and Saudi Arabia may mean that in these countries UTAUT is not working cleanly or be due to the relatively small sample sizes of India and Saudi Arabia.

Table 4: Kruskal-Wallis test for UTAUT constructs

	Chi-Squared	DF	Asymp. Sig.
Performance	76.25	8	r0.000
Effort	144.21	8	0.000
Attitude	189.27	8	0.000
Social	145.22	8	0.000
Self-efficacy	158.59	8	0.000
Anxiety	174.43	8	0.000

4.3 Analysis of means of UTAUT constructs

Because different UTAUT constructs emerged as having more influence (explaining more variance) in some countries sampled than others, it is interesting to see if the differences are significant. It was not possible to assume that the samples were parametric in nature, so the more conservative Kruskal-Wallis test was run instead of ANOVAs. Table 4 gives the results for the Kruskal-Wallis test, and shows that all the mean differences for each of the UTAUT constructs was significant in the nine countries presented here. However, given the large sample sizes used, this result should be interpreted with some caution. Large sample sizes, like the one here, can show significant differences even when these are not entirely interesting or meaningful. Further research and analysis, such as Kruskall-Wallis post tests, is needed to determine the direction of the differences, establish if the differences found here on UTAUT are meaningful to cross-cultural acceptance, and can be translated into guidelines or recommendations for design.

5. DISCUSSION

The results presented here clearly show that the UTAUT tool is robust enough to withstand translation and to be used cross-culturally, outside its original country and language of origin. This finding is useful, as it enables HCI researchers and practitioners to use the tool in an international context without concern for its cross-cultural validity. Our analysis seems to indicate that the UTAUT tool will uncover cultural differences at least in the constructs it measures. Our analysis also gives an initial indication that the UTAUT tool may be useful in providing insight into cross-cultural technology acceptance differences. This is a particularly useful result, as the current trend for explaining such differences relies heavily on the use of cultural models that have not been validated in the HCI field [11]. Future analysis of the tool would be useful with more and different countries as those covered here are by no means exhaustive.

The Anxiety measure not loading on the omnibus factor could be caused by several aspects of the research. It could be an artefact of the changes made to the UTAUT questionnaire; it could be because participants are asked to reflect on their previous decisions and use, and are therefore emphasising their anxiety more in hindsight; it could be caused by some particular aspect of how people reflect on the use of websites as opposed to other technologies. All these possibilities would benefit from further and more in-depth exploration.

Alternatively, the problem with Anxiety may only be due to one question, since the others all load on the omnibus factor at or around the 0.3 level. This is similar to the exceptional questions in the Effort and Self-Efficacy constructs. It is possible that all these slight anomalies are due to the rewording and realignment of the UTAUT tool to query website use retrospectively. If the tool was used as a *predictive* measure of acceptance, the concern of the missing questions may not be an issue. It is likely that the missing questions simply do not hold as much sway or as much explanatory power when being used with a technology such as websites. If the tool were used with the intent to query the acceptance of a specific office software application, say, or even a specific web site the concerns noted here may not arise.

6. ACKNOWLEDGMENTS

The authors would like to thank Dr. V. Venkatesh for allowing the use of the UTAUT. A great amount of gratitude is owed to those who helped translate and gather data in the countries sampled, unfortunately too numerous to list here; thank you!

7. REFERENCES

[1] Anderson, J. and Schwager, P., SME Adoption of Wireless LAN Technology: Applying the UTAUT Model. *Proceedings 7th Conference of the Southern Association for Information Systems (SAIS),* 39–43, 2004.

[2] Barnett, G. A. & Sung, E., Culture and the Structure of the International Hyperlink Network. *Journal of Computer-Mediated Communication.* 11(1), 217–238, 2005.

[3] Cleary, Y., The impact of subjective cultural issues on the usability of a localized Web site: The Louvre Museum Web site. In Bearman, D. and Trant, J. (eds.) *Museums and the Web 2000.* 153–162, 2000.

[4] Day, D., Cultural Bases of interface acceptance: foundations. *Proc. of BCS HCI'96.* 35-47, 1996.

[5] De Angeli, A., Athavankar, U., Joshi, A., Coventry, L. and Johnson, G. I., Introducing ATMs in India: A contextual inquiry. *Interacting with Computers.* 16(1), 29–44, 2004.

[6] Evers, V., Cross-Cultural Applicability of User Evaluation Methods: A Case Study amongst Japanese, North American, English and Dutch Users. *CHI'02 extended abstracts on Human Factors in computing systems.* 740–741, 2002.

[7] Evers, V. and Day, D., The role of culture in interface acceptance. In Howard, S., Hammond, J. and Lindegaard, G. (eds), *Proc. of INTERACT'97,* 260–267, 1997.

[8] Kline, P., *An Easy Guide to Factor Analysis.* Routledge, New York, 2002.

[9] Kruger, T. and Roodt, G., Hofstede's VSM-94 Revisited: Is it reliable and valid? *South African Journal of Industrial Psychology.* 29(1), 75–82, 2003.

[10] Maitland, C. F. and Bauer, J. M., National level culture and global diffusion: The case of the Internet. In Ess, C. & Sudweeks, F. (eds.), *Culture, Technology, Communication Towards an Intercultural Global Village.* State University of New York Press, Albany, NY, 87–128, 2001.

[11] Oshlyansky, L., Cairns P. and Thimbleby, H., A cautionary tale: Hofstede's VSM revisited. *Proc. of BCS HCI 2006. vol 2,* 11–15 2006.

[12] Neuman, W. L., *Social Research methods: qualitative and quantitave approaches 4th edition.* Allyn and Bacon, Boston, 2000.

[13] Shimaneni, J. S. and Dunckley, L., Users' Satisfaction — An African Perspective. *Proc. of BCS HCI, vol 2,* 167-172. 2005.

[14] Spector, P. E., Cooper, C. L. and Sparks, K., An International Study of the Psychometric Properties of the Hofstede Value Survey Module 1994: A Comparison of Individual and Country/Province Level Results. *Applied Psychology: An International Review.* 50(2), 269–281, 2001.

[15] Straub, D., Keil, M. and Brenner, W., Testing the technology acceptance model across cultures: A three country study. *Information & Management.* 33(1), 1–11, 1997.

[16] Venkatesh, V., Morris, M., Davis, G. B. and Davis, F.D., User Acceptance of Information Technology: Toward a Unified View. *MIS Quarterly.* 27(3), 425–478, 2003

Voice Art: Investigating Paralinguistic Voice as a Mode of Interaction to Create Visual Art

Dharani Perera	R. T. Jim Eales	Kathy Blashki
School of Engineering and IT	School of Computing Science	School of Engineering and IT
Deakin University, Melbourne,	Middlesex University, London,	Deakin University, Melbourne,
Australia	NW4 4BT, UK	Australia
++44 20841 14850	++44 20841 14396	+61 438 328 266
deehansika@gmail.com	j.eales@mdx.ac.uk	Kathy.blashki@gmail.com

ABSTRACT

In this paper, we report on our investigation into people's ability to use the volume of their voice to control cursor movement to create drawings. Early analysis of the results show changing the volume of the voice as an interaction method is a concept that is easily understood by users. People find changing the volume of their voice comfortable, natural and intuitive. With motivation, training and practice use of volume to control drawing tasks shows great promise. This is especially hopeful for artists with upper limb disabilities who show remarkable endurance, patience and determination to create art with whatever means available to them. We have also identified several design recommendations that may improve the control and performance of such a system. We believe that volume control has wider implications beyond assisting artists with upper limb disabilities. Some possible implications may be: as an alternative mode of interaction for disabled people to perform tasks other than creating visual art or for hands busy environments and as a voice training system for people with speech impairments.

Categories and Subject Descriptors

H.5 Information Interfaces and Presentation (e.g., HCI), H.5.2 User Interfaces, *Voice I/O*

General Terms

Human factors, Design, Experimentation

Keywords

Voice, volume, visual art, interaction, people with upper limb disabilities

1. INTRODUCTION

Visual art is an important activity for many people with physical disabilities. It provides a vehicle for creative expression, communication and sometimes financial independence. People with upper limb disabilities demonstrate remarkable endurance, patience and determination to adapt their remaining capabilities such as facial gestures, voice or foot movements to create various forms of art. Creating art

using existing tools can be a tedious and time-consuming process. One significant advantage of digital tools for disabled artists is that they require little or no help from a human assistant when compared to artists who use non-digital tools [8,9]. Research into alternative forms of digital input would suggest that there are significant opportunities to design and develop new ways in which artists with upper limb disabilities can be supported by digital technologies [3, 6, 7].

Voice recognition technologies have proven to be a particularly promising mode of interaction. However, speech commands lack sophistication when it comes to creating visual art. Artistic expression generally requires an interaction style that can support a certain freedom of movement.

"With dragon dictate you have to remember very precise commands, and it's very slow and restrictive in what you can say...I don't have the patience for it. And when I am planning my art work I don't want to be thinking about every word I say." Tom Yendell (personal communication).

Vocal paralanguage are the general sounds people make that do not have speech elements, for example laughter, whistling and hissing. It can be characterised by numerous properties such as volume, pitch, phase and timbre. The user may intentionally change these properties that may be mapped to different actions. Most people with upper limb disabilities have vocal paralanguage abilities; unlike speech recognition it is not governed by a need for a language model and is universal for all languages.

Lately, there has been significant research interest in audio to visualisation mapping. Various strategies have been employed to establish novel mapping techniques between visual properties and voice characteristics. Al Hashimi [1], Igarashi and Hughes [4] and Sporka *et al.* [11] have successfully investigated paralinguistic voice interfaces for control of cursor movement, scrolling, clicking on icons and control of output devices such as plotters.

This paper presents an innovative design for a drawing system that may be controlled by varying the volume of different sounds made by people. The aim of this research was to investigate people's ability to control the volume of their voice to create drawings on the screen for artistic expression.

2. Design Concept

Our design concept is based on people's ability to change the volume of the sounds they make. People often change the volume of their voice in day to day communication and are able to do it intentionally [2, 5, 10]. Volume is also a continuous vocal characteristic that goes beyond the capabilities of discreet speech commands. Therefore it may be better suited for artistic expression which generally requires a certain freedom of movement. This study investigated if people are able to change the volume of their voice to control the direction of motion of the cursor to create drawings on a screen.

2.1 Prototype Design

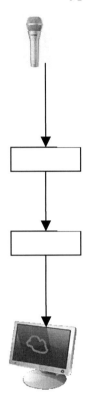

Figure 1. Overview of the system.

Figure 1 shows the overview of the system. The users make sounds into the microphone. The voice signal captured by the microphone is analysed using the Fast Fourier Transformation (FFT) algorithm. The algorithm transforms the voice signal into frequency-based data. The prototype is programmed to compare the volume levels (energy transfer) at each frequency band. The highest volume level is mapped to the direction of motion. The mapping is based on a circular gauge, such as a speedometer. The mapping allows the user to control the full range of 360 degrees. The lower volumes are mapped to lower angles and higher volumes to higher angles. The volume range is set to the users' comfort range (described further in section 2.1.2.1). The range is divided into equal steps which will be mapped to equally divided angles. A voice sample is averaged over 2000 counts, as this proved to be the best reaction time during development. As no noise cancellation is built in, the described prototype is effective only for environments with low background noise.

2.1.1 Experimental setup
The prototype was installed on a machine with an Intel® Pentium® M 740 processor, 1.73 GHz and 512 MB of system RAM. An Electret® condenser microphone was used to capture the voice. Figure 2 shows the interface.

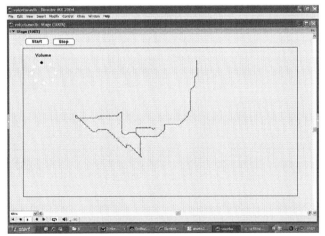

Figure 2. Screen capture of the interface.

In the top left corner of the screen the participants were provided with a circular gauge that showed them the direction their voice was currently controlling. The cursor started to move from the middle of the screen. The "Start" and the

"Stop" buttons started and stopped the voice capture. If at any point the participant stopped the voice capture in the middle of the drawing, the cursor remained in the current position and continued to move from there when the voice capture was started again. A video camera was set up to capture the screen and the sounds made by the participants and the recordings were later used for analysis.

2.1.2 Procedure
The experimental process consisted of three parts. The participants first filled out a preliminary questionnaire that was used to gather some basic personal information such as gender, age and any voice impairments. Then they completed the experiment (section 2.1.1.1). After the experiment the investigator asked a few open ended questions about thoughts and feelings on the system. These interviews were tape-recorded. The recordings were transcribed later for analysis. Four males and two females, aged 20 to 65 years, were used to test the system. None had upper limb disabilities nor speech disorders or vocal training. Only one participant had experience with a speech recognition based system.

2.1.2.1 Experiment
The investigator explained the purpose and procedure of the experiment. Then, the participants were given 10 to 15 minutes practice time with the system. During the practice time they were exposed to several previously set volume ranges and were asked to choose the range that best suited their voice. Once they were comfortable with the experimental setup the testing started. The participants were exposed to four experimental conditions (Table 1). For example the 8 directions allowed the participants to move in steps of 45 degree angles, while the 20 directions allowed movement in steps of 18 degree angles. The participants completed four tasks under the four experimental conditions, 16 tasks in all. Table 1 shows the experimental conditions and the tasks.

Table 1. Experimental conditions and tasks

Experimental condition	Tasks for each condition
8 directions	Draw square
12 directions	Draw circle
16 directions	Draw triangle
20 directions	Draw cloud

The participants were told that any sound they made would be captured by the system and result in a modification of the drawing. The participants completed all the tasks for one experimental condition and then moved on to the next experimental condition in the order shown in Table 1. The participants were allowed to take breaks anytime during the experiment and ask questions from the investigator. There was no time limit set to complete the tasks. On average participants took approximately 30 minutes to complete the experiment.

3. Results and Discussion
3.1 Input strategies
The participants used two input strategies to control the drawing task.

Strategy One: Control via changing the volume of a single sound. Only one participant used this method. The "Ahhhhhhhh"-sound was used. During the practice session the participant learned how to lower and increase the volume of this sound to control the direction.

Strategy Two: Use of multiple sounds to control direction. During the practice sessions the participants experimented with several sounds and identified three to four sets of sounds that would control the four main directions (up, down, left, right). The participants would then change the volume of the identified sounds to acquire neighbouring directions.

Both strategies worked with equal merit. However, two participants who used the second strategy got confused during the testing as the identified sounds wouldn't always result in the desired direction. This could be due to the fact that the same sound can be produced at different volumes and control of the volume takes more practice.

Generally the participants were quick to understand the concept behind the design. They identified ways to change the volume to control the directions and found varying the volume of their voice comfortable and intuitive.

However, volume control using both strategies suffered the following drawbacks.

- It is very difficult to produce the correct volume level to obtain the desired direction at the initial burst of the sound. In most cases the participants made a sound that they thought would result in the desired direction but then had to correct the volume. Since the drawing continued during this correction time it resulted in undesired curves.

- It is difficult to hold the volume of the voice within a constant volume range. The volume oscillated between the ranges resulting in incorrect drawings on the screen. The oscillations were more frequent in higher angles as higher angles resulted in narrower range values.

- The participants found it difficult to hold the desired volume for a long period of time. The volume level dropped over time, especially for higher volumes. In many instances to the human ear it seemed like the participants were holding the same volume level, but the volume level captured by the system recorded a drop. This may be due to the fact that the microphone captures the varying pressure waves in the air and converts them into different electric signals. Over time the pressure caused by the voice may drop, the system was more sensitive to these drops than the human ear. This led to a lot of confusion among the participants.

3.2 Visual Feedback

The system provided two types of visual feedback: the drawings on the screen and the circular gauge in the top left corner of the screen (Figure 2). Participants were divided on the use and the usefulness of the visual cues. Three out of the six participants only used the drawing on the screen for visual guidance. Out of the 3 participants who used the circular visual gauge, one used it extensively during the experiment, the second one mainly during practice session as a tool to identify the sounds that would control a desired direction and the last took it as an added aid to monitor oscillations and drops in volume. All participants, while performing the task, produced volumes out of the selected range. The system provided no feedback for this situation which confused the participants.

3.3 Shapes

The square shape was best drawn with the eight direction experimental condition. While all participants found it difficult

to control the volume to draw a perfect square, many were able to draw a shape that closely resembled it.

It was very difficult to obtain a smooth circle shape. Most participants drew a shape that closely resembled a "puddle of water". The circle shape was best drawn with the 20 direction experimental condition.

The triangle proved to be the most difficult to draw. None of the experimental conditions seemed to be of any particular help. The participants found it especially difficult to control diagonal directions. They had more control over the four main directions. This may be due to the fact that during the practice sessions they spent time mainly learning to control these directions.

Participants were most comfortable with drawing the cloud shape. The oscillations and the dropping of the volume complimented the task. Most participants deliberately oscillated the volume of their voice in a playful manner to obtain the cloud shape. The shape was best drawn in the 20 direction condition.

3.4 Number of Directions

The eight directions experimental condition was best to draw square shapes.

As the number of angles increased, it was easier to draw circular and irregular shapes. The undesired "jaggies" caused due to oscillations and dropping of the volume were smoother for higher number of angles.

However, a higher number of angles resulted in frequent oscillations as the bandwidth of the volume ranges was narrower.

3.5 Fatigue

All participants reported that performing the tasks was not tiring and the number of tasks was not overwhelming. They agreed that the opportunity to rest during the task helped considerably. However, the video recordings showed that most participants got tired trying to hold the high volumes.

Heavy breathing and sighing when the microphone was close to the mouth was picked up by the system and modified the drawings. Coughing, sneezing didn't affect the system as most participants used the "Stop" button in these situations.

3.6 Guidance, learning curve and practice

Initially, the investigator didn't give any guidance to the participants. However, if the participant sought assistance to perform a certain task the investigator suggested several strategies as a help.

During the 10 to 15 minutes practice time they were able to identify ways to control their voice to move in the four main directions. However, it is evident that a lot more training and practice is needed to obtain a level of control that is needed to create accurate drawings of the given shapes. Most participants agreed that they would improve with time.

4. Implications for Technology

Changing the volume of the voice as an input method is a concept that is easily understood by users. People find changing the volume of their voice, comfortable, natural and intuitive. With motivation, practice and training, use of volume to control drawing tasks shows great promise. This is especially hopeful for artists with upper limb disabilities who show remarkable endurance, patience and determination to create art with whatever means available to them [9].

When developing voice based systems better averaging functions should be built-in to control the undesired oscillations of voice. The system should also have improved functions to cancel out unwanted noise such as heavy breathing and sighing.

The visual feedback of the drawing is sufficient for direction control. However it would be useful to provide a visual gauge that shows the dropping of volume, oscillations in volume and instances where volumes outside of the set volume ranges are made.

A microphone that captures the sound signals in a different mechanism to the vibration of air; such as a throat microphone may be less prone to capturing volume drops and may provide more intuitive control. Therefore it will be useful to test the system with different types of microphones.

It is very difficult to produce the correct volume level to obtain the desired direction at the initial burst of the sound. In most cases the participants made a sound that they thought would result in the desired direction but then had to correct the volume. Since the drawing continued during this correction time it resulted in undesired curves. A possible design solution could be to let the user first obtain the desired direction and then move the cursor to create the drawing. In the event the voice drops below the desired volume range the drawing will stop and the user will get chance to set the direction. This method may be most useful for drawing straight lines and may hinder the drawing of curvy lines and the deliberate rise and drop of volume to create more abstract shapes like a "cloud".

It is important to give users a choice to select different modes that may suit different situations. A few of such choices could be:

- Fixing the direction to draw straight lines or no fixing for more curvy and abstract shapes.
- Number of directions 8, 12, 16, 20, ... N.
- Preferred volume range.

The use of two microphones, one to control the angles in the right and one for the left may provide more intuitive control of direction. This would also reduce the need to use very high ranges of volume that most participants had trouble with.

5. Conclusions and future directions

We have investigated people's ability to use the change of volume to control the direction of motion to create drawings in a digital medium. The study captured the instant usability of the system. However on reflection it seems that with motivation, training and practice use of volume to control drawing tasks shows great promise. We believe this is more relevant for artists with upper limb disabilities who have much more time to develop their skills. In the future we plan to build the suggested design recommendations into the system and test it for long term learnability. Volume is a continuous vocal characteristic that goes beyond the capabilities of discreet speech commands. Therefore it is better suited for artistic expression that generally requires a certain freedom of movement. We also believe that volume control has wider implications beyond assisting artists with upper limb disabilities. Such possible implications may be: as an alternative mode of interaction for disabled people to perform tasks other than creating visual art or for hands busy environments and as a voice training system for people with speech impairments.

6. REFERENCES

[1] Al Hashimi, S, Blowtter: a Voice-Controlled Plotter, in *Proceedings the 20th BCS HCI Group Conference in Cooperation with ACM*, London, UK, 2006.

[2] Banse, R. and Scherer, K. R. 1996, Acoustic profiles in vocal emotion expression, J *Pers Soc Psychol, 70, 3,* (1996), 614-36.

[3] Gorodnichy, D. C., Malika, S., and Roth, G. Nouse: Use your nose as a mouse -a new technology for hands-free games and interfaces, in *Proceedings of the International conference on vision interface (VI'2002)*, Calgary, Canada, 2002, 354-361.

[4] Igarashi, T. and Hughes, J. F. 'Voice as Sound: Using Non-verbal voice input for interactive control', in *Proceedings of the 14th Annual Symposium on User Interface Software and Technology UIST'01*, ACM Press, Orlando, Florida, USA, 2001, 155-156.

[5] Nass, C. and Brave, S. *Wired for speech: how voice activates and advances the human-computer relationships.* MIT Press, Cambridge, UK, 2005.

[6] Oviatt, S., and Cohen, P. Multimodal interfaces that process what comes naturally. *Communication of the ACM 42,* 3(2000), 45-53.

[7] Oviatt, S., DeAngeli, A., and Kuhn, K. Integration and synchronization of input modes during multimodal human-computer interaction, in Proceedings of the SIGCHI conference on Human factors in computing systems, (Atlanta, Georgia, United States, 1997), ACM Press, 415-422.

[8] Perera, D., Blashki, K., and Li, G. Visual art for the disabled: A user requirement study on the needs of visual artists with upper limb disabilities, in Proceedings of the 2006 IRMA International Conference, (Washington, DC, USA, 2006).

[9] Perera, D., Eales, R. T. J., and Blashki, K. The Drive to create: An investigation of tools to support disabled artists, to appear in the Proceedings of the Creativity and Cognition 2007, (Washington, DC, USA, 2007), ACM Press.

[10] Scherer, K. R. 1986, Vocal Affect Expression: A Review and a Model for Future Research, *Psychological Bulletin, 99,* 2, (1986), 143-165

[11] Sporka, A. J., Kurniawan, S. H. and Slavik, P. Acoustic control of mouse pointer, *Universal Access in the Information Society, 4,* 3,(2005), 237-245.

Interaction Design in the Wild

Dorothy Rachovides, David Frohlich
Digital World Research Centre
University of Surrey
Guildford GU2 7XH, UK
{d.rachovides, d.frohlich} @surrey.ac.uk

Maxine Frank
VOICES
9th Cross, 1st Stage, Indiranagar
Bangalore, 560038, India
maxine.frank@gmail.com

ABSTRACT

The StoryBank project in the UK is exploring the application of digital storytelling technology to information sharing in the developing world. A multidisciplinary team of interaction designers, ethnographers and computer scientists are adopting a user-centered approach to the design of a system which should be useful to a specific rural community in South India. This paper discusses some of the challenges that the interaction designers met and how these shaped the design process.

Categories and Subject Descriptors

H.5.2 [**Information Interfaces and Presentation**]: User Interfaces – *Prototyping, User-centered design, control structures.*

General Terms

Design, Human Factors.

Keywords

Digital divide, ICT4D.

1. INTRODUCTION

The UK Engineering and Physical Sciences Research Council in the UK recently funded four ICT-for-development research projects. All these projects are multidisciplinary with partners in some of the poorest parts of the world. They are strongly committed to a participative design process which leads to a sustainable technology intervention of real value to end users. This paper presents some of the design challenges that the StoryBank project has met and how they have been addressed. This is done through a case study with the work carried out early in 2007.

2. BACKGROUND
2.1 The Location

StoryBank has partnered with VOICES, a local NGO (Non-Governmental Organization) in Bangalore who provide media infrastructure to facilitate communication within local communities. With UNESCO funding, VOICES in partnership with Myrada (an other NGO) have set up a community radio station, *Namma Dhwani* ('*Our Voices*') in the village of Budikote in Kolar. The radio station is hosted in the village ICT (Information and Communication Technologies) resource

centre, where a variety of programs are made both by staff and the wider community. These radio programs are broadcasted over the cable TV network, or narrow cast, using the village Public Address speakers. The narrow cast extends to two neighboring villages. Radio programs are also used at meetings of self help groups and sold over to other community radio stations in the region. Budikote is on the borders of Karnataka, Andhra Pradesh and Tamil Nadu, and as a consequence a mixture of three local languages (Kannada, Telugu, Tamil) is spoken giving a local dialect. The village population is about 3000, which is typical of rural Indian villages. It is the head village of the area, so the local government offices, Panchyat, Health Centre, primary and secondary schools are located there.

Due to the radio station which was setup in 2001, the village has attracted interest from westerns and the community is very friendly and helpful. Although the majority of the population is illiterate and many have not traveled further than Bangarpet, which is a 30 minute ride on the bus, they are very open to the use of technology. Despite the limited power supply, 2 hours a day, most homes have TV sets. Some people have mobile phones, but until recently the village had no mobile phone coverage, so this was a luxury of the few who travelled frequently outside of the village.

The ICT resource centre, run by Myrada, is a community hub that hosts many self help group meetings, and provides IT courses for the community. This was the obvious choice of venue for our base, both for the social functionality and the technical infrastructure available. The staff has embraced the project and has proved to be an extra valuable resource.

2.2 The StoryBank Concept

StoryBank is inspired by the digital storytelling movement which has demonstrated the power of short two-minute audiovisual stories for compelling communication and empowerment within local communities in the west [1] [2]. This audiovisual format seemed to us to be ideal for giving a voice to those in the developing world who are disenfranchised from self-expression, internet use and other forms of written information sharing because they cannot read or write.

Hence one aim of the project is to make audiovisual story creation and sharing accessible to poor rural communities, and to test its value for empowerment and information sharing. What we have in mind is a kind of YouTube system for development, which extends initiatives that already provide local internet information in village ICT centers [5].

3. THE STORYBANK INTERFACE
3.1 Initial Prototype

From the very first discussions about the interface it was clear that we would opt for the completely visual option. The reason behind this was the high level of illiteracy in the area, and the variety of languages. As we are trying to look at the bigger picture, that at some point more villages, further afield could use this system, audio tagging would be of no benefit, as there would have to be a language translation for different regions. Additionally, users from the west should be able to interact with the system, as one of the aims of the project is to give us an insight to the needs and lives of the developing rural communities.

Our choice of device to capture and edit stories was mobile camera phones. The reason being, the versatility of the technology both to capture the story and to communicate it. Originally Multimedia Short Messaging (MMS) was the chosen technology, but after our first trip to the village, this was reconsidered as there was no GSM coverage. Additionally we found out that MMS is in general very problematic and not supported in all regions of India. This seemed to be a problem originally but, made us think of other alternative solutions, using WiFi and Bluetooth. Another observation that made us rethink our approach was the sense of community. When we visited the village the ICT resource centre staff showed us around and talked about the functions of the centre. Through-out our visit a swarm of people passed by, whether to find out about the next meeting of their self help group, or to assist in making a radio program, or attend an IT class, or just to say hello and see who we were. The building consists of two floors, with an office/ meeting room downstairs and upstairs a large patio, and three small rooms, one is a studio, one the editing room and the small IT classroom. The patio has a blackboard on the wall and is used for meetings and gatherings of various kinds. Essentially this area is the community hub. The buzz that was created by our visit brought on the idea of a situated display that would make the content of the StoryBank repository accessible to the community.

With all these observations and considerations we designed the first version of the system. The main purpose of this design was to provide a technological probe, and an interface to use in the second trip. A Nokia N80 camera phone with a very basic demo of the system, and a laptop with a wall mounted touch screen with an interface to access the repository which was populated with a number of existing radio programs and photographs from the village were taken to the village on the second trip. We present in the form of a case study the use of the camera phone and other prototyping artifacts as probes to engage the community in discussions on the design of the interface . Lessons learned and Future work which has been informed by this study are also discussed.

3.2 Using the Prototype as a design probe

The second trip took place late January early February 2007. Our experiences in the village resembled those described by [6]. We had a bit of a slow start which was a good reflection of the laid back Indian life. The setup of the situated display was delayed due to the power cuts, giving us a day to interact with the local community in a more informal way. Once the touch screen was up and running it instantly became a point of interest for the community as shown in figure 1.

Figure 1 Community interacting with situated display

As it was constitution day and various activities were taking place in the village, the ICT resource centre was buzzing with visitors. The Manager who is very cooperative was proud to be involved with the project and that we were there to design with the community for the community the StoryBank interface. When the visitors left he gathered the resource centre and Namma Dhwani staff to be our first focus group. This meeting was important in formulating our methodology. The resource centre manager gave an introduction about the project and its importance for the village. After the introduction they were presented with the situated display interface. At this very early stage it became evident, that the icons that had been chosen for the story categories were not identified within the Indian culture. This was an issue that was anticipated; however their function was very important, as described in 3.2.1. The discussion of the camera phone interface and interaction followed. From the observation of how the focus group received the situated display interface, and their questions, a number of last minute changes were made to the methodology of these sessions. Additionally, it was decided that the focus groups would first have the session on the camera phone, which would be followed by the use of the touch screen. The main reason was that it was easier to explain the content and the interaction in the camera phone session. Over the 7 days that the study took place 8 focus groups were held in formal sessions. As these sessions took place on the patio, the number of participants increased, as friends of the participants who were passing by came up to see what was happening. These focus groups had 4-15 people and were of various educational levels, castes and financial status. As the sessions took place in the ICT resource centre, it was easy to have groups from various castes, as this is considered to be a neutral ground. The groups consisted of: resource centre and Namma Dhwani staff, farmers, women, Health workers, the a small group of people who speak English and are regarded to have a higher education than the others and school children.

3.2.1 Methodology

The focus group sessions were carried out on the patio area which had become our office space, as shown in figure 2, as we had access to electrical power from the UPS (Uninterrupted Power Supply) in the lab and radio station, and was visible to all the community, which as explained later on is also influenced our study. Our local researcher, who speaks all three languages of the village, and therefore can understand the local dialect, was the interpreter and cultural advisor in these sessions. The Interaction designer was the main facilitator. The same methodology was followed in all focus groups. With the exception of some of the radio station staff, most participants were not familiar with digital stories. The full understanding of digital stories was essential both for the interaction and design feedback from these sessions, but mainly to engage the community with the project by considering potential uses. The first day of our visit we prepared two photo narrative digital stories, one about the interaction designer, and one about a local child. The first consists of 5 photographs and 35 seconds of narrative in English. The second was made from photographs from three pictures that a local child drew about his home and favorite things, and a 44 second voice recording in the local dialect talking about them. These two simple stories were used to demonstrate the simplicity and versatility of digital stories.

Figure 2 Focus group session

The sessions would typically start with a brief introduction about the project, followed by an introduction to digital storytelling, and the showing of the two stories. This prompted discussions of the potential stories that the participants could create. For example, the health workers immediately found great potential in making health education stories, which due to their small duration (maximum length 2 minutes) would not be tiring for the audience and would be simple and easy to create. Once the scope of the project was clear it was much easier to discuss the interface and the interaction. This was broken into two main parts: *Icon identification* and *Interaction.*

Icon identification. In the early stage of the first prototype design the Indian partners pointed out that only computer literate users would understand some of the icons we were planning to use. This is very much in line with observations made by G. Marsden in South Africa [3], [4]. The use of a set of icons to provoke a discussion and bring suggestion was agreed on, but due to the Indian culture it was stressed that the participants might be too shy to tell us their opinion or to disagree with our choice. One option to overcome this problem was to ask the participants to draw images that they thought would be functional was considered. This was almost immediately dismissed as too time consuming and could possibly limit the number of participants, as they could feel intimidated if their drawing skills were not particularly good. Icon identification seemed to be the obvious choice. Each of the icons used was presented full screen on a laptop. These were all clipart images, widely available, and considered to be easily identifiable in the European culture. Figure 3 shows the original icon set.

Figure 3 Original Icon set

These icons represented the story categories and user groupings. The last two icons were functional icons, for story capture and viewing. The participants were presented with the icon and asked to identify what it represented. At this point there was usually silence especially with the first icon that represented agriculture. The majority of the participants thought it was a man cleaning the street. They pointed out that farmers in India do not wear hats, but tie a cloth on their head, and that they wear a specific outfit which is easily identifiable. One of the participants drew a sketch of a farmer, which the others immediately recognized. In all focus groups this proved

to be the least identifiable icon. The icon identification proved to be very successful as it was a good ice-breaker, giving the participants the opportunity to say their opinion without the danger of offending us, which was one of the cultural issues. The community had embraced us and did not want to appear to be disrespectful, consequently they would not say that they did not like something if asked their opinion. But identifying an icon was completely different as there was no issue of agreeing with us or offending us.

The discussions that sprung from this exercise gave us a clear picture of what the community preferences were. The main comment was that all icons had to relate with the rural Indian life style. For example, the news icon should be a person reading a local newspaper, the education a female teacher in a sari, with a ruler in her hand in front of a <u>black</u> blackboard with letters of the Kannada alphabet. The school children category icon, although identifiable, would be preferred to show a child in local school uniform. It was interesting to see that even though some icons were more easily identified, the participants would ask them to be more culture specific. By the time that the third icon was discussed the participants had overcome their original inhibitions and voiced freely their opinions. The Interaction designer had begun to understand the body language displayed by the participants and even though there was a strong language barrier, she could get the jest of the discussions taking place between the participants and the Indian researcher. There were times that the participants would get carried away and ask for great detail in the icons. That is where the N80 with the prototype came in to play, as by showing them the original icons on the phone they got an understanding of the size and detail that the icons would originally take. It is no surprise that this level of detail was requested by the community, as this is the first time that most of the participants will interact with a system through an icon representation, unlike western cultures where using a metaphor, or even a dead metaphor in some cases (such as the desktop) is the norm. From the outcome of these discussions a new set of icons was later developed, as shown in figure 4.

Figure 4 New Icon set

Interaction For this part of the discussion a sequence of cards with the suggested interface was used. The interface was described by the interaction designer and the cards were distributed among the participants. Each card was a cut out of the camera phone with the interface which was discussed at the moment at a 130% scale (figure 5). At the same time the interaction designer had the same interface on the laptop and went through the interaction process, while the Indian researcher translated using the actual camera phone as reference. As the semantic issues had been resolved this part of the conversations evolved around the actual interaction and the use of the interface. The original design had a log on screen, where the user was required to identify what group of user he or she belong to. These groups were identical to the story categories. The participants found this step just an extra burden, and of no relevance as there were various overlappings, as for example a child could also be a farmer. They also commented that the least possible steps would be preferable. Additionally, the community asked for a category on self help groups to be added Overall the interface was well accepted and the interaction understood and was picked up with minimum training.

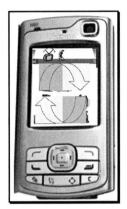

Figure 5 - Interface mock up card

Using the camera phone as a probe, even though the prototype was not fully functional, gave a good insight to the participants of how the system would function. Most of the participants had not used a mobile phone previously, and found the interaction straightforward, with the exception of the login screen. The participants also suggested that the navigation inside the application to capture or view a story. These suggestions were all taken on board and resulted in a complete design overhaul, where the capture, view and transfer functions are separate applications.

4. DISCUSSION

This part of the StoryBank project informed the design of the interface that will be tested and evaluated in the late summer. Additionally the experience from these focus groups and how they were held has helped us plan the testing and evaluation.

4.1 Lessons Learnt

Although the work carried out in this phase of the project seems to be very practical some very interesting research lessons were learn:

Work in open groups: this allowed people to join in the focus group activities when they felt comfortable, by first observing from a distance or getting reassurance from their peers that it was interesting and worth their time.

Use of combination of Hardware and Software props: As most of the community has not used mobile phones previously the combination of the camera phone to demonstrate the appearance of application with the sample stories and more detailed interface on the laptop gave the community a more concrete understanding of the system, resulting in discussions that formulated the current design. Additionally the card cut outs allowed the participants to envision how they could

possibly interact with the device, removing the fear of damaging the device itself.

Finding ways of opening up creativity: Using open ended questions, discovery and recognition, made the participants to use their creativity. By using the icon identification method, the participants felt at ease and engaged with the creative part of the exercise, suggesting alternative icons.

5. FUTURE/CURRENT WORK

Since this study was carried out content generation activities have been run by the Indian researcher and the community. We have gathered about 20 stories dealing with village life, its people and the problems that they face in their every day lives. The StoryBank application has been redesigned and is on schedule to be tested and evaluated in the end of the summer.

6. CONCLUSION

The StoryBank project aims to provide a tool for a rural Indian community which will enable them to disseminate stories of their everyday life and experiences. Additionally it can be a powerful educational tool, which due to its portability can be used to take the stories to remote locations, with no power supply. The local community has embraced the project, and its participation has driven the design. At the time of writing, the revised design is being developed and its evaluation is planned to be carried out in the summer.

7. ACKNOWLEDGMENTS

The StoryBank project is funded by the UK Engineering and Physical Sciences Research Council. Staff includes David Frohlich, Dorothy Rachovides, Matt Jones, Will Harwood, Eran Edirisinghe, Dhamikke Wickramanayake, Mounia Lalmas, Paul Palmer, Arthur Williams, Roger Tucker, Ram Bhat and Maxine Frank.

8. REFERENCES

[1] BBC Capture Wales: Digital Storytelling http://www.bbc.co.uk/wales/capturewales/

[2] Lambert J. *Digital Storytelling. Capturing lives: Creating communities.* Digital Diner Press, 2003.

[3] Marsden G. *Mobile Blog – Literacy* http://web.mac.com/hciguy/iWeb/udev/Under%20Develop ment/D8958C04-257E-414C-849B-A61F6E43C92B.html

[4] Marsden, G. *"Using HCI to leverage communication technology"* Interactions, Volume 10(2), ACM press, pp.48-55, 2003.

[5] OKN: http://www.openknowledge.net/

[6] Ramachandran, D., Kam , M.,Chiu, J., Canny, J., and Frankel J. L., *Social Dynamics of Early Stage Co-Design in Developing Regions.* In *Proceedings of the SIGCHI conference on Human factors in computing systems (CHI '07)* (San Jose, California, USA, April 28-may 3, 2007). ACM Press, New York, NY, 2007.

Meaningful Personalization at a Self-Service Kiosk

Jamie Sands
NCR Financial Solutions
Group Ltd.
3 Fulton Road
Dundee, DD2 4SW,
Scotland
+44 (0)1382 714045

jamie.sands@ncr.com

Graham Johnson
NCR Financial Solutions
Group Ltd.
3 Fulton Road
Dundee, DD2 4SW,
Scotland
+44 (0)1382 718321

graham.johnson@ncr.com

Professor David Benyon
HCI Group, Napier
University
10 Colinton Road
Edinburgh, EH10 5DT,
Scotland
+44 (0) 131 455 2736

d.benyon@napier.ac.uk

Dr Gregory Leplatre
HCI Group, Napier
University
10 Colinton Road
Edinburgh, EH10 5DT,
Scotland
+44 (0) 131 455 2709

g.leplatre@napier

ABSTRACT

Personalization of a self-services kiosk or ATM may provide the user with an efficient means of obtaining new appropriate services with the degree of immediate gratification consumers now require. Successful personalization relies on many factors including acceptance of the services provided and the way these services are delivered. This paper presents a summary of the results from a recent investigation of personalized services at a self-service kiosk and the use of avatars as a potential interface style. Results indicate that users – in particular younger users - would accept personal information being used and would accept new services such as news headlines and budgeting advice at a self-service kiosk.

General Terms

Experimentation, Security, Human Factors

Keywords

Personalization, ATM, Public Technology, Security.

1. INTRODUCTION

By using personal information, a kiosk may be able to better anticipate and deliver the services the user requires, increasing transaction efficiency, ensuring consumer satisfaction and often creating an improved customer/company relationship [1]. Personal information may also be used to broaden the range of tailored services and bring new services to the users' attention, satisfying the demand for greater functionality and a more effective use of the consumers' time.

Appropriate interface design is a critical aspect of the acceptance of any personalized, public, self-service kiosk to facilitate the speedy, secure, trustworthy and easily understandable acquisition of desired options. The use of personal information in determining applications or menu options may lead to confusion about how resulting options were chosen and what information has been applied. One approach is to use an avatar or companion to change the interaction into a realistic dialogue between the user and the avatar. However, the choice of companion and dialogue style is equally important in

matching the expectation of the consumer's experience.

Reeves and Nass [3] suggest that human-computer interaction is akin to normal social interaction. In simple terms, same social rules apply, and users will react to a personified computer as they would a real person, similarly they have expectations about how the computer will behave because of the expected social rules. In the example of a bank teller, a formal and business like interaction would therefore be expected for both a human bank teller and a cash dispensing ATM. However this theory does not take into account the use of personal information. Simple withdrawals, either from the ATM or teller are impersonal (other than a courteous smile), but (hypothetically) a teller offering insurance for their holiday (because they are aware a holiday has been purchased) may not expect such an impersonal dialogue. The appropriate level of dialogue is unclear.

Previous work has investigated alternative interface styles using an informal companion - 'Granny' interface offering personalized informal assistance and services and comparing these with an existing formal ATM interface and a real cashier [4]. interface delivered instruction and advice as a real Granny may do, offering personal reminders about bills, important dates, local information and even horoscope information. Results indicated that 'Granny' was perceived primarily in terms of social and aesthetic values where as the ATM and real cashier was considered in terms of function.

The perceived personality of an interface is also influenced by the tone of the dialogue used in the interaction. A perceived formal interface may be influenced not only by the look of the interface, but also the way in which instructions and communication is conducted. A recent study [5] investigated users perceptions of the tone of dialogue (TOD) used by a virtual ATM while offering a range of unfamiliar services including a train booking service and share trading. Results showed that users rated the importance of TOD significantly higher than their awareness of it. Users also rated their preference for a brief tone highest followed by instructional and re-assuring with a personal tone least desired. The results indicate that even for new services, consumers' reluctance to waste time is paramount; however formal instructional and re-assuring information is also necessary for new services. A personal/informal style appears to be least accepted dialogue style.

The acceptance of personal information in order to provide new services is not solely linked to the way in which the services are provided to the user. Many consumers are reluctant to allow personal information to be used for a number of reasons, primarily over concerns about security through an increased risk of putting sensitive information at risk and through a mistrust of how information will be used and who will be in control of its use [6] and a reluctance to spend the time setting up or providing personal information [7]. However personal information can also be used to improve accessibility [8] and provide the individual with tailored appropriate services. One particular study [9] investigated consumer's opinions of self-service kiosks and ATMs and examined consumer's opinions of financial and e-commerce services that could be conducted through a self service kiosk. Personalization has the potential to benefit the consumer in more ways than a greater customer/business relationship. Through knowledge of the user, the system can offer tailored services, recommend products, remind users of important events and even give advice about the users financial behaviors. Conceivably personal information can also be used to improve security, as personal information is particular to each user. Using personal information can be a quick and memorable way of verifying a user's identity.

2. METHOD

To investigate users' opinion of the use of personal information, new services, security and novel interface styles a prototype self-service kiosk was developed. The prototype was run from a laptop and displayed using a touchscreen interface. The laptop and touchscreen was incorporated into a purpose built kiosk, allowing the set-up to appear like a real self-service kiosk. The aim of the investigation was to implement new services and features, seamlessly into a transaction, using personal information to drive information, new services and security of the transaction.

Participants were asked to perform a number of transactions using a self-service kiosk. The investigation looked at users' perception of five new services that could be offered at an ATM type kiosk: budgeting advice; on-line product purchases; EBay™ auctions; restaurant booking services; and news headlines. These services were personalized through the application of user information. Prior to the start of each test, participants were asked to provide some personal information in the form of favorite music and film genres, food and interest in current affairs and sport. This was done using the touchscreen interface. This information was used to generate appropriate news headlines and as a method of identity verification where participants were identified by selecting the correct option from a menu to authorize certain additional services.

Figure 1. Example of non-avatar interface used (a) transaction pane, (b) logo/avatar pane (replaced with avatars in the avatar conditions, (c) instruction pane and (d) scrolling news headline bar.

Three different interface designs were used. The overall interface is shown in Figure 1. In the avatar conditions, pane (b)

was replaced by either the formal avatar (Figure 2 (a) or the informal avatar (Figure 2 (b)).

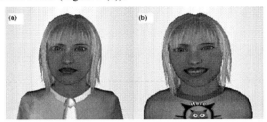

Figure 2. Examples of avatar conditions, (a) formal avatar and (b) informal avatar

The avatar conditions audibly spoke the written transaction instructions to the user. The formal avatar used the same formal instructional dialogue as used in the non-avatar condition, whereas the informal avatar referred to themselves in the first person and provided more informal instructions. Examples of the formal and informal dialogue can be seen below.

Style	Example
Formal	'Your account has been debited successfully, would; you like to perform any other services?
Informal	'I have debited your account; can I help you with anything else?'

Each experiment session included pre-test instructions and information gathering session, three transactions and a posttest online questionnaire evaluation. Each test took approximately twenty minutes to complete.

A within subject design was used, whereby all participants performed all of the tasks. After performing each of the tasks, participants were asked to rate their level of agreement with statements using 5-point Likert scales (Agree (A), Slightly agree (SA), undecided (U), slightly disagree (SD) and disagree (D)). New services were addressed in terms of usefulness, appropriateness and their willingness to use and accept the service. Evaluation of the interfaces focus on statements regarding people's perception of characteristics of the interface (see Table 3).

Each task was preceded by a written scenario. For example one scenario required the user to withdraw £40 to go out for the evening, but when they tried to do this a budgeting service interrupted saying that it was recommended to withdraw only £30. Another scenario required them to check their account balance. This was accompanied by a news headline concerning their favourite football team. In this way personalization and new services were combined and presented through each of three interfaces. The first task included an online purchase, the second an EBay™ auction and the third was a restaurant booking service. After completing the tasks, users completed the online evaluation designed using QuestionPro on a laptop computer (www.questionpro.com). Responses were automatically saved anonymously online.

3. RESULTS

For all results percentages have been rounded up to the nearest round figure. Acceptance is defined as a combined measure of usefulness, appropriateness and willingness. 54 volunteer participants were recruited from the staff, student and visitors to Napier University where the experiment took place. 65% were male, 45% were aged 25-34, 22% were younger and 33% older; 28% visited an ATM once a week and 48% 2-3 times a week. New services are presented in Table 1.

Table 1. Level of acceptance for each new service

	A	SA	U	SD	D
News Headlines	22%	30%	6%	4%	38%
	52%		6%	42%	
EBay™	11%	19%	16%	10%	44%
	30%		16%	54%	
Online Purchases	15%	24%	19%	11%	31%
	40%		19%	41%	
Restaurant booking	19%	20%	12%	15%	34%
	39%		12%	49%	
Budgeting advice	53%	27%	8%	4%	8%
	80%		8%	12%	

Three main results can be obtained from table 1 above. Budgeting advice is highly accepted with 80% of participants in favour. For most services (budgeting advice aside) there is almost a 50/50 split between those accepting and rejecting all services, no service has more than 19% of undecided participants. These results suggest that users would like to see budgeting advice at the self-service kiosk, however the population is split between accepting and rejecting other services, those who would accept them do not feel as strongly about accepting them. Participant's perception of the use of personal information is summarized in table 2.

The results in table 2 show that only 28% of participants did not think personal information should be used to provide enhanced services at the self-service kiosk where as 63% of participants saw the use of personal information as a means of increasing security at the self-service kiosk. These results suggest that not only is it acceptable for personal information to be used to provide additional services, but it can also be used to provide increased security measures.

Table 3. User perceptions towards the interface styles used

I felt in control of this interface	A&SA	85%	74%	74 %
	U	6%	7%	9%
	SD&D	9%	19%	17%
This interface is appropriate	A&SA	91%	52%	52%
	U	2%	17%	17%
	SD&D	7%	31%	31%
I could trust this interface	A&SA	91%	63%	56%
	U	5%	14%	18%
	SD&D	4%	22%	26%
I felt this condition was secure	A&SA	80%	54%	52%
	U	15%	19%	17%
	SD&D	6%	28%	31%
I would use this interface	A&SA	90%	39%	43%
	U	5%	17%	16%
	SD&D	5%	44%	41%
This interface was Formal	A&SA	72%	52%	18%
	U	24%	37%	28%
	SD&D	4%	11%	54%
This interface was Personal	A&SA	43%	54%	60%
	U	39%	28%	25%
	SD&D	18%	18%	15%
Most suitable		76%	9%	15%
Preferred		67%	5%	28%

Table 3 shows that most participants consider all the interfaced designs to provide a high level of control and are appropriate, trustworthy and secure; however the non-avatar interface is consistently rated higher on all of these factors

Table 2. Level of acceptance of the use of personal information and perceived benefit to security

	A	SA	U	SD	D
Personal information is ok to be used	22%	26%	24%	13%	15%
	48%		24%	28%	
Personal information increases security	22%	41%	22%	7%	7%
	63%		22%	14%	

The non-avatar interface is considered the most likely to be used interface with almost 90% agreement, with avatar conditions gaining around 40% acceptance. Further investigation showed that when comparing interfaces, the non-avatar interface is considered both most suitable and most preferred, interestingly the informal avatar in considered higher on ratings of suitability and preference to the formal avatar condition. These results suggest that when using avatar conditions, users perceive an element of control, trust and security to be lost, although not completely. Users prefer to use interfaces without avatars at the self-service kiosk when using personal information, however if an avatar condition was to be employed, an informal personality would be better received than a formal avatar.

To further investigate differences between identified groups, Spearman's non-parametric correlations were performed to investigate for connections between factors. Statistical significance levels are indicated as (..) significant to 0.01, and (.) significant to 0.05, 2 tailed.

Table 4. Correlation relationships between age and new services

	Age			
	Useful	Appropriate	Would Use	Would accept
News Headlines	..	..	..	n/a
EBay™	.		.	n/a
Online purchases				n/a
Restaurant booking	..	.		n/a
Budgeting advice	..		..	

Table 4 shows that age is significantly correlated with many aspects of new services; most notably age is correlated with the acceptance of news headlines and budgeting advice. Examination of the correlations shows that as user get older they are less likely to accept the services indicated above. Frequency of ATM use did not correlate with any new services or perceptions of the use of personal information.

Table 5 shows significant correlations for each service and its associations with other services. It can be seen that almost all services significantly correlate with each other. Suggesting that acceptance of one service is indicative of a tendency to accepting other services. Only user intention to use a News headline service is not significantly indicative of user acceptance of a restaurant booking service.

Table 5. Correlation relationships between participants' perceptions of each new service

		News			EBay™			Online			Restaurant		
		Useful	Appropriate	Would Use	Useful	Appropriate	Would Use	Useful	Appropriate	Would Use	Useful	Appropriate	Would Use
News Headlines	U												
	A	..											
	W	..	..										
EBay™	U	..	..	..									
	A	..	..	..	..								
	W	..	..	..	..	..							
Online purchases	U			..	..	..	..						
	A	..	..	..	..	..	..	..					
	W			.	..	..	..	..	..				
Restaurant Booking	U	..	..		..	..	.	..	..	..			
	A	..			..	..		..	.	..	..		
	W	..	..		..	..	..	..	..	..	..	..	

4. CONCLUSIONS AND FUTURE WORK

In summarizing the results, there is a split in opinion about the acceptance of new personalized services. However if new services were to be implemented, users would most desire budgeting advice. Younger users would also tend to accept budgeting advice than older users; they would also like to have news headline information displayed at self-service kiosks.

No overwhelming support exists for using personal information in providing new services; however the majority of users agree that the use of personal information can improve security. Users see avatars as both not suitable and not preferred as a choice of interface, however if an avatar condition was used, most users would not find this detrimental to their perception of the transaction as secure, trustworthy and controllable. A choice between formal and informal avatars favours the informal.

A more detailed examination of the results shows that age correlates with some aspects of acceptance for most new services, suggesting that the sample of younger users is responsible for a large element of those accepting new services. However it is also clear that age is not the only factor, as age shows no correlation with acceptance of online purchases, yet the general level of acceptance for this service shows a similar split. The general correlation of all services with each other also indicates that there is a sample of participants who are willing to accept all new services. Therefore this indicates that from the sample used, a split on opinion is evident and not based solely upon age. It is interesting to note the sample used, a university sample is predominantly university employees and staff who may be expected to have a higher incidence of technology experience. Therefore further investigation of occupation difference was conducted. Chi Squared test investigated differences between occupation groups and new service acceptance. Significant differences were only found for willingness to use news headline and budget advice, indicating a higher proportion of student participants accepting these services. Interestingly professionals were again split between accepting and rejecting news headlines and slightly in favor of budgeting advice suggesting that a split in opinion is not a direct result of occupation differences.

Further examination is warranted to investigate reasons behind the apparent split in user opinion of acceptance of new services. This split seems to exist irrespective of occupation, with age playing a role in determining a degree of support for acceptance of new services. Potential areas for further study not addressed in this study would be user's familiarity with new technologies and their tendency to personalize other technologies.

5. ACKNOWLEDGMENTS

We are to the DTI (Department of Trade and Industry, UK) for their support of this work under the auspices of the KTP (Knowledge Transfer Partnership) initiative. Thanks are also due to Darren Grant for his work in prototype development, Napier University for hosting the experimental work and NCR for provision of the ATM/Kiosk model.

6. REFERENCES

[1] Blom, J., Personalization Psychological implications of Personalized User Interfaces. *Doctoral Thesis*. Department of Psychology. University of York (August 2002)

[2] Reeves, B. and Nass, C. *The Media Equation*. New York: Cambridge University Press. (1996)

[3] De Angeli, A., Lynch, P., Johnson. G., Personifying the e-Market: A Framework for Social Agents. *Proceedings of IFIP INTERACT'01: Human-Computer Interaction* (2001) 198-205

[4] Ward, J., Sands, J. and Johnson, G. The Effect of 'Tone of Dialogue' on Users' Interactions with Self-Service. *Contemporary Ergonomics. London: Taylor and Frances.* (2007)

[5] Briggs, P., Simpson, B. and De Angeli, A. Does personalisation affect trust in online advice? *CHI2003 Workshop Designing Personalized User Experiences for eCommerce: Theory, Methods, and Research, Fort Lauderdale, Florida.* (April 2003)

[6] Neilsen, J., *Personalisation is over rated.* Jakob Neilsen's Alertbox, (Oct 1998). http://www.useit.com/alertbox/981004.html

[7] Coventry, L., Johnson, G. and De Angeli, A. Achieving accessibility through personalization. *People and Computers XVI – Memorable yet invisible. Proceedings of HCI 2002*, London: Springer Verlag (2002)

[8] Costa, B., Ditzion, S., Kschwendt, G., Nogales, J., Schmitt, A. and Wang, J. The 2000 Study of Web-ATMs and Kiosks. The Consumer Proposition. *Dove Consulting – Executive summary.* (August 2000)

[9] QuestionPro. Online Survey Software. www.questionpro.com

A Pattern-Based Usability Inspection Method: First Empirical Performance Measures and Future Issues

Martin Schmettow
University of Passau
Information Systems II
94032 Passau, Germany

schmettow@web.de

Sabine Niebuhr
University of Kaiserslautern
Software Engineering Research Group (AG SE)
67663 Kaiserslautern, Germany

sabine.niebuhr@iese.fhg.de

ABSTRACT

The Usability Pattern Inspection (UPI) is a new usability inspection method designed for the added downstream utility of producing concrete design recommendations. This paper provides first empirical evidence that UPI measures up to the established inspection method Heuristic Evaluation (HE) regarding defect identification. It is shown that there is also some potential for synergy between UPI and HE. The further research plan of measuring UPI is presented.

Categories and Subject Descriptors

H.5.2 [**User Interfaces**]: Evaluation/ methodology

General Terms

Measurement, Human Factors.

Keywords

Usability Inspection, Experiment, Evaluation, Usability Patterns.

1. INTRODUCTION

In the development of usable interactive software applications, inspection methods play a major role for the early identification of usability defects. Whereas the evaluation of inspection methods has always been of interest in usability research, two major topics have been raised in the last years: Improved approaches for valid measurement of method performance have been triggered by harsh criticism on previous evaluation studies [9] (see section 1.2). In response to the "Five users is (not) enough" debate, advanced models for predicting and monitoring evaluation processes have been explored (e.g. [7, 8]). In contrast, there have been few efforts to enhance methods or design new ones in order to resolve principal issues with existing methods.

One such issue is, that common inspection methods lack support for redesign. This was uncovered by a longitudinal study investigating the value of usability defect reports for the actual fixing of these defects. The alarming result was, only few previously reported defects were adequately fixed [5]. This might be overcome by integrating design recommendations into inspection methods. A more recent study has shown that reporting design recommendations has the potential of

replacing traditional defect reports [11], as they are at least comparably informative and convincing to "downstream" software developers.

The Usability Pattern Inspection (UPI) method was explicitly designed for reporting concise design recommendations together with the defects, facilitating effective problem fixing in the user interface [15].

1.1 Pattern-based usability inspection

Usually, an inspection method supports experts with a particular set of guidelines for identifying possible defects. For example, the Heuristic Evaluation (HE) - the most common inspection method - supports defect identification with a set of 10-12 heuristics, which have once been acquired from usability experts [14]. One major property of the Usability Pattern Inspection is to provide the inspector with a very rich set of guidelines (usability patterns) on the level of interaction design. These patterns were collected from several widely known collections, e.g. [16, 18]. It was assumed that the following properties make patterns valuable for usability inspection: First, they are problem-oriented in that they describe the context and specific forces of recurring usability design problems. Second, they are on an intermediate range of abstraction which makes them applicable for a wide range of applications and platforms. And third, they describe established design solutions in detail and confirm them with rationales. This enables the inspector to rationalize on the design level - as opposed to the task or user level. As argued earlier [15], there is a need for evaluation methods, which can efficiently be applied by non-experts in small and medium enterprises (as opposed to highly specialized usability experts in large companies). We believe a design-oriented approach to be more natural for common software practitioners than more abstract guidelines, like heuristics. The focus on design is also the main source of UPI's downstream utility, in that the inspection results contain concrete design recommendations beyond mere defect identification.

Whereas the guidelines employed in UPI are focused on design solutions, the walkthrough procedure provides a strong notion of user goals and inter-action. First, the inspection process is guided by a predefined set of critical user tasks, which can, for example, be derived from requirements documents. Another UPI sub-procedure was explicitly designed to let software experts take the perspective of the common user on the level of singular interaction events: The inspector permanently monitors his/her own activities according to a set of 16 predefined abstract user activities. This self-monitoring is further encouraged to facilitate pre-selection of applicable patterns from the pattern repository via a search interface, as patterns have been classified to those user activities.

In brief, the UPI inspection procedure is as follows:

1. The inspector selects a user task and starts doing it. *Example: Search facility of mobile phone's address book is inspected.*

2. Whenever the inspector monitors a change in his current user activity, it is time to inspect. *Example: After initial orientation the inspector searches for a specific entry.*

3. A pre-selection of matching patterns is received from the pattern collection. *Example: The inspector selects all patterns about searching.*

4. Patterns that match the current situation based on dialogue configuration and user interaction are compared with the current design. *Example: The inspector considers patterns "List Browser" and "Continuous Filter" to match the situation (both from [18]).*

5. If the current design deviates from the pattern's proposed solutions, this is a possible usability defect and ... *Example: The inspector notes that "List Browser" is implemented, but no feature to filter address entries is present.*

6. ... a recommendation for improvement is given according to the pattern. *Example: The inspector notes that adding a "Continuous Filter" allowed for efficient search on small screens.*

1.2 Assessing inspection methods

The primary goal of assessing a usability inspection method is to prove its performance in validly identifying those misconceptions in the UI design that are liable for usage problems. After the criticism above the poor validness of effectiveness studies before 1999 [9], several researchers have established a canonical model of measuring the effectiveness of usability evaluation methods [6, 10]. The basic measures of an evaluation experiment resemble the categories known from the signal detection theory: *Hit* - a true defect was detected, *false alarm* - a defect is denoted with no usage problems truly arising, *correct rejection* - an element is correctly identified as defect-free, and *miss* - a true defect was not identified. The basic performance criteria are derived from these measures as:

$$\text{Thoroughness} = \frac{\text{number of hits}}{\text{number of real defects}}$$

$$\text{Validity} = \frac{\text{number of hits}}{\text{number of hits} + \text{number of false alarms}}$$

$$\text{Effectiveness} = \text{Thoroughness} \times \text{Validity}$$

For exact signal detection measures, complete knowledge of the true defects - those that are liable for observable usage problems - is required. In case of incomplete knowledge, thoroughness is prone to overestimation and validity to underestimation. As complete knowledge of usability defects is very expensive to acquire, two variants of usability testing can be employed to estimate the performance measures efficiently. With *falsification usability testing*, the defects identified in an inspection experiment are challenged with a focused test design (focused tasks, predefined observation set) in order to identify false hits [2]. *Asymptotic usability testing* is employed to estimate the total number of existing defects without the need to identify them all. Whereas the identification of false alarms is required for the computation of validity, it is not necessary to know the complete number of defects if the goal is a comparison of two methods. Thus, the experiment presented below is complemented by a falsification usability test only. Previously undetected defects were also recorded to get a rough idea of the absolute measures for thoroughness.

1.3 Hypotheses

Whereas the performance of HE has been assessed in numerous studies and is known to be fair, UPI is a newly developed method with unknown performance. While this method was designed with added down-stream utility in mind, it still has to show that it is comparable to HE in the amount of true defects detected:

Hypothesis 1: The thoroughness with UPI is at least as good as with HE.

UPI's main feature for identifying defects is to evaluate an existing design against established design solutions. It can thus be argued that a considerable amount of false alarms can be expected with UPI as there might be a design that is working well, although it was not yet captured as a usability pattern. However, the complete procedure of evaluating a solution supports a strong user perspective and additional decision points to mitigate this problem. Additionally, HE is also known to produce a considerable amount of false alarms [1], thus:

Hypothesis 2: The validity of UPI is at least as good as with HE.

The UPI method provides guidelines quite different from HE and thus might have qualitatively different capabilities and limitations to capture defects and produce false alarms. From the perspective of signal detection, this method-specific detection profile cannot be efficiently broadened with larger inspection groups. In contrast, it is necessary to mix methods with different profiles in order to average out the method-specific bias. Thus, if there exists a method-specific detection profile:

Hypothesis 3: Mixed method inspection groups perform better than pure method groups.

2. METHOD

2.1 The inspection experiment

To gather the inspection performance data, we asked 10 persons (male computer science students and researcher, aged between 25 -34) to evaluate a bibliography management tool. Randomly divided into two groups, they were given three typical user tasks for evaluation (add reference, search for reference and export list of references). Only one participant had previous experience with usability evaluations and was assigned to the HE group which is conservative regarding our hypotheses. The settings for both groups were the same, except the usability inspection method: the first group performed UPI (n_{UPI}=4), the second group performed HE (n_{HE}=6) as a control group[1]. At the beginning, we gave both groups a short introduction to the usability inspection method and bibliography management tool. The main part was evaluating the tool with the introduced inspection method which ended after 1 hour (controlled time). The participants had to report their findings in a structured template, comprising the defect description, dialog element, heuristic or pattern applied and additional comments. Also, a few questionnaires were presented to obtain participants personal data and impressions of using the method[2].

2.2 The falsification test study

The falsification test study followed the procedure described by [2] with some enhancements towards adaptive testing. A small set (2-6) of observable usage problems was compiled for each defect. A set of tasks was then prepared to challenge each predicted defect at least twice. During the test, a structured observation protocol was used by the observer to record each

---

[1] Uneven group size due to appointment conflict of a participant

[2] These results will not be presented here

time a predicted usage problem was observed. As it suffices to verify each defect only once[3], the observation protocol could be adaptively reduced after each session. After the second session, some "exhausted" tasks could be replaced to stress on the remaining defects. The observer also collected new defects in a separate protocol. Because defect identification in usability tests is an asymptotic process [17], a stop rule had to be defined for adding further sessions. We decided to finish the study when a session gained no more than one new verified defect, which happened with the fourth session. All four participants had an academic background but did not have any previous experience with this particular bibliography management tool.

3. RESULTS

During the inspection experiment, 48 individual defects were proposed by the participants, 22 in the UPI group and 28 in the HE group. Via falsification testing, 35 defects could be validated, whereas 13 were considered as false alarms. Additional 35 defects were identified in the falsification test, which have not been detected in either of the inspection groups. Table 1 shows the basic defect detection measures on the group level. Note that counting true rejections is not applicable here, as there is no data available on the negative decisions of the inspectors. The larger HE group identified slightly more defects but also produced more false alarms. Both groups missed a considerable number of defects.

Table 1: Basic defect detection measures for the two inspection groups

	Hits		False Alarms		Misses	
	UPI	HE	UPI	HE	UPI	HE
Group Count	22	28	5	11	50	44
Intersection	15		3		37	

The three performance criteria will be compared using the means of individual inspector performance. As the sample size is quite small, no statistically relevant differences could be found via comparison of means (t-test) or variances (F-test). As was argued above, the thoroughness reported here is a comparative measure as no asymptotic usability testing was conducted. The set of 70 defects identified in the experiment or the falsification test is the reference for the thoroughness measures reported here.

Table 2: Comparison of performance measures for the two methods per individual inspectors

	Thoroughness		Validity		Effectiveness	
	UPI	HE	UPI	HE	UPI	HE
Mean	.144	.150	.834	.843	.121	.128
SD	.058	.052	.039	.084	.0522	.050

As table 2 shows, individual thoroughness is quite low in both methods, but there is no considerable difference, in mean or in variance (or standard deviation). The validity measures were obtained with the set of proposed defects that remained unverified after the falsification testing. Table 2 shows, that both methods perform equally well in avoiding falsely predicted defects. However, it might be the case that there are larger individual differences with HE. This also shows up in the larger number of overall introduced false alarms, which summed up to 11 in the HE group. But this effect is far from being statistically verifiable. Both methods perform equally well in terms of the derived measure of effectiveness.

---
[3] Only during mere identification, more observation needed for severity estimation

The third hypothesis stated that HE and UPI differ in the types of defects they capture, so that mixed method groups perform better than pure method groups. This was analyzed by simulating all possible inspection groups with four inspectors from the whole sample. This results in pure HE ($n_{HE4}=15$) and UPI groups ($n_{UPI4}=1$) and mixed groups, with 1, 2 or 3 inspectors from each condition ($n_{MIX4}=194$). For each single group, the hits, misses, and false alarms were combined. Table 3 shows the resulting performance criteria of the three conditions in the simulation. As expected from the previous analysis, there is only a marginal difference between the pure groups. But indeed, there appears to be a slight advantage of mixed groups, mostly caused by a gain in thoroughness.

Table 3: Performance measures (means) from simulated groups of four inspectors

	Thoroughness	Validity	Effectiveness
UPI	.306	.815	.249
HE	.322	.761	.253
Mixed	.350	.788	.276

4. DISCUSSION

We have conducted a comparative method evaluation study, which adhered to recent standards regarding study design and performance criteria. However, the study is only preliminary because the sample size was much too small to gain any statistically relevant results.

We achieved quite low values for the thoroughness of both methods, which would not satisfy real applications (about 10 inspectors were needed to capture 80% of the defects with a thoroughness of .15). This may be due to the experiment being conducted under restricted laboratory conditions. The participants were non-experts, introduced to the method and tested application in only one hour, and had just another hour for the inspection. Especially UPI has quite a detailed procedure and also a large body of guidelines, which is usually trained in at least half a day. It can be expected that a more thorough training and supervised practice would enhance the performance significantly. Yet, validity was fair in our study.

Regarding the performance comparison, there were no considerable differences between the new UPI method and HE regarding thoroughness, validity and effectiveness on an individual level. To draw a careful conclusion: our study provides no arguments for practitioners to hesitate using UPI instead of HE and, in turn, benefit from the additional downstream utility of design recommendations.

We also found preliminary advantages in using a deliberate mixture of methods in inspection processes. In our simulation of inspection groups, a mixed method seemed to broaden the perspective. More different defects were detected, without sacrificing the validity too much, which was recently reported as a problematic side effect of employing larger inspector groups with a single method [1]. This result also supports our hypothesis that UPI and HE have differing detection profiles and serves as one starting point for the further research agenda, which will be outlined below.

5. FURTHER RESEARCH

This experiment was our first effort to systematically evaluate UPI. But the results are far from being sufficient to employ the method based on precise economical considerations. To prove the value of UPI (or other evaluation method), it has to be assessed under more realistic conditions (e.g. by modifying the laboratory procedure). For more ecological validity, our studies have to be complemented by a few industrial case studies. These will also challenge the assumed downstream value of design recommendations.

A general limitation lies with the foundations for measurement of inspection performance. The measures gained with typical inspection experiments suffice to compare two methods if they are assessed under completely equal conditions. But they suffer from severe restrictions regarding generalizability. It is a lesson learned from the "Five users is (not) enough" debate; simple probability measures for defect detection capability of a method are not a reliable base for predicting the outcome evaluation processes, e.g. [7]. But predictability is a necessary precondition for giving (credible) guarantees to stakeholders who request a usability evaluation. A strikingly simple measure for the predictability of inspection processes is the variance in performance between inspectors [8]. For UPI currently a study with a larger sample size is in progress for comparing it to HE regarding performance variance. The hypothesis is that UPI produces less variance because it provides a better defined procedure and detailed guidelines to the inspectors.

The claim for predictability is also tightly connected to the problem of reliability of evaluation methods. It was recently argued that high reliability might not be desirable, because it sacrifices the inspector's different viewpoints as a source of thoroughness [10]. Regarding process predictability, this is, in our opinion, a problematic argument, unless the method-independent contribution of each inspector is known (e.g. from individual performance tests), valid, and deliberately assembled. A better alternative is probably to have different reliable but limited-in-scope evaluation methods at hand. This would allow for a purposeful mixture of several methods in the inspection process in order to gain a broad defect identification profile. A similar approach of separating perspectives has already proven successful for perspective-based inspections in Software Engineering [4]. A further study is currently planned to examine the advantages of inspection processes where UPI is complemented by another evaluation method.

For usability evaluations, it has recently been observed that specific perspectives (or kinds of knowledge) contribute differently to detection performance [3]. It is likely that UPI has a specificity for defect types in that it provides design knowledge in the first place. A study is currently planned to investigate the performance profile of UPI regarding different defect types. A first candidate for defect classification is the Usability Problem Taxonomy [12], but recent efforts of the MAUSE initiative [13] will also be considered. A defect type related performance profile will allow practitioners to deliberately choose (or avoid) a particular method for certain kinds of expected defects.

The goals of measuring and profiling UPI are quite ambitious but they may eventually foster new measurement approaches and deeper insights regarding the anatomy of usability inspection processes in general.

6. REFERENCES

[1] Alan Woolrych, and Gilbert Cockton. Testing a conjecture based on the DR-AR model of usability inspection method effectiveness. In Proceedings of HCI 2002, Vol. 2.

[2] Alan Woolrych, Gilbert Cockton, and Mark Hind-march. Falsification Testing for Usability Inspection Method Assessment. In Proceedings of HCI 2004 (2004).

[3] Alan Woolrych, Gilbert Cockton, and Mark Hind-march. Knowledge Resources in Usability Inspection. In Proceedings of HCI 2005 (2005).

[4] Basili, V. R., Green, S., Laitenberger, O., Lanubile, F., Shull, F., Sorumgard, S., and Zelkowitz, M. V. The empirical investigation of perspective-based reading. Empirical Soft-ware Engineering 1, 2 (1996), 133–164.

[5] Bonnie E. John, and Steven J. Marks. Tracking the Effectiveness of Usability Evaluation Methods. Behaviour & Information Technology 16 (1997), 188–202.

[6] Cockton, G., Lavery, D., and Woolrych, A. Inspection-based evaluations. In The human-computer interaction handbook: Fundamentals, evolving technologies and emerging applications, J. A. Jacko and A. Sears, Eds. Lawrence Erlbaum Associates, 2003, pp. 1118–1138.

[7] David A. Caulton. Relaxing the homogeneity assumption in usability testing. Behaviour & Information Technology 20, 1 (2001), 1–7.

[8] Faulkner, L. Beyond the five-user assumption: Benefits of increased sample sizes in usability testing. Behavior Research Methods, Instruments & Computers 35, 3 (2003), 379–383.

[9] Gray, W. D., and Salzman, M. C. Damaged merchandise? A review of experiments that compare usability evaluation methods. Human-Comp. Interaction 13,3 (1998), 203–261.

[10] Hartson, H. R., Andre, T. S., and Williges, R. C. Criteria for evaluating usability evaluation methods. Int. Journal of Human-Computer Interaction 15, 1 (2003), 145–181.

[11] Kasper Hornbæk, and Erik Frøkjær. Comparing usability problems and redesign proposals as input to practical systems development. In Proceedings of CHI '05 (NY, USA, 2005), ACM Press, 391–400.

[12] Keenan, S. L., Hartson, H. R., Kafura, D. G., and Schulman, R. S. The usability problem taxonomy: A framework for classification and analysis. Empirical Softw. Engg. 4, 1 (1999), 71–104.

[13] Law, E.L-C., Hvannberg, E.T., Cockton, G., Palanque, P.A., Scapin, D.L., Springett, M., Stary, C., Vanderdonckt, J. Towards the maturation of IT usability evaluation (MAUSE). In INTERACT (2005), M. F. Costabile and F. Paternò, Eds., Vol. 3585 LNCS, Springer, 1134 – 1137.

[14] Nielsen, J. Enhancing the explanatory power of usability heuristics. In Proc. of CHI '94, 152–158.

[15] Schmettow, M. Towards a pattern based usability inspection method for industrial practitioners. In Proc. of the Workshop on Integrating Software Engineering and Usability Engineering (held at Interact 2005) http://www.se-hci.org/bridging/interact2005/03_ Schmet-tow_Towards_UPI.pdf

[16] Tidwell, J. Designing Interfaces. O'Reilly, 2005.

[17] Virzi, R. A. Refining the test phase of usability evaluation: How many subjects is enough? Human Factors 34, 4 (1992), 457–468.

[18] Welie, M. v. Patterns in interaction de-sign, 2003. http://www.welie.com/

Usability – Not as we know it!

Paula Alexandra Silva
Lancaster University
Computing/Infolab21
Lancaster, LA1 4YR, UK
+44 1524 510319
palexa@gmail.com

Alan Dix
Lancaster University
Computing/Infolab21
Lancaster, LA1 4YR, UK
+44 1524 510319
alan@hcibook.com

ABSTRACT

YouTube has been the Internet success story of 2006. However, when subjected to conventional usability evaluation it appears to fail miserably. With this and other social Web services, the purpose of the user is fun, uncertainty, engagement and self-expression. Web2.0 has turned the passive 'user' into an active producer of content and shaper of the ultimate user experience. This more playful, more participative, often joyful use of technology appears to conflict with conventional usability, but we argue that a deeper 'usability' emerges that respects the user's purposes whether acting as *homo ludens*.

Categories and Subject Descriptors

H.5.5 [**Information Interfaces and Presentation**]: HCI

General Terms

Design, Human Factors

Keywords

YouTube, user experience, Web2.0, Evaluation, Design

1. INTRODUCTION

YouTube was last year's Web success story. A website that allows users to store and share personal videos, subsequently, linked, searched and/or rated, has gone from zero to 60% of all online viewing in just 18 months [1]. Its huge and sudden popularity made it the Internet phenomenon of 2006.

However, when analysed with conventional usability heuristics it fails many. So is the popularity in spite of this – the draw of the content meaning that YouTube can afford poor usability? Or is it more fundamental, conventional usability neglects or conflicts with the more ludic aims of the site? We have become used to debates or even argument between user experience design and more Taylorist usability engineering. However, Web2.0 sites, such as YouTube, add more complexity to this picture as the user becomes the producer.

In this paper, we explore some of these issues, first analysing YouTube from a conventional usability standpoint and then exploring the reasons why this does not give a true indication of the real 'usability' of the system and how conventional conceptions may need to change… and where they do not.

Paula Alexandra Silva and Alan Dix, 2007
Published by the British Computer Society
Volume 2 Proceedings of the 21st BCS HCI Group
Conference
HCI 2007, 3-7 September 2007, Lancaster University, UK
Devina Ramduny-Ellis & Dorothy Rachovides (Editors)

2. THE YOUTUBE PHENOMENON

YouTube became the Internet phenomenon of 2006, in the sense of a site, idea or arguable 'meme' that spreads with extreme speed due to the size and/or often social interconnectedness of the internet [9].

According to Alexa's website[1], YouTube is the fourth most visited website, and the first if we do not include search engines (see Figure 1). Also, if we look at the Web ratings by country, we realise that YouTube is also quite popular, for instance, it is the 5th most accessed site in the US, Portugal and Spain, the 6th in Canada and Japan and the 8th in the UK.

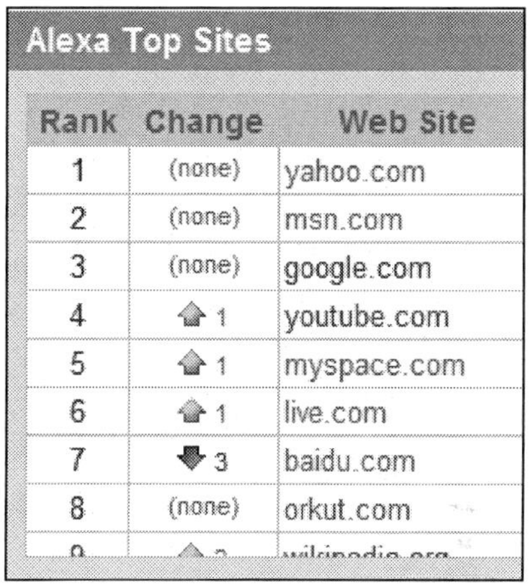

Alexa Top Sites		
Rank	**Change**	**Web Site**
1	(none)	yahoo.com
2	(none)	msn.com
3	(none)	google.com
4	⬆ 1	youtube.com
5	⬆ 1	myspace.com
6	⬆ 1	live.com
7	⬇ 3	baidu.com
8	(none)	orkut.com
9	⬆ 2	wikipedia.org

Figure 1: Alexa top sites (22-05-2007)

YouTube is the type of site a user accesses when he or she has some spare time, and just feels like 'hanging around' the Web, or when someone, usually a friend or colleague, sends him or her a link to an interesting video. So, we are here referring to a particular kind of public that includes Web surfing among its hobbies and that, in some way, socialises via the Web.

These phenomena have been recognised in other Web services, such as MySpace, Blogger or Flicker. Interestingly, these sites obey the 1% rule: for each 100 people online, just 1 will create content, 10 will interact[2] with it and the remaining 89 will only view it. For YouTube, each day, there are 100 million downloads and 65, 000 uploads, that is 1,538 downloads per upload (Antony Mayfield cited in Arthur [1]).

Finally, placing ourselves in the role of Web designers and/or evaluators, when we consider YouTube from a usability point-of-view, it seems poorly designed, or maybe has no design at all: just a chaotic, cluttered website. However, as we

---

[1] Alexa (www.alexa.com) provides information on web traffic to other websites collected from users of Alexa Toolbar.

[2] Interact here includes commenting or contributing somehow with improvements.

understand this phenomenon we find that, maybe, it is not at all a case of bad design. This leads us to reflect: What is changing in Web interaction? What type of user are we now dealing with? If the Web has adopted new roles? What must consequentially change in web evaluation and (re)design?

3. EVALUATING YouTube

How do we evaluate YouTube? How would YouTube perform if we evaluate it according to conventional usability metrics? In this section, we will try to answer these questions, by reflecting on and providing some examples of usability problems, as well as giving our own thoughts and suggestions about it.

3.1 Conventional YouTube evaluation

One of the most common, popular and advantageous usability evaluation techniques is Heuristic Evaluation [2, 3], which allows experts to critique an interface by verifying its agreement with general and simple heuristics[3] or principles, such as clarity, consistency or fluidity of navigation. Following the list of the ten Nielsen's recommended heuristics [2, 8] for a usable interface design we can audit YouTube's usability. Our general evaluation is shown by a ↑ – positive, ↓ – negative, ↔ – present but unsatisfactory.

Visibility of system status – ↑ – Concerning this guideline, YouTube performs generally well, as it keeps the user informed about what the system is doing, by providing information about loading and total video times.

Match between system and the real world – ↔ – This heuristic verifies to what extent the language of the interface respects the user's familiar language and concepts. On the one hand the video controls, similar to domestic video players, respect real-world conventions, but on the other hand, there is a vast amount of unclear terminology and associated functions, such as: *quicklists*, *featured videos* or *channel names*[4].

User control and freedom – ↑ – This is the principle in which YouTube performs the best. In fact, the use of the conventional video commands allows full control and freedom to the user who then uses the interface skilfully.

Consistency and standards – ↓ – In contrast, this is where YouTube performs worst. Two examples are: i) Navigation history is lost when the user logs into the system, so, for instance, the loss of videos watched, quicklists, etc; and ii) Comments are frequently chats between users, but as these are not presented over a linear, dated logic, the context and understanding are mislaid.

Error prevention – ↓ – This guideline is not observed; for example, when watching a video in a channel page, a table of contents is shown, although every time the user clicks in any of the other videos, the user is directed to a standard page losing any previous contextual information. In order to re-access it, being obliged to use the back button. The same happens when you are visualizing the comments and several other basic tasks.

Recognition rather than recall – ↓ – Interfaces should not rely on user's memory, making actions visible to the user. Interfaces

should not rely on the user's memory, by making actions immediately visible to the user. Besides the not obvious terminology, the page's layout on lower resolution screens requires the user to navigate with the scroll bar to vital components such as the search box. These are often fundamental if the user is purposely looking for specific content on the site, instead of following a link sent by a friend or lingering around. This requires the user to recall the position or location of such functions, instead of merely recognizing them.

Flexibility and efficiency of use – ↔ – The user has full mastery of the video controls, but there are various functions in which the system performs poorly. An important example refers to the retrieved search results that cannot be ordered or organised under any criteria, such as date or rating.

Aesthetic and minimalist design – ↓ – If we consider the quantity of images, videos and other types of information available on YouTube pages, we are temped to state that this heuristic is simply not considered. In fact, the first general reaction to YouTube pages is of chaos.

Help users recognize, diagnose, and recover from errors – ↔ – This heuristic gives direction on how to express error messages. These are only present when the user is signing up.

Help and documentation – ↔ – While, arguably, a system should be usable without documentation, help and documentation are necessary! YouTube has FAQ-style help, but less in terms of 'how-to do it' documentation.

In summary, from the list of ten recommended Nielsen's heuristics, YouTube respects only two, with the rest failing or unsatisfactory. From these results, we can say that YouTube appears to fail miserably when evaluated with a conventional usability evaluation technique. Moreover, if we consider the most precious usability metrics, total task completion time, total number of clicks and total number of errors, YouTube, definitely fails. However, YouTube's clear success means there must be something really good that makes users go back and back again.

3.2 YouTube evaluation – not as we know it

Having examined how it fails, we now consider why YouTube succeeds focusing on the website purpose, content, and design.

3.2.1 Reasons for success

As we demonstrated in section 3.1, YouTube is a disaster from a conventional usability evaluation point-of-view. Thus, users were not expected to return to reuse the system, and definitely not to make it such as show-case of success. So what are the reasons for its success? We identified three possible answers: its users, its content and its design.

Users

Current Web users are very different from those of the '90's. We now have also a generation of users that grew up on and together with the Web and its technology. Therefore they are reasonably literate in all that concerns the Web, its tools, services, etc, and use them just as any other artefact in their everyday life. Additionally, they access YouTube because they want to or just happen to have some free time. Finally, partly as a consequence of the latter, these users are content designers themselves, communicating and socialising via the Web.

Content

YouTube content is largely responsible for YouTube success. First there is the aspect of personal broadcasting of a user that wants to communicate and extend him or herself via the web. In fact, there is not unusual to find users simply broadcasting their

---

[3] A heuristic is a guideline, general principle, or rule that describes properties of a usable interface. It can be used to guide the design or to critique a decision [2, 7, 8].

[4] Channel titles are not always meaningful. For instance, names as *brokensonnet2* are probably helpless for a novice user, and therefore will not help on deducting what is under a channel with such name.

daily routines, as a kind of digital diary, or their participation in a conference. These are then shared with a vast community of friends, relatives or anyone potentially accessing the Web. Then, and being particularly relevant, we have all the amateur videos as well as movies and television series that have not yet being released. These videos are sometimes illegal.

(Apparent bad) Design

Without forgetting any of the faults reported in section 3.1, we now emphasise specifically four of them – aesthetic and minimalist design, error prevention, total number of clicks and task completion time – because, as we will explain, these may, in fact, constitute the smart features of the YouTube interface.

We will start by explaining why **task completion time** is so relevant for YouTube, but from a totally opposite perspective to the one of the past! In fact, as YouTube is mainly supported by advertisement the longer we keep the user hanging out the better, so it is important for users to be able to accomplish their tasks but not in the shortest possible time. For the same reason, the **total number of clicks** should not be reduced to a minimum, because the more pages the user browses, the more he or she is likely to be subjected to more ads!

The **error prevention** is another form, almost cruel, of keeping the user in the system. In effect, the user is permanently losing the interaction context, and forced to use the back button, or, if unlucky, restart the navigation.

Finally, concerning **aesthetic and minimalist design,** we need only to consider the major and permanent information clutter. Image and text chaos is evident when we access and browse YouTube (see Figure 2 and Figure 3).

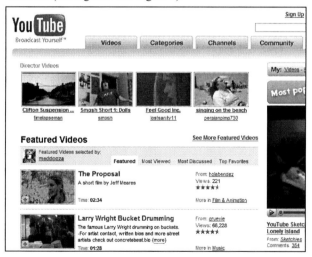

Figure 2: YouTube main page

To comprehend this, we recall Miller's [6] magical number seven and Hicks law[5] [4]. How many chunks of information does a user have to deal with when browsing YouTube? How many choices does the user have available in each YouTube page? Certainly, these two metrics are large and, inevitably make demands on the human perception and reasoning systems. Various images concurrently catch the attention of user that

---

[5]This law describes the time it takes for a user to make a decision. Given n equally probable choices, the average reaction time T required to choose among them is approximately $T = b\ log_2(n + 1)$ where b is a constant that can be determined empirically by fitting a line to measured data (for a particular individual and context).

clicks one and another image and, interminable and subsequently, watches the videos associated with them. The pace is defined by how fast the user's eye is captured by a different image and the user's attention and interest are released from the previous video.

YouTube success has proven that none of the (apparently) bad design features here presented have prevented the increasing use of YouTube; indeed, we think they have favoured it, being responsible for it. So, we wonder: How would YouTube be if "well" designed? How would it perform? Would it still achieve its purpose? Would it yet be a success?

3.2.2 Crucial features

Having presented the possible reasons for YouTube success, we now reflect on the interface features contributing for this intriguing interaction experience.

User control and freedom

The design features discussed above might not have survived, nor indeed YouTube itself, if they were not balanced by an excellent interaction feature – user full sense of control and freedom of the system. This matter is well achieved by the YouTube interface and is extremely important from a user interaction point-of-view. The conventional video controls, similar to domestic video players, allow users full control and freedom when interacting with the system. It is easy to choose a video just by looking at its image, title and short description. But also, if the video does not correspond to the user expectations, it is equally easy to immediately choose and change to another video among the nearest bit of clutter.

Interaction in YouTube is as easy and similar to the use of any common remote control while zapping through your endless television channels. Another similarity with television zapping is the "syndrome of the unfinished movie"; we always think we should watch it a bit longer just in case it gets more interesting or it has a surprising ending. So we keep on prolonging our experience expecting something better to appear.

Engagement

Another wise feature of YouTube is related to the way the system manages to keep the user engaged with the system. This is achieved as follows. First, when the user is accessing the main YouTube page (Figure 2), he or she is helped in the selection of videos by visual clues to: i) featured, ii) most viewed, ii) most discussed; and iv) top favourites videos.

Then, after having selected a video and when in a YouTube video viewing page (Figure 3); ie: before, while and after watching the video, the service provides a set of information about the video such as i) related, ii) more from this user, and iii) playlists or i) about the video, ii) rating, iii) views, iv) comments and v) favorited. These seduce users' curiosity and tempts them to jump from one movie to another and yet another. This creates a cycle that together with unexpectedness and sense of surprise creates a remarkable engagement.

The homo ludens

In the 1950's, Huizinga coined the term *Homo Ludens* [5], defining humans as playful creatures and suggested play was crucial to the generation of culture. Play includes acting, games, fun – activities that require human action (maybe performance) and engagement. YouTube clearly addresses this basic human need and indeed is rapidly creating its own cultural shifts.

Huizinga particularly emphasises that play is for itself and of all activities most about freedom – just because it is superfluous (see [5] pp.7, 8). However, he also shows how play permeates the 'serious' business of life from law to war, from poetry to philosophy. As well as just 'having a good time', the freedom of the 'playful' element in YouTube allows users to express (or portray) themselves and do the serious work of identity and sociality.

Figure 3: YouTube video viewing page

4. SO DOES USABILITY MATTER?

If YouTube violates so many usability principles and yet is still so successful, does usability matter at all, especially for the channel-hopping, iPod-shuffling generation brought up with pervasive technology and incessant media?

4.1 Fitness for Purpose

Usability is always part of a broader agenda of designing things that are fit for purpose. There are always conflicts here, for example we often trade usability for security. There are also conflicts between fitness for purpose for a user and for the supplier, for example, Amazon forbids reviews with URLs to avoid links to rivals – good for the user but bad for Amazon.

In traditional GUI systems the users' purpose is assumed to be to attain some goal and the purpose of the designer to help them do so. Usability guidance, such as Nielsen's Heuristics, embodies this assumption. In YouTube the users' purpose is explore, have fun, and enjoy the 'route' as much as the goal. Not surprisingly 'usability' guidance should change accordingly.

4.2 Designers and Users

YouTube has two (overlapping) classes of end users: those who browse and those who produce content. In 'producer' role, their purpose and goals are closer to traditional systems – to upload a video, change some setting. Here traditional usability principles still apply and indeed in recent discussions with a group of relatively computer-naïve end-users, they cited YouTube's instructions for video upload as an exemplar of good practice. Similarly when a browsing user wants something specific: to subscribe to a video producer or look in their history for a recently seen video – here again conventional advice applies.

More problematically YouTube and such sites have two (potentially non overlapping) classes of designers: the professionals and the end-users configuring their own pages (the second class of users above). The purpose of the second class, the user-as-designer, includes self-expression, publicizing videos, maybe directing visitors towards specific content. The purpose of the 'professionals', is then both to make it easy for user-as-designer and for the result to be fit for purpose for the browsing users. In YouTube the freedom of the user – as designer – is relatively limited, so the browsing users have a similar structure across the site. In other Web2.0 sites such as MySpace, this becomes a more major issue – how do you create frameworks that allow expression and yet have some level of overall usability (in its broadest sense)... and how do you help (or educate?) users-as-designers to use these most effectively.

5. DISCUSSION AND FURTHER WORK

A more detailed study about YouTube-like websites, such as Wikipedia, Flicker, Blogger or MySpace, would allow us to validate some of our assumptions, for instance with respect to the reasons why a user accesses this type of services and for how long? Furthermore, information gathered would permit a better understanding of these Web Phenomena, its services, purposes, design and evaluation. So far, the similarities we identify make us conclude that the Web is approaching or already going through a new stage, in which the increasing number of young but literate web users will play a major role. This user wants and is able to manipulate playful, participative and joyful Web services. This new context requires new and sharp usability evaluation approaches that we, as researchers and/or academics, should include in our repertoire. From this study we learnt that the user's sense of control and freedom, engagement and playfulness are critical qualities for success.

6. REFERENCES

[1] Arthur, C.. What is the 1% rule? *The Guardian*, July 20, 2006 (accessed 22-01-2007) http://technology.guardian.co.uk/weekly/story/0,,1823959,00.html

[2] Dix, A., Finlay, J., Abowd G. and Beale, R. *Human–Computer Interaction*. Pearson/Prentice-Hall, 2003.

[3] Ellis, P. and Ellis, S. *Measuring User Experience*. 2001 http://www.webtechniques.com/archives/2001/02/ellis/

[4] Hick, W. On the rate of gain of information. *Quarterly Journal of Experimental Psychology*, 4 (1952), 11–26.

[5] Huizinga, J. *Homo Ludens: A Study of the Play Element in Culture*. Boston: The Beacon Press, 1950

[6] Miller, G. The Magical Number Seven, Plus or Minus Two: Some Limits on Our Capacity for Processing Information. *The Psychological Review*, 63 (1956), 81–97.

[7] Nielsen, J. *Usability Engineering*. USA, Morgan Kaufmann Publishers, Inc., 1993

[8] Nielsen, J. Heuristic Evaluation. useit.com. (accessed 12/04/2000) http://www.useit.com/papers/heuristic/. Please see also related links.

[9] http://en.wikipedia.org/wiki/Internet_phenomena (accessed 22-01-2007)

Names and Reference in User Interfaces

Harold Thimbleby
Swansea University
Wales
SA2 8PP
United Kingdom
+44 1792295393

harold@thimbleby.net

Michael Harrison
Informatics Research Institute,
Newcastle University
NE1 7RU,
United Kingdom
+44 191 246 4938

michael.harrison@ncl.ac.uk

ABSTRACT

This short paper argues that references in user interfaces, in particular names and the values they denote, are often designed in a way that is incomplete and inconsistent thereby causing problems for users. This paper explores names and values through illustrations in order to clear the way for a more systematic approach to the design of names and reference.

1. INTRODUCTION

People use computers to achieve things with greater ease, effectiveness, reliability, or enjoyment that they could not do, or could not do so well, without them. *Naming*, in particular, allows an activity, a specific set of features or a routine task to be exploited or invoked repeatedly with no more effort than it takes to use its name once. Names can also refer to ideas and objects that are not present in the "here-and-now"; they facilitate remembering, planning, explaining, and communicating. Names are frequently used for distinguishing objects that are otherwise indistinguishable. In practice, names are of course ubiquitous in computing: objects like computer servers are given names so that they can be distinguished by people and by internet name servers. Clarity, memorability, and consistency are key principles that apply to naming schemes.

An important aspect of interactive systems is how reference and naming is designed. Typically interactive systems are complex and are used in many ways, ways unforeseen from the early stages of design. This paper will argue that problems often occur in the use of interactive systems because of a lack of clarity about the mechanisms for naming and referencing.

Confusions arise for a variety of reasons. Some of these reasons have been explored relatively thoroughly: for example the issues associated with mode confusion in interactive systems. Others are less well understood in the context of interactive systems, even though they have been studied relatively thoroughly in other contexts. Naming issues become more important as mobile devices become more available as a platform for applications. This diversity leads to a richer set of mechanisms for referring to items and the requirement for consistency across a range of different interfaces for the user to the same device in different locations, different devices in the same location, and so on.

This paper will discuss how naming in particular and reference in general are being used in a number of designs and will reflect upon the problems that these create. The purpose of the paper is to explore what analysis is most appropriate for the design. In general it is important is to have theories or frameworks that can raise key design issues *before* systems are built, and, moreover, that raise issues that can be addressed analytically and systematically. Analytic insight into design is particularly important for safety- and mission-critical systems, where certain sorts of use experience may be too rare or too costly to evaluate by conventional UCD techniques.

Names and their meaning were explored in programming language design forty years ago [3,5,6], and concepts such as binding, assignment, environments, scope, encapsulation, and so forth are established and remain stable. While programming problems related to names (for example problems with aliasing) are well understood, similar problems in user interface design have attracted little attention and continue to be dealt with on an ad hoc basis. Most research activity has been in relation to naming schemes (for example [1, 2]), particularly concerned with psychological issues. This paper, in contrast, argues that there are also engineering issues relating to the structure and consistency of naming systems in interfaces that have an important impact on the usability of a particular design.

Names *bind* to objects and then refer to those objects. Hence, for example, "Thinkbridge" is a name bound to an object that happens to be a laptop computer. This is not the only name that is bound to this particular object. The computer is also bound with an IP number, a MAC number, plus other names that might be used by the software installed in the system. These different names will be used in different task contexts for the same object (the laptop); some names are known by the user, some are hidden. Furthermore, in the case of "Thinkbridge," the name binds to a computer with its *own* namespaces, which themselves are complex, partly hierarchical naming structures.

In user interfaces it is possible to refer to objects by name, as in the case of a programming language, but alternatively the interface may allow pointing at objects as a means of reference, or a combination of naming and pointing as in the case of "Put that there" [1]. Hence names like "that" and "there" are generic names that are made specific references when combined with other mechanisms (here, pointing) for reference. In user interfaces names can be organised hierarchically and systems can be moded as a result. Consider for example, an example from unix where invoking the command `cd papers/naming` followed by `emacs hci07.tex` refers to a file name that is part of a hierarchical naming structure. The effect of changing the directory using "cd" was to change the context or mode in which the file name is used.

The systematic analysis of reference and naming in HCI is a non-trivial, and probably long-term endeavor. This paper aims to start the process by providing a number of illustrations to indicate the range of problems. Users can be confused by a number of aspects of bindings between reference and object. They can be confused because the extent and nature of the binding is not clear. They can be confused because actions that appear to be intuitive cannot be performed in the way that one would expect using the reference.

We describe four types of issue that are problematic in the design of interfaces. We do not intend to be complete, rather to indicate the kind of framework that would be of value in design. These issues are concerned with:

1. The binding between a name (or other reference) and its denotation
2. What the interface supports in terms of that binding, and how it is understood by the user.
3. Transparency of reference, and the extent to which denoted objects can be replaced by references.
4. Mode transparency and confusion.

Note that the terms "binding" and "transparency" are standard [5].

2. REFERENCE AND DENOTATION

Mac OS X provides facilities for dealing with the mobility of a device. OS X allows the user to name the settings required to access the internet from a variety of locations the computer's owner might occupy. A pull-down menu selects a location as current. It is shown below selecting "Swansea University," which denotes a preset location and information for a particular office.

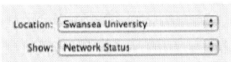

In other words, "Swansea University" is a name that *in this scope* is bound to various internet parameters. If the user moves to another location, they select it from a menu:

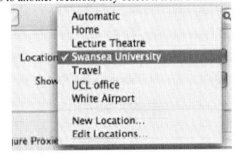

The system provides a menu of different locations so that the user can choose by name what settings are relevant to the current location. However, a setting may need changing, and this provides a simple illustration of a naming confusion.

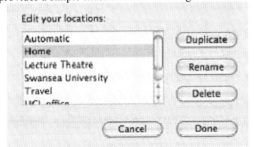

Selecting "Edit Locations..." from this menu means editing the *names* of locations not editing the values of the names, that is the internet *settings* of locations, as might be intuitively expected by the user. Thus a user can duplicate an

existing name; if "Duplicate" is selected, the user can obtain a new location name, "Home Copy," for instance, with the *same* settings as "Home" currently has. If the user wants to change "Home Copy" to some other name, such as "Holiday" then they now need to rename this location. Typically, the user would then change some or all of the internet settings of "Holiday"; the advantage being that "Holiday" has been initialized to have the same settings as "Home" has, and therefore this process is easier than entering all the holiday settings by hand.

The name "Swansea University" can be changed to be, say, "My office," but the IP number associated with it *cannot* be changed here. This interpretation of "Edit Locations" cannot be achieved at this level by deleting the existing location and then adding a new location with the intended name; IP numbers (the values of these names) are set or changed at a different level in the menu hierarchy.

As it happens, Mac OS provides an alternative view of these bindings, which enables a sophisticated user to shortcut this user interface. The network names are stored in an XML file called `preferences.plist`, which can be edited using the Property List Editor, so, in this case, the name `UserDefinedName` would be associated with `Home`:

```
<key>UserDefinedName</key>
<string>Home</string>
```

The file also defines what settings are associated with that name, and these settings can be edited directly. Therefore there is a means by which the intuitive meaning of "Edit locations" can be achieved, but it isn't a meaning supported by the normal interactive user interface. The point of mentioning XML in this paper is to emphasise that, technically, the user interface could have been different: the XML can represent "any" changes to names, bindings and values, so any constraints are purely user interface design choices.

Given the tasks that are being performed using these locations, it would seem natural to allow a user to refer to the names in other contexts, say to send an email to a technician to get help, or to email it to someone else who wants to edit the location to their own requirements. Unfortunately, location names only have meaning in the very restricted context of the menus described above. Emailing "Home" to anyone else sends nothing other than the word; the binding is lost (and it doesn't even surprise us that this is so). Indeed, the binding is lost even if the user cuts-and-pastes from any of the location dialog boxes. Worse, it is actually very tedious to determine what the name Home is bound to; its value (the IP numbers and so on) are spread over many windows and dialog boxes.

Eudora (a popular email client) illustrates another issue in relation to the binding between names and objects. For Eudora, `<Dominant>` is the name of the unique, default email account. Whereas all names can be edited — for instance, if a user wants to change the spelling of a name — the special name `<Dominant>` is fixed and cannot be edited. If a user changes their lifestyle and wants to change which account is dominant, they are *unable* to modify the dominant account, rename it to another account name, or rename an existing name as dominant. An obvious solution to this problem is that the dominant property should not be a property of the name spelling, but one of its values. Certainly the choice of name itself should not affect whether the user can change it. For example, each account name could have a check box "Dominant?" that the user can set to make it the dominant account. (Obviously, the program would ensure exactly one name had the associated dominant property.) In other words, dominance should not be a property of the name but of the denotation thereby making it possible to have a more uniform naming scheme.

3. NAMING THE RIGHT OBJECTS IN DESIGN

Our next example relates to the fact that interfaces may have concepts within them that are understood in the user's model, but which that may not be capable of being referenced directly. Issues of naming are often resolved using task analysis techniques (see [2] for a careful summary). Consider the following example. The Casio HS-8V is a basic calculator with a single memory. The calculator provides the keys MRC, M– and M+ to handle its memory. Formally, these are names denoting operations that have an effect on the memory. However this set of operations is not complete in terms of the user's mental model of how the calculator works. For example the user is quite likely to want to use the memory explicitly (why else are there buttons for it?) as a location in which a value is saved for future use. This cannot be done easily. If by chance, the memory is already zero, the user can press M+ to add the number to be saved to memory. If the memory is not zero, however, there is no obvious way to save any number.

The labeling of functions limits the means of use of the calculator and should therefore reflect typical mental models of the device, thereby making it easier to carry out actions that would seem to be intuitively obvious.

Again we see the use of names in a user interface that seem to be routine, but which conceal rather obscure issues — and not just technically obscure issues, but issues that affect users and the tasks they are able to achieve.

4. REFERENTIAL TRANSPARENCY

A number of issues in the design of interactive systems are associated with referential transparency and other issues that relate more specifically to mode confusion.

Key buttons are names that denote calculator functions. Consider calculating $10^{-\pi}$ (which should be about 0.00072) on the Sharp EL-531VHB calculator. Keying 10^x–π ± produces "Error" while 10^x 2 ± produces 0.01. So the names π and 2 behave differently.

Storing π in memory A, by pressing π STO A should make it possible to use A for the value of π: indeed, pressing π or RCL A both produce the same results. Yet 10^x RCL A± produces 0.00072, even though 10^x π ± is an error.

In these examples the key named π (which denotes 3.14159...) is not treated the same way as the key labeled 2 or A. There is no referential transparency. Different sorts of names, different sorts of numbers (i.e., Arabic names of numeric values) are apparently bound to very different things.

Consider now the following further example of a different lack of referential transparency. If a user enters just =, the last expression is re-evaluated; if a user enters a binary operator, ANS (a name representing the value of the last calculation) is automatically inserted as its left operand. These interface accelerations increase the power of the calculator: consider, say, the expression ANS+1 (or equivalently, +1, which gets the ANS name inserted automatically) which turns the calculator into a counter where every press of = calculates ANS := ANS+1. Unfortunately the abbreviation mechanism creates a feature interaction with names. If the user enters ANS+RCL A =, they as anticipated get the last answer added to the value of A. If they enter RCL A+ANS = different things happen. First, RCL A is treated as a query to find the value of A: immediately the calculator shows A's value. When the user presses the +, the calculator inserts ANS as its left operand, which in fact will be equal to the value just displayed, namely A. But when the user explicitly enters ANS, *that* ANS will be the last value

displayed which is of course now A, rather than the intended answer.

The rules by which ANS works is as follows:

1. A missing operand defaults to the last answer. This makes writing + 2 a shorthand for ANS + 2.

2. Asking the value of a name straight after using = *immediately* gets the value. So RCL A immediately gets A's value (and hence changes ANS), saving the user writing RCL A = which would be the obvious way of finding A's value.

Each of these features makes some sense in isolation, but they interact with each other and names with the unfortunate consequence that they compromise the calculator's mathematics — spelt out more abstractly, the example is equivalent to the surprising $a+b \neq b+a$. The meanings of names such as ANS and A depend on exactly when they are used.

5. MODE CONFUSION

The final issue we explore in this paper is associated with modes, mode confusion and mode transition. Issues of mode confusion have been extensively studied (see [8] for review). The Canon EOS350D digital SLR camera has a mode selection dial so that the photographer can select how much control they have over photography or how much the camera performs automatically. A variety of parameters, such as aperture, shutter speed, exposure measurement, choice of object to focus on, whether to use flash, set the ISO speed, white balance, and others can either be set by the camera automatically or, depending on mode, different subsets of parameters can be specified by the photographer (the camera's computer sorts out unspecified parameters depending on prevailing conditions). By design, there are seven basic modes where the photographer chooses a type of photograph — such as portrait, scenery, macro or sport — and the camera selects all parameters fully automatically. There are also five so-called "creative" modes where the photographer overrides parameters. For example, in the creative mode named Av, the photographer can control the aperture, leaving the camera to automatically adjust the shutter speed to maintain the same exposure. In all creative modes, the photographer can also control the flash, ISO speed, focus sensors, exposure sensors, and the white balance.

The icons in the figure above are names that refer to the sets of photographic parameters, as well as the functions that are performed on them. The symbols therefore denote camera functions, in much the same way as the M+ button in the calculator example represented a calculator function. This time, however, the automatic processes of the camera use environmental conditions to fill in the remaining parameters. This makes sense, as often the user is more interested in changing or adjusting a value rather than specifying one outright; that is, instead of setting the aperture to f/5.6 (say) the user may prefer to set it to be so-many stops larger or smaller than whatever the camera suggests.

Suppose a photographer uses the basic portrait mode to photograph somebody's face. The camera will select all appropriate photographic settings. Now suppose the photographer wishes to do a portrait but wants to control the aperture; they must change to Av creative mode. Unfortunately, now the camera will use all the previously user-defined settings — such as ISO speed and white balance — and none of the automatically determined values that were being used a moment earlier in the portrait mode. Worse, the many settings are distributed around the menu hierarchy of the camera, and are not easy for a user to locate.

Hence in the mode transition, none of the parameters that were calculated automatically in the previous mode are carried over. The user is required to fill all the parameters explicitly, which are tedious to check or change. The more usual issues of mode confusion that arise because a user is unaware that controls mean something new because they have not observed the transition are not of concern here. Instead a new problem of mode is indicated: in the process of transition the previously-named state, and therefore potentially time-saving information, is lost. The underlying name/reference problem is similar to the internet setting problem we reviewed earlier: the name (an internet location; a mode of photography) is bound to settings which are inaccessible to the user.

An obvious solution would be something like the following. The mode selection knob can be pressed and, in so doing, the complete set of settings is saved. The creative modes then adjust with respect to this saved setting. Hence the user can opt to save the information in the transition. In conventional terms, pressing the knob performs an assignment from the current setting to the default setting, to be used in the creative modes. Of course, assignment is well-known in computing; one wonders why the interaction designer did not support this technically trivial solution.

Another solution is to separate modes from what can be changed. For example, as currently designed it is physically impossible to be both in portrait mode and to control the flash manually, because these choices are in different locations on the same knob. Alternatively, knobs may refer to function rather than a mode. The knobs themselves may compute automatically or be user-defined, and this choice could be selected by the photographer. There are many possibilities.

6. CONCLUSIONS AND AGENDA FOR FUTURE WORK

Reference and in particular names raise non-trivial user interface design issues. Designers need better support in understanding the naming implications of their design.

(1) A framework is required for describing reference mechanisms (including names and naming structures) so that designers can use it to consider design options and, in particular, a framework would enable appropriate schemes for linking an application to appropriate platforms.

(2) Principles for reference are required that would enable user interface consistency and ease of use. There are many in programming language design [5], but they have not been carried over and validated in the interactive case.

(3) The principles that are adopted should be clear and easy to explain or interpret to users.

(4) The semantics of names and reference is well-understood in programming, and this can be a creative (and consistent) source of user interface features.

In conventional programming, the concepts alias, binding, environment, scope, inheritance, extent and so on are well defined, and their combined use and interplay has been worked out thoroughly. The same concepts are not applied uniformly in user interfaces, and (at least as implemented) they interact in complex and non-intuitive ways. Studying these issues and knowing that corresponding abstract operations are possible in user interfaces will encourage interactive system implementers to make more consistent, more powerful, and more reliable systems — and ones where standard user interface design principles, such as undo and help, would be implemented correctly, consistently and generally. Thus a more thorough understanding of references, names and binding, much has already been developed and used for many years in relation to programming languages, will clarify many interaction design issues in user interfaces. An understanding would provide a clear and well-defined way to discuss user errors and confusions in relation to many user interface problems. However, user interfaces introduce many ideas that go beyond conventional programming languages, and this will be a substantial research project.

A further research project would be to determine appropriate models of reference, naming and scope specifically relevant to interactive usability that would be valid from the perspective of usability; this would make it possible for designers to reason about and conceptualize their user interface designs. With such a framework, for instance, it would become possible to redesign a camera and analyze experimentally the effect that it has had on the user's model of the system and their understanding and use of the design.

7. ACKNOWLEDGEMENTS

Tim Bell, Paul Cairns, Peter Mosses, and Will Thimbleby made many helpful suggestions.

8. REFERENCES

[1] Carroll, J. M., *What's in a Name? An Essay in the Psychology of Reference*, Freeman, 1985.

[2] Johnson, P., "Human Computer Interaction: psychology, task analysis and software engineering". McGraw Hill, 1992.

[3] Landin, P. J., "The Next 700 Programming Languages," *Communications of the ACM*, **9**(3):157–166, 1966.

[4] Nigay, L. & Coutaz, J., A design space for multimodal systems: concurrent processing and data fusion. Proceedings of the SIGCHI conference on Human Factors in Computing Systems. ACM Press pp. 172–178. 1993

[5] Strachey, C., "Fundamental Concepts in Programming Languages," *Higher-Order and Symbolic Computation*, **13**(1/2):11–49, 2000.

[6] Tennent, R. D., *Principles of Programming Languages*, Prentice-Hall, 1981.

[7] Gow, J., Thimbleby, H.W. & Cairns, P. "Automatic critiques of interface modes" In Gilroy, S. W. and Harrison, M.D. Interactive Systems: Design, specification and verification (DSVIS 2005). Springer Lecture Notes in Computer Science. No. 3941. 2006. pp. 201-212

Internalist and Externalist HCI

Harold Thimbleby
Swansea University
Wales
SA2 8PP
+44 1792295393

harold@thimbleby.net

Will Thimbleby
Swansea University
Wales
SA2 8PP
+44 1792295393

will@thimbleby.net

ABSTRACT

The history of technology, as a discipline, supports alternate points of view termed *internalist* and *externalist*, which terms highlight an approximately similar division in points of view within HCI. Conventional HCI is externalist, rightly concerned with human-centered issues; but externalism risks ignoring important internalist issues. A successful human-computer system is better if it is successful from *both* perspectives.

This discussion paper argues that the externalist view, while necessary and immensely useful, is not sufficient—and in the worst case, risks eclipsing innovation from internalist quarters.

1. INTRODUCTION

David Nye's review of the history of technology [14] uses the clear terms *internalist* and *externalist*, applying them to styles of historical analysis.

Why did the internal combustion engine triumph over the alternatives, horse, steam and electric? An internalist might emphasize the power-to-weight ratio of the internal combustion engine; an externalist might emphasize the lower cost of the Ford Model T and the dramatic impact cost had on a growing market. An internalist, then, considers the technology as such.

- **Externalism** is focused on the world external to the user interface: *human*-interaction and e.g., observation, evaluation, cognition, etc.

- **Internalism** is focused on the world internal to the user interface: *computer* interaction and e.g., logic, engineering, computation, etc.

An example illustrating human-computer interaction issues is Tracy Kidder's classic *The Soul of a New Machine* [10]. The book traces the development of a computer, the Data General Eclipse MV/8000, all the technical issues, right up to the point that the finished product is brought to market. Then the book ends, just when the external world of the computer and its possible use starts to get interesting. The book takes an internalist view.

Of course both views are needed in a balanced discussion, and indeed Nye provides a masterful analysis. We believe Nye's internalist/externalist terms from the history of technology have value in distinguishing major styles in the way HCI is viewed, presented and undertaken.

Clayton Lewis proposed a similar, but, psychological distinction for HCI, that of *inner* and *outer HCI* [13]. Here, inner and outer refer to cognitive processes and human behavior respectively. Lewis emphasizes the potentially fruitful interplay of inner and outer HCI. Curiously, while his the terms "inner" and "outer" might at first seem to cover everything, Lewis *excludes* the computer (or other interactive system)—he simply does not mention it in his conception of HCI! It is as if the interactive system is a given, taken for granted, rather than a legitimate object of study in its own right.

Similarly in the "Kittle House Manifesto" [3] Carroll suggests that academic psychology has had no impact on interactive design practice, and that major innovations in practice (e.g., Sketchpad, an innovative graphics program) have made no explicit use of psychology. He bemoans the fact that HCI does not use science, or that if it does the relation is haphazard. Yet, curiously, he overlooks that computer science is science too, and in fact underlies the major contributions he describes as driving innovation. While it seems to us quite right to try to promote psychological science and explore why it is in some sense under-rated or used haphazardly, it seems counter-productive to the wider purpose of HCI to overlook computational science. Carroll's more recent collection [4] sees HCI as something computer scientists need to be taught, as something quite other than computer science, rather than something that can draw on computer science *as well as* human sciences.

This externalist emphasis of the HCI field is routinely found in the standard HCI textbooks, of which most take externalist points of view—indeed, [5] suggests that teaching HCI should cover the computer science which standard HCI textbooks omit.

Barnard, May, Duke and Duce remind us of "syndesis," binding together systems that contain interacting subsystems, such as people and computers. They introduce the terms "Type 1 theory" and "Type 2 theory," referring to approaches that go *deeper* or that go *across* interaction respectively. They warn that we are not very good at establishing Type 2 connections, and this weakness may lead to "the fragmentation and demise of HCI as a coherent science" [1].

It seems that HCI needs terminology to discuss these issues. Our internalist/externalist distinction is analogous to the Lewis inner/outer HCI distinctions, but from the point of view of the computer rather than the human. Without repeating Lewis's arguments here, we too see the great potential of fruitful interplay between internalist and externalist perspectives.

Just as a brain-computer interaction (BCI) researcher would certainly wish to go deeper into the "inner HCI" than Lewis does, so also our "internalist" perspective has a rich internal structure—it isn't just "the computer" set against the wide range of standard HCI disciplines, anthropology, psychology, social science, economics, marketing, design; the internalist sees algorithms, complexity, information theory, proof, requirements, hardware, graphics, databases, and so forth … a rich science contributing to HCI.

1.1 The Authors' Perspective

Both authors of this paper have an internalist background, and it is unashamedly from this perspective that this paper has been written. The paper has a twofold purpose: to name and introduce a useful distinction for HCI, and to stimulate debate on the balance—or the lack of balance—in HCI as practiced, and hence stimulate thinking on strategies for doing better.

We believe the internalist/externalist distinction allows a constructive discussion about the methodologies of HCI, without diminishing either internalist or externalist points of view. By naming the distinction, we suggest that there are different *and valid* views about how HCI, and particularly HCI research, can and should be done. Nevertheless, we believe internalist HCI tends to be under-valued by the more dominant externalist point of view, and this paper therefore makes an enthusiastic case for internalism.

HCI could not exist without programming computers, which is an internalist perspective, and also HCI could not exist without the human context and study, which is an externalist perspective. Singly, internalist and externalist perspectives are monocular and lack depth and perspective. Both are needed.

2. HOW WE GOT HERE

The HCI community's traditional emphasis of externalist perspectives to some extent eclipses internalist perspectives. Historically, existing externalist methodologies were ready when they were needed: there was and still is a very substantial resource of experimental psychology that was applied and works to a high standard. In contrast, it might be said that most early internalists did not know what they were doing; see below when we comment on the Therac-25.

A second, crucial, reason for the current emphasis on externalist methods in HCI is that external experimental methods can be used independently of the specifics of internalist details. Every HCI system has very different internals, and requires investment in specific programming and design; in contrast, the externalist methods (e.g., cognitive walkthrough, think aloud, eye tracking) work on all systems. Experimental designs, statistical methods and so on, can be applied to a word processor or to a graphics package with little modification. In contrast, a new contribution to HCI by an internalist might take years of work that has no other application. It is noteworthy that most externalist studies of programming in HCI design use trivial programs, because programming real user interfaces is too slow. Inevitably, few internalists contribute to mainstream HCI.

Perhaps the HCI community has changed too. As fewer internalists contribute at the same rate as externalists, the peer community becomes dominated by externalist values. If an internalist submitted a result to a conference or journal now, most referees calling themselves members of the HCI community would be externalists.

ACM CHI, the major international HCI conference, is primarily externalist. In contrast one of the major internalist conferences, *DSVIS* (Design, Specification and Verification of Interactive Systems) has only a hundredth of the participants. This reflects a difference in the sizes of the communities. Thus, internalists face higher hurdles to participate in the development of the field. Then, as the externalists operate in a community

dominated by externalists, it appears reasonable to *require* externalist criteria for contributing to that community: possibly even a hegemony—being defined as the emphasis of cultural beliefs, values, and practices to the dismissal and over-looking of others.

3. SAMPLE SYSTEMS

3.1 Therac-25

Horrific stories of bad HCI abound. The Therac-25 was a medical device that killed patients as a result of "operator" error (actually system design error). It is primarily an example of inadequate internalist HCI, an argument for better internalist HCI rather than fixing design problems with externalist HCI. Bad programming killed people.

Although the Therac-25 story is an extreme example, the case illustrates how important it is for user-centered design to react against sloppy programming practices—this paper is not arguing internalism is a panacea! Given that many programmers are not computer scientists, UCD *is necessary* to improve things.

One could argue that iterative design gained prominence to compensate for the difficulty of writing good software, particularly given the typical programmer skills available to industry.

3.2 Calculators

By considering logic programming, Runciman and HThimbleby introduced an analytic concept, *equal opportunity* [15]. HThimbleby used equal opportunity to constrain the design of a new user interface, choosing a calculator, as this is a well-researched artifact. Background research revealed how conventional calculators were badly designed, an internalist criticism of their poor technology [16]. Somehow this critical observation had escaped externalist research on calculator user interfaces.

We question the point of externalist research when it ignores the *intrinsic failure* of the technology; what point is iterative design or working with users when the conceptual problems of the user interface are so hard, complex and broken? HThimbleby made a technically improved calculator available to the community in 1986. However, it was not till 2004 that it had any externalist evaluation [2]. More recently, WThimbleby generalised the calculator, and made its user interface recognize handwriting [17,18,19]. This calculator has had a modest externalist evaluation [17].

The new calculator was developed entirely by internalist considerations. Specifically, it should do mathematics properly [19]. Few externalist considerations drove its design, yet it is very successful. The calculator was exhibited at Royal Society Summer Science Exhibition, 2005; at the exhibition, several thousand people used it. 90% of respondees said they really liked it or loved it. But despite the unusually large scale of the survey and feedback we gained no new ideas from users that would contribute to iterative design improvements.

Some feedback from users at the exhibition is listed below:

- "It visualizes the internal workings of abstract calculations, fun, as it is wonderful! Fun! Engaging and importantly visible!"—University Professor

- "Calculators seem clumsy and hard to use—the new method is genius!—when can I buy one in the shops (If I had had one I would have done A level maths)"—A–Level Student

- "Engagement, excitement, interactivity, seamless, more visually appealing and easier to use!"—Teacher

- "I've never seen anything that's brought a smile to my face while doing addition, but this has. For that reason alone, I want one!"—Artist

The point we would like to make is that an internalist design program has produced a good user interface, recognized as such by users. Yet by conventional externalist HCI criteria, the work would not be acceptable for publication.

3.3 Graphics Programs

The calculator is an example of an internalist HCI research program, spanning twenty years before it resulted in a user interface that attracted attention. In contrast WThimbleby conceived, designed and built a vector graphics editor within two years, as a purely internalist project.

The resulting program, Lineform, was fully formed on its initial release. No early focus on users, no empirical design, no iterative design [7] informed its development—though of course computer science and HCI principles did inform and direct its development.

The quality of the design was recognized by the award to WThimbleby of the 2005 Apple Student Design Award. Arguably, this shows the user interface design was better than of thousands of others (i.e., the number of competitors)—which, had they been realistically entered into the review, should have been excellent programs in their own right.

Lineform is sold by Freeverse Software and has been commercially successful. The program has been reviewed in commercial magazines and web sites. Its reception has been uniformly favorable.

Below are some sample quotes from reviews. They are included to support the claim that the HCI in Lineform is successful, regardless of its lack of externalist methodology. Like the facts we presented about the calculator, the evidence supports our view that HCI contributions can be good despite the lack of externalist, practices.

- "Lineform from Freeverse Software claims to be the solution for modern drawing and illustration. It is. Winner of a 2006 Apple Design Award, Lineform is not only easy to use, but the interface design makes the application so intuitive, Mac users need no explanation to start illustrating."—*CreativeMac* (Feb 2007)

- "It's not often that you find a product you literally have to gush over ... but Lineform, for me at least, is that product."—*AppleGazette* (Jan 2007)

- "Lineform has two other selling points. First, its speed: the program launches in a couple of seconds and shames Illustrator throughout in its responsiveness. Second, its ease of use. The simple interface alone makes it easier to find things."—*MacUser* (Issue 22 Volume 22)

An internalist design program produced a very good user interface, recognized as excellent by the market and critical reviewers. Yet by conventional externalist HCI criteria, the work would not be acceptable for publication.

3.4 Google

On any measure Google is an extremely successful user interface, with a value to users that exceeds most conventional user interfaces studied in HCI. Google is in fact just a text field with a substantial algorithm behind it [12]: its user interface is successful because it has a good internalist design. First, the

internalist algorithm *then* the user interface. *Once* Google works it *then* makes sense to evaluate it and refine it from an externalist point of view: what services do users want given that Google works, and how can they be made better? However, the original, key HCI innovation was internalist.

Few of the services Google now offers would have made any sense to users or anyone else until after the basic algorithm worked, and had been demonstrated working well. Although externalism is now essential to Google, it was not how it started.

4. SAMPLE ISSUES

4.1 Anecdotes

If Jo is using a system, and this is reported in a research contribution, then an externalist wishes to know in what way Jo is typical of the population and to what extent, if at all, the particular interaction is typical. Jo may be idiosyncratic; the experimenter may have misdirected Jo. If we wish, ultimately, to design better interfaces for anybody other than Jo, we need reliable, generalizable knowledge. Statistics is a good way to characterize reliable generalization, and a one-off experiment with a unique individual would be hard-pressed to be reliable.

From an internalist perspective things look very different. Internal arguments are independent of the user. For example, computability could show that certain tasks are impossible. Not just for Jo, but for *anybody*—impossible for the whole human population, martians, dogs and bacteria. One hardly needs to recruit conventional experimental methods to make such claims reliable. This is not an anecdotal claim, but an analytic claim.

The confusion of these two methodologies undermines communication. It is our experience that internalist papers submitted to journals and conferences have been rejected because the referees have interpreted our analytic descriptions as "anecdotal."

The desire that contributions to HCI must include sufficient (and valid) externalist content before they are acceptable, increases the burden on the internalist researcher. Few researchers are able to span the internal/external bridge; different skills, different theory, different methods are required. Moreover, in the way of things, externalist work can only follow after internal work—or simulate it (e.g., with paper prototyping, which has no internalist content). Perhaps this is *the* gulf of HCI? An internalist has to do twice as much work?

4.2 Reproducibility

The systems mentioned in this paper are fully working systems and can be downloaded by interested researchers (www.freeverse.com/lineform for the graphics program, www.cs.swansea.ac.uk/calculators for the calculator, and labs.google.com for an API). From an internalist perspective, the research these systems embody is reproducible. That is, the claims we make about the quality and design can readily be checked by any interested researchers; because the claims are user independent.

From the perspective of the present paper, of emphasizing internalist HCI, it seems a great advantage that exactly what we have contributed—the underlying science, the programs, and so forth—are completely available to any researchers who wish to build on or critique our work. This level of reproducibility is very rarely the case with externalist HCI research.

4.3 Opposition or complimentarity?

At the BCS HCI 1995 conference, what we would now call an internalist/externalist debate was presented by an externalist in a keynote, metaphorically, as an actual *war*: "Which trench are you shooting from?" [6], illustrated with pictures of carnage. Another keynote at the same conference [8] suggested that "in a nutshell ... what I see is a need to get away from the computer at centre stage, and a need for methods of description that make themselves useful ..." If it's a war, consider [21], which starts off, "If you want to make software developers squirm..." and sets out to create the impression that developers don't know what they are doing. Some don't, no doubt, but most have a hard enough job getting systems to work at all, and they should not be blamed for problems that arise through poor management expectations and requirements that *nobody* understood until their systems were working.

Landauer's *The Trouble with Computers* [11] blames programmers for being "arrogant" (p173)—not designing for users, testing, evaluating, and so on. Programmers have "fantasies" he says. Yet he also mentions that Stu Card "a leading expert in HCI" was "confident" that a new word processor would be "vastly" better—but was proved wrong. Thus he makes rhetorical distinctions whose effects are to discredit the internalist perspective in HCI: internalists are "arrogant" whereas equally wrong externalists are "leading."

We surely need more balanced views, particular as both internalist and externalist share the same goals for the user. A first step in being more balanced is to name the imbalance.

Grudin, one-time editor of the *ACM Transactions on Computer-Human Interaction*, presented a mature view of the diversity of the HCI community [9], based on his experience as editor and final arbiter between conflicting referee and author points of view. A non-partisan view is [20], which argues how easy it is for differences to escalate to unconstructive conflict.

5. CONCLUSIONS

This paper has proposed a distinction between externalist and internalist approaches to HCI. The distinction helps clarify the nature of HCI research and practice, as well as preferred approaches within the HCI research community.

This paper described a selection of very different products of internalist HCI. None have been developed through or supported research that would have met conventional externalist HCI criteria, indeed none followed any recommended externalist HCI development cycles—yet all are successful. Of course the systems beg a wide range of externalist questions, but the fact that one can now do externalist work does not mean it was necessary to do it for the overall work to form a valid contribution to HCI.

Our purpose is not to dismiss externalist approaches, but to recognize that an internalist approach to HCI can be very effective and lead to good user interface design. Internalist design and research can be valid without any externalist evaluation.

Given that the computer science community argues that design should start with a mathematically rigorous specification, and then refine to implementation—almost the opposite of the externalist HCI view of design—there are new questions to be asked. Can internalist approaches lead to quality HCI, and if so, to what extent and under what assumptions? This paper has shown that internalist HCI can. We need to see more internally-driven HCI, and we need to explore when and why it is successful.

6. REFERENCES

[1] Barnard, P., May, J., Duke, D. & Duce, D., systems, Interactions, and Macrotheory, *ACM Transactions on Computer-Human Interaction*, **7**(2):222–262, 2000.

[2] Cairns, P., Thimbleby, H. & Wali, S., Evaluating a Novel Calculator Interface, *Proceedings BCS HCI Conference*, **2**:9–12, 2004.

[3] Carroll, J. M., Introduction: The Kittle House Manifesto, *Designing Interaction*, J. M. Carroll, ed., pp1–16, Cambridge University Press, 1991.

[4] Carroll, J. M., ed., *HCI Models Theories and Frameworks*, Morgan Kaufmann, 2003.

[5] Cockburn, A. & Bell, T., Extending HCI in the Computer Science Curriculum, ACM International Conference Proceeding Series, **3**, *Proceedings of the 3rd Australasian conference on Computer Science Education*, 113–120, 1998.

[6] Gasen, J. B., Support for HCI Educators: A View from the Trenches, Proceedings BCS HCI Conference, 21–36, 1995.

[7] Gould, J. D. & Lewis, C., Designing for usability: key principles and what designers think, *Communications of the ACM*, **28**(3):300–311, 1985.

[8] Green, T. R. G., Looking Through HCI, Proceedings BCS HCI Conference, 21–36, 1995.

[9] Grudin, J. "Crossing the Divide," *ACM Transactions on Computer-Human Interaction*, **11**(1):1-25, 2004.

[10] Kidder, T., *The Soul Of A New Machine*, Back Bay Books, 2000.

[11] Landauer, T., *The Trouble with Computers*, MIT Press, 1995.

[12] Langville, A. N., Meyer, C. D., *Google's PageRank and Beyond*, Princeton, 2006.

[13] Lewis, C., Inner and Outer Theory in HCI, in *Designing Interaction*, J. M. Carroll, ed., pp154–161, Cambridge University Press, 1991.

[14] Nye, D. E., *Technology Matters*, MIT Press, 2006.

[15] Thimbleby, H. & Runciman, C., Equal Opportunity Interactive Systems, *International Journal of Man-Machine Studies*, **25**(4):439–451, 1986.

[16] Thimbleby, H. Calculators are Needlessly Bad, *International Journal of Human-Computer Studies*, **52**(6):1031–1069, 2000.

[17] Thimbleby, W., A novel pen-based calculator and its evaluation, *Proceedings ACM Nordic Conference on Human-Computer interaction*, 445–448, 2004.

[18] Thimbleby, W. & Thimbleby, H., A Novel Gesture-Based Calculator and Its Design Principles, *Proceedings BCS HCI Conference*, **2**:27–32, 2005.

[19] Thimbleby, H. & Thimbleby, W., Mathematical Mathematical User Interfaces, *DSVIS 2007*, in press.

[20] Thimbleby, H., Supporting Diverse HCI Research, *Proceedings BCS HCI Conference*, **2**:125–128, 2004.

[21] Udell, J., Capturing user experience closes the feedback loop, *InfoWorld*, www.infoworld.com/article/04/06/04/23FEuser_1.html 2004.

Acknowledgements. Thanks to Ann Blandford, Richard Harper and Matt Jones.

Designing Educational Software Inline with the Creative Learning Process: Just how Important is the Preparation Phase?

Sylvia M. Truman
Knowledge Media Institute
The Open University
Milton Keynes, MK7 6AA
+44 (0)1908 645771

s.m.truman@open.ac.uk

ABSTRACT

A question gaining widespread interest in education today is 'how can learning tasks be structured to encourage creative thinking in the classroom?' This has a number of implications for the design of educational software. Numerous scholars have suggested that the processes of 'learning' and 'creativity' share many similarities. Extending upon this a generative framework of creative learning is presented here. This framework exists as a design support tool to aid the design of educational software. In order to demonstrate how this framework can be applied in practice, a music composition program called 'SoundScape' has been developed in accordance with the framework. This paper reports upon study conducted with SoundScape within a school with 96 children aged 11. The study focused upon two objectives, firstly, identifying differences in explicitly supporting the "preparation" phase of the creative process as opposed to not explicitly supporting the "preparation" phase. Secondly, the study compared differences in using real-world metaphors at the interface compared to using visual abstract representations at the interface.

General Terms

Design, Theory, Verification.

Keywords

Constructivist learning theory, constructionism, creativity, collaboration, music learning

1. INTRODUCTION

This paper emphasises the importance of designing educational technology inline with the creative process. In particular this paper focuses upon the importance of designing technology to explicitly support the 'preparation phase' of the creative process. In order to investigate this, this paper reports upon a study using the music composition program SoundScape. The design of SoundScape was guided by the generative framework

of creative learning [1]. This paper reports upon the findings of the study.

2. THEORETICAL BACKGROUND: CREATIVIY & REPRESENTING MUSIC

2.1 The creative process

Wallas (1926) formalised the four stage model, representing the creative process [2]. This model consists of four stages; preparation, incubation, illumination and verification. Preparation concerns immersing one's self within a domain and developing a curiosity about a particular problem [3]. At this stage, an individual will also consciously accumulate knowledge and draw upon influences from previous experience. During the incubation stage, conscious thought pertaining to the problem is rested and left to the unconscious mind [4]. Illumination occurs when one experiences a sudden flash of insight [5]. Finally, verification concerns forming judgements pertaining to the creative artefact produced. A number of scholars have continued to apply the four stage model as a basis for understanding creativity [6] [7], while others have extended upon it [8] [9].

2.2 Specifying musical representations

Visual imagery is widely acknowledged as a crucial element of creative thinking [10], therefore, it is common sense to incorporate visual imagery into the design of creative learning environments. In relation to music composition software, music has been typically specified using staff notation. However, more recent studies into musical representations have reported that music notation may act as an inhibitor of musical creativity [11] [12] [13] [14], owing to the mis-match between the sound properties of music and the visual specification of staff notation.

3. A generative framework for creative learning

Drawing on the above, a framework which represents a distillation of creativity theory is presented, focusing upon education. This framework is presented in the form of a generative framework, which exists as a design support tool to assist the design of creative educational experiences for the classroom (see figure 1). Wallas's four-stage model has been adapted as the fundamental basis for this framework, with the processes of preparation, generation and evaluation represented laterally across the framework. The vertical dimensions reflect individual (denoted here as personal) and social components of creativity. The 'social' level refers to others, peers and society. Whereas, 'personal' levels reflect explicit and tacit levels of thinking.

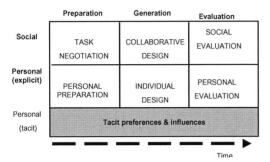

Figure 1. A generative framework for creative learning

With regard to figure 1, the processes of preparation, generation and evaluation are three integral concepts of the creative process. Every creative act involves the preparation of ideas. At a personal level, an individual will develop a curiosity or a desire to create. Once this desire has been established, information is consciously accumulated from the external environment and thoughts may be discussed with others on a 'social' level which the individual can reflect upon. If working in a collaborative setting, group-wide negotiations of the task will also take place. Inevitably, the way in which an individual prepares for the task will be influenced by their past experiences [15].

The generation process of the framework encompasses social and personal design. Within this process ideas are generated which can involve negotiation between the individual and peers in their environment. Additionally, idea generation is assisted partly by a continuous dialogue which occurs between conscious thought at the personal explicit level and sub-conscious processing at the tacit level. The evaluation process concerns reviewing early creative ideas through to evaluating the final artefact. Evaluation may occur at a personal level, or at a wider (community) level. It is emphasised that the framework does not commit to a strict linear route, rather the creative process is cyclic in nature. Therefore, the review of creative ideas may result in a need to revise ideas which may result in further preparation, or evaluation or further generation and so on. The processes of the framework are not mutually exclusive, as in some instances processes within the framework may overlap. The framework can be used as a design support tool to facilitate creative thinking in the classroom by ensuring that preparatory materials are scaffolded to the six component boxes of the framework.

4. RESEARCH QUESTIONS & PLANNING THE STUDY

Extending upon the theoretical background and the generative framework, two questions were raised. Firstly, what different outcomes may arise when the software explicitly supports / does not support the preparation phase? Secondly, what different outcomes may arise when real-world metaphors are used to specify music as opposed to abstract representations? In order to investigate these questions, four different prototypes of SoundScape were designed.

4.1 SoundScape prototypes

With prototype one, students prepare for the task by specifying their 'composition' object by associating real-world metaphors with pre-recorded music samples. After creating eight objects students then progress to the composition screen whereby objects are placed on the composition background using drag and drop functionality (see figure 2). This prototype has been designed to explicitly support preparation whilst using real-world metaphors to specify music. With Prototype two, preparation is not explicitly supported and students enter the program at the generation phase (i.e. composition screen) and create a composition using pre-selected objects. Prototype three uses abstract representations to specify music, similar to those used in off the shelf programs such as the E-Jay range. Preparation is supported by allowing students to select eight music samples to use for their composition. After selecting eight music samples students progress to the composition screen and place the objects on the screen using drag and drop functionality (see figure 3). Prototype four does not support preparation and students enter the program at the composition screen using pre-selected objects which are abstract representations of music is with prototype three.

Figure 2. Screen shots of prototypes 1 and 2

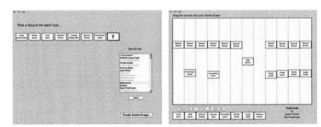

Figure 3. Screen shots of prototypes 3 and 4

4.2 Experimental conditions

In order to investigate the research questions, each prototype was assigned to one of four experimental conditions as show in table 1. Ninety six school children participated with the study, all eleven years of age. Twenty four participants were allocated to each of the conditions, with twelve pairs of students in each condition. The study conducted with one pair at a time to allow participants to work free from distraction. Prior to interacting with SoundScape, participants were instructed: "working as a pair, create a piece of music using SoundScape. There is no right or wrong way of carrying out this task. Spend as long as necessary until you feel you have completed the task.

Table 1. Experimental conditions used in study

CONDITION	PREPARATION SUPPORT?	REPRESENTATION USED
V-P	Yes	Visual metaphor
V-NP	No	Visual metaphor
NV-P	Yes	Abstract representation
NV-NP	No	Abstract representation

Data was collected during the participant's session both by the program and behaviour analysis. Outcomes of the study are now discussed in terms of: time on task, manipulation of composition objects used, and points of pair-wise discussion.

5. RESEARCH FINDINGS ARISING FROM THE STUDY

Outcomes were compared across the four conditions in terms of the time spent on the composition task, the number of composition objects moved during the session, the number of musical bars used, the number of the eight available objects used, the number of discussion points made about individual sound samples, the number of discussion points made about individual pictures, and the number of discussion points made about mapping (i.e. the association between the music samples and pictures).

5.1 Time on task

Results indicate that those working within preparation conditions V-P and NV-P spent significantly longer on the task than those in non-preparation conditions V-NP and NV-NP. Findings also indicate that those working with visual metaphors to specify music (i.e. V-P and V-NP) spent significantly longer on the task than those using abstract representations (i.e. NV-P and NV-NP).

5.2 Object manipulations

Results indicate that those using visual metaphors moved significantly more objects than those using an abstract representation to specify music. No significant differences were reported between preparation and non-preparation conditions. Those using visual metaphors to specify music used significantly more musical bars than those using abstract representations. Again, no significant differences were reported when comparing preparation and non-preparation conditions. With regard to the number of the eight available composition objects used, those using visual metaphors to specify music used significantly more of the 8 objects than those using abstract representations. When comparing preparation and non-preparation conditions, those working within the preparation conditions used significantly more of the 8 objects.

5.3 Pair wise discussion points

In terms of discussions that took place within the pairs as student worked on their compositions, results indicate that those using the abstract representation to specify music made significantly more sound comments than those using visual metaphors. No significant differences were identified when comparing preparation and non-preparation conditions. With regard to discussion points concerning individual pictures (i.e. metaphors used), those within the preparation condition (V-P) made significantly more comments concerning pictures as opposed to those within the non-preparation condition (V-NP). With regard to mapping discussion points, those in the preparation condition (V-P) made significantly more mapping

discussion points than those within the non-preparation condition (V-NP). These findings are summarised in table 2.

Table 2. Summary of findings

OUTCOME	TASK SUPPORT	REPRESENTATION
Time on task	Those in preparation conditions spent longer on the task.	Those in visual metaphor conditions spent longer on the task.
No. of composition objects moved	No significant differences.	Those in visual metaphor conditions moved more objects.
No. of available bars used	No significant differences.	Those in visual metaphor conditions used more of the musical bars.
No. of eight composition objects used	Those in preparation conditions used more of the eight available objects.	Those in visual metaphor conditions used more of the eight objects.
No. of sound discussion points	No significant differences.	Those in abstract representation conditions made more sound comments.
No. of picture discussion point	Those in the preparation condition made more picture comments.	N/A
No. of mapping discussion points	Those in the preparation condition made more mapping comments.	N/A

6. CONCLUSIONS: PULLING THE THREADS TOGETHER

In answer to original question: *"How can learning tasks be structured to encourage creative thinking in the classroom"?* This study has attempted to provide a solution through the presentation of the generative framework.

The design of educational technologies can be assisted by this framework, which can be applied to differing domains of the curriculum. This paper has also demonstrated the application of the framework in practice through the music composition program SoundScape which has been used as a vehicle through which to address the research questions. Outcomes of the study suggest that preparation is a crucial element of the creative process and that supporting task preparation during system design can help to encourage creative thinking. Outcomes also suggest that the use of visual imagery is a useful tool for learning, especially where imagery used is consistent with real-world artefacts.

7. ACKONWLEDGEMENTS

The author acknowledges and extends appreciation to Ben Hawkridge (Knowledge Media Institute, The Open University) for his assistance with developing the SoundScape program.

8. REFERENCES

[1] Truman, S.M & Mulholland, P. Designing educational software to enhance the creative learning experience: An integrative framework. In *Proceedings of HCI 2006 Engage*. 11th – 15th September. Queen Mary, University of London, 2006

[2] Wallas, The Art of Thought. Jonathan Cape [republished in 1931]. London. 1926

[3] Getzels J.W. Creative Thinking, Problem-Solving, and Instruction. In E.R. Hilgard (Ed), Theories of Learning and Instruction. University of Chicago Press. Chicago. 1964

[4] Claxton, Hare Brain Tortoise Mind: Why Intelligence Increases When you Think Less. Fourth Estate Limited. London. 1998

[5] Poincare (1913) in Leytham, G (1990) Managing Creativity. Peter Francis Publishers. Norfolk.

[6] Osche R. Before the Gates of Excellence: The Determinants of Creative Genius. Cambridge University Press. 1990

[7] Goswami A. Creativity and the quantum: A unified theory of creativity. Creativity Research Journal. 9. p 47 – 61. 1996

[8] Amabile T.M. Creativity in Context. Westview. Boulder, CO. 1996

[9] Runco M.A & Dow, G Problem Finding. In Runco, M.A & Pritzker, S.R (Eds) Encyclopedia of Creativity. (Vol. 2). P 433 – 435. Academic Press. San Diego. 1999

[10] Gruber H. E. & Wallace, D. B The case study method and evolving systems approach for understanding unique creative people at work. In Sternberg, R. J (Ed) *Handbook of Creativity*. pp 93 – 115. Cambridge UK; Cambridge University Press. 1999

[11] Walker R. Auditory-visual perception and musical behaviour. In Colwell, R. (Ed) *Handbook of Research on Music Teaching and Learning*. New York; Schirmer Books. 1992

[12] Auh M. Prediction of musical creativity in composition amongst selected variables for upper elementary students. (Doctoral Dissertation, Case Western Reserve University, Cleveland, Ohio, USA, 1995). *Dissertation Abstracts International*. 56, 3875A. 1996

[13] Auh M. Prediction of musical creativity in composition among selected variables for upper elementary students. *Bulletin of the Council for Research in Music Education, 133*, 1-8. 1997

[14] Auh M. Effects of using graphic notations on creativity in composing music by Australian secondary school students. *Proceedings of the Australian Association for Research in Education Conference*. Australia 2000.

[15] Schank R. What we Learn when we Learn by Doing. *Technical report* Northwestern University, Institute for Learning sciences. 1995

Is an Apology Enough? How to Resolve Trust Breakdowns in Episodic Online Interactions

Asimina Vasalou

Electrical and Electronic Engineering
Imperial College
SW7 2BT, London, United Kingdom
a.vasalou@imperial.ac.uk

Astrid Hopfensitz

Swiss Center for Affective Sciences
University of Geneva
1205, Geneva, Switzerland
astrid.hopfensitz@cisa.unige.ch

Jeremy Pitt

Electrical and Electronic Engineering
Imperial College
SW7 2BT, London, United Kingdom
j.pitt@imperial.ac.uk

ABSTRACT

This paper addresses what kind of system allows the victim of a trust breakdown to fairly assess an unintentional offender who is also a benevolent member. Two systems were compared: a system that displayed the offender's unblemished reputation score as obtained in previous interactions with other members, and a system that also had a communication channel which displayed the offender's expressed apology and regret over the offence. The findings of this study suggest that the system which also endorses apology, as well as records reputation, allows the victim to recover his/her trust in the unintentional offender. However, trust is repaired only when the offender validates the apology with a reparative action.

Categories and Subject Descriptors

H1. Models and Principles: User/Machine Systems

General Terms

Design, Economics, Experimentation.

Keywords

Apology, Forgiveness, Trust, Reputation, Repair.

1. INTRODUCTION

Researchers have considered anti-normative behaviour in computer-mediated communication (CMC) from two different angles. One stream of research has been concerned with how to engender trust, thus preventing trust breakdowns. For instance, it has been shown that when placed in a social dilemma, members are more likely to cooperate with others over rich media such as video or audio as opposed to being pseudonymous [1]. In online auctioning, buyers can choose which sellers to trust with a transaction on the basis of sellers' historical behaviour as captured by reputation systems [6]. Media theorists on the other hand, have researched trust breakdowns usually by regarding the offender's behaviour as a frequent and intentional act. For example, "trolls" are seemingly genuine members who often post taunting messages in newsgroup forums, in truth meant to spark disputes by challenging the group's beliefs [2]. In this paper we identify a topic that has not been accounted for in these two existing approaches: a trust breakdown may occur as a result of an *unintentional* offence of an otherwise *benevolent* member of the

community. In everyday life, such offences are inevitable but not unforgivable. Apologies for one can evoke empathy towards the offender and in turn facilitate the process of forgiveness [4]. But in anonymous, episodic interactions which are part of many online settings the resolution of such offences can become increasingly complex. This is partly because the narrow timeframe of each interaction combined with the impoverished communication channel constrict the cues of trustworthiness one can acquire on another member (e.g. identity, integrity, willingness to comply to institutions, benevolence; [8]). At the onset, this establishes interactions that are perceived as more risky, thus building barriers that may stand in the way of resolution if trust breaks down. Even more, reputation systems which have been widely employed to sustain trust in episodic interactions are not necessarily able to repair trust. Reputation systems convey members' ability and performance, hence all the rational reasons for initiating a transaction in an online auction or for accepting a member's advice in an online forum. Yet, when trust breaks down, it is not known if a static reputation score can motivate the victim of an offence to forgive, while at the same time indicating the offender's good intention and willingness to repair. In a recent effort to address this problem, eBay launched a feature called the "mutual feedback withdrawal" by which users can contest the reputation score they received. Only if both the victim and the offender agree to engage in this process, the resolution of the issue is taken offline. Later, the victim may retract and improve the offender's online reputation score. At heart, eBay offers an online offender an outlet through which to apologize, elaborate on his/her intentions and repair, subsequently allowing the victim of the offence to restore the trust by removing the original low reputation rating.

This paper contrasts a reputation system to a reputation system that also includes an apology channel, parallel to the eBay approach. The aim of this research is to reveal which of the two systems may motivate the victim of a trust breakdown to forgive and once again to trust an unintentional and infrequent offender during a episodic interaction.

2. A DEFINITION OF TRUST FOR CMC

The work presented in this paper was informed by a definition of trust proposed by [7][8]. This definition describes trust in CMC as an *asymmetric* and *asynchronous* relationship between two parties, the trustor and the trustee. Asymmetry results as the trustor only assumes risk in anticipation of an asynchronous fulfilment from the trustee. This relationship can be broken down into two sequential moves. In the first move, the trustor assesses the trustee's perceived trustworthiness. On the basis of this judgment, the trustor may or may not decide to take some risk over an interaction that can have an uncertain outcome. From his part, the trustee, who is the second mover, may either fulfil or violate the first mover's trust. This high level definition applies to numerous online interactions each of which may present different types of risk. For example, members of online emotional support forums post private information expecting empathy in return. In online auctioning, buyers pay before receiving the goods.

3. STUDY

3.1 Overview

The study conducted captured the asynchronous and asymmetric definition of trust with the trust game [7] which has been used as a research paradigm in previous CMC studies (e.g. [9]). The trust game assigns one player to be first mover (trustor) while a second player is the second mover (trustee). The payoffs of the game we used were taken from [3]. The first mover starts with 150 points, 50 points more than the second mover. The first mover may choose to transfer his extra 50 points to the second mover or to withdraw from the risk. If the first mover transfers the points, they are multiplied by 6 before they are given to the second mover. The second mover has the option to confirm the first mover's trust by sharing the fair half of the gains (cooperate), or to keep the full amount (defect). Figure 1 displays the players' moves and the possible payoffs.

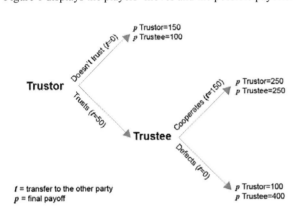

Figure 1. Trust game dilemma.

This research aimed at investigating which of two mechanisms (reputation or reputation with apology) was most effective for resolving and alleviating a trust breakdown (defection in the trust game). The offender (trustee) was a member with an unblemished historical track, who breached the norm (defected in the game) as a result of an error, experiencing and expressing regret thereafter. In exploring this particular scenario, it was important to retain control over the offender's profile across the two treatments. Thus, trustees were simulated in this study and participants were always assigned to the trustor's role.

We expected two main outcomes, the first related to forgiveness and the second concerned with the restoration of trust. Firstly, apology has been shown to predict forgiveness by evoking the victim's empathy for the offender [4]. As such, participants who viewed the offender's apology online were expected to report increased forgiveness towards him/her as compared to participants viewing the offender's reputation score only (Hypothesis 1). In the second set of outcomes we expected that participants, who had viewed the offender's apology and had presumably forgiven the offender, would once again trust the offender. Trust was indirectly measured by reputation and cooperation. In online auctioning, users trust members whose reputations are high [6]. This finding was inversed and applied to the case of trust restoration. If participants' trust in the offender is repaired, they should give the offender higher reputation scores directly after the offence and also in any future interactions (Hypothesis 2). Furthermore,

it has been shown that members whose trust in others is high are more likely to cooperate with them [1]. Therefore, participants whose trust in the offender has been restored should be more willing to cooperate with the offender given a future interaction (Hypothesis 3).

3.2 Participants and Procedure

An email announcement for participation was sent across four different departments of a UK university promising monetary reward. In total, forty-two participants responded and took part in this study. It was made clear in the announcement that proficiency in English was a requirement for attending. All participants were enrolled in undergraduate studies and were between 18 and 24 years of age.

Participants arrived in three groups of twenty-one. They were then taken to a quiet room and each one of them seated by a computer. None of the participants faced one another and it was ensured they could not see each others' screens. The trust game was played using a web-based application. In making the game appear believable, participants were led to believe they were assigned to either first movers (trustor) or second movers (trustee) by a random draw. However, participants were always first movers and faced the dilemma of trusting the second mover by giving the 50 points or withdrawing from the risk involved by keeping the 50 points. The second mover was always simulated in each round with a new non-gender indicative pseudonym. Participants were instructed that in each round they were playing with a new remote player from the University of Geneva. To avoid end-game effects (i.e. decreased trust in the final rounds of the game), usually observed in these kinds of games (e.g. [1]), participants were told they would randomly play up to 10 rounds of the game. After each round, an onscreen notification informed them whether they would proceed to the next round. In the experiment, the rounds played were set to six rounds in total.

A "starred" reputation system was embedded in the trust game application; one star signalled the lowest reputation score obtainable and five stars the highest. The stars summarise the mean of reputation scores received in previous transactions, similar to the Amazon auctioning reputation system [6]. Second movers' reputation scores in each round were simulated and held constant for all participants; however participants were instructed that reputation scores were calculated on the basis of other players' ratings and were constantly updated. The same reputation mechanism was made available to participants for rating the second mover, whenever they made the initial trust move.

In the first four rounds of the game participants played with a different simulated second mover. To make the second movers believable, each one displayed a different reputation score ranging from two, the lowest, to five, the highest; the second mover of round one had no reputation score displayed since he had not been previously rated. During the first four rounds, if trusted, the second movers always reciprocated the initial trust move by returning the fair amount. In round 5, the second mover for the first time betrayed the participant's trust by returning nothing. At this stage, participants received one of two treatments: reputation or reputation with apology (see Section 3.3). At the end of round 5, participants were asked to assign a reputation score to the second mover. Immediately after, they filled out a questionnaire measuring forgiveness. At the beginning of round 6, participants were informed they were randomly assigned to the same player again, i.e. to the offender of round 5. The reputation score given to the offender in round

5 by the participant, was averaged into the second mover's displayed reputation in round 6. If trusted with the initial 50 points, the second mover repaired the trust breakdown by returning the fair half of the gains. At the end of round 6, those participants who had made the initial trust move were asked to assign a reputation score to the second mover. The game ended after round 6. Participants received their earnings calculated from the points earned, one point equalling 0.5 pence, with an average of £7.50 per participant. To investigate treatment effects on forgiveness and trust restoration, we will discuss measures from the offence (round 5) and the subsequent interaction (round 6).

3.3 Experimental Design

Following the trusted offender's defection in round 5, forty participants received one of two treatments; two participants did not make the initial trust move in round 5 and were omitted from the data.

- **Reputation** (N=20) — in round 5, a reputation score of 5 stars demonstrated the offender's good standing in previous interactions with other players.
- **Apology** (N=20) — this treatment was identical to the reputation treatment. In addition, a written apology from the offender was simulated. The apology read: "Hey [first mover ID]. I am sorry for transferring nothing back. I accidentally clicked on zero absentmindedly - realised it when it was too late. Sorry! I promise I will be more careful next time."

Three measures were collected:

- **Cooperation** — in the round after the offender's defection (round 6) participants had the choice to trust the offender with the initial 50 or to keep the points and withdraw from the interaction. Cooperation was assigned a "1" if participants chose to trust and "0" if they didn't.
- **Reputation score** — directly after the offence (round 5) and after the subsequent interaction (round 6) participants rated the offender with a reputation score ranging from 1 (low) to 9 (high). If participants withheld the 50 points in round 6, we assumed that their judgment, and thus reputation score stayed constant and use the value from round 5 in the analysis.
- **Forgiveness** — to our knowledge there was no forgiveness measure available for episodic interactions such as those concerned in this research. Therefore, forgiveness was measured with an adapted version of the twelve-item questionnaire, "transgression-related interpersonal motivations inventory" (TRIM). TRIM was originally designed to evaluate forgiveness in interpersonal relationships [4]. The first five questions measure revenge towards the offender and the remaining seven questions measure avoidance. Higher scores of revenge and avoidance indicate lower levels of forgiveness. The questions were extended to reflect the tone of episodic interactions. For example, the question 'I keep as much distance between us as possible' was reformulated to 'if I were to play with him/her again, I would keep as much distance between us as possible'. Each item was rated on a scale of 1 (strongly disagree) to 5 (strongly agree).

4. RESULTS
4.1 Validation of forgiveness measure

A principle component analysis of the modified twelve-point forgiveness questionnaire showed two factors with Eigenvalues greater than 1.0, presumably one for revenge and one for

avoidance. An examination of the communalities table (Varimax rotation) suggested that four items be omitted as they loaded on both factors (>0.4). The remaining items all met the threshold criteria of 0.4 on one of the two factors. The final eight-point questionnaire consisted of four questions measuring revenge and four questions measuring avoidance (Appendix A).

4.2 Analysis

A multivariate analysis was performed with condition as a factor (reputation or apology) on the following measures: reputation score after round 5, reputation score after round 6, cooperation and forgiveness. Table 1 summarises the results.

	Condition N=20	M	SD
Cooperation	Reputation	0.70	0.47
	Apology	1.00	0.00
Forgiveness	Reputation	25.65	7.47
	Apology	23.10	7.39
Reputation score after round 5	Reputation	1.90	1.68
	Apology	2.95	2.08
Reputation score after round 6	Reputation	4.20	3.20
	Apology	6.70	2.20

Table 1. Summary of results.

The main effect of condition (reputation, apology) was non-significant (F (4, 35) = 2.48, $p>0.05$). After round 5, participants completed a measure of forgiveness. Participants in the apology condition as compared to those in the reputation condition did not report more forgiveness (F (1, 38) = 1.17, $p>0.05$). The first hypothesis was not supported. After the offender's defection in round 5, participants in the apology condition gave reputation scores to the offender that were not significantly higher than the scores given by participants in the reputation condition. However, the trend was in the predicted direction (F (1, 38) = 3.06, $p=0.09$). In round 6, once the offender had shared the fair half of the gains, participants of the apology (F (1, 38) = 8.26, $p<0.01$) condition assigned significantly higher reputation scores to the offender as compared to participants of the reputation condition. The second hypothesis was partly confirmed: participants who received an apology assigned higher reputation scores but only after round 6 when the offender had cooperated. Finally, in support of the third hypothesis, in round 6, participants in the apology condition made the initial trust move by transferring the 50 points more frequently than participants in the reputation condition (F (1, 38) = 8.14, $p<0.01$).

5. DISCUSSION

Participants, who viewed the offender's reputation score only, compared to those who also received an apology, demonstrated lower trusting behaviours towards the offender. The offender's displayed reputation score in the round previous to the offence was the highest obtainable, thus signalling the offender's prior benevolence to others. This, in combination with the offender's gesture to return the fair amount in round 6 did not express the offender's low intention when defecting and high intention when repairing. As a result, participants' trust in the offender was not restored. This can be seen by the low reputation scores participants assigned after the offender's return of the fair amount in round 6. Even more, participants of the reputation condition frequently withheld the initial trust move in the round after the offence. The risk involved in the trust move was only

25 pence. Hence, it appears plausible that some participants withdrew from the transaction as a consequence of retaliation rather than only due to a lack of trust. These conclusions taken together suggest that a victim's trust in an unintentional offender cannot be restored with a reputation system only, while misattributions may be made that lead to retribution.

This study further compared the reputation system to a system that also displayed the offender's apology to the victim. We anticipated that the latter, would elicit higher degrees of forgiveness and an increase in trust for the offender. The results found partly confirmed this prediction. When viewing an apology from the offender directly after the offence, participants did not immediately report increased forgiveness. Similarly, participants' trust towards the offender was not restored; this can be seen in the low reputation scores they assigned. By contrast, in round 6, the offender's apology, as compared to viewing the offender's impeccable reputation score only, motivated victims to always cooperate with the initial trust move. After round 6, when the offender had corroborated his/her apology with the reparative move, participants in the apology condition assigned higher reputation scores than those who had not viewed the apology. Given the apparent restoration of trust in round 6, we postulate that participants also forgave the offender; retrospectively, the forgiveness measure should have been included also after round 6. Nonetheless, this research does not give a clear answer on why the offender's apology did not repair the offence directly after it occurred in round 5. Was it due to the lack of a prior history between the two parties? Or was it because of the lack of non-verbal cues online, e.g. blush, which make it more difficult to discriminate between a truthful account and one that is deceitful? In summary, it appears that online apologies can restore trust but only when the offender has acted on his/her words of regret. In this sense, the eBay "mutual feedback withdrawal" forum prompts both parties to sustain the interaction, thus allowing the offender to repair his or her actions which in turn can restore the victim's trust. However, this approach does not shield both parties from the initial dismay resulting from the offence. On the one hand, the victim may feel deceived and thus experience anger towards the offender. Conversely, the offender may also experience anger due to the unjust low rating. In a panel of users collected before the introduction of the "mutual feedback withdrawal" feature, eBay sellers who received negative feedback were 25% less likely to post new products than sellers with only positive feedback; this effect was attributed to users' feelings of injustice when receiving an unfair punishment [4]. This short paper does not undertake the task to propose specific solutions that address this issue. It is important though to note that [10] have investigated ways for proactively facilitating forgiveness in social systems.

To conclude, this work set its focus on understanding whether reputation systems are able to repair trust as well as they sustain it and furthermore, whether apologies as given online are sufficient to motivate repair. As expected, it was found that reputation systems cannot repair trust breakdowns. By contrast, an apology from the offender restored the victim's trust, although only after the offender had proven his/her intent by correcting his/her future behaviour. We end this discussion with some open questions for social system designers. Is it always feasible for a benevolent member who has unintentionally transgressed a norm to repair his/her actions? If not, should systems take upon themselves the role to resolve the trust breakdown? Furthermore, should social systems allow for the

unfair punishment of a benevolent member or should the system safeguard such a member in the first place?

6. APPENDIX A
"I wish that something bad will happen to him/her in the game", "I want him/her to get what he/she deserves in the game", "If I get the opportunity in the game, I'm going to get even", "I would like to see him/her hurt and miserable in the game", "If I play with her/him again, I will pretend like he/she doesn't exist, isn't around", "If I play with her/him again, I will avoid him/her", "If I play with her/him again, I will cut off the relationship", "If I play with her/him again, I will withdraw from him/her".

7. ACKNOWLEDGMENTS
Jens Riegelsberger (Google) is acknowledged for his comments on an earlier draft of this paper. We thank Amjad Hanif (eBay) for his advice on the eBay system. We further acknowledge Arvind Bhusate, Tom Carlson and Daniel Ramirez who assisted in the experiment. This research was funded by the HUMAINE Network of Excellence.

8. REFERENCES
[1] Bos, N., Olson, J. S., Olson, G. M., Wright, Z. and Gergle, D. Rich media helps trust development. In *proceedings of the SIGCHI conference on Human Factors in Computing Systems* (CHI2002) (Minneapolis, Minnesota, 2002), ACM Press, New York, NY, 2002, 135-140.
[2] Donath, J. Identity and Deception in the Virtual Community. In M. Smith and P. Kollock (eds.) *Communities in Cyberspace*. London, Routledge, 1998.
[3] Hopfensitz, A. and Reuben, E. The importance of emotions for the effectiveness of social punishment. *Discussion Paper TI 2005-075/1*, Tinbergen Institute, 2005.
[4] Khopkar, T., Li, X. and Resnick, P. Self-Selection, Slipping, Salvaging, Slacking, and Stoning: the Impacts of Negative Feedback at eBay. In *proceedings of the ACM Conference on Electronic Commerce (EC 05)* (Vancouver, Canada, 2005), ACM Press, New York, NY, 2005, 223-231.
[5] McCullough, M. E., Rachal, K. C., Sandage, S. J., Worthington, E. L., Jr., Wade-Brown, S. and Hight, T. Interpersonal forgiving in close relationships II: Theoretical elaboration and measurement. *Journal of Personality and Social Psychology*, 75 (1998), 1586-1603.
[6] Resnick, P., Zeckhauser, R., Friedman, E. and Kuwabara, K. Reputation Systems. *Communications of the ACM*, 43, 12 (2000), 45-58.
[7] Riegelsberger, J., Sasse, M.A. and McCarthy, J.D. The researcher's dilemma: evaluating trust in computer-mediated communication. *International Journal of Human-Computer Studies*, 58, 6 (2003), 759-781.
[8] Riegelsberger, J., Sasse, M.A. and McCarthy, J.D. The mechanics of trust: a framework for research and design. *International Journal of Human-Computer Studies*, 62, 3 (2005), 381-422.
[9] Vasalou, A., Joinson, A. and Pitt, J. The role of shame, guilt and embarrassment in online social dilemmas. In *proceedings of the British HCI Conference (HCI 2006)* (London, UK, 2006), 108-112.
[10] Vasalou, A., Pitt, J. and Piolle, G. From theory to practice: offering forgiveness as a way to repair online conflicts in CMC. In *proceedings of the iTrust conference* (Pisa, Italy, 2006) Springer, Berlin/ Heidelberg, 397-411.

Use Study on a Home Video Editing System

Hans Weda
Philips Research Europe
High Tech Campus 34
5656 AE Eindhoven, The Netherlands
+31 40 2747939

hans.weda@philips.com

Marco Campanella
Philips Research Europe
High Tech Campus 34
5656 AE Eindhoven, The Netherlands
+31 40 2747899

marco.campanella@philips.com

ABSTRACT

To help consumers dealing with their growing amount of home video, we have developed the Edit While Watching (EWW) system. It is designed to automatically create an edited version of a home video and then allow the users to modify and refine it in an easy, intuitive and lean-back way. To measure the ease of use, ease of learning, and effectiveness of the EWW system, we have performed a use test by means of giving participants tasks to do and interviewing them. The use test was focused on four main aspects: functionality, usability, pleasantness, and user satisfaction. The test was performed with eight participants, and was located in the Philips HomeLab, which resembles a home environment as much as possible. The results show that the system provides rather limited control of the editing functions, and the overview of the video material is unsatisfactory. However, the participants judged the system as an easy to learn and easy to use video editing tool. They expressed their pleasure in working with it.

Categories and Subject Descriptors

H.5.2 [**Information Interfaces and Presentation**]: User Interfaces – *User-centered design, evaluation/methodology.*

General Terms

Design, Experimentation, Human Factors, Verification.

Keywords

Intelligent user interfaces, user experience evaluation, home video editing.

1. INTRODUCTION

In recent years, more and more people capture their experiences in home videos. While the market of digital camcorders is stable, the number of gadgets with an embedded camcorder is rapidly increasing: nowadays almost every mobile phone has a camcorder that can shoot medium to good quality videos.

Although the technology for capturing home videos is becoming cheaper and more efficient, the tools for enriching and editing the users' videos are still basic. Because video media consists of both a visual and an audio stream, and each stream contains many frames every second, video media is intrinsically complex and difficult to process, manipulate, and

share with others. This makes video editing a difficult and time-consuming task [5].

To resolve this issue, the Edit While Watching (EWW) system has been developed [3]. It has been designed to automatically create an edited version of a home video and then allow the users to modify and refine it in an easy to use and lean-back way. After uploading the raw video material, the video is indexed, segmented, shortened, and combined with proper music and editing effects. This is based on content analysis [4][9]. The result is an automatically generated edited version of the home video that is shown to the user. While watching it, users can indicate by using a remote control whether they like certain content, so that the system will adapt the edited version to contain more content that is similar or related to the displayed content. EWW does not require a complex user interface: a TV and a few keys of a remote control are sufficient.

To assess the degree of ease of use and ease of learning of the design we have performed a use test on the EWW system. The test consisted in giving the participants practical tasks to do (i.e. editing a home video) and interviewing them. The focus was on four main aspects: functionality, usability, pleasantness of the system, and the user satisfaction while working with the system.

This article is structured as follows. The next section describes the EWW system in more detail. Section 3 is devoted to the definition of the objective of the test. The implementation of the use test is discussed in Section 4. The results and conclusions of the use test are dealt with in Sections 5 and 6 respectively.

2. EDIT WHILE WATCHING SYSTEM

Existing tools for video editing can be mapped onto two main categories: fully manual, frame-accurate video editing software programs[1] and fully automatic summarization tools. A host of fully manual PC-based home video editing programs such as Adobe Premiere [2], and Pinnacle Studio [8] are already available on the market. These tools are based on low-level editing operations, but, to achieve nice results, users need to acquire quite some technical skills, have knowledge of the technical structure of a video document (frames, shots, transitions, filters) and invest a lot of time and effort. These solutions are ideal for people who want to have full control of their video to obtain a perfect result, but discourage most of the common users.

On the other side of the spectrum, some fully automatic solutions are present. In these software packages, the technical

---

[1] There are also video editing tools on devices such as hard disk recorders, for example [11]. These tools usually have limited automation, and therefore require considerable effort to use.

details are hidden while users can still convey their own style and wishes through a simplified editing process. An example of these is Muvee autoProducer [7] or the function "smart movie" of Pinnacle Studio. After investigation and experiencing these systems, we found out that they do not provide enough control on the editing choices and processes. Users can only choose which raw material to use, specify the duration of the final result, and select a desired "style" (e.g. music video, romantic, slow-paced), then the tool produces the final video of the defined length. This final video consists of automatically selected parts of the raw material. Depending on the original duration of the selected raw material and the desired output length, the raw material is either partially used, or repeatedly shown. Users have no idea what the consequences of their choices are and cannot influence the "hidden" editing operations.

The EWW system we have developed overcomes the disadvantages of the existent solutions, by giving back control to the user via an easy to use interaction paradigm while hiding unnecessary technical details [3]. This is achieved by applying content analysis and film grammar rules to translate high-level users' choices into low-level editing operations. The EWW concept is targeted at the niche that is not yet occupied: easy home video editing in the living room.

The EWW system takes the raw video data as input. It extracts low-level features from the material such as camera motion, contrast, and luminosity. Based these low-level features the raw video data is segmented into short segments of typically 1-10 seconds. Each segment gets a numerical suitability score based on the mentioned low-level features. The segments with the highest scores are selected for the initial edited version, and shown to the user. The selected segments that are contiguous in time form a *shot*. Each editing operation affects one shot at a time.

Even the best automatic algorithm will never fully meet the desires of the user, since the relevance of a certain video scene is subjective and depends on the user's mood and taste, the experience recorded and the recipient of the video. Therefore, we aim at reaching the best edited version of the video using a synergy of human and machine abilities, providing the user with efficient interaction functionalities to refine the video.

The EWW system is not PC-based: the user interacts with it using a remote control and a TV-set. While watching, the user can press the pause button and select one of the following options (see Figure 1):

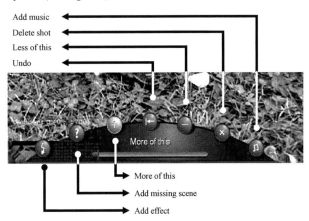

Figure 1. A screenshot of the user interface that appears at the bottom of the screen when the user presses 'pause' on the remote control to start editing.

- **Add music** to the current shot: shows a menu with different pieces of music to include in the current shot. Presently the option is limited to only five different music pieces. The idea is that, in a next version of EWW, the user can also upload his own music.

- **Delete the current shot**: deletes all segments of the current shot from the edited version.

- **Less of this**: deletes one segment (with lowest suitability score) of the current shot.

- **More of this**: adds one segment (with the highest suitability score) to the current shot.

- **Add missing scene**: shows a menu with different scenes not yet included in the edited version.

- **Add effect**: shows a menu with different video effects which can be applied to the current shot. Presently the effects are limited to about a dozen colour effects.

With the *more* and *less of this* functions the user can add or remove video content about a specific part by just pressing a button. The system will automatically add or remove video segments concerning that event from the edited version of the video.

By pressing the *add missing scene* button, the user is prompted with the thumbnail panel shown in Figure 2. Each thumbnail represents a scene of the raw material that is not included in the edited version. The user can browse these thumbnails and select the desired one.

Figure 2. Screenshot of the "Add missing scene" menu

The button *Undo*, shown at the centre of the menu, is not yet implemented. Besides these listed editing options, we have implemented some navigation options in the version used for the use test. The options consisted of 'play' (at normal speed) and 'pause'. Furthermore the user can jump one shot ahead or back by using the arrow keys on the remote control.

Details on the technical implementation can be found in [3].

3. OBJECTIVE OF THE TEST

The objective of the use test described here is to assess whether EWW really enables the easy home video editing mentioned above. With respect to the functionality, we address the question if the system has sufficient options and functionalities for (basic) home video editing. Concerning the usability of the system, we investigate if the user understands the options and knows how to use them. Furthermore we investigate if the feedback of the system is clear to the user.

We also study the satisfaction of the user when working with the EWW system. Do the users like to work with the system, and are they satisfied with the functionalities and the results?

4. TEST DESIGN

To answer the mentioned research questions we have divided the test in three parts: first we investigate the user behaviour and experience with respect to home video capturing, editing and sharing. In the second part of the test, the user is invited to try and use the system. We did not provide a full explanation of the functions. Therefore, initially the user is left as much time as needed for learning and getting acquainted with the system and its functions. Successively, the user is given a list of specific editing tasks to perform, like adding more video content about a certain event or delete the scene with an unwanted event. When the tasks are completed, the user is left as much time as wanted to freely edit this material according to his or her creativity. In the third part of the test, the user can give feedback on the system by means of a questionnaire and Likert scales [6], and an interview with the test leaders.

Since the EWW system is designed to be used in a home setting, we have selected the Philips HomeLab as test environment [1]. The HomeLab contains a living room with video cameras that recorded the test for later reference. A remote control and a TV set have been used for the interaction. A picture of the setup can be seen in Figure 3. All the operations done on the EWW program are logged for future reference. The test has a maximum duration of 60-90 min.

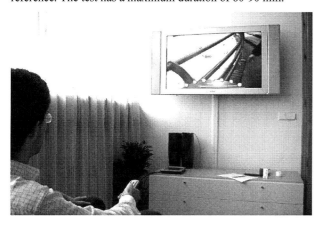

Figure 3. A picture of the test setup.

We have decided to use the same video material, which consisted of a home video of a Zoo visit, for all participants. The clear advantage is that all participants used the same material, and we can assign to the users specific editing tasks to perform, like adding more of the panthers and less of the bears in the final edited version. This allows us to evaluate the system with respect to particular tasks, which correspond to well-defined user requirements. The underlying assumption is that we know and understand how the system will typically be used. A disadvantage is that the test may seem artificial to the participant: he does not feel involved with the provided material. As a consequence, we cannot precisely investigate what the user needs are in editing his own material. However, from the test we found that the users considered the task scenario realistic. Therefore we feel confident about using the same video material for all users.

A usability test with four or five participants will expose 80 percent of the problems of the system, and this 80 percent represents most of the major problems [10]. To be certain to find the most apparent problems, and to gain some confidence, we invited eight participants.

5. RESULTS
5.1 User Profile

Eight students and employees from Philips Research in Eindhoven, with some experience in home video capturing, participated in the test: three females, and five males. None of the participants were working on related topics. Their age varied between 22 and 29, most of them capture video four or five times a year (range 2-100 times a year). When capturing video, six of the eight participants (6/8) use a digital still camera, or occasionally a camcorder (5/8). All of the participants own a digital still camera with video capturing functionality, half of them own a cell phone with video capturing functionality, and only two own a camcorder.

The captured video is rarely or never edited (7/8). Adobe premiere is the most used program for editing (2/8). When editing is done, it takes a lot of time, 1 hour – 1 day for 1 minute of edited video. Some participants have no video editing experience at all (3/8). The video is mostly watched directly after capturing with friends, and only rarely shared or watched later. The explanation could be that usually unedited video is unattractive for these purposes, and video editing is too long and difficult to do.

5.2 Questionnaire

After the practical editing tasks, the user is asked to fill in a questionnaire on the functionality, usability, pleasantness, and user satisfaction with respect to the usage of the system. The questionnaire was printed on paper and involved twelve statements. The answers to these statements were given on Likert scales, ranging from 'false' to 'true'.

The results show that most participants agreed that the EWW system enables fast and easy editing. Furthermore, they mostly liked working with the system, and judged the task scenario as realistic. However, the final edited version did not convincingly satisfy the participants. The probable reasons are that the current editing functions are too limited and do not provide enough control. Additionally, the results show that there was a demand for more editing functions to further enrich the edited version. Furthermore, some users remarked that they would like to personalize the video by adding text, and inserting special transitions between the shots. Most of the participants do not outspokenly want to have the system, or to use it for their own home video.

5.3 Remarks of the participants

We have asked the participants to think aloud during the test. During their experience with the system and the final interview, users also expressed a number of free comments and remarks on the advantages and the deficiencies of EWW. Their comments and actions have been written down, and recorded on video. We have grouped and analysed the records. Based on this analysis, the following main results have been extracted.

Many users found the "more" and "less of this" functions too inadequate for their needs and difficult to understand. In general users were not satisfied by the fact that the system was automatically choosing which video segments to add or to discard for each more or less of this operation. Five over eight users would like to be able to decide whether to shorten or grow a scene from the beginning or from the end, three over eight would like to select how many seconds of video to add or to discard.

The system proved to have easy and effective navigation functionalities, all users but one found out how to navigate among the scenes by using the arrows. However, 4 over 8 users observed that fast-forward and rewind functionalities are missing and would be needed. Three over eight users expressed the lack of an overview of the whole raw footage, for example a key-frames panel or a timeline. They were, in fact, unfamiliar with the raw material and had difficulties to get acquainted to that using only the "add missing scene" functionality.

The "add missing scene" functionality was too limited to easily find a missing scene. One of the practical tasks consisted of adding a specific scene to the edited version that was not yet there. Five of the eight users expressed their difficulty in finding this specific scene.

As general remarks, 6 users were willing to use EWW or an improved version of it to edit their own video material. Everybody agreed that EWW is easy to learn and use, however 4 users clearly said that the system is too rigid and that they would like to have more control on the parameters of the editing operations and more editing functionalities.

5.4 Log-files analysis

During each test, we kept trace of the operations that users performed on the system by saving them into log files. From these files, some characteristics of the usage of the system can be extracted. The users employed on average 9 minutes (range 6 – 16 minutes) to get acquainted with the system and to feel ready to start the tasks. These tasks were completed on average in 14 minutes (range 10 – 18 minutes). The average time in which the users enjoyed editing the video according to their own creativity was on average 8 minutes (range 3 – 15 minutes).

Participants spent on average a large time using the system, dealing with it in a very personal way. The average time dedicated to creatively edit the video is about as long as the time which is spent on getting acquainted with the system. This fact, combined with the results from the questionnaire, seems to suggest that the users liked the system and enjoyed trying it out and spending time on it.

Users executed the tasks quite effectively, and all of them managed to complete them correctly. Only one or two users needed more time for completing some of the tasks. As expected, the two most used editing operations are "more" and "less of this". These were used more than twice as much as any other operation.

6. CONCLUSIONS

We have performed a use study on the EWW system. This system was designed as an easy to learn and use video editing system using just a remote control and a TV-screen. The test was performed with eight participants, who all had some experience in capturing video. The participants regarded the use and task scenario as realistic. They judged the system as an easy and fast video editing tool. It took the users a short time to try and learn all the functionalities implemented in the system. With regard to this aspect, the requirements of easiness and simplicity of EWW are met.

However, most users did not feel to be in control of the system. The lengthening and shortening of scenes seemed random to them, and they could not control the start and end of the added

music precise enough. Furthermore they missed an overview of the material. It was regarded as difficult to easily see which parts were included and where, and what was left out. This could also be caused by the fact that the material was not their own, and consequently they were not familiar to all the content. Still the system was judged as reasonably 'fun' to work with. The users liked the system and liked to try it out and spend time on it.

Since the participants have a technical background and are highly educated, there is the danger of bias in the results. Participants with such a profile are typically fast learners and easy adopters. Furthermore they may tend to accept less surprises and unpredictability in the system, and would like to have more overview and control. On the other hand, all the non-technical people we have initially approached for the test were excluded due to lack of video capturing experience. Therefore the participants may be the interesting group to target with such systems. Therefore we think that the main deficiencies of the system found during the use test, are valid and relevant.

In the design of video editing systems, there seems to be a trade off between the ease of use and the amount of user control. Currently, systems allowing the user to edit video on frame level are difficult to learn and use. On the other hand, fully automatic systems are easy to use, but users cannot control all the details in the editing. With respect to these points, an optimal video editing system should try to optimize the balance between ease of use and user control. Thus, in an improved system, the ease of use, and ease of learning of EWW should be carefully preserved, while the user control and overview should be improved. Future work will therefore be concentrated on providing an easy to understand and use overview based on intuitive timelines, and on controllable trimming, deleting and adding of video.

7. REFERENCES

[1] Aarts, E., and Diederiks, E. (Eds.), *Ambient Lifestyle, from concept to experience*, Kluwer Academic Publishers, 2007.

[2] Adobe Premiere, http://www.adobe.com/products/premiere/

[3] Campanella, M., Weda, J., and Barbieri, M. Edit while watching: home video editing made easy. In *proc. SPIE vol. 6506, 65060L, 2007.*

[4] Furht, B., and Marques, O. (Eds.), *Handbook of video databases: design and applications*, CRC Press, 2004.

[5] Lienhart, R., *Abstracting Home Video Automatically*, Proc. ACM Intern. Multim. Conf., part 2, pp. 37-40, 1999.

[6] Likert, R. A Technique for the Measurement of Attitudes. *Archives of Psychology 140*, 55 (1932).

[7] Muvee autoProducer, http://www.muvee.com/

[8] Pinnacle Studio, http://www.pinnaclesys.com/

[9] Rosenfeld, A., Doermann, D., and DeMenthon, D., (Eds.), Video Mining, *The International series in Video Computing*, Kluwer Academic Publishers, 2003.

[10] Rubin, J. *Handbook of usability testing*. John Wiley & Sons, 1994.

[11] Yasutaka, N., and Kyoko, T., Patent application, EP 1 276 110 Pioneer Corp., 2003, http://gauss.ffii.org/PatentView/EP1276110

Student Papers

Visualising Bluetooth Interactions: Combining the Arc Diagram and DocuBurst Techniques

Daragh Byrne, Barry Lavelle, Gareth J. F. Jones, Alan F. Smeaton
Centre for Digital Video Processing & Adaptive Information Cluster
Dublin City University
Dublin 9, Ireland
+353 1 7005262

{daragh.byrne, gareth.jones, alan.smeaton@computing.dcu.ie},{barry.lavelle@eeng.dcu.ie}

ABSTRACT

Within the Bluetooth mobile space, overwhelmingly large sets of interaction and encounter data can very quickly be accumulated. This presents a challenge to gaining an understanding and overview of the dataset as a whole. In order to overcome this problem, we have designed a visualisation which provides an informative overview of the dataset. The visualisation combines existing Arc Diagram and DocuBurst techniques into a radial space-filling layout capable of conveying a rich understanding of Bluetooth interaction data, and clearly represents social networks and relationships established among encountered devices. The end result enables a user to visually interpret the relative importance of individual devices encountered, the relationships established between them and the usage of Bluetooth 'friendly names' (or device labels) within the data.

Categories and Subject Descriptors

H.5.2 [Information Interfaces and Presentation (e.g., HCI)]: User Interfaces;

General Terms

Design, Human Factors

Keywords

Bluetooth, friendly name, mobile phones, mobile computing. visualisation, DocuBurst, Arc Diagrams.

1. INTRODUCTION

Bluetooth is a short-range wireless protocol by which enabled devices can exchange content. Each device is identified with a 12-digit hardware ID, unique to an individual device, and a user determined short string known as a 'friendly name.' Bluetooth can be used with a wide variety of devices from home computers to portable laptops, PDAs, mobile phones, keyboards, mice and headphones. We can easily encounter hundreds of devices as we go about our daily routine: from traveling on the bus to sitting at a desk at work and being surrounded by colleagues' phones and laptops.

In our previous work, we observed that a mobile user may

encounter several thousand devices within a month and that these encounters may include several hundred unique friendly names [7]. The amount of data that Bluetooth encounters yields in even a short period is also overwhelming, especially for large groups of people. For example, in previous study [7] we recorded Bluetooth device encounters at 10 second intervals and this yielded over 200,000 recorded encounters with devices across 6 participants in just 24 days.

Chen [2] states that information overload "*becomes a common problem in the exponential growth of widely accessible information in modern society.*" This is certainly the case, in our experience, with Bluetooth. The data can rapidly grow within the first few days to the point where gaining an overview of the dataset quickly and easily is virtually impossible. In this paper, we explore the combination of Arc Diagram techniques [15,6,8] and the DocuBurst space filling radial diagram [3,4] as a means by which we can explore the interactions recorded for a Bluetooth device by providing an at-a-glance overview to more effectively and intuitively visualise the wealth of Bluetooth data that can be garnered from just one device. Such a visualisation has practical applications for designers and developers working with Bluetooth as well as in the domains of social networking and human digital memory (or lifelogging).

2. RELATED WORK

2.1 Bluetooth and Familiarity

Nicolai [9,10] popularized the concept of familiarity of devices within the Bluetooth space. He suggests that there are 3 main types of devices that are encountered: those that are well known, regularly encountered and *familiar* to you; those that are somewhat known, encountered at semi-regular intervals (known as a *familiar stranger*) and those which are infrequently encountered and generally unknown (known as *strangers.*) His work demonstrated that social context could be drawn from general encounters with devices. In [7], we extended Nicolai's work and examined a more robust mechanism for calculating a measure of familiarity for an encountered device. Our mechanism provides a cumulative score based on a device's presence relative to the others by dividing each day into intervals at which presence and duration of presence is examined.

2.2 Arc Diagrams

The Arc Diagram is a concept developed by Wattenberg [15] for visualising complex repetition in string data. Documents such as DNA sequences, music, programming code or HTML pages contain sequences, and each sequence may have repeated subsequences. Arc diagrams are especially suited to conveying these complex patterns and we can see an example of how an Arc Diagram describes a document in Figure 1. Related sequences are simply represented using an arc which connects any two sequences, however, extra information can be conveyed based on the width and opacity of the arc. It is also important that all arcs are somewhat transparent to ensure that all crossings are clearly identifiable.

Figure 1. An Example Arc Diagram Showing String Repetition in a HTML Page

Alternative applications of the Arc Tree approach include ArcTrees [8] and Thread Arcs [6]. ArcTrees are used to visualise relationships within Hierarchical data such as structured documents. Thread Arcs are used to visualise relationships between threaded emails over time. The Arc representation of these threads was used to enhance a user's understanding of the chronology and relationships between email messages allowing them to interpret the type of conversation or discussion present within the thread.

2.3 DocuBurst

Figure 2. An Example DocuBurst Diagram

The DocuBurst visualisation [3,4] is used to explore the lexical content of documents and is designed to provide a rich overview of the concepts contained within the document. It leverages the relationships between the individual words in a document to higher-level concepts through a semantic lexicon, WordNet. It uses a radial space filling layout technique based on the previous work of [14]. The centre of the diagram contains a circle which represents the root node. Spanning out from the centre are a series of child nodes. Children are represented as a wedge connected to its parent. The size of the wedge is determined by the child's overall importance within the document and is proportional to the size of its parent. Figure 2. demonstrates how children are displayed within concentric rings spanning out from the root node. This visualisation technique, like Arc Diagrams, makes use of opacity displaying frequently occurring items as opaque with infrequent items appearing transparent.

3. DATA COLLECTION & PROCESSING

Bluetooth activity data can be recorded from a range of applications. In our laboratory, we have developed a Java ME based mobile application specifically designed to record Bluetooth interactions, at a high sampling frequency (every 10 seconds) than other available tools. This tool runs on a mobile phone and saves recorded data to an online database [7,1]. Alternative solutions to recording Bluetooth activity include the ContextLogger application developed by the University of

Helsinki [11]. The ContextLogger is designed to record a wide range of mobile phone activity data including incoming and outgoing calls, contact information and Bluetooth. It is in use in a wide range of projects including those of the Reality Mining Project [5].

After collection, the data is automatically processed to extract information on each Bluetooth enabled device encountered by the logger. First, a measure of the encountered device's relative familiarity to the logger is calculated using methods described in [7]. This yields a score of an encountered device's overall presence within the dataset and allows a determination of how well they are known to the owner to be made. A list of periods at which each device was encountered is also extracted. As a device can move in and out of range thereby missing an individual poll, a small window for reappearance was allowed. This lets a device be re-encountered within a 5-minute window without considering it to be a new period of encounter for the device. This is based on Nicolai's [9] approach to dividing Bluetooth activity into individual periods of encounter. For each period of encounter, a list of collocated devices is also gathered. Finally all friendly names found for the given device are located and used to aggregate the devices.

4. VISUALISATION

Shneiderman [12] states that every information-seeking visualisation should seek to provide "overview first, zoom and filter, then details-on-demand." This statement has become the principle tenet and base design requirements for any information visualisation. At the core of this concept is the need to provide a visualisation which is effective in providing a high level overview of the data set as well as allowing detailed exploration of a specific area of interest within the data. Spense [13] also believes that an important aspect of the visualisation is to provide insight and understanding through engagement and that the person must be informed by the visualisation. Below we outline a means by which a user can gain a detailed understanding and an at–a-glance overview of the complex relationships contained within day-to-day Bluetooth interactions. We integrate the Arc Diagram concepts into a radial space-filling layout, which was designed with these concepts very much in mind. The size of the diagram also provides an immediate visual cue to the amount of the data and the number of devices that it represents.

4.1 Displaying Familiarity

Figure 3. Visualising familiarity by transparency.

In our visualisation, we represent each device as a node within a concentric radial layout. As the hardware ID of the device is unique, we use this to identify it within the visualisation, despite the fact is it not designed to be human readable. It is however chosen instead of a friendly name as if the encounters are too low for a given device, there may be no recorded friendly name, or as friendly names may be changed at any point, there may be more than one to choose from. As such, employing the friendly name to label and identify a device within the visualisation could present problems in selecting the a representative name for that device.

Familiarity represents a device's overall presence within mobile interactions and gives a measure of how important it is relative to the other devices. This is an extremely significant item of information to convey within the visualisation and to express it we use opacity and shading. The most familiar devices appear as solid black nodes, while those, which are determined to be unfamiliar, are displayed highly transparent and faded (see Fig. 3.). This allows familiar, unfamiliar, and familiar strangers to be visually determined and clearly distinguished.

4.2 Displaying Collocation

Typically devices are not encountered in isolation. For example, if you attend a meeting with John and Mary, you will encounter both John and Mary's Bluetooth devices. As their devices have been encountered at the same time we can infer a relationship between them. If you attend regular meetings with John and Mary, and hence regularly encounter both of their devices, they will form a strong "bond". We may then expect that if I encounter John, I will also encounter Mary. From the familiarity scoring of devices, we understand the strength of the relationship I have individually with John and with Mary, but there is a need to present the relationships within the encounters to give a more complete understanding of the data.

In a similar approach to Kerr [6], we extended Arc Diagrams to visualise presence of devices relative to one another allowing users to visually interpret the social relationships between the individual devices they have encountered. Within the inner area of our radial diagram an arc will connect an encountered device to another if they have been encountered at some point at the same time, i.e. they were encountered proximal to one another. The more collocated encounters, the stronger the weight of the line and the less transparent the arc. Conversely if a device has only been collocated infrequently with another, it will be represented as a thin transparent line. The inner area in Figure 4 illustrates this concept.

4.3 Displaying Friendly Names

A device's friendly name can be changed by the user at any point in time, and potentially many times over short periods of time. We have previously observed that there is a large degree of overlap between the friendly names used where we recorded encounter data for 6,181 unique devices, while only 1566 unique friendly names were found [7]. This demonstrates that considerable overlap exists between friendly names in the Bluetooth space. This is mainly attributable to approximately 25% of users opting to use the devices default, manufacturer specified, name e.g. Nokia 6230i. We leverage this in our visualisation. Instead of representing individual device's friendly names as nodes we aggregate friendly names, which occur across multiple devices, and display them as a wedge in the radial diagram, in a style identical to that of DocuBurst. The device hardware IDs are ordered based on the occurrence and overlap of friendly names, and so align with the friendly name wedges appropriately. Any devices within this wedge which have further overlap are recursively subdivided until all friendly names have been displayed.

The display of friendly names adapts the DocuBurst technique to the domain, but preserves the visual richness of the technique (see Figure 4.) In our approach the depth of child nodes conveys the number of friendly names recorded for a given device. This provides visual insight into the frequency of change for friendly names, an infrequent but important occurrence. Additionally, the wedged radial approach provide an excellent means to rapidly gain an overview of friendly name usage within the dataset and the amount of overlap that exists between encountered devices' friendly names. Large friendly name wedges represent friendly names which are commonly found within the dataset and which span multiple devices. Overlapping friendly names can cause difficulty in identifying the intended device for interaction [7] and the visualisation allows the viewer to visually determine how problematic this may be within the dataset. Also, gaps in the radial burst will indicate where no friendly name has been

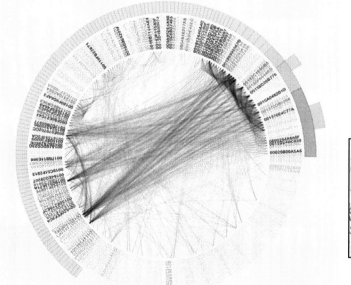

Figure 4. A Bluetooth Visualisation displaying 10 days data for one device. (Inset: tooltip to inquire on the friendly name)

encountered. Finally, we also make use of opacity to represent a friendly name's relative important within the dataset.

5. FUTURE WORK

Currently the visualisation is static in nature as it was designed to provide an at-a-glance overview of the dataset. We would like to extend the current visualisation to include some level of interaction. For example, selection of a particular device within the visualisation might highlight the arcs representing collocation for that device. It would also be useful to provide some focus+context techniques [13,14] for exploring the data set. This might include the ability to select a date range for the data being displayed, thereby allowing the viewer to focus the visualisation on periods of particular interest.

We also would like to examine extending this visualisation to provide more detailed information to a user on the Bluetooth interactions occurring with devices. This could include expanding the visualisation to allow the representation of Bluetooth encounter data recorded on multiple devices and the resulting social network between those devices. Additionally, enhancing the DocuBurst technique within the current visualisation could be very useful. Employing some automatic lexical analysis of the data would allow for the aggregation of not only exactly matching friendly names but also friendly names containing similar attributes or words. This may serve to provide a more effective overview of the friendly names contained within the dataset. It may also allow us to automatically classify the type of friendly name which has been encountered, e.g. use's a model name, a manufacturer name, a persons name etc.

Finally, colour and hues might be used within the visualisation to indicate and distinguish particular types of links between the encountered devices or perhaps the classification(s) or type(s) of friendly name(s) which has been encountered for a particular device.

6. CONCLUSIONS

In this paper we have presented a combination of the Arc Diagram and the DocuBurst visualisation techniques for visualising device encounters within the Bluetooth-enabled mobile space. Our visualisation technique allows the relationships between encountered devices to be quickly established by providing an understanding of the relative importance (or familiarity) of an encountered device as well as visually representing the relationships between and collocation for encountered devices. Finally our technique provides an understanding of the relative overlap and overall usage of Bluetooth '*friendly names*' for the encountered devices. The Bluetooth Visualisation is a unique tool for interpreting interactions within the mobile space. It provides a one-dimensional overview of the Bluetooth encounters and affords a user rapid cognition of an overwhelmingly large data set.

7. ACKNOWLEDGMENTS

We would like to thank the Irish Research Council for Science, Engineering and Technology and Science Foundation Ireland under grant number 03/IN.3/I361 for support.

8. REFERENCES

[1] Byrne, D., Lavelle, B., Doherty, A.R., Jones, G.J.F., Smeaton, A.F. Using Bluetooth & GPS Metadata to Measure Event Similarity in SenseCam Images, Proceedings of the 5th International Conference on Intelligent Multimedia & Ambient Intelligence (Jul 2007).

[2] Chen, C. Information Visualization: Beyond the Horizon. 2nd edition. Springer, London, 2004.

[3] Collins, C. DocuBurst: Document Content Visualization Using Language Structure. Proceedings of IEEE Symposium on Information Visualization, Poster Session. Baltimore (2006).

[4] Collins, C. DocuBurst: Radial Space-Filling Visualization of Document Content. Technical Report, KMDI, University of Toronto, 2007. Retrieved from: http://kmdi.utoronto.ca/publications/documents/KMDI-TR-2007-1.pdf

[5] Eagle, N. "Using Mobile Phones to Model Complex Social Systems", O'Reilly Network. (June 2005). Retrieved from: http://www.oreillynet.com/pub/a/network/2005/06/20/MIT medialab.html

[6] Kerr, B.J. Thread Arcs: An Email Thread Visualization. Tech. Rep. RC22850, IBM Research, Cambridge, MA, USA, 2003.

[7] Lavelle, B., Byrne, D., Jones, G.J.F., Gurrin, C., Smeaton, A.F., Receive Data From?...A mechanism for determining familiarity amongst Bluetooth devices. Submitted to Mobile HCI 2007, Singapore (2007)

[8] Neumann, P., Schlechtweg, S., Sheelagh, M. & Carpendale, T. ArcTrees: Visualizing Relations in Hierarchical Data. In EuroVis 2005, pages 53–60, 319. Eurographics, 2005.

[9] Nicolai, T., Behrens, N., Yoneki, E., "Wireless Rope: Experiment in Social Proximity Sensing with Bluetooth", *PerCom 2006, Pisa, Italy*

[10] Nicolai, T., Yoneki, E., Behrens, N. & Kenn, H. Exploring Social Context with the Wireless Rope. 1st International Workshop on MObile and NEtworking Technologies for social applications (MONET'06), Montpellier, France.

[11] Raento, M., Oulasvirta, A., Petit, R. & Toivonen, H. ContextPhone: a prototyping platform for context aware mobile applications. IEEE Pervasive Computing 2005 4(2), 51-59.

[12] Shneiderman B., The eyes have it: A task by data type taxonomy for information visualization, Proceedings of 1996 IEEE Symposium on Visual Languages, Boulder, Colorado, September 1996, pp. 336-343

[13] Spence R., 2001 Information Visualization, Addison-Wesley, Essex UK.

[14] Stasko, J.T., Zhang E. Focus+Context Display and Navigation Techniques for Enhancing Radial, Space-Filling Hierarchy Visualizations. In Proc. InfoVis'00 (Oct. 2000), IEEE Press, pp. 57–65

[15] Wattenberg, M. Arc Diagrams: Visualizing Structure in Strings. In Proc. InfoVis'02, pages 110–116. IEEE Press, 2002.

Breaking the Campus Bubble:
Informed, Engaged, Connected

Nick Day
Lancaster University
Computing Department
LA1 4WA
+44 (0) 1524 510492

nick@njday.com

Motoko Toma
Bosch Japan
SAP

+81 (0) 806567 2484

motoko.toma@jp.bosch.co

Corina Sas
Lancaster University
Computing Department
LA1 4WA
+44 (0) 1524 510318

corina@comp.lancs.ac.uk

Chris Bevan
University of Bath
Computer Science and
Psychology
+44 (0) 7770 640406

bevan.chris@gmail.com

Alan Dix
Lancaster University
Computing Department
LA1 4WA
+44 (0) 1524 510319

alan@hcibook.com

Dave Clare
17 Millthrop
Sedbergh
LA10 5SP
+44 (0) 7811 7044474

dave_clare_millthrop@hotmail.com

ABSTRACT

This paper introduces UniVote, a system supporting mobile phone-based interaction with public displays. The case study carried out at Lancaster University indicates that the campus "bubble" in which students live can lead to feelings of isolation within an insular community cut off from the outside world. UniVote makes use of a voting system to help elicit user involvement, keep users informed of campus- and world-wide events and news and create a sense of community. Findings of this preliminary study suggest that the campus "bubble" can indeed be broken, and the voting component of the system particularly fosters interaction and human connectedness.

Keywords

Interacting with public displays, mobile phones, expressing opinions, human connectedness, voting.

1. INTRODUCTION

Across the Lancaster campus there is an ongoing deployment of public displays designed to enable pervasive interaction as well as broadcast more traditional multimedia content. This infrastructure offers an opportunity to explore ways in which technology can improve student quality of life on university campuses.

Our work is driven by the ever-increasing levels of stress and work experienced by university students, with students' anxiety levels being particularly high during their first year at university [6]. Students therefore have very little time to explore new things [10] and often have a general lack of interest in anything that is not directly related to student life.

This often produces insular and self-centred behaviour which can easily develop into a feeling of isolation, particularly on the Lancaster campus which is physically isolated from the city itself. This lends itself to the notion of students living in a "bubble", with students becoming more and more detached from the world outside of the university campus. Students at the university are aware of this problem, as the following quote suggests:

"Campus is a place cut-off from the rest of the world... Students are disinterested and often blatantly unaware of what's going on around them."

It is this issue of student isolation from the outside world and each other that we would like to address by developing the UniVote system, through understanding campus life and exploring ways in which technology can assist in making the campus more responsive to student needs. Two concepts are particularly relevant here: *user engagement* and *human connectedness*, which are considered throughout the entire design process.

People in general have a desire to be involved in meaningful social relationships, a topic which has been explored in relation to technology by Agamanolis during his development of nine *human connectedness* principles [1]. These principles explore how such essential relationships are built, maintained or enhanced by technology [2], and as such can assist in designing effective public displays that encourage acceptance and entice interaction through building and maintaining a *relationship* with the user. To build this relationship a public display must *engage* its users and encourage interaction. A phenomenon coined as the *honey pot effect* was observed by Brignull and Rogers [5], which describes the *social buzz* produced by an increasing number of people gathering in the proximity of a public display, attracted by its interaction potential and the social payoff of congregating. Such displays would only need to attract the critical mass of people before the social facilitation of the display would maintain a high level of users' engagement and interaction with the display. However, there are no accounts of how such phenomena would evolve over time, particularly once the novelty of the display wears off.

Through the study of ambient displays Mankoff and Dey [8] identified that the information source is a crucial factor in user adoption and acceptance of a display. Since interaction with public displays is usually short (even for users interested in its content) the display has to ensure a transition from the users periphery to the focus of their attention. It is hoped that by providing information of interest to students (broadening their awareness of the outside world) and asking them to provide their input, the display will be woven into the fabric of students' interests and needs and will help to increase both acceptance and interaction. In addition an aesthetically pleasing front end will help to entice interaction in situations where the content on the display does not speak directly to the interests of students.

We hope to reduce the feeling of isolation on campus by keeping students better informed of campus- and world-wide events and allowing them to voice their own opinions on such matter through a voting procedure. Given that interaction with public displays often encounters resistance from a public audience [5], we feel that a voting system will help to elicit audience involvement as it has proven to do so in radio and TV. This research is particularly relevant given that there has been little work exploiting voting as an activity that can successfully promote interaction with public displays [13][12]. Opinionizer [5] includes similar voting capabilities to UniVote based on open-ended questions, however a serious limitation is that it does not provide anonymity to voters and cannot allow for simultaneous interaction by multiple users due to its use of a keyboard for input. The mobile phone interaction of UniVote will overcome these limitations and will consist of closed multiple-choice questions to ensure that the threshold to participation is perceived as low, so that the benefits of interacting outweigh the perceived costs [5].

Our work focuses on the use of mobile phones to act as a display and input for larger public displays to leverage on the strengths of both components: the personal control and market saturation of mobile phones (particularly in a predominantly student-centred environment); and the larger presentation space, and greater computational power and bandwidth of public displays [12]. It is hoped that the combination of the rich media potential of public displays and the communications possibilities of mobile phones, will produce a truly interactive system to entice user interaction and try to build a sense of community on Lancaster campus.

2. THE UNIVOTE SYSTEM

The UniVote system and further screenshots can be downloaded from *www.univote.co.uk*. The system has been developed and tested on a Nokia 6230 and Mac OS 10.4.

2.1 Needs Analysis

Our needs analysis involved both questionnaire and observation of students on campus. The questionnaire was administered to 31 students and captured factual data including: access to television, radio and Internet; level of interest in campus, local, national and international news; news categories of interest; level of knowledge about current affairs; and level of interest for a campus news system. The findings suggested that campus residents used the Internet as their main source of information (partly due to inadequate TV and radio signal on campus) and as a result residents were insufficiently informed about current news and events – supported by an overall poor level of knowledge in factual questions. Off-campus students preferred national news, politics and sport, whereas campus-based students were more interested in information about social events on a campus level. Both on- and off-campus students

have a strong interest for knowledge of these areas, despite being uninformed, and responded enthusiastically to the proposed system. Naturalistic observation found that while there were many paper-based notices and advertisements along common campus routes, people rarely stopped to read them. Focussing on observing the natural patters of peoples' movement throughout campus will inform the decision of where the UniVote displays should be located.

2.2 System Architecture

UniVote is based on a client-server model (Figure 1) and has been designed with multiple campus installations in mind.

Figure 1. System Architecture

Each UniVote display will require its own Mac running the server application and front end. The components of the system are described below.

2.2.1 Client Application

The client application was designed to run on any J2ME and Bluetooth enabled mobile phone and is distributable over the air using a WAP connection. It uses the standard J2ME API to ensure it inherits the look-and-feel of the host mobiles' operating system, and operates in a step-by-step linear manner to ensure maximum usability (Figure 2). Users must have this application running on their phone before they can cast a vote. Users are connected to the server application nearest to their location (as determined by the Bluetooth protocol) which is highly likely to be the UniVote public display they are intending to interact with. On the development phone (Nokia 6230) it takes on average 16 seconds to cast a vote (including starting the application).

2.2.2 Server Application

The server application coordinates communication between client devices and the central database. It accepts incoming connections, retrieves the questions from the database (applicable to the display the user is interacting with) and sends them to the user's mobile phone. It also sends users' votes to the central database where they are saved.

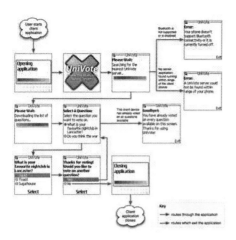

Figure 2. Client Application

2.2.3 Front End

The front end application (Figure 3) running on the public displays shows a scrolling news headlines feed and two-minute headline summary; cycles through the questions, inviting users to cast a vote and displaying a voting outcome; displays information on how users can cast a vote; and provides immediate feedback of new incoming votes by means of an animated bar chart. The front end application was implemented using Director, a common choice for delivering content on large public displays [5][13].

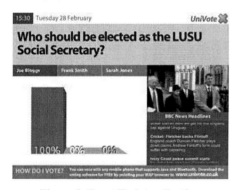

Figure 3. Front End Application

2.2.4 Central Database & Web Service

A central MySQL database and PHP-based web service are remotely hosted at *univote.co.uk* to allow screens to be deployed around campus wherever an Internet connection is available. The central database contains the questions, screen configuration settings and votes, and the web service provides a compatibility layer for passing data to the Director front end.

2.2.5 Web Administration Site

The web administration site allows university staff to manage the UniVote system. A central bank of questions is available to which staff can add, edit or delete questions. Questions comprise of a single question statement and three fixed answers and can be assigned start and expiry dates/times. Questions from this central bank are then assigned to *question groups*. Each screen around campus has a unique name and is assigned specific *question groups* to show: only questions from the central bank which belong to those groups will be shown on this screen. Screens have three configuration options: colour scheme (red, green, blue, black); question change interval (10, 20 or 30 seconds; 1-5 minutes); and voting information interval (1-10 questions) which controls how frequently the front end shows more detailed and eye-catching instructions on how to cast a vote. Voting statistics (for any screen around campus)

can be viewed remotely by university staff as well as a timeline to show how voting is spread throughout any given 24-hour period. There is also a simulator for university staff to test a screen configuration before physically deploying it to an on-campus display.

2.3 Information Sources

There are two sources of information used in UniVote: *news* (displayed on the front end) and *questions* (on which users vote). The BBC was chosen as the source of news data because they provide an XML and two-minute RealVideo feed of the latest news headlines. The XML feed (parsed by the web service, and presented as a vertical scrolling marquee) and the two-minute video summary are embedded into the front end.

At this stage of the development it was decided that the questions would be added to UniVote by university staff and not by students directly, partly due to the proof-of-concept nature of this work. However, giving students the capability to manipulate campus displays in real-time could have negative consequences for the campus community through the posting of offensive or nonsensical questions (cf. "Error prevention and user control" [8]).

This notion of control also ensures that the questions posted on UniVote are neither highly controversial nor have right or wrong answers, so people do not feel defensive or inhibited in expressing their opinions. Public expression of opinions or attitudes for which people hold strong beliefs is often problematic [3][4][9] and can lead to the "spiral of silence" effect [11] in which those who hold minority opinions will choose to remain silent because of fear of isolation from the majority [14]. Given we are trying to increase the feeling of community and diminish the sense of isolation, this is certainly something we wish to avoid – if people perceive support for their opinions from a social network, they are more willing to express them [7].

3. EVALUATION

UniVote was evaluated by means of a lab-based evaluation session comprising of 23 first year undergraduate Computer Science students – 21 male, 2 female, with an average age of 20. Only 21% of participants had prior experience of public display systems such as UniVote. The front end of the system was projected at the front of the room.

Participants were given a brief presentation as an introduction to the system and the context in which it would be used in a real-world situation. Participants were asked to complete two tasks and were given an incentive for their participation.

The first task required participants to use the web administration site for posting their own questions, as a means of gaining familiarity with how the system works. Qualitative and quantitative data was collected from participants through a worksheet. The second task required participants with Java- and Bluetooth-enabled mobile phones to download the client application and cast a vote, and complete another worksheet based on their interaction experience with the voting functionality of UniVote.

Initial reactions to the system after the first task were positive, with 87% of participants reporting they would use such a system if it was deployed around the university campus. All participants found it easy to use. Over two thirds thought it suitable for deployment around campus, with one student particularly liking the idea of anonymous voting, and another suggesting that their real-world usage would very much depend on the types of questions available on it. As previous discussed this is crucial to the success of the system – participants suggested topics including campus-related topics (where to build more parking spaces, new bus routes); student topics (student elections particularly); current events; or just anything fun or useful. Two usability issues were identified during this phase. A few students pointed out that the scrolling news feed would be difficult to read on smaller screens, suggesting the need for different "themes" of the front end which are optimised for certain screen resolutions. While the immediate feedback of the animated bar chart was thought advantageous, one student noted that the bar chart would be continually animating during periods with high voting levels. This suggests the need for scheduling of screen updates, for which further research would have to be conducted to find the optimal trade-off between immediacy of feedback and system capacity.

Despite the positive initial reaction, only 39% of participants were able to complete the second task (despite 70% having compatible phones). This was due to two factors. There were major problems downloading the client application: although 91% of participants had WAP-enabled mobile phones only 4% had experience using it. This suggests that WAP is not the ideal distribution method for such applications and a more convenient method such as SMS should be considered. Secondly, implementations of the J2ME API do vary between mobile phone manufacturers which caused runtime errors for some participants: further testing is required here.

Aside from these usability and technical problems, the general consensus of the system was highly positive and the majority of students would use such a system if deployed around campus.

4. DISCUSSION & CONCLUSION

Despite its prevalence, the lab-based evaluation session has limitations that need to be acknowledged. Ethnographic studies on future versions of UniVote running "in the wild" for a long period of time will undoubtedly capture aspects of the system's success that we cannot foresee at this stage. While the evaluation session showed a positive reaction to the system, a longer-term evaluation would be required to measure the system's success in terms of both human connectedness, and whether the system would outlast the novelty effect and recreate the *honey pot effect* to ensure continued interaction.

There are two features that we feel are very important to include in the next version of UniVote (given the evaluation findings) to help encourage interaction. Firstly, the system should handle questions with more than three answer options. This would be essential for using UniVote in student elections – a key usage area identified by the study participants and during the needs analysis. Secondly, a "points system" could be used to reward frequent voters with gifts and vouchers from the student union, who would be identified by the unique Bluetooth address of their mobile phone.

The outcomes of this study highlight that interaction with shared displays has a lot to offer through encouraging users to express opinions by casting votes on topics of interest, and our preliminary findings suggest that the campus "bubble" can indeed be broken. A series of real-world testing and evaluations would have to be conducted to confirm this with respect to human connectedness principles. Unsurprisingly we replicated the general finding that a strong well-founded rationale for developing an interactive system is the best

predictor for its success, particularly when this is matched with users' greatest interests and needs.

5. REFERENCES

[1] Agamanolis, S. Designing Displays for Human Connectedness. In O'Hara K., Perry M., Churchill E., Russell D., *Public and Situated Displays: Social and Interactional Aspects of Shared Display Technologies*, pages 309-334, Kluwer Academic Publishers, 2003.

[2] Agamanolis, S. New Technologies for Human Connectedness, *ACM Interactions*, 12, 4 (July - August 2005), 33 – 37.

[3] Anderson, J.A. *Communication theory: epistemological foundations*. New York, NY: The Guilford Press, 1996.

[4] Borovoy, R., Martin, F., Vemuri, S., Resnick, M., Silverman, B. and Hancock, C. *Meme Tags and Community Mirrors: Moving from Conferences to Collaboration*, 1998.

[5] Brignull H. and Rogers Y. Enticing People to Interact with Large Public Displays in Public Spaces. In Proceedings of INTERACT'03 (Zürich, Switzerland, Sep. 2003), 17-24.

[6] Cooke, R., Bewick, B.M., Barkham, M. Bradley, M. and Audin, K. Measuring, monitoring and managing the psychological well-being of first year university students. *British Journal of Guidance and Counselling* 34, 4, (2006), 505-517.

[7] Hayes, A.F., Shanahan, J. and.Glynn, C.J. Willingness to express one's opinion in a realistic situation as a function of perceived support for that opinion, *International Journal of Public Opinion Research,* 13, 1, (2001), 45-58.

[8] Mankoff, J. and Dey, A.K. From Conception to Design: A Practical Guide to Designing Ambient Displays. In O'Hara K., Perry M., Churchill E., Russell D., *Public and Situated Displays: Social and Interactional Aspects of Shared Display Technologies*, pages 210-230, Kluwer Academic Publishers, 2003.

[9] Miller, K. Communication theories: perspectives, processes, and contexts. (2nd ed). New York, NY: McGraw-Hill, 2005.

[10] Newton, F.B. (1998). The stressed student, *About Campus*. (May-June 1998), 4-10.

[11] Noelle-Neumann, E. The Spiral of Silence. Chicago: University of Chicago Press, 1993.

[12] O'Neill, E., D. Woodgate and V. Kostakos, 2004, "Easing the wait in the Emergency Room: designing public information systems". ACM Designing Interactive Systems, Boston, MA.

[13] Scheible, J. and Ojala, T. MobiLenin combining a multi-track music video, personal mobile phones and a public display into multi-user interactive entertainment. In *Proceedings of ACM Multimedia* 2005, 199-208.

[14] Shoemaker, P.J., Breen, M. and Stamper, M. Fear of isolation: Testing an assumption from the spiral of silence, *Irish Communications Review,* 8, (2000), 65-78.

Teaching Severely Autistic Children to Recognise Emotions: Finding a Methodology

Salima Y Awad Elzouki
Leeds Metropolitan University
Headingley Campus
Leeds LS6 3QS, UK
+44 113 283 2600

s.elzouki@leedsmet.ac.uk

Marc Fabri
Leeds Metropolitan University
Headingley Campus
Leeds LS6 3QS, UK
+44 113 283 2600

m.fabri@leedsmet.ac.uk

David J Moore
Leeds Metropolitan University
Headingley Campus
Leeds LS6 3QS, UK
+44 113 283 2600

d.moore@leedsmet.ac.uk

ABSTRACT

This paper presents part of our wider research project concerning the design, development and evaluation of computer systems for children with autism. Research currently being carried out concerns how children with autism recognise human facial expressions of emotion and how the use of computer-based animated characters might help them in this recognition. The context for the research is a primary school unit of children with severe autism and moderate to severe learning difficulties. We present results of a preliminary study designed to establish a baseline for the abilities of each child, and describe the methodology considerations that arose during and after the study. The merit of participant observers is discussed, and links to action research are pointed out.

Categories and Subject Descriptors

H.1.2 [User/Machine Systems]: Human factors, Human Information Processing

General Terms

Measurement, Experimentation, Human Factors

Keywords

Autism, Emotions, Avatars, Social Networking

1. INTRODUCTION

The literature has different views about what precisely "Autism" is. Leo Kanner in 1943 invented the label "early infantile autism" to describe children who "had never been participants in that social world" [8]. Hans Asperger in 1944 used the term "autistic" or "autism" to describe the more able children who "found it difficult to fit in socially" [8]. This less severe form of autism is since referred to as Asperger Syndrome (AS). The National Autistic Society recognises several subgroups of autism. Having an autistic spectrum disorder (ASD) is a "complex lifelong developmental disability" [21].

The deficit of social proficiencies is still considered as one of autism's specific concerns and one of the common views of the nature of autism. For example Aarons & Gittens [1] think that the "social disability is the essence of autism". Many students with Autism or ASD have learning difficulties or learning disabilities [16][21]. This might explain the suggestion of Baron-Cohen & Bolton [6] that to the general public, autism is often perceived as a "mental handicap". Wing [26] proposed that the social difficulties that characterise children with autism ban best be described as a "Triad of Impairments". These impairments are as follows:

1. Firstly there is a communication impairment: people with autism tend to have difficulty understanding and also using verbal and non verbal communication

2. Secondly a social impairment: autistic people find it difficult to join and sympathize with other people.

3. Thirdly there is an impairment of social imagination. People with autism have rigidity in language, thinking and manners.

Howlin et al. [14] suggest that this triad of impairments is underpinned by a "Theory of Mind deficit" (ToM) which is the ability to mind-read and surmise the thoughts, beliefs, desires and intentions of others. Peterson et al [20] argue that the understanding of desires precedes the understanding of beliefs. Therefore, understanding that other people have desires and emotions is also an important part of ToM.

The incidence of autism and its related behaviours is increasing. In 2004 the Autism Society of America estimated autism to occur in 2 - 6 per 1,000 births, with boys being affected four times that of girls [2]. However, more recently the reported incidence rose to 1 per 150 in the US [3] and to 1 per 100 in UK [21]. Autism is not limited to the Western world. However, many developing countries do not recognise autism. Libya, for example, has only recently recognised autism as a separate diagnosis but figures for incidence are not yet available.

2. EDUCATION AND TECHNOLOGY FOR PEOPLE WITH AUTISM

The reason behind the rise of autism incidences is unknown but it is clear that there is an urgent need for help and intervention. Education is seen as the key solution to overcoming autism impairments and it is also seen as the most important part of any attempt to help people with autism attaining a good base to live a better and more cheerful life [1][18][20]. Recently, there has been an interest in research using computer approaches with people with autism [19]. This is partly based on the fact that people with autism are naturally attracted to and interested in computer approaches [19][22][25]. This might be due to the beneficial characteristics that computer environments might offer to people with autism. Computers can, for example, provide individualised tutoring where the instructions could be repeated to the user or the student without tedium and without potentially counter-productive human intervention [19][24][20]. Much of recent research concerns social skills education for autistic people as well as addressing ToM problems. However, it has been argued that there is an urgent need for more programs that directly address autism specific impairments. [20][19][4]. Also there is little work looking at the more severe end of the spectrum [17] which is where the work reported in this paper comes in. Bosseler and Massaro [7], for example, confirmed that children with autism can successfully use computer-based animated characters to increase their vocabulary.

Whether children with severe autism can use such characters to improve their knowledge of emotions is the key question behind this research. We are investigating whether and how children with severe autism can recognise, or learn to recognise, emotions from human facial expressions. These emotions are presented by real people (photographs) as well as computer-generated characters and the work builds on work by Fabri's [11] investigation of using emotionally expressive avatars for social networking. The ultimate aim of the current work is to engage children with autism in social networking systems to help them overcome some of their social impairments in a safe environment. In this paper we present preliminary results of a study designed to establish a baseline for emotion recognition.

3. CHILDREN CASE STUDIES

The research is being conducted in a special unit at a local school (Leeds, UK) for children with severe autism and moderate to severe learning difficulties. Before outlining our actual work and experimental study, we believe it is crucial to present the diversity of the children in the school, and illustrate how wide the spectrum of autism is. Realising and responding to this had a major impact on our research methodology.

The total number of children in the unit is 11, divided into two classes: In Key Stage 1 (KS1) there are 6 children (5 boys & 1 girl) aged 6 to 8 years. In Key Stage 2 (KS2) there are 5 children (4 boys & 1 girl) aged 9 to 11 years. In the unit, these children follow a tightly organised daily routine in an attempt to maintain a predictable environment and minimise sudden changes in their behaviour. That does not mean, however, that unexpected changes do not happen, and in reality some children find it hard to cope even with this predictable and familiar environment depending on their mood at certain times and on certain days.

Due to the ethical considerations when working with children in general, and impaired children in particular, all parents were asked for consent after being fully informed of the aims and procedure of the study (see section 5 below). Parents for 8 children agreed for their children to participate (5 from KS1, 3 from KS2). In the next section we present characteristics of these 8 children. The names are not their real names.

Kareem, 7 years
Kareem has a severe language impairment as a result of which he finds it hard to communicate with others. He usually points to objects he wants, uses symbols available in the classroom, or says words in his own language. Kareem likes using a computer and is focussed and interested in the computer whenever he has the opportunity to play with it. However, he does not like sharing the computer with others.

Moftah, 7 years
In addition to autism Moftah's behaviour is sometimes aggressive and challenging. Moftah has a good articulation and pronunciation when compared to Kareem. While he cannot formulate full sentences, he can say what he wants very clearly in singular words. He sometimes becomes incomprehensible though and appears to talk to objects close to him, followed by giggling. Moftah is interested in computers and does not like to share the computer with other children.

3.1 Jamal, 8 years
Jamal is on a language level similar to Moftah. He can say clearly what he wants in one or two words. Jamal is sometimes aggressive and scratches other children or teaching staff in the face. Somewhat untypical for severely autistic children, Jamal maintains good eye-contact with who he talks to. He exposes the "Echolalia" feature of autism where he repeats what other people say to him. Jamal likes to draw, in particular animals. He has a talent to copy what is placed in front of him in a matter of minutes and to near perfection. Children with such unusual abilities are often referred to as "savants". Jamal has no interest in computers and does not know how to use one.

3.2 Nahla, 8 years
Nahla is the only girl in the KS1 class. Her diagnosis changed recently from autism to "attachment disorder". Compared to the other KS1 children, Nahla is the most able child with regards to communication. She acts "neuro typical" (NT) in the school environment where she likes to join in the class activities. Occasionally, Nahla is very aggressive and is then difficult to calm down if she does not get her way. This may culminate in her slapping other children or teaching staff. Like Jamal, Nahla has no interest in computers.

3.3 Nasser, 6 years
Nasser is the youngest child in the KS1 class. He joined the unit only recently. In class Nasser would usually be in his favourite corner of the room. He rarely moves from there unless he needs something. While in "his" corner, Nasser makes clicking noises with his mouth, a unique behaviour in the class. Nasser is generally well behaved and non-aggressive. When there is something he does not like his response is usually to cry. He can say what he wants in singular words, like Jamal and Moftah. Nasser has no interest in computers but likes watching videos and DVDs.

3.4 Tarek, 9 years
Tarek's visible behaviour is different from the other children. He shows some very typical features of autism e.g. keeping his ears blocked most of the time, turning his face away from people near him or flapping hands or objects around him [cf. 26]. He spends most of his time in class standing on his own, in a certain spot in the room, moving away only when he needs something. Tarek likes to hum and sing parts of movie songs to others, or sometimes with others. He is interested in computers and his typical behaviour when using one is to stand in front of the screen, close one of his ears with one hand, and play with the mouse or keyboard with the other hand. He likes to listen to songs on the computer and he can move the mouse, minimise, maximise and close down computer windows.

3.5 Yzan, 10 years
Yzan is a quiet boy whose voice is rarely heard in class. He has problems communicating and is in the early stages of learning to speak. He is aloof most of the time in class, and likes being on his own, looking thoroughly at walls and glass windows. Yzan likes to play computer games, jumping from one scene to another without finishing any game task. When he loses interest he will immediately turn off the computer. He may repeat this pattern several times during one day. Tarek likes the sounds coming from the computer and he often puts up the volume to highest setting.

3.6 Nabeel, 9 years

Nabeel has autism with moderate learning difficulties. He has good speaking abilities compared to the other children. Nabeel can construct full sentences and say what he wants very clearly. However, he sometimes utters words and sounds that cannot be understood, and appears to be talking to some invisible person or object next to him – in a similar way to Moftah. Sometimes he stays aloof from the others and spends the time sitting in front of the window, or he lies down on the floor. Nabeel is interested in computers and spends time sitting down and playing games. He uses the mouse and follows links in order to win a game or complete a task

3.7 Reflection

As evidenced above, behaviours and abilities under the umbrella of the Autistic Spectrum Disorder are wide and varied. Looking at each child individually was crucial to inform our methodology and study design, and it also helped us to set the preliminary results of our work into context. In the next section we describe what methodology we used and how we arrived there.

4. METHODOLOGY

Based on the above we realised that these children were special and individual in many ways. The debate about which methodology to use for an in depth investigation into how these children could be helped to overcome some of their impairments represented a major part of the initial research. Due to the small number of children, quantitative data was not expected to be statistically relevant. In any case, the individual differences between the children, and the inherently social and personal nature of autism called for detailed qualitative research methods. In the next sections we describe our "journey" to identify the right methodology which we hope is of interest to other practitioners.

4.1 Participation during observation

In research, observation is a fundamental method of gathering data, aiming to gather first hand information in a naturally occurring situation. We initially intended to use non-participant observation where the observer is a neutral outsider, commonly used to avoid the observer influencing the events taking place. For a number of weeks the children were observed within the daily basic sessions at school to get to know how they behaved in their daily routine. Some of the case study characteristics mentioned above were the output of these observations. However, it became obvious that to engage the children in any experimental activity, one had to become part of their daily routine. Further, it was difficult to stay neutral due to the small group size and it was during this time that the primary author started to sympathise with the children. Towards the more severe end of the autistic spectrum it seems to be impossible to observe without getting to know the child over a longer period of time if any type of response from, or interaction with, the children is to be achieved.

In HCI, "co operative user observation" is considered a most suitable method to evaluate prototype interfaces with children [9]. We argue, therefore, that to apply this method with this user group the observer requires detailed knowledge of each child's needs. Indeed, familiarity between the child and the observer is important to avoid distress or upset during any computer intervention. A combination of both participant (neutral observer) and non-participant (involved observer) observations was adopted, and a detailed case study profile was created for each child. The observer effectively became a

teaching assistant in order to create a sufficient level of familiarity and trust.

4.2 Relationship to Action Research

It could be argued that there is a loop of cycles within above approach which is related to the Action Research method [12]. In action research, one goes through several cycles namely a) observe events occurring in real life, b) reflect on these and identify that there is a problem, c) plan how the problem could be solved or the situation improved on, and finally d) act and start observing again. We argue that on an individual child's basis, we can follow a similar cycle and apply interventions in order to assess the child's abilities and observe any development or learning taking place as a result. The study described below is the first intervention and it aimed to establish a baseline for what the participating children were able to do, and where the next cycle could lead them.

5. RECOGNITION STUDY

The literature concerning children with autism and emotional understanding suggests that these children have difficulty in creating and producing emotional expressions, they are also poor in reading and understanding other's facial expressions [14][15]. This might explain their weaknesses in understanding other people's mental states i.e. the Theory of Mind (ToM) impairment [5]. To overcome this impairment, [14] considered recognising human facial expressions from photographs as the first level of acquiring emotional understanding. The range of impairments, abilities and preferences of the children participating in this research meant that there could not be one single piece of software that would suit all children. To establish a baseline for what each child is capable of, we followed the approach taken by [14] who presented children with pictures of people showing facial expressions of emotions corresponding with *happy, sad, angry* and *frightened* (see Fig 1 below).

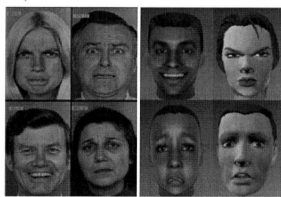

Figure 1. Material used in Stages 1 and 2

5.1 Procedure

The place, time and the date of the study had been agreed with the teacher before starting any stages of the study. Participating children were put in a familiar and predictable environment in order to make the experiment part of their daily routine as much as possible. A laptop was used and all sound was recorded using a digital recorder.

At the time of the study, the children were asked individually by the staff if they like to work on the computer. The ones who were interested came to the workstation area and sat down. A red "wait" symbol that is usually used by the staff to encourage turn-taking during computer usage was used in the study.

Each child was shown the photos in a 2x2 matrix on a computer screen ([14] used laminated paper) and asked the same question about each emotion, e.g. "can you point to the happy face?". After being shown the first set of photographs (identical to the black & white photographs Howlin [14] used), the children were in stage 2 presented with screen shots of computer generated faces showing expression for the same set of emotions, as created and validated by [11]. In a third stage, the children were shown the same set of computer-generated faces from stage 2 after rotating them and with different genders representing the emotions, to avoid order and gender prototyping problems.

By studying pre-validated emotion representations with such a user group, we are arguably testing the standard in extremis, and hence potentially enabling the standard to be strengthened. Lessons from the use of the technology in extraordinary human computer interaction might then lead to helpful development of the technology for "general" use [cf. 13].

5.2 Results

Results were inconclusive. Only one child (Moftah) recognised all expressions. While Kareem recognised all of the photographs, he struggled with the computer-generated faces. Interestingly, Nahla's results were reversed, indicating a possible link with her attachment disorder. Nabeel was successful only during stage 2. Several children did not co-operate at all, or only during some stages.

6. CONCLUSIONS AND FURTHER WORK

The results obtained in the recognition study show that each child is individual in their ability to recognise emotions. The number of instances of non-cooperation during the experiment indicates the difficulties that working with such children can involve, even when the children know the observing researcher well. Further, the case studies revealed that because of their severe autism, the children have significantly different abilities of social interaction and communication. Based on both the quantitative and qualitative data we will now create a programme for each child, aimed at their current level of ability and taking advantage of their individual interests. Jamal's interest in animal drawings, for example, could provide a way to get him interested in the facial expressions when they are somehow related to animals. Nahla, who had difficulty recognising the human photographs, could be presented with computer-generated faces with a higher degree of realism than the ones used so far. Eventually we hope to evidence progress for each child, at their level, and potentially be able to identify patterns in their behaviour that recur across several children.

7. REFERENCES

[1] Aarons, M., Gittens, T. (1998). Autism: A social skills approach for children and adolescents. Oxford: Winslow

[2] Autism Society of America (2004). Statistics for 2004. http://www.autism-society.org

[3] Autism Society of America (2007). Statistics for 2007. http://www.autism-society.org

[4] Beardon, L., Parsons, S., & Neale, H. (2001). An interdisciplinary approach to investigating the use of virtual reality environments for people with Asperger syndrome. Education & Child Psych. 18(2), 53-62.

[5] Baron-Cohen, S. (1996). Psychology in action; Autism

[6] Baron-Cohen S. & Bolton B. (1993), Autism: the facts, Oxford

[7] Bosseler, A., Massaro, D.W. (2003). Development and Evaluation of a Computer-Animated Tutor for Vocabulary and Language Learning, Journal of Autism and Development Disorders, 33(6), 653-672.

[8] Cumine V, Leach J and Stevenson G. (2000), Autism in the early years: a Practical Guide.

[9] Dix, A. , Finlay, J., Abowd, G., Beale, R. (1998). Human-Computer Interaction, 3rd edition

[10] Ekman and Friesen (1975). Pictures of Facial Affect. CD-ROM, University of California

[11] Fabri (2006). Emotionally Expressive Avatars for Collab. Virtual Environments. PhD Thesis. Leeds Met University

[12] Herr, Kathryn and Anderson (2005). The Action Research Dissertation. London. Sage

[13] Hobbs, D.J., Moore, D.J. (1998) Human computer interaction. FTK Publishing, London

[14] Howlin, P., Baron-Cohen, S., Hadwin, J. (1999) Teaching Children with Autism to Mind-Read, A Practical Guide for Teachers and Parents, John Wiley and Sons

[15] Irish Autism Society (1995). A Story of Autism. Booklet

[16] Jordan, P. Jones, G. Morgan, H (2001), The Foundation for People with Learning Disabilities.

[17] Moore (2007). Computer Systems for People with Autism; Internal Report, Leeds Met University

[18] Moore D, McGrath P, Thorpe J (2000) Computer Aided Learning for People with Autism Innovations in Education and Training International, 37(3), 218-228

[19] Moore D, Cheng Y, McGrath P, Powell N (2004). CVE Technology for People with Autism; Internal Report, Leeds Met University.

[20] Moore D, Taylor J (2000) Interactive multimedia systems for people with autism. J. Educ. Media, 25, 169-177

[21] The National Autistic Society, http://www.nas.org.uk

[22] Parsons, S., Mitchell, P. (2002). The potential of virtual reality in social skills training for people with autistic spectrum disorders, J of Intell. Disab. Res., 46, 430-443

[23] Peterson, C.C., Wellman H.M. & Liu D. (2005). Steps in Theory- of-Mind Development for Children with Deafness or Autism. Child Development, 76(2) 502-517.

[24] Silver, M., & Oakes, P. (2001). Evaluation of a new computer intervention to teach people with autism or Asperger Syndrome to recognise and predict emotions in others. Autism, 5(3), 299-316.

[25] Tucker L (1997). Primary Education, Communication, Winter, pp13-15

[26] Wing, L. (1996) The Autism Spectrum: A Guide for Parents and Professionals, London, Constable

MARPLE Investigates: An 'Adversarial' Approach to Evaluating User Experience

Jane Holt
Lancaster University
Computing Department
Infolab 21
+44 (0) 1524 510311

holtj1@comp.lancs.ac.uk

Simon Lock
Lancaster University
Computing Department
Infolab 21
+44 (0) 1524 510304

lock@comp.lancs.ac.uk

ABSTRACT

User experience of interactive systems has always been difficult to assess due to its subjective nature. In this paper we present a new approach to the evaluation of pleasure as an aspect of user experience. This multi-lateral approach, entitled MARPLE, is based upon an adversarial courtroom metaphor.

Categories and Subject Descriptors

H1.2 User/Machine Systems; H5. Information Interfaces and Presentation.

Keywords

User Experience, Interactive, Subjective, Evaluation, Adversarial.

1. INTRODUCTION

The last ten years has seen a growth of interest, within the Human-Computer Interaction (HCI) community, towards User Experience. User experience is concerned with the 'quality of the process' that the user *feels* during interaction. User experience typically includes such aspects as fun [4, 22], creativity [3, 15], playfulness [14] and aesthetics [15]. Efforts are currently being made to design and evaluate systems which take these aspects into account. However, this is a challenging prospect due to the emotional aspects of user experience.

The term 'emotion' is in itself difficult to define. There are many differing opinions as what emotion is and how it functions, from such fields as psychology [6, 7, 9, and 11] and neuroscience [19]. What appears to be a repeating theme though, is that emotion is seen as 'a mental state that does not arise through free will, and that is often accompanied by physiological changes' [9]. These states can be triggered by either an internal or external stimulus, e.g. a pleasant memory or a perceived threat, which can then manifest themselves as an increase in heart rate and breathing, changes in facial expression or tensing of the muscles. There are said to be six basic emotions that we all experience, such as anger, disgust, fear, joy, sadness and surprise [6], though the number and type varies amongst psychologists [6, 7, 9 and 11].

Emotional states are both fleeting and unpredictable, and are open to individual interpretation which can also be subjective. What is interesting to note is that historically, emotions were seen in a negative aspect, as self-limiting and obstructive as compared to a logical, rational approach. However, due to research undertaken into the field of affective computing, emotions have come to the forefront with the emphasis now on ensuring systems are enjoyable as well as usable.

Incorporating this into the design process is problematic, and this equally applies to evaluation. Usability has long established

methods in order to determine whether a system is efficient, effective and satisfying. Conversely, user experience is a relatively new area which is focused upon developing frameworks and approaches [3, 8, 12], which will include evaluation guidance. Experiments have been conducted into this type of evaluation [1,] which draw upon existing usability techniques, such as questionnaires [5, 18], interviews, [5, 18], heuristics [18] and 'think aloud' protocols [17]. These are well used techniques, in both academia and industry, which appear to provide reliable data.

However, user experience is a wide ranging area of research which has engendered a variety of approaches. Many researchers are adopting a 'holistic' approach by focusing on the subject as a whole [3, 8], whereas others have chosen to concentrate on single aspects such as fun [22, 4], enjoyment [17], play [15] and motivation [8].

2. EXISTING APPROACHES

Currently there appears to be no single standard approach to the issue of evaluating pleasure, as part of user experience. Discussion is centred around whether to rework 'old' or existing methods of evaluation, specifically for user experience, or to develop new techniques. Another option is that of combining techniques from usability with user experience thereby assessing both task performance and emotional impact.

What is recognized by many researchers is the challenge of designing a common methodological approach [3] for this purpose. It has even been suggested that this may be an insurmountable problem due to the imprecise and ambiguous nature of emotions. However, we have already mentioned that there is a growing awareness of the importance of emotions during user interaction and so efforts are being made to find ways of assessing their impact.

We have already mentioned that some researchers have chosen to use existing usability techniques, such as interviews – both structured and semi structured [5, 18] and questionnaires [5,

18]. These and other usability methods are frequently used throughout the usability community and as such can be said to be tried and tested though not entirely conclusive. This may be more of an issue with qualitative methods which tend to rely upon interpretation of data rather than pure statistics [18].

As well as these, other approaches are being used: one approach uses bio sensing or physiological measures. These are metrics which allow us to obtain physiological data in order to assess user emotion and stress [14]. Sometimes used in cognitive psychology, this includes measuring heart rate via an Electrocardiogram (ECG) or the conductivity of the skin via Galvanic Skin Response (GSR). Increases in heart rate or the temperature of the skin can indicate periods of stress and anxiety experienced by the user during interaction.

Another is that of 'pastiche scenarios', which a team at the University of York have been using as a form of evaluation. These are short narratives which borrow from other texts to show how a user might interact with a device. Similar to a diary yet also closely allied to persona creation, they aim to capture emotionally rich data from everyday occurrences [2].

A more structured method is advocated, based upon an experiential value scale which measures user responses via a seven point scale. Based upon marketing research, it uses nine indicators, for example, intrinsic enjoyment, that are then used against a series of statements related to user experience. These statements are measured via this scale according to their levels of agreements [21].

Other new methods have been proposed, for example, 'cultural probes' in which users self report about their interaction experience via a package consisting of a diary, camera and task cards, which records their actions, thoughts and feelings [1, 10]. The use of 'anticipation' interviews in which users are encouraged to keep voice note diaries, followed by a reflection interview [20], and a multiple method which uses in situ observations, 'obstacle cards' and interviews, at various stages in order to assess customer behaviour for an e-commerce website [16].

We have highlighted a few of the various approaches, for user experience evaluation, which are drawn from both the qualitative and quantitative domains. What is interesting to note is that some of these use a single technique for evaluation whereas others suggest a multiple approach. Which are better for user experience evaluation? Both of these approaches have advantages and disadvantages which are discussed in the next section.

3. COMPARISON AND CRITIQUE

The use of a single technique, for example, a questionnaire, may be considered perfectly appropriate for user experience evaluation. These have been and are used on a regular basis in both academia and industry: a single technique could be particularly beneficial when both time and money are subject to constraints, for example, conducting an 'expert walkthrough' [18]. On the other hand, if undertaking a protracted series of evaluations, then the utilisation of several techniques may be more profitable. In either case, a systematic approach seems to bring dividends – when determining usability. Usability is often focussed upon the achievement of specific criteria [18] within a context of use, so having what appear to be clearly defined goals and objectives can make things easier.

However, the application of a rigid 'checklist' approach to what can be a fluid, unpredictable and sensual process may not be

ideal. It may be more beneficial to use a range of techniques which are based upon interpretation rather than metrics, for example, combining interviews with video observation and/or photography, or cultural probes followed by an interview. As we are dealing with qualitative measures, a single technique might not be strong enough or reliable enough to accurately capture data. So it may be more worthwhile to use several of these techniques together in order to provide a solid justification when discussing the results.

4. THE MARPLE METHOD

MARPLE stands for the Multi-lateral Assessment and Review of Pleasure Laden Experiences and is a methodology which is currently being developed as a response to the issue of evaluating pleasure as part of the user experience. Due to its interpretative nature, we are devising a largely qualitative approach which is both systematic and integrated. It is still at an early stage, though it will undergo further refinement over time via testing and feedback. It will use several existing techniques e.g. interviews, video observation etc, as a means of gathering evidence, which is then used in a post-session discussion. As illustrated in figure 1, MARPLE will aim to provide a framework which drives these individual approaches, integrates their results and supports the building of cases to argue about specific aspects of user.

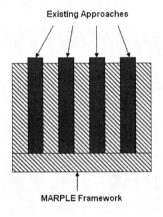

Figure 1. The MARPLE integrated approach

In keeping with the name and the 'adversarial' metaphor, this methodology aims to build a case for the assessment of user experience, from which it will be decided if it was pleasurable or whether in fact, it was 'displeasurable'. It will use these techniques, in conjunction with each other, to gather evidence, which is then offered as proof at the post session discussion. A single piece of evidence could be seen as too flimsy and not capable of fully capturing the emotional aspects whereas several pieces of evidence, used together could help reinforce an argument.

We also advocate the use of two investigators who will take up positive and negative stances, or in reference to the adversarial metaphor, the 'prosecution' and the 'defence'. These investigators will be looking to determine if the interaction was pleasurable or not and the reasons why. The rationale behind this stance is that they may be able to counter accusations of personal subjectivity and bias. One will argue for the positive determinants of a pleasurable interaction and the other will argue for the negative aspects. Then, the two will swap roles and continue the discussion until a final judgement is reached via a third party. The MARPLE Method is strongly based upon a prosecuting/defence investigator stance which we think makes it a novel approach to the issue of user experience evaluation.

MARPLE will consist of two halves: one half is the theoretical background and the other is the development of a 'toolkit' which can be used to conduct evaluation of interaction experiences. This toolkit will include a set of guidelines as to what to consider during evaluation, a tutorial which outlines the pleasure evaluation process, from the initial setting up of the equipment through to data analysis and post session discussion, and a case study. Its systematic approach includes obtaining participants, the setting up of the test situation, the evaluation session using video and interviews, data analysis and then the post session discussion with the prosecuting/defence stance. The post session discussion will be followed by the production of an evaluation report.

The MARPLE process model provides an overall framework for structured evidence gathering, analysis and interpretation. This model starts with the setting up of the system, the interaction itself and evidence gathering, through to data analysis, the post session discussion and the creation of a case for a positive or negative experience.

MARPLE will be used at various stages throughout the design cycle, where evaluation needs to be undertaken, e.g. low fidelity stage, and, after implementation, before the system is released into the public domain. It is also designed to complement current usability methods.

5. EVALUATION: HCI 2006

MARPLE was first trialled at the Re (Actor) workshop, as part of HCI 2006, in which it assessed the pleasurability of an interactive installation. In order to do this, we set up a 3D interactive installation (illustrated in figure 2) which used two anthropomorphic interface agents, a games console and two unusual input devices. The two unusual input devices - a couple of children's dolls were chosen as firstly, the theme of the workshop was 'playful/clubbing environments'; secondly, we thought they epitomised 'play' as well as being amusing and thirdly, that they would engender a pleasurable experience.

Figure 2. Interactive Installation (HCI 2006)

We set up the interactive installation in an area in which other types of 'playful' devices were displayed. During the conference intervals, e.g. lunch, delegates could wander around and try out the devices. The installation was based upon users being able to emotionally interact with the two agents, by manipulating the two dolls. He/she could express a single emotion which the agents would respond to from a pre-defined range of actions. For example, if the user wished to show 'anger', he/she would shake the dolls violently or use them to

perform 'punching' actions towards the agents who would respond by 'punching' back towards the user. The agents always had a default 'start' position in which they were standing still facing the user. The installation involved the user performing a single action with the dolls to which the agents would respond accordingly and then return to the start position. The user would perform another action; the agents would respond again, assume the start position and so on. The agents, one male and one female, were constructed using Poser 4 - 3D character modelling software, and the interactivity was enabled using Java and the console's basic motion capture system.

Due to time constraints, we were able to perform 'quick and dirty' evaluations with five users only. These users were mainly from the performing arts/digital arts domains and were evenly balanced in terms of gender, age and expertise. Each user would sit in front of the installation and would emotionally interact with two 3D interface agents via the doll input devices. These dolls were attached via retractable wires to a games console which the user could manipulate in any way they saw fit – see Figure 2. Each session involved an informal interview with video observation and photography and lasted, on average, around five to ten minutes.

This was followed by data analysis of the interview transcripts and a post session discussion. The data analysis involved grouping the stills into a linear sequence or 'storyboards', to ascertain a pattern of interaction and any distinguishing features. The video footage was viewed in much the same way, with the emphasis on looking at facial expression, gesture and body language in order to highlight positive/negative aspects.

Similarly with the interview transcripts: these were analysed in order to look for repeating words or emerging patterns of behaviour. As the interviews themselves were short, this meant a limited amount of user feedback, though we still managed to elicit some useful comments. The results showed that overall, the users enjoyed the interactive installation, with such words as 'playful', 'funny' and 'good' which suggest that this was a positive experience. There were a few suggestions for improving the installation, such as the 'time lag' between the user's action and the agent's reaction.

The resulting data was then open to discussion by both investigators who adopted the prosecuting and defence lawyer stance. One investigator argued in favour of a positive experience by describing various features which they felt supported this; such as expressive body language, smiling face etc, whereas the other investigator opposed this by pointing out indicators of a negative experience. Eventually, agreement was reached on a variety of issues though it was suggested that a neutral party might be needed.

This initial trial was fairly successful in that it elicited positive and useful feedback. It also raised a number of important issues relating to the evaluation of user experience in general. One such issue is the problem of interpreting photographic evidence, and as such, can not be taken as conclusive. Also, one aspect of MARPLE still open to debate is the friendly, 'chatty' and yet semi structured interview or 'stealth interviewing' which is designed to be unobtrusive and still obtain useful feedback. We have designed a series of suggested interview questions, which are concerned with conceptual issues rather than issues of 'how do you do this', 'what did you expect to happen' and so on. There is the tendency to slip into usability interviewing, particularly if the investigator has previous experience in this area and so there needs to be an awareness of this issue.

The MARPLE Method is still in its infancy and so further work needs to be undertaken before advocating its adoption by both academia and industry. This means a look at other multi-faceted approaches, an appraisal of the techniques we have chosen and why, and, its suitability and appropriateness as a means of evaluating user experience.

6. REFERENCES

[1] Axelrod, L and Hone, K.S. *Affectemes and Allafects: a novel approach to coding user emotional expression during interactive experiences.* Behaviour and Information Technology, Vol. 25, No 2, March-April 2006, pp 159-173.

[2] Blythe, M. *Pastiche Scenarios.* Interactions, September + October 2004.

[3] Blythe, M; Wright, P; McCarthy, J and Bertelsen, O.W. *Theory and Method for Experience Centred Design.* CHI 2006, April 22-27, 2006, Montreal, Quebec, Canada.

[4] Carroll, J.M. *Beyond Fun.* Interactions, September 2004.

[5] Dix, A; Finlay, J; Abowd, G.D; and Beale, R. *Human-Computer Interaction: Third Edition.* Pearson Prentice Hall, Essex, England, 2004.

[6] Ekman, P. *Facial Expression and Emotion.* 1992 Award Address. American Psychologist, April 1993, Vol 48, No 4, pp 384-392.

[7] Ekman, P. *Basic Emotions.* Chapter 3, Handbook of Cognition and Emotion. Sussex, UK. John Wiley & Sons Ltd, 1999.

[8] Forlizzi, J and Battarbee, K. *Understanding Experience in Interactive Systems.* DIS2004, August 1-4, 2004, Cambridge, Massachusetts.

[9] Goertzel, B. *A General Theory of Emotion in Humans and Other Intelligences.* DynaPsych Table of Contents. http://www.goertzel.org/dynapsyc/2004/Emotions.htm.

[10] Jaasko, V and Mattelmaki, T. *Observing and Probing.* DPPI '03, June 23-26, 2003, Pittsburgh, Pennsylvania, USA.

[11] James, W. *What is an Emotion?* Classics in the History of Psychology. An internet resource developed by Christopher D. Green, York University, Toronto, Ontario. http://psychclassics.yorku.ca/James/emotion.htm.

[12] Knight, J and Jefsioutine, M. *The Experience Design Framework: from Pleasure to Engagability.* Conference HCI, the Arts and Humanities, 2003, University of York, UK. http://www-users.cs.york.ac./~pcw/KM_subs/Knight_Jefsioutine.pdf.

[13] Mandryk, R.L; Atkins, M.S and Inkpen, K.M. *A Continuous Objective Evaluation of Emotional Experience with Interactive Play Environments.* Proceedings of the SIGCHI conference on Human Factors in computing systems, Novel Methods: Emotions, Gestures, Events (CHI 2006), (Montreal, Quebec, April 22-27, 2006).

[14] Mandryk, R.L; Inkpen, K.M and Calvert, T.W. *Using psychophysiological techniques to measure user experience with entertainment technologies.* Behaviour and Information Technology, Vol 25, No. 2, March-April 2006, pp 141-158.

[15] Myers, D. *What's good about bad play?* Proceedings of the Second Australasian Conference on Interactive Entertainment, 2005, Sydney, Australia 2004.

[16] Petre, M; Minocha, S; and Roberts, D. *Usability beyond the website: an empirically-grounded e-commerce evaluation instrument for the total customer experience.* Behaviour & Information Technology, Vol 25, No 2, March-April 2006, pp 189 – 203.

[17] Picard, R.W. *Affective Computing for HCI.* Ergonomics and User Interfaces 1999.

[18] Preece, J; Rogers, Y; and Sharp, H. *Interaction Design: Beyond Human-Computer Interaction.* Wiley, USA, 2002.

[19] Simon, V.M. *Emotional Participation in Decision-Making.* Psychology in Spain, Vol 2, No. 1, pp 100-107.

[20] Swallow, D; Blythe, M and Wright, P. *Grounding Experience: Relating Theory and Method to Evaluate the User Experience of Smartphones.* Proceedings of the 2005 Annual Conference on European Association of Cognitive Ergonomics, Chania, Greece. Session: On theories, methods and techniques. Vol. 132, 2005, pp 1- 98.

[21] Toms, E.G; Dufour, C and Hesemeier, S. *Measuring the User's Experience with Digital Libraries.* JCDL '04, June 7-11, 2004, Tucson, Arizona, USA.

[22] Wiberg, C. *Usability and Fun: An overview of relevant research in the HCI community.* http://www.sics.se/~kia/evaluating_affective_interfaces_/Wiberg_2.doc.

Designing for Photolurking

Haliyana Khalid

Lancaster University
Computing/Infolab21
Lancaster, LA1 4YR, UK
+44 1524 510349
h.khalid@lancaster.ac.uk
http://www.lancs.ac.uk/postgrad/khalid/index.htm

Alan Dix

Lancaster University
Computing/Infolab21
Lancaster, LA1 4YR, UK
+44 1524 510319
alan@hcibook.com
http://www.hcibook.com/alan/

ABSTRACT

This paper describes our early work on design and development to support photolurking. Photolurking is browsing and looking at people's photographs without participating in discussion or addressing the owner of the photographs or photologs, whilst still discussing them in other avenues. We suggest several recommendations, including supporting ad-hoc instantaneous sharing, having remote and live discussion with groups of friends, and fostering collaborative experience. Having said that, the aim of this paper is not to propose an ideal application for supporting photolurking, but rather to provide an instance of how findings and analysis from ethnographic studies can feed into practical design.

Categories and Subject Descriptors

H.5.5 [**Information Interfaces and Presentation**]: HCI

General Terms

Design, Human Factors

Keywords

Photo sharing, photolurking, user experience, social networking

1. INTRODUCTION

There are many web-based public image sharing applications such as Flickr and Fotopages. In addition other social network applications, such as MySpace, Friendster, Facebook and blogs, offer photo sharing facilities as well. With this proliferation of opportunities to upload images, there are often too many photographs to look at and too many to choose from.

User experience in photo sharing has changed dramatically since the advent of digital photographs. Traditionally, personal photographs were shared among family members and friends, kept carefully in photo albums or stored in boxes and tins. Sharing was face to face or through the post. Art photography was shared through exhibition, magazine or books. However, just as technology has changed the nature of photography, so also has it changed the user experience of sharing.

This growing interest in public image-sharing applications and

photologs was, for many, based on a desire to share experiences with remote friends and acquaintances, or to share skills and photography techniques. However as they have developed and become more 'public' they also become a ways of showing your skills, your interests and yourself to the world.

Apart from photologgers (those who actually post images), visitors swamp into photologs for different reasons. Some are browsing to catch up with friends' and families' updates, some are searching for information like photography techniques, recipes and gossip, while others are just fulfilling their curiosity and boredom. Visitors and photologgers form an online community around the photolog; a new community that unites through photography. As one would expect, there are two types of visitors in online communities; active and passive. From our findings, active visitors frequently participated in the discussion column of a photolog, often acknowledgeable by the photolog owner. On the other hand, the passive visitors or as we named them, photolurkers [7,9] do not offer any comments to the photolog yet often visited them.

Whilst the term 'photolurker' has a pejorative sound, but in fact our studies show this is not a negative experience. Photolurkers often communicate outside the photolog about the images they find within it and indeed photolurking is a valuable part of their social relationships. We therefore are looking at ways in which technology could be used to support this behaviour.

While studies of this sort often are regarded as having 'implications for design' [4], it is less common to see these implications worked through into actual design. In this paper we describe the early stages in the process of taking some of the findings of this research and pushing them into specific design concepts. These design concepts are currently being added into an existing web application Snip!t so that it can support discussion amongst photolurkers.

We will begin by briefly describing our ethnographic studies on the user experience in photologs that began in 2004, where we uncovered many interesting findings including the phenomenon of photolurking. This is followed by a few of the design recommendations which have arisen from this work, and which form the focus of this paper. We will then introduce Snip!t; an existing bookmarking tool, that allows one to snip a portion of the page content which can be stored and organized, but in addition can be passed to other web applications [3]. Methodologically this is important as real design is typically not ex nihilo, but instead builds on some existing platform, application or infrastructure. This base point often forms an additional constraint on the final product. We are using a scenario-based approach and we illustrate with a short scenario and how this is going to be integrated into Snip!t.

2. BACKGROUND STUDY

Our analysis based on user-experience studies on photologs since 2004 has focused attention on several interesting issues. Using various forms of ethnography, we have seen how personal memories of some people and other kinds of photographs are now freely shared on photologs. From our empirical studies, photos are shared on the application because of its mass-sharing capacity, responsibility to family and friends and to share techniques on photography and other skills. Apart from photologgers, photolog applications attract large number of viewers; both acquaintances and strangers. This combination of photologger and visitor has created the online community of the photolog. The visitors include silent visitor whom we described as 'photolurker' [7].

The word photolurker is derived from the word 'lurker' which means "one of the 'silent majority' in an electronic forum who posts occasionally or not at all but is known to read the postings of the group regularly" [8]. Our qualitative studies showed that our participants are more active photolurkers than photologgers. They visited people's photologs almost every day, often motivated or inspired by professional photographers or other people's photographs, which explains their frequent photolurking. We have suggested photolurking as term to describe this behaviour of browsing and looking at people's photographs without participating or acknowledging the owner of the photographs or photologs.

Personal attributes like shyness, being afraid to be recognised, lack of confidence with the language used and not having time to write are some of the reasons that prevent people from participating in discussions in photologs. However, our findings revealed that photolurkers do find other avenues to discuss the photographs. Encounters with photographs that trigger their interest are quickly considered, remembered and shared as this vignette from our studies demonstrates:

A group of friends are having breakfast together. As usual, they started to chat, catching up with stories like other friends would do. Then, one of them started to tell stories about a stranger and her photographs. Apparently, this stranger is no stranger to them, as most of them have seen her photos in her photolog. This group is reminiscing almost everything that they saw in the stranger photolog; her trip to Disneyland, her brother's convocation and who she's dating. Then the conversation flow to other people's photologs and gossips.

None of them has participated in the column discussion in the owner's photolog. However, discussions are made outside the photolog with a certain circle of friends in various ways such as face-to-face meetings (as in the above vignette), instant messaging or telephone conversation.

3. DESIGN RECOMMENDATIONS

As the focus of this paper is the movement from ethnography to design, we only present some specific findings here which suggest a potential for design. Briefly we need features that support user's desire for instantaneous sharing triggered by other people's photographs, and that allow remote discussion about those photographs privately with certain group of friends. The envisioned design also would benefit from synchronous communication and social interaction features. In the following, the ideas are broken down and further described.

3.1 Supporting ad-hoc feeling to share

Photolurking involves browsing and looking at people's photographs without participating openly in the discussion box or acknowledging the owner of the photographs. To date, there are thousands of photologs that display collections of

146

photographs. This amount does not include social network application like MySpace and Facebook or weblog and newspapers that contains pictures.

Certain photographs elicit emotions to certain people. While browsing, people might encounter photographs or photologs that really interest them or reminded them of some occasions. Any encounters of photographs that trigger their interests are quickly thought, remembered and shared. Thus, photolurking deals with ad-hoc feelings and curiosity of people that further motivates shared experience. In our study;

"I was photolurking one night, when I spotted one celebrity's photolog. I've got very excited to see her photos and stories. I send message to all my friends in the block, and they rush to my room, and we look at the photologs together... We talk and then after that, everybody resume to their room."

This discussion was face to face and requires no explicit support. However, it demonstrates a user need to instantly share with others outside of the photolog itself to encourage further discussion and exploration. At the present, some photologs and other applications such as Friendster allow people to notify their friends about photos of their interest through email, but this communication channel does not support user need to share impulsively.

3.2 Remote Discussion and Synchronous Communication

One of the most common and enjoyable uses for photographs is to share stories about experiences, travels, friends and family [2]. However, with the advent of photolog, people don't just talk about their families and friends, but strangers as well. Interestingly, the life of a stranger (that could be seen through his photolog) can be an object of obsession and talked about to certain groups without them participating in the owner's photolog. From our findings, the discussion usually happened in face-to-face meetings, telephone and instant messaging.

Having a design that offers a remote discussion with synchronous communication channel immediately after seeing a photo would help to improve their shared experience. This also will help in communicating the context in which such photos are to be understood. Simultaneous discussions with selected friends encourage social interaction in the application.

Such an envisioned design would take advantage of instant messaging technology, but needs to be tied closely to the photos being discussed.

3.3 Demonstrating social interaction

While social networking sites share the basic purpose of online interaction and communication, specific goals and patterns of usage vary significantly across different services [5]. For example, MySpace allows for sharing profiles, LinkedIn for finding work, YouTube for video sharing and LiveJournal for sharing blogs.

Supporting photolurking that involves groups of users may benefit from creating a social network application. Unlike other social network application, the design will foster discussion about photographs and other articles on the Internet. This idea suggests many designs and user interface issues. Design challenges include ways to invite some friends to the discussion while also have the ability to save and to re-tell stories in the future. The design could also benefit from features allowing for invitation to the network, locating and discovering friends and connecting through different media.

These recommendations represent an instance of how the qualitative results study generated through ethnography can potentially 'inform' design. However, we would like to see these lead to far more specific design concepts.

4. INTEGRATING THE RECOMMENDATIONS INTO SNIP!T USING SCENARIOS

One of the considerations in our designing for photolurking is that we are integrating our design strategies into an existing social bookmark tool called Snip!t. Snip!t was chosen as the authors have access to its developers and it already has some of the features that make it suitable as a basis.

As noted in the introduction real design rarely starts with a blank sheet. For similar reasons to a more commercial design process building a full application from scratch would not be effective in terms of time involved and by leveraging an existing platform we will be able to create a deployable system that can both act as a concept demonstrator for the results of existing studies and a technology probe [6] for future investigations.

4.1 Existing features of Snip!t

Snip!t is a web-based application that acts as a form of social bookmarking and also includes 'intelligent' features. A Snip!t user can select a portion of a web page and 'snip' it using a bookmarklet. The snipped portion together with the URL, title etc. are then saved in the web application and can be categorized, searched, and shared with others through email or public channels. In particular, the snipped part of the web page may include images (see Fig. 1), so this forms an initial way in which images can be selected form different photo sharing sites in order to be discussed.

In addition, Snip!t uses various patterns and heuristics in order to analyse the snipped area and web page. It looks for things like names, post codes, or telephone numbers and then suggests things which can be done with the matched areas; for example, a name might be looked-up in web-based people finders or an IP address checked in spam black-lists. The url of the page is also analysed so that, for example, the ISBN can be extracted from an Amazon page so that it is easy to use other services to find the book in a local library.

This feature means it would be possible to create patterns for popular photo-logs so that if the user snips a photo-log page this can trigger further rules to extract data, such as the title of the picture, from the page

4.2 Scenario-based design

Having Snip!t in mind, we are adopting scenario-based design methods to assist us with the process. This approach although perhaps the simplest design representation, is often considered one of the most flexible and powerful [1].

In this work, we are designing with a particular goal in mind – supporting photolurking, especially remote discussion about other people's photos. However, we also need to create designs that can be potentially integrated with the existing application. The flexibility of scenarios is particularly important as a more generative approach (e.g. driving design form a task analysis) would run the risk of producing designs which whilst in theory good would not be deliverable in practice.

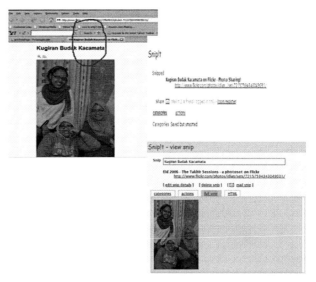

Figure 1. Snip!t used to snip an image

An example of short scenario to show an envisioned user task is as follows;

A is a frequent user of Snip!t. She uses Snip!t as a book marking tool and also to store interesting images that she notices while photolurking through photologs. She invites some of her friends to join Snip!t, and adds some friends who are already in Snip!t to join her network. One day, A found an image that really struck her emotion and would like to share it with her friends. She snips the picture to save it and sends an alert/message to some of her friends in her network to look at the image. A discussion box is supplied to allow them for discussion.

As is common, these scenarios are accompanied by sketches, and the design ideas. Critically the scenario above both sets itself into the context of Snip!t use (mentioned 4 times!) as well as photolurking. However, it is not limited to existing Snip!t features but adds functionality such as a network of friends and discussion areas.

One of the tensions in doing this work has been to create scenarios that are both (i) sufficiently unconstrained by the existing application that they suggest new design directions, but are also (ii) not so open that they are unimplementable! In practice, though we have lent towards an open design as the main aim of the scenarios is to explore detailed requirements not produce a final design.

4.3 From scenarios to system

As noted the scenarios suggest features not present in the exiting application as well as making use of current features. In addition in moving from the scenarios to a detailed design we looked extensions to that would be generally useful to Snip!t users as well as supporting photolurking.

The first element from the above scenario that is missing form the current systems is support for groups of friends. This is a common feature of such systems and has obvious benefits to the broader Snip!t users. Currently categories of snips can be either private to the user or public to everyone on the web.

Adding networks of friends will mean that it is possible to share snips (of web pages as well as images) with selected people.

The other key element in the scenario is the discussion box. The first design idea, based on the above scenario, was to have an instant messenger style chat box attached to each snip. To allow slow discussions we decided this should be persistent and would be rather like comments on existing photologs except it would be private to a group.

However, further scenarios, themselves based on our previous studies of photo sharing, suggest that conversation would move form photo to photo, so the model of a conversation per photo would breakdown. From this, the conceptual model changed from one where chat was per picture, to one where pictures were moment-to-moment the topic of a chat.

Figure 2 shows a sketch of this with an area (1) for the current photo being discussed, a chat area (2) that includes both the typed contributions of the members of the chat group and also embedded thumbnails (3) when a new picture was introduced as the topic. Also at the bottom (4) is an unshared area for the user to collect images they would like to introduce into the chat.

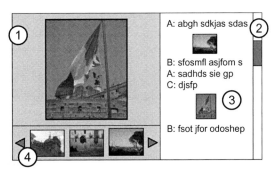

Figure 2. Potential photo chat

5. CONCLUSIONS

In this paper, we have described our initial work on the design and development of a tool to support photolurking. The design draws on our ethnographic studies of user experience in photologs. Building on Snip!t's existing ability to snip photographs and link to them from its web application, we are adding community and discussion facilities. These are each relatively simple, but together, we hope, will help answer users' ad hoc feelings and curiosity and the need for instant sharing and discussion. The flexibility of scenario-based methods have been crucial to balancing the goals of photolurking with the constraints of the existing application.

The choice of Snip!t was largely pragmatic based on our ability to influence its evolution. One alternative would be to alter an existing open-source image gallery. If we had done that, we would have been able to show how the design would fit into an existing photo-sharing site. However, actual deployment would have revealed little unless we had attracted a huge user base (unlikely!). In contrast, the Snip!t design builds off the presence of existing photo-sharing sites. Another alternative would be to use the API of one of the large sites to develop an application. However this would have been limited to a single site whereas Snip!t can allow discussion of multiple sites. It is interesting that these advantages of the proposed design were

'accidents' of the constraint to use Snip!t, but it has frequently been our observations that apparently arbitrary constraints lead to design innovation.

The ultimate aim of this phase of work is to deliver a deployable prototype. This will be given to subjects who we know already engage in both individual photolurking and also collective discussions, as described in section 3. We expect that the observations of logs and other observation techniques from protracted use will reveal other aspects of photolurking as well as further validate existing results.

6. ACKNOWLEDGMENTS
The study described in this paper was partially supported by Peel Trust Studentship, Lancaster University.

7. REFERENCES
[1] Benyon, D,. Turner, P. and Turner. S, Designing *Interactive Systems*. Pearson Education, 2005.

[2] Chaflen, R., *Snapshot versions of life*. Bowling Green State University Press. 1987.

[3] Dix, A., Catarci, T., Habegger, B., Ioannidis, Y., Kamaruddin, A., Katifori, A., Lepouras, G., Poggi, A., and Ramduny-Ellis, D.. Intelligent context- sensitive interaction on desktop and the web. In *Proceedings of the International workshop in conjuction with AVI2006 on Context in advanced interfaces*. 2006. Venice, Italy. ACM Press, New York, NY, 2000, 526–531.

[4] Dourish, P. 2006. Implications for design. In Proceedings of the SIGCHI Conference on Human Factors in Computing Systems (Montréal, Québec, Canada, April 22 - 27, 2006). R. Grinter, T. Rodden, P. Aoki, E. Cutrell, R. Jeffries, and G. Olson, Eds. CHI '06. ACM Press, New York, NY, 541–550.

[5] Gross, R. and Acquisti, A. Information revelation and privacy in online social networks. In *Proceedings of the 2005ACM Workshop on Privacy in the Electronic Society WPES '05*. 7 November, Alexandria, Virginia. 2005.

[6] Hutchinson, H., Mackay, W., Westerlund, B., Bederson, B. B., Druin, A., Plaisant, C., Beaudouin-Lafon, M., Conversy, S., Evans, H., Hansen, H., Roussel, N., and Eiderbäck, B. Technology probes: inspiring design for and with families. In *Proceedings of the SIGCHI Conference on Human Factors in Computing Systems (Ft. Lauderdale, Florida, USA, April 05 - 10, 2003). CHI '03*. ACM Press, New York, NY, 2003, 17–24.

[7] Khalid., H. and Dix, A.. From selective indulgence to engagement: exploratory studies on photolurking. In *Extended Abstract of the British HCI 2006 Conference*. Queen Mary, University of London, 11–15 September,2006.

[8] Nielsen, J. *Participation Inequality: Encouraging More Users to Contribute* Alertbox, October 9, 2006. www.useit.com/alertbox/participation_inequality.html

[9] WordSpy. Photolurker (definition and press references). Accessed 27 May 2007, available at: www.wordspy.com/words/photolurker.asp

Mapping the Demographics of Virtual Humans

Rabia Khan

School of Informatics
The University of Manchester

PO Box 88, Manchester M60 1QD
United Kingdom

Tel: +44 161 306 1291
E-mail:
Rabia.Khan@postgrad.manchester.ac.uk

Antonella De Angeli

School of Informatics
The University of Manchester

PO Box 88, Manchester M60 1QD
United Kingdom

Tel: +44 161 306 1291
E-mail:
Antonella.De-angeli@manchester.ac.uk

ABSTRACT

This paper presents a census of 147 virtual agents, by examining and reporting on their physical and demographical characteristics. The study shows that the vast majority of agents developed are from a white ethnic background. Overall, female agents tend to be more photo realistic than their male counterparts who are more cartoon like. These findings highlight current stereotypes in relation to agents and contribute to a deeper understanding of virtual worlds.

Categories and Subject Descriptors

Human Factors

General Terms

Design and Human Factors.

Keywords

Embodiment, agents, age, gender, race.

1. INTRODUCTION

In the last few years, virtual bodies have become increasingly prevalent in HCI (for example, embodied conversational agents, ECA's, and avatars). ECA's are defined as being synthetic characters (full body, graphical or physical simulations of people) that can maintain a conversation with a user [1]. An ample amount of research on ECA's has been concerned with how to emulate human conversation following the assumption that ECA's will have the same properties as humans in face to face conversation [2]. This line of research has led to the definition of relational agents, as computational artifacts designed to build long term, social-emotional relationships with their users [3]. There are many domains which could benefit from the deployment of relational agents; such as in online shopping, e-learning, advice giving, behavioural change therapy, helping people to stop smoking or dieting, counseling, or coaching them [4].

The debate on anthropomorphism and its implications in designing agents with more human-like qualities has been going on for quite some time. Walker et al. [5] found that people spent more time interacting with a talking face display

than text-only interface. Sproull et al. [6] showed that users were more positive in their response to a face by spending more time with it than with a text only version, where users quickly got bored. Reeves and Nass [7] clearly identify several benefits of the anthropomorphic approach by concluding that people respond to computer agents in fundamentally the same social ways as they would to another person.

A recent trend in anthropomorphic design has seen an increase in research on the effect of demographic and physical appearance variables of virtual agents. According to De Meuse's [8] taxonomy, a number of non-verbal variables affect face-to-face communication. These variables can be broken up into those cues that are behavioural in nature and those which are not. Non behavioural actions are *demographic variables* (ethnicity, age and gender) and *physical appearance variables* (clothing/attire, bodily and facial attractiveness). Demographic variables are not under an individual's control, whereas physical appearance cues can be subject to rapid change. Hence, cues such as hair/eye colour, cosmetics, clothing style can all affect social reactions to an individual's or an agent's. [9].

When looking at the importance of such demographic elements in embodiment, studies have shown that users prefer interacting with agents that either match their own ethnicity, or agents that are young looking [9]. The design of pedagogical agents' ethnicity and gender do influence learner perception of agent personality, motivational qualities, and perceived influence on the learning process. Students also perceived agents of the same ethnicity to be more engaging and affable. In particular, African-American learners were more likely to choose a pedagogical agent of the same ethnicity, and have a positive attitude towards this chosen agent after the lesson [10].

Baylor and Kim [11] draw attention to the impact of demographic variables and realism of pedagogical agents on learners. The findings suggest that students had a greater transfer of learning when agents were more realistic, and when the agents were represented non-traditionally (as black versus white) in the 'expert' role. The more realistic looking agents positively affected transfer of learning. Students which worked with the Black Expert agents found this quite novel, and thus paid more attention to the black agents than the white expert counterpart (the 'novelty effect').

As regards to gender, Hone [12] suggests that a female agent is more effective than a male agent in reducing frustration. Hence, frustration reduction is improved when an agent is embodied. Furthermore, a study showing female agents acting as a non-traditional engineer (e.g. very attractive and outgoing) significantly enhanced student interest in engineering as compared to a more stereotypical 'nerdy' version (e.g. homely and very introvert) [13]. Female learners have been reported to

149

prefer and choose a cartoon like pedagogical agent (as opposed to realistic looking agents) more often than their male counterparts [10]. Despite this growing corpus of evidence suggesting a significant role of physical variables of virtual embodiments, at present, little research has evaluated the demographic characteristics of existing agents. In this paper, we report a census of virtual agents by looking at physical characteristics of existing ones. The main aim of this study was to determine what type of demographic and physical variables were commonly or rarely being assigned to agents.

2. METHOD

A database of 147 virtual faces was analysed. These faces were collected by conducting internet searches in online journals and conference proceedings (ACM library and Science Direct), search engines (Google Scholar) and Conference sites (IVA: Intelligent Virtual Agents conference from 2003) using the following keywords: Embodied Conversational Agents (ECA's), Synthetic Agents, Social Agents, Conversational Agents, Virtual Agents, Virtual human, Agents and Avatars. Several e-mails were also sent to mailing lists (British HCI, CHI Announcements, CHI Students) and individual researchers to invite them to share pictures of Agents/Avatars they had utilised in their research.[1]

Agents were selected based on the following criteria: (a) Human like (No animal characters), (b) Frontal view only, and (c) Good quality image (at least 10 x 10 cm). Each agent was assigned a unique ID and recorded in a database system (Microsoft Access). The following attributes were researched and recorded in relation to each agent: Gender, Age, Ethnicity, Dressing Style, Profession, Anthropomorphism level, and Name. A coding/classification system was developed by the authors for each of the mentioned attributes. The source of each agent was recorded including details of the paper and authors who utilized/developed them in their research.

2.1 Framework of analysis

The framework of analysis was developed following an iterative process to accommodate different agent characteristics. Categories were refined and modified during the process. Double coding was conducted for 20% of the database yielding a reliability of almost 90%. All faces were coded according to a number of demographic and physical appearance variables [8]. Gender was divided into two categories: *Male and Female*. The remaining variables are discussed as follows:

Age consisted of four distinguished categories:

- *Child* – An individual between birth and puberty;
- *Young Adult* – An individual between puberty/teens and the age of 30;
- *Adult* – An individual between ages of 30 and 50; and
- *Older Adult* – An individual over 50.

Ethnicity consisted of 4 categories:

- *White* – Faces originating from Caucasian/European background;
- *Black* – Faces originating from African background;

- *Asian* – Faces originating from South Asian background; and
- *Oriental* – Faces originating from the Far East.

Dressing style was divided into 4 groups:

- *Casual* – Informal clothing and not dressy;
- *Formal* – Designed for wear or use in certain occasion/event or role;
- *Uniform* – A job specific outfit; and
- *Missing* – No outfit is visible, only face and neck displayed

Embodiments were also clustered into four broad categories according to their **level of anthropomorphism**:

- *Cartoon* – faces which do not represent real people. They can be sketches, or humorous images often displaying some exaggeration of facial characteristics (caricatures);
- *Drawing* – 2 dimensional representational images featuring human-like faces;
- *Mannequin* –3 dimensional representational images of human-like faces; and
- *Photo realistic* - Pictures of real human beings or artificial faces which are extremely human like, so that they could be erroneously attributed to a real person.

Profession consisted of 5 main roles (the role source was where the agents were retrieved from as described in the paper):

- *Pedagogical Agent* – Agent that facilitate the learning process;
- *Actor* – Performs the role of a character within a scenario;
- *Storyteller* – A narrator of anecdotes, incidents, or fictitious tales;
- *Assistant* – Agent who assists, supports, guides and helps the user; and
- *Presenter* – Agent which presents/read out the daily news and weather forecast.

Name was classed into two groups:

- *Name* – Agent with a personal human like name (such as Peter, and Lucia); and
- *No Name* – Agent with no human like name.

3. RESULTS

Queries were used in order to collect data. The focus was on gender in comparison to the other attributes previously stated. Virtual embodiments were evenly divided between males (n=73) and females (n=74). Table 1 reports the frequency values for male and female agents as a function of their ethnicity. The vast majority of these agents were white (84%). The remaining ones were Black (n=17), Oriental (n=1), and Asian (n=5).

---

[1] The reason for concentrating on academic sources is due to the need for limiting the scope of our project, and looking at innovative design solutions which will constitute the future internet populations of virtual avatars.

Table 1. Gender by Ethnicity frequency distribution

	Male	*Female*	*Total*
Whites	61	63	124
Others	12	11	23
Total	**73**	**74**	**147**

A trend analysis indicated that non-white agents started to appear in 2004 [14], and are growing fast in number since then [10, 15].

Table 2 compares the frequency values for male and female agents as a function of their Age. It appears that the bulk of agents are young adults. There is an interaction between age and gender, where Adults and Older Adults are largely made up of males, and Young Adults are predominantly female.

Table 2. Gender by Age frequency distribution

	Male	*Female*	*Total*
Child	7	4	11
Young Adult	46	62	108
Adult	11	5	16
Older Adult	9	3	12
Total	**73**	**74**	**147**

Data on Dressing Style are summarised in Table 3. Agents were chiefly in Casual dress with no specific gender effect. An equal number of male and female agents could not be attributed any Dress Style (Missing), while only 2% of agents were dressed in a uniform.

Table 3. Gender by Dressing Style frequency distribution

	Male	*Female*	*Total*
Casual	42	46	88
Formal	13	11	24
Uniform	2	1	3
Missing	16	16	32
Total	**73**	**74**	**147**

A vast number of agents (75%) did not possess a name. Leaving 25% of agents with names, out of which almost half were assigned a role and the other half without. When looking at Age by Role it was surprising to see that over 90% of Child agents were Actors. Amongst Young Adults, Adults and Older Adults, the Pedagogical role was the most frequently assigned. Investigating Age by Anthropomorphism level highlighted over 90% of Child agents having a Cartoon like face. Amongst the other three age groups, each of the Anthropomorphic levels were distributed evenly.

Figure 1 illustrates frequency values for male and female agents as a function of Anthropomorphism. It is evident that a larger number of male agents are Cartoon like in comparison to female agents. Conversely, the number of female agents significantly increases as the realism of an agent increases.

Photo realistic agents are primarily female thus showing a specific gender effect.

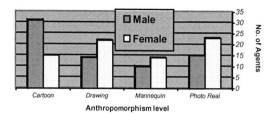

Figure 1. Gender by Anthropomorphism

Figure 2 represents agents that had a role assigned to them. Almost 46% of agents had no defined role showing no specific gender effect. The most common profession for a virtual agent is that of a tutor. The roles which are least common are those of a Storyteller and Presenter.

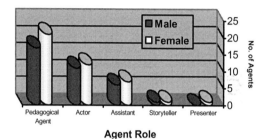

Figure 2. Gender by Role

4. CONCLUSION

The findings of our study add to a growing body of literature on the effect of agents' demographics on user perception, by presenting a census of this virtual world. This census can give an insight into the stereotypes of virtual agents held by their designers and is useful to predict biases and difficulties in the interaction with these virtual agents.

Our study indicates that females are in general more photorealistic and anthropomorphic than their male counterparts who are usually represented as cartoon like agents. This suggests that more emphasis is focused on the female appearance. Studies have shown [16] that the physical attractiveness stereotype is more potent when applied to women than to men, and females are generally seen as being more attractive than males. Thus the real-life bias which expects females to look more attractive than males may lead to the reason why the female agents are more realistic than the male counterpart.

Earlier research has shown [9, 10, 17] that users in general prefer to interact with agents of a similar ethnicity to their own. The results in this study clearly show that the vast majority of agents are from a white background, leading to a large mismatch between potential users and available agents. This may be due to the bulk of designers coming from a principally white background, as we have only analysed publications in English. Yet, we believe that this finding highlights a prevailing ethnocentric approach to agent design, which may strongly hamper their global adoption.

A point designers need to consider is that the presence of a wholly white agent world with a handful of agents from other ethnic backgrounds could increase the tendency of racist behaviour towards the non white agents. Long ago, social psychology has posited a clear link between discrimination and minorities. More agents from various ethnic backgrounds should be developed in order to counteract this issue.

The vast majority of agents are young adults, and only a handful are classed as children. The reason for developing more younger adult agents may be the designer's view that the vast majority of users are also young adults who may prefer to interact with agents of a similar age group, backing Cowell et al. study [9]. On the contrary, these days users range from nursery children to the old aged pensioners. Ideally, these age groups should also be considered when developing agents. Yet, the results in this study indicate a minimal number of child and older aged agents being used.

The most prevalent type of role assigned to an agent is that of a pedagogical one. Perhaps this is the role researchers see most fitting for an agent; as a tutor, advisor and guide. Agents can play far more diverse roles, rather than being cocooned into the pedagogical role. Further work needs to be done to assign more agents to other roles and professions like a news/weather presenter, storyteller, online sales assistant and so on. This study highlights Child like agents predominantly playing an acting role; researchers should be aware of the benefits of assigning other roles to them (such as a kindergarten tutor or storyteller). The implications of these findings for design are:

- The function and role of an agent must be acknowledged and high on the functional spec agenda before commencing the development of an agent. Different embodiment may fit different roles, and it is important to clarify this relationship.

- What kind of user will be interacting with the agent? For example, are the users young or old? What is their gender as well as their cultural and ethnic background? Thus, agents can be modified according to the users that will interact with them.

- Allowing the user to choose from a drop down list of options as to what age, gender, and race they would prefer their agent to possess before interaction. This is more crucial in light of HCI's commitment to interfaces that are equally accessible and acceptable to all intended users.

- Agent designers should take greater care when choosing how to represent the agent's ethnicity, gender, and realism.

Further research will be conducted into the effects of the physical appearance of agents on user behaviour. In particular, the effect of agent facial attractiveness on the user perception has yet to be investigated

ACKNOWLEDGMENTS
We thank the many researchers who helped in the construction of our agent data-base by contributing their exemplars.

5. REFERENCES
[1] Olivier, P. (2004). Gesture Synthesis in a Real-World ECA, In: Elisabeth André, Laila Dybkjær, Wolfgang Minker, Paul Heisterkamp (Eds.): Affective Dialogue Systems, Kloster Irsee, Germany, *Proceedings.*

[2] Cassell, J. (2000). Embodied Converstional Interface Agents. *Communications of the ACM*, 43, 70-78.

[3] Bickmore, T. (2003). Relational Agents: Effecting Change through Human-Computer Relationships, MIT Ph.D. Thesis.

[4] Bickmore, T. and Picard, R. (2005) "Establishing and Maintaining Long-Term Human-Computer Relationships" *ACM Transactions on Computer Human Interaction (ToCHI)*, 12(2): 293 – 327.

[5] Walker J. et al. (1994). Using a Human Face in an Interface. *Proceedings of CHI '94*, ACM Press, 85-91.

[6] Sproul et al. (1996). When the interface is a face. *Human-Computer Interaction,* 11, 97-124.

[7] Reeves, B., & Nass, C. (1996). The Media Equation: How people treat computers, television, and new media like real people and places, *Cambridge: Cambridge University Press.*

[8] De Meuse, K. P. (1987). A Review of the Effects of Nonverbal Cues on the Performance Appraisal Process. *Journal of Occupational Psychology*, 60, 207- 226.

[9] Cowell, A. J. & Stanney, K. M. (2005). Manipulation of non-verbal interaction style and demographic embodiment to increase anthropomorphic computer character credibility *International Journal of Human-Computer Studies, Volume 62, Issue 2, Pages 281-306*

[10] Baylor, A. L., Shen, E., & Huang, X. (2003). Which Pedagogical Agent do Learners Choose?The Effects of Gender and Ethnicity. Paper presented at the E-Learn (*World Conference on E-Learning in Corporate, Government, Healthcare, & Higher Education*), Phoenix, Arizona.

[11] Baylor, A. L. & Kim, Y. (2004). Pedagogical Agent Design: The Impact of Agent Realism, Gender, Ethnicity, and Instructional Role. *Presented at International Conference on Intelligent Tutoring Systems*, Maceio, Brazil, p 592-603.

[12] Hone, K., (2006). Empathic agents to reduce user frustration: The effects of varying agent characteristics. *Interact. Comput.* 18, 227–245.

[13] Baylor, A. L. (2004). Encouraging more positive engineering stereotypes with animated interface agents. Unpublished manuscript.

[14] Morency, L. P., and Darrell, T. (2004). From Conversational Tooltips to Grounded Discourse: Head Pose Tracking in Interactive Dialog Systems, *International Conference on Multimodal Interfaces*, pp. 32-37, College State, PA, October

[15] Cassell, J., & Miller, P. Is it Self-Administration if the Computer gives you Encouraging Looks? (in press) In F.G. Conrad & M.F. Schober (Eds.), *Envisioning the Survey Interview of the Future.* New York: John Wiley & Sons.

[16] Cross, J. F., & Cross, J. Age, sex, race, and the perception of facial beauty. *Developmental Psychology,* 1971, 3, 433-439.

[17] Moreno, R., & Flowerday, T. (2006). Students' choice of animated pedagogical agents in science learning: A test of the similarity-attraction hypothesis on gender and ethnicity. *Contemporary Educational Psychology*, Volume 31, Issue 2, Pages 186-207

Design in Evaluation:
Reflections on Designing for Children's Technology

Emanuela Mazzone
ChiCI Group
University of Central Lancashire
Preston PR1 2HE (UK)
+44 1772 895152

EMazzone@uclan.ac.uk

Diana Xu
ChiCI Group
University of Central Lancashire
Preston PR1 2HE (UK)
+44 1772 895301

YFXu@uclan.ac.uk

Janet C Read
ChiCI Group
University of Central Lancashire
Preston PR1 2HE (UK)
+44 1772 893285

JCRead@uclan.ac.uk

ABSTRACT

This paper reflects on the design value that emerges from evaluation methods used in the field of child computer interaction.

The work is based around an evaluation study of a tangible game prototype for children. The prototype and the evaluation techniques used are described. The authors provide a reflection on the analysis of results from one of the methods and use this analysis to propose a direct connection with design tools.

Categories and Subject Descriptors

H.5.2 User Interfaces – Evaluation/Methodology, Theory and methods, User-centred design; I.3.6 Methodology and Techniques - Interaction techniques;

General Terms

Performance, Design, Experimentation, Human Factors, Theory, Verification.

Keywords

User-Centred approach, Children technology design, Evaluation methods, Design methods.

1.   INTRODUCTION

The term 'design' in a Human-Computer Interaction context can assume many different meanings and perspectives depending on the design goals and resources.

[14] defines design as three main comprehensive connotations:

- The redesign to solve problems on existing systems;
- The development of new system to support current activities;
- The envisioning of novel application that could support emerging human activities.

This latter emergent level of design has been addressed by several researchers within the context and description of future technologies [22,21] and it aims at freeing the creativity from

constraints and the biases due to experience and background culture. In this creative process users are considered to play a significant role.

From a User-Centred approach, it is agreed to refer to the whole design process as iterations of different cycles from concepts generation to product prototyping, evaluation and implementation. In traditional approaches [19], users were consulted mainly at the end of the process to evaluate and validate an almost-finished product. It is now becoming common practice to include users at any stage of the progress, according to different techniques and purposes.

Following the same principle, the tradition of involving children when designing and producing technology for them as users has being growing in the last decade or so [i.e. hence the origin of Interaction Design and Children conferences]. Studies have classified their roles as users, testers, informants or design partners [6], according to the degree of contribution and the stage of their intervention throughout the design process.

Within these broad categories many studies have developed, through investigating and experimenting new methods or validating and adapting existing ones [12]. At the same time, many principles and guidelines have been derived and produced from a comprehensive tradition of research in the field.

Investigation of methods, as seen in [10], normally focuses on a specific context or design purpose.

Given its broad sense of encompassing the whole process, in this paper the meaning of the term 'design' refers to the specific phase of concept generation which feed the development of the product or its prototypes.

With regards to the design phase, two of the most interesting ways that allow children to be significant contributors to the design process are informant design and cooperative enquiry. The term informant was first used by [20] and describes a process by which children contribute their ideas to the overall design of a product but are not considered as design partners. Participatory design and cooperative enquiry [7], which are closer to the ideal of design partner, suggest greater equality between children and adult designers, together with more involvement by the children, and a democracy of ideas.

Many difficulties still need to be overcome in the application of informant and cooperative design methods, and several studies are looking at novel approaches to get more value from sessions with children.

On the other hand, concerning the evaluation phase, methods involving children as users can be divided into two main categories [3]: inquiry, which aim to elicit information and opinions by questioning the users after their interaction with the system; and observational methods, carried out during the user performance. This last category includes techniques like Think Aloud protocol, Constructive Interaction [15], Cooperative Evaluation, Peer-Tutoring [9] and Problem Identification Picture Cards (PIPC) method [4].

This paper refers to a study [23] designed with the intention of determining the ease of use and effectiveness of four combined user-based evaluation methods to discover problems and detect flaws when children interact with tangible technology.

After a brief description of the four methods (two for the observation and two for the inquiry) chosen for the evaluation study of the two tangible game prototypes, this paper will briefly present the study and then focus its reflection on the results of the two inquiry methods.

2. METHODS

The two methods selected for the observation during the user activities were: Co-discovery, Peer Tutoring.

Co-discovery (or constructive interaction) intends to let the users collaborate with each other in order to learn how to interact with the system. This method is supposed to facilitate discussion between the subjects and provide information on their understanding of the interaction [16]. It is proved to be more effective in encouraging children verbalizing their thoughts than simply trying to prompt them to think aloud while performing the task [2, 15].

In the Peer Tutoring method [9], children teach their friends how to use the technology after they have interacted with the product. This technique is useful to see how children have understood the product and how they are able and willing to communicate this to their peers

The inquiry methods employed after the user tasks were Questionnaire and Drawing Intervention [24].

When it comes to children, questionnaires are a useful and quick source of information [17], but they still need thoughtful planning when designing them, paying particular attention to the length, language or other implicit biases that are likely to compromise the response.

Drawing Intervention is a novel and more informal evaluation method, inspired by the natural school classroom settings. According to it, after the children completed the tasks, they draw anything related to what they have done. Drawing is an activity they are very familiar with and normally used in classroom to express themselves. The rationale behind this method is that children feel more relaxed and less inhibited to talk to each other when drawing while the researchers are able to discover their real thoughts about their experiences.

3. THE STUDY

The study took place in an educational suite of a local primary school, involving 24 children from a Year 5 (aged 9-10) classroom. The children participated to the activities during a normal school day.

Groups of four children at a time were brought into the room and asked to play together the two games set up for the study. Following the games, they were asked to sit at a table and fill in the evaluation sheet, consisting either of the questionnaire or of the Drawing Intervention. Each group session lasted between 15 and 20 minutes.

The two games were based on a very simple principle, which was to interact with a tangible interface to find 8 correct items

amongst 16 shuffled pieces. The team to gather more food items would win the game. Two prototypes were created, one for the tabletop and one for the room. Both implementations were coded in Visual Basic and used the Phidgets® technology.

The game was designed to be played across two different dimensions of interaction, both involving a screen displayed feedback. One, called TableTop (Figure 1.a), was constrained to a wooden board and used light sensors, the other, Box-based (Figure 1.b), involved loose pieces that could be located anywhere in the space, in this case they were scattered in a box together with decorative objects and tagged with RFID technology. While this paper focuses on a specific aspect of the results of two of the evaluation methods, a detailed description of the games can be found in [23].

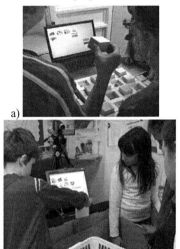

Figure 1. the groups playing at the games: TableTop (a) and box-based (b)

To allow a comprehensive combination of the evaluation methods, the first group was asked to have a turn at the games and learn to play them, while they were observed during the Co-discovery approach. In this instance of play, the children were asked to split spontaneously in two teams of two, playing one team against the other.

After both game had been played, the children sat at a table to complete a paper evaluation sheet (Figure 2).

Figure 2. Children completing evaluation sheets

On completing the session, one of the two pairs of children (randomly chosen by tossing a coin) was sent back to the classroom while the other pair was asked to come back with two new class mates, to re-form another group of four children. According to a Peer tutoring approach, the two children (experts) who have played before guided the second two (novices) in the play of the game, based on their previous understanding.

For the inquiry methods evaluation, two paper forms, Drawing Intervention and questionnaire were alternated in order to give the 'peer tutors' the chance to complete a different one each time.

At this point all the four children were then sent back to the classroom and a new group of four children entered the room to start again the process.

4. DISCUSSION

Two researchers conducted the study, one mainly interacting with the children, while the other focussing more on the observation, taking notes and video recording the playing.

For the purpose of this paper, the focus will be on the analysis of the two inquiry methods.

Being a study about the effectiveness of evaluation methods in discovering problems when interacting with technology, the selected inquiry methods were designed in order to make the children focus on the same question through two different approaches.

In both cases children were asked to think of what they would like to add and to change about the game they had just been playing. In the questionnaire sheet they had some blank space to write add-ons and changes for each of the games, in the Drawing Intervention sheet they had one blank box to draw anything they wanted to add and change on one or both of the games. It has been shown that children find it more difficult to express their ideas with words while drawing is a more effective tool for communication for them [6] and so it was expected that these methods would produce different results.

It was also supposed that the amount of i

deas that resulted from the Drawing Intervention would be greater from that gathered from the questionnaires, and this was the case. In addition, the Drawing Intervention activity provided results that were also richer in details and creativity than those from the questionnaire. For example, the suggestions written in the questionnaire mainly concerned addition of sound/music feedback or change in the topic of the pictures. In many cases they also answered that they did not want to add or change anything to the actual game. On the other hand, all the children that had the chance to draw their thoughts did offer more than one idea and in more than one design aspect (content, multimedia feedback, mode of interaction, input modality).

Furthermore, in the same way as the children that completed just one of the evaluation exercises, even the children that had the chance to complete both the questionnaire and the Drawing Intervention (those who had tutored in the peer tutoring activity) responded to the same question with a completely different perspective, being much more imaginative and detailed in the drawing activity compared to the writing one. Figure 3 gives an idea of the difference in amount of information given by the same child in the two different methods.

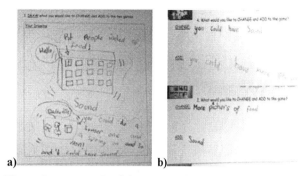

Figure 3. an example of the output of Drawing Intervention (a) and Questionnaire (b) from the same child

5. CONCLUSION

In many cases drawing has been shown to be useful as a form of low-tech prototyping to allow children (and not only children) to envision and visualise their ideas [6, 21, 11, 22]. In the case described in this paper, drawing proved to be also a very effective evaluation tool, providing feedback on children's likes and dislikes of the specific technology as well as information about their interactions with the technology.

Although evaluation was the main purpose for this specific study, the method referred to as Drawing Intervention in this study acted as a design tool at the same time. The output from the Drawing Intervention can be considered not only useful for the evaluation of the game but at the same time it provides potential requirements for the following iteration of the design cycle.

Since evaluation and not design was the main goal of the study, no constraints were given to the children in that respect. Therefore, in the case of using these results as design requirements, they would contribute towards an open-ended or emergent, future technology approach [14,21,22].

Nevertheless, the outputs of the drawing activity have added value in term of design and requirements gathering as a first hand insight and a rich source of information of the children concept and understanding of the technology interaction.

This study has provided several ideas for further work. The first one being the redesign of the tangible game including children design contributions concerning content, interactive functionalities and different type of multimedia inputs and outputs. Other directions to take could be to examine other evaluation methods and investigate their potential for use in design; or also to explore if design methods can similarly be used for evaluation.

A study is currently ongoing to discover new design methods for use with children and this work is contributing to a greater understanding of designing for and with children of several ages.

6. ACKNOWLEDGMENTS

Our thanks go to the children and staff of Hesketh with Becconsall All Saints C.E. Primary School (UK), who participated in the study, and to J and J who kindly worked on building the wooden TableTop prototype.

7. REFERENCES

[1] Alborzi, H., A. Druin, J. Montemayor, M. Platner, J. Porteous, et al. "Designing StoryRooms: interactive storytelling places for children". *ACM SIGCHI 2000*

Symposium on Designing Interactive Systems (Brooklyn, 2000), ACM Press.

[2] Als, B.S., Jensen, J.J., and Skov, M.B. Exploring verbalization and collaboration of constructive interaction with children, in *Proceedings of Interact Conference* (Rome, Italy, 2005)

[3] Barendregt, W., *Evaluating fun and usability in computer games with children*, Ph.D. Thesis, Eindhoven University of Technology, Eindhoven, 2006

[4] Barendregt, W. and M.M. Bekker. Development and Evaluation of the Picture Cards Method in *Proceedings of Interact 2005, Tenth International Conference on Human-Computer Interaction* 2005. Rome, Italy

[5] Borgers, N., J. Hox, and D. Sikkel, Response Effects in Surveys on Children and Adolescents: The Effect of Number of Response Options, Negative Wording, and Neutral Mid-Point. *Quality and Quantity*, 38(1): 2004.17 - 33.

[6] Druin, A., Ed. *"The Design of Children's technology"*, Morgan Kaufmann Publishers, Inc. 1999

[7] Guha, M.L., Druin, A., Chipman, G., Fails, J.A., Simms, S., Farber, A. Working with Children as Technology design partners, *Communications of the ACM*, January 2005, vol.48, no.1, special issue Interaction Design and Children, 39-42

[8] Hanna, E., et al., The Role of Usability Research in Designing Children's Computer Products, in *The Design of Children's Technology, A. Druin, Editor. Morgan Kaufmann: San Francisco. (1999). 4-26.

[9] Hoysniemi, J., P. Hamalainen, and L. Turkki, Using peer tutoring in evaluating the usability of a physically interactive computer game with children. *Interacting with Computers*, 2003. 15(2): p. 203-225

[10] Jensen, J., Skov, M. A Review of Research methods in Children's Technology Design, in *Proceedings of IDC Conference 2005* (Boulder, USA 2005)

[11] Kelly,R., Mazzone,E., Horton, P., Read, J. "Bluebells: A Design Method for Child-Centred Product Development". in *Proceedings of NordiCHI 2006* (Oslo, 2006), ACM Press.

[12] Markopoulos, P and Bekker, M. (2003b) On the assessment of usability testing methods for children. *Interacting with Computers*, 15(3), 227-243.

[13] Markopoulos, P. and M. Bekker. How to compare usability testing methods with children participants. in *Proceedings of Interaction Design and Children'02.* (Eindhoven, Netherlands, 2002)

[14] Marti, P., Rizzo, A. Levels of design: from usability to experience, in *Proceedings of HCI International* (Crete, 2003) Lawrence Erlbaum Associates

[15] Miyake, N. Constructive Interaction and the Iterative Process of Understanding. Cognitive Science, vol. 10(2), 1986. pp. 151 -- 177

[16] Nielsen, J. *Usability Engineering*, Morgan Kaufmann Publishers Inc., San Francisco, CA, 1993

[17] Read, J.C. and S.J. MacFarlane. Using the Fun Toolkit and Other Survey Methods to Gather Opinions in Child Computer Interaction. in *Interaction Design and Children, 2006* (Tampere, Finland, 2006) ACM Press.

[18] Read, J. C., MacFarlane, S. J., and Casey, C. What's going on? : Discovering what Children Understand about Handwriting Recognition Interfaces, in Proceedings of IDC2003 (Preston, England, 2003) ACM Press

[19] Rubenstein, R. and H. Hersh, "The Human Factor: Designing Computer Systems for People", Digital Press, 1984.

[20] Scaife, M., & Rogers, Y. Kids as informants: Telling us what we didn't know or confirming what we knew already. A. Druin (Ed), *The design of children's technology*, Morgan Kaufmann, San Francisco, CA, 1999, 27-50.

[21] Stringer, M., Harris, E., and Fitzpatrick, G. Exploring the space of near-future design with children. In *Proceedings of NordiCHI2006* (Oslo, Norway, 2006)

[22] Vavoula, G. N., Sharples, M., & Rudman, P. D. Developing the 'Future Technology Workshop' method. In *Proceedings of IDC 2002*, ACM Press (2002), 65-72

[23] Xu, D., Mazzone, E., Read, J.C. Designing and Testing a Tangible Interface Prototype for use in the Evaluation Study with Children in *Proceedings of Interaction Design and Children 2007*, Denmark, ACM Press (2007)

[24] Xu, D., Read, J.C., Mazzone, E., MacFarlane, S., Brown, M. Evaluation of Tangible User Interfaces (TUIs) for and with Children – Methods and Challenges in *Proceedings of International HCI Conference 2007*, (Beijing, China, 2007) LNCS, Springer (in press)

Posters

How Effective is it to Design by Voice?

Mohammad M. Alsuraihi
Department of Computing
University of Bradford
Bradford, West Yorkshire, BD7 1DP
0044 1274 236830

mmnalsur@bradford.ac.uk

Dimitris I. Rigas
Department of Computing
University of Bradford
Bradford, West Yorkshire, BD7 1DP
0044 1274 235131

d.rigas@bradford.ac.uk

ABSTRACT

Previous studies on usability of crowded graphical interfaces that are full of widgets like menus, buttons, palette-tools etc, have shown evidence that they create a fertile environment for information overload and usability problems. In this paper, we investigate the use of multimodal interaction metaphors (visual, vocal and aural) for improving effectiveness of learning functions and completing tasks in one of the most graphically crowded user-interfaces, the user-interface of IDEs (or Interface Design Environments). This investigation was done empirically on two experimental interface design toolkits (TVOID and MMID) which were built especially for the study. Assessment of the visual and multimodal interaction metaphors was carried out by two independent groups of users (A and B) of which each consisted of 15 users. Results showed that the use of speech for input and output along with limited use of the mouse was more effective than interacting visually only using the typical common graphical metaphors: pull-down menus, toolbar, toolbox, properties-table and status-bar.

Categories and Subject Descriptors

H.5.2 [Information Interfaces and Presentation]: User Interfaces

General Terms

Measurement, Performance, Design, Experimentation.

Keywords

Interface design, Multimodal interaction, Speech recognition, Effectiveness, Usability.

1. INTRODUCTION

Crowding the interface with graphical widgets that allow visual interaction only with no involvement of other senses like the auditory system exposes the user to experience information overload [1]. This causes important information around the interface to be missed [2]. Another problem with visual-only interaction is the high potential for usability problems with graphical metaphors to occur. There are two root-problems from which all usability problems branch: interface intrusion into task [3] and closure [4]. The key solution to enhancing usability of graphical interfaces is to lessen the visual workload on the visual channel, which negatively affects effectiveness of

task-performance [5]. In order to enhance usability of a user-interface, more than one modality has to be involved in interaction. In this paper, we investigate the use of multimodal interaction metaphors (visual and auditory) for improving effectiveness of interface design toolkits. The paper presents a multi-group study comparing effectiveness of speech as input and output means for designing user-interfaces against effectiveness of the common typical GUIs that can be used for the same purpose. The study targeted novel computer users who had limited knowledge in using Interface Design Environments (IDEs). In order to fulfill the aim, two interface design toolkits were built from scratch (TVOID and MMID) to be tested empirically. The following sections present an overview of the related work and put more light on the experimental toolkits, design of the experiments and discussion of the results obtained.

2. RELEVANT WORK

Previous researchers recommend the addition of non-speech sounds (earcons [6, 7] and auditory icons [8, 9]) to interfaces in order to improve their performance and increase their usability. However, in order for perception and right interpretation of non-speech sound to be successfully achieved, a high level of concentration and the development of a perceptual context are required by the users [7, 10]. This causes the users to incorrectly interpret the non-speech messages sometimes, because of lack of concentration and distraction with other events or messages in the interface [10]. Processing natural language (speech) feedback in the interface has been recognized as bringing many benefits to human-computer interaction [11]. Rigas et al [10, 12] investigated the use of speech along with non-speech sounds, and found that combining earcons with synthesized speech was a successful and effective approach for communicating information to the users. In addition, a study by Vargas and Anderson showed that the users' performance was better in terms of time, number of keystrokes, errors, and workload when used speech along with earcons [13].

The work by Bolt [14], which introduced the approach of processing speech and gesture for moving graphical objects on an interface, was pioneer and promising for researchers to investigate the use of speech as an input utility for enhancing efficiency of the user-interface. Cohen, Oviatt and others [15-19] have strongly recommended employment of speech recognition for utilizing the user interface. Recent studies have shown the potential of this interaction metaphor for enhancing performance of interaction between the user and the interface [20-24]. However, all these studies have discussed effectiveness of speech recognition with caution due to recognition errors that emerge from sensitivity toward noise and inaccurate pronunciation of words. These errors are tamable and can be tolerated [17, 25], especially if limited vocabulary was used [26]. Also, the impact of such errors can be dramatically reduced if the speech-recognition system being studied was compared to a counterpart visual-only graphical system in regard to usability measures. Our review of the previous related work has revealed a strong need for such comparative usability studies. In this study we measure effectiveness of vocal instruction against effectiveness of visual-only instruction for designing interfaces using two experimental Interface Design toolkits (TVOID and MMID).

3. EXPERIMENTAL TOOLKITS

Two experimental toolkits were developed using Microsoft Visual C#: Typical Visual-Only Interface Design (TVOID) and Multi-Modal Interface Design (MMID) toolkits. TVOID imitates the style of interaction implemented in most of the existing interface-design environments like Microsoft Visual C# and Java NetBeans IDE. It interacts with the user visually-only with no involvement of other senses like the auditory system. This interaction takes place in six areas in its main interface: menus, toolbar, toolbox, workplace, properties-table, and status-bar. Figure 1 shows a screenshot of TVOID.

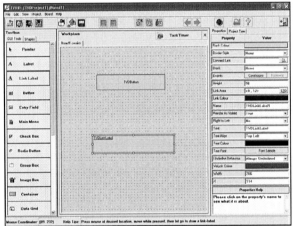

Figure 1: A screenshot of TVOID's main interface

MMID provides a combination of visual, vocal and aural interaction metaphors. It is a speech-recognition and text-to-speech based environment that allows limited use of the mouse and the keyboard. It allows the user to interact with it from the position of the mouse-cursor. In this environment, there is no need for the user to use any of the graphical metaphors implemented in TVOID. The system command receptor in this environment is represented by a friendly character (MS Agent) that listens to commands and interacts with the user via speech and facial expressions. Vocal commands are in the form of simple one to three English-words. Figure 2 shows a screenshot of MMID.

4. DESIGN OF THE EMPIRICAL STUDY

The empirical study aimed at measuring effectiveness of learnability (or the ability to learn functions from first time use) of TVOID and MMID. The toolkits were tested independently by two groups of users (A and B). Each group consisted of 15 users. The participants were computer users who had limited experience in using interface design environments. Each user attended a 10-minute training video for using the toolkit he/she was assigned to test. Both groups were asked to complete the same tasks (10 tasks). Each task consisted of one to three functions. The tasks were designed to be increasing in complexity and covering all expected functionality (activating

menu-command functionality, selecting tools, drawing objects, and setting properties). Effectiveness was measured by calculating the percentage of functions learned in absence of additional help and percentage of tasks completed successfully (i.e. within task-completion criterion time). In order to obtain these percentages, efficiency of the two experimental toolkits was first measured by timing learning functions and completing tasks for each user under the two conditions (visual-only and multimodal).

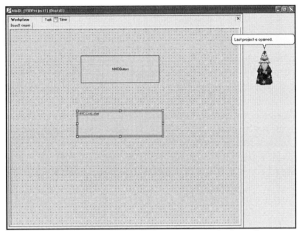

Figure 2: A screenshot of MMID's main interface

5. DISCUSSION OF RESULTS

During the experiments, it was noticed that the users who tested TVOID (Group A) expected how to do most of the functions. This environment looked familiar to them because they had previous experience with similar environments that provided with similar interaction metaphors. This experience made them primarily rely on their memory. Before doing a task, the users of TVOID spent time on recalling how to do functions in the similar systems they were used to, to be able to do them using this environment. Expectations of how to do functions were incorrect sometimes, which caused the users to find out how to do these functions. In this way, the users of TVOID did two things to learn functions: remembering or expecting, and exploring in case of incorrect expectation. This was not the case with the users who tested MMID (Groups B) as they were not familiar to voice-instruction, and thus they headed directly to exploring. Although MMID was more prone to errors than TVOID because of sensitivity toward noise and accurate pronunciation of words, it must be recalled that it was tried for the first time and that frequent use could lessen the number of errors and make it more usable.

Figure 3 shows the variances between the two environments in regard to task accomplishment (learning and completion) time. These variances have mainly taken place because of the methods used to learn functions. Another factor behind this result was that MMID limited the use of the mouse and decreased the user-reliance on the visual sense. Significance of the difference was tested using the t-test. The difference was found significant (t = 2.64, P = 0.02). Gathering all commands in one location (e.g. one list) in MMID helped the users in Group B to locate the required commands for doing functions in a faster way than their counterparts in Group A, who looked for these commands in different locations around the interface. Also, the use of one interaction metaphor (voice-instruction) in MMID with limited use of the mouse and the keyboard saved the time for the users to think where to go to activate the required command within the many encapsulated widgets in the interface (menus, toolbar, drawing tools, properties, etc) as in TVOID. For example, In order to draw an object in TVOID, the user must select it at first from the tool-box, while in MMID the user can draw directly by saying the tool's name on the required location. Also, learning how to set properties was done through interactive training simulations in MMID, while in TVOID was done textually. Enabling the user to specifically learn what he/she needs to learn using interactive training as in MMID saves the time for thinking of the appropriate keywords, looking for them, and reading about them as in TVOID.

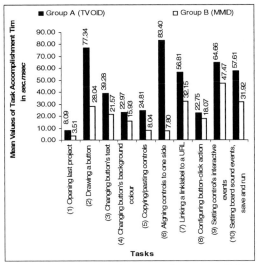

Figure 3: Mean values of time taken for accomplishing 10 tasks for the first time using TVOID (Group A) and MMID (Group B)

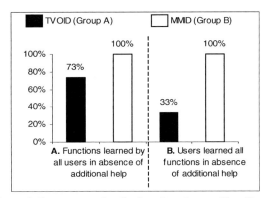

Figure 4: Percentages for the functions learned by all users and users who learned all functions in absence of additional help using TVOID and MMID

An efficient system that helps the user to learn functions within the least possible time is considered to be effectively learnable because the probability that all required functions would be learned by all users is high. Similarly, the probability that all users would learn all functions if the system is pretty efficient is also high. Figure 4.A and Figure 4.B reinforce this finding. This also applies for effectiveness of task completion in terms of percentages of tasks completed successfully (i.e. within threshold time) by all users and the percentage of users who complete all tasks successfully as can be seen in Figure 5.

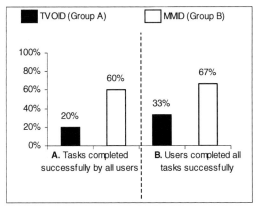

Figure 5: Percentages for (A) the tasks completed successfully by all users and (B) the users who successfully completed all tasks using TVOID and MMID

6. Conclusion

In this paper, we provided with a comparative study done by two independent groups of novel users who had limited knowledge in using IDEs. The study aimed at measuring effectiveness of two interface design toolkits: typical graphical and visual-only toolkit (TVOID), and a speech input and output toolkit (MMID). TVOID interacted with the user through six areas comprising pull-down menus, toolbar-buttons, drawing tools, workplace (form being designed), properties table and status-bar. On the other hand, MMID interacted with the user through one area only, which is the workplace. All the other graphical interaction metaphors were replaced by vocal commands. From results, it can be concluded that in order to shorten task accomplishment time and, hence, enhance effectiveness of task accomplishment, a design environment should aim at enabling the user to do all actions from inside the workplace area with no need to leave it to other areas. The more visual interaction metaphors an environment provides the more time will be spent in thinking where to find the appropriate ones for accomplishing jobs, and the vice-versa is correct. The use of voice-instruction as a way of interaction was found to be more effective than the use of several visual interaction metaphors, in terms of shortening function learning and task-accomplishment time. This study opens a research door toward substituting the well-known graphical interaction metaphors used in IDEs, namely, menus, toolbar, toolbox, properties-table and status-bar with vocal commands in order to enhance usability of the user-interface of ID systems.

7. Future work

The empirical work covered in this paper investigated the usability parameters: efficiency and effectiveness for the two experimental environments from one angle: learnability or the ability to accomplish tasks from first time use. Further experiments will take place for measuring Experienced User Performance (EUP) using the same experimental toolkits. More than 30 users will be recruited for each environment to make the samples more representatives of the target population. In addition, user-satisfaction with the interaction metaphors provided in each environment will be empirically evaluated.

8. ACKNOWLEDGMENTS

Our thanks to ACM SIGCHI for allowing us to modify templates they had developed.

9. REFERENCES

[1] Brewster, S. A., "Using Non-Speech Sound to Overcome Information Overload," Displays, vol. 17, pp. 179-189, 1997.

[2] Oakley, I., McGee, M. R., Brewster, S., and Gray, P. D., "Putting the feel in look and feel," In ACM CHI 2000 (The Hague, NL), pp. 415-422, 2000.

[3] Brewster, S. A. and Clarke, C. V., "The Design and Evaluation of a Sonically Enhanced Tool Palette," ACM Transactions on Applied Perception (TAP), vol. 2, pp. 455-461, 2005.

[4] Dix, A., Finlay, J., Abowd, G., and Beal, R., Human-Computer Interaction, Second ed: Prentice Hall, 1998.

[5] Brown, M. L., Newsome, S. L., and Glinert, E. P., "An Experiment into the Use of Auditory Cues to Reduce Visual Workload," In proceedings of ACM CHI '89, Austin, Texas, USA, pp. 339-346, 1989.

[6] Rigas, D. I. and Atly, J. L., "The Rising Pitch Metaphor: An Empirical Study," International Journal of Human-Computer Studies, vol. 62, pp. 1-20, 2005.

[7] Rigas, D., Memery, D., Hopwood, D., and Rodrigues, M., "Using Non-Speech Sound to Communicate Information in User Interfaces," In Applied Informatics 2000, Innsbruck, Austria, pp. 357-362, 2000.

[8] Gaver, W., "Auditory Interfaces," in Handbook of Human Computer Interaction, vol. 1, M. G. Helander, T. K. Landauer, and P. V. Prabhu, Eds. Amsterdam: Elsevier, 1997, pp. 1003-1041.

[9] Cohen, M., "Throwing, Pitching and Catching Sound: Audio Windowing Models and Modes," International Journal of Man-Machine Studies, vol. 39, pp. 269-304, 1993.

[10] Rigas, D. I. and Memery, D., "Utilising Audio-Visual Stimuli in Interactive Information Systems: A Two Domain Investigation on Auditory Metaphors," In International Conference on Information Technology: Coding and Computing, pp. 190-195, 2002.

[11] Manaris, B., "Natural Language Processing: A Human-Computer Interaction Perspective," Advances in Computers, vol. 47, pp. 1-66, 1996.

[12] Rigas, D., Yu, H., and Memery, D., "Experiments Using Speech, Non-Speech Sound and Stereophony as Communication Metaphors in Information Systems," In proceeding of the 27th Euromicro Conference, Warsaw, Poland, pp. 383-390, 2001.

[13] Vargas, M. L. and Anderson, S., "Combining Speech and Earcons to Assist Menu Navigation," pp., 2003.

[14] Bolt, R. A., "Put-that-there: Voice and Gesture at the Graphics Interface," In proceedings of the 7th annual conference on Computer Graphics and Interactive Techniques Seattle, Washington, USA, pp. 262-270, 1980.

[15] Cohen, M. and Ludwig, L. F., "Multidimensional Audio Window Management," International Journal of Man-Machine Studies, vol. 34, pp. 319-336, 1991.

[16] Cohen, P. R., Johnston, M., McGee, D., Oviatt, S. L., Clow, J., and Smith, I., "The Efficiency of Multimodal Interaction: A Case Study," In proceedings of the International Conference on Spoken LAnguage, Sydney, Australia, pp., 1998.

[17] Cohen, P. R. and Oviatt, S. L., "The Role of Voice Input for Human-Machine Communication," In proceedings of the National Academy of Sciences, pp. 9921-9927, 1995.

[18] Mellor, B. A., Baber, C., and Tunley, C., "Evaluating Automatic Speech Recognition as a Component of a Multi-Input Human-Computer Interface," In proceedings of the International Conference on Spoken Language, 1996.

[19] Cohen, P. R., Johnston, M., McGee, D., Oviatt, S. L., Pittman, J., Smith, I., Chen, L., and Clow, J., "QuickSet: Multimodal Interaction for Distributed Applications," In proceedings of the Fifth ACM International Multimedia Conference, New York, pp. 31-40, 1997.

[20] ElAarag, H. and Schindler, L., "A Speech Recognition and Synthesis Tool," In proceedings of the 44th Annual Southeast Regional Conference, Melbourne, Florida, pp. 45-49, 2006.

[21] Adler, A. and Davis, R., "Speech and Sketching for Multimodal Design," In International Conference on Computer Graphics and Interactive Techniques, Boston, Massachusetts, pp. 214-216, 2006.

[22] Jung, J. H., Looney, C. A., and Valacich, J. S., "Fine-Tuning the Human-Computer Interface: Verbal versus Keyboard Input in an Idea Generation Context," In proceedings of the 40th Hawaii International Conference on System Sciences (HICSS'07), pp. 27c, 2007.

[23] Begel, A. and Graham, S. L., "An Assessment of a Speech-Based Programming Environment," In Visual LAnguages and Human-Centric Computing (VL/HCC'06), pp. 116-120, 2006.

[24] Desilets, A., Fox, D. C., and Norton, S., "Voce Code: An Innovative Speech Interface for Programming-by-Voice," In Extended Abstracts of the 2006 Conference on Human Factors in Computing Systems (CHI 2006), Montereal, Quebec, Canada, pp., 2006.

[25] Oviatt, S. L., "Taming Recognition with Multimodal Interface," Communications of the ACM, vol. 43, pp. 45-51, 2000.

[26] Lahtinen, S. and Peltonen, J., "Enhancing Usability of UML CASE-Tools with Speech Recognition," In proceedings of IEEE Symposium on Human Centric Computing Languages and Environments, pp. 227-235, 2003.

Ten Emotion Heuristics: Guidelines for Assessing the User's Affective Dimension Easily and Cost-Effectively

Eva de Lera
Universitat Oberta de Catalunya
Avinguda Tibidabo 39-43
08003 Barcelona
+34 3 253 23 00

edelera@uoc.edu

Muriel Garreta-Domingo
Universitat Oberta de Catalunya
Avinguda Tibidabo 39-43
08003 Barcelona
+34 3 253 23 00

murielgd@uoc.edu

ABSTRACT

Emotional appeal is a key dimension in user experience that often goes unmeasured in most user-centered design projects. This paper presents preliminary work for developing a set of guidelines for efficiently, easily and cost-effectively assessing the users' affective state by evaluating their expressive reactions during an interface evaluation process. The evaluation of this dimension complements the analysis of the objective and quantitative data gathered through usability tests and the subjective feedback provided through post-test questionnaires.

Categories and Subject Descriptors

H.5.2 [Information interfaces and presentation] User Interfaces

General Terms

Measurement, Documentation, Design, Experimentation, Theory.

Keywords

Affective computing, human-computer interaction, evaluation, usability testing, emotions, heuristics, user-centered design.

1. INTRODUCTION

Emotion is a key aspect in user experience since measuring it helps us understand the user's level of engagement and motivation. As Spillers [20] writes, "emotions govern the quality of interactions with a product in the user's environment and relate directly to appraisal of the user experience. Users generate emotion as a way to minimize errors, interpret functionality, or obtain relief from the complexity of a task."

Therefore, accounting for emotional cues during an interface evaluation process provides usability practitioners, researchers and interactive designers with valuable information. Nowadays, there are several software applications that automatically capture facial expressions and eye gaze which provide key information to the practitioner. However, this paper defines an observational system to help evaluate interactions in an easier, time and cost effective manner through observation of the users.

© Eva De Lera & Muriel Garreta-Domingo, 2007
Published by the British Computer Society
Volume 2 Proceedings of the 21st BCS HCI Group Conference
HCI 2007, Lancaster University, 3-7 September 2007
Devina Ramduny-Ellis & Dorothy Rachovides (Editors)

Our tool allows researchers and practitioners to take into account emotional measures such as gestures and oral expressions without the requirement of extra software and hardware. Measuring user's emotion is both difficult and costly [3, 11], therefore, most interface evaluation efforts focus on cognitive and subjective aspects, neglecting the affective dimension. To date, usability practitioners have mainly relied on performance user test data and on the subjective information from the post-test questionnaire to measure user satisfaction and emotions. Measuring errors, time and other objective measures provides key but partial information. Feedback surveys or questionnaires provide only partial and often unreliable data, especially considering that users tend to give a positive evaluation to avoid blaming the person who developed the application or simply to minimize the time spent on the evaluation. Moreover, analyzing a questionnaire is a subjective measure of the user's feelings and emotions; therefore it is not a dependable methodology to measure affect. As a result, most common evaluation methods (not considering facial recognition software and other advanced techniques as common methods) have some limitations, as objective data is mostly cognitive and a questionnaire's subjective data provides the evaluator's with the user's perception of his/her emotions and not actual state(s) during the test.

Human emotions and affect are essential to understanding users, as these can facilitate the development of persistence and deep interest in a subject or goal. The analysis of this affective dimension in empirical user-centered design (UCD) methods helps us ensure that our users will be engaged and motivated while using our systems. Therefore, analyzing and evaluating emotional cues will provide practitioners with a third dimension of analysis for collecting user data, supplementing typical and common evaluation methods and resulting in a more accurate understanding of the user's experience.

Nowadays, there are few techniques and methodologies for gathering affective data without asking the users what and how they feel. We can give computers affective perceptual abilities and measure physiological and behavioral signals such as body-worn accelerometers, rubber and fabric electrodes, for example [17]. We can also evaluate users' eye gaze and collect electro-physiologic signals, galvanic skin response (GSR), electrocardiography (EKG), electroencephalography (EEG) and electromyography (EMG) data, blood volume pulse, heart rate or respiration and, more recently, facial recognition software. As we have already seen, most of these methods have limitations as they can be intrusive for the user, costly and most require specific skills and additional evaluation time.

Our aim was to find a non-invasive, cross-cultural, cost-efficient and easy to carry out method to help gain further understanding about the affective state of a person during an interface evaluation with users. This observational technique does not replace the current and most common methods used during a UCD process, but complements the objective and subjective data gathered, therefore adding a third dimension to the evaluation process.

2. FACIAL EXPRESSIONS AND HUMAN-COMPUTER INTERACTION

Emotions are best treated as multifaceted phenomena consisting of behavioral reactions, expressive reactions, physiological reactions and subjective feelings [6]. However, to date, most instruments measure one component at a time or a group of specific components, such as facial recognition software, that does not yet gather other body gestures or vocal data. An exception is the AMUSE tool which helps practitioners to conduct interface evaluations by collecting and aggregating different sources of data including psychological and navigation data [2]. This approach is similar to ours in the sense that mixes different data from more than one source. In summary, our study aims at providing an observation instrument that helps account for affective events during common usability evaluations, providing more data than the one obtained through an intuitive and unstructured observation but without using a more complex, expensive, and costly technique.

Focusing on the expressive reactions component, facial expressions are central in the area of emotional research [1]. The first major scientific study of facial communication was published by Charles Darwin in 1872 [5], who concluded that many expressions and their meanings (e.g., for astonishment, shame, fear, horror, pride, hatred, wrath, love, joy, guilt, anxiety, shyness, and modesty) are universal. Other studies indicate that the facial expressions of happiness, sadness, anger, fear, surprise, disgust, and interest are universal across cultures [7]. Therefore, using facial expressions as a tool to evaluate the emotional dimension is a cross-cultural tool.

Several studies on emotions and human-computer interaction are based on the analysis of facial expressions. Nevertheless, most focus on the analysis of physiological data or facial recognition, omitting other non-verbal communication aspects. Hazlett [10] describes how facial EMG sensors were used to detect facial emotional responses while the subjects performed tasks on websites. Partala and Surakka [16] studied the effects of affective interventions by recording facial EMG responses from the muscle sites that control smiling and frowning. Branco et al. [1] approach was closer to ours in the sense that it complements the traditional methods of software usability evaluation by monitoring users´ spontaneous facial expressions as a method to identify the moment of occurrence of adverse events. However, they too used EMG sensors to do the monitoring. All of the above-mentioned methods are costly, require specific skills and are time consuming, a limitation for most usability and human computer interaction practitioners.

Our technique is based in observation and does not require extra implementation effort since most interface evaluations are conducted observing and recording the user as he or she interacts with the interface. In such a scenario, facial and body expressions are often observed and recorded, but generally not measured in a structured manner.

Another approach used to evaluate emotion is the instrument developed by Desmet [6]. PrEMO is a non-verbal self-report instrument that measures 14 emotions that are often elicited by product design. This tool requires respondents to report their

emotions with the use of expressive cartoon animations. This method is closer to the self-assessment questionnaires at the end of the user test than to the analysis of emotions we had envisioned. The information gathered through this method is still subjective and does not provide and accurate understanding of the user's emotions.

3. THE 10 HEURISTICS

The ten emotion heuristics are based on theories that relate expressive reactions to distinct emotions. The heuristics are guidelines to help measure the affective state easily, cost-effectively and cross-culturally. One of the theories in which our work is based is the Facial Action Coding System (FACS) [8], currently a well-known standard to systematically categorize the physical expression of emotions. The Maximally Discriminative Facial Moving Coding System (MAX) [12] is another theory that links expression features to specific emotions.

Using these theories and other research as a starting point, we selected a subset of features that allowed us to partially assess the emotional reaction of the users as they interacted with an application. These set of features were identified from previous user evaluations and helped us build a list of the most common expressions taking place during user evaluations. We correlated the emotional cues identified with an emotional state and ensuring that these could be easily identified and measured during a user evaluation. A total of 10 emotional cues were selected. Better than any body parts, our faces reveal emotions, opinions, and moods. However, we use all of our body to communicate nonverbally. Thus, our list of heuristics includes some features that are not directly related to facial expressions. Our study focused on recording one measure for the 10 emotional cues, as more work and experimentation would be required to provide a specific measure for each cue. The goal of this study was to provide a positive, neutral or negative value to the overall user experience.

Again, it is important to note that this emotional data needs to be analyzed in conjunction with the user evaluation's other objective measures (time, errors, etc.) as well as the subjective measures gathered through the feedback questionnaire. In conclusion, the ten heuristics focus on taking into account the user's instantaneous emotional reactions, while the performance and navigation data provides objective data and, the *a posteriori* self-assessment provides the user's perception of his/her emotional state.

The 10 heuristics help measure the affective dimension when the product designers are looking for a neutral and relaxed interaction with the application. Therefore, these do not apply when evaluating a game or music website, for example. The smile heuristic included in this method represents the goal of the evaluation: to see a user with relaxed facials, therefore, without experiencing negative reactions or frustration.

1. **Frowning.** Frowning can be a sign of a necessity to concentrate, displeasure or of perceived lack of clarity. Darwin [5] wrote about how frowning is one of the signs of deep and "perplexed reflection". In their study, Partala and Surakka [16] found that the frowning activity attenuated significantly after the positive interventions than the no intervention condition.

2. **Brow Raising.** Brow raising should also be considered a negative expressive reaction. To lift the arch of short hairs above the eye is a sign of uncertainty, disbelief, surprise and exasperation [9].

3. **Gazing Away.** The gazing away from the screen may be perceived as a sign of deception. For example, looking down tends to convey a defeated attitude but can also reflect guilt, shame or submissiveness [9].

4. **Smiling.** A smile, or elevation of the cheeks, is a sign of satisfaction. The user may have encountered an element of joy during the evaluation process. Partala and Surakka [16] found that smiling activity was significantly higher during the positive condition.

5. **Compressing the Lip.** Seeing the user compress his or her lips should be perceived as a sign of frustration and confusion. Lip and jaw tension clearly reflects anxious feelings, nervousness, and emotional concerns. [9]

6. **Moving the Mouth.** If the user is seen mouth gesturing or speaking to himself / herself, this is associated with a sign of being lost and of uncertainty.

7. **Expressing Vocally.** Vocal expressions such as sighs, gasps, coughs, as well as the volume of the expression, the tone or quality of the expression may be signs of frustration or deception.

8. **Hand Touching the Face.** Elevating the hand that is placed on the mouse to his / her face is a sign of confusion and uncertainty, generally a sign of the user being lost or tired.

9. **Drawing Back on the Chair.** The user may be experiencing negative or refusing emotions. By drawing back the chair, he / she may be showing a desire to get away from the present situation.

10. **Forward Leaning the Trunk.** Leaning forward and showing a sunken chest may be a sign of depression and frustration with the task at hand. Like with the previous heuristic, the user might be encountering difficulties but instead of showing refusal, leaning forward is a sign of attentiveness, of "getting closer".

4. OUR PILOT STUDY

Our pilot study aimed at demonstrating the validity of the 10 heuristics as a one measure observational system to help evaluate, besides the traditional data gathered in user testing, a set of expressions or emotional cues that a user may demonstrate while interacting with a system. The 10 heuristics are easy to identify during a typical user evaluation and can be quickly analyzed in conjunction with the other gathered data. Each of these cues was assigned a positive, neutral and negative value and they are primarily aimed at evaluating the negative or frustrated emotional state [19]. For example, as mentioned, frowning is related to obstacles while the movement of the cheeks with pleasantness [18]. However, since the study did not experiment with each heuristic individually, the result of our evaluation is either that the user had a positive user experience, a neutral or negative one. In the study, identifying five negative heuristics provided a negative experience value that would later be evaluated in conjunction with the other data gathered.

In order to begin evaluating our methodology, we conducted a test with 8 participants. Four participants were assigned to carry out some tasks at an intentionally frustrating online supermarket, and 4 other participants were asked to carry out the same exact tasks at a much less frustrating online supermarket. This helped us identify whether the emotional cues gathered were in fact related to the difficulty of the task (frustration event) or another variable. Our study gathered the objective data (time, errors and number of clicks) and the

values for the emotional cues we noted in the 10 emotional heuristics guideline (positive, negative and neutral). At the end of the test, users were also asked to fill in a feedback questionnaire that included questions about the difficulty of the accomplished tasks and their overall satisfaction.

Our pilot study had a total of eight participants aged from 28 to 47. Half were men while the other half were women. All participants used computers on a daily basis and had not previously conducted their home shopping online. Half of the participants carried out the tasks in one supermarket while the other half in another online supermarket. While this is an initial study and further research and testing needs to be done to fully validate this technique, the results showed that the emotional cues identified always accompanied moments of errors or difficulty and, most importantly, that sometimes the emotional cues would come unrelated to a specific negative event providing us with new information about the user experience that we would not have collected if we were just gathering the other common data. When this happened, we would evaluate the event as negative, and when five of these events would happen during the user evaluation we would give the evaluation a negative measure for user experience.

For our usability laboratory, we used Morae software [15]. Using this software, we captured a video image mixing the PC screen and the participants' faces. Additionally, Morae saved all clicks and keyboard actions in a file. Capturing the user's video and audio allowed us to review specific moments as needed, and to involve other observers that could not be present at the time of the evaluation.

5. RESULTS AND FUTURE WORK

The interface evaluation analysis considered the three dimensions. The cognitive dimension was analyzed through the number of clicks, the time needed to accomplish the task, and the number of errors. The user's emotional perception was gathered through the feedback questionnaire and the affective dimension was observed through the 10 emotional cues. Users' expressions and comments were also noted to support the evaluation results. The tests were observed by a multidisciplinary team; one user experience director, one psychologist and one graphic designer.

The observers' analysis of both the interactions and observations recorded concluded that the emotional cues, together with the objective data, provided a more accurate understanding of the user experience and level of satisfaction than the questionnaires completed at the end of the test. Participants that encountered errors and took longer time showed signs of frustration (emotional cues) during the evaluation but did not mention them in the users' feedback questionnaire. Often participants want to please the practitioner, avoiding criticism, and they do not want to provide an overall negative evaluation. Besides, they tend to think that the cause was their lack of ability, instead of it being a design problem.

The analysis of these signals or emotional cues also showed consistency of emotional state throughout all participants as they all expressed frustration in similar ways. However, these cues were harder to identify when the participants did not display many facial or bodily expressions. Some participants were more expressive than others but the emotion heuristics allowed us to provide a positive, neutral or negative value for their overall experience. Identifying several emotional cues during the user evaluation helped us understand if the participant had an overall emotionally positive or negative experience.

In summary, and considering this as preliminary work that requires further evaluation, measuring the affective dimension with our observational system in conjunction with the other data provided a better understanding of the user's experience. At the same time, it is important to note that not all emotions can be identified through facial or bodily movements, so we may not be able to evaluate all moments of frustration, anxiety, or satisfaction, but the overall experience. Further research should be conducted in evaluating emotions when these occur without expression [4].

Our pilot study aims at providing a preliminary guideline to help conduct a structured observation to evaluate the emotional dimension during a user evaluation. The 10 emotion heuristics provide researchers and practitioners with a set of guidelines that can help them to begin incorporating the affective dimension in their user evaluations.

6. ACKNOWLEDGMENTS

This work has been partially supported by the Campus project promoted by the Generalitat de Catalunya (www.campusproject.org) and by the Universitat Oberta de Catalunya (www.uoc.edu).

7. REFERENCES

[1] Branco, P., Firth, P., Encarnao, L. M. & Bonato, P. Faces of emotion in human-computer interaction. In *Ext. Abstracts CHI 2005* (Portland, OR, April 2-7,2005), ACM Press, 1236-1239.

[2] Chateau, N. and Mersiol, M. *AMUSE: A tool for evaluating affective interfaces*. Unpublished paper. Retrieved on 15 February, 2007 from http://www.sics.se/~kia/evaluating_affective_interfaces/Chateau.pdf

[3] Chin, J.P., Diehl, V.A., & Norman, K. Development of an instrument measuring user satisfaction of the human-computer interface, in *Proceedings of CHI 1988* (Washington DC, May 1988), ACM Press, 213-218.

[4] Dalgleish, T. and Power, M. (Eds.). *Handbook of Cognition and Emotion*. John Wiley & Sons, Ltd., Sussex, U.K., 1999.

[5] Darwin, C. *The expression of the emotions in man and animals*. Oxford University Press, New York, NY, 1872/1998.

[6] Desmet, P. M. A. Measuring emotions: Development of an instrument to measure emotional responses to products. In Blythe, M.A., Overbeeke, K., Monk, A.F. and Wright, P.C. (Eds.), *Funology: from usability to enjoyment*. Kluwer Academic Publishers. Dordrecht, Boston, London, 2003.

[7] Ekman, P. and Friesen, W. V. Constants across cultures in the face and emotion. *Journal of Personality and Social Psychology*, 17(2) (1971) 124-129.

[8] Ekman, P. and Friesen, W. V. *Facial Action Coding System: A technique for the measurement of facial movement*. Consulting Psychologists Press, Palo Alto, CA, 1978.

[9] Givens, D. B. The nonverbal dictionary of gestures, signs and body language cues http://members.aol.com/nonverbal2/diction1.htm#The%20NONVERBAL%20DICTIONARY.

[10] Hazlett, R. Measurement of User Frustration: A Biologic Approach. *Ext. Abstracts CHI 2003* (Florida, FL, April 5-10, 2003), ACM. Press, 734-735.

[11] Ives, B., Olson, M. H., and Baroudi, J. J. The measurement of user information satisfaction. *Communications of the ACM*, 26 (1983) 785-793.

[12] Izard, C. E. *The Maximally Discriminative Facial Movement Coding System (MAX)*. Newark: Instructional Recourses Centre, University of Delaware, Newark, DL, 1979.

[13] Mahlke, S. and Minge, M. *Emotions and EMG measures of facial muscles in interactive contexts*. Unpublished paper. *Retrieved on 24 February, 2007 from www.bartneck.de/workshop/chi2006/papers/mahlke_hcif06.pdf*

[14] Mandryk, R.L., Atkins, M.S. and Inkpen, K.M.. A continuous and objective evaluation of emotional experience with interactive play environments. In *Proceedings CHI 2006* (Montréal, Québec, Canada, April 22-27, 2006), ACM Press, 1027-1036.

[15] Morae Techsmith: Usability Testing for Software and Websites, http://www.techsmith.com/morae.asp

[16] PartalaT. and Surakka, V. The effects of affective interventions in human-computer interaction. *Interacting with Computers*, 16 (2004) 295-309.

[17] Picard, R. W., and Daily, S.B. *Evaluating affective interactions: Alternatives to asking what users feel*. Presented at CHI 2005 Workshop 'Evaluating Affective Interfaces' (Portland, OR, April 2-7,2005).

[18] Pope, L. K. and Smith, C. A. On the distinct meanings of smiles and frowns. *Cognition and Emotion*, 8 (1994) 65-72.

[19] Scherer, K., Wallbot, H.G. and Summerfield, A. *Experiencing Emotion. A cross-cultural study*. Cambridge University Press, Cambridge, MA, 1986.

[20] Spillers, F.: *Emotion as a Cognitive Artifact and the Design Implications for Products That are Perceived As Pleasurable*. Retrieved on 18 February, 2007 from http://www.experiencedynamics.com/pdfs/published_works/Spillers-EmotionDesign-Proceedings.pdf

Challenges of Evaluating the Information Visualisation Experience

Sarah Faisal, Paul Cairns, Ann Blandford
University College London Interaction Centre (UCLIC)
Remax House, 31/32 Alfred Place
London WC1 E7DP, UK
+44 (0) 207 679 5225
{s.faisal, p.cairns, a.blandford} @cs.ucl.ac.uk

ABSTRACT

Information Visualisation (InfoVis) is defined as an interactive visual representation of abstract data. We view the user's interaction with InfoVis tools as an experience which is made up of a set of highly demanding cognitive activities. These activities assist users in making sense and gaining knowledge of the represented domain. Usability studies that involve a task-based analysis and usability questionnaires are not enough to capture such an experience. This paper discusses the challenges involved when it comes to evaluating InfoVis tools by giving an overview of the activities involved in an InfoVis experience and demonstrating how they affect the visualisation process. The argument in this paper is based on our experiences in designing, building and evaluating an academic literature visualisation tool.

Categories and Subject Descriptors

H5.m. [Information interfaces and presentation] (e.g., HCI)

General Terms

Human Factors

Keywords

Information Visualisation, User Experience, Evaluation.

1. INTRODUCTION

Information Visualisation (InfoVis) is the visual representation of abstract data of a specific domain on a computer screen. We consider user's interaction with InfoVis systems to be an experience, due to the activities that users are engaged with in addition to the knowledge being gained. This experience is made out of a combination of cognitive activities which are related to making sense and gaining knowledge of the visually represented domain, and a set of activities which are related to interacting with the interface. Standard HCI usability measures rely mainly on capturing the usability of the interface with no clear manner with which to capture domain related cognitive knowledge. Hence by merely relying on standard HCI usability measures, insight into an experience is fragmentary, since only the usability of the interface is captured. In this paper we argue that in order to evaluate InfoVis tools, we need to take into account both of these activities due to their interconnectivity. In other words,

we need to capture the user's visualisation experience as a whole. The argument we make is based on our experiences in designing and evaluating an academic literature visualisation tool, drawing on observations and analysis from a pilot study.

2. THE INFOVIS EXPERIENCE

Spence [9] describes InfoVis as a cognitive activity with which users are engaged with the potential of gaining an insight and an understanding of the represented data. This participation of the user in a cognitive activity leads not only to gaining domain related knowledge but is the substance of the user experience with the visualisation. In addition to this knowledge gaining activity, the user is also involved with activities that are essential to interacting with the represented tool. It is the combination of both that forms the user's visualisation experience. Hence when it comes to evaluating InfoVis tools it is essential to capture the experience as a whole. The user's visualisation experience, whether it is related to the gaining of domain knowledge or interacting with the interface, has a cognitive nature related to mental images of the domain and user's mental model of the interface. The interconnectivity and cognitive nature of the user's mental image and interaction model makes the user experience hard to measure.

3. THE COGNITIVE ACTIVITIES

The main user role in the InfoVis process is a cognitive one. The user interprets the visual representations of the data and builds mental images from which knowledge of the domain is gained. The visual representations are the only means with which domain related knowledge can be communicated to the user. Users need to make sense of these visual representations, hence engaging in cognitive activities. Some authors claim that InfoVis has moved out of the mind and onto the computer screen [10]. This is true in the physical sense, however, the activities involved from the user are still very much in the mind. In addition to users' engagement with these visual representations, users must also interact with the interface itself, in order to do so they rely on mental models that they develop of the system. This concept has been thoroughly covered in HCI literature and reflected in standard usability measures. However, when it comes to the building of domain related knowledge, there is a substantial lack in the literature. Hence, this forms the main challenge when it comes to the evaluation of InfoVis tools.

3.1. Mental Models: InfoVis and HCI

Both InfoVis literature and HCI literature refer to cognitive activities that users engage with in order to gain knowledge and interact with a system. This is reflected by the concept of building mental images of abstract domains or models of the interface. However, there are crucial differences between InfoVis and HCI literature when it comes to defining these concepts. In InfoVis literature, mental images represent the

Published by the British Computer Society
Volume 2 Proceedings of the 21st BCS HCI Group Conference
HCI 2007, Lancaster University, 3-7 September 2007
Devina Ramduny-Ellis & Dorothy Rachovides (Editors)

images that people construct of a particular domain, whereas in HCI, it represents the models that people develop of a system [7]: from this point forward we will refer to this HCI model as the interaction model. We argue that mental images and interaction models cannot be separated since they both take part in the user's InfoVis experience, and hence must take part in the evaluation process of InfoVis tools. The visualisation activity is seen as that of building an internal interface [10] that cannot be printed or seen by anyone other than the user. It is through this act that users gain knowledge and insight of the represented domain.

3.2. InfoVis Mental Images is the Challenge

When it comes to mental images, in the context of InfoVis, there is no right or wrong: it is how people make sense of something they interact with. Since it is their belief, it is not susceptible to rigorous tests. The capturing and validating of mental models is a difficult task. In addition, it is a controversial one: Rogers et al [8] have proven that merely trying to make people talk about their mental model may in fact affect and change these models, proving its delicacy. In order for users to create mental images of the domain whilst interacting with an InfoVis system, they engage in a number of activities such as: interpretation of the visual cues, building associations, identifying similarities, etc. In addition, users rely on the models they build of the system's interface in order to interact with the InfoVis. Whilst in this interaction process they are engaged in the process of building domain related models. Interaction models and the building of mental images of the domain are interrelated and hence must take part in the evaluation process of InfoVis tools. Ideally, interaction models should not interfere with the building of domain related mental images; on the contrary, they should complement it. Users face challenges when interacting with InfoVis tools which rely on the fact that information cannot be seen: it is interpreted by users from the represented data.

4. EVALUATING INFOVIS TOOLS

In InfoVis the raw data itself is not the goal, it is the information it conveys. It is important to note that information and data are not equivalent. Information is derived from the data as Spence [9] indicates. By looking at the visually represented data, in other words browsing through the representation, interesting information is revealed. This exploration results in gaining higher levels of knowledge at the semantic level. However, before such knowledge can be gained users must interact with the interface at a syntactic level through a set of visual tasks, such as: identifying individual entities, categorizing entities, identifying clusters, etc. In order to evaluate InfoVis tools we should target knowledge at both the syntactic and semantic levels through a set of low and high level tasks. Usability in general is not a standard practice when it comes to designing and building InfoVis tools. Of the studies that do exist we categorize them according to the level of knowledge that they target, in other words, whether they target knowledge at the syntactic level or the semantic level.

4.1. Syntactic-Knowledge: Low-level tasks

Low-level tasks represent the tasks performed by users at the syntactic level of the InfoVis user experience. The low-level tasks evaluate whether or not the user understands the syntax of the visual language. Zhou and Feiner [11] identified a visual task taxonomy from which domain independent visual tasks were identified. Examples of these tasks are: identify, locate, rank, generalize, correlate, etc. Morse el al [6] used these low-level tasks to devise specialized tasks which were used to evaluate visualisations at the syntactic level of knowledge.

4.2. Semantic-Knowledge: High-level tasks

The high-level tasks correspond to the tasks used to evaluate the visualisation at the semantic level. They are tightly coupled with the visualized domain, unlike the low-level tasks. Evaluating the visualisation using these tasks assists in determining whether the visualisation design corresponds to the requirements of the tool. However, unlike the low-level tasks, where the primary tasks are generated regardless of the represented domain, the high level tasks are generated from user requirements. Kobsa [5] argues that simply giving users low-level tasks, such as searching for a specific entity, or performing counting tasks makes it easier to identify the usability issues, since tasks such as these are rarely executed by users in a real InfoVis experience situation. When it comes to InfoVis systems there is more than one way of executing a task; as a result they emphasize that testing for high-level tasks is of great importance. We completely agree with this argument, as we discuss next. However, we strongly believe that both the low-level tasks and the high-level tasks are interconnected, since in order for users to execute the high level tasks they must go through a set of low-level tasks. Tasks at both of these levels represent activities that take part in the building of domain related mental images, they however do not target interaction related knowledge.

5. THE ACADEMIC LITERATURE VISUALISATION TOOL

The challenge of evaluating an information visualisation has been made concrete for us by our work in visualising academic literature [2]. This domain consists of the literature data within an academic context. It includes information such as: authors, papers, citations, journals, etc. Users of such information are mainly researchers in an academic field since it is important for them to keep track of the literature. In addition, they also need to create a complete and global understanding of the community. Literature data is complex due to its size and interrelations that appear between the entities, e.g.: citation trails where a paper cites another paper which in turn cites another, etc. Researchers would need to keep track of thousands of literature items ranging from the authors of the publications to the detailed ideas presented in each publication. The diversity and individualism of academic literature users formed one of the main challenges in the design and evaluation of the associated visualisation tool.

5.1. The Design

Prior to designing the literature visualisation tool we conducted a qualitative study [2] to capture users' experiences whilst interacting with academic literature. The qualitative study revealed the subjectivity of the literature domain. The participants' literature knowledge depended heavily on their background, knowledge and goals at the time of interacting with their academic literature. Hence, the goal is to give the user the freedom to explore and manipulate the visualisation through multiple interactive activities. In addition, users need to be given the ability to personalize their experiences. We developed a preliminary prototype of a literature domain [3] (Figure 1). The data we visualized was the dataset used for the InfoVis'04 contest which includes the complete metadata of 8 years for all InfoVis conference [4]. The data layout and interactive activities were based on users' literature experiences.

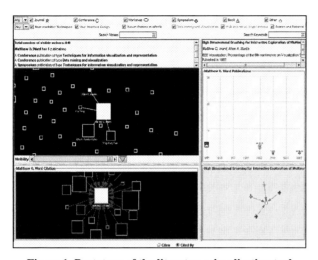

Figure 1. Prototype of the literature visualisation tool

5.2. The Evaluation

As discussed earlier, we believe that InfoVis tools must be evaluated at the syntactic level before they can be evaluated at the semantic level through a set of low-level tasks that target the visual syntax. The generated low-level tasks must fit within the context of the interface, since it is through interacting with the interface that any InfoVis knowledge can be learned. Therefore, we took a similar approach as Morse et al [6], where we devised tasks based on Zhou and Feiner [11] visual taxonomies.

Table 1 Difficulty level and its associated visual task

Difficulty	Visual Task
Primitive	Locate, identify, associate
Intermediate	Categorise/rank, compare/distinguish, reveal, cluster, Correlate
Complex	Generalise

Based on our system's design rationale we decided that the following low-level tasks best represented our needs: locate, identify, associate, categorise, rank, compare, distinguish, reveal, cluster, correlate and generalize. Unlike Morse el al [6], we ranked these tasks into three levels of difficulty (Table 1). The difficulty levels we identified were based on the primitiveness of the actions that the users had to engage with in order to accomplish the specific task, which in turn related to the complexity of the visual language syntax. The reason for doing so is that we are interested in identifying usability problems which are related with the visual syntax, in addition to the user's interaction model. For each of the actions we devised a set of tasks. These tasks were based on the results of the qualitative study we conducted [2].

Primitive tasks

We identified the following actions as primitive:

Locate tasks: assist us in determining whether or not the user understands the visual data layout since it is essential that they are able to locate specific entities. For example: Locate [author_name]'s 2001 paper, what are its keywords?

Identify tasks: assist us in determining whether the user is able to understand the visual encodings, such as shape and color, which are used to encode the data. For Example: Of the

papers that have been published by [author_name] which has been cited the most?

Associate tasks: assists us in determining whether the user understands the relationships between the various visual entities. For example: Which research interest is associated with more authors?

Intermediate Tasks

From these primitive actions more complex actions were identified based on Zhou and Feiner [11] visual taxonomies: categorize/rank, compare/distinguish, reveal, cluster and compare. We base our categorization on the fact that in order for the user to be able to accomplish any of these actions one or more of the primitive action must be executed. For example: The 1996 [paper_title] by [author_name] cites another paper by [author_name], who does the latter paper cite? This is an intermediate revelation task since it is made out of various primitive actions, which are: *locate* and *identify*. In order for the user to accomplish this task the user must first *locate* the particular author, *identify* the specific paper and then reveal its citation information.

Complex

Complex tasks lean more towards the high-level tasks since they are based on users' exploration of the visualisation and not on specifics. They are less controlling compared to the primitive or the intermediate tasks in terms of the actions that the user must execute, and the answers they provide. Complex tasks are related to the '*generalize*' visual tasks since users reach generalized conclusions on the entities being explored. An example of a complex task: What is the relationship between the following authors [author_name] and [author_name]? In this task the users are given the freedom to explore the visualisation to identify the relationship. Comparing this task with an intermediate task such as: [author_name] cites [author_name], how many papers did they co-author? In this task the users are restricted in the way they would explore the visualisation since the grounds of the relationship are specified. However, with the complex tasks different users can reach different results in various ways. A few users identified a relationship between the authors that we had not previously come across despite extensive knowledge of the dataset.

5.3. Case Study: Test of Evaluation

In order to evaluate our evaluation approach, we conducted a pilot-study which took the form of a standard HCI task-based evaluation study which was based on the tasks devised. The tasks were given by order of difficulty: primitive, intermediate and complex. In total a set of 22 questions were given to the participants. During the course of the study the researcher was taking notes in addition to measuring the time participants needed to answer each question. Prior to beginning the study demographic information was gathered in addition to participants' knowledge and experiences with InfoVis tools in general and literature visualisation tools in particular. Users' interaction satisfaction was captured using the Questionnaire of User Interface Satisfaction (QUIS) [1]. There were seven participants in total. Six of them had at least two years experience in doing research. Two of these participants did not know what InfoVis was. One participant was an expert in the field of InfoVis. None of the participants had ever worked with literature visualisation tools. The questionnaire helped us identify some minor usability issues that needed improvement.

6. WHAT WE LEARNT

This study did not reflect anything that relates to the users' InfoVis experience. This was expected since the aim of the study was to capture the users' syntactic knowledge and interaction model. However, a lot was learnt in relation to the evaluation of InfoVis tools.

6.1. Low-level Tasks: Usability not Experience

A controlled task-based usability study assisted us in evaluating whether or not the system's interaction model fitted the users' interaction model which, as we discussed earlier, is an essential part in evaluating InfoVis tools. However, it said nothing about the visualisation or the experience as a whole. In fact it seemed to hinder such an experience. The study revealed that following a standard task-based evaluation method restricted users' experiences. For example, one of the participants commented: *"I liked the system but I was trying to complete tasks given – it might mean more if I used it for research and saw interesting relations in papers that was meaningful to me"*.

We merely got a glimpse of the users' experiences with the visualisation tool through the comments that the users gave and the observations the researcher captured during the study. We argue that relying on quantitative measures proved to be insufficient. We strongly believe that relying on higher-level tasks and the combination of qualitative and quantitative analysis will assist us in capturing users' InfoVis experiences more effectively.

6.2. Efficiency: Physical Activities rather than Time

Users were timed during the pilot-study as they answered each of the questions. After analyzing this data there was not a straight correlation between how well the users did and the time it took them to do it. In fact, it seemed that the more time they spent on each of the tasks the better they did. However, due to the number of participants we cannot unequivocally assert the claim. But we can claim that, from our observation of the users' performances and experiences during the study, there was a direct relation between the number of physical activities that they engaged with and their overall satisfaction, which reemphasize our argument that the execution of the interaction model should complement and not interfere with the creation of the domain related mental images. We observed that the more they had to engage with physical activities as: constantly clicking, or zooming in and zooming out to accomplish something specific the more they were frustrated, as observed by the researcher through: the comments that they gave, the facial expressions or gestures they performed. They seemed to want to have the information they needed, that related to a specific task, with the least number of physical activities. We hypothesize that the amount of physical activities users engage with whilst accomplishing a specific task might be a better measure of efficiency rather than relying on the time it takes users to accomplish a task.

6.3. Experience is the Essence

Interestingly, all complex questions were answered correctly by the participants. This might be due to the fact that these tasks come last in the list of questions given to participants. In addition, it might be due to the fact that these complex tasks, as expressed earlier, are less restrictive compared to the primitive and intermediate tasks. As a result they give users the freedom to explore the InfoVis interface, hence allowing for a better experience. This is not an assertion but a hypothesis that needs to be further investigated. One of the participants commented*: "It got easier to use with more practice, also became more adventurous…"*. From here we identified interesting questions: What makes it *"more adventurous"*, what makes it a better experience? This is what we would like to capture and understand.

7. CONCLUSION

Where does HCI lie when it comes to evaluating InfoVis tools? It assisted us in successfully identifying usability issues related to the user's interaction models. However, the InfoVis experience is not just made out of the interaction models but it also relies on the building of domain related mental images. Mental images are built as the user interacts with the visualisation at the syntactic and semantic levels of knowledge. From our pilot-study we argue that in order to evaluate the InfoVis we need to capture the experience as a whole, which remains as a challenge to the field of HCI. In addition, we also demonstrated that efficiency in the InfoVis tool cannot be captured using time and suggested the use of physical activities instead.

8. REFERENCES

[1] Chin, J., Diehl, V., Norman, K. (1988) 'Development of an instrument measuring user satisfaction of the human-computer interface', Proc of SIGCHI conference on Human factors in computing systems, 213-218.

[2] Faisal, S., Cairns, P., Blandford, A., (2006) 'Developing User Requirements for Visualisations of Literature Knowledge Domains,' 10th International Conference on Information Visualisation (IV'06), 264-269.

[3] Faisal, S., Cairns, P., Blandford, A., (2007) 'Building for Users not for Experts: Designing a Visualisation of the literature domain,' to be presented at 11th International Conference on Information Visualisation (IV'07).

[4] Ke, W., Borner, K. and Viswanath, L (2004), InfoVis04 Contest MS-Access Database, Indiana University, School of Library and Information Science and School of Informatics, <http://ella.slis.indiana.edu/~lviswana/iv04-contest.mdb>

[5] Kobsa, A. (2001) 'An Empirical Comparison of Three Commercial Information Visualisation Systems'. IEEE Symposium on Information Visualisation 2001, 123-130.

[6] Morse, E., Lewis, M. and Olsen, K. A. (2000) 'Evaluating Visualisations: Using a Taxonomic Guide', *International Journal of Human-Computer Studies*, **53**(5), 637-662.

[7] Norman, D. (1988) *Psychology of Everyday Things.* Basic Books

[8] Rogers, Y., Rutherford, A., and Bibby, P. (1992). *Models In the Mind - Theory, Perspective, and Application.* London: Academic Press.

[9] Spence, R. (2001) *Information Visualisation,* first edition ACM Press Books, Edinburgh Gate, Harlow, Essex, UK.

[10] Ware, C. (2000). Information Visualisation: Perception for Design: Morgan Kaufmann.

[11] Zhou, M., Feiner, S. (1998) 'Visual task characterization for automated visual discourse synthesis', Proceedings of the SIGCHI conference on Human factors in computing systems, 392-399.

Mental Health Issues and Pervasive Computing

David Haniff

ActivityComputing.com

Oldbrook, Milton Keynes, MK6 2XT

+44 (0)1908 236 379

davejhaniff@hotmail.com

ABSTRACT

This poster describes work being undertaken in the use of pervasive computing for the treatment of mental health problems. The use of technology to help patients with psychological issues such as depression are explored and preliminary investigations are discussed.

Categories and Subject Descriptors

J.3.3 [Life and Medical Sciences], H.5.2 [User Interfaces]

General Terms

Design, Human Factors.

Keywords

Mental Health, Pervasive Computing, Ubiquitous Computing.

1. INTRODUCTION

This poster presents preliminary investigations into the issue of pervasive computing and mental health. Research has been carried out on the use of computers to diagnose and provide aid to patients suffering from mental illness [5], as well as providing tasks for patients outside of psychotherapy sessions [7]. Mental health problems can be defined as disorders within the mind that effect the normal life of an individual. One in four people suffer from a mental health problem within a year, severe mental health problems are, however more rare. The problems can be crippling for the person but is often neglected because it is within the mind and not a physical problem. They can be distressing for the individual and for those around them. There are a range of treatments for various mental illnesses such as medication, electric shock treatment and cognitive therapy. Pervasive computing rather than replacing these treatments can be used to support the individual with the problem. The aims for the research are to investigate how pervasive technology can support clinical psychologists in the treatment of mental illness, to examine the type of information that is appropriate for the patient with the mental illness and to build and evaluate the use of pervasive technology for mental illness. There are many types of mental illness suffered by patients, however, the illnesses addressed by this research are those where cognitive therapy can be useful, such as depression, and Obsessive Compulsive Disorder (OCD).

2. DEPRESSION

Depression is a state of mind where the individual feels low which can be caused by negative thoughts. Depression can have a profound effect on people's lives leading to symptoms ranging from lethargy to some in extreme cases to commit suicide. There are a number of treatments for depression such as anti-depressants, for example, Prozac, which is intended to lift the mood of the patient. Cognitive therapy can also be used to alter the way the patient thinks. Negative thoughts that can cause depression can be replaced by positive thoughts or challenged by the patient. Negative thoughts for some people are caused by seeing an insurmountable problem and having a feeling of hopelessness, they can be taught to break down a problem into smaller components and rewarding themselves when the smaller problem is solved. The causes of the depression need to be identified by the patient, the thoughts that trigger this emotion can then be worked upon. Another method for combating depression is to structure the day with activities that lift the patient's mood, for example, chatting to a friend or doing exercise. Furthermore, depression can also be helped by the use of physical exercise which can release Serotonin into the brain. This helps to relax the mind and can lift the mood of the patient.

Pervasive computing can aid the patient by providing reminders about activities that are beneficial to the mood of the patient. This can take the form of a Personal Digital Assistant (PDA) and voice output gently reminding the patient about tasks that they should be doing through out the day. Technology can also be used to identify particular thoughts through the patient verbalising a key word and presenting a challenge to that thought when it occurs. The computer can use speech recognition to identify a particular word associated with the thought and the challenge to the thought presented by the computer can be decided in co-operation with a cognitive therapist. These types of applications will be further explored by the research.

With regard to exercise, an exercise routine can be presented to the user through a PDA and when targets have been met these can be ticked off on the computer, having a structured routine will help their mental and physical health. The software could calculate the routine for them, setting small targets initially in order to gain a sense of achievement. This routine has to be agreed by their doctor. Furthermore, technology can be used to remind people when to do exercise [2]. In addition, wearable computers have been used for sports training, providing feedback on their performance [4], this can be used as a personal training device for the patient. Words of encouragement can be presented to the user from the system when personal goals have been achieved, this will encourage the patient and give them confidence which may lift their mood further.

In addition, reminders of people in the patients life can lift their mood, for example their wives or children. A PDA can be used to provide images, speech and video to distract the patient and help them think about the things that are important in their

Published by the British Computer Society

Volume 2 Proceedings of the 21st BCS HCI Group Conference

HCI 2007, Lancaster University, 3-7 September 2007

Devina Ramduny-Ellis & Dorothy Rachovides (Editors)

lives. Figure 1 shows an example of an application which was written in Java 2. When the patient is low these media files can be used to trigger positive thoughts and lift their mood.

Figure 1: An Application that presents pictures, voice, words and video of a patients daughter.

3. OBSESSIVE COMPULSIVE DISORDER

Obsessive Compulsive Disorder (OCD) is a mental illness that causes the sufferer to mentally or physically repeat irrational actions, internally or physically. "Obsessive compulsive disorder (OCD) is a common mental health condition that affects 2% of the population." [6]. To the patient these actions can be seen as completely rational, what separates these actions from 'normal' actions is the culture in which the person is nurtured. There are rules and conventions that determine what is appropriate human behaviour. The treatment for such a condition has been conventionally through medication and/or cognitive therapy. Certain anti-depressants are credited to ease this illness by acting on the repetitive nature of this action. The cognitive therapy indicates appropriate techniques and mental actions to reduce or cure the occurrence of this inappropriate behaviour.

Using an analogy with computer programming the internal processing of information is akin to the execution of a 'while' loop without a condition stopping the repetitive loop from its process. For example, there are many cases of OCD patients who wash their hands constantly without due course. The sufferers wash their hands to an extent that the skin becomes raw when they know that this detrimental to their person. The mind is caught in a loop without rational thought to stop the action. There have been cases whereby the sufferer performs a certain ritual that certifies their well being even though there is no causal relationship between performing the act and the consequences of the act. For instance, repeating certain words to ensure a loved ones safety.

This poster suggests that the treatment of this mental illness by the use of technology embedded within the environment can prove fruitful. The technology adapts in a unique way whereby ubiquitous computing responds to the mental state of the user. As with a pace-maker, technology is used to aid the patient but instead of being solely a personal device the technology is distributed within the environment too. Wearable computers and external sensors have been used for the visually impaired, there has however not been widespread adoption of this technology for those with various needs. This project hopes to stimulate discussion within the HCI community about the use of technology and in particular ubiquitous computing due to its pervasiveness and adaptability to situations to treat mental

illness. OCD often manifests itself in reaction to situations that the individual might find them self in, pervasive computing can be situationally-aware (using sensors to provide contextual information) and can therefore provide the flexibility required by the sufferer. For some sufferers the condition worsens under stress, a state of anxiety can be detected through various on-body sensors and appropriate information can be given to counteract the anxiety. A particular object or situation can trigger anxiety, pervasive computing can sense these objects and situations and provide help for the sufferer, for instance RF tags could be used to identify disturbing objects to the patient. The help could well be auditory, for example, words of comfort or instructions on what to do next may be spoken to the user. Sensors have been used in medical applications, for example, Kientz and Abowd [3] describe the use of toy-embedded sensors to collect data concerning developmental milestones in the early detection of autism in children. Ebrahimi et al. [1] describe brain computer interfaces whereby signals from the brain can control external devices. One possible way of detecting OCD is to monitor brain patterns and a computing device can therefore respond appropriately.

The pervasive systems developed can be integrated with cognitive therapy which in many ways attempts to change the way someone thinks in order to relieve the individual from the symptoms of the condition. In some cases a cure may be achieved as certain actions become automatic, however, the potential for this technology to rid the sufferers of this illness needs to be explored.

4. CONCLUSION

The research described within this poster aims to examine and provide technology based solutions to the increasing quantity of the population effected by mental illness. The illnesses to be investigated by this research are depression and obsessive compulsive disorder. The research is very much at an early stage and can potentially greatly influence the lives of people suffering from mental problems.

5. REFERENCES

[1] Ebrahimi, T., Vesin, J. & Garcia, G. (2003) Brain Computer Interface in Multimedia Communication. IEEE Signal Processing Magazine, February 2003.

[2] Fogg, B. (2002) Persuasive Computing. Morgan Kaufm.

[3] Kientz, J.A., Abowd, G.D. (2006) Designing Technology to Aid in the Early Detection of Developmental Delay in Children. UbiHealth 2006.

[4] Knight, J. F., Schwirtz, A., Psomadelis, F., Baber, C., Bristow, H. W., Arvanitis, T. N. (2005) The Design of Sunvest. Personal and Ubiquitous Computing, 9 (1) 6-19.

[5] Marks, I. (1999) Computer Aids to Mental Health Care, Canadian Journal of Psychiatry, 44, 548-555.

[6] NHS Direct. (2007) http://www.nhsdirect.nhs.uk/articles/article.aspx?articleID=266.

[7] Sa, M. D., Carrico, L., Antunes, P. (2007) Ubiquitous Psychotherapy, IEEE Pervasive Computing, 6(1), 20-27.

Interaction Manifolds: Theory from Experiments

Cecily Morrison
Cambridge University
William Gates Building
15 JJ Thomson Avenue
Cambridge CB3 0FD UK
(+44) 1223 763 783

Cecily.Morrison@cl.cam.ac.uk

Alan F. Blackwell
Cambridge University
William Gates Building
15 JJ Thomson Avenue
Cambridge CB3 0FD UK
(+44) 1223 763 783

Alan.Blackwell@cl.cam.ac.uk

ABSTRACT

This poster builds on comparative ethnographic work of a multi-disciplinary medical team using a paper-based and a computer-based patient record system. It describes the design and preliminary results of an experiment aimed to help articulate an analytical construct that would describe the trade-offs between a technological setup and a group's ability to negotiate an interaction among themselves.

Categories and Subject Descriptors

H.5.3 [**Group and Organization Interfaces**]

General Terms

Performance, Design, Human Factors, Theory

Keywords

CSCW, Interaction Manifold

1.   INTRODUCTION

In a previous ethnographic study [1], we examined how a multi-disciplinary medical team negotiated interaction amongst themselves while using a patient medical record to decide on future treatment. We compared how the physical interactions, (or non-verbal behaviours), changed when a paper-based system was used as opposed to a computer-based one. The result of the work suggested a need for an analytical construct that identifies the trade-offs between the configuration of a technological setup and the abilities of a group to negotiate interaction. As a first step in developing this construct, *the interaction manifold*, we are preparing a number of experiments. Using a motion capture system that enables us to track the position of participants' entire bodies in 3-dimensional space that is linked with video, we are able to evaluate a group's physical interactions in a given circumstance both qualitatively and quantitatively. After summarizing the research questions posed by our previous study, we will describe the experiment and preliminary results.

2.   BACKGROUND

The ethnographic study that this work builds on compared interaction around a paper-based patient medical record system to a computer-based one in an intensive care unit. We specifically looked at physical interactions – that is: group formation, upper-body orientation, gesture manipulation, object manipulation and posture. Analysis of the paper-based system usage demonstrated the importance of physical interactions in seamlessly negotiating conversation. It also showed that Kendon's F-formation [2], a framework describing non-verbal behaviour in group interaction, fits well. However, this was not the case with the computer-based system where the group was forced to split due to the position of the display, as shown in figure 1, causing a break down in communication.

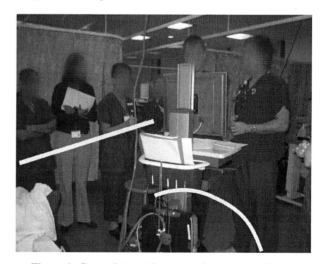

Figure 1: Group interaction around a computer-based medical record system

The split removed physical interactions as a viable means of communication, blocking members from participating in the interaction. The inability of group members to monitor each other's physical (non-verbal) interactions caused a reduction in parallel work and less integration with those switching between reviewing, taking notes and the group conversation. The solution to static display devices is generally mobile devices which allow people to configure themselves as need be. However, it is not clear from our ethnographic research whether this will solve the problem. We conjecture that -- looking at different content, no central source of orientation, and an inability to monitor what information that others are using -- will decrease group cohesion and thus, the effectiveness of the interaction. The experiment described below aims to understand more precisely whether mobile handheld devices, such as Emanotech's new device *MedTab* [3], can solve the problems articulated above. We would therefore like to test how physical interactions differ when a group of 3 performs a cooperative task using a large, wall-projected display versus having a shared screen displayed on a personal handheld device that each participant holds individually.

3. EXPERIMENTAL DESIGN

3.1 Setup

Each participant wears a hat, one glove, a belt, a shoulder pad, and shoe covers fitted with reflective dots whose 3-dimensional coordinates can be tracked by a *Vicon* motion capture system within a 3 x 3 meter area, illustrated below in figure 2.

Figure 2: Experimental Setup

The large display is projected 50 cm in front of the motion capture space. The handheld displays are standard PDAs running VNC. In both cases, the display will be created through a java program running on the main computer and projected or sent as appropriate.

3.2 Task

Participants cooperatively control one on-screen pen with their body movements in a drawing program. Each participant can manipulate either the x-component, y-component, or speed of the direction vector by changing the angle of their hand to their hip and the colour, width, or alpha value by moving in space.

They are asked to do the following two exercises: (1) draw their dream house; (2) draw an animal that is a cross between their three favourite animals. The order of exercises and display types are randomised.

4. EVALUATION

Participants will be videoed and log files kept of their head, torso, and foot movements as well as their absolute position in space. Using this data, we will analyse the following:

(1) changes in group formation by visualizing each participant's position and orientation;
(2) completion times;
(3) number of times and degree that participants turn their heads, upper torso, or whole body (feet) towards each other;
(4) conversation analysis.

Visualisations will be rendered to examine each of the above categories individually as well as, all data will be fed into *Replayer*, an application that allows simultaneous viewing of different media at any given timestamp.

5. PRELIMINARY RESULTS

As of the writing of this paper, a preliminary experiment has been completed to test the usability of the drawing program and provide initial feedback from the participants. 2 pairs of students used the program with the wall projection. Both pairs found the program very enticing and after 1.5 hours we had to request that they finish. The students, even the non-mathematical ones, had no problem controlling the system, taking about 10 minutes to adjust. We saw very different styles of cooperation and therefore different postures, body orientations and speech styles. It became clear that cooperation styles will need to be accounted for in the analysis of the full experiment.

6. ACKNOWLEDGMENTS

We are grateful for the support of Papworth Critical Care Unit, Papworth Anaesthetic Research, and head consultant Alain Vuylsteke, who initiated this project. This research is sponsored by Boeing Corporation and IMDsoft, and is being conducted in collaboration with David Good and Alice McGowan (Social and Political Science) and Matthew Jones (Judge Business School).

7. REFERENCES

[1] Morrison, C. Blackwell, A. F. (2007). Manifolds of Social Interaction in Physical-Digital Environments. (work-in-progress)

[2] Kendon, A. (1990). Conduction Interaction: Patterns of Behavior in focused encounters, Cambridge University Press, Cambridge, UK.

[3] Emano Tec Inc. (2007). www.emanotec.com/medtab.htm

Interactive Experience

The Emotion Sampling Device (ESD)

Linda Hole
Bournemouth University
School of Design, Engineering & Computing

Talbot Campus
Poole, Dorset BH12 5BB
+44(0)1202 965251

lhole@bournemouth.ac.uk

Oliver M. Williams
Bournemouth University
School of Design, Engineering & Computing

Talbot Campus
Poole, Dorset BH12 5BB
+44(0)1202 965503

owilliams@bournemouth.ac.uk

ABSTRACT

The emotion sampling device (ESD) has been developed in the light of ever-increasing interest in the area of affective computing, and out of a need to better understand the effect that electronic products have on the emotions of their users. A study of emotion theory and current sampling techniques revealed a need for a method of a different nature, one that does not rely upon the traditional forms of emotion representation. Therefore, the ESD aims to satisfy this need, being a tool that can not only accurately sample the multi-faceted human emotional experience, but also blend seamlessly into our world in the true spirit of ubiqitous computing.

Categories and Subject Descriptors

H.1.2 [**Models and Principles**]: User/Machine Systems - *human factors, human information processing.*

General Terms

Measurement, Design, Human Factors, Theory

Keywords

Affect, Appraisal, Experience, Interface Design, Mobile Devices, Event-based, Emotion Sampling Device

1. INTRODUCTION

Development of the ESD follows an earlier study to consider theoretical models from psychology which could be effectively applied to the field of emotion sampling. The following aims have been present during the development process:

- to identify to what extent the theory can be applied to experience sampling;

- to improve the experience sampling process through the use of event-based reporting;

- to develop the emotion sampling device and its ability to collect emotion information from a heterogeneous population;

- to map ESD information to traditional representation styles and to incorporate these styles into the ESD.

The emotion sampling device has thus far been developed in a laboratory setting and will soon undergo initial testing to verify

its core architecture and to begin to validate the first two aims listed above.

2. FEELINGS, EMOTION AND COGNITON

As previously stated an earlier study had identified emotion theory not previously used in the area of emotion sampling. In support of the use of this method we take reference from the work of Lang [cited in 1: 125] who concluded that emotion and its processes manifest themselves in the visceral, behavioural and verbal states. Norman [3] develops this further to suggest that the visceral and behavioural states exist in the subconscious space, while the verbal state exists in the conscious space, and only there do we achieve emotion. With this in mind, we have identified a conceptual model of emotion processing to describe the transfer from feeling to emotion and the importance of cognition in the emotional process. This model, shown in Figure 1, underpins this research and provides placement for our approach.

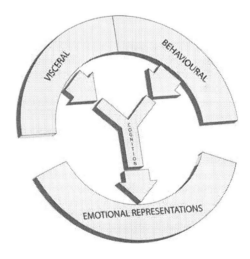

Figure 1. Conceptual Model of Emotion Processing.

3. APPRAISAL THEORY OF EMOTION

From the analysis of existing methods, we have identified evidence to suggest that that there is a space following the cognitive process, but before representations are applied, in which a new method could be placed. Methods used to sample emotion in the pre-cognitive space require extra abstraction to fill in the blanks that would normally be filled by the process of cognition, and thus only succeed to measure *feeling* not *emotion*. Post-cognitive methods can be biased by a subject's knowledge of emotional expression and the bearing of the method towards specific representation types such as language or imagery.

CleverTracker software framework is distributed as an open source project hosted on SourceForge[1], under the BSD license.

2. FRAMEWORK DESIGN

The framework is based on the client-server model. The server component stores data permanently to a relational database for later analysis. It is written in Java and can be configured to support any database with a JDBC driver. This allows the server component to be set up and run on any operating system. The client component is a library which is used in the code of the application under evaluation. As such there are multiple client libraries to match the various programming languages that applications may be written in. Currently, these include Java (for desktop applications) and JavaScript (for web applications). The interaction data is transferred from the client libraries to the server component in the form of HTTP messages, making it easy to extend the framework to support additional technologies in the future. Each message represents a single event generated from the application under evaluation and is sent by the client with the fields listed in Table 1. The "messageId" field acts as the unique identifier for each message. All unique identifiers are generated locally on the client side, with the help of UUID generators. This makes it possible to use the framework in partially connected environments where internet access may not always be available.

Table 1. Description of the parameters of the log method.

Parameter	Description
messageId	The messageId serves as a unique identifier for messages sent from any client to the server and logged in the central repository.
sessionId	The sessionId stands for a single run of the application providing the interaction data.
userId	The userId anonymously identifies a user of the software application.
messageType	The messageType provides an extra categorisation of the generated messages.
eventOrigin	The attributes eventOrigin describes the source in the application that triggered the message generation, eg: `brunel.Converter.buttonClicked`
eventMessage	A free text field that can contain any data which is relevant to the researcher.
timestamp	A record of when the message was passed from the software application to CleverTracker client.

The "userId" field is also automatically generated by the client libraries as a sequence of characters which cannot be directly traced back to the users' details. This field then allows aggregating and analysing usage data for individual users, while respecting their anonymity. Unlike the "userId" field which remains the same, the "sessionId" field is generated for each run of the application. It can be used to identify for how long people use an application, or what functionality is used during each session. The "messageType" field can be set in advance to provide some categorisation of messages, for example an "INFO" message or "BUTTONCLICK" message. This field is free text. The actual information which is recorded

is passed as free text using the "eventMessage" field. This allows any type of textual data to be passed in the form of a string. The eventOrigin allows locating the source of the message. It is a hierarchical classification which identifies the user interface element which triggered the message. In Java desktop applications this is automatically captured as the package name, class and method name which generated the event.

2.1 Message Flow

The intended message flow (Figure 1) between the clients and the server for this framework is the following: A user interacts with an application, through some input device, such as keyboard or mouse. The application then responds to this input by executing some method or procedure. Additional code should be inserted at this point which interacts with the CleverTracker library and captures the event. The library then checks whether the user has allowed the tracking of data and sends the events to the server component. If the server is not reachable the messages are queued locally and resent later once the server is available. When the server receives the message it is stored in a database. The server then sends a response to the client to confirm the storage of the message. A researcher may then access the database directly and perform detailed analysis of interaction data using their chosen technique. Such analysis may be achieved, for example, using data mining tools or custom defined SQL queries. To provide a degree of fault tolerance, the client is designed to continue sending the same message to the server, until it receives an acknowledgement, thus compensating for loss of messages. The server checks the "messageId" field of every incoming message and only stores each message once, even if it is received multiple times.

3. USING CLEVERTRACKER

3.1 Server Component

The server component runs as a J2EE application, and is designed to be compatible with most Servlet containers (such as Apache Tomcat or Jetty). The database connectivity can be set up by editing an XML configuration file on the server. This file contains the individual SQL statements that are used to insert and select data, and as such the server component may be configured to work with any database engine which provides a Java driver.

3.2 Client Libraries

An application that wants to make use of CleverTracker has to be customized by a software developer to call the programming interface of the appropriate client library. The following code snippet is a sample method called "buttonClicked" from a currency converting application (Figure 4). This application is written in Java and hence makes use of the Java CleverTracker client library. This code illustrates a call to the programming interface of the library to log the amount money and the currency type which a user wishes to convert.

```
private void buttonClicked() {
1. double amount = getAmount();
2. String currency = getCurrency();
3. double converted =
      exchange(amount, currency);
4. recorder.logMessage("User converted " +
      amount + currency, "INFO");
}
```

---

[1] For the source code and documentation see
http://clevertracker.sourceforge.net/

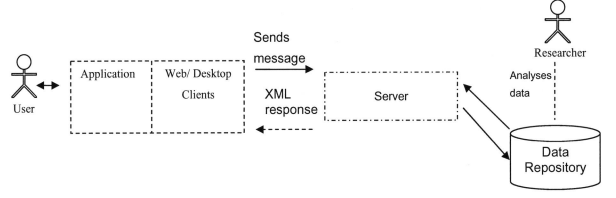

Figure 1. Message Flow.

The client library is called in line 4 and two pieces of information are passed separated with a comma. The first part is the "eventMessage" field, while the second part is the "messageType" field. Once this information is passed to the client library and it has been confirmed that the user has allowed data collection, the rest of the fields are automatically generated. Then the message is sent to the server. The sending of the messages is processed separately while the application is running, and as such including this code does not produce any noticeable delay. The presence of this additional code is transparent to the user. A sample logged message in the database record is illustrated in Figure 2.

---

messageId = 05135554-a343-4de3-b017-44121e129823-1

messageType = INFO

userId = f795b2e5-95e3-4eda-adc5-0cbbaca1090e

sessionId = 05135554-a343-4de3-b017-44121e129823

eventMessage = User converted 10USD

eventOrigin = clevertracker.DriverGui.buttonClicked

timestamp = 2007-05-24 3:42:59.000000921

Figure 2. Example of a recording.

4. VISUAL CONTROLS

CleverTracker provides additional user interface elements, which allow users to be in control of the recording process. When the application makes its first attempt to log data, the user is prompted that the application is going to collect data and asks for their consent. If the user is happy to allow this action, data collection begins and visual controls are provided as a small system tray icon with a right-click menu (Figure 3). This menu allows the user to monitor the status of the data collection process, which could be either "Started" or "Paused". By clicking on the "View Recorded Data" button, a sample of the logged data from the current session is displayed to the user. Another important menu option is "Why is data being recorded?". It allows the researcher to provide further information on what type of data is being collected as well as external web resources, where the user can read more about the study. This menu button for example could also lead to a discussion forum, where the user can post questions and communicate with the researcher directly.

The "Start Recording" and "Pause Recording" options allow users to pause the data collection for a single session and restart

it at a later stage. On the other hand, the "Stop and Exit" button stops the recording functionality for an entire session. The "Opt-out" option permanently disables the CleverTracker functionality; hence the user can choose to leave the study.

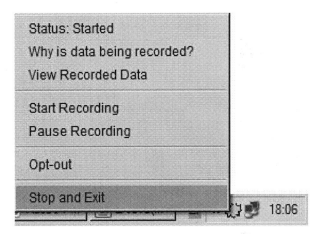

Figure 3.User Visual Control Menu.

5. USABILITY EVALUATION

An initial usability evaluation of the framework was conducted, which aimed to evaluate clarity and usability of the user controls provided by the CleverTracker client libraries. In order to evaluate the visual interface of the clients, a series of informal semi-structured interviews were conducted. The interview questions were centred on the ethical requirements, which were the focus of the CleverTracker framework. Five participants took part in the study. They were all undergraduate students in their last year of their Computer Science degree and they were between 20 and 26 years old.

After given a short introduction on the tasks which they need to fulfil, the participants had to use both a web and desktop currency converter application (Figure 4). The complexity of the application was relatively simple, as participants had to enter a value, select a currency, and press the convert button to get the value in Euro. After completing their task, participants where interview in a short debriefing session. The interview questions covered key issues such as the alerting system, the clarity of information provided and the usability of the visual controls.

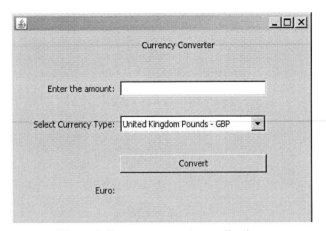

Figure 4. Currency converter application.

A number of interesting observations were made. All of the participants seemed confident in using the "Start Recording", "Pause Recording", "View Recorded Data" and "Opt-out" options. Almost all participants realised immediately that data was being collected from the two applications, which meant that the alerting system seemed to work as expected. Some of the participants liked the fact that the alert pop-up comes when they actually used the functionality of the web application. In their opinion this helped them distinguish the data collection alert from other spam message which according to them were frequently seen, while browsing the web. In the desktop application, the alerting pop-up with the opt-out feature seemed also clear, however some of the users did not seem to notice immediately the system tray icon for the visual menu, even though there was an information pop-up indicating that there was a menu there. A potential way to overcome this problem in future editions of this platform might be to convert the system tray menu into a floating window appearing next to the application or even it could be part of the application window itself.

When asked whether they would feel comfortable participating in studies that was tracking data about their use of a web or desktop applications, most participants were rather positive about it. Although a few mentioned that they seemed more at ease if they were participating in a web based study instead of their desktop machines. Overall, the evaluation study showed encouraging results. A further step would be organising a similar more hands-on session with developers and researchers to gain an understanding of what features they believe need further improvement.

6. LIMITATIONS AND DISCUSION

One limitation of the JavaScript CleverTracker client became apparent when the client library was tested with a web browser, which had its pop-up blocker on. In that case the CleverTracker JavaScript alert asking users for their consent to collect data was blocked, which resulted into having the collection process paused for the entire user session. Another important issue, which has not been yet addressed, is the collection of sensitive data with the framework. This could be an important issue if the application under evaluation stores passwords or credit card details. Currently, CleverTracker does not apply any filtering on what data is collected from the user. This has been left to the

discretion of the researchers. They decide what data is actually recorded. Still, with the View Recorded Data option, users will be in the position to see what type of data is recorded, making the recording process transparent. This awareness might help them to understand when to use the Start Recording and Pause Recording functionally when participating in study which records their actions.

7. FINAL REMARKS

We believe that this software will allow researchers to better understand how people interact with software. Given that this is one of the first tools that spans on both web and desktop platform, it could also allow an interesting comparison between the two technologies. During every stage of the development process, it was aimed to create a reliable and extensible system, which is easy to configure and support. Naturally, taking into consideration the size of the project, there are a few areas that deserve further improvement. From functionality point of view, it would be interesting to extend further the opt-out feature. Users could be given the choice to opt out only from specific types of recording and to give them an opportunity to participate in other. Another key area of improvement might be an automatic data removal feature. This would allow the complete removal of already collected users' data from the database on request. Potential future work could also involve gathering more user feedback on how users perceive the usability of the visual controls of the framework. We equally hope to receive feedback from researchers and developers on what could be further improved in this framework. Future work could also focus on developing clients to support more programming languages, and developing software for research to extract and analyse the interaction data in data repository.

8. REFERENCES

[1] Brinkman, W.-P., HCI 2006 workshop report interaction tracking. In *Proceedings of the 2006 Workshop on Computer Assisted Recording, Pre-Processing, and Analysis of User Interaction Data*. Lulu, Morrisville, NC, 2006, 93-95.

[2] Fine, N. Personalising Interaction using Profiled User Interface Skins. In *Proceedings of HCI 2005*, vol. 2, 194-196

[3] Hilbert, D. M., and Redmiles, D. F. Large-Scale Usage Data to Inform Design. In *Proceedings of INTERACT 2001* (Tokyo, Japan, July 9-13, 2001). IOS Press, Amsterdam, The Netherlands, 2001, 569-576.

[4] Renaud, K., and Gray, P. Making sense of low-level usage data to understand user activities. In *Proceedings of SAICSIT'04*. South African Institute for Computer Scientists and Information Technologists, Stellenbosch, Western Cape, South Africa, 2004, 115-124.

[5] Tang, J. C., Liu, S. B., Muller, M., Lin, J., and Drews, C. Unobtrusive but invasive: using screen recording to collect field data on computer-mediated interaction. In *Proceedings of CSCW '06*. ACM Press, New York, NY, 2006, 479-482.

Panels

HCI 2.0? Usability meets Web 2.0

Alan Dix
Computing Department, InfoLab21
Lancaster University
Lancaster, LA1 4WA, UK
+44 1524 510 319

alan@hcibook.com

Laura Cowen
User Technologies, IBM UK Ltd
MP 095, Hursley Park
Winchester, SO21 2JN
+44 1962 815622

laura_cowen@uk.ibm.com

http://www.hcibook.com/papers/HCI2007-HCI-2.0-panel/
http://lancs.facebook.com/group.php?gid=2390506988

panellists: Elizabeth Churchill (Yahoo!), Pat Healey (Queen Mary, University of London),
Nadeem Shabir (Talis), Paula Gomes da Silva (Lancaster University)

ABSTRACT
The web has already dramatically changed society, but the web itself is changing. Web2.0 sites mean that users have become the producers of content and the designers of each others' viewing experience. Technologies such as AJAX combined with public Javascript libraries have allowed applications to be deployed that once would have required extensive programming. Open APIs and mashups make it difficult to tell the difference between a service, and application or a web page. So what are the challenges for HCI when every user is designer, and every menu a different behaviour, when experience outranks efficiency, and connectivity replaces consistency?

Categories and Subject Descriptors
H.5.5 [Information Interfaces and Presentation]: HCI

General Terms
Design, Human Factors.

Keywords
Web 2.0, user experience, end-user programming, AJAX, social networking

1. INTRODUCTION
Anyone working in human-computer interaction, whether an academic or a practitioner, will lead a life infused if not dominated by the internet and the web. In society more broadly, internet shopping has become ubiquitous and the web has ceased to be a matter of news and has become simply the normal way in which we find out the train time or fill in a tax return.

However, the web itself is changing; young people live in the world of MySpace and Facebook; applications that once ran on the desktop are now running interactively online. Whether this is a step change or simply an evolution, something is

happening, and whether it is over-hyped or under-studied, certainly Web2.0 is hot news .

In HCI we cannot afford to neglect this phenomenon. As practitioners we need to know how to design effectively for changing technology and changing use patterns. As academics we need to distil which things are simply old problems in new clothes and which are fundamental shifts that we need to study, not just because they are "this year's story" but because they are the current manifestation of long-term issues.

This panel will bring together a selection of practitioners and academics, some with answers and all with questions, trying to make sense of this emerging picture.

2. WHAT IS WEB 2.0
The term Web2.0 was coined by O'Reilly Media [9] to describe a change in emphasis in web applications and technologies. They used a number of pairwise comparisons to visualize the differences: Wikipedia vs. Britannia online, taxonomies vs. folksonomies etc.

Part of this is a technological view: the "web as platform" changing the ways applications are delivered and, perhaps, become services rather than applications in the process. Part is a social view where the web is seen much more as created from the 'bottom' up by the individual users, rather than top down from large companies.

The two sometimes get confused and it is not clear whether these are two separate phenomena or in some way linked. However, certainly in the growth of mashups, these come together as applications are chopped and diced and remixed by savvy users.

Web 2.0 gets linked occasionally with the Semantic Web, although the two are almost the antithesis in terms of spirit and ethos. While the Semantic Web emphasizes rigid standardised semantics, Web 2.0 is more abut emergent phenomena. This is perhaps epitomised by that central Semantic Web concept of the RDF ontology, in contrast to the proliferation of very individual tagging schemes of Web 2.0 applications and their emergent folksonomies.

However, the Semantic Web and Web 2.0 both share common ultimate goal in making the web a more open platform with interchangeable services. Indeed there is ongoing work on mining folksonomies to find emergent ontological structure within them (for example [5]), so it may even be that Web 2.0 and the Semantic Web converge.

3. HCI ISSUES FOR WEB 2.0
3.1 Social Experience as Product
Issues of user experience have taken centre stage over recent years, not least because the web has been gradually transforming former software products into services. Wherever end users have choice, user experience becomes critical. In addition, many Web 2.0 sites are about social networking, personal identity. Functionality is important, but the function may be fun, meeting someone or 'hanging around' … click counts do not give adequate measures!

It is important when considering this to understand the difference between 'chocolate bar' and 'baked bean' products. If you have a room full of children, you can give them baked beans knowing at least most will be satisfied – baked beans are good enough. However, if you give 100 children pocket money and let them loose in a sweet shop they all will get something different – if a chocolate bar is 'good enough' no one will buy it, it has to be *best* for at least someone. Traditional application design has followed the 'baked bean' model looking at broad user groups and often purchased at a corporate level. With low barriers to entry and broad choice, web products have to be the best for some, not good enough for all.

3.2 The User as Designer
In social networking sites such as YouTube, MySpace or Facebook, the page you see is the product of not just the site itself, but also of the owner of the page. Some sites are quite uniform in their appearance, differing mainly in personal content. Other sites, however, allow personalisation ranging from simple re-skinning and colour schemes, to more radical configuration, and in some cases full HTML and Javascript content. Even when we know what 'usability' means for such sites: How do the site owners design usability into a radically configurable site? What about consistency? How do we effectively communicate with 10 million end-user designers?

3.3 AJAX and Toolkits
While distancing ourselves from some of the AJAX = Web 2.0 confusions, the two do have connections; not least in that AJAX has been an essential technology in allowing web-based applications to compete with their desktop cousins. However using AJAX means that every application becomes a distributed application with all the potential usability issues that this entails [3] and the complications of programming asynchronous systems. Also virtually every web page designer ends up effectively designing their own widgets. For 20 years the ubiquity of a small number of windowing platforms has meant that the issues of fine design in simple widgets could be ignored by all but a few system developers. Now we all need to learn these lessons again to avoid the horrors of jumping Javascript menus [4]. As every web page becomes a user interface: How do we effectively communicate appropriate usability advice? Can widely used Javascript toolkits such as MIT Prototype library or Yahoo! YUI 'build in' usability so that end-developers need to know less?

3.4 Democratisation of Media
Increasingly events are being reported using and through personal images: the shaking video of the dust- and panic-filled fall of the Twin Towers, or the approaching tsunami. Now, through YouTube and blogs, our individual and personal recordings become the shared memory and history escapes the hegemony of the media barons and government propaganda. But is there a danger in these democratised, but fragmented, images and vignettes; do we risk losing the threads that have traditionally been provided by the established media?

The UK Education Minister, Alan Johnson, recently recommended using Wikipedia in schools sparking widespread debate on the scholarship and reliability of open-authorship media. In HCI are we also too reliant on web sources … even Nielsen gained his notoriety through a newsfeed!

4. WEB 2.0 DEBATE
There is a growing recognition of the need to understand how usability and Web 2.0 phenomena interact and whether we need to change some of our conceptions of usability in order to meet the challenges of Web 2.0. The topic has already sparked several panels at Web conferences and sessions on related topics at CHI [2] and DIS [6]. There have also been recent articles in Interfaces [11] and Interactions [7] and we can expect many more to come. Perhaps predictably Nielsen has complained that Web 2.0 is 'neglecting good design' [1], but work reported in this conference [10] suggests that some apparently 'bad usability' in Web 2.0 sites is actually good design! Nielsen's remarks have triggered substantial comment from the Web20 community and even a comic strip [8].

We hope this panel will contribute to this debate and if not answer every question at least expose crucial issues for the future … for your say join the debate in facebook.

5. REFERENCES
[1] BBC News. *Web 2.0 'neglecting good design'.* 14 May 2007 (reporting Jakob Nielsen) http://news.bbc.co.uk/1/hi/technology/6653119.stm

[2] Degler, D., Henninger, S., and Battle, L. Semantic web HCI: discussing research implications. In *CHI '07 Extended Abstracts.* ACM Press, 2007, 1909–1912.

[3] Dix, A. Que sera sera – The problem of the future perfect in open and cooperative systems. In *Proc. of HCI'94.* Cambridge University Press, 1994, 397–408.

[4] Dix, A. Chapter 3: Human-Computer Interaction and Web Design. In *Handbook of Human Factors in Web Design.* Robert W. Proctor and Kim-Phuong L. Vu (eds). Lawrence Erlbaum, 2005, 28–47

[5] Dix, A., Levialdi, S. and A. Malizia, A. Semantic Halo for Collaboration Tagging Systems. Workshop on Social Navigation and Community-Based Adaptation Technologies, *Proc. of Workshops of AH2006*, Dublin: National College of Ireland, 2006, 514–521

[6] Galloway, A., Brucker-Cohen, J., Gaye, L., Goodman, E., and Hill, D. 2004. Design for hackability. In *Proc. DIS'04.* ACM Press, New York, NY, 2004, 363-366.

[7] Interactions Special Issue: Web technologies. *Interactions*, 14, 2 (Mar–Apr 2007), 33–39.

[8] Mehta, H. *Usability Guru Vs. Web2.0 Community.* 7 June 2007. http://comicstick.com/?p=12

[9] O'Reilly, T. *What Is Web 2.0: Design Patterns and Business Models for the Next Generation of Software,* O'Reilly Media, 30th Sept. 2005, (accessed 23/06/2007) http://www.oreillynet.com/pub/a/oreilly/tim/news/2005/09/30/what-is-web-20.html

[10] Silva, P. and Dix, A., Usability – Not as we know it! In *Proc. of the 21st BCS HCI Group Conference, HCI2007, Volume 2.* British Computer Society, 2007.

[11] Tse, O., England, D. and Nimoy, J. What's your view on Web 2.0? *Interfaces* 69 (Winter 2006), 8–9.

A Conference Panel – but not as we know it!

Tom McEwan (Chair)
Napier University Edinburgh
Edinburgh, EH10 5DT, UK
t.mcewan@napier.ac.uk

David England
Liverpool John Moores University,
Liverpool, L3 3AF UK
d.england@ljmu.ac.uk

Eamonn O'Neill
University of Bath
Bath BA2 7AY, UK
eamonn@cs.bath.ac.uk

Nick Bryan-Kinns
Queen Mary, University of London,
Mile End, London. E1 4NS
nickbk@dcs.qmul.ac.uk

Janet Finlay
Leeds Metropolitan University
Leeds LS6 3QS, UK
j.finlay@leedsmet.ac.uk

ABSTRACT

This panel will take the form of a public debate about whether the conference of which it forms part has a future. Academic conferences are increasingly hard to cost-justify and growing awareness of the environmental impact adds to the negative aspects – especially when the HCI community have developed so many tools and techniques to afford virtual collaboration, dissemination and critique. Yet participants continue to enjoy conferences and some would seem them as vital to the sustainability and coherence of the discipline. It is chaired by the chair of HCI2005 [3], and features as panellists the chairs of HCI2003 [1], HCI2004 [2], HCI2006[4], HCI2008, and is intended to feature vibrant contributions from other delegates. The motion to be debated is **"This conference believes that the conference has no future after Sept 5th 2008"**.

Categories and Subject Descriptors

K.7.2 Organizations

General Terms

Human Factors.

Keywords

British HCI Conference.

1. Introduction

1.1 "British HCI ... what is it good for?"

The British HCI Series of conferences have been running annually for over 20 years, occasionally merging with Interact. It has established a reputation as an international conference - more than half the papers are from overseas, and the social programme is usually much enjoyed. Attendees, however, are mainly UK lecturers and professors - the proportion of industrial attendees has been in steady decline since 2000. Delegates typically come from around 25 countries, but around

80% are UK-based.

There is an ongoing debate as to whether, academically, it is an excellent conference or merely a very good. It is certainly a very competitive conference to gain acceptance for - the committee typically reject 70% of submissions. Reviewers' comments and ratings, at least in 2005, indicate that there are very few totally incompetent submissions (certainly fewer than some we receive to review for higher profile international HCI conferences). There remains consistently, however, disappointingly few contributions from what used to be called 5-star HCI experts, who appear to save their work either for CHI, or for more specialised conferences.

There is also a debate about its impact. The 2006 Volume 1 proceedings, the last to be published by Springer, had only a single citation in the entire volume of any paper from any previous British HCI conference. Is this a write-only conference?

As university budgets tighten there are fewer institutions willing to pay for a student, let alone an academic to attend to present only a poster or a short paper. Given the growth of online communities, and the pressures to minimise carbon footprints, is there still a case for 2-300 people to travel from around the world to spent 15-30 minutes describing their work?

The conference budget is precarious as well. Is there still a case for public money to be used to pay £60 a head for a lavish dinner every year? Would academics pay for their own food if they had to? Should the meal be declared as a taxable benefit? Each year 12 doctoral consortium students and 15-20 student volunteers receive free entry to the conference, accommodation and the full social programme, all of which has to be paid by the full-price delegates (a dwindling band of around 100). This (and the fact that other student delegates can attend at marginal cost price) is thought to be an investment to build the HCI community of tomorrow - but how many of these individuals do go on to publish in HCI?

The contrary view is that nothing beats face-to-face in sustaining a community. People who are overloaded with email and unresponsive can be much more open and available over coffee or a glass of wine. Books get launched, research consortia get assembled, teaching ideas get exchanged, serendipitous conversations unlock doors and remove barriers. Additionally as more "spin-off" conferences emerge in specialist areas of HCI – mobile, user experience, interaction design, ambient, tangible – if there is not a single annual expression of the "wide church" of HCI, does HCI itself have a continued coherence?

1.2 Panel structure

The panel chair will be a roaming moderator seeking out contributions and questions from the floor, after each of the panellists have put forward their positions in 5-minute statements at the start. Panellists will be encouraged to give short responses (less than 60 seconds) to each question from the floor.

The final twenty minutes of the panel will consist of three minute summary statements each, by Finlay and England in favour of the motion and by O'Neill and Bryan-Kinns against, after which those present will vote on the motion.

2. Position Statements

2.1 Janet Finlay (Chair, HCI2004)

Twenty-one years ago, when the conference started, human-computer interaction was a fledgling discipline with a multi-disciplinary but fairly coherent community. In those early days the conference sustained and facilitated the growth of that community at a time when attendees had little support for their curious obsession with user-centredness outside. It was also a time of plenty in academia, when budgets for conference attendance did not have to be justified above the demands of other "core activities". Times have changed.

The community has grown and fragmented and most now have their own specialisms - mobile, CSCW, ubiquity, design, education etc. – with their own conferences of choice. HCI is now the primary community for very few. And with ever tightening purse strings for both academics and practitioners, it is becoming more and more difficult for many to justify attendance or involvement.

I have been attending HCI regularly since 1991, was conference chair in 2004, programme chair in 2002, local chair in 1996 and have been involved in the organisation of several others. From a personal perspective I enjoy this conference as many of us do. But an annual "jolly" for a dwindling community does not a conference make. The HCI conference in its current form has no future – we need to look at alternatives before it is too late

2.2 Dave England (Chair, HCI2008)

Some words that stuck with me from my first Mechanical Engineering tutor were "Engineering is about improving the quality of life". That led me to take an interest in HCI in 1984.

The question is, whether HCI is still improving the quality of life in 2007, or more specifically is our conference making a significant contribution?

Have most of the general problems been solved by the adopting of industry and marketing standards? And have most of the user population simply adapted to those standards, no matter how sub- optimal they may be? And has the quest for "hard science to drive out soft" led to more papers with good methodology that say more and more about less and less? If we did a meta-analysis of papers with good stats versus the most cited papers would we find a correlation?

To paraphrase Don Norman, should p<.05 be considered harmful to the wider picture and potential contribution of HCI? Should we instead look to the Arts and Humanities to ask the "big picture" questions even though the answers may be, in the short term, less clear?

2.3 Eamonn O'Neill (Chair, HCI2003)

At first glance, the British HCI conference seems to be very successful. It has run for a couple of decades – in HCI terms, since the dawn of time. A large proportion of the papers, typically more than half, are international.

There are a healthy number of submissions and the acceptance rate is low. So what's going wrong? Industrial attendance has waned in recent years but that is true of many similar conferences around the world. These are primarily academic conferences and the British HCI Conference holds its own amongst them.

But there's a clue to the problem in the name: the conference shoots itself in the foot by calling itself the British HCI conference. Delegates are overwhelmingly UK academics: given restricted budgets, overseas researchers are perhaps not being attracted to attend. At the same time, some leading UK based academics are more attracted to other conferences, often overseas. Calling it the British conference makes it seem parochial and risks having less international impact. Similarly, the lack of online publication has reduced impact and correspondingly discouraged high quality submissions. Online publication is now a reality.

Internationalise the branding and we may well have a successful conference for many more decades.

2.4 Nick Bryan-Kinns (Chair, HCI2006)

As far as I understand it, in the dim and distant past HCI started out as an innovative blend of Computer Scientists, Psychologists, and Ergonomicists. Excitement and drive came from establishing a new field in which to park our campervans and pitch our tents of knowledge to shed new light and understanding on how we use these things we call computers. But, innovation needs change.

Yes, of course there is a need examine problems in depth - navel gazing if you like - this helps us to be sure that our tents are pitched in the right field, and that there isn't some huge bull about to come charging in. But tents and campervans are inherently movable. They need to move or they become rusty and mouldy. In the past people have moved to find new fields such as CSCW and UbiComp.

We need to keep on moving. HCI is becoming like Stonehenge - people return once a year to conduct mystical ceremonies with high priests, but if all the high priests' campervans become rusty and immovable who will come, and how will they get here?

3. REFERENCES

[1] O'Neill, E., Palanque, P., & Johnson, P. (Eds.) (2003) People and computers XVII: Designing for society. Proceedings of HCI 2003. London, UK: Springer-Verlag.

[2] Fincher, S., Markopoulos, P., Moore, D., & Ruddle, R. (Eds.) (2005). People and computers XVIII: Design for life. Proceedings of HCI 2004. London, UK: Springer-Verlag.

[3] McEwan, Tom; Gulliksen, Jan; Benyon, David (Eds.) (2006). People and Computers XIX - The Bigger Picture. Proceedings of HCI 2005. London, UK: Springer-Verlag

[4] Bryan-Kinns, N., Blandford, A., Curzon, P., Nigay, L. (Eds.) (2007) People and Computers XX – Engage. Proceedings of HCI 2006. London, UK: Springer-Verlag.

Organisational Overviews

HCI and Creative Problem-Solving at Lancaster

Tom Ormerod, Linden Ball
Lancaster University
Department of Psychology
Lancaster, LA1 4YF, UK
+44 1524 593164 / 593470

{t.ormerod;l.ball@lancaster.ac.uk}

Alan Dix, Corina Sas
Lancaster University
Department of Computing
Lancaster, LA1 4WA, UK
+44 1524 510319 / 510318

{alan@hcibook.com; c.sas@lancaster.ac.uk}

ABSTRACT

The Creative Problem-Solving Research Group (CPSRG) at Lancaster University is a collaboration between psychologists and computer scientists conducting research into creativity, problem-solving and design at the interface between humans and computer systems. Our aim is to develop theoretical understandings and practical interventions that address how creative individuals and groups manage conflicting demands of novelty and divergent thinking versus constraint, domain relevance and minimization of task load. Current projects include creative design in virtual and ubiquitous environments, developing methodologies for inspirational design, and impacts of expert reasoning on creative problem-solving.

Categories and Subject Descriptors

I.2.8 [**Problem Solving, Control, Methods, and Search**]: Heuristic Methods. I.5.2 [**Design Methodology**]. H.5 [**Information Interfaces and Presentation**]

General Terms

Management, Design, Experimentation, Human Factors.

Keywords

Creativity, problem solving, design, innovation, insight, investigative expertise.

1. INTRODUCTION

The CPSRG was initiated by Tom Ormerod in 2004 to facilitate interdisciplinary research on creativity, problem solving, expertise and design. With four academics from Psychology and Computing, and eight researchers reading for PhD or enrolled in post-doctoral research, this group provides a critical mass of interdisciplinary expertise and a forum for weekly seminars. The Psychology Department performs world-leading research into the nature, acquisition and support of design expertise; the development and evaluation of design processes and support tools for innovative design; and in particular creative-problem solving in work situations. The Computing Department conducts internationally recognized innovative research into the design of collaborative interactive systems, the development of methods and tools for supporting creativity in design, innovative methods for learning design together with cognitive

models for skill acquisition. Computing is also involved initiatives at the boundary of arts and technology that intersect with CPSRG's focus on technical innovation and creativity.

2. RESEARCH TOPICS & PROJECTS

2.1 Studying Creative Problem Solving

Creative problem solving in design raises significant research questions. How do people solve complex and ill-defined problems? What makes a problem appear insoluble? How does insight arise? What role does analogizing play in finding and understanding problems as well as in generating and evaluating solutions? For example, we have also investigated how humans produce solutions to the travelling salesman problem, an optimization problem of key importance in industrial and commercial settings. We also developed cognitive ethnography as a methodology for studying creative expertise [3], and studied processes that facilitate design problem-solving [4, 5].

2.2 Modelling Creativity

Cognitive and computational models of planning behaviour in ill-defined problems [13, 14] and creative designing from a situated cognition perspective [1] further refine our theoretical understanding of creativity. Central to creativity is the interplay between more convergent analytic modes of thought and the role of imagination, and an off-shoot from this concern has led to preliminary results suggesting that a computational model of regret can be used to improve machine learning [6].

2.3 Supporting Creative Design

One research topic with arguably the highest impact on creative design processes and outcomes is that of developing tools, methods and practices to support creativity in design [16]. We are interested in studying methods of 'extreme design' where arbitrary constraints (such as limited time) can lead to radical ideas [21] and also ways of inspiring divergent thinking such as BadIdeas [7]. We are considering how tools could support better articulation of creative ideas, for example in the BadIdeas technique. Issues regarding creative environments for design range from virtual environments allowing manipulation of real-world constraints and their impact on creativity [11] to socio-organizational aspects that foster creative cultures.

2.4 Innovation in Teaching/Learning Design

Challenges for teaching or learning creative design appear throughout the design process, starting from problem specification, continuing with the relevant feedback that students need to receive, to the assessment of design-related activities and outcomes [17]. We have implemented new approaches to the teaching of interaction design, ranging from students' direct exposure to practitioners in the field [18], to alternative design briefs such as finding new applications for existing technologies [20]. We have also explored reduced-cost routes for knowledge transfer consisting of addressing a business problem through student assignments [19].

2.5 Supporting Expert Problem-Solving

In addition to design, the group conducts research on creative problem-solving in other applied domains. For example, we are interested in ways in which expert criminal investigators come up with creative ways of testing their suspicions [12]. We also are currently exploring novel ways to design health and safety support systems for the construction industry [2]. We also have an ongoing interest in how expert users of shared information repositories can capitalize upon facets of embodied cognition in supporting tasks of information storage and retrieval [15].

2.6 Connecting with Arts and Design

While the central focus of the group is on more technical and problem oriented creativity, members of the group are also involved in connecting areas in arts, user experience design and product design. We have been part of several recent and ongoing AHRC/EPSRC networks in this area including LeonardoNet, NonPlace and Branded Spaces and past work has included formal models of the interactive performance and space as well more philosophical pieces.

In collaboration with the Cardiff School of Art & Design, we are currently leading one of the Designing the 21st Century projects, DEPtH [8], which is looking at issues of physicality in design, building on ongoing work on this area and including the Physicality 2007 workshop at this conference.

3. EDUCATION IN THE CPSRG

In addition, our interest in technological creativity is reflected in our practical teaching, most notably the research carried out by students on our Masters by Research in HCI. This EPSRC-funded programme is a joint venture focusing on the development and evaluation of interactive systems. It also offers an opportunity for experimenting with innovative teaching/learning techniques for the study of collaborative design.

Outside of Lancaster we have presented the concepts of teaching innovation in Singapore [9], used BadIdeas in teaching to the USI programme at the Technical University, Eindhoven, and Paula Silva, one of the groups' PhD students, chaired the 2007 HCI Educators Conference in Aveiro, Portugal [10].

4. PEOPLE

The work of the group is only as good as the people within it. As well as the authors this includes David Alford, Alex Sandham, Genovefa Kefalidou, Maria Jemicz, Lorna McKnight, Ben Short, and Ut Na Sio. We are also grateful to many outside the group whose work impinges and inspires us, in particular Jenn Sheridan and .:thePooch:. for their various 'Scrapheap' events.

5. REFERENCES.

[1] Ball, L.J., Evans, J.St. B., Dennis, I.& Ormerod, T.C. (1997). Problem-solving strategies and expertise in engineering design *Thinking and Reasoning*, **3**, 247-270

[2] Ball, L.J., & Alford, D. (2007). What determines the acceptability of deontic health and safety rules? D. McNamara, & G. Trafton (Eds.): *Proc. 29th Annual Conf. Cognitive Science Society*. Alpha, NJ: Sheridan Printing.

[3] Ball, L.J. and Ormerod, T.C. Putting ethnography to work: The case for a cognitive ethnography of design. *International Journal of Human-Computer Studies, 53* (2000), 147-168.

[4] Ball, L.J. and Ormerod, T.C. Structured and opportunistic processing in design: A critical discussion. *International Journal of Human-Computer Studies, 43* (1995), 131-151.

[5] Ball, L.J., Ormerod, T.C. and Morley, N.J. Spontaneous analogising in engineering design: A comparative analysis of experts and novices. *Design Studies, 25* (2004), 495-508.

[6] Dix, A. The adaptive significance of regret, 2005. http://www.hcibook.com/alan/essays/

[7] Dix, A., Ormerod, T.C., Twidale, M., Sas, C., Gomes da Silva, P.A. and McKnight, L. (2006). Why Bad Ideas are a Good Idea. *HCI Educators Workshop*.

[8] DEPtH, Designing for Physicality, 2007. http://www.physicality.org/

[9] Dix, A. Teaching innovation (keynote). at *Excellence in Education and Training convention*. Singapore, 2002. http://www.hcibook.com/alan/talks/singapore2002/

[10] HCI Educators 2007 – Creativity[3]: Experiencing to educate and design. Aveiro. Portugal, 2007. http://www.bcs-hci.org.uk/hcied2007/

[11] McKnight, L. (2007). Creativity in Second Life: Exploration versus Constraint. The 6th Creativity & Cognition Conference, Graduate Symposium.

[12] Morley, N.J., Ball, L.J., & Ormerod, T.C. (2006). How the detection of insurance fraud succeeds and fails *Psychology, Crime, and Law*, 12, 163-180.

[13] Ormerod, T.C. (2005). Planning and ill-defined problems. Chapter in R. Morris and G. Ward (Eds.): *The Cognitive Psychology of Planning*. London: Psychology Press.

[14] Ormerod, T. C., MacGregor, J. N. & Chronicle, E. P. Dynamics and Constraints in Insight Problem Solving. *Journal of Experimental Psychology Learning, Memory, and Cognition*, 28 (2002), 791-799

[15] Ormerod, T.C., Morley, N., Mariani, J., Lewis, K., Hitch, G., Mathrick, J. & Rodden, T. (2004). Doing ethnography and experiments together to explore collaborative photograph handling: *In A. Dearden & L. Watts (Eds.) Proc. HCI2004: Design for Life, Volume 2,pp. 81-84.* 6-10th September 2004, Leeds.

[16] Ormerod, T.C., Mariani, J. Ball, L.J. & Lambell, N. (1999). Desperado: Three-in-one indexing for innovative design: *Interact -Seventh IFIP Conference on Human-Computer Interaction*. IOS Press, London.

[17] Sas, C. (2006). Learning Approaches for Teaching Interaction Design. *HCI Educators Workshop*.

[18] Sas, C. (2006). Teaching Interaction Design through Practitioners' Praxis. *Proceedings of the 7th Annual Conference of the Higher Education Academy*. poster

[19] Sas, C. (2007). Engaging Higher Education Institution in regional development: A case study for Human Computer Interaction discipline. *Engaging HEIs in business and the community: A learning perspective Symposium*. Lancaster University Management School.

[20] Sas, C. and Dix, A. (2007). Alternative Design Brief for Teaching Interaction Design: Finding New Applications for Existing Technologies. *HCI Educators Workshop*.

[21] Silva, P. and Dix, A. Chindogu and Scrapheap Spirit as Creativity Triggers. In *Proc. of The First International Symposium on Culture, Creativity and Interaction Design, CCID 2006*. LeonardoNet, 2006, 97–101.

Introducing the Companions Project: Intelligent, Persistent, Personalised Interfaces to the internet

David Benyon
Centre for Interaction Design
Napier University, Edinburgh
+44 131 455 2736

d.benyon@napier.ac.uk

Oli Mival
Centre for Interaction Design
Napier University, Edinburgh
+44 131 455 2438

o.mival@napier.ac.uk

ABSTRACT

The Companions project is a 4 year, EU funded Framework Programme 6 project involving a consortium of 16 partners across 8 countries. Its aim is to develop a personalised conversational interface, one that knows and understands its owner, and can access resources on the Internet. It does this whilst nurturing an emotional, psychological and social involvement from its owner (user seems an inappropriate term in this context). In doing this it will change interactions to relationships. On a technical level it intends to push the state of the art in machine based natural language understanding, knowledge structures, speech recognition and text to speech.

Keywords

Agents, personalization, relationships.

1. COMPANIONSHIP AND THE ELDERLY

Companionship is a concept that is familiar to all, yet defies simple explanation. Psychology considers it a central need, yet balks at a concise definition of what constitutes a companion beyond "a relationship…with mutual caring and trust" [2], p467. What is clear, is the importance of companions to emotional well being. Indeed the loss of companions is considered a primary cause of depression among older people [6]. The erosion of social networks inevitably leads to the loss of companions and is often accompanied by an experience of emotional impoverishment, not infrequently experienced by the elderly as a pervasive depression "without a reason" [3].

With consideration of this natural decline in human companionship, the potential value of developing artificial companionship becomes distinctly apparent. On a simple level, older people have relationships with companions, be they pets, friends or care assistants. But what constitutes the difference between an interaction and a relationship? To form a relationship, the user needs to care about the interaction, to invest emotion in it. The artificial companions evoke the emotional investment through replicating recognizable real world behaviour. From this it may be suggested that the difference between a tool and a companion is a set of characteristics, a personality, which transforms an interaction into a relationship and evokes an emotional investment.

The medical benefits of pet ownership are well documented [3]. Pet ownership can lead to an enhanced emotional status and provides significant support in reducing emotional trauma following bereavement. Not only emotional health but also physiological health is enhanced through contact with animals, particularly in the elderly. Furthermore, studies have shown that when animals enter the lives of older patients afflicted with Alzheimer's disease or arteriosclerosis, the patients will laugh and smile more, are more socially communicative and less hostile to their care workers [1,5]. However, some older people live in accommodation which does not allow pets or may suffer from psychological or physiological deterioration that make pet ownership problematic and potentially unsafe for the animal. In situations such as these, the use of artificial pets may be an alternative.

It is interesting to note that pets are at the non-specific purpose end of the companionship spectrum. A cat serves no other function than to be a cat. Yet as discussed above, by simply being a cat it can affect the health and well-being of its owner. People take delight in its activities, and it is purely from its behaviour that the benefits are derived. Cats cannot read email to you, struggle as a webcam and do not react to guidance from a computer. They are autonomous objects driven by their own goals. Kaplan suggests that this autonomy, this non-functionality is an important design consideration when developing artificial pets, he suggests they should "be designed as free 'not functional' creatures" [4].

It is the intention to use these insights to drive the interaction design elements of the major new FP6 EU project Companion.

2. INTRODUCTION TO THE COMPANIONS PROJECT

The Companions project's vision is a personalised conversational, multimodal interface to the Internet, one that knows its owner, is implemented on a range of platforms, indoor and nomadic, and based on integrated high-quality research in multimodal human-computer interfaces, intelligent agents, and human language technology [7]. This project is an ECA (Embodied Conversational Agent) which differs from the ECA state of the art by having large-scale speech and language capacity; it also differs significantly from the standard "big engineering" approach to this area, by offering relatively simple architectures with substantial tested performance, based on extensive application of powerful machine learning methods.

Companions will learn about their owners: their habits, their needs and their life memories. This will allow them to assist with carrying out specific Internet tasks, which will be facilitated by having complex models of their owners, by which we mean whole-life-memories, or coherent autobiographies, built from texts, conversations, images and videos. Some of this will already be in digital form, but some will be information gleaned from conversations with the Companion, information relatives and friends will want later, after the owner's death, but might never have been able to ask, such as "where did you and your husband first meet?"

The objectives of the proposal are to develop autonomous, persistent, affective and personal interfaces, or Companions, embedded in the Internet environment, with intelligent response in terms of speech and language, integrated with the manipulation of visual images and their content.

An early implementation of a Companion is PhotoPal [8]. PhotoPal allows people to view their photos and talk about them with their Companion. Photos are automatically tagged with the relevant dialogue allowing PhotoPal to build up a rich representation of the person's activities and relationships. This allows PhotoPal to sort, style and send photos and for people to reminisce with their Companion.

3. CHARACTERISTICS OF COMPANIONS

There are clearly many challenges for 'companion technology'. Bickmore and Picard [9]) argue that maintaining relationships involves managing expectations, attitudes and intentions. They emphasize that relationships are built over time through many interactions. Relationships are fundamentally social and emotional, persistent and personalized. Citing Kelley they say that relationships demonstrate interdependence between two parties – a change in one results in a change to the other. Relationships demonstrate unique patterns of interaction for a particular dyad, a sense of 'reliable alliance'. It is these rich and extended forms of affective and social interaction characteristics of relationships that we are trying to tease apart. We are looking at the characteristics of companions in terms of utility, form, personality, emotion, social aspects and trust.

3.1 Utility

Utility is concerned with the allocation of function between two participants in a relationship. Companions are needed to filter large amount of information and conflicting views and ideas on the internet. They need to take the initiative and be pro-active in starting some new activity, but only when appropriate. They may be conversational rather than task-focused.

3.2 Form

The form that a companion takes refers to all the issues of interaction such as dialogues, gestures, behaviours and the other operational aspects of the interaction. It also refers to the representational aspects such as whether it is 2D, graphical 3D or true 3D, whether it has a humanoid, abstract or animal form, and the modalities that is uses. The many aesthetic issues are also considered under this heading. The form and the behaviours of the companion are likely to vary widely between different owners. The careful construction of a mixture of interface characteristics result in people enjoying the interaction and attributing intelligence and emotion to the Companion.

3.3 Emotion

Designing for pleasure and design for affect are key issues for companions [11]. Attractive things make people feel good which makes them more creative and more able [11]. Relationships provide emotional support. Emotional integration and stability are key aspects of relationships [9]. Emotional aspects of the interaction come through meta relational communication, such as checking that everything is all right, use of humour and talking about the past and future. Another key aspect of an interaction if it is to become a relationship is empathy; empathy leads to emotional support and provides foundations for relationship-enhancing behaviours.

3.4 Personality and Trust

Personality is treated as a key aspect of the media equation by Reeves and Nass [12]. They undertook a number of studies that showed how assertive people prefer to interact with an assertive computer and submissive people prefer interacting with submissive devices. As soon as interaction moves from the utilitarian to the complexity of a relationship, people will want to interact with personalities that they like. Trust is "a positive belief about the perceived reliability of, dependability of, and confidence in a person, object or process" [10]. It is a key relationship that develops over time through small talk, getting acquainted talk and through acceptable 'continuity' behaviours. Routine behaviours and interactions contribute to develop a relationship that emphasize commonalities and shared values.

3.5 Social attitudes

The social side of relationships such as group belonging, opportunities to nurture, autonomy support and social network support are all important. Relationships also play a key role in persuasion. The rather controversial idea of 'persuasive technologies' [10] is based on getting people to do things they would not otherwise do. In the context of companions, though, this is exactly what you would hope a companion would do — providing it was ultimately for the good. A Health and Fitness companion, for example, should try to persuade its owner to run harder, or train more energetically.

4. ACKNOWLEDGMENTS

This work is funded by the European Commission under contract IST 034434.

5. REFERENCES

[1] T Garity, L Stallones, M Marx, M. & P. Johnson, Pet Ownership and Attachment as Supportive Factors in the Health of the Elderly. *Anthrozoos.* 3 (1) pp 35-44 (1989)

[2] H. Gleitman, Psychology. Oxford University Press (2000)

[3] K.L. Gory, & K. Fitzpatrick, The effects of environmental contexts on elderly depression. Journal of Aging and Health, 4(4):459-479 (1992)

[4] F. Kaplan (2001) Free creatures: The role of uselessness in the design of artificial pets. In Proceedings of the CELE-Twente workshop on interacting agents (2001)

[5] O. Mival S. Cringean, and D. Benyon Personification Technologies: Developing Artificial Companions for Older People, ACM Press, 1-8. (2004)

[6] C. Sluzki, The extinction of the galaxy: Social networks in the elderly patient. New York: Family Process (2000)

[7] Y. Wilks, Artificial Companions as a new kind of interface to the future internet. Oxford Internet Institute, Research Report 13, October 2006

[8] www.napier.ac.uk/companions

[9] Bickmore T. and Picard R. Establishing and maintaining long-term human-computer relationships. ACM Trans. on Computer-Human Interaction (TOCHI), 12 (2) (2005)

[10] Fogg, B. J. (2003) Persuasive Technologies. Morgan Kaufman

[11] Norman, D. (2004) Emotional Design Basic Books

[12] Reeves B. and Nass, C. (1996) The Media Equation CSLI Publications; Stanford, CA.

Workshops

3rd International Workshop on Ubiquitous and Collaborative Computing (iUBICOM)

Rahat Iqbal
Faculty of Engineering and Computing
Coventry University
Priory Street, Coventry
+44 24 7688 8225

r.iqbal@coventry.ac.uk

Jacques Terken
Department of Industrial Design
Technische Universiteit Eindhoven
Eindhoven
+31 40 247 5254

j.m.b.terken@tue.nl

ABSTRACT

It is recognised that the traditional methods of requirements capture are not suitable when applied to ubiquitous and collaborative systems. With these sorts of systems what is important is an understanding of the social characteristics of work itself as well as the people who operate in the work environment. User-centred design and evaluation approaches have been used to do this however these approaches may not be straightforward in situations where perceptive technology is involved. The purpose of this workshop is to bring multi-disciplinary researchers together in order to discuss different models and theories that can be used to design and evaluate ubiquitous and collaborative systems. Particularly, the focus of the third International Workshop on Ubiquitous and Collaborative Computing (iUBICOM) is on user-centred design and evaluation of ubiquitous and collaborative computing including ethnography.

Categories and Subject Descriptors

H.5.3 [**Information interfaces**]: Group and organization interfaces – Collaborative computing - Computer-supported collaborative work; J.4. [**Computer applications**]: Social and behavioural sciences – Sociology.

General Terms

Design, Human Factors, Design, Human Factors, Theory, Verification

Keywords

User-Centred Design, Formative and Summative Evaluation.

1. INTRODUCTION

Mark Weiser [1] put forth a vision of ubiquitous computing, according to which people and environments are augmented with computational resources which provide information and services whenever and wherever required. Achieving this vision required communication and interoperability between different applications and devices. The availability of information through a wide range of media including mobile devices and sensors has given a new momentum to collaborative computing by providing people with new opportunities to communicate with geographically dispersed teams and to conduct business.

The development of ubiquitous and collaborative systems requires a significant understanding of the cooperative work taking place in real world as the system interface moves into the world of work. The desire to service this need encapsulates the problems for the traditional forms of requirements capture as ubiquitous and collaborative systems moves beyond the individual user to recognise the socially organised character of work that should be included within the requirements engineering process. To acknowledge the fact that work has a social dimension to it, researchers need to move literally as well as metaphorically from the laboratory to the field to inform both ubiquitous and collaborative systems.

Research shows how and why many large-scale projects in the past have failed [2]. One of the key reasons for their failure is inadequate analysis of user requirements. Most importantly, social, political and cultural factors have not been considered during the development of these systems. For example, the failure of 'office automation' systems to support a group of individuals in the workplace was due to concentrating on the functional requirements of the tasks rather than the group dynamics affecting how well they performed them. It is in this respect that traditional analytic approaches are found wanting, representing an intrusion of the 'engineering mentality' into areas where it is inappropriate. To get a better idea of how different researchers are dealing with the issue of user requirements, we have provided an overview of different methods in [3].

In the following section, we will briefly talk about several large-scale projects in Europe and the United States that focus on supporting human-human communication and collaboration. Following that issues and questions to be addressed in the workshop are outlined. In the last section, theme of the workshop is highlighted. Contributions to this workshop are mainly expected to be from colleagues involved in large-scale projects. Of particular importance are people working in multi-disciplined teams involving different levels of collaboration

2. CURRENT PROJECTS

Developments in perceptive technologies (most notably computer vision and speech recognition) and the availability of multi-user devices (like non-desktop devices and portable devices) have triggered renewed interest in supporting communication and collaboration. The ability to maintain a context model through perceiving what is going on has opened possibilities for services that anticipate people's needs and can take action to support people's communication and collaboration in a contextually and socially appropriate way.

Recently, a number of research projects have started to actively investigate these issues, for example the EU-funded Integrated Projects Computers in the Human Interaction Loop [4], Augmented Multiparty Interaction [5], the Canadian Network for Effective Collaboration Technologies through Advanced Research [6], The MeetingManager [7], InterSpace project at the Fraunhofer Institute [8] and Organizes [9].

Rather than just driving developments from the technology perspective, user-centred design and service evaluation are central concerns in these projects. For more conventional interaction design, the User-centred Design philosophy has been well established. In the early stages of the design process, information is obtained from the users through simulations (i.e. low-fi prototypes such as drawings, sketches, interactive PowerPoint simulations etc) that help the designers to obtain requirements and elaborate the concept in an iterative fashion. Also, in most cases the evaluation metrics are straightforward. However, the design for ubiquitous and collaborative computing is more complex and therefore the traditional forms of requirements capture are found wanting.

3. ISSUES AND QUESTIONS TO AD-DRESS IN THE WORKSHP

Applying user-centred design approaches to the development of ubiquitous and collaborative systems to support human-human communication and collaboration is more complex. Building simulations is already a major effort and involves many decisions without proper guidance from user data, in the awareness that the decisions will strongly affect the user experience. Also, many of the perceptual components cannot easily be simulated. Therefore, formative evaluation is a slow and laborious process, which runs counter to the ideas underlying User-centred Design, namely to obtain the information in the early stages of the design process. Similarly, extensive summative evaluation is a challenging task.

Against this background, we propose a workshop on ubiquitous and collaborative computing focusing on user-centred design and evaluation with the aim to bring together researchers from different backgrounds to share experiences. Building on our previous workshop that has been organised on user-centred design and evaluation (http://www.industrialdesign.tue.nl/ ICMI/ eval-workshop/) and our ongoing workshop on ubiquitous and collaborative computing (http://www.coventry.ac.uk/dsm/ iUBICOM/), the main goals are, to exchange information about the design and development of ubiquitous and collaborative systems to support human-human communication and collaboration. The main questions to answer are given below:

- What are proper methodologies and metrics for formative and summative evaluation?

- What is the role of theory in conducting evaluations and what are the theoretical frameworks that different researchers employ?

- What is the role of ethnography to inform system design and how it could be achieved in an effective and efficient way?

We expect that the discussion will help to construct, elaborate and refine a framework for formative and summative evaluation that can be used for ubiquitous and collaborative systems.

4. THEME OF THE WORKSHOP
The main theme of this workshop is User-Centred Design and Evaluation for Ubiquitous and Collaborative Computing. In this workshop, we invite contributions from researchers whose interests lie in the area of user-centred design of ubiquitous and collaborative computing. Contribution on summative evaluation using formal concepts or pragmatic approaches is particularly welcome.

5. REFERENCE

[1] Weiser, M. (1993): 'Some Computer Science Issues in Ubiquitous Computing', *Communications of the ACM*, 36, 75-84.

[2] Goguen, J.A., and Linde, C. (1993): 'Techniques for Requirements Elicitation, Requirements Engineering', *IEEE Computer*, pp. 152-164.

[3] Iqbal, R., Sturm, J., Kulyk, O., Wang, C., Terken, J., (2005): "User-Centred Design and Evaluation of Ubiquitous Services", Proceedings of the 23rd annual international conference on Design of Communication: Documenting and Designing for Pervasive Information, ACM SIGDOC, pp. 138-145, ISBN: 1-59593-175-9.

[4] CHIL; http://chil.server.de/servlet/is/101)

[5] AMI; http://www.amiproject.org

[6] NECTAR; http://www.nectar-research.net) and Cognitive Agent that Learns.

[7] Oh, A., Tuchinda, R. and Wu, L. (2001): 'Meeting Manager: A Collaborative Tool in the Intelligent room', *Proceedings of Student Oxygen Workshop*, 2001.

[8] http://www.m4project.org

[9] CALO; http://www.cse.ogi.edu/CHCC/Projects/CALO .

2nd International Workshop on
Formal Methods for Interactive Systems

Paul Curzon
Department of Computer Science, Queen Mary,
University of London
Mile End
London, UK. E1 4NS
+44 20 7882 5212

pc@dcs.qmul.ac.uk

Antonio Cerone
Int. Inst. for Software Technology, United Nations
University
Macau SAR China

antonio@iist.unu.edu

ABSTRACT

This workshop is the second in a series that is intended as a focused forum for researchers from academia and industry interested in the application of formal methods to interactive system design. Topics of interest include, for example, the development of formal tools, techniques and methodologies based on cognitive psychology results, the development and use of formal user models, case studies applying formal methods to interface design, and formal analysis of the design of the wider socio-technical systems.

1. INTRODUCTION

Reducing the likelihood of human error in the use of interactive systems is increasingly important: the use of such systems is becoming widespread in applications that demand high reliability due to safety, security, financial or similar considerations. Interactive systems are also becoming increasingly ubiquitous and being used in new and more complex situations. Consequently, the use of formal methods in analyzing properties of and verifying the correctness of interactive systems should also include analysis of human behaviour in interacting with the interface as well as with the wider socio-technical system.

2. AIMS

The aim of the workshop is to provide a focussed forum for researchers with an interest in both formal methods and interactive systems to discuss how formal methods can be applied to interactive system design. Topics of interest include, for example, the development of formal tools, techniques and methodologies based on cognitive psychology results, the development and use of formal user models, case studies applying formal methods to interface design, and formal analysis of the design of the wider socio-technical systems. The scope of HCI issues covered extends to all aspects of applying formal methods to interactive systems, including usability, user experience, human error, etc.

Application areas considered are intentionally wide and include but are not limited to:

- safety-critical systems,
- high-reliability systems,
- shared control systems,
- mobile devices,
- embedded systems,
- digital libraries,
- eGovernment,
- pervasive systems,
- augmented reality,
- ubiquitous computing, and
- computer security applications.

3. ORGANISATION

The workshop is organised by Paul Curzon of Queen Mary, University of London and Antonio Cerone of UNU-IIST, Macau SAR China, in conjunction with the QMUL-UCL Human Error Modelling Project.

The Programme Committee for the workshop is international in breadth:

- Bernhard Beckert, Germany;
- Ann Blandford, England;
- Judy Bowen, New Zealand;
- Howard Bowman, England;
- Paul Cairns, England;
- Antonio Cerone, Macau SAR China;
- Josè Creissac Campos, Portugal;
- Paul Curzon, England;
- Alan Dix, England;
- Gavin Doherty, Ireland;
- Michael Harrison, England;
- C. Michael Holloway, USA;
- Chris Johnson, Scotland;
- Peter Lindsay, Australia;
- Philippe Palanque, France;
- Fabio Paternò, Italy;
- Chris Roast, England;

- Rimvydas Ruksenas, England;
- Siraj Shaikh, Macau SAR China;
- Daniel Sinnig, Canada;
- Harold Thimbleby, Wales

FMIS consists of a mixture of long and short presentations together with discussion and working sessions. Papers accepted for long presentation will be published as post-proceedings as well as in the participants' proceedings available at the workshop. Papers accepted as short presentations will be published in the participants' proceedings only. Accepted papers will be made available to participants electronically prior to FMIS to increase the potential for detailed discussion at the Workshop. It is expected that the post-proceedings will be published by Elsevier in the series Electronic Notes in Theoretical Computer Science (ENTCS). This is to be confirmed, however.

4. ACKNOWLEDGMENTS
The Human Error Modelling Project is funded by EPSRC on research grants GR/S67494 and GR/S67500.

Design, Use and Experience of E-Learning Systems

Willem-Paul Brinkman[1,2]
[1]Delft University of Technology
Melkweg 4, 2628 CD Delft, The Netherlands

willem.brinkman
@brunel.ac.uk

Annette Payne[2] and Nayna Patel[2]
[2]Brunel University
Uxbridge, Middlesex UB8 3PH, UK

{Annette.payne,nayna.patel}@brunel.ac.uk

Darren Griffin
University of Kent
Canterbury, CT2 6NZ, UK

d.k.griffin
@kent.ac.uk

Joshua Underwood
London Knowledge Lab, IOE, 23-29 Emerald Street
London WC1N 3QS, UK

j.underwood
@ioe.ac.uk

ABSTRACT

The use of computer applications to support learning and assessment is becoming more common, along with a growing body of research focusing on the pedagogical effectiveness of these applications. However, until recently less research attention has been given to the design of learning technology with regard to their usability, actual use, and the way they motivate and engage learners. Learner centred design [7] looks beyond the technological possibilities such as distance learning, virtual reality, and computer assisted assessments by focussing on learners in their learning contexts, and how their interaction with these applications can help and stimulate them to apply deep learning strategies. However, what are the best and most effective ways to accomplish this? Can lessons learned in the field of HCI be directly applied, or do e-learning applications have their own set of design guidelines? The workshop plans to bring together individuals with an interest in the design and use of e-learning systems with the aim of improving and understanding the learning experience. The workshop will be a platform to discuss new ideas and to share experiences, but also to identify new research challenges and potential solutions.

Categories and Subject Descriptors

K.3 [**Computers and education**]: Computer Uses in Education – *collaborative learning, computer-assisted instruction (CAI), computer-managed instruction (CMI), and Distance learning.*

General Terms

Design and Human Factors.

Keywords

e-learning, computer assisted training, computer assisted assessment, web-based learning, educational technology, learner centred design, usability, usage.

1. INTRODUCTION

The use of technology to support learners in the classroom, the office, workplace, at home or on the move has become an everyday phenomenon. Educators use online learning environments to distribute their material, set quizzes, answer student

questions posted on discussion boards, collect student coursework assignments, etc. Where traditionally the learning experience was limited to classroom and text books, e-learning environments allow learners to conduct experiments in a simulated lab [3], watch videos in which instructors solve mathematical problems [1], engage in scientific enquiry using handheld and remote sensors and advanced visualisation tools [10] or practice a second language online with native instructors on the other side of the world [4]. Much of the success of these educational technologies depends on their ease of use, ability to engage the learner and to adapt to their needs, for example to be accessible at the right time and in the right place, to match the learners' existing knowledge of the material, learning style, culture, etc. Well designed systems should also discourage learners from applying surface approaches to learning, which do not lead to in-depth understanding of the material, but simply mimic learning behaviour, e.g. clicking through a series of online quizzes without consideration of the question, rote learning to pass an exam, or simply staying away from classroom sessions expecting that a last minute look before the exam at the e-learning environment will substitute these sessions. Badly designed educational technologies can even become an obstacle to learning when they are hard to use. Even if learners manage to operate such environments, boredom or frustration can prevent them from learning. Educational technology designers are left with difficult questions about how best to create systems that are usable and appealing whilst simultaneously engaging users in learning, which may itself be difficult and require effort.

1.1 Design guidelines

Educators use learning theories, such as constructivism, behaviourism, cognitivism, Piaget's developmental theory, humanistic oriented theories, and learning styles to develop their curriculum, module, lesson plans etc. How effective are these theories for the design of e-learning? And how do they relate to HCI inspired practices and design guidelines suggested by for example Nielsen [8] and Norman [9]. Are such guidelines alone sufficient to guide the design of successful learning systems? Or do we need a set of guidelines tailored for these types of applications? Fortunately research on the design of e-learning systems is making progress. For example at previous BCS-HCI conferences work was presented that explored student diversity (such as cognitive styles [12]) and the use of learning systems [2], or the use and attitude towards computer-adaptive tests [5, 6] and the design of educational software to support creative learning [11].

1.2 Research Methods

Studying the use of e-learning systems might require a specific research approach. Systems could be evaluated for example in the lab under controlled conditions. Because of time limitations this might only provide a small snapshot of the initial use of these systems. Field studies provide a more advanced understanding of the actual use of the entire system during a training course. Offering or withholding system elements to understand their effect on the learning process whilst providing a very robust experimental design might not always be possible because of pedagogical and ethical considerations. The latter often needs special attention because of the potential position of power between the learner and the researcher, who might at least be perceived as closely associated with the educator even if they are not the same individual. Furthermore, what is the value of data collected from interviews or questionnaires with learners? Are learners able to understand the learning process or can they only comment on the learning experiences?

2. WORKSHOP FOCUS

Workshops that focus on the intersection of HCI and e-learning systems are not new, for example CHI 2003 hosted a workshop on Designing for Learning[1], and INTERACT 2005 hosted a workshop on eLearning and Human-Computer Interaction[2]. This workshop wishes to continue this tradition and additionally look at new developments in this area such as: designing for inclusion, personalisation, blended learning, and consistency in computer assisted marking. Possible topics include but are not limited to:

- Design guidelines and patterns for e-learning and computer assisted assessment

- Research methods to study the design, learnability, and use of e-learning systems

- The learner's experience of e-learning systems

- The design of personalised and adaptive e-learning systems

- E-learning tools such as video, quizzes, discussion board and dynamic voting.

- The design of novel educational technologies such as VR, AR, mobile learning and games for learning.

The workshop intends to attract researchers, designers, and educators that are interested in understanding good design and the learner experiences of e-learning systems. Workshop participants could come from a variety of backgrounds such as HCI, psychology, design, and education. The main objective of the workshop is to establish a community of individuals with an interest in this area, allowing a lively exchange of ideas, and a joint exploration of current problems, as well as discussion leading to the proposal of possible solutions.

3. WORKSHOP FORMAT

This is a full-day workshop. The morning session will consist of short presentations and discussion of participants' position papers. Participants will be encouraged to demonstrate e-learning systems or evaluation tools that they might use or have developed. In the afternoon session, participants will break into small groups depending on their main interest and discuss topics such as research methodology, designing usable and engaging e-learning environments, while exploring new research questions, unsolved problems, potential solutions and new research directions. At the end of the workshop, the small groups will report back, which will form the basis for a plenary discus-

sion. The workshop will also be supported by a website (http://disc.brunel.ac.uk/HCI2007elearningworkshop) hosted by Brunel University. The draft position papers will be posted here in advance, and participants' slides will also be made available on the website before the workshop. After the workshop position papers and minutes from the workshop discussions will be published in the proceedings of the workshop.

4. WORKSHOP COMMITTEE

Willem-Paul Brinkman[1,2], Nayna Patel[2] and Annette Payne[2]
[1]Delft University of Technology, The Netherlands, [2]Brunel University, UK,
Darren Griffin, University of Kent, UK
Darren Pearce and Joshua Underwood, London Knowledge Lab, University of London, UK
Enric Mor Pera, Universitat Oberta de Catalunya, Spain
Hilary Smith, University of Sussex, UK

5. REFERENCES

[1] Brinkman, W.-P., Rae, A., and Dwivedi, Y.K., Web-based implementation of the Personalised System of Instruction: A case study of teaching mathematics in an online learning environment. *Int. J. of Web-based Learning and Teaching Technologies 2, 1* (Jan.-March 2007), 39-69.

[2] Chrysostomou, K.A., Chen, S.Y., and Lui, X. Mining users' preference in an interactive multimedia learning system: a human factor perspective. In *Proc. of HCI2006, Vol. 2* (London, UK, Sept. 11-15, 2006), 118-122.

[3] Gibbons, H.J., Evans, C., Payne, A., Shah, K., and Griffin, D.K., Computer simulations improve university instructional laboratories? *Cell Biology Education, 3* (2004), 263-269.

[4] LaPointe, D.K., and Barrett, K. A., Language learning in a virtual classroom: synchronous methods, cultural exchanges. In *Proceedings of conference on computer support for collaborative learning (CSCL'05)* (Taipei, Taiwan, 2005), 368-372.

[5] Lilley, M., and Barker, T., The use of item response theory in the development and application of user model for automatic feedback: a case study. In *Proc. of HCI2005, Vol. 2* (Edinburgh, UK, Sept 5-9, 2005), 99-104.

[6] Lilley, M., and Barker, T., Student attitude to adaptive testing. In *Proc. of HCI2006, Vol. 2* (London, UK, Sept. 11-15, 2006), 123- 127.

[7] Luckin R, Underwood J, du Boulay B, Holmberg J, Kerawalla L, O'Connor J, Smith H and Tunley H., Designing Educational Systems Fit for Use: A Case Study in the Application of Human Centred Design for AIED. *Int. J. of Artificial Intelligence in Education 16*, (2006) 353-380

[8] Nielsen, J. *Usability Engineering*. AP Professional, Boston, MA, 1993.

[9] Norman, D.A. *The Psychology of Everyday Things*. Basic Books, New York, NY, 1988.

[10] Smith H, Luckin R, Fitzpatrick G, Avramides K, and Underwood J. ,Technology at work to mediate collaborative scientific enquiry in the field. In *Proc. of AIED* (2005), 603-610.

[11] Truman, S., and Mulholland, P., Designing educational software to enhance the creative learning experience: an integrative framework. In *Proc. of HCI2006, Vol. 2* (London, UK, Sept. 11-15, 2006), 133-136.

[12] Uruchrutu, E., MacKinnon, L., and Rist, R. Designing the learning interface using cognitive styles. In *Proc. of HCI2005, Vol. 2* (Edinburgh, UK, Sept 5-9, 2005), 105-110.

---

[1] http://www-personal.umich.edu/~sjul/learning03/

[2] http://www.dis.uniroma1.it/~lhci/default.htm

Usability of User Interfaces:
From Monomodal to Multimodal

Silvia Abrahão[1,2]

[1]Departament de Sistemas Informàtics i Compu-
tación, Universidad Politècnica de València
Camí de Vera s/n – 46022 València (Spain)
34-96 3877350

sabrahao@dsic.upv.es,
abrahao@isys.ucl.ac.be

Jean Vanderdonckt[2]

[2]Belgian Lab. of Computer-Human Interaction (BCHI),
Louvain School of Management (IAG), Université ca-
tholique de Louvain,
Place des Doyens, 1 – B-1348 Louvain-la-Neuve
(Belgium)
+32 10/478525

jean.vanderdonckt@uclouvain.be

ABSTRACT

This workshop is aimed at reviewing and comparing existing Usability Evaluation Methods (UEMs) which are applicable to monomodal and multimodal applications, whether they are web-oriented or not. It addresses the problem on how to assess the usability of monomodal user interfaces according to techniques involving one or several modalities, in parallel or combined. In particular, how to synchronize results provided by different UEMs producing various types of results (e.g., audio, video, text, log files) is concerned. It also addresses the problem on how to assess the usability of multimodal user interfaces according to techniques based on multiple modalities. In particular, the question of generalizing the applicability of existing UEMs to these new types of user interfaces is concerned.

Categories and Subject Descriptors

D.2.2 [**Software Engineering**]: Design Tools and Techniques – *Computer-aided software engineering (CASE)*, *Evolutionary prototyping, Structured Programming, User Interfaces*. H.5.2 [**Information Interfaces and Presentation (e.g., HCI)**]: User interfaces – *Graphical user interfaces, Interaction styles, Input devices and strategies, Prototyping, Voice I/O*.

General Terms

Measurement, Performance, Design, Experimentation, Human Factors, Standardization, Languages.

Keywords

Accessibility, Automated evaluation, Monomodal applications, Multimodal user interfaces, Multimodal web interfaces, Usability engineering, Usability evaluation method, Usability testing, Usability guidelines, Web engineering.

1. MOTIVATIONS

Today, existing applications tend to shift their locus of interaction from the graphic channel to other channels such as speech, gesture, and haptic, to name a few. For instance, new markup languages exist today for developing multimodal web applica-

tions, such as VoiceXML, X+V, SVG. The W3C Multimodal Interaction Framework offers multiple ways of implementing multimodal web applications, also leaving several degrees of freedom to the designer and the developer. This new locus of interaction poses unprecedented challenges for assessing the usability of such applications. It is not because we are able to technically develop these multimodal user interfaces that we can guarantee their usability. Existing usability evaluation methods (UEMs) which mainly consider the graphic channel cannot be directly reused for other modalities of interaction. Moreover, UEMs which are applicable for one modality only (e.g., speech) may become inappropriate for applications combining several modalities (e.g., speech and haptic). In the other way around, UEMs which are particularly suited for one modality may become of some interest for other channels if they bring some new ideas on how to assess the usability. For instance, eye tracking techniques may be used to detect the visual paths of a user on a screen, a web page, even if eye tracking is not used as an input modality.

The motto of this workshop is that we need to evaluate multimodal user interfaces as a whole and not as the sum of pieces involving a combination of individual interaction modalities. Therefore, this workshop is intended to examine existing UEMs for individual modalities (e.g., graphic, speech) as well as for combined modalities. This does not mean that it should be restricted to multimodal applications only: UEMs valid for monomodal applications would be also very interesting for being transferred to the multimodal domain. Therefore, monomodal or multimodal UEMs would be considered for monomodal and multimodal applications, whether they are intended for the web or not.

2. TOPICS OF INTEREST

In this one-day workshop, we invite contributions, which discuss methodological, technical, application-oriented and theoretical aspects of the usability evaluation of monomodal and multimodal user interfaces. These topics include, but are not limited to:

- Adaptation and identification of ergonomic/HCI criteria and principles to multimodal interfaces
- Application of any existing UEM or modified one to one or several case studies recommended by the workshop
- Classification of usability models, methods, notations, and tools
- Evaluation of user's performance in a multimodal context of use
- Experimental studies conducted on multimodal interfaces
- Experimentation with cognitive models of user interaction for multimodal interfaces

- Tools for automatic or computer-aided usability evaluation of multimodal interfaces
- Tools for capturing usability knowledge for monomodal and multimodal
- Usability and accessibility guidelines for monomodal and multimodal interfaces
- Usability evaluation method for monomodal and multimodal interfaces
- Usability evaluation of multimodal web interfaces (e.g., speech and gestures)
- Usability factors, criteria, metrics, rules, recommendations
- User experience in multimodal dialogue systems
- Validity of models

3. METHODOLOGY OF WORK

Prior to the workshop, a first draft of the white paper will be distributed as a working document to be discussed and expanded during and after the workshop. Based on papers accepted for the workshop and existing experience, this document will discuss a matrix comparing models, methods, notations, and tools existing in the field. Second, participants will be encouraged to apply partially or totally one of their UEM to one or many of the 3 case studies recommended for the workshop. It is expected that by comparing the results provided by different methods on the same case study, significant similarities and differences will emerge. Based on a questionnaire to be filled by workshop participants prior to the workshop, the document will raise significant questions to be addressed by researchers and practitioners belonging to all communities. Discussion groups will be organized around key questions and topics that arise from the accepted papers. It is hoped that these groups can be multidisciplinary, including designers, developers and usability experts.

3.1 Format

The first part of the workshop will be dedicated to the presentation of some selected papers accepted for the workshop along with their results on the 3 case studies and limited discussion. The second part will be devoted to a discussion in sub-groups and a plenary session to complete the matrix to be obtained during this workshop. Given our outcomes, we need to use the first part for participants to present their individual understanding of the research problems in this area. The second part will be used to pull together these individual insights into a common framework and to update the first draft of the white paper.

3.2 Potential participants

Ideally, 15 to 20 participants will take part in the workshop. All the participants will be asked to submit a 8 pages position paper (maximum) or a 14 pages full paper (maximum). We will encourage papers that address the aforementioned challenges, that present any aspects of a UEM for a monomodal or multimodal interface. We will particularly appreciate for acceptation papers attempting to use their UEM on one or several of the three case studies recommended by the workshop:

1. A multimodal conversational agent, coming from the eNTERFACE'06 workshop (Similar).
2. A multimodal navigation into 3D medical images developed on top of the OpenInterface platform.
3. A multimodal game with two players, one being deaf the other one being mute, developed at eNTERFACE'06 under the lead of Dimitrios Tzovaras (Univ. of Tessaloniki).

These three case studies will be delivered in a packaged form to be downloaded from the workshop web site.

3.3 Submission procedure

Authors of papers must submit their papers themselves by APRIL 15th, 2007. All submissions must follow the Journal of Multimodal User Interfaces format (JMUI - http://www.open interface.org/JMUI/) and be submitted electronically in PDF format to the workshop co-chairs at iwumui@similar.cc. All submissions must be maximum 15 (fifteen) pages according to this format. Authors are requested to prepare submissions as close as possible to final camera-ready versions. The submission should clearly emphasize the discussion aspects relevant to the workshop. Members of an international program committee will review all submissions. For the rigorousness of the reviewing process, authors may also submit additional material such as screen dumps, images (e.g. PNG files), videos (e.g., MPEG, AVI files), demonstrations (e.g., Camtasia, SnagIt, Lotus ScreenCam) of software. Some instructions will be put on-line for this purpose. If accepted, this material can also be published on the web site upon agreement of the authors. For questions and comments, please contact the workshop co-chairs at iwumui@similar.cc.

3.4 Publication

All papers accepted for the workshop will be first published in the workshop proceedings. Provided that accepted papers are substantive both in quantity and quality, a special issue of the Journal of Multimodal User Interfaces (JMUI - http://www. openinterface.org/JMUI/) has been already agreed. The white paper that will be edited by the workshop co-chairs will be the introducing paper of this special issue. The description of the implementation of the three case studies will then be provided in appendix.

4. ACKNOWLEDGMENTS

The workshop is mainly sponsored by the European COST Action n°294 MAUSE (Towards the Maturation of IT Usability Evaluation, www.cost294.org) and by SIMILAR, the European research task force creating human-machine interfaces similar to human-human communication (http://www.similar.cc). Several members of this network of excellence and of this COST action are members of the above Program Committee and guarantee a large geographical and topical coverage of the workshop. It is also supported by the OpenInterface Foundation (www.openinterface.org) supported by FP6-IST4 and the UsiXML Consortium (www.usixml.org).

5. REFERENCES

[1] Law, E., Hvannberg, E., Cockton, G., Palanque, Ph., Scapin, D., Springett, M., Stary, Ch., and Vanderdonckt, J. Towards the Maturation of IT Usability Evaluation (MAUSE). In *Proc. of 10th IFIP TC 13 Int. Conf. on Human-Computer Interaction INTERACT'2005* (Rome, 12-16 September 2005). Lecture Notes in Computer Science, Vol. 3585, Springer-Verlag, Berlin, 2005, pp. 1134-1137.

[2] Law, E., Hvannberg, E., and Cockton, G. (eds.). *Maturing Usability: Quality in Software, Interaction and Value.* HCI Series, Springer-Verlag, Berlin, 2007.

[3] Mariage, C., Vanderdonckt, J., Pribeanu, C. *State of the Art of Web Usability Guidelines.* In "The Handbook of Human Factors in Web Design", Proctor, R.W., Vu, K.-Ph.L. (eds.), Chapter 21. Lawrence Erlbaum Associates, Mahwah, 2005, pp. 688–700.

[4] Vanderdonckt, J. Development Milestones towards a Tool for Working with Guidelines. *Interacting with Computers* 12, 2 (December 1999) 81–118.

Towards a UX Manifesto

Effie Lai-Chong Law
University of Leicester, UK
Computer Science
University Road,
Leicester,
LE2 4UN
+44 116 2717 302
elaw@mcs.le.ac.uk

Arnold P.O.S. Vermeeren
TU Delft, NL
Industrial Design
Engineering
Landbergstraat 15
NL 2628 CE Delft
+31 15 2784218
a.p.o.s.vermeeren@tudelft.nl

Marc Hassenzahl
University of Landau, DE,
Economic Psychology
Fortstraße 7
76829 Landau
+49 6341 280 261
hassenzahl@uni-
landau.de

Mark Blythe
University of York, UK
Computer Science
Heslington, York
YO10 5DD
+44 190 4434764
mblythe@cs.york.ac.uk

ABSTRACT

In this workshop we invite researchers, educators and practitioners to contribute to the construction of a coherent Manifesto for the field of User Experience (UX). Such a UX manifesto should express statements about issues like: Fundamental assumptions underlying UX (principles), positioning of UX relative to other domains (policy) and action plans for improving the design and evaluation of UX (plans). The UX manifesto can become a reference model for future work on UX.

1. BACKGROUND & MOTIVATION

Is the research and practice on User Experience (UX) maturing since it has popularized the HCI community and the industry more than a decade ago? Is there a unified view about **principles** of UX? Are there any well-defined **policies** where to position UX in a map of the Information Technology (IT) landscape, which is populated by usability, human factors, interaction design, software engineering, marketing, and other domains? Are there any sound **plans** how to refine methodologies on designing for, evaluating and teaching UX? In fact, such set of Principles, Policies and Plans constitute what we coin «**UX Manifesto**», which is deemed important for the maturation of this emerging domain by providing the foundation, objectives, and action plans for the future work of UX. Principles inform the formation of policies, which in turn feed into plans as courses of action.

1.1 Principles

The term "Principles" denotes fundamental assumptions underlying UX. It addresses questions of what an experience is (in the context of interactive products and software), how it can be described or - from a designer' perspective - how it can be fabricated?

Two seemingly exclusive positions emerged from discussing these questions: one phenomenological/pragmatist and one inspired by experimental psychology. The former is exemplified by McCarthy and Wright's notion of 'felt experience' [4]. It is based on Dewey's pragmatist view of experience. They argue against abstract models of experience and place emphasis on the situatedness and uniqueness of experience. In contrast, approaches inspired by experimental

psychology tend to deconstruct experience into single components (e.g. motivation, trust, aversion, hedonics, fun, etc). The collection of components is further supplemented by processes, which address, for example, the temporal aspect of experience or the dynamicity of psychological states, and modulate experience. The concomitant questions are: Is there a core set of UX components (if yes, what are they)? Are these components orthogonal, hierarchical or causally linked? How does the relevance of each UX component vary with the particularities of a context? What are boundary conditions for a component-based UX model and what are the alternatives?

Although proponents of both approaches tend to overemphasize differences in the approaches, both are important and far from mutually exclusive. The pragmatist perspective advocates the detailed analysis of experience, offering rich insights into specific interactions, which can surely be used by designers. However, some in the field of HCI feel uncomfortable with relying solely on very small - but detailed - samples of experiences on which the design or evaluation of an interactive product is based. They rather look for more general principles and mechanisms – a few categories of "average" experiences. The strength of an approach based on aggregated knowledge is the potential simplicity of the resulting models. However, at the same time this – per definition – implies a reduction. This reduction has costs. First, the average model may not be predictive for any real user and his/her experience. Second, averaged data and accordingly abstract principles are not vivid; they may appear shallow and may thus not be very inspiring for designers.

Obviously, to be fruitful in the field of HCI UX, it is a must to have both: ways to describe experiences in detail and all their complexity – especially as an inspiration for designers - and ways to average experiences, to build models to reduce complexity and to guide the detailed enquiries. In other words, integrating the advantages of both approaches rather than treating them as mutually exclusive is the challenge of future UX theorizing.

1.2 Policy

The term 'Policy' primarily addresses the positioning of UX relative to other closely related but distinct domains. For instance, distinctions between usability and UX have been drawn [2]. Usability is a necessary but insufficient condition to make a user smile, but UX, when desirable, can do so. Positioned in this way, usability is subsumed by UX. But some argue that UX is just an extension of usability to accommodate fuzzy quality attributes such as emotion and fun. The link between UX and software engineering lies in the definition of quality models that address a mesh of functional and non-functional quality factors (e.g. reliability, security, accessibility) determining user acceptance. There is also a link to the domain of industrial (electronic) product design which traditionally focuses on integrating sub-outcomes of attributes and consequences into the overall value of a product. As noted by Cockton [1], UX can be considered at least as one of these sub-outcomes. While usability standards (e.g. ISO 9241) have some visible impacts on the research and practice of usability, questions concerning the necessity and utility of such standards are recurrent. Hence, whether specific standards for UX should be developed is debatable. Besides, as UX has added a new dimension to HCI and interactive product design, it should be explored how UX can effectively be taught as well.

1.3 Plans

Theoretically UX is incoherent; methodologically UX is not yet mature either. Questions like "How to design for UX?" and "How to evaluate UX?" are easy to ask but difficult to answer. Answers may be sought in terms of devices that may improve the UX (see the articles by Timco et al., Følstad, and Hole in [3]) and of techniques (see Geven's article in [3]) and tools (e.g. TUMCAT [see Vermeeren & Kort's in [3]) for analyzing, designing, engineering and evaluating UX. In brief, developing theoretically sound methodologies should be high in the UX research agenda. Besides, there are critics that UX is only used as a marketing slogan. It is intriguing to gather real case studies to illustrate how UX is actually handled in the professional world of interactive product design in terms of requirements analysis, design, engineering and evaluation.

2. THE MAIN GOAL AND OBJECTIVES

The overarching goal of the workshop is to invite inputs for the construction of a coherent **UX Manifesto** constituted by the three pillars: Principles, Policy and Plans. This goal is divided into a number of objectives:

- To work on a unified view on UX by integrating different theoretical perspectives (Principles)
- To develop a generic UX model comprising the structure (i.e. core components; static) and process (i.e. situational factors; dynamic) of UX (Principles)
- To identify boundary conditions under which a generic, component-based UX model is applicable and identify alternatives otherwise (Principles)
- To identify the transversal relationships between UX and the related fields by fleshing out their communalities and distinctions (Policy)
- To understand the role of UX in the means-end chains between product attributes, usage consequences and product values (Policy)
- To explore the necessity and potential utility of developing UX standards (Policy)
- To identify effective teaching strategies for UX (Policy)
- To develop theoretically sound methodologies for analyzing, designing, engineering and evaluating UX (Plan)
- To understand UX in practice through case studies, thereby identifying factors that may facilitate or hinder the incorporation of UX into interactive products (Plan).

3. PARTICIPANTS

Maximum: 25. Generally, contributions from researchers, educators and practitioners working on UX and related areas are invited. Specifically, the participants of earlier UX workshops (DAC'05, CHI'06 and NordiCHI'06) and members of the MAUSE SIG-UX (http://www.cost294.org) are strongly encouraged to partake in the Workshop to substantiate the ideas explored. UX experts will be invited to be panelists.

4. WORKSHOP PROCEDURE

All submissions will be peer reviewed by members of the program committee. For each submission, authors are required to include a "Reflection Section" to derive from their analytic or empirical work their own version of Principles, Policy and Plans as constituents of a UX Manifesto. Participants may understand the three terms differently, and our challenge is to negotiate and consolidate the divergences to draw a consensus. Prior to the workshop, a Green Paper will be drafted based on ideas to be extracted from the submissions of this workshop and those from the earlier UX workshops. It will then be distributed to the workshop participants for comments and further inputs. In the workshop, the following activities will be conducted:

(i) Presentation of the Green Paper
(ii) Presentation of 'personal' UX Manifesto by the main author of each accepted submission
(iii) Group Discussions: The audience will be divided into groups of four or five to consolidate a group-based UX Manifesto and discuss other topics of interest (to be listed in the Green Paper).
(iv) Plenary Reporting: Each group presents their UX Manifesto
(v) Panel Discussion: Invited UX experts will hold a panel to discuss the group Manifestoes and address the future development of UX

5. PROGRAM COMMITTEE

- Mark Blythe, University of York, UK
- Gilbert Cockton, University of Sunderland, UK
- Asbjørn Følstad, SINTEF, NO
- Marc Hassenzahl, University of Landau, DE
- Paul Hekkert, Delft University of Technology, NL
- Effie Lai-Chong Law, University of Leicester, UK
- Gitte Lindgaard, Carlton University, CA
- Virpi Roto, Nokia, FL
- Arnold Vermeeren, Delft University of Technology, NL
- Peter C. Wright, Sheffield Hallam University, UK

6. EXPECTED OUTCOMES

- Accepted papers will be published in the workshop proceedings, both online and printed versions.
- Selected papers will be invited to submit an extended version to a special issue of a prestigious HCI journal
- Interested participants are invited to join the MAUSE SIG-UX to sustain the collaborative efforts of the workshop.
- To publish a draft UX Manifesto on a designated website, inviting further comments and input.

REFERENCES

[1] Cockton, G. (in press). Putting value into e-valu-ation. In E. Law, E. Hvannberg & G. Cockton (Eds.), *Maturing usability: Quality in software, interaction and value.* London: Springer.

[2] Hassenzahl, M., & Tractinsky, N. (2006). User experience – a research agenda. *Behaviour & Information Technology, 25*, 91-97.

[3] Law, E., Hvannberg, E. & Hassenzahl, M. (2006). *Proc. of the workshop "User Experience – Towards a unified view"* in conjunction with NordiCHI' 06, 14-18. October, Oslo. Online at: http://www.cost294.org/

[4] Wright, P. C., McCarthy, J., & Meekison, L. (2003). Making sense of experience. In M. Blythe, C. Overbeeke, A. F. Monk, & P. C. Wright (Eds.), Funology: From Usability to Enjoyment (pp. 43-53). Dordrecht: Kluwer.

Designing Human Centred Technologies for the Developing World: HCI but not as we know it

Rose Luckin
London Knowledge Lab
23-29 Emerald Street
London WC1N 3QS
+44 (0)20 7763 2176

j.underwood@ioe.ac.uk

Lynne Dunckley
Thames Valley University
Wellington Street
Slough SL1 1YG
+44 (0)1753 697739

Lynne.Dunckley@tvu.ac.uk

Andrew M. Dearden
Sheffield Hallam
Howard Street
Sheffield S1 1WB
+44 (0)114 225 2916

a.m.dearden@shu.ac.uk

ABSTRACT

ICT could be a powerful tool for development, but how appropriate are developed-world HCI methods? Should we 'parachute in' foreign methods, do we have more to learn than to teach?

Categories and Subject Descriptors

H.5.2 [**User Interfaces**]: Evaluation/methodology, Graphical User Interfaces, Input devices and strategies, Interaction styles, Prototyping, Screen design, Standardization, Style guides, Theory and methods, User-centered design

General Terms

Measurement, Documentation, Design, Reliability, Experimentation, Human Factors, Standardization.

Keywords

Development, developing world, Africa, Asia, participatory design

1. INTRODUCTION

With huge investments being made in ICT for development (ICT4D) and education (e.g. "$100 laptop," UN programmes etc.) and high expectations being raised, it is critical to ensure that ICT developments are in fact usable, useful, appropriate and well adapted to the communities and contexts in which they are intended to be used. This requires well designed solutions, which in turn requires appropriate human-centred design methods. However, it is unclear that methods largely developed for and with users in the developed world will prove appropriate in the developing world. This workshop aims to bring together interested parties and strengthen the User-centred design for development (UCS4D) community, as well as contribute to the body of knowledge about designing for and with communities in the developing world.

2. GOALS OF THE WORKSHOP

- Share experiences of Human Centred Design in the

developing world;

- Identify key issues and patterns;

- Learn from each other's experiences;

- Explore new, alternative and modified methods for human centred and participatory design of Development Technologies;

- Develop new partnerships - particularly international partnerships;

- Disseminate learning from this workshop through online and and offline publication; and

- Strengthen the HCI in Development Technology community.

3. LIKELY PARTICIPANTS

We hope to attract participants from varied backgrounds, not just designers of ICT. Agriculture and technology, ICT for education, development and community action. We also expect particpants from UK based 'Bridging the Global Digital Divide' projects and ICT for Development community. Our own backgrounds are in HCI, education, internationalisation, and technology and social action.

4. CALL FOR PAPERS

ICT4D is currently a 'hot research topic' in many fields with recent conferences (for example, eLearning Africa), conference tracks (CAL 07 ICT4D) and workshops (AI in ICT for Development Workshop) dedicated to the theme. However, until recently less attention has been paid to the specific difficulties of designing for and with communities in the developing world (see UCD4ID). How appropriate are developed-world participatory and human-centred methods? Should we be 'parachuting in' foreign methods and experts, or focusing attention on building local HCI expertise? Do we in fact have more to learn than to teach?

To participate in this workshop submit a two-page position paper. Possible themes are:

- Case studies of user-centred design and participatory experiences in the developing world - both successes and failures;

- The difficulties of separating development and research objectives;

- Design of educational technology for development;

- Participatory methods from community action, education, agriculture, technology design, theatre, etc..;

- Innovative methods for designing for and with communities with diverse needs; or

- Managing expectations in particpatory design projects.

5. BEFORE THE WORKSHOP

The workshop organisers will invite short position papers. These will be reviewed by committee. Accepted papers will then be made available online on workshop blog. Comments on papers will be enabled and participants will be encouraged to post comments to the blog Key issues arising from papers and comments will be identified prior to the conference. Outcomes from other recent workshop will also be linked from the blog and issues for discussion may also be drawn from there.

6. AT THE WORKSHOP

Facilitators will make short presentations around the key issues & challenges identified before the workshop.

Participants will then make short presentations, and will be encouraged to address specific comments from the blog. If appropriate permissions are given we will record the presentations (and/or stream them live using Elluminate if possible) in order to broaden participation beyond those that are able to travel to the conference.

This will be followed by discussion. Participants will break in to small groups to discuss a subset of these issues and challenges with a facilitator.. Each group will summarise its discussions to the workshop as a whole.

We will produce a poster and presentation to summarise the workshop activity and outcomes.

7. AFTER THE WORKSHOP

The blog will act as a record of the workshop, and also the hub for a community in UCD4D. We will collect the output of the workshop and edit into a journal special issue, or book, as appropriate. We will also disseminate our findings in relevant networks, communities and organisations.

8. ORGANISATION

8.1 Coordinators

Andy Dearden (point of contact for communication) is a participatory designer with a background in human computer interaction. His recent work has investigated tools to support distributed forms of participation in design and the design of ICT systems to support 'social action' in voluntary and community groups, NGOs and 'civil society'.

Lynne Dunckley, Ph.D. (Birmingham), is Professor of Information Technology at the Institute for IT at Thames Valley University. Prior to her academic career she worked for central and local government organizations, specialising in database design and project management. In addition she has

worked as a usability consultant for cross-cultural design and interoperability. She has carried out consultancy for numerous e-Commerce companies and published work in the Journal of Decision Systems, Interacting with Computers, Interact, International Ergonomics Applications and major international conferences in Europe and USA. She is the author of a textbook on Multimedia Databases (2003) and a book for database practitioners on application development using rich media in Oracle (2007). She has chaired an international conference on the internationalisation of products and services.

Rosemary Luckin is Professor of Learner Centred Design at the London Knowledge Lab. Prior to this she was director and co-founder of the Interactive Digital Educational Applications Lab and the Human Centred Technology Research group at Sussex. She is an experienced project manager and has held a range of EU/EPSRC and ESRC grants. She is a member of several journal editorial boards and conference program committees in the area of educational technology, including those of the International Association of Artificial Intelligence in Education. She has numerous peer reviewed journal and conference publications and has acted as a consultant to various organisations including the BBC and the DFES. She has worked with schools in Brazil, has close working relationships with many UK schools and set up the Sussex Education Skills Exchange to foster exchanges of knowledge and skills between with practitioners.

8.2 Committee

Jose.Abdelnour-Nocera, Thames Valley University

Souleymane Camara, Thames Valley University

Liz Fearon, Aptivate

Cecilia Oyugi, Thames Valley University

Joshua Underwood, London Knowledge Lab

Tim Mwololo Waema, University of Nairobi

Kevin Walker, London Knowledge Lab

8.3 Contact

Kevin Walker

London Knowledge Lab

23-29 Emerald Street

London WC1N 3QS

+44 (0)20 7763 2170

k.walker@ioe.ac.uk

The End of Cognition?

Phil Turner
Centre for Interaction Design
School of Computing, Napier University, Edinburgh
+44 (131) 455 2700

p.turner@napier.ac.uk

ABSTRACT

Cognition has long been a central conceptual pillar for human-computer interaction (HCI) but with the current emphasis on interaction design and user experience, this position may now be in doubt.

This workshop considers whether cognition still has relevance for the "post experience" generation.

Categories and Subject Descriptors

H5.m Information interfaces and presentations (e.g. HCI): Miscellaneous.

General Terms

Theory.

Keywords

Cognition, "Second Wave HCI".

1. INTRODUCTION

Carroll [1] in the introduction to his edited volume HCI Models, Theories and Frameworks notes that, "the initial vision of HCI as an applied science was to bring cognitive-science methods and theories to bear on software development. Most ambitiously, it was hoped that cognitive-science theory could provide substantive guidance at very early stages of the software development process." What Carroll has described as the "golden age of HCI" saw this come to fruition. Human computer interaction (HCI) has successfully developed numerous such methods which have ranged from model-based design approaches [2] to the use of formal methods [3]. Cognitive models and psychologically-plausible engineering models of human behaviour have also been derived [4] [5] [6] which, to a greater or lesser extent, have proved to be able to model the behaviour of people using interactive systems and devices. Some of these have even proved to be of practical value [7].

Add to this cognitive work analysis [8], cognitive ergonomics [9] and cognitive engineering [10] and the importance of cognition in all things interactive becomes apparent. Cognition has also given us metaphor, mental models and guidelines urging us to, for example, respect the constraints of memory by designing for recognition not recall [11]. And where would the

latest offerings from Microsoft© and Apple© be without the all-but-ubiquitous desktop metaphor? Though the desktop is still the primary means by which we interact with computers, the means by which we go about designing interactive technology has changed dramatically, particularly in the last 10 years.

2. INTERACTION DESIGN AND USER EXPERIENCE

Interaction design and interest in user experience have emerged as the foci for much of what once would have called itself HCI. Interaction design was first proposed by Moggridge and developed into what we would recognize now by people such as Crampton-Smith at the Royal College of Art. Moggridge describes his early treatment of the subject as *Soft-face* which comprised " … a combination between software and user-interface design." [12].

Interaction design which has a distinct product design feel to it, also emphasizes the importance of aesthetics [13], fun [14], pleasure [15], affect [16] and so forth. And all of this is for the current generation of desktop users who most likely do not realize that the desktop is based on a metaphor.

This has been parallel by research into user experience as exemplified by [17], the appearance of new conferences such as DUX and the profession of "user experience designer".

All of which begs the question as to whether cognition remains the most appropriate conceptual basis for the design of interactive systems and devices? Indeed does cognition still have a role in HCI? If so what? For example, how much and what kind of cognition is involved using an iPod, a smart phone or making an e-purchase? These activities might better be described as skilful coping [18]. Perhaps any discussion of cognition should be limited to specialist applications such as the monitoring of complex and safety critical systems?

But, all may not be lost. Our understanding of cognition has evolved dramatically in the last twenty years and is no longer seen as merely a set of processes taking places in an individual's head. Cognition is now recognized to be situated [19], distributed [20][21], embodied [22] and even collective [23][24].

3. THE THEME OF THIS WORKSHOP

This workshop is concerned with evaluating whether cognition still has a contribution to make to the current "Second Wave of HCI". It will also consider whether these re-conceptualization of cognition are sufficient to bridge the gap left between the traditional view and the next generation of interactive systems and devices.

4. REFERENCE

[1] Carroll, J. (2003) Introduction: Towards a Multidisciplinary Science of Human-Computer

interaction. In J. Carroll (Ed.) *HCI Models, Theories and Frameworks*. Morgan Kaufmann.

[2] Dix, A. and Runciman, C. (1985) Abstract models of interactive systems. In P. Johnson and S. Cook (Eds.) *People and Computers: Designing The User Interface*. Cambridge, UK: Cambridge University Press, 13-22.

[3] Palanque, P. and Paternó, F. (Eds) (1997) *Formal Methods in Human Computer Interaction*. London: Springer-Verlag.

[4] Payne, S.J. (1991) A Descriptive Study Of Mental Models. Behaviour and Information Technology, 10, 3-21

[5] Payne, S.J. (1992) *On Mental Models And Cognitive Artefacts*. In Y. Rogers, A. Rutherford and P. Bibby (Eds) Models In The Mind. London: Academic Press.

[6] Hollnagel, E. and Woods, D. (1983) Cognitive Systems Engineering: New Wine In New Bottles. *International Journal of Man Machine Studies*, **18**, 583-600.

[7] John, B.E. and Kieras, D.E. (1996) Using GOMS For User Interface Design And Evaluation: Which Technique? *ACM Transactions on Human Computer Interaction*, **3(4)**, 287-319.

[8] Vicente, K.J. (1999) *Cognitive Work Analysis*. Laurence Erlbaum Associates, Mahwah, NJ.

[9] Shackel, B. (1986) Ergonomics in design for usability. Proceedings Of The Second Conference Of The British Computer Society, Human Computer Interaction Specialist Group On People And Computers: Designing For Usability, 44-64.

[10] Watson, M., & Sanderson, P. (2007). Designing for attention with sound: Challenges and extensions to Ecological Interface Design. *Human Factors*, **49(2)**, 331-346.

[11] Gardiner, M.M. and Christie, B. (1987) Applying cognitive psychology to user-interface design. John Wiley & Sons, Inc. New York, NY, USA

[12] Moggridge, B. (2007) *Designing Interactions*. MIT press.

[13] Petersen, M.G., Iversen, O.S., Krogh, PG and Ludvigsen, M. (2004) Aesthetic Interaction: A Pragmatist's Aesthetics of Interactive Systems. *Proceedings of the 2004 Conference on Designing Interactive Systems*, Cambridge, MA, 269 – 276.

[14] Blythe M.A., Monk A.F., Overbeeke K. and Wright, P.C. (2003) (Eds.) *Funology: From Usability to Enjoyment*. Kluwer Academic Publishers.

[15] Jordan, P. W. (1998) Human Factors For Pleasure In Product Use. *Applied Ergonomics*, **29**, 25 - 33.

[16] Picard, R.W. (1998) Affective Computing. MIT Press.

[17] McCarthy, J. and Wright, P. (2004) *Technology as Experience*. MIT Press.

[18] Dreyfus, H.L. (1996) The Current Relevance of Merleau-Ponty's Phenomenology of Embodiment. *Electronic Journal of Analytic Philosophy*, **4 (Spring)**, no pages numbers.

[19] Suchman, L.A. (1987) Plans and Situated Actions: The Problem of Human-Machine Communication. Cambridge, Cambridge University Press.

[20] Hutchins, E. (1995) *Cognition in the Wild*, MIT Press.

[21] Rogers, Y. and Ellis, J. (1994). Distributed Cognition: an alternative framework for analysing and explaining collaborative working. *Journal of Information Technology*, **9(2)**, 119-128.

[22] Dourish, P. (2001) *Where the action is*. MIT press.

[23] Engeström, Y. (1987) *Learning by expanding: An activity-theoretical approach to developmental research*, Helsinki: Orienta-Konsultit.

[24] Engeström, Y. (1999) Expansive visibilization of work: an activity theoretic perspective, *CSCW*, **8(1-2)**.

Emotion in HCI

Christian Peter
Fraunhofer Institute for
Computer Graphics
Joachim Jungius Str. 11
0049 381 4024 122

cpeter@igd-
r.fraunhofer.de

Russell Beale
School of Computer
Science
University of Birmingham
Edgbaston
Birmingham
+44 121 414 3729
R.Beale@cs.bham.ac.uk

Elizabeth Crane
University of Michigan
Division of Kinesiology
401 Washtenaw Ave.
Ann Arbor, MI 48108
USA
bcrane@umich.edu

Lesley Axelrod
Department of Information
Systems and Computing
Brunel University
UB8 3PH, UK
+44 (0)1895203397 x 3822
lesley@axelrod.co.uk

ABSTRACT

An increasing number of conferences, symposia, workshops, journals and books address the subject of emotions and their role in Human-Computer Interaction, including workshops at the last two HCI conferences. The need for discussion, exchange of ideas, and interdisciplinary collaboration is ever-increasing as the community grows. This workshop will meet the requirements of individuals working in fields affected by emotion, giving them a podium to raise their questions and work with like-minded people of various disciplines on common subjects. It will focus around four sessions, and will use predominantly small group work, rather than being presentation-based.

Categories and Subject Descriptors

C.5 Computer System Implementation, D.2 Software Engineering, H1.2 User/Machine Systems, H5.m. Information interfaces and presentation

General Terms

Algorithms, Management, Measurement, Performance, Design, Economics, Reliability, Experimentation, Human Factors, Languages, Theory, Legal Aspects, Verification.

Keywords

Emotions, Affective Computing, Design, Applications, Sensing, Theories, Human-Computer Interaction, Emotion Recognition

1. INTRODUCTION

Emotion plays an important role in our interactions with people and computers in everyday life. Emotions, some believe, are what make our interactions human. Rosalind Picard's fundamental publications [1, 2, 3, 4] on affective computing

increased awareness in the HCI community of the important role of emotion in human-computer interactions. Since then, researchers have also become increasingly aware of the importance of emotion in the design process [5]. This recent affective awareness is leading designers and HCI researchers to try and understand the subtleties of emotion and its effect on our behaviours. This is encouraging for a young field of research, and there exists many exciting directions where this field may be expanded.

Emotion theory, however, is not grounded in the HCI discipline. Studying emotion within the HCI discipline is an inherently interdisciplinary task. The specific areas of interest span recognition and synthesis of emotion in face and body, emotion sensors, speech specifics, and the influence of emotion on information processing and decision-making. Despite these different areas of interest, there are common obstacles each of us face in our work. Given that we ask similar questions about emotion and could benefit from learning about solutions others have devised, a workshop at HCI 2007 will serve as a good format for discussion.

There have been workshops on the role of emotion in HCI at the last two conferences [6, 7]. They proved to be a good meeting place for like-minded people investigating several aspects of emotion in the wide field of HCI. As such, they had a fairly wide basis and participants worked collaboratively on selected topics, with tangible results [8]. Building on the last workshops' success, this year's workshop aims at bringing the community further together and continuing the consolidation process. As participants last year suggested and contributors to the mailing list [9] confirmed, this year's workshop will be more focussed on selected topics based on the contributions.

Contributions are encouraged to the following topics:

- How do applications currently make use of emotions?

- What makes applications that support affective interactions successful?

- How do we know if affective interactions are successful, and how can we measure this success?

- What value might affective applications, affective systems, and affective interaction have?

- What technology is currently available for sensing affective states?

- How reliable is sensing technology?

- Are there reliable and replicable processes to include emotion in HCI design projects?
- What opportunities and risks are there in designing affective applications?

With the workshop being very interactive and focused on selected topics, it is expected that the outcome of the workshop will be even more tangible than its two predecessors, which themselves resulted in a Springer book to be published this year. We aim for citable outputs this year as well.

2. WORKSHOP PROCEDURE

We will solicit submission of position papers related to the subject. Case study papers describing current applications or prototypes are strongly encouraged. As a way of bringing the domain to life, presentations of products or prototypes that participants have been involved in are highly encouraged. The call for papers will be submitted to relevant newsgroups and mailing lists, within relevant European Networks of Excellence such as emotion-research.net, and published on the workshop's website. Papers will be reviewed by the workshop's committee members.

A short reading list of online papers will be prepared for all accepted participants, to allow them to acquaint themselves with the basics of the domain, so that the workshop sessions can assume a common baseline and be as productive as possible.

The format of the workshop is designed to encourage interaction between participants. The workshop will be divided into a very short introductory part; four thematic working sessions allowing the participants to acquaint themselves with their group and to work collaboratively on selected themes; and a concluding part to consolidate findings and generate tangible outputs.

This year's workshop will have a strong emphasis on small group work. For this, the introductory part will be kept very short with the participants being asked to prepare a short biography bullet list to be circulated before the workshop.

The focus of the workshop is on discussions and group work on selected themes. The general topics for the individual working sessions will be prepared in advance. Participants will be divided into groups for the thematic working sessions. After each session participants will join a new group for the next session. This will facilitate the wish of many participants to be able to work with many people and on more than one subject over the day, as expressed last year.

The anticipated outline is as follows:

Introduction: The organizers will introduce themselves and review the goals and format of the workshop. Each participant's biography will be presented for 30 seconds with the individual having a chance to comment.

Demos: A slot for demonstrations of working prototypes of affective applications, sensors, data analysis tool and other related work.

Review session: Key concepts will be reviewed and discussed. The purpose of this short session is to set the foundation for the rest of the activities and discussion.

Working groups:

Session 1: Participants will be asked to identify both their expertise and their gaps in knowledge in terms of emotion in HCI. The purpose of this session is to allow to identify common research issues and possible solutions, and to foster communication after the workshop.

Session 2: Participants will discuss topics related to designing for an affective response, detection of affect, and modeling affect. The purpose of this working group is to discuss theoretical issues, to identify the current state of knowledge, and to discuss the possibilities and pitfalls of affective computing.

Session 3: Participants will discuss adding affect to an existing system. The purpose of this working group is to discover the range of possibilities for adding affect, to identify issues related to adding affect, and to discuss possible solutions to those issues.

Session 4: Participants will discuss selected topics identified by the organizers in the position papers. The purpose of this working group is to discuss issues directly related to the participants of this workshop.

Create outputs: By debating the findings of the working groups, we will aim to develop tangible deliverables such as joint publications on issues identified in the workshop, collaboration efforts, networking activities or grant proposals.

3. REFERENCES
[1] Picard, R.W. Affective Computing. M.I.T. Press, Cambridge, MA. (1997).

[2] Picard, R. W, Healey, J. Affective Wearables, Personal Technologies Vol 1, No. 4 , (1997), 231-240.

[3] Picard, R.W. Affective Computing for HCI. Proc. of the 8th International Conference on Human- Computer Interaction: Ergonomics and User Interfaces-Volume I. Lawrence Erlbaum Associates, Inc. (1999).

[4] Picard R.W., Vyzas E., Healey J. Toward Machine Emotional Intelligence - Analysis of Affective Physiological State. IEEE Transactions on Pattern Analysis and Machine Intelligence, Vol 23 No. 10. (2001).

[5] Norman, D.A. Emotional Design: Why we love (or hate) everyday things. Basic Books. (2003).

[6] Peter C., Blyth, G., 2005. The Role of Emotions in Human-Computer Interaction. A workshop held at the 2005 HCI conference, Edinburgh. Proceedings of the HCI 2005 Conference, vol.2. (2005) , pp. 295-298.

[7] Peter C., Crane E., Axelrod L., Beale R.. Engaging with Emotions – the Role of Emotion in HCI. In Fields et al.(Eds.). Proceedings of the HCI 2006 Conference, London, volume 2, British Computer Society (2006). pp 270 - 272. ISSN 1470-5559.

[8] C. Peter, E. Crane and R. Beale (2006) The role of emotion in human-computer interaction. Interfaces 69, Winter 2006, ISSN 1351-119X.

[9] Emotion-in-HCI Mailing list (2007). http://lists.emotion-in-hci.net/cgi-bin/mailman/listinfo/public

From HCI to Media Experience: Methodological Implications

Elizabeth F. Churchill
Yahoo! Research
2821 Mission College Boulevard
Santa Clara, CA, 95050, USA
+1 408 349 4591

churchill@acm.org

Jeffrey Bardzell
Indiana University
1900 E. 10th Street
Bloomington, IN 47406
+1 812 856 1850

jbardzel@indiana.edu

ABSTRACT

The landscape of interactive technology design and evaluation is expanding. In the past, usability and task efficiency were the main focus for research in human computer interaction; evaluation methods worked from single user data over constrained tasks. This kind of work remains central to our discipline. However, new issues are complicating this scenario. For example, how do we design for quintessentially elusive concepts like "experience"? Especially when that experience is not singular, but social, where data are spread across many people, potentially many platforms and devices, and many settings. Where the lab test cannot shed light on ways that experience unfolds over time. The units of analysis and the data to be gathered are contested. In this workshop we invite discussion of interactive media experience and how to design for and evaluate it.

Categories and Subject Descriptors

A.1 [**Introductory Survey**]

General Terms

Design, measurement, theory

Keywords

Workshop; design; social media; experience; engagement; methods; evaluation; measurement; amateur multimedia; games

1. INTRODUCTION: FROM INTERACTION TO EXPERIENCE

HCI as a discipline has tended to focus on designing to increase efficiency and reduce frustration at the single user, single interface, or task and session level. However, the advent of internet-based social media, and increasing complexity in digital information itself (conversational interface agents, collaboratively editable video, massively multiplayer online games and self-referential animations and videos at sites such as Newgrounds and YouTube) has signaled a gap in design in and evaluation thinking. Use of rich social media content is not instrumental to another task, as use of a word processor is instrumental to the composition of a legal brief; instead, its "use" is the social experience it affords, and its ostensible content is often almost incidental. This dynamic can be seen,

for example, in the spectacular success of certain viral videos, which can have downloads in the tens of millions, international news coverage, and production and distribution costs approaching zero. The meaning of a viral video is not the information it transmits, but rather how different social networks position themselves relative to it, disseminate it, and iteratively build on its expressive language.

From digital marketing to interactive media, there appears to be a deep shift from interaction with information to experience. Epistemologically, experience is harder to understand, represent, and search than information; these difficulties are affecting most if not all of the information sciences and have wide-ranging implications for IT businesses.

2. ADDRESSING EXPERIENCE

Understanding experience transforms not just research methods, but also the units into which we divide the phenomena we set out to study.

Addressing this shift, in this workshop we address the increasing focus on designing "experiences" – which includes of course characterizing, perhaps measuring, and certainly offering guidelines for crafting compelling and memorable experiences. This shift is reflected in recent publications [3] and in conferences (for example, ACM's DUX, Designing the User Experience, conference), as well as in conversations and presentations. Recent memes include "experience prototyping", "experience mining" and "experience analysis".

Critiques of established HCI practice for addressing this broader notion of experience acknowledge that usability studies have established goals and tried and tested methods for gathering and analyzing data on important issues such as time to task completion, error rates, time to select a target on screen, usability surveys, think-aloud use protocols, etc. However, these methods and measures are not geared to evaluating, reflecting or representing people's lived *experience* [5]. And we need to account for socially constructed experiences, not for individual reactions to presentations of information; we need to glean a sense of experiences as it occurs across platforms (from desktop to mobile to public spaces), and across physical locations. Video and pervasive game design is one place where the issue of experience design is actively discussed, but even here we see little evidence of systematic game design research, which would include the elaboration of new methodologies and evaluative measures (but see[1][4]).

3. CROSS-DISCIPLINARY EXPLORATIONS

The humanities offer mature critical vocabularies to describe experiences, from the philosophical pragmatism of John Dewey to the literary theory of Mikhail Bakhtin and Wolfgang Iser as well as the film theory of Christian Metz and Laura Mulvey (see [2]). Common to these approaches is an interpretive examination of the intersections between experiences and aesthetics, often as they originate in complex cultural expressions. Interactive media have become cultural expressions, and our responses to them are often aesthetic. Yet useful as these humanist vocabularies are as tools of criticism, they do not, at least directly, provide means of measurement, scientific evaluation, or prediction.

A major issue, then, is *how to operationalize critical categories into nuanced yet verifiable scientific methods*.

And, on the other hand, we need to *ask how do we make sense of data that are gathered into meaningful reflections of people's experience*? We see use of detailed data from sensors, audio and video recordings, psycho-physiological readings combined with survey, interview and eye gaze data in attempts to characterize common and individual responses to events.

4. WORKSHOP DETAILS

4.1 Workshop questions

In this workshop we invite participants to address:

What is an experience? Where does an experience begin and where does it end? And how do such bounded, singular experiences contribute to *experience as culturally embedded knowing* – which is what people bring to the events and setting we, as designers, are creating and evaluating. As posed above, how can we operationalize critical categories into nuanced yet verifiable scientific methods?

What are the ways in which qualitative and quantitative measures can weave together? What are the challenges we face in mapping data from multiple data sources into a coherent understanding of the user's experience? How do we aggregate disparate data into meaningful units of analysis? And further, what language do we have for sharing our findings about experience?

What skills are needed if one is to be an "experience designer"? It is clear that the kinds of skills required to be an experience designer are not those typically taught in HCI classes where the emphasis is often on (negative) experience prevention, and in the absence of irritation we assume there will be a positive experience. What are required skills as they would be listed on job sites?

4.2 Workshop solicitation and application

Workshop participants will be invited to submit a four-page page proposal or position paper outlining their current research areas, and approach to media experience research and design. We will ask submitters to outline their aims and goals, their currently used methods and any limitations of their current methodologies. We encourage submission of novel and innovative methods with some consideration of the underlying inspirations and potential for further development. We will actively solicit cross-disciplinary perspectives. We are particularly looking for artful conceptualizations of methods that yield data that can be gathered to offer cross-setting comparisons.

Submissions will be actively solicited by emailing members of the HCI, CSCW, Pervasive Gaming and WWW communities; by the creation of a workshop specific website for information sharing; and by emails sent to related conference lists.

4.3 Workshop outline

Workshop participants will be introduced to each other before the workshop itself, and position papers made available for pre-workshop reading. Each participant will be asked to summarize the central points of the position paper at the workshop rather than give a long presentation. In addition, workshop participants will be asked to bring some data from an ongoing study, or simulated data reflecting a proposed study. These data will be shared and discussed in terms of the issues that are raised in terms of the project goals, the data collection methods, the data organization and analysis methods and the final outcome of the representation or reflection of experience in the context of the project goals.

We anticipate the workshop morning session to be an introduction and data sharing session, and the workshop afternoon to be a set of methods sharing exercises around a previously agreed upon set of design exercises.

Our intended outcome from this will be to create a repertoire of methods and data analysis techniques that are currently in use and that are being created to address issues in media experience analysis, as well as a list of issues and gaps that need to be addressed in the field. Given our approach is a tool-box of methods approach, we will attempt to also lay out the limitations as well as the benefits of methods. Finally, we will explore the ways in which these newly evolving methods challenge contemporary teaching and data gathering methods within university curricula and within traditional usability laboratory set-ups.

4.4 Workshop outcomes

We propose inviting the best submissions to extend based on workshop conversations for a special issue of a journal. Potential journals include the Journal of Computer Mediated Communication and the Journal of Human Computer Studies. Journal editors will be approached if the workshop proposal is successful.

4.5 A/V requirements.

We require a projector, and extension chords for laptops. Workshop participants will be asked to bring their own laptops for presentations. We would like a set of speakers for showing video clips with audio (these can also be provided by the workshop organizers if necessary). In addition, we would also like 3 or 4 flipcharts and some post-its with markers if possible (again these can also be provided by the workshop organizers if necessary).

5. REFERENCES

[1] Bell, M., Chalmers, M., Barkhuus, L., Hall, M., Sherwood, S., Brown, B., Rowland, D., Benford, S. and Hampshire, A., Interweaving Mobile Games with Everyday life. Proc CHI 2006, pp. 417-426. ACM Press.

[2] Braudy, Leo & Marshall Cohen, eds. (2004). Film Theory and Criticism. 6th Ed. Oxford: Oxford University Press.

[3] McCarthy, J. and Wright, P. Technology as Experience, MIT Press, 2004.

[4] Taylor, T.L. Play Between Worlds: Exploring Online Game Culture. The MIT Press, 2006.

[5] Turner, V.W. and Bruner, E. The Anthropology of Experience, University of Ilinois Press, 1986

Supporting Human Memory with Interactive Systems

Denis Lalanne
DIVA group
Department of Informatics
University of Fribourg,
Fribourg, Switzerland
denis.lalanne@unifr.ch

Elise van den Hoven
User-Centered Engineering Group
Industrial Design Department
Eindhoven University of Technology
The Netherlands
e.v.d.hoven@tue.nl

ABSTRACT

The major goal of this workshop is to explore how interactive systems can support human memory, using novel technologies and innovative human/machine interaction paradigms, such as tangible interaction. We believe this is important since memory and attention are becoming critical resources for our wellness, e.g. with regard to a continuously increasing information overload. The goal of this workshop is not only to support personal information management but also daily life activities, e.g. adapted to user preferences and specific contexts. Where current multimedia search engines are designed for large user communities and their applications, this workshop targets the support of individual's personal memory in everyday life.

1. MOTIVATION

Human memory is central in our daily life activities, not only to build relationships with friends, create our identity or reminisce about the past [2] but also to drive our attention towards the most important tasks to perform and to manage our lives [1]. Information overload, memory and attention lacks are crucial challenges to solve, not only for elderly people but also for the rest of the society.

Numerous elderly have memory and attention problems, without speaking about Alzheimer disease [8][11], which hinder their daily lives. Not only do they have difficulties remembering appointments and tasks that need to be done, such as buying bread or milk twice the same day, they might lose their glasses, they have trouble remembering people and places, which can result in insecurity, unsafe situations and melancholic feelings.

Younger people also face memory problems, especially with the constant increase of information a person owns and handles. Not only the information amount is growing fast, it is dematerializing and thus, people are often experiencing the "lost-in-infospace" effect. Our documents are multiplying in very large file hierarchies, our pictures are no longer stored in photo-albums, our music CDs are taking the form of mp3 files, movies are stored on hard-drives. Google and Microsoft recently tried to solve the "lost-in-infospace" issue by providing, respectively, a desktop search engine and a powerful email search engine, in attempt to minimize the effort needed by people to organize their documents and access them later by

browsing. However, in order to find a file, one still has to remember a set of keywords or at least remember its "virtual" existence. If one does not remember having a certain document, browsing could be helpful, since it can reveal related keywords and documents. Those, in turn, can help you remember by association, like our human memory does [1][10].

The process of "remembering" usually starts with a sensory cue which gives you access to an associated memory. For example, we may see a picture of a place visited in our childhood and the image cues recollections associated to the content of the picture and trigger an emotional reaction simultaneously. This information is generally easier to retrieve if it is associated to a strong emotional experience [9] or when it is rehearsed often which can be facilitated by having physical objects related to memories, such as souvenirs or photographs [4]. Therefore tangible interaction systems seem to have potential for supporting everyday human memory (e.g. [3][5][12]). Furthermore, it appears that humans easily access and retrieve information when it is linked to other related information or objects [7][13], either information or sounds, smells, images, etc. which supports the idea of cross-modal indexing [6].

This workshop proposes to explore possible ways to support memory, by means of interactive systems, to improve the wellness of people suffering from memory or attention lacks or just everyday people in everyday situations.

2. AIM OF THE WORKSHOP

The aim of the workshop is to bring people together to discuss ongoing studies on human memory, both user centred and technology driven, and to address some of the following questions:

Human Memory: What human memory knowledge is needed to create optimal memory support? What are the known drawbacks of our memory?

Target group: Which groups of people could benefit most from human memory support? Can we support people suffering from Alzheimer and dementia? How can potential users be involved in the analysis, design, implementation and evaluation process?

Evaluation: How do we evaluate memory support from the perspective of the target group, interaction or interface design and supporting technologies? What has been done in terms of evaluation thus far and what did the results teach us?

Supporting Technologies: Which kind of technologies can be used to support human memory? Which multimodal technology can help best supporting memory? For which tasks and target group? And what is the context of use?

Tangible Interaction: Why is tangibility important? How can we assess tangibility? What kinds of tangible objects are suitable for supporting remembering, i.e. how does tangible object design relate to human memory? Are personal tangibles more suitable than generic tangible objects for the memory field?

Emotion-oriented interfaces: How can emotion-oriented computing help supporting memory? How can a machine detect emotions and link it with related information? How can a machine generate emotions and recall memories? Can we use the knowledge that memories and emotions are closely linked?

Personal Information Management and Visualization: Which novel information mining and retrieval strategies are necessary to index and retrieve memories? How to adapt and extend multimedia search engines to handle personal memories? How to deal with the cross-modal nature of personal memories and information?

3. PARTICIPANTS

We aim at a mix of researchers and practitioners working on (including but not limited to) tangible user interfaces, multimodal interfaces, system designers, sensing technologies, cognitive sciences, personal information management or information visualization. These participants could be originating from diverse fields, including HCI, computer science, (interaction) design, psychology, sociology and ethnography.

4. WORKSHOP PROCEDURE

In case you are interested in participating in this workshop you should submit a 4-page position paper on any of the above-mentioned or related topics using the ACM-template (http://www.acm.org/sigs/pubs/proceed/template.html). Papers will be selected based on the quality, the relevance and on the diversity, since we are aiming at discussing work from different backgrounds, such as HCI, computer science, cognitive science. We will have to limit the number of presentations to no more than 15, due to time limitations. The total number of participants is limited to 25 to keep the workshop interactive.

The full-day workshop will consist of a morning program including an introduction and position paper presentations (of approximately 10 minutes each). We want to divide the participants in the afternoon session according to the themes mentioned in the previous section. These themes and the related questions raised in the workshop will be used to start discussions and brainstorms in small discussion groups. Later these groups will present their results to the other workshop participants. We would like to end the workshop with a group discussion on possible future directions. This is a rough first schedule of the day:

9	Welcome & Intro	13-14	Lunch/brainstorming in groups
9-11	Position papers	14-16	Brainstorm. in groups
-	15 min. break	16-17	Group presentations
11-13	Position papers	17-17.30	Wrap up & future

5. FUTURE WORK

Plans for publishing the workshop proceedings with Springer-Verlag or electronically on ACM Digital Library will be studied in advance. However, we also want to discuss the follow-up possibilities during the workshop: a forum, a wiki, a mailing list, a book or a special issue in an international journal. In addition we are confident that this workshop will facilitate future collaboration and continuing discussions.

6. REFERENCES
[1] Baddeley, A. (1997). Human Memory: Theory and Practice, Psychology Press (UK).

[2] Cohen, G. (1996). Memory in the real world, Hove, UK: Psychology Press.

[3] Glos, J.W. and Cassell, J. (1997b). Rosebud: A Place for Interaction Between Memory, Story, and Self, Proceedings of the 2nd International Conference on Cognitive Technology (CT'97), 88.

[4] Hoven, E.A.W.H. van den (2004). Graspable Cues for Everyday Recollecting, Ph.D.-thesis at the Department of Industrial Design, Eindhoven University of Technology, The Netherlands.

[5] Hoven, E. van den, and Eggen, B. (2004). Tangible Computing in Everyday Life: Extending Current Frameworks for Tangible User Interfaces with Personal Objects, Markopoulos et al. (Eds), proceedings of EUSAI 2004, LNCS 3295, Nov 8-10, Eindhoven, The Netherlands, pp. 230-242.

[6] Lalanne, D. and Ingold, R. (2005). "Structuring Multimedia Archives With Static Documents." In ERCIM News: "Multimedia Informatics", vol. 62, n° 62, July 2005, pp. 19-20.

[7] Lamming, M. and Flynn, M. Forget-me-not: intimate computing in support of human memory. In: FRIEND21: International symposium on next generation human interface, Meguro Gajoen, Japan, 1994, 125–128.

[8] Morris, M.E. (2005). Early Detection of Cognitive Decline with Embedded Assessment. Alzheimer's and Dementia, Volume 1, Issue 1, Supplement 1, July 2005, p. 107.

[9] Ochsner, K.N. and Schacter, D.L. (2003). Remembering emotional events: A social cognitive neuroscience approach. In: Handbook of Affective Sciences, R. J. Davidson et al. eds., Oxford University Press, pp 643-660.

[10] Rigamonti, M., Lalanne, D., Evéquoz,, F. and Ingold, R. (2005). "Browsing Multimedia Archives Through Intra- and Multimodal Cross-Documents Links." In Renals S. & Bengio S., eds., Machine Learning for Multimodal Interaction II, LNCS 3869, Springer, pp. 114-125.

[11] Rusted, J.M. and Sheppard, L.M. (2002). Action-based memory in people with dementia: A longitudinal look at tea-making. Neurocase, 8, 111-126.

[12] Ullmer, B., Ishii, H. (2000). Emerging frameworks for tangible user interfaces, IBM Systems Journal, 39, 915-931.

[13] Whittaker, S. Bellotti, V. and Gwizdka, J. (2006). Email in Perso nal Information Management. In Communications of the ACM, 49(1), 68-73.

Second International Workshop on Physicality

Devina Ramduny-Ellis
Computing Department, InfoLab21
Lancaster University
Lancaster, LA1 4WA, UK
+44 1524 510501

devina@comp.lancs.ac.uk

Alan Dix
Computing Department, InfoLab21
Lancaster University
Lancaster, LA1 4WA, UK
+44 1524 510319

alan@hcibook.com

Steve Gill
PDR
University of Wales Institute Cardiff
Western Avenue, Cardiff, CF5 2YB
+44 29 2041 6732

sjgill@uwic.ac.uk

www.physicality.org/physicality2007

ABSTRACT

When designing purely physical products we do not necessarily have to understand what it is about their physicality that makes them work - they simply have it. However, as we design hybrid physical/digital products we now have to understand what we lose or confuse by the added digitality - and so need to understand physicality more clearly than before. This multi-disciplinary workshop will seek to construct a fundamental understanding of the nature of physicality: how humans experience, manipulate, react and reason about 'real' physical things and how this may inform the design process and the design of future innovative products.

Categories and Subject Descriptors

H.1.2 [**Models and Principles**]: User/Machine Systems – *human factors, human information processing, software psychology.*

General Terms

Design, Human Factors, Theory.

Keywords

Physicality, digitality, product design, design process, design techniques, tangible interfaces, ubiquitous computing.

1. INTRODUCTION

We live in an increasingly digital world yet our bodies and minds are naturally designed to interact with the physical. From electric kettles that switch themselves off when boiling, to washing machines, TV remotes and in the future increasingly automated homes, the products of the 21st century are and will be syntheses of digital and physical elements – and for the user, these will become indistinguishable just as we do not consciously think of the wire between a light switch and bulb.

The pace of change is such that waiting for craft understanding to develop is untenable, hence the need for more radical and fundamental understandings, informed by and informing praxis. As we design hybrid physical/digital products we have to recognise what we lose or confuse by the added digitality.

© Devina Ramduny-Ellis, Alan Dix & Steve Gill, 2007
Published by the British Computer Society
Volume 2 Proceedings of the 21st BCS HCI Group
Conference
HCI 2007, 3-7 September 2007, Lancaster University, UK
Devina Ramduny-Ellis & Dorothy Rachovides (Editors)

As well as commercial and technological pressures, there are also research agendas which are predicated on the increasing digital infiltration of day-to-day objects, in particular tangible user interfaces, mixed reality and the Weiser vision of ubiquitous computing [1]. Despite the rush of research in this area the large majority is focused on technological proof of concept, with occasional user evaluation, but little systematic design knowledge construction.

2. BACKGROUND

This workshop follows on from the successful 'First International Workshop on Physicality, which was held at Lancaster University in 2006 [2]. The workshop showed that the importance of the topic is recognised widely and attracted contributions from disciplines including design, computing, sociology and music.

In April 2007, we started work on the 'DEPtH: Designing for Physicality' project which is part of the Designing for the 21st Century Initiative[1]. Both the timeliness of the topic and the substantial possibilities it offers, give good reasons for holding a second workshop this year. This workshop is supported by the DEPtH project[2].

3. AIMS

The aim of this workshop is to provide a forum for researchers to discuss how the move from physical to digital or hybrid products affect our understanding of the technology and more importantly, how people interact with them and eventually adopt, shape or are shaped by them.

The workshop also offers a unique opportunity for participants to draw and consolidate a wider perspective of physicality from an interdisciplinary group.

Application areas that address physicality are intentionally wide and include but not limited to:

- design at the physical-digital frontier;
- the philosophy of physicality;
- artefact-focussed social interaction;
- physically-inspired interaction in virtual worlds;
- creativity and materiality;
- interactive art and performance.

---

[1] http://www.design21.dundee.ac.uk/Phase2/P2_Projects.htm

[2] http://www.physicality.org/

4. PARTICIPANTS

This workshop is intended to bring together a multidisciplinary group of researchers from industry and academia – including product designers, interaction designers, researchers in ubiquitous computing, tangible interface and cognitive, social and philosophical fields, and indeed all excited by this new challenge of the third millennia.

5. ORGANISATION

The workshop is organised by Devina Ramduny-Ellis and Alan Dix from Lancaster University and our collaborators on the DEPtH project, Steve Gill and Joanna Hare who are affiliated with the National Centre for Product Design & Development Research at the University of Wales Institute in Cardiff.

The Programme Committee for the workshop is international and covers a wide breadth of disciplines:

- Monika Buscher, Dept. of Sociology, Lancaster Univ., UK

- Hans Gellersen, InfoLab21, Lancaster Univ., UK

- Gabriella Giannachi, Performance and New Media, Univ. of Exeter, UK

- Masitah Ghazali, Information Systems Dept., Universiti Putra Malaysia, Malaysia

- Eva Hornecker, Pervasive Interaction Lab, Open Univ., UK

- Caroline Hummels, Department of Industrial Design, Technische Universiteit Eindhoven, The Netherlands

- Simon Lock, InfoLab21, Lancaster Univ., UK

- Gareth Loudon, National Centre for Product Design & Development Research, UWIC, UK

- Ann Morrisson, Information Environments Program, School of ITEE, Univ. of Queensland, Australia

- Mark Rouncefield, InfoLab21, Lancaster Univ., UK

- Paula Alexandra Silva, InfoLab21, Lancaster Univ. UK

- Jennifer Sheridan, BigDog Interactive, UK

- Lucy Suchman, Centre for Science Studies, Lancaster Univ., UK

- Steve Viller, Information Environments Program, School of ITEE, Univ. of Queensland, Australia

6. PROCEDURE

The Call for Papers for the workshop will be distributed to relevant mailing lists to solicit submission of 4-6 page position papers. We would also like to encourage contributions in other forms such as demonstration, artwork, performance, etc.

A website will be developed to support the workshop and will provide up-to-date information to prospective participants.

All submissions will be peer-reviewed and judged on the basis of originality, contribution to the field, technical and presentation quality, and relevance to the workshop. All accepted contributions will be published in the workshop proceedings.

The workshop will run over two days and will include invited talks, short individual presentations, and group activities. The latter will be designed to encourage interaction among participants and discussion on selected themes. The workshop will conclude by consolidating the findings over the two days and generate some tangible outputs.

We are also planning to have a slot for some prototype demos that exemplify the issues surrounding physicality.

The DEPtH project will fund two speakers to give a keynote address on their viewpoints on physicality to the workshop. We are looking for renowned researchers to stretch our conceptions of physicality, for example with a philosophy, sociology or emerging technologies background.

Building from this workshop and the previous one, we are planning a journal special issue and would hope that some of the workshop contributions will be expanded for submission to this.

7. ACKNOWLEDGMENTS

The DEPtH: Designing for Physicality Project is jointly funded by AHRC/EPSRC on research grant AH/E507646.

8. REFERENCES

[1] Weiser. M. The computer for the 21st Century. Sci Am 265(3), 1991, 99-104.

[2] Ghazali, M., Ramduny-Ellis, D., Hornecker, E., Dix, A. (Eds) Proceedings of the First International Workshop on Physicality, Physicality 2006 (6-7 February 2006), Lancaster University, UK, ISBN: 1862201781, http://www.physicality.org/physicality2006/Physicality2006Complete.zip.

Tutorials

Using Personas Effectively

Peter Bagnall
SurfaceEffect
18a Castle Park
Lancaster, UK
+44 (0)1524 39145

pete@surfaceeffect.com

ABSTRACT

Personas are a powerful design and communication tool to help all those involved in the creation of interactive systems to better focus their efforts on their users. A persona is a fictional character made to represent an archetypal user, and is best derived from field research. They help direct design, and communicate both to marketing and engineering teams.

Keywords

Personas, Empathy, Design Methodology

1. TUTORIAL OVERVIEW

Personas have become an increasingly common tool in the interaction designer's armoury over the last five years. But while many are using personas, few are getting the full benefit of the technique. While using personas may appear straightforward, there are a number of subtleties, which can substantially increase their effectiveness. There are also a number of non-obvious applications, which will help delegates get more from the method.

For any design project, understanding your users is clearly of vital importance. Personas are a highly effective, easy to use, method for ensuring that understanding is infused into the design throughout the development lifecycle.

Peter has substantial experience using personas. He worked for two years at Cooper, Alan Cooper's firm in Silicon Valley, which is credited with inventing the persona methodology. His research also includes persona methodology, specifically examining where the technique breaks down. He has taught the technique on Lancaster Universities MRes course for the last two years.

2. KEY LEARNING OUTCOMES

- How to collect relevant data for persona creation
- How to create personas, including from user interview data
- How to use personas to generate and guide an evolving design
- How to use personas to manage client expectations and requirements
- Why personas work, and the limits of their utility

3. TUTORIAL SCHEDULE

3.1 Segment 1 (90 minutes)

Lecture: Creating Personas
What is a persona?
How to create personas
    User research
    Persona generation
Lecture: Using personas
How are they used (in design, evaluation and communications)
    Primary, secondary and negative personas, and walk-on roles
Avoiding common design pitfalls
    elastic users
    self referential
Client Management through Personas

3.2 Segment 2 (90 minutes)

Practical exercise: User Research
After a demonstration, delegates will interview each other as a way of collecting a body of user research aimed at designing a Cinema guide system. This interview information will then be collated amongst the group, and between 2 and 4 personas generated from the interview data as group exercise directed by the tutor. A primary persona will then be selected for the exercise in segment 3.

3.3 Segment 3 (90 minutes)

Practical exercise: Persona Guided Design
In this exercise the design for the Cinema guide system will be derived from the personas. Delegates will be guided through a group exercise (3-4 delegates per group) to create scenarios that aim to address the primary persona's goals. These scenarios will then be used to form a conceptual design of the system, and set of functions the system must support. The emerging design will be tested against the persona to ensure it is appropriate.

3.4 Segment 4 (90 minutes)

Lecture: Persona Theory
Why do Personas work?
Persona Overload
    The purpose of the Primary Persona
Empathic Distance
Solutions to Persona Overload
Solutions to reduce Empathic Distance
Persona Reuse - Risks

Discussion & Questions
The last 30 minutes of the day will be reserved for discussions arising out of the exercises, and delegates specific questions about how the technique might be applied in their organisations.

Introducing HCI: A Practitioner's Guide

Steve Cummaford
IMG Media
McCormack House
London
W4 2TH

steve.cummaford@imgworld.com

John Long
University College London
Gower Street
London
WC1H 0AP

j.long@ucl.ac.uk

ABSTRACT

HCI continues to grow in popularity amongst commercial practitioners, many of whom have no formal training or education in HCI. Conferences, such as HCI 2007, offer an attractive means for practitioners to increase their knowledge and skills. However, many such practitioners can find it difficult to understand how research presentations relate to their specific needs. They often fail to make the most of their attendance at conferences and can struggle to pull through knowledge from the HCI research reported into their own practices, due to their lack of HCI training. This tutorial presents an introduction to the discipline of HCI in the form of a practitioner's guide, and so seeks to help delegates identify conference sessions, which offer the most promise for delivering value to the commercial practitioner. In so doing, it suggests ways in which the research can be pulled through into their practices, so increasing their engagement with HCI.

1. INTRODUCTION

Discussions with attendees at various conferences (including the HCI series) have indicated that this lack of HCI training reduced the benefit of conference attendance. In particular, they welcomed support in orienting themselves to the general theme of the conference, relative to their goals, and then selecting specific sessions to attend. The tutorial therefore meets the aims of the stated conference theme by supporting a better understanding of 'HCI not as we know it' by introducing such practitioners to 'HCI as we know it'. In addition, the tutorial offers first time conference attendees support in maximising the value of their attendance, and thus encouraging their future attendance at the HCI conference series.

The tutorial presents an overview of the historical and theoretical foundations for HCI, followed by an overview of the UCD lifecycle. The UCD approach is then used to illustrate how the research, reported at conferences, can be pulled through into practice. The specific knowledge requirements of the participants will be identified via practical exercises. Audience participation during the tutorial will be via small group exercises, conducted during the sessions.

2. LEARNING OBJECTIVES

The learning objectives are:
- To understand the historical development of HCI as a discipline.
- To review and agree the theoretical foundations of HCI and the UCD development life-cycle.
- To identify how HCI research knowledge can better support their own practices.
- To identify sessions and presentations in the conference programme, which offer most promise for uptake in the participants' future work.

Following tutorial attendance, participants should be able:
- To define HCI activities with reference to the theoretical foundations of HCI.
- To understand the relationship between (academic) research and (commercial) practice.
- To identify HCI techniques, which address their specific needs in current and future work.
- To plan their conference attendance in the light of their learning requirements.

The tutorial is designed for practitioners with little or no formal training or education in HCI, who wish to make the most of their attendance, with reference to their specific knowledge requirements. Prerequisites for attendance are therefore: an interest in understanding HCI and how it can be integrated into participants' own work, to increase the effectiveness of their design activities, and to facilitate effective pull-through of research knowledge into their own practices.

3. OVERVIEW BY SESSION

3.1 History and theoretical foundations of HCI

Session 1 presents an overview of the development of HCI as an academic and commercial discipline, from early time and motion studies through to World War 2 Ergonomics of sonar and radar systems to the present day, via the advent of the PC and interactive computing, virtual reality; mobile telephony and the notions of usability, user experience and affective interaction, that is, including the new frontiers, associated with the theme of HCI 2007. The theoretical foundations for HCI are defined, focusing on the need to specify successful design in terms of achieving performance targets, based on frameworks, modelling and notions of process. The theoretical foundations are presented in order to orient participants to the concepts presented later in the tutorial. The relationship between academic research and commercial development is presented using timelines, to illustrate the status of current research programmes as drivers of future commercial practice.

3.2 Overview of HCI in the system development lifecycle

Session 2 presents an overview of HCI methods, in context of the system development lifecycle. The 'prototype and test' approach of usability engineering is contrasted with the HCI engineering approach of using models of the user, device and domain during design. The benefits of this approach are demonstrated via examples taken from recent work undertaken by the tutors. The practical component of the session involves the selection of specific methods for hypothetical design projects, and justification of the resources required in order to undertake these methods during the design process.

3.3 Relations between HCI research and practice

The first afternoon session explores the relationship between HCI research knowledge, and HCI techniques to support requirements definition, design, and evaluation. Examples of established HCI knowledge and techniques are related to their research antecedents, in order better to understand the potential for research knowledge to support future HCI practice. Examples of research knowledge to be presented at the conference will then be discussed in the light of this relationship.

The session will be illustrated with a case study of the redesign of a high-traffic website, conducted by one of the tutors. The case study is intended to support delegates in mapping HCI research knowledge and design techniques to domains with which they are likely to be familiar, thus enabling a better understanding of the pull through of research knowledge into practice.

3.4 Conference programme review

The final session will review the conference programme in terms of the practitioner's introductory guide to HCI, in order for the participants to identify the most promising sessions for the specific needs of the participants. The session will commence with a practical exercise, in which the participants will, in the manner of UCD user requirements, exposed and agreed in Session 2, identify their key knowledge requirements, and goals for conference attendance. The conference programme will then be reviewed, in the light of participants' needs identified during the practical exercise. The aim of the session is to identify the conference presentations and interactive sessions, which offer the most promise for incrementing participants' knowledge and meeting their specific requirements. Delegates will be encouraged to identify the relations between the conference programme and their specific needs, both in terms of Conceptual and Detailed Design, in the manner of Session 2. Thus, they will put their new understanding of the discipline of HCI to work. The application will facilitate more effective participation in the conference generally. It is hoped that such a perspective will result in greater knowledge transfer from HCI research into practice, thus achieving the conference's general aims of exploring the new frontiers of HCI.

3.5 ABOUT THE PRESENTERS

Steve Cummaford worked as a Research Fellow in the Department of Psychology, investigating the design of effective e-commerce interfaces, before being appointed Lecturer in HCI, University College London (UCL). He continues to be active in teaching and research. He was a founding partner of Amberlight Partners, a leading HCI consultancy based in London, designing and evaluating websites for clients including Autotrader, AOL, Ask Jeeves, MSN and Yell. Steve is now at IMG Media, where he designs and produces websites and mobile applications, for clients including Manchester United, FIFA, The Open Championship, O2, Vodafone and Miss World.

Emeritus Professor John Long worked for Shell International as a line-manager. He then joined the Medical Research Council's Applied Psychology Unit, Cambridge conducting HCI research and managing major consultancy projects. He was Director of the Ergonomics & HCI Unit (UCL), where he supervised and mentored both students and members of academic staff. He has authored/co-authored over 200 publications and managed more than 40 grants. He has acted as consultant to numerous companies, on a wide range of practices. He was awarded the Bartlett Medal for research and received the IEA's Outstanding Educator Award. He is currently Emeritus Professor at the UCL Interaction Centre.

Old Cards, New Tricks:
Applied Techniques in Card Sorting

William Hudson

Syntagm Ltd

10 Oxford Road

Abingdon, UK OX14 2DS

+44 1235 522859

whudson@acm.org

ABSTRACT

Card sorting is an extremely useful technique in the design of interactive systems. However, it is under-used in practice – often through a lack of understanding and the complexities of cluster analysis. This half-day, hands-on tutorial uses concrete examples taken from live web sites to guide participants through the analysis, design and execution of card sorting activities, particularly as they apply to web navigation. Specific topics presented include open and closed sorting, rapid data collection using bar codes, cluster analysis and extensions to traditional analyses using quality of fit metrics and measures of deviation.

Categories and Subject Descriptors

H.5.2 [**User Interfaces**]: Evaluation/Methodology; Theory and methods.

General Terms

Design, Human Factors.

Keywords

Card Sorting, Cluster Analysis, Dendograms, Dendrograms, Topography, Navigation Design.

1. INTRODUCTION

(This brief paper provides a flavour of the content of the tutorial. It is based on a longer article written for ACM interactions [1]).

Card sorting is a knowledge elicitation technique often used by information architects, interaction designers and usability professionals to establish or assess the navigation hierarchy of a web site. The items are typically menu entries or hyperlinks while the groups are categories or headings. The process involves asking participants to sort items into meaningful groups. In open card sorts the number and names of groups are decided by each participant while in the closed card sorts these factors are fixed by the researcher in advance.

2. CARD SORTING ANALYSIS

© William Hudson, 2007

Published by the British Computer Society

Volume 2 Proceedings of the 21st BCS HCI Group Conference

HCI 2007, 3-7 September 2007, Lancaster University, UK

Devina Ramduny-Ellis & Dorothy Rachovides (Editors)

Analysis of card sorting results range from simple counting of the number of times items were grouped together to the rather intimidating monothetic agglomerative cluster analysis (known simply as cluster analysis in most cases). Unfortunately, no single technique provides everything a researcher needs to know, especially if convincing evidence is needed to persuade colleagues or customers of the effectiveness of a proposed design.

2.1 Convincing Evidence

The evidence we need falls into three categories:

- Participants. Are these the right participants for our site? Are they all thinking about the items and their groupings in a similar way? Do they have a clear understanding of the card sorting task itself?

- Items. Are the item names well-understood by participants? Are there alternatives that should be considered – perhaps terms users are more familiar with?

- Groups. For closed card sorts, have we chosen the right number of groups and names for each? For open sorts, are participants largely in agreement about the number of groups needed? How well do participants feel the items fit into their groups?

Happily, the answer to this last question – how well participants feel the items fit into their groups – can also help us with many of the other issues listed. Coupled with a few data collection guidelines and alternative presentations of results, we can collect fairly comprehensive evidence about what is and what is not going to work in our navigation hierarchies.

2.2 Quality of Fit by Item

So let's examine this last question in some more detail: How well do participants feel the items fit into their groups? It is possible to argue that this question is redundant; that the items must fit into their groups relatively well in any given set of results, because that is how the participant decided to group them. However, practical experience says otherwise. In many cases, participants place items into groups that are "good enough" but not necessarily ideal (satisficing versus maximizing behaviour). By asking participants to provide a "quality of fit" measure the cluster analysis can be extended to include the strength of relationship between items. Furthermore, analyzing quality of fit by participant or by item can give us useful insights into the some of the thought processes behind the sorting activity. For example, *figure 1* shows quality of fit averaged by item[1] for a closed card sort based on wines. The highest quality of fit in this example is

---

[1] Quality of fit is indicated by participants on the following scale: fair (1), good (2) or perfect (3). If an item is omitted by a participant, its quality of fit is 0.

Claret while the lowest is Beaujolais. They are both red so it seems a little curious that the graph shows such dis The answer lies in the group names that were assig advance: full-bodied reds, dry whites and spa Participants were happy to put both Claret and Beaujola "full-bodied reds" even though they apparently kne Beaujolais was not full-bodied and despite instructio they were to omit items they felt did not fit into any grou

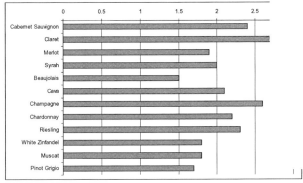

Figure 1: Mean quality of fit by item

In this case the quality of fit metric has allowed participants to express their dissatisfaction with Beaujolais (in the full-bodied reds group) while acknowledging their reluctance to discard the item entirely.

2.3 Alternatives to the Dendogram

Card sorting results are traditionally shown using a tree-like figure known as a dendogram. Unfortunately, in many applications, dendograms hide more information than they show. A simple alternative that is explored in the tutorial is a simple surface map of the underlying proximity matrix used for cluster analysis (each cell in the matrix is the frequency with which card pairs appeared in the same groups weighted by average quality of fit for the pair). An example, produced using Microsoft Excel, is shown in *figure 2*.

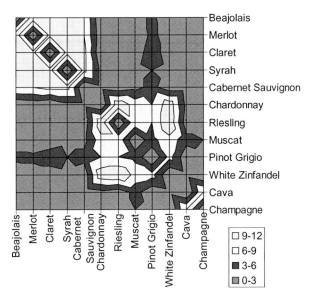

Figure 2: Surface map of the weighted proximity matrix

The map shows three distinct groups with anomalies centred on Pinto Grigio. Further investigation brought to light a terminological confusion: participants were not generally familiar with Pinot Grigio (white) and were associating it with Pinot Noir (red). Consequently, participants grouped Pinto Grigio with red wines almost as frequently as they did white. While a hint of this problem would have been discernable in a traditional dendogram, it would not have been as dramatically obvious.

3. REFERENCES

[1] Hudson, W. Playing your cards right: getting the most from card sorting for navigation design. *interactions*, 12(5), 2005, 56–58.

AJAX[1] Design and Usability

William Hudson
Syntagm Ltd
10 Oxford Road
Abingdon, UK OX14 2DS
+44 1235 522859

whudson@acm.org

ABSTRACT
AJAX, and related approaches that enable greater levels of interaction within web pages, have the potential to both help and hinder usability. This half-day interactive tutorial examines the issues, providing examples and guidance on appropriate application of these technologies.

Categories and Subject Descriptors
H.5.2 [**User Interfaces**]: Graphical User Interfaces; User-centred design.

General Terms
Design, Human Factors.

Keywords
AJAX, Change Blindness, Attentional Gambling, Flow.

1. INTRODUCTION
At its inception, the World Wide Web used a page-based model with most changes of content requiring that a new page be loaded from the host site. This approach introduced a number of usability problems relating to users' inabilities to notice changes to content (change blindness) or, in the case of completely new pages, uncertainty over where their attention should be focused (attentional gambling). The move away from the page-at-a-time model afforded by client-side scripting, the Document Object Model and AJAX[1] can help to address these issues when used appropriately. However, they can easily introduce a large variety of usability problems instead of or in addition to those just described. The purpose of this tutorial is to introduce attendees to the issues, provide guidelines on the appropriate use of AJAX from a usability perspective and to review a case study of a sample AJAX implementation.

2. ATTENTIONAL ISSUES
2.1 Change Blindness
Change blindness occurs when the movement normally associated with change is temporarily masked. With the traditional page-at-a-time model, this masking occurs every time a new page is loaded[1]. For example, in the tutorial, the image shown in figure 1 is alternated with one that includes a

non-trivial difference. Because of a 250 ms grey field that separates the two images in time, many participants often do not find the change at all.

Figure 1: Change Blindness Example

A related issues, inattention blindness, where users do not see even very large changes because their attention is elsewhere on page, can The more dynamic nature of AJAX can help to avoid these issues when used appropriately, but designers must be careful to address 'mud splash blindness' (where a visual distraction can mask change) and attentional gambling, where users simply guess incorrectly where they should be looking on the page.

2.2 Attentional Gambling
Attentional gambling[2] refers to the choices that users must make when viewing a page. For example, in completing a single column form, users will tend to work in left-to-right, top-to-bottom order. Messages or controls that appear in the periphery of the screen will tend to be ignored unless special steps are taken – such as animation – to make them more apparent. The more dynamic approach to page updates allowed by AJAX can improve the success with which users will see intended feedback but only when account is taken on where attention is likely to be focussed.

A general example is shown in figure 1. After adding an item to their shopping basket, users will focus their attention on A (at the Add button) but the site in question updates the basket details at B (in the top right corner). Consequently, users tend not to notice that information.

---

[1] Asynchronous JavaScript And XML.

Figure 2: Attentional Gambling Example

3. FLOW

AJAX technologies can also be used to improve flow – a user's engagement and sense of immersion in an interaction. Again, as with attentional issues, designers must optimise feedback so that users feel in control without the frustration of excessive interruptions.

4. CASE STUDY

The tutorial concludes with a case study of a simple AJAX application that follows web design standards:

- Separation of content (HTML), presentation (CSS) and behaviour (scripting)

- Graceful degradation / progressive enhancement

The application demonstrates these basic principles and allows participants to understand the basic issues of the technology itself; the simple HTML and JavaScript used are fully explained.

5. REFERENCES

[1] Hudson, W. Designing for the Grand Illusion. *SIGCHI Bulletin*, 33, 2001, 8.

[2] Hudson, W. Attentional gambling: getting better odds from your web pages. *interactions*, 11(6), 2004, 55-56.

Managing Iterative Projects More Effectively: Theories, Techniques and Heuristics for HCI Practitioners

John Long
University College London
Gower Street
London
WC1H 0AP

j.long@ucl.ac.uk

Steve Cummaford
IMG Media
McCormack House
London
W4 2TH

steve.cummaford@imgworld.com

ABSTRACT

Most HCI specialists are involved, in one way or another, with iterative project management (IPM), as opposed to HCI, on a day-to-day basis. However, few specialists have any systematic training or exposure to IPM. Further, market pressures highlight the importance of HCI iterative and adaptive planning and development to meet changing conditions, associated with novel technology and customer change. This tutorial is intended to fill these gaps. IPM is characterised in terms of its theory, its methods and heuristics to support its practice. Exercises and mini-practicals support the integration of HCI into the heuristics, methods and theory of IPM. In the light of our recent experience, participants' IPM effectiveness, as either managers or as team members, is expected to increase as a result.

1. INTRODUCTION

Most HCI system development takes place within the context of the project, whether embedded, cash point, fun, web site or complex systems. Such projects are conducted by project managers and carried out by project teams. Most projects are iterative. As a result, HCI specialists are involved with iterative project management (IPM) on a day-to-day basis, including the iteration of the HCI/User-Centred Design (UCD) contributions, for which they are responsible. However, very few such specialists have any systematic training or exposure to IPM. Further, the increasing pressure of the introduction of novel technology and of the market place, constraining budgets, while shortening deadlines, ensures there is an ever-greater need to manage projects iteratively and to plan adaptively, consistent with both IPM and HCI/UCD constraints. Otherwise, the potential for IPM error will increase too. Changing plans, including those of UCD, within a fixed budget, has become a routine IPM requirement; but one, which is all-too-often carried out ineffectively. This tutorial supports both managers and team members in meeting this requirement, as well as filling the training/educational gap.

2. LEARNING OBJECTIVES

The learning objects for the participants are threefold:

- To understand the scope; theory; and practice of IPM, as they relate to HCI.
- To become acquainted with, and selectively to practise, UCD methods, in relation to IPM.
- To become familiar with IPM guidance, in the form of heuristics, which they can integrate into IPM and HCI methods.

Following tutorial attendance. Participants should be able:

- To follow up further their interest in IPM via the literature, the web and other sources.
- To make IPM issues explicit in their own UCD activities and to suggest approaches to them.
- To contribute to IPM best practice, within their own HCI projects.
- To become a more effective HCI member of the IPM team.

3. PARTICIPANTS

The tutorial is of interest to anyone involved in, or indeed concerned by, HCI/UCD, including: human factors and software engineers; project managers; usability specialists; user experience architects; designers; graphic artists; web services teams; project sponsors; marketers; financers etc. The pre-requisites for the tutorial are either that participants have some experience of IPM projects, either as managers or as HCI/UCD team members, or that they have an interest in HCI and IPM, directly or indirectly, that they would like to develop further.

4. OVERVIEW BY SESSION

4.1 IPM theory

The question of what is IPM, as it relates to HCI/UCD, is answered by proposals, concerning: its definition (What is iterative? What is IPM?); its concerns (resources; effort; people/teams; and risks); its discipline: (research; tools; case-studies) and practice (iterative; incremental; evolutionary; and adaptive); and the requirement for IPM, as it relates to HCI/UCD (common managers' problems and common team members' problems). IPM knowledge is reviewed in terms of: Waterfall problems; research; standards; experts; and business cases. IPM practice is characterised by: its types (risk-driven; client-driven;); its methods (planning; development; and Agile); and its development cycle (pre-production; production; maintenance; and evaluation), as concerns HCI/UCD practice.

4.2 IPM method

IPM planning and development methods are reviewed. A web site development method is selected for particular address and is used to illustrate the nature of IPM and HCI/UCD practice. However, its general aspects are emphasised. The major phases and stages of the method are described and illustrated. These comprise: pre-production – project clarification; solution definitions; and project specification; production – content; design; construction; testing, launch and hand-over; maintenance; and evaluation. HCI and UCD practice and methods are situated with respect to the IPM method.

4.3 IPM practice

Heuristics have been culled from a wide range of different sources, both published and experienced. The heuristics are organised around the following topics: project management: planning; iterating; environment; requirements; and testing. All topics are illustrated and exemplified. Participants practise mapping the heuristics (3) to the methods (2) in the light of theory (1), as they concern HCI/UCD practice.

5. REVIEW

The tutorial is well suited to presentation at HCI 2007.The level is introductory to intermediary. It is accessible to participants, newly involved or interested in IPM and so, introductory. The tutorial provides definitions of IPM, surveys IPM knowledge, and reviews the need for IPM, as it relates to UCD. It is also intended to improve IPM practice of participants with some experience of IPM and so, intermediary. It addresses issues such as: contingency planning; overlapping project activities; multi-team and multi-site working; and risk assessment. It is not intended for experienced IPM managers, managers of very large and complex projects or team members, operating within mature and well-structured practice.

The purpose of the tutorial is to increase awareness of IPM and to contribute to IPM and UCD best practice in participants' future projects. The significance of the tutorial is to fill a gap for both HCI project team members and managers. As such, it is entirely suitable for HCI 2007, fitting well with the theme of 'exploring new frontiers'.

5.1 ABOUT THE PRESENTERS

John Long initially worked for Shell Oil International, as a manager, before joining the Medical Research Council's Applied Psychology Unit, Cambridge, as a researcher in Human Factors and HCI. He moved to UCL and led a research group for 20 years. He is currently Emeritus Professor of Cognitive Engineering at UCL. He has authored and co-authored over 200 publications and has acted as an external consultant to many companies, government agencies and universities. He has extensive experience in managing large HCI projects. He was awarded the Outstanding Educator Award by the IEA. He has wide interests, including: usability engineering; applied psychology; office and high street systems; command and control systems; distributed work; and telecommunications-supported work.

Steve Cummaford worked as a Research Fellow in the Department of Psychology, investigating the design of effective e-commerce interfaces, before being appointed Lecturer in HCI, University College London (UCL). He continues to be active in teaching and research. He was a founding partner of Amberlight Partners, a leading HCI consultancy based in London, designing and evaluating websites for clients including Autotrader, AOL, Ask Jeeves, MSN and Yell. Steve is now at IMG Media, where he manages the design and production of websites and mobile applications for clients including Manchester United, FIFA, The Open Championship, O2, Vodafone and Miss World.

Introduction to Social Network Analysis

Panayiotis Zaphiris
Centre for HCI Design
City University, London EC1V 0HB
+44-20-7040-8168
zaphiri@soi.city.ac.uk

Ulrike Pfeil
Centre for HCI Design
City University, London EC1V 0HB
+44-20-7040-4214
u.pfeil-1@city.ac.uk

ABSTRACT

Online communities and social software are revolutionizing the way we interact with the web. Analysing the interactions that take place there is complex. Social Network Analysis (SNA) is a powerful way of doing such analysis. This tutorial provides a detailed introduction to SNA. The theory is backed up with a number of practical case studies.

Categories and Subject Descriptors

H4.3. Information System Applications: Communication Applications; K4.2. Computers and society: Social issues

General Terms

Design, Experimentation, Theory.

Keywords

Social Network Analysis, Online Communities, Online Research Methodologies

1. Motivation

Social network theory views a network as a group of actors who are connected by a set of relationships. Social networks develop when actors meet and form some kind of relation between each other. These can be of an informal as well as of a formal nature. Hereby actors are often people, but can also be nations, organizations, objects etc. Social Network Analysis (SNA) focuses on patterns of relations between these actors. It seeks to describe networks of relations as fully as possible. This includes teasing out the prominent patterns in such networks, tracing the flow of information through them, and discovering what effects these relations and networks have on people and organizations. It can therefore be used to study network patterns of organizations, ideas, and people that connected via various means in an online environment. Figure 1 shows an example of SNA visualization (sociogram).

Although social network analysis could be extensively used to analyze current topics of interest in the area of HCI, e.g. human-human interactions in online communities or the connectivity of organizations on the internet, unfortunately this is very rarely used. We believe that this tutorial at HCI 2007 would be a valuable contribution to the HCI community as it will make the topic more widely known to HCI researchers and practitioners who will find it of use.

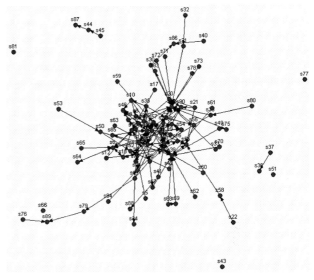

Figure 1: An example of an SNA sociogram

2. Benefit

This tutorial provides an overview of this analytic technique and demonstrates how it can be used in HCI (especially Computer Mediated Communication and CSCW) research and practise. This topic becomes even more important these days with the increasing popularity of social networking websites (e.g. youtube, myspace, MMORPGs etc.) and the research interest in studying them. As people increasingly use online communities for social interaction, new methods are needed to study these phenomena. SNA is a valuable contribution to HCI research as it gives an opportunity to study the complex patterns of online communication.

3. Learning Outcomes

Upon completion of this Full-day tutorial, participants should:

o   Be able to understand the basics of social network analysis, its terminology and background (part 1)

o   Be able to transform communication data to network data (part 1)

o   Know practically how social network analysis (SNA) can be applied to HCI (especially CMC) analysis (part 2)

o   Understand the different possible presentations of social networks (e.g in a matrix or a sociogram)

o   Get familiar with the use of standard SNA tools and software (part 2)

o   Be able to derive practical and useful information through SNA analysis that would help design an innovative and successful online community. (part 2) o   Part 1 will be delivered in the morning and part 2 in the afternoon.

4. Content

This is a full day tutorial and its content is divided into two parts, each of which is structured in small groups to maximize the interaction among participants.

In the first part, we participants will be exposed to the introduction of SNA and online research methodologies, get familiar with the terminology and definitions of SNA. Additionally to the presentation of lecture material, small informal exercises and discussion will be held in order to encourage interaction. This will include:

o   Introduction to Online Research Methodologies

o   Introduction into the components and characteristics of social networks

o   Information about relational data that is used for SNA along with the different ways that the data can be presented

o   Presentation of the different measurements of network characteristics within SNA

o   Discussion of different approaches towards SNA

The second part will address the practical uses of SNA. Through a series of interactive exercises, a number of case studies will be demonstrated and discussed. Case studies will be draw from diverse areas (e.g. use of SNA to study age differences in CMC, use of SNA in universal design and research). Ways of using SNA to study new forms of CMC such as MMORPGs, Wikis, blogs etc. will also be discussed.

Furthermore, exercises will take part to encourage the participants to think about the application of SNA in their work or research area. As SNA is a flexible method that can be applied in different ways, we think it is important to create space in the tutorial for discussing and elaborating on the possibilities of SNA to the research or working areas of the participants. This will be further supported through demonstrations of popular SNA tools (e.g. netminer, pajek)

5. Target Audience

We welcome practitioners and academics interested in computer mediated communication, universal design, especially researchers and practitioners who are interested in

domains that social network analysis can be applied. As the tutorial will be introductory, no background knowledge about Social Network Analysis or statistics is required.

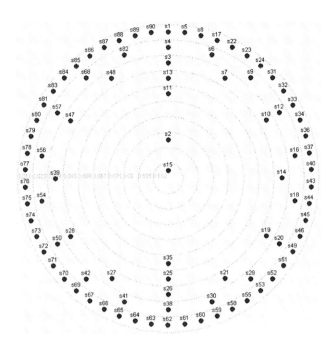

Figure 2: A characteristic SNA centrality diagram

6. Past Delivery of this Tutorial

A similar tutorial has been accepted at HCII 2007 and will be delivered this summer in China. The content of the tutorial is also delivered as part of two lectures of the Inclusive Design module of the Human-Centred Systems course we have at City University. The presenters of this tutorial have published extensively in this area including a paper in TOCHI on SNA, a full paper at CHI 2007 on empathic online communities, a chapter on online communities in the HCI handbook (by Sears and Jacko), two special issues on computer games and HCI (with strong emphasis on communities around computer games). In addition the authors are currently editing a special issue of the ACM Transactions on Accessible Computing (TACCESS) on online communities for people with disabilities.

HCI Practice Day

Information Architecture with IBM Task Modeler

Colin Bird
IBM United Kingdom Limited
Hursley Park
Winchester SO21 2JN
+44-1962-816025

colinl_bird@uk.ibm.com

Mark Farmer
IBM United Kingdom Limited
Birmingham Road
Warwick CV34 5JL
+44-1926-465232

farmerm@uk.ibm.com

ABSTRACT

The IBM Task Modeler supports the rapid creation and analysis of hierarchical task models, thereby providing a valuable and naturally visual tool for information architects. Task Modeler not only facilitates the essential processes of design, validation, and modification but also enables an information architect to develop and apply schemes for information classification.

Categories and Subject Descriptors

H.5.2 [**Information Interfaces and Presentation (e.g., HCI)**]: User Interfaces - *Graphical user interfaces (GUI), Interaction styles*. D.2.10 [**Software Engineering**]: Design Tools and Techniques - *Evolutionary prototyping*.

General Terms

Documentation, Design, Experimentation, Human Factors.

Keywords

Modelling, Task Analysis, DITA, Visualization.

1. INTRODUCTION

On the alphaWorks web site, the overview describes Task Modeler as a "tool for modeling human activity as a hierarchy of tasks and related elements." [1] In our accompanying paper, we demonstrate how Task Modeler enables analysts to develop their task model representations visually and rapidly create, explore, analyse, and share these models [2]. One can fairly easily transform the alphaWorks description to a "tool for information architecture." Information architects work from goal-oriented models of the way in which users will interact with the content, so Task Modeler provides a naturally visual medium for realizing the architectural design.

The information provided by IBM about its solutions and products includes Eclipse-based information centers, for which DITA (the Darwin Information Typing Architecture [3]) is used to author the content as topics and the navigation scheme as a set of maps.

In this paper we consider how the design process can be assisted by visual representation with Task Modeler. Our context for this study is a repository of guidelines and best practices, presented as an information center for use by the

Information Development groups at IBM Hursley.

1.1 The information repository

The basic aim of this repository can be stated as "to encourage commonality between groups by sharing guidance about good practice." The interface to the repository is an Eclipse-based information center, with the content being authored in DITA.

1.2 Modelling DITA

Task Modeler uses the hierarchical task analysis (HTA) approach that models human activity as a hierarchy of goals, tasks, and subtasks. Originally developed for the conceptual design of interactive systems, Task Modeler has evolved to comprise several different dialects. The dialect that we shall be considering uses the DITA Modelling perspective. We follow the basic approach described by Larner in his tutorial [4].

2. MODELLING THE REPOSITORY ARCHITECTURE

The use model for the information repository envisages members of the information development groups wanting to find out and/or understand aspects of practice related to procedure, policy, and the infrastructure.

Task Modeler provides a naturally visual medium so, in the early stages of representing this use model as an information architecture, we adopt the radial diagram view to capture the essential components without implying any particular sequencing. Our initial view, as shown in Figure 1, comprises a conceptual description of the organisation and its roles and responsibilities, and three high-level ('container') tasks:

- Understanding the tools and technologies used in User Technologies

- Maintaining this repository

- Delivering consistent information

Working with this radial diagram, we decide to alter the initial sequence and to expand the 'Delivering' container task. At this stage, we change to the Indented List view, because its format most closely corresponds to the structure of the DITA map that

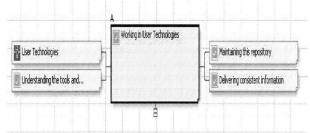

Figure 1, The radial diagram view of the initial representation of the repository use model

will be the formal representation of our architecture. Figure 2 shows the Indented List view of the architecture at this stage. Tasks 3 through 6 replace "Delivering consistent information".

We then evolve the architecture in Task Modeler by creating nodes of different types to reflect the kind of information required to describe the tasks derived from the use model.

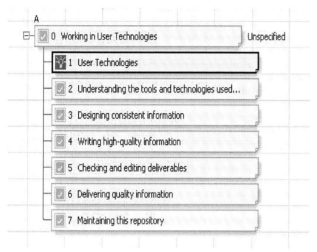

Figure 2. The indented list view of the evolving information architecture

3. TASK MODELER FACILITIES FOR INFORMATION ARCHITECTURE

In addition to the options for working with DITA maps and topics that Larner describes in [4], Task Modeler provides the following facilities:

- Creating a new information center. Moreover, the next version of Task Modeler will enable the table of contents to be edited and the resulting changes to be written back to the source DITA maps.

- Assembling information components into solutions with the use of DITA anchor and navref elements. Henry & Fell describe the use of these elements in [5]

- Creating a new map from a template that embodies information architecture best practices

- Visualizing property values, particularly the 'Href status' property

- Visualizing the links in relationship tables

4. TASK MODELER AS A TOOL FOR INFORMATION CLASSIFICATION

DITA enables topics and topic collections to be classified with the taxonomy specialization [3, 6]. A fundamental aspect of the classification process is the design, construction, and maintenance of the taxonomy. The DITA Modelling perspective and the hierarchical nature of the models created make Task Modeler an ideal vehicle for working with taxonomies in DITA.

The next version of Task Modeler is planned to include support for the DITA taxonomy specialization. In this paper we shall be presenting and illustrating early results from work on taxonomies for use with information centers sourced with DITA.

5. REFERENCES

[1] *IBM Task Modeler Overview*, http://www.alphaworks.ibm.com/tech/taskmodeler

[2] Farmer, M. and Bird, C, *Creating and Analysing Models in IBM Task Modeler*, HCI 2007

[3] *DITA (Darwin Information Typing Architecture)*: http://dita.xml.org/

[4] Larner, L., ISTC Communicator, Autumn 2006, pp.14-17

[5] Henry, C. and Fell, J. *Best Practices*, Volume 8, Issue 5, October 2006

[6] Hennum, E., Anderson, R. and Bird, C. *Subject classification with DITA and SKOS*, http://www-128.ibm.com/developerworks/xml/library/x-dita10/

Creating and Analysing Models in IBM Task Modeler

Mark Farmer
IBM United Kingdom Limited
Birmingham Road
Warwick, CV34 5JL
+44-1926-465232

farmerm@uk.ibm.com

Colin Bird
IBM United Kingdom Limited
Hursley Park
Winchester, SO21 2JN
+44-1962-816025

colinl_bird@uk.ibm.com

ABSTRACT
We illustrate the basic constituents of a model and demonstrate how the facilities of Task Modeler, such as the visualization options, enable the rapid creation, analysis, and communication of the model

Categories and Subject Descriptors
I.6.5 [**Model development**]: Modeling methodologies

General Terms
Documentation, Design, Human Factors.

Keywords
Modelling, HTA, Task Analysis, DITA

1.   INTRODUCTION
IBM Task Modeler is a tool for creating rich models of human behaviour.

Originally developed to support pure task analysis techniques, as described by John Annet [3], Task Modeler allows an overall goal to be decomposed into tasks, and further into subtasks. The result is a Hierarchical Task Analysis (HTA). Later versions also support the development of hierarchical models other than the classic HTA.

In this paper we demonstrate how Task Modeler enables analysts to develop their task model representations visually and "rapidly create, explore, analyse, and share these models. [1]"

2.   CREATING A MODEL
A model is developed to decompose and organize a complex area of interest until it is more fully understood. For example, an HTA can be created to understand the user's tasks during software development; or a DITA map [2] can be created to model the structure and content of an online help system [4]. Task Modeler supports the creation of models of different types through *dialects*.

2.1   Dialects
When creating a model in Task Modeler, you are asked which style of model to create. Task Modeler comes with a set of pre-defined modelling styles, each of which is defined by a Task Modeler dialect. Version 5 provides the following dialects: DITA maps, Roles and Goal models, Question Option Criteria (QOC) models, a use case analysis, mind maps and site maps.

A dialect includes templates and sample models, allowing models to be created and further developed with concrete examples. Dialect-specific method and modelling help is also included, and presented to the user throughout development. These dialect contents help the creation of new models, and aid the model's continued development.

2.2   Nodes and Properties
Each model dialect defines the model elements and metadata that construct the model, where Task Modeler represents each model element as a *node*, and each item of metadata as a *property*.

Once a model style is selected, a model can be created by hierarchically creating and arranging instances of the available node types, and setting property values.

As an example, to create a use case analysis model, a *Use Case* node is added to represent each use case. Use cases are decomposed into steps, by adding child *Step* nodes, which are further described by child *Actor Action* and *System Response* nodes. See Figure 1.

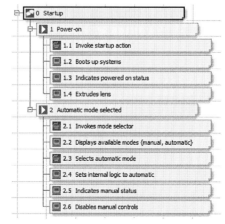

Figure 1: A use case decomposed into steps, actor actions and machine responses.

Each node type also provides a distinct set of properties to more fully describe the model. For example, a Use Case can define the *actors* that it applies to, and the *trigger* that is the source for the use case; a Step can be linked to by a source *Requirement* node, and document step-specific *issues*. The list of properties can also be customized and extended, making Task Modeler a flexible modelling tool.

Each property is of a certain type, examples of which are: free-form text, integer, real number, constrained keyword, date, and an external file reference.

The property type serves two purposes, firstly to constrain the possible values, where appropriate, and secondly to allow analysis of the model's property values, in a type-specific way. This property analysis is described below.

Task Modeler has a highly visual modelling interface, allowing nodes to be created and added to the model efficiently and clearly. This is enhanced with intuitive keyboard shortcuts, based around the standard arrow keys, to rapidly add nodes relative to the selected node.

Nodes can be dragged to other parts of the model, allowing for rapid moving and copying of nodes. This promotes a hands-on and low-commitment modelling experience, very similar to using a stack of sticky notes.

The model editor automatically lays out the model hierarchically, ensuring the model structure is always clear during editing, but supports alternative model views. This allows analysts to concentrate on modelling, rather than ensuring the model is correctly and sensibly laid out.

3. ANALYSING A MODEL

A model is only as good as the information it contains. An incomplete or incorrectly structured model, or a model containing erroneous property values, can cause more serious and expensive problems later in the development process. Therefore it is important to get the model right. Task Modeler provides mechanisms for ensuring the accuracy of a model, as early in the development process as possible.

3.1 Visualization

To ensure property values are accurate and complete, Task Modeler can visually show them on the model. Property values can be viewed either as symbols, colours, label contents, emphasis and network lines. See figure 2.

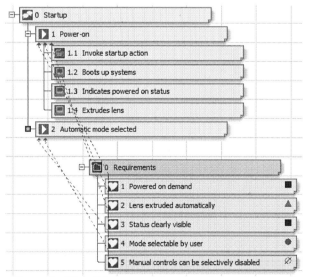

Figure 2: Visualizing properties as symbols, colours, and network lines

Recent versions have improved these visualization facilities, allowing the model to talk-back to the user. This provides a powerful way to ensure the model is fully and accurately documented. It also highlights hotspots and trends within the model, and areas that might need further work and analysis.

3.2 Managing a Complex Model

Typically the models can quickly become large and unmanageable, making them difficult to use effectively. Task Modeler provides facilities for selectively hiding and showing parts of the hierarchy, allowing the user to focus on just the area of interest.

Task Modeler allows particularly large models to be split across multiple files, which are linked in a variety of ways. Task Modeler can then show the entire model, by visually *embedding* the linked models within their linking model, allowing the model to still be viewed, analysed and used as a whole.

3.3 Validation

Version 5 of Task Modeler provides embedded model-specific validation, by presenting a list of model problems on the analyst's request. This further ensures that the structure and content of the model are complete and accurate.

4. REUSING MODELS

Along with ensuring that a model is accurate, it is important to understand where it fits in the overall development process. The resulting models are not the end of the work, and are used as inputs to the next phase of development, or as a working document that is constantly referenced and updated as development continues.

As the model continues to be central to development, Task Modeler provides facilities for using and reusing the model content. Models can be exported in a variety of ways, for example use case models can be exported as HTML Use Case reports, which document the relationships between use cases, requirements and development line items, or as a simpler development plan to use as development progresses.

5. REFERENCES

[1] *IBM Task Modeler Overview*, http://www.alphaworks.ibm.com/tech/taskmodeler

[2] *DITA (Darwin Information Typing Architecture)*, http://dita.xml.org/

[3] Annett, J. Hierarchical Task Analysis. In *The Handbook of Task Analysis for Human-Computer Interaction* Lawrence Erlbaum, New Jersey, 2004.

[4] Bird, C. and Farmer, M, *Information Architecture with IBM Task Modeler*, HCI 2007

Eye Tracking in Practice

J.A.Renshaw
Leeds Metropolitan University
Usability North
Caedmon Hall, Beckett Park
+44(0)1138128608

t.renshaw@leedsmet.ac.uk

N.Webb
Amberlight Partners Ltd
58 Bloomsbury St.,
London WC 1B 3QT, UK
+44(0) 2027307779

Natalie@amber-light.co.uk

ABSTRACT

This paper describes the practical side of eye tracker use in the field of human computer interaction. The paper relates to usability evaluations in practice covering those topics of primary importance to practitioners including the business case for eye tracking and the technique's benefits and limitations. The authors describe techniques, based on practical experience, to be deployed to ensure success with eye tracking and provide some useful links and references for those contemplating adoption of the technique. Ideas on future practical areas of deployment are discuss.

Keywords

Eye tracking, application, evaluation.

1. INTRODUCTION

The purpose of this paper is to describe proposals for a presentation to be given by the authors, as part of the HCI Practice track, on the more practical side of the use of eye trackers in the field of human computer interaction. This will primarily cover usability but there will be references to other areas which are of topical interest. The presentation will not cover the psychological or physiological theoretical concepts behind eye tracking unless these issues are raised by questions from the audience.

2. PRESENTATION OUTLINE

- Background
- What it is the audience is going to get out of this presentation
  - o The financial case for eye tracking
  - o Some FAQs about Eye Tracking
  - o Wider benefits of eye tracking
  - o What makes a successful eye tracking based evaluation
  - o Areas of Application
- Useful books and links
- Summary

3. BACKGROUND

The problem with eye tracking is that when something is detected in a study the recipient of the information invariably says "I knew that already" or "a questionnaire would have picked that up!"

However, in reality it is doubtful that observers would be able to describe where players look whilst playing first shooter/racing car games and how their fixations are distributed over the screen, or what influence a film directors use of frames, camera angle or depth of focus has over eye movements, or where most of the audience look frame by frame when viewing a film. Everyone knows that an expert will faithfully recall the secret short cuts/areas of interest he/she uses when working with an application, or where a child's eyes are looking as you re-read a sentence of a story to them. Or do they? The determination of these things is possible with eye tracking but difficult with the more conventional evaluation tools.

The point being made is that the trick of getting eyetracking the recognition it deserves is to get the eye tracker to provide answers to questions that interviews and questionnaires have not a hope of answering economically if at all. Hopefully by the end of the current presentation the audience will have ideas about what those questions could be.

3.1 The Financial Case for Eyetracking

A state of the art eye tracker costs less than £20000 in a ready-to-use state. The equipment is very easy to use, robust and versatile for, in addition to eye movements, it records and time stamps mouse clicks, key depressions, web pages visited and can be also used as a normal computer terminal. Used in combination with a webcam it is a real productivity aid saving both analysts' time and adding to a study's accuracy. Participant processing rates can exceed 2 per hour for a moderately complex study.

Of course expense is a relative thing, some might prefer to replace the accountant's company car, some may not mind loosing a couple of contracts a year because their business could not offer the services a client wanted, some may not really appreciate the time spent at the coalface taking notes and/or wracking the analyst's memory for the context a particular note taken during an interview.

It is possible that an investment of this nature could be recouped within 18 months or less.

3.2 Table 1.Some FAQs about Eye Tracking

Question		Response 1		Response 2
What does eye tracking tell me that other techniques don't?		Quickly, easily and reasonably reliably where people look in real time and where they don't. For how long/fleetingly they look at specific areas or where they don't. The sequences of their gazes		
Well if they are so marvellous why haven't they caught on more?		More than what? Are you sure you know for certain how many leading edge usability consultancies **_don't_** have one?	But also because	The concept was new. Before technological improvements were made the techniques was perceived as invasive (one had to be in a lab and wear helmets), unreliable and temperamental and ROI uncertain.
Do you need much training to run an eye tracking session?	No	Operating the equipment and conducting the all important calibration process has been made very easy by the manufacturers	and yes	As with any evaluation using human beings it is important to plan ahead. The design of the study needs to be thought through if meaning full results are to be obtained.
Do evaluations take long to do?	No	It's a bit like "how long is a piece of string". But eye tracking yields a lot of data very quickly. Sensible results can be derived in as little as 15 minutes per participant. Visual renditions of the data are almost instantaneously available. Data is easily exported to spreadsheet applications	and yes	Large volumes of data can be generated. Interpretation of the data requires some knowledge of the theory behind visual perception, attention and statistics. For qualitative studies it takes time to match visual patterns to user behaviour.
Can eye tracking be incorporated into normal evaluation processes?	Yes	A modern state of the art eye tracking can be integrated into a website evaluation at any stage in the process and given that the eye tracker can record urls visited, mouse clicks and keyboard depressions it can be seen as a great productivity aid.	and no	Long eye tracking sessions may generate large data files which can be difficult to manage and may lead to system crashes. Java elements will not be shown in some renditions of the gaze data
Do clients like the outcomes?	Yes	An eye tracker quickly generates authoritative visually appealing outputs	and no	Clients want concise clear answers, they give the impression of not wanting to hear about complexity, probability and statistical significance.
Can clients view eye movements live?	Yes	Clients can view eye movements live on a separate screen	But	There are some technical restrictions.
Can eyetracking do everything including making the tea?		Eye tracking is not a silver bullet. It augments other techniques rather than being a panacea for all ills. There are still a few technical limitations e.g. showing fixations and scan paths over the Flash element of a website is, at the time of writing, not possible.	No	They don't make the tea!

3.3 The Wider Benefits of Eye Tracking

- Users' attention/inattention to specific areas can be demonstrated
- Some indication of strategies in problem solving can be elicited
- Permits exploration of problems with menus, navigation link issues and/or status indicator salience
- The data collected is not dependant on a participant's memory
- A large volume of objective quantifiable data can be collected
- Some eye movement patterns are involuntary being natural reactions to the visual scene and consequently less prone to participant bias
- Visual summaries of participant behaviour are quickly and easily rendered and data exported to databases or spreadsheets within a few key strokes
- The equipment used can be unobtrusive
- Complements other evaluation techniques and can be used to triangulate findings

3.4 What Makes for a Successful Eye Tracking Evaluation?

The following suggestions are made with the intention of ensuring success in conducting an eye tracking based evaluation. They have been gleaned by the authors from several years of practical experience

- Careful selection of the problem to be resolved in terms of playing to the strengths of the eye tracking technique and the economics of getting to an answer through other methodologies.
- Thinking through the possible outcomes and expected results.
- Careful planning, selection and rehearsal of the tasks to minimise the occurrence of an unexpected event and to make sure that the tasks are sufficiently demanding and relevant to avoid breeches of eye tracking theory.
- Careful and accurate calibration of the equipment to each participant. Many participants change their seating position after calibration it is important that this potential risk is avoided by getting them comfortable and in their normal posture before calibration starts.
- Allow time for analysis
- Use the recording of the eye movements as a prompt to memory during subsequent post evaluation interviews
- Use a microphone to record user reaction during and after the eye tracking evaluation and to inform post evaluation analysis of same.
- Make sure the evaluation is conducted within the relevant environmental ambiance.

3.5 Areas of Application for the Technique

- Evaluations of websites and productivity applications: the assessment of placement, salience and organisation of menus, advertisements, help buttons, system status advice
- Efficacy of search engine results displays
- User reaction to variations in advertising location and format
- Behaviour differences between experts and novices in (for example) reading, mammogram examination and location of metal fatigue in aircraft airframes
- Analysis of game playing and film viewing behaviours.

4. USEFUL ARTICLES and LINKS

Eye tracker manufacturers' websites: ASL, SMI and Tobii

Usability Practitioners: Amberlight; Bunnyfoot, Usability North to name but a few.

http://www.poynterextra.org/eyetrack2004/main.htm

http://www.cs.tufts.edu/~jacob/papers/ecem.pdf

5. SUMMARY

In this paper supporting the presentation the authors have delivered details about eye tracking as an evaluation tool albeit only in outline. Interest in this topic is growing. Both the advantages and limitations of this technique have been presented no punches have been pulled. Overall the technique is a cost effective, technologically advanced, accurate, robust, mobile, versatile evaluation tool; a more than useful addition to a practitioner's usability repertoire. The technique demands forward planning, vigilance against confounding effects, staff training in its use and data analysis skills. So what's new? All the techniques used in a practitioner's business make similar demands... don't they?

6. REFERENCES

[1] Goldberg, J.H. and Wichansky, A.M. (2003) In The Mind's Eye: Cognitive and applied aspects of Eye Movement Research (Eds. J.Hyona, R. Radach and H.Deubel. Oxford, Elsevier Science)

[2] Renshaw, J.A. and Webb, N. (2006). Getting a measure of satisfaction from eye tracking in Practice. CHI 2006 Workshop, Montreal, Canada.

[3] Webb,N. and Renshaw,J.A. (2006). Adding Value with Eye tracking. UPA 2006 Workshop, Omni Interlocken Broomfield, Colorado, USA.

[4] Renshaw,J.A. and Webb,N., (2005) Commercial Uses of Eye Tracking . HCI 2005 Workshop, Edinburgh, Scotland.

[5] Duchowski, A.T. (2003). Eye Tracking Methodology: Theory and Practice, Springer.

Doctoral Consortium

The Role of Input Devices in the Gaming Experience

Eduardo H. Calvillo Gámez
UCLIC
University College London
Remax House/Alfred Place 31-32
London, WC1E 7DP UK
+44-20-7679-5214

e.calvillo@ucl.ac.uk

ABSTRACT
This paper reports on my doctoral work done at UCLIC that looks at how novel input devices affect the gaming experience. The paper presents the motivation, question, methodology, expected contributions, partial results and time line to complete the thesis.

Categories and Subject Descriptors
H.1.2 User/Machine Systems

General Terms
Human Factors

Keywords
User Experience, Videogames, Input Devices.

1.MOTIVATION
During the last decade, Human Computer Interaction (HCI) has had an influx of new input devices that aim at providing a more real interaction between users and computers. Examples of these real interaction applications are Tangible User Interfaces, Ubiquitous Computing, Lightweight interfaces, and so on [4]. Although the nature of what makes an input device more real or surreal can be questioned, the projects that developed these new devices claim that the new devices provide a better interaction and are in general more usable. Without questioning the methodology used, it is not clear if the users of these new devices like them because of the novelty of the device or because they provide a better experience. The methodology of these projects is not questioned because it relies on an overall goal of providing a more usable application, if the user can perform a task more efficiently and effectively then the application is good. The aim in providing *reality based* interaction styles should be driven by the objective of providing the user with a better experience, not just a more usable system. Although there is a strong relationship between usability and user experience, as a poorly usable interfaces can indeed mar the experience of the user, an application made to the highest

usability standards does not necessarily imply a good user experience.

For the interaction styles the difference between usability and experience becomes wider when users after experiencing the new styles decide to go back to their legacy systems. What is the point, then, in creating Tangible User Interfaces if the user would just put away and go back to the mouse and keyboard to perform the exact same task? Narrowing the scope of interaction styles to only the input devices, this thesis aims at understanding how input devices affect the user experience. User experience is defined, for this work, as a function of the elements that affect the task. User narratives are the main source of experience. The nature of user experience is discussed below. Videogames provide an approachable application domain since their main objective of any videogame is to provide its users with a positive user experience. The user experience while playing videogames is then referred to as the gaming experience.

2.THE QUESTION
The question that is driving this research is: *What is the role of input devices in the gaming experience?*

Finding the answer to this question requires work in three different research domains: Input Devices, User Experience and Videogames. Regarding input devices, this work, rather than aiming at building or modeling new input devices, looks at the previous work for existing novel input devices, the testing methodologies used, and the motivation behind their design. The role that the input devices have on the experience of users is studied in the emerging area of user experience. Standard HCI books [7] define user experience as the subjective feeling of the user while interacting with an application. It is usually associated with aesthetics or flow. Until recently, User Experience was just a black box of something that surrounded usability [3]. However, there is a trend of new research (e.g. [1, 2, 5, 6, and 9]) that tries to identify what the user experience is, mechanisms to assess it, and how to design for it. This research uses the existing contributions in User Experience in order to answer the question, and will investigate mechanisms to assess and design for experience.

Finally, videogames were chosen as the application domain because their nature is to provide users with a positive user experience. Also, videogames use different input device, such as different types of pads, mouse and keyboard, steering wheels, etc. therefore, videogames made a natural match to find the answer to the above question. It is important to notice that this research does not aim at developing new games, or methods to evaluate videogames. It looks at the experience of videogames, and how input devices affect it.

Regarding the methodology, the nature of the question leads to an empirical/design approach to answer it. The approach taken looks at defining the gaming experience, understand methods to assess experience, and finally design and evaluate for experience. The methodology is discussed in more detail below. One path not followed in this research was to do a comparison between input devices and ask users to rate them. This was due to two factors, one trivial and one of depth. The trivial one is that we don't have access to the input devices developed at other schools. It is because of the second factor, which although an effort could have been made to collect them, there is not enough evidence that the design of the new input device was in order to create a better user experience.

3.EXPECTED CONTRIBUTIONS

The major contributions are expected in the area of User Experience. The expected results would enrich the literature of user experience and the way it is understood. It would also provide a methodology to design for and evaluate user experience and input devices. Another contribution would be a working prototype of a videogame that uses novel input device and standard ones.

4.METHODOLOGY

The research question poses an easy to describe inquiry, "What is"; finding its answer, in the other hand, is not easy to describe and an empirical approach using a mixed methodology was followed. The methodology used benefits from cases studies, ethnographies, experience narratives, experiments and design.

The approach followed began by defining the concept of "gaming experience", a somehow common term but in the best of cases its definition was taken for granted or it was just ill defined. The methodology used was Grounded Theory [8]. The data used was commercial over the counter magazines and websites that reviewed videogames. The underlying questions were "How are videogames described?" and "Which elements of the videogame affect the experience?" After the theory was constructed, a series of interviews with game designers, players and reviewers were conducted to validate the results.

Once gaming experience was defined, the next step was to understand how it could be evaluated. Although there is a wide literature on experience and user experience with technology, there is not a clear or established method to conduct experiments and assess the experience. The path taken in this research was to invite participants to play or interact with videogames in different ways, and then ask about their experiences. With the obtained results a preliminary framework was developed with the idea of helping in the final evaluation.

The following step is to observe how participants interact with games that use other means of interaction, such as board games and videogames. An ethnographic study is planned which involves first observing how players interact with the game, and then modifying the way of interacting. The lessons learned from the study will inform the design of a videogame that uses new input devices. Only the interaction style of the game will be designed, and a standard off the shelf videogame is going to be used as a platform. The final step will be to evaluate the new system and compare it with a system that only uses mouse and keyboard.

5.SETBACKS

The key setback found so far is the multidisciplinarity of HCI. The literature on User Experience is heavily based in philosophy, and the empirical methods are imported from psychology. Neither of those two areas are part of my forming background. And although there is great support from my Supervisors, it is not easy to discern when it is necessary to understand everything completely or just the key points.

The other problem is the overload of information. Papers keep coming in from Google scholar, user experience and input devices are topics that are still being heavily researched, hence the constant flow of new papers, sometimes without proper references. Just as the previous problem, the solution relies on being able to stop reading and concentrate in the developmental part of the project, but every new paper seems crucial to my research.

6.RESULTS AND TIMELINE

Most of the literature review has been finished. The elements of the gaming experience have been identified, and a preliminary framework to understand and evaluate experience has been formulated. The next steps are to start the ethnographic studies on board game players and videogame players. Design the input devices for the videogame and formulate the evaluation study. The ethnographic studies are due to be finish by August 2007, the design process by December 2007, and the evaluation study by April 2008. The thesis should be submitted by June 2008.

7.ACKNOWLEDGEMENTS

Eduardo Calvillo Gámez doctoral studies are sponsored by PROMEP/SEP and he is also a faculty member, on leave, of Universidad Politécnica de San Luis Potosi, México.

8.REFERENCES

[1] Blythe, M.A.; Monk, A.F.; Overbeeke, K. & Wright, P.C. (ed.) *Funology: From Usability to Enjoyment.* Kluwer Academic Publishers, 2003, 3

[2] Hassenzahl, M. & Tractinsky, N. User experience--a research agenda. *Behaviour & Information Technology*, Taylor & Francis, 2006, 25, 91-97

[3] ISO 9241-11. Ergonomic requirements for office work with visual display terminals (VDTs) - Part 11: *Guidance on usability* (1998).

[4] Jacob, R.J.K.; Girouard, A.; Hirshfield, L.M.; Horn, M.S.; Shaer, O.; Solovey, E.T. & Zigelbaum, J. Reality-based interaction: unifying the new generation of interaction styles. *CHI '07: CHI '07 extended abstracts on Human factors in computing systems*, ACM Press, 2007, 2465-2470

[5] Lindley, S.E. *The Effect of the Affordances Offered by Shared Interfaces on the Social Behaviour of Collocated Groups.* Ph.D. Thesis, University of York, 2007

[6] McCarthy, J. & Wright, P. *Technology as Experience.* The MIT Press, 2004

[7] Preece, J.; Rogers, Y. & Sharp, H. *Interaction Design - Beyond Human Computer Interaction.* John Wiley & Sons, 2002

[8] Strauss, A. & Corbin, J. *Basics of Qualitative Research: Techniques and Procedures for Developing Grounded Theory.* SAGE Publications, 1998

[9] Sulaiman, S. User Haptic Experience: Transferring Real World Tactile Sensation of Drawing Tools into Haptic Interfaces. Ph.D. Thesis, University College London -- University of London, 2006

Figuring Configuration: "Everyday" Users and End-User Configuration of Pervasive Computing Environments

Thom Heslop
Dept. of Informatics
University of Sussex
Falmer, Sussex.
T.T. Heslop@sussex.ac.uk

ABSTRACT

The research outlined investigates strategies that non-programming or "everyday" users may take in interaction with a Pervasive Computing Environment within relevant domains specified by them using a novel probe methodology developed with reference to theories of appropriation of technology and Vygotsky's "Tool and Result" methodology. A hypothesis of configuration policy styles is tested and types of everyday user styles and likely task domains are identified and discussed.

Categories and Subject Descriptors

H.1.2 [**Models and Principles**]: User / Machine Systems – *human factors.*

General Terms

Design, Experimentation, Human Factors.

Keywords

Pervasive, Ubiquitous, User-centered design, configuration, methodology, interaction design, Natural Language.

1. RESEARCH PROBLEM

With the advent of computer technologies embedded in a variety of devices and the convergence of wireless technologies with the Internet has come the possibility of a *ubiquitous* or *pervasive* computing environment involving many interacting complex systems. There is a growing recognition among researchers that people are likely to feel the need to control these environments - studies show that people can feel at the mercy of ubiquitous systems (Edwards [6], Barkhuus [1]) rather than in control of them. If this is the case then it would mean that the configuration of Pervasive Computing Environments (PCEs) is most likely to be in control of non-computing / programming, or "everyday" individuals and groups, especially within the domestic and public sphere. This poses a number of challenges for HCI research:

- Greenfield [7] points out that interacting with PCEs will involve new modes that are radically different to what most domestic users used to. What strategies are they likely to adopt when configuring these environments?

- As noted above, people can feel uncomfortable with ubiquitous systems. Researchers such as Rogers [11] also point out that these systems may not be suitable for all situations. It is therefore important to identify which areas of their lives and routines everyday users can envision an application for PCEs. Which domains will be relevant to

them?

- There is a growing body of research into interfaces for end-user configuration (examples can be found in [4] [8] [10] and [13]. On the main, these are primarily *policy based* (where the user specifies conditional rules for the operation of the system) and tend to conceive of policy composition as either the connection of devices to enact the users wishes or one of definition of goals and tasks with reference to the functionality of the system. However, ethnographic work [3] has shown that people do not conceive of their goals in terms of device behavior but rather their needs. Furthermore goal and tasks within the domestic area are often unclear. It can be argued that the interfaces mentioned above are therefore too low-level for most everyday users to operate successfully. What is the level that they will feel comfortable with?

- Finally, with the present state of incomplete or as yet undefined systems, what methodology can we use to evaluate these important issues?

2. CONTRIBUTION TO HCI RESEARCH

Identification and classification of configuration styles (in the form of policies) most likely to be used by non-programming users and task domains the use of the systems would be most appropriate for, contribution to understanding of the sort of language likely to be used by non programming users, (important as one of the main modes of interaction with PCEs is likely to be via Natural Language Interfaces). A novel probe methodology for discovering the suitability of a proposed computational model for real users.

3. PROPOSED SOLUTIONS

Pilot studies carried out as part of a research project into the configuration of a PCE using policies defined in Natural Language [14] at the University Of Sussex produced the hypothesis that the range of NL utterances would fall into the following styles: *Trigger policies* where activity is initiated when a particular event occurs, (otherwise known as event-condition-action rules), *Refinement policies* where defaults are set or overwritten and *Deontic policies* which specify circumstances when a service is allowed or place constraints on possible values in a request. It was further predicted that the knowledge of devices and services available would influence style and constrain the content of these policies. However, these studies were limited to a discrete domain (office printing), where goals would likely be clear to the user. Part of this research proposes to test this hypothesis over the broader and far less well defined domestic domain where these PCEs are likely to be in operation.

In order to gather examples of policies garnered from "everyday" users studies were needed. The design of these user studies presented the following challenges

- Most existing methodologies for User studies are based in the discipline of User Centred Design, which concentrates on the goals and tasks of the user. The system on which the required user studies are centred may be unfamiliar to the interviewee, who is unlikely to have any clearly defined goal or tasks within its domain.

- There is as yet no fully operational PCE running on the computational model under investigation. This would rule out an observational or ethnographic approach.

In order to overcome these problems a multi-stage Vygotskyan "tool and result" methodology [9] was designed, where the results of the previous stage of the study are used as tools or support in the next stage. It is my hypothesis that the methodology described in the next section will produce two results: a) it will identify likely use domains allowing us to anticipate where technology likely to be suitable and b) help users to conceive of and express goals and tasks that technology can be used for, allowing us to identify types of policies.

4. METHODOLOGY

Proponents of theories of the appropriation of technologies (such as Dourish [5] and Carroll [2]) argue that in order to make use of a new technology, users must make it "meaningful" to themselves by placing it within their own practices. As shown in the studies by Davidoff [3] and Tolmie [12]. people think of their domestic lives in terms of routines rather than discrete goal or tasks. In order to get useful policies from the interview subjects it was decided to leverage their conception of their daily routines and, in particular, how they would envision how these could be supported by a PCE in the form of a 'Virtual Noticeboard' system. This would show useful information from a variety of different sources and would have screens located in a number of locations around a domestic setting as well as mobile devices and sites outside the home (car, office). Over the series of studies, 20 people were interviewed. They were all professional people between the ages 35 – 50, with normal everyday technical experience (i.e. non-programming) and who are used to running households containing a number of people. It is envisioned that this demographic will form the likely users for this sort of PCE.

There were three stages to the series of studies:

- The first stage of interviews concentrated on discovering likely routine domains – what domestic routines the technology would be most likely used to support. The interviewees were introduced to the 'Virtual Noticeboard' system using a mock-up of a likely on-screen layout showing the output from different information sources. The interviewer then explained the concept of a PCE and services, the underlying model of configuration via policy definition and the conditional nature of policies, with examples. The interviewee was asked to consider where this technology may be of use in supporting their daily life routines and, if possible, to formulate some policies of their own.

- In the second study the interviewees were re-introduced (if they had taken part in the first stage) or introduced (as in the first stage) to the system and the concept of policies. The routine domains identified from the first stage were outlined, and the interviewees were supplied with lists of possible services that would carry out policies relevant to each domain.

- For the third stage of interviews the methodology was as before, using the same scenario and materials with the addition of focused goals in the guise of small scenarios (derived from analysis of interviews for Stage Two)

encapsulated by a high level "goal-oriented" phrase, such as "Maintain my heating". The interviewees were then asked to try to break these down into more specific policies over a number of task domains again derived from ones commonly occurring in the Stage Two interviews.

5. CURRENT STATUS

I am currently formalising the methodology described above preparing the final studies as described in the "Future Work" section.

6. INTERIM CONCLUSIONS

6.1 Identified Task Domains

No usable policies were forthcoming in first stage from any of the interviewees, indicating that more support for policy formulation than just the idea of the technology was needed (in keeping with the idea of Appropriation). However, three commonly re-occurring high-level areas were identified at this stage: Child, Food / Meal and Home Maintenance. These were used as the basis for the second stage of interviews.

The second stage gave a finer grained picture of task areas that cropped up regularly: Media Control, Child / People care, Food & Meals Maintenance, Calendar co-ordination and Heating & Energy Control. These were used as the basis of the focused goals used in the third stage, where the majority of the policy corpus was formed.

6.2 Policies Styles

A corpus of 184 policies was collected and analysed to test the validity of the style hypothesis.

80% of the policy corpus conforms to the predicted types of policy: 38% Trigger and 21% each Refinement and Deontic However it was noted that there are sub-types of Trigger policies - as well as the expected event-based ones, there were also a number of time-based policies (example: *"From 1st July 2005 to 6th July 2005 collect all key stage three articles on "the chartists" and file in Chloe's school folder"* and state-based polices (example: *"Using the set of stock cupboard articles, keep me informed if I'm running out".*)

20% lay outside of the original classification schema. Other styles identified are:

Time-dependent default overwrites (example: *"At 6PM the temperature in Bedroom 3 should be x and at 7.30PM it should be changed to x-3 degrees".*)

Requests: this involves asking the system to provide information or offer a solution based on a given criteria, such as *"Suggest favourite recipes depending on the weather forecast for tomorrow at 8pm".* This style is mostly found in the policies formed in the Food Maintenance area.

Aggregation or "Pipe" policies: essentially a combination of styles - specific actions that become an event that triggers other actions which in turn will trigger actions, set defaults or specify circumstances (example: *"Check diary for destinations in the next 24hours, search for best route and transfer information to navigation system."*)

Rather than the being constrained and influenced by knowledge of the devices and services, the style and language of the collected policies often have no discernable reference to either, supporting the contention that users tend to think of their goals in terms of their needs.

Finally, the task domains made no real difference to types of policies formed but some users showed a particular bias to Deontic and Refinement policies while others were more likely to define Trigger policies bringing up the issue of "personal style" in defining policies.

7. FUTURE WORK

A tentative plan for further work would include:

a) proper formalisation of methodology, b) further investigation of the prevalence of task type within domains to build up a richer picture of application of PCEs, c) policy style – see if we can get users to specify policies with explicit references to services / devices: use this to test both the level at which "everyday" users are comfortable using the technology and the formalized methodology.

8. REFERENCES

[1] Barkhuus, L., Dey, A.,: Is Context-Aware Computing Taking Control away From The User? Three Levels Of Interactivity Examined

[2] Carroll, J., (2004), Completing Design In Use: Closing The Appropriation Cycle, White Paper, (University Of Melbourne), www.dis.unimelb.edu.au/oasis/AppropnWPaper.pdf

[3] Davidoff, S., Lee, M.K., Yiu, C., Zimmerman, J., Dey, A.K, Principles Of Smart Home Control. Dourish, P., Friday, A., eds, *Ubicomp 2006* Berlin Heidelberg: Springer Verlag pgs 19-34 2006,

[4] Dey, A., Hamid, R., Beckmann, C., Li, I., Hsu, D., *a CAPpella*: Programming by Demonstration of Context-Aware Applications. In *CHI 2004*, April 24-29, 2004, Vienna, Austria pgs 34-40

[5] Dourish, P. Where the Action Is: The Foundations of Embodied Interaction. MIT Press, Cambridge: 2001. [6] Edwards, K., Grinter, R., (2001) At Home With Ubiquitous Computing : Seven Challenges. In UbiComp 2001

[7] Greenfield, A. (2006), Everyware: The Dawning Age Of Ubiquitous Computing, Berkeley: New Riders Press

[8] Humble, J., Crabtree, A, Hemmings, T., Akesson, K-P., Koleva, B., Rodden, T., Hansson, P., "Playing with the Bits" User-configuration of Ubiquitous Domestic Environments, http://ubicomp.org/ubicomp2004 2003

[9] Newman, F and Holzman, L., Lev Vygotsky: Revolutionary Scientist, Routledge Press, London 1993.

[10] Newman, M., Sedivy, J., Neuwirth, C.M., Edwards, W.K., Hong, J.L., Izadi, S., Marcelo, K., Smith, T.F., Designing For Serendipity, www2.parc.com/csl/projects/speakeasy/papers/dis02.pdf

[11] Rogers, Y., Moving On From Weiser's Vision of Calm Computing: Engaging Ubicomp Experiences, in Dourish, P., Friday, A., eds, *Ubicomp 2006* Berlin Heidelberg: Springer Verlag pgs 404-421 2006

[12] Tolmie, P., Pycock, J., Diggins, T., MacLean, A., Karsentty, A. (2002) Unremarkable Computing, Conference On Human Factors in Computing Systems , *SIGCHI Minneapolis pgs 399-406,* 2002.

[13] Truong, K, Huang, E., & Abowd, G., (2004), CAMP: A Magnetic Poetry interface for End-User Programming of Capture Applications for the Home. *Proceedings of the Sixth International Conference on Ubiquitous Computing (Ubicomp 2004; Nottingham, UK)*

[14] Weeds, J., Keller, W., Weir, D., Wakeman, I., Rimmer, J., Owen, T, Natural Language Expression of User Policies in Pervasive Computing Environments, *OntoLex, Lisbon, Portugal, May 2004.*

Facilitating the Communication between Malaysian Grandparents and Grandchildren Living Abroad through Computer-Mediated Communication

N. Jomhari
University of Manchester
Manchester Business School
Oxford Road
+440161 200 3074

nazean@gmail.com

ABSTRACT
The main focus of this research is to design a Computer-Mediated Communication system that is easily used bygrandparents (GP) and grandchildren (GC) separated by physical distance. An effective and usable design solution requires an understanding of its users and context, and therefore this project also aims to understand the nature of the communication failures and successes in GP-GC relationship and how physical distance and technology change this relationship, especially in Eastern (more specifically Malaysian) culture, which has not been studied extensively in published GP-GC communication literature.

Categories and Subject Descriptors
H.5.3 [**Information Interfaces and Presentation**]: Group and Organization Interfaces – *synchronous interaction, evaluation.*

General Terms
Design, Human Factors.

Keywords
Usability evaluation, human computer interaction, synchronous communication, older person.

1. INTRODUCTION
Everybody, including older persons, naturally would like to see their family members regularly. Chen reported that 17% of older persons felt that they would like to see more of their families [1]. However when they are separated by distance, the cost of communication can be high, which could be unaffordable for some older persons on small pension. Perhaps one way to overcome this problem is through computer-mediated communication (CMC) system such as video conferencing or instant messaging, which incur lower costs than traditional long-distance phone calls.

2. PROBLEMS
Based on the interviews with nine Malaysian grandchildren aged between 2-12 years old living in the UK, the researcher discovered that these children usually use telephone as a way of communicating with their grandparents in Malaysia, even though they are very familiar and comfortable with CMC technology such as Instant Messaging. There are two reasons why Malaysian grandparents do not want to use CMC. Firstly, they hesitate to change their communication method (changing this behaviour is beyond the scope of this paper). Secondly, the software available may not be fit for use for older persons. If the second reason is the main barrier of adoption of alternative way of communicating with grandchildren living abroad, then HCI can contribute in mediating this problem.

At present, most Malaysian older adults do not use the Internet extensively. The majority of Internet subscribers are students and working professionals. A statistic from Malaysian Communications and Multimedia Commission (MCMC) in 2006 showed that there was no older person subscribed to the Internet service [5]. One of the reasons is perhaps the fact that many Malaysian older people live with extended families [6] who are the subscribers of the Internet services. This is evident when this statistic is linked to the data that suggests that the majority of older people live in a house with computer and Internet connection [7]. So even though many grandparents do not have Internet services or claimed to be novice users, it is feasible for them to use CMC with the help of other family members. Therefore, the research focused on the investigation on how to design and evaluate a usable CMC.

3. MAIN CONTRIBUTION TO HCI
There are various ways of ensuring that older persons can utilize the Internet. One possible solution is through applying guidelines that would make the user interface more ageing friendly. Many such guidelines on other interactive systems are available for public use, such as those for digital TV [2], web page [3] and electronic bulletin board [4]. However, very few published guidelines are available for CMC. Therefore, the first contribution of this project is a set of guidelines that can be readily used by designers and evaluators of CMC for older persons to make their user interface more ageing-friendly.

The second contribution of this project relates to the understanding of the nature of GP-GC communication in Eastern culture when separated by physical distance and how distance and technology change the nature of this communication. This knowledge can inform the design of CMC in general and systems for intergenerational communication in particular (or even more specifically, design of CMC for users from Eastern culture).

Finally, the project also contributes in the form of the ageing friendly CMC system itself, that has been evaluated in controlled experiments (as to measure error rate and capture usability problems) as well as in context.

4. PROPOSED SOLUTION

There are three objectives of this study. First is to understand the nature of the relationship between grandparents and grandchildren. Second is to identify the effectiveness of CMC technology to mediate long-distance relationship. Lastly is to design and evaluate better CMC technology to support long distance communication between grandchildren and grandparent, especially those from Eastern culture.

5. METHODOLOGY

This study will engage with Malaysian children in the UK and their grandparents in Malaysia have easy access to the Internet. All respondents will be interviewed about their Internet usage and the nature of communication with their grandparent. They will also be observed on how they are handling the CMC application using their computer. The same process will be performed with respective grandparents. In addition, the grandparents are required to accomplish some specific tasks during their experience in using three CMC applications: Yahoo Messenger (YM), Windows Live Messenger (WLM) and Skype. These applications were chosen based upon the best three choices put forward by the grandchildren in an online survey [8]. The grandparents will be asked to perform tasks such as registering, installing, logging in, adding contact, text chatting, sending file, using webcam and using emoticons to observe the nature of communication.

This study also aims at investigating the interaction between grandparents and social helpers, which in this case would be other family members. After the interview sessions, there will be training sessions over four days on using three CMC systems (YM, WLM and Skype) with the help of other family members.

During these demonstration sessions, the interaction between the GP and the family members who will be the assistant will be video recorded for later analysis to see the role of social helpers for older persons, in general.

The problems and likes/dislikes revealed during these sessions will inform the initial design of the CMC system, which will then be evaluated in controlled experiments and in-context with GP and GC at a later stage. The interaction between them will be recorded and computer screen activities will be captured, too. These grandparents will be visited twice a week and each visit will last no longer than two hours to minimize fatigue.

6. CURRENT STATUS

Currently, I have already completed interviewing nine grandchildren (and also their mother to get more information on the GP-GC relationship). Majority of them are computer literate and their grandparents in Malaysia have easy access to computer. The objective of the interview is to know and compare their relationship with grandparents before and after coming to England, and also to gauge their experience while communicating with their grandparent through computer. The majority of them preferred Yahoo Messenger (YM) (with Windows Live Messenger (WLM) and Skype in the second and third places) and the researcher identified seven active areas that the grandchild usually access when communicating through YM: webcam, photo, text chat, audibles, IMVironment, emoticons and image or avatar. The researcher will be going back to Malaysia to interview the nine grandparents in Malaysia in June 2007.

7. FUTURE WORKS

The researcher will analyze the interview, the video recordings, the saved text chats and the evaluation of three CMC systems and then start the design of ageing-friendly CMC system that can facilitate GP-GC communication.

8. REFERENCES

[1] Chen, P. C. Y. (1987). "Family support and the health of the elderly Malaysian." Journal of Cross-Cultural Gerontology V2(2): 187-193.

[2] Evaluating digital 'on-line' background noise suppression: clarifying television dialogue for older, hard-of-hearing viewers", Dr. A. Carmichael, Neuropsychological Rehabilitation, 14(1/2) (2004), Psychology Press Limited, pp.241-249. ISBN: 1841699608.

[3] Kurniawan, S.H., Evans, D.G. King, A., Blenkhorn, P. Personalizing Web Page Presentation for Older People. Interacting with Computers 18, 2006, 457-477

[4] Morell, R.W., Park, D.C., MAyhorn, C.B., and Echt, K.V. (1995). Older adults and electronic communication networks: Learning to use ELDERCOMM. Paper presented at the 103 Annual Convention of the American Psychological Association. New York, New York, August.

[5] Malaysian Communications and Multimedia Commission (2007). "Statistic and Records." Available at http://www.cmc.gov.my/facts_figures/stats/index.asp.

[6] Malaysian Population and Family Survey. National Population and Family Development Board, Kuala Lumpur; 1994.

[7] Jomhari, N. and S. H. Kurniawan (2007). "Exploring the Opportunity for Malaysian Grandparent to Communicate with Their Grandchildren through Computer." Postgraduate Research in Arts, Social Science and Humanities (PRASH) 2 April 2007.

[8] Grandparent-Grandchildren Relationship Survey, available at http://windev.humanities.manchester.ac.uk/surveys/TakeSurvey.asp?SurveyID=8LL8mmMM7ml0I

Interaction Manifolds:
Understanding Behaviour Around a Shareable Interface

Cecily Morrison
Cambridge University
William Gates Building
15 JJ Thomson Avenue
Cambridge CB3 0FD UK
(+44) 1223 763 783

Cecily.Morrison@cl.cam.ac.uk

ABSTRACT
This poster presents a suggestion for how ethnography of shareable interfaces might be used to inform subsequent design decisions by creating an analytical construct that we name *the interaction manifold*. We first describe and summarize results of our research to date in a medical intensive care unit. We then propose why and how an analytic construct might prove useful for design of shareable interfaces.

Categories and Subject Descriptors
H.5.3 **[Group and Organization Interfaces]**

General Terms
Performance, Design, Human Factors, Theory

Keywords
Shareable Interfaces, CSCW, Interaction Manifold

1. INTRODUCTION
The term, Sharable interfaces [1], has been proposed to describe a number of recent technology configurations that support collocated groups working with or around the same content but have little theoretical underpinning. One common example is interactive displays. The term also applies to medical environments where staff frequently gather around displays of patient medical records to discuss future treatment. In a recent study, we compared the non-verbal means with which the medical staff negotiate the interaction between themselves during the daily ward rounds while using a paper-based medical record and later a computer-based one. The result was a rich analysis of how the tenuous interaction between nurses and doctors, with a clearly hierarchical relationship, is accomplished in these two settings. Below we summarize the research and suggest that it can be generalized to support the design of sharable interfaces through articulating a concept we define and then refer to as the interaction manifold.

2. BACKGROUND
Medical situations necessitate a large number of staff coordinating their actions and communicating their findings.

This is generally done with the help of the patient medical record. During the ward round, the medical record at the end of each bed, either in its paper form on the nurse's table or in its digital form displayed on a monitor, becomes the center piece of a complex interaction of ten or so staff of different ranks. The large number of people, and their different knowledge and rank require careful negotiation between the members to ensure that all useful information is revealed but the conversation is kept as short as possible. By negotiation we mean how a group mutually decides: (1) who can speak and (2) what the topic of conversation is [2]. Interaction negotiation is usually done non-verbally through what we refer to as physical interactions: group formation, upper-body orientation, gesture and object manipulation, and posture. Our analysis compares how physical interactions are used in negotiating who speaks and what is discussed during a ward round using the paper-based medical record and the computer-based one, highlighting the effect each type of record has on the communication.

3. ANALYSIS
The analysis of the group usage of the paper-based record showed how each of the physical interactions listed above played a role in determining who spoke and about what. We highlighted in particular, the ways the consultant (head doctor) directed the conversation and how the nurses contributed. Much of what we found fit into Kendon's framework describing group behaviour, the F-formation [3]. The computer-based record on the other hand, produced very different ways of communicating. The placement of the screen split the group formation into two, leaving only the aural channel connecting the members. This had the effect of requiring group members to use other means than physical interaction to negotiate the interaction: either interruption or through the technology (eg. leaving notes). There was a notable decrease in the amount of interaction between the nurses and the doctors. As different means of interacting are used in the computer-based record, Kendon's analysis does not seem to provide a sufficiently complete account for use as a basis for design decisions.

F-formation analysis assumes that the interaction content is expressed through social mechanisms expressed in the moment, verbally and bodily. In the computer-based scenario that we describe, device interaction becomes more prominent as an external motivating "force" that tends to modify the formation from outside this immediate social context. The interaction design of the computer-based system, together with the available structures for navigation of the online records, create trajectories of collaboration that are both visible and invisible. The available channels cross between the world of data relations "behind" the screen, and the configuration of actors who read and interact with the screen and each other. Our concern is to describe these more diverse structures in ways that take account of their inter-dependence rather than drawing misleading boundaries that might divide closely couple phenomena.

4. FUTURE WORK

That neither ethnography of the non-digital version of the shareable interface nor Kendon's analytic construct proved useful in understanding behaviour around the digital shareable interface, indicates the need for an alternative analytical construct to support the design of this shareable interface. The interaction manifold, as we would call it, would describe the tradeoffs of group negotiation abilities (ie. how different members of the group can enter the conversation and how the topic can be changed) depending on the number of displays, their size, their placement in place, the staticness of information on them, and the interaction possibilities. The analytical construct would provide designers a means to judge design decisions when creating a shareable interface, similar to Cognitive Dimensions [4] with notational design.   I am currently working on this theoretical perspective.

Once the interaction manifold has been clearly developed, I plan to look at ways that motion captured data of movement during interaction might be used to support the analytical claims made.   In order to demonstrate the power of the interaction manifold as an analytic construct for design, I will design a technology space, in which users can manipulate digital data projected on the wall through TUIs, while interacting with each other.

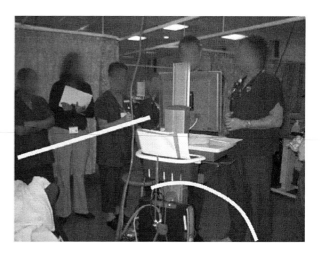

Figure 1. Group interaction around a computer-based medical record system

5. ACKNOWLEDGMENTS

We are grateful for the support of Papworth Critical Care Unit, Papworth Anaesthetic Research, and head consultant Alain Vuylsteke, who initiated this project. This research is sponsored by Boeing Corporation and IMDsoft, and is being conducted in collaboration with David Good and Alice McGowan (Social and Political Science) and Matthew Jones (Judge Business School).

6. REFERENCES

[1]   Shareable Interface Workshop 2007
       http://mcs.open.ac.uk/pm5923/si2007/

[2]   Suchman, L. (1986): Plans and Situated Actions, Cambridge University Press, Cambridge, UK.

[3]   Kendon, A. (1990): Conduction Interaction: Patterns of Behavior in focused encounters, Cambridge University Press, Cambridge, UK.

[4]   Blackwell, A. F. Green, T.R.G (2003): "Notational Systems – the Cognitive Dimensions of Notations framework." In J.M. Carroll (Ed.) *HCI Models, Theories and Frameworks: Toward a multidisciplinary science.* Morgan Kaufmann.

Social Support in Empathic Online Communities for Older People

Ulrike Pfeil
Centre for HCI Design
City University
London, EC1 0HB
U.Pfeil-1@citv.ac.uk

ABSTRACT

The goal of my PhD is to investigate how older people exchange social support in empathic online communities. This will be achieved through an in-depth investigation of online communities for older people. The results of my work will shed light on the characteristics of empathy exchanged among older people in online communities opposed to their offline communication. This is a valuable contribution to the research area of HCI, as it shows how empathic online communities can be used to support older people in their daily lives. I have published the preliminary findings of my work as a full paper at CHI 2007.

Categories and Subject Descriptors

H4.3. Information System Applications: Communication Applications; K4.2. Computers and society: Social issues

General Terms

Design

Keywords

Older people, online communities, empathy, support, communication, social interaction

1. INTRODUCTION

1.1 Problem statement

Between 2000 and 2004 the degree of internet usage by people aged 65 and older has increased by 47%. Currently, 28% of older British people go online [4]. Similar numbers can be found in USA, as 22% of American older people use the internet and this figure is estimated to continue growing [3]. A lot of work has been done to establish guidelines and standards to make the internet accessible for older people. However, the focus has so far been mainly on making information on websites accessible. Does this account for all activities that can be performed online?

In recent years, activities on the internet expanded from mainly retrieving information to participating in virtual social settings, where people interact with each other to socialise [7] and/or to collaborate [6]. Empathic online communities are one such example where people meet online. They offer a place for

people that experience a similar life situation to share information and to support each other [7].

However, little is known about how older people interact and socialise in online communities. How does the exchange of support among older people differ between online and offline settings? What are the motivations for older people to participate in online communities? How could online communities for older people be designed to encourage their participation and support them in their daily lives? To answer these questions, I am studying the characteristics and patterns of support in empathic online communities for older people.

1.2 Aims and objectives

The overall aim of my research is to study the facilitation of empathy and social support in online communities for older people. Online and offline empathic communication will first be investigated separately. Differences and similarities between the two will be highlighted. The acquired knowledge will then be applied in a detailed ethnographic study of an online community for older people. The following steps are proposed:
I. Identify the characteristics of online and offline empathic communication and the social networks that evolve around it.

II. Investigate possible methods that allow gathering of the necessary data (e.g. virtual ethnography).

III. Based on the findings of objectives I. and II., develop a methodological framework for studying empathic online communities for older people.

IV. Apply the framework to study an online community for older people in detail. This includes the investigation of the content, the social network and the evolution of the online community over time.

2. RELATED STUDIES

Studies of empathic online communities have so far been mainly focused on health-related online communities for people suffering from an illness and/or for their caregivers. Findings show that factual information about the disease, practical tips about how to handle the situation, and emotional support are the major topics of online empathic communication [7]. People value to talk to others that are in a similar situation and turn to the online community for support when they face problems.

As older people often share a similar life situation (e.g. retirement) it is likely that they develop online communities that entail a high degree of emotional support. As social interaction correlates positively with the perceived well-being of older people [1], it is believed that participation in empathic online communities can prevent isolation and enhance the quality of life for older people. Furthermore, studies have shown that regular computer usage encourages older people to keep mentally and socially active [2].

Only few studies have so far investigated social interaction in online communities by older people. Wright [9] studied the exchange of social support within SeniorNet, an online community for older people. Findings show that valuing the community, giving advice based on one's own experiences and sharing life experiences are the major online community topics. Members value both, informational and emotional support [9]. The more time older people spend in online communities, the higher is their satisfaction with their received support and the larger is the number of people they are in contact with [8].

3. COMPLETED WORK

I have applied qualitative content analysis to messages of an online discussion board within SeniorNet to study the occurrence of empathy. Through an iterative process in which message postings were reduced to concepts and patterns, I developed a code scheme that captured the prevalent themes of the discussion. The findings were contrasted to characteristics of offline empathy. The work was published in a full paper at CHI 2007 [5] and another part of it is currently under review by the *Universal Access in the Information Society* journal.

Furthermore, Social Network Analysis (SNA) was performed with the data of the discussion board. SNA aims to understand the structure of relations between members of a social system that are characterised by information exchange between these members [10]. I applied SNA to investigate the impact of the communication content on the social network and relations between the participants of the online discussion board.

In order to investigate if the characteristics of online empathy are valid for a broader variety of online communities for older people, I generalised the code scheme across three additional discussion boards for older people with different topics. Furthermore, I conducted interviews with older people in order to capture their experiences of social support offline. I compared the findings with online support to see how older people's view of supports fits into the code scheme that was developed from the online discussion boards (see objective I).

4. FUTURE WORK

The findings from my completed work will be used to investigate the differences and commonalities of social support for older people in online and offline environments. The pre-studies will conclude in a methodological framework that can be applied to study online communities for older people (see objective III). This framework will be used to study an online community for older people over a long period of time and in-depth (see objective IV).

Virtual ethnography will be used to study the facilitation of empathy in an online community for older people. A multi-method triangulation will be applied, as different methods will be used to study the online community and the combination of the findings will allow for an in-depth investigation of the communication patterns and community structures of the online community for older people. The application of different methods in the pre-studies will help to judge their applicability in the main study (see objective II.). Methods that will be applied in this research include, but are not limited to:

I. Content analysis will be used to understand the components and characteristics of the content within an empathic online community for older people.

II. SNA will be applied to investigate the characteristics of the network that is developed through the communication and to spot and study key-members within the online community.

III. Query-based techniques will be used in order to gather experiences and opinions from older people. If necessary, interviews and questionnaires will be conducted online.

5. FUTURE CONTRIBUTION

The conclusions of my research will help to assess the opportunities and challenges of online communities for older people as a means of supporting them in their daily life. By clarifying how older people exchange social support in online communities, I will investigate in depth the components of online support and the network structure that develops around it. Investigating the advantages and problems of online communication for older people, my research will give insights in how the accessibility of the social aspect of the internet can be improved for this user group. This will contribute significantly to the analysis and evaluation of online communities and can also feed back into their design. Understanding the needs and preferences of older people concerning empathic online communication helps us to find technologies and concepts that support these. Thus, online communities that nurture supportive communication among older people can be designed more successfully.

6. REFERENCES

[1] Czaja, S.J., Guerrier, J.H., Nair, S.N., and Laudauer, T.K. Computer communication as an aid to independence to older adults. *Behaviour and Information Technology*, 12, 1993, 197-207.

[2] Eilers, M.L. Older adults and computer education: Not to have the world a closed door. *International Journal of Technology and Aging, 2,* 1989, 56-76.

[3] Fox, S. *Older Americans and the Internet.* Washington, DC: Pew Internet & American Life Project, 2004.

[4] Office of Communication. *Consumers and the communications market: 2006.* Ofcom Consumer Panel, 2006.

[5] Pfeil, U. & Zaphiris, P. Patterns of empathy in online communication. To appear in *Proceedings of CHI 2007 – the ACM Conference on Human Factors in Computing Systems* (San Jose, CA, 28. April - 03. May 2007).

[6] Pfeil, U., Zaphiris, P., Ang C.S. (2006). Cultural Differences in Wiki Collaboration. *Journal of Computer Mediated Communication*, 12(1), article 5.

[7] Preece, J. & Ghozati, K. Observations and Explorations of Empathy Online. In. R. R. Rice and J. E. Katz, *The Internet and Health Communication: Experience and Expectations.* Sage Publications Inc.: Thousand Oaks, 2001, 237-260.

[8] Wright, K. B. Computer-mediated support groups: An examination of relationships among social support, perceived stress, and coping strategies. *Communication Quarterly, 47*(4), 1999, 402-414.

[9] Wright, K. B. The communication of social support within an on-line community for older adults: A qualitative analysis of the SeniorNet community. *Qualitative Research Reports in Communication, 1*(2), 2000, 33-43.

[10] Zaphiris, P., Sarwar, R. (2006) Trends, Similarities and Differences in the Usage of Teen and Senior Public Online Newsgroups. *ACM Transactions on Computer-Human Interaction (TOCHI), 13*(3), 2006, 403-422.

Interaction Designers' Use of Their Repertoire in Meetings with Clients

Per Sökjer
Human-Centered Systems
IDA, Linköpings universitet
581 83 Linköping, Sweden
+46 (0) 28 26 09

perso@ida.liu.se

ABSTRACT

An important part of an interaction designer's work is meeting with clients during design sessions. It is of great importance that the designers participate in establishing some level of common ground. This research aims at investigating how designer's repertoire, in terms of facts, skills and examples, can help establishing common ground between designers and their clients. The research method is inspired by cognitive ethnography. Initial results from workshops, where interaction designers work together with participants from the Swedish Enforcement Authority, indicate that the interaction designers use examples from several design levels to establish common ground with clients and each other. Our future research aims to show how interaction designer and client work together in multidisciplinary teams.

Categories and Subject Descriptors

H.5.2 User Interfaces - User-Centered Design, K.6.1 Project and People Management - Systems analysis and Design

General Terms

Management, Documentation, Design, Human Factors, Theory

Keywords

Repertoire, objects, clients, procurement

1. INTRODUCTION

A designer participates in many communicative contexts. One critical and rather central situation is meetings with clients. We know that when a designer communicates with other designers the dialogue is facilitated by previous experience. This previous experience is sometimes called a repertoire and could be described as the facts, skills and examples available to the designer. A significant aspect of becoming a good interaction designer is building and maintaining this repertoire. This includes analyzing artifacts, using different tools for visualization depending on purpose and audience and getting experience working in projects [1]. Building and maintaining a repertoire should be part of every interaction designer's central competence since it's a cognitive resource for defining problem

spaces and working towards solutions [3].

Common ground is the shared understandings that participants in a joint activity build their communication on [2]. One way to think about designer's common ground is in terms of shared repertoire. When meeting clients during design sessions it is of great importance that the designers help the session participants establishing some level of common ground. We believe that the repertoire of the designers play an important role in this activity. The question is what that role is, and how to study it. In the study described here we will investigate how designer's repertoire can help establishing common ground between designers and their clients.

2. RESEARCH ISSUES

In my research I want to develop a theoretical and empirical understanding of how interaction designers use their repertoire depending on situation and purpose. Initially I have chosen to focus on how designers use repertoire for communication, and to establish common ground, with clients. More specifically, the initial research perspective is to study the conceptual and material objects created, maintained and proposed by the interaction designers during these designer-client meetings. Objects evolve and resonate in this setting providing clues regarding repertoire in use.

3. CONTRIBUTION

This research has significance for HCI since it focuses on how the quality of multidisciplinary teamwork in design can be improved. By providing empirical evidence how the repertoire of the interaction designer contributes to establishing common ground between designer and client we can assess how this aspect influences the outcome of these meetings.

4. METHOD

To accomplish this research, a method inspired by cognitive ethnography will be used [5]. This framework provides perspectives that help capturing the dynamic and distributed nature of the multidisciplinary activities being observed. Video, interviews and participant observation are techniques that will be utilized.

This research is a part of an ongoing project where multiple organizations and institutions are involved. The project's main focus is to develop a design-oriented IT procurement organization. Swedish authorities are required by the government to work in a "clear delineation between procuring and developing department structures" The Swedish Enforcement Authority is involved in the project regarding the development of their procurement organization [6][4].

Published by the British Computer Society
Volume 2 Proceedings of the 21st BCS HCI Group Conference HCI 2007, 3-7 September 2007, Lancaster University, UK
Devina Ramduny-Ellis & Dorothy Rachovides (Editors)

One part of this project lets team members from the procurement organization meet and work together with interaction designers in a series of workshops. The aim of these workshops is to allow the different competences to work together as teams. In the workshops the interaction designers provide tools and methods for defining problems, work toward possible solutions and present methods how to capture problems, important use qualities etc.

Researchers captured team activities using pen and paper and video for off site analysis. Material and objects produced during the workshops (sketches, models, user profiles etc) were also saved for later analysis.

The recorded material will be analyzed using methods and tools for video analysis. Different object definitions will be utilized when trying to capture the dynamic use and evolution of objects.

5. CURRENT STATUS

The workshops were carried out successfully during the autumn 2006. Members from the Swedish Enforcement Agency worked together with representatives from Swedish interaction design consultancy firms. The specified task the groups worked on was based on detailed work processes. These work processes were developed as part of the Swedish Enforcement Agency's reorganization process.

Data were collected through observation, video recording and still imaging by researchers present at the workshops. The data are for the moment being organized and transcribed.

6. PRELIMINARY RESULTS

Initial results indicate that the participating interaction designer's use examples from multiple design levels proposed by Markensten (business, activity, interaction and technology) [7] to establish common ground during the workshop sessions. These design levels are used when trying to define system requirements.

Results also indicate that objects shift "status" during the workshops and convey different properties, meanings and purposes to the participants at different stages of the process; an explorative visualization of different tasks evolves into a user interface concept.

7. ACKNOWLEDGMENTS
This research was made possible through a grant from VINNOVA, the Swedish innovation agency, in the project Enabling technology through usability and organizational change with focus on the procurers terms (2001-05131). I would like to thank my advisor Stefan Holmlid, Ann Lantz, Mattias Arvola, Jakob Tholander and Henrik Artman. Additional thanks to the participants from the Swedish Enforcement Authority and from the participating design companies.

8. REFERENCES

[1] Schön, D.A. (1987). Educating the Reflective Practitioner: Toward a New Design for Teaching and Learning in the Professions. San Francisco, CA: Jossey-Bass.

[2] Clark, H.H. (1996). *Using Language*. Cambridge, England: Cambridge University Press.

[3] Löwgren, J. and Stolterman, E. (2004). *Thoughtful Interaction Design. A Design Perspective on Information Technology*. Cambridge, Mass.: MIT Press.

[4] Holmlid, S. and Lantz, A. (2006). *Developing e-services in a government authority: Different views on design in procurement and system development*. NordiCHI workshop on User involvement and representation in e-Government projects. Oslo, October.

[5] Hollan, J.D., Hutchins, E.L. and Kirsh, D. (2000). *Distributed Cognition: Toward a New Foundation for Human-Computer Interaction Research*. In ACM Transactions on Computer-Human Interaction, Vol. 7, No. 2.

[6] Artman, H. and Andersson, F. (2006). *Communicating the Future Business: A Procurement Organizations Understanding of their Role in Systems Development*. In A. Følstad, H. Artman, J. Krogstie (eds.) User Involvement and representation in e-Government projects. NordiCHI, Oslo, Oct. 15, 2006

[7] Markensten, E. (2005). *Mind the Gap: A Procurement Approach to Integrating User-Centered Design in Contract Development*. Licentiate Thesis. Stockholm, Sweden: Royal Institute of Technology.

The Design and Evaluation of an Assistive Multimodal Interface

Philip Strain
Sonic Arts Research Centre
Queens University, Belfast
BT7 1NN
+44 (0)28 90974829

p.strain@qub.ac.uk

ABSTRACT

A requirements capture carried out with thirty blind and visually impaired participants has outlined many issues visually impaired people face when accessing the Web using current assistive technology. One key finding was that spatial information is not conveyed to users. An assistive multimodal interface has been developed that conveys spatial information to users via speech, audio and haptics. Additionally, techniques for evaluating assistive technology with visually impaired participants are discussed.

Categories and Subject Descriptors

H.5.2 User Interfaces: auditory feedback & haptic I/O; H.5.2. Evaluation/methodology; K.4.2 Social Issues: assistive technologies for persons with disabilities

General Terms

Design, Human Factors.

Keywords

Accessibility, audio and haptics, evaluation/methodology

1. INTRODUCTION

The Web has the potential to enhance the way visually impaired people lead their daily lives. However, due to limitations in current assistive technology, this potential is not being realized. For instance, it is estimated that the web is three times easier to use for sighted users than for the visually impaired [1]. Various factors have been identified to explain this – for example many web sites have not been designed with accessibility in mind and the linear access model employed by screen readers is constrained by user's short-term memory.

A requirements capture consisting of a questionnaire with 30 respondents, several focus groups and observational studies have highlighted some of the issues visually impaired people face when accessing the Internet [4]. Many participants requested access to spatial information. Screen reader models have been categorized as being linear, conversational, hierarchical or spatial; however current screen reader technology only employs a linear model.

This research is thus concerned with the design and evaluation of an assistive multimodal interface that mediates spatial

information to visually impaired users via non-speech audio, haptics and speech.

2. DESIGN

An initial prototype was designed that provides access to Web pages via audio, haptics and speech. Input is provided via a force-feedback mouse. Visually impaired users cannot use a standard mouse, due to a lack of feedback, however it was hypothesized that by augmenting a mouse with haptics and audio, users would be able to gain a sense of position on a page. Haptic effects and auditory icons were associated with links, images and the page border. A "torch effect" was employed that informed users if there was an element in the vicinity of the mouse cursor - the location of the element was conveyed via non-speech audio. An initial evaluation [8] of the system found that users were able to develop a spatial representation of a web page. However the distance moved by the mouse did not correspond to the distance moved by the cursor, users were unaware of their position in the context of the page, and one user stated that additional feedback to provide additional awareness of the position of the cursor would be beneficial.

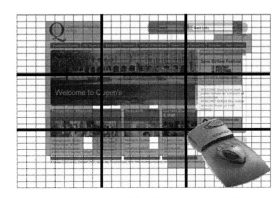

Figure 1 – 27x27 grid with page segmentation

In the second iteration of the system, a 3x3 grid was overlaid unto the webpage [7]. As users moved over each segment, the current location of the cursor in relation to the grid was conveyed to the user via speech. An evaluation of the system within a collaborative context was carried out [3]. It was found that the addition of the grid enhanced users positional awareness and led to an average of 17.3 second reduction in task completion timings. In addition, users found the concept of a grid easy to learn.

Current work focuses on the expansion of the grid concept to incorporate finer grids, such as a 27x27 grid (Figure 1). This will improve the mapping between the user's mouse movements and the movement of the cursor on screen by providing additional feedback. In addition, the page could be segmented, reducing the perceivable resolution of the screen, providing a simplified interface.

Future work will look at segmenting the page horizontally, enabling users to explore smaller sections of the page using a left to right strategy. A keyboard shortcut will be provided to enable the user to move up and down the page. This separation of horizontal and vertical exploration is hypothesized to enhance the usability of the system.

3. EVALUATION

Stevens et al [4] have outlined the difficulties involved in evaluating assistive technology. The second part of this research will examine techniques for evaluating assistive technology, with a focus on systems which convey spatial information. Key areas of interest will be participant profiling, training, elicitation of user's mental models, and the logging of users cursor movements.

Recruitment is an important issue with studies involving visually impaired participants. It is vital to ensure a homogeneity of variance across participant profiles. Typically blind and visually impaired users will be categorized into congenitally and adventitiously blind, blind and visually impaired, expert and novice users. However there is a wide variance within these subgroups, e.g. there are many different conditions that may render a person visually impaired, and spatial ability may vary significantly within these sub-groups. Thus the effect of a participant's spatial ability on results will be determined.

Participant training before studies is important to ensure it is the interface is being tested and not the participants' interaction with the device. Currently, training techniques and duration vary widely among studies. Research into the factors influencing adequate training will be carried out.

Another key challenge is the elicitation or externalization of user mental models. Various techniques are available - this research will focus on think-aloud, drawing and two-dimensional reconstruction.

It has been recognized that adaptations are required to the think-aloud protocol to enable effective usage with visually impaired participants [7]. Such adaptations focus on the testing environment, where the auditory interface, participant and moderator dialog contribute to create a complex auditory environment. This research will look at the spatial language used by participants to describe their spatial model.

Researchers in way-finding typically encourage participants to draw the models they have generated of an area. Kitchin et al [2] describe four drawing techniques that can be used, depending on the data required.

Two-dimensional reconstruction has been used by psychologists studying the development of spatial awareness in visually impaired children. Typically, blocks are used to build up a tactile environment that reflects user's current spatial model. However this can be a slow and unfamiliar process for participants. Many visually impaired people play specially adapted board games for entertainment, e.g. chess and Sudoku. By using this familiar framework, it is hypothesized more accurate results will be gained more quickly. Bi-linear regression can then be used to analyze the differences between the original model and the model externalized by the user. Results from previous evaluations have shown that it was

difficult to record and track the users' spatial movement and exploration through the system. Thus in addition to typical usability measures, such as time-on-task, task completion rate and error rate, the users' path through the system will be recorded. From this it will be possible to track areas where the user has paused or changed direction, providing an additional insight into the user's interaction with the system. It may be possible to analyze these visualizations using eye-tracking methodologies, as the mouse enables the user to "scan" the page as a sighted user would.

The evaluation framework developed will then be used to evaluate future versions of the assistive multimodal interface.

4. CONCLUSION

This research will provide three main contributions to HCI – i) a greater understanding of the issues visually impaired people face when accessing the Web ii) guidelines for the development for assistive multimodal systems and iii) a framework for evaluating assistive technology that conveys spatial information.

5. ACKNOWLEDGEMENTS

Thanks to Emma Murphy, Ravi Kuber, Graham McAllister, Wai Yu for their advice and assistance.

6. REFERENCES

[1] Coyne, K. and Nielsen, J. (2001). Beyond ALT text: making the web easy to use for users with disabilities. Fremont, CA: Nielsen Norman Group

[2] Kitchin, R.M. and Jacobson, R.D. (1997) Techniques to collect and analyze the cognitive map knowledge of people with visual impairments or blindness: Issues of validity, Journal of Visual Impairment and Blindness. July-August, 360-376.

[3] Kuber, R., Murphy, E., McAllister, G., Strain, P., and Yu, W. "Evaluation of an Assistive Web Interface: A Collaborative Approach", in Press, 2007.

[4] Murphy, E., Kuber, R., McAllister, G., Strain, P., Yu, W., (2007) "An Empirical Investigation into the Difficulties Experienced by Visually Impaired Internet Users" accepted for publication *Universal Access in the Information Society Journal, 2007*

[5] Stevens, R., and Edwards, A. An approach to the evaluation of assistive technology. In ASSETS'96, pages 64–71. ACM Press, 1996

[6] Strain, P., McAllister, G., Murphy, E., Kuber, R. & Yu, W., 2007: A Grid-Based Extension to an Assistive Multimodal Interface. In *Proceedings of CHI '07 Extended Abstracts*, San Jose, California, USA, 28 April - 3 May, 2007,

[7] Strain, P., Shaikh, A. D., and Boardman, R. 2007. Thinking but not seeing: think-aloud for non-sighted users. In *CHI '07 Extended Abstracts on Human Factors in Computing Systems* (San Jose, CA, USA, April 28 - May 03, 2007), 1851-1856.

[8] Yu, W., Kuber, R., Murphy, E., Strain, P., and McAllister, G. 2006. A novel multimodal interface for improving visually impaired people's web accessibility. *Virtual Real.* 9, 2 (Jan. 2006), 133-148

Issues with the Construct of Quality

Nele Van den Ende[1], Jettie
Hoonhout[1] & Lydia Meesters[2]
[1]Philips Research
HTC 34, NL - 5656AE Eindhoven

[2]Eindhoven University of
Technology
Den Dolech 2
NL – 5612AZ Eindhoven

{nele.van.den.ende,
jettie.hoonhout}@philips.com
l.m.j.meesters@tue.nl

ABSTRACT

This paper proposes an outline for a framework that aims to give a comprehensive view of perceived video quality, including physical characteristics, perceptual attributes and cognitive factors.

Keywords

theoretical framework, quality research, perceived video quality

1. INTRODUCTION

When testing subjective video quality, it is relatively easy to manipulate or vary physical characteristics and ask people for a response. This response should then be straightforward and relatively easy to interpret. Unfortunately, things are not as easy and straightforward as that. For example, perceptual attributes of video such as blockiness and jerkiness can influence each other, but the influence of attribute A on B is not necessarily the same as the influence of attribute B on A.

An example might help to clarify why perceived quality is not as straightforward as it may seem: think of the quality of food, say tomatoes. The way tomatoes are displayed in a grocery-shop influences your memories and associations of their taste: all jumbled together, they might have blemishes, but lined up like soldiers they could be prime quality. Then there are people who do not like tomatoes: no matter the way tomatoes are displayed, they will still not like them and will probably not be inclined to sample them. Another part is that a nice big red tomato can make you think that it is juicier and tastier than its neighbor, which is not as big and not a nice equal red. Interaction can be found as well, because tomatoes go very well together but basil, but most people would probably think twice before eating peanut-butter and tomatoes.

For video quality, there are similar problems. When watching multimedia, people might not like the shown video sequences and therefore judge the video quality as lower than someone who does like them. A good question that has been used for quite some time is to ask "What is video quality?". What do experts who ask about video quality mean, and what do they expect from it? What do they intend video quality to mean to laypeople? We postulate that "video quality" is often used to indicate an internally represented construct. This internal representation is, among other things, influenced by experiences and can fluctuate over time.

2. FRAMEWORK OUTLINE

Janssen [4] has defined image quality as a useful attribute of an image, which expresses how well the observer is able to employ the image as a source of information about the outside world. So the quality of an image is determined by the adequacy with which the image can serves as input to visual perception. Specifically, the adequacy of said image as input to visual perception is determined through discriminability and identifiability of items depicted in said image. There are other image quality models that it would be possible to continue with, but video is another context, which does not always have the same applications and uses.

Gulliver & Ghinea [3] devised a framework where Quality is divided between Quality of service, which focuses only on technical aspects, and Quality of Perception (QoP), which focuses on the subjective level of quality. QoP uses the level of information transfer and user satisfaction to find out subjective opinions. User satisfaction especially asks about two different things: presentation quality independent of content and enjoyment of multimedia content. Here, quality is already determined on several levels, but there are only 3 cognitive constructs that are allowed to explicitly contribute to user judgment.

Visual perception, from the human visual system to cognitive process, is not entirely understood yet. A lot is known about the early stages of human visual perception, from the light going in to the retina, from the cells discriminating between orientation of lines. However, there is no consensus yet about what happens later on in the brain with the interpretation of images [8].

Physical characteristics in the material are not the only influence; there is a top-down interaction to reckon with as well. Top-down interaction is defined here as coming from people their preconceived notions about quality, their expectations, the kind of television they are used to, motivation and external information about visual details based on incoming light (in the eye). On top of that humans need focused attention to notice changes in visual scenes.

3. DISCUSSION AND FUTURE WORK

Obviously, the framework as outlined in figure 1 is far from finished. A lot of work has been done on the influence of the physical characteristics (such as change in frame rate, quantization levels and chrominance levels,...) and the perceptual attributes (such as jerkiness, blockiness, blurring, ringing, colour bleeding, ...), but the real challenge will be in combining the top-down and bottom-up approach.

Many studies will be needed to provide input to work out this framework in more detail. The first step that we consider next is looking at the influence of involvement on perceived image quality. Involvement of users into the content could be tested by using an experimental and a control group. The control group would see pictures and would have to judge the perceived quality of the pictures. The experimental group would see the same pictures, but in such a way that they form a story and give participants a way to be drawn in the story, to give them an intrinsic motivation for watching and judging perceived image quality.

4. ACKNOWLEDGMENTS

Thanks to Don Bouwhuis, Klaus Kursawe, Matthias Krause and Paul Shrubsole for their support and comments.

to watch television, attention they are actually giving to the material, ... There seem to be a lot of factors that contribute to subjective video quality and it is currently unclear whether or how these factors influence users' judgment (see figure 1 for a way to look at the interaction between top-down and bottom-up factors).

When testing subjective video quality, there is another "layer" to keep in mind, experimental design. External and internal judgment scales are not comparable, it has been proven that internal judgment scales are influenced by the choice of the rating scale given (do you ask for quality or impairment, and in which way?), in which order the material is offered and video or image content shown [5]. Furthermore, voice quality research has shown that, when given more external benchmarks for the scale (options to listen to what the researchers think is a medium rough voice, for example, and compare it to the given sample), external standards are more constant [2].

So, people device a judgment strategy based on a number of factors, one of which is the experimental procedure itself and another is the video content [1]. In addition to those factors, people tend to watch video and multi-media for a reason: so there is the motivation and attention with which they watch video. Video content also plays a role in deciding whether or not they will continue to watch said video content. Other constructs that could play a role are challenge, engagement, overall enjoyability, future use, situational factors, aesthetics of the CE-application (television, mobile phone, PDA, ...), expectations and presence [7]. These constructs are not easy to test, however. For example, expectations cannot really be assessed after watching video material, because it is likely that they will have changed already. Self-rapportage is not always the best way to research expectations.

Rensink [6] also proposes that visual perception of a scene on a display is related to internal information based on knowledge

REFERENCES

[1] de Ridder, H.(2001). Cognitive issues in image quality measurements. *Journal of Electronic Imaging*, vol. 10, no. 1, pp. 47-55

[2] Gerratt, B. R., Kreiman, J., Antonanzas-Barroso, N., and Berke, G. S.(1993). Comparing Internal and External Standards in Voice Quality Judgments. *Journal of Speech and Hearing Research*, vol. 36 pp. 14-20, 1993.

[3] Gulliver, S. R. and Ghinea, G. (2006). Defining user perception of distributed multimedia quality. *ACM Transactions on Multimedia Computing, Communications, and Applications (TOMCCAP)*, vol. 2, no. 4, pp. 241-257

[4] Janssen, T. J. W. M. (1999). Computational Image Quality. Eindhoven University of Technology

[5] Meesters, L. M. J. and Martens, J.-B. (2000). Influence of processing method, bit-rate, and scene content on perceived and predicted image quality. 3959, 45-55. SPIE Conference on Human Vision and Electronic Imaging.

[6] Rensink, R. A. (2002) Internal vs. External Information in Visual Perception. 24, 63-70. ACM Press. SMARTGRAPH '02: Proceedings of the 2nd international symposium on Smart graphics.

[7] Schickenberg, B. and Hoonhout, H. C. M.(2003). Development of a rating scale to determine the appeal of enriched content to users. Philips Research

[8] Solso, R. L. (1995) *Cognitive Psychology*, 3d ed. Boston: Allyn & Bacon

Safer Prescribing in Intensive Care: Designing a System to Reduce Errors

Kathryn Went
University of Dundee
Queen Mother Building
Dundee DD1 4HN
+44 (0)1382 388084

kwent@computing.dundee.ac.uk

ABSTRACT

Prescribing in intensive care is a complex process involving a number of disciplines working in a highly stressful clinical environment. Within the National Health Service this process is generally written down manually. Errors are made each year as a consequence of illegible or incorrect prescriptions.

This research investigates engaging users from multi-disciplines in the design process to result in a system that is usable and demonstrates a reduction in prescribing errors

Keywords

User-centred design, evaluation, user interfaces, prototyping

1. INTRODUCTION

The National Programme for IT in the NHS, which is expected to exceed £12bn [1], has been widely criticized for running behind schedule and producing solutions that have not always been deemed as satisfactory. One of the reasons for this alleged failure is not engaging with the clinicians during the initial stages of the design [1].

This research looks at involving users throughout the development of an electronic prescribing system to result in a successful end product which is not only usable but reduces the errors made in prescribing in intensive care.

2. BACKGROUND

Approximately 200 million prescriptions are generated in NHS hospitals each year in the UK [3]. The majority of these prescriptions are handwritten.

The Department of Health estimates that one in 10 patients admitted to NHS hospitals will be unintentionally harmed, with medication errors being the second highest reported cause of harm. [2]

A medication error is defined as a mistake, slip or lapse made when medicines are prescribed, dispensed or used.

It is currently estimated that between 44,000 – 98,000 deaths per year are attributable to medication errors in America [4] and an unknown number in the UK [2] which is likely to be comparable.

Medication errors are believed to be a significant problem in the intensive care unit. Patients are frequently prescribed a large number of drugs, often in complicated combinations. This complexity increases the risk of medication errors, which may have catastrophic consequences. [3]

It is therefore imperative that in such critical environments there is an appropriate prescribing system in place to ensure accuracy and provide a clear audit trail.

3. PROCESS

The Intensive Care Unit (ICU) at Ninewells Hospital Dundee approached the University of Dundee to request the investigation of replacing the paper based prescribing system used in the ICU ward with an electronic version.

3.1 Identifying the errors made

Initially a survey, to identify the prescribing errors that occur in the ICU, was carried out. This allowed an understanding to be formed of how these errors could be prevented.

The survey took place over a 15 week period, 21 November 2005 until 7 March 2006. In this time 90 prescription charts were viewed and surveyed for 68 different patients. The survey consisted of checking the chart against 15 standards and documenting whether these standards were met or not. The standards were derived from the local hospital Safe and Secure Handling of Medicines Policy [5].

All of the charts viewed contained at least one non-compliance. Of the 1,921 individual medical prescriptions viewed 30% contained at least one deviation, with some prescriptions containing several.

3.2 Involving the users

It is commonly accepted that involving users in the development process results in a successful end product.

To ensure that the software created catered for the needs of the clinicians, nurses and pharmacists a clinical development team was established consisting of a consultant in anesthesia and intensive care, a consultant in anesthesia, an intensive care fellow, the principal clinical pharmacist for critical care, the intensive care specialist liaison nurse and the practice education facilitator.

To encourage and then later maintain engagement and buy-in by the clinical staff, monthly meetings were held with the team to discuss and evaluate the development of the prototype. These meetings consisted of the members of the clinical development team and a group from the University of Dundee and were led by the author. Meeting agendas were circulated in advance of meetings providing an opportunity for items to be added. The agendas were well received by the team as they allowed the meetings to be structured and thus were very productive.

3.3 System design

The aim of the design was to produce an error-free interface that captured the users' requirements and produced a positive user experience.

The system design employed an iterative approach, using rapid prototyping, responding to feedback from the regular meetings of the multi disciplinary team, to inform changes and additions to the design.

After observing staff in ICU the preliminary design was created using paper prototypes. Once evaluated this design was implemented as a working prototype. Rapid prototyping was employed to ensure that usable prototypes were produced whilst maintaining the engagement of the users. Many design iterations were completed as a result of the feedback given from the 30 evaluation sessions held.

Discussions during these sessions often resulted in the identification of new requirements, which may not have been discovered if this approach was not taken. Due to the number of new requirements identified it was suggested by a member of the team to create a wish list of requirements that could be developed at a future stage. This was suggested as the system was being developed as part of a PhD research project and whilst it was important to implement requirements that would make a direct impact on patient safety not all would necessarily reduce errors.

3.4 Evaluation

Evaluation sessions held with the clinical development team consisted of a cognitive walkthrough of the software followed by a feedback session chaired by the author.

To gain feedback from users' outwith the group, several drop-in sessions were held. To accommodate with the ICU staffs busy workload, these sessions took no longer than half an hour comprising of a walkthrough of the software followed by a series of open-ended and closed questions.

A member of staff from the School of Computing performed 3-monthly heuristic evaluations on the design to allow any usability issues to be highlighted.

An evaluation was carried out, with 22 prescribers outwith the team, which compared errors made with the paper system against the electronic system. Initial results suggested that the electronic system not only reduced non compliances made in the prescription process but was favoured by the users, who considered it "very user friendly and intuitive". Figure 1 shows the output of the evaluation for one of the subjects on both the electronic and paper system.

Engaging the users of the system during the design process resulted in a working prototype which users considered "very clear and familiar" and "a lot better" than the current procedure.

Adopting this iterative and responsive approach to the design of the evolving prototype resulted in the users developing a strong sense of ownership for the developed prototype.

4. SUMMARY

By applying usability techniques and involving the end users in the design it is hoped to show that the solution produced reduces errors made in Intensive Care prescribing in addition to creating a piece of software which the users accept and enjoy using.

The main contribution to the HCI field that this study is making is confirming that genuine buy-in and involvement is crucial to the development of a new error-free system accepted by the users.

5. FUTURE PLANS

Preliminary findings show that there is a reduction in errors with the electronic system but this will need to be demonstrated when used in the real life setting. The feedback received about the electronic system has been very positive but once again will need to be evaluated when used with actual patients in Intensive Care.

6. ACKNOWLEDGMENTS

My PhD supervisors, Prof Peter Gregor and Prof Ian Ricketts. The team of users at Ninewells Hospital, Dundee: Patricia Antoniewicz, Deborah A Corner, Dr. Judith Joss, Ann Mathewson, Dr. Shaun McLeod, Dr. Alfred J Shearer

7. REFERENCES

[1] Cross, M. Benefits of £12bn IT programme in NHS are "unclear," MP s say. *BMJ* 2007;334(7598):815

[2] Department of Health. *A safer place for patients: Learning to improve patient safety*. London: The Stationery Office, 2005.

[3] Department of Health. *Building a safer NHS for patients: Improving Medication Safety*. London: The Stationery Office, 2004.

[4] Kohn, L., Corrigan, J., Donaldson M. (1999). *To Err is Human: building a safer health system*. Washington, D.C.: National Academy Press, 1999

[5] Royal Pharmaceutical Society. The safe and secure handling of medicines: a team approach. London: RPSGB, 2005.

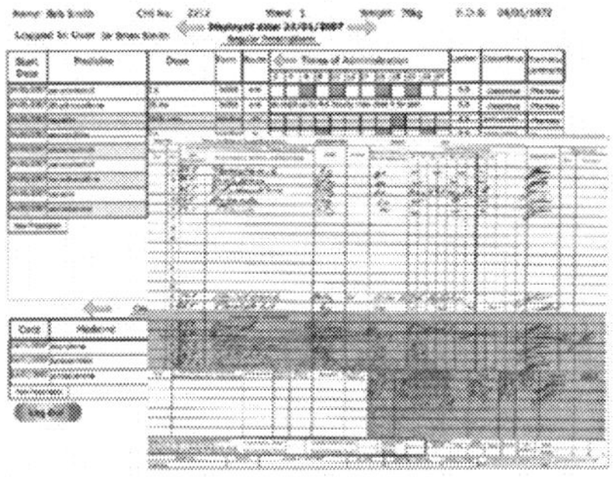

Figure 1. Electronic and paper system

Keyword Index

Author Index